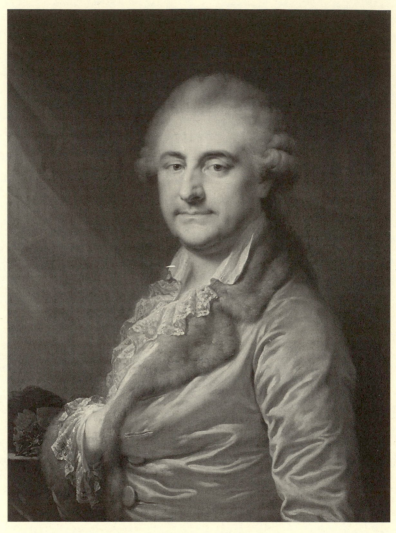

G. B. Lampi the elder, *Stanisław August*, *c.*1790.

POLAND'S LAST KING AND ENGLISH CULTURE

Stanisław August Poniatowski
1732–1798

RICHARD BUTTERWICK

CLARENDON PRESS · OXFORD
1998

Oxford University Press, Great Clarendon Street, Oxford OX2 6DP
Oxford New York
Athens Auckland Bangkok Bogota Bombay
Buenos Aires Calcutta Cape Town Dar es Salaam
Delhi Florence Hong Kong Istanbul Karachi
Kuala Lumpur Madras Madrid Melbourne
Mexico City Nairobi Paris Singapore
Taipei Tokyo Toronto Warsaw
and associated companies in
Berlin Ibadan

Oxford is a trade mark of Oxford University Press

Published in the United States by
Oxford University Press Inc., New York

British Library Cataloguing in Publication Data
Data available

Library of Congress Cataloging in Publication Data
Data applied for

ISBN 0–19–820701–8

1 3 5 7 9 10 8 6 4 2

Typeset by Graphicraft Typesetters Ltd., Hong Kong
Printed in Great Britain on acid free paper by
Biddles Ltd., Guildford & King's Lynn

Kochanej Małgosi

PREFACE

Vous m'avez assez bien connu pour scavoir que le redressement de l'état Politique de ma Patrie, et le développement du Génie de ma Nation sont les principaux buts de mon ambition. Ceci vous dit combien je désire de revoir une fois l'Angleterre.

Stanisław A. Poniatowski to Charles Yorke, 1755.

This book was researched and written during six momentous years of Polish history. When the subject was first suggested to me, early in 1989, I could not have imagined its current relevance. Studying the influence of foreign models in a 'new creation of the Polish world' two centuries ago, I witnessed similar phenomena and similar controversies, as Poland was transformed around me. There is another analogy, a more foreboding one—the sudden recovery of national sovereignty in 1788 and 1989. Will Poland's present independence be one more interlude in a pattern of Russian domination that stretches back to the early eighteenth century, or will it lead to the permanent replacement of that pattern? Now as then, the successes and failures of the Poles themselves count for less than the attitudes of the great powers. Such analogies make a book more exciting to write; they may even make it more interesting to read. They are also dangerous. The Polish world of two centuries ago was very different from that of today, for all the striking analogies, and the perils of anachronism are nowhere more obvious than in the minefield of nomenclature.

The English historian of early modern Poland–Lithuania may legitimately envy his French colleague the relative ease with which he may render official terminology and place and personal names. The use of French as the international language of diplomacy and high society in the seventeenth and eighteenth centuries has bequeathed a comprehensive French nomenclature, which may be employed (almost) without fear or favour. Contemporary Englishmen, confronted with the same names and terms, wavered between the French, Latin, and German versions. The wholesale adoption of eighteenth-century English nomenclature, if indeed a 'received' version could be culled from maps, books, letters, and despatches, would be as confusing to the modern English reader as the bowdlerized Polish terminology (such as 'voivod') and modern place-names (like Szczecin) used in histories translated into English in Poland. Unable to be at the same time consistent and comprehensible, I have striven to avoid anachronism, even at the price of upsetting national sensibilities. I have anglicized those institutions and offices best able to bear the change, such as tribunal for 'trybunał'. I have preferred 'envoy' to 'deputy' for 'poseł', because 'deputaci' were the elected judges of the tribunals. Although it conveys the dominant ideology of Poland–Lithuania, the rendering of 'Rzeczpospolita' as 'Republic' (as was usually done in the eighteenth century) prejudges the question of the nature of the Polish–Lithuanian state. 'Commonwealth', the seventeenth-century English translation of 'res publica', is an acceptable and neutral alternative. As all sources are quoted without modernization, orthographic mistakes included, I have used the old spelling 'Seym' instead of the modern 'Sejm'. I do not regard it as more difficult than 'Diet'. I have naturalized Seym, hetman, and starosta, but otherwise I have retained italics and Polish plurals. For towns, except for Warsaw and Cracow, I have used the language of the dominant inhabitants. In most cases, this means the Polish version. Thus Wilno, not Vilnius or Vilna, and Lwów, not L'viv or Lvov. However, the names of cities with Germanophone patriciates are given in German: Danzig, Thorn, and Elbing, rather than Gdańsk, Toruń, and Elbleg. I have Anglicized or Latinized the names of provinces and palatinates; thus Great Poland for Wielkopolska, Mazovia for Mazowsze, and Volhynia for Wołyń. The palatinate of Ruthenia (Ruś) comprised the land known as Red Ruthenia and later as East Galicia, not the entire territory inhabited by the non-Great Russian eastern Slavs. The eighteenth century usually referred to it as the 'palatinate of Russia'(!). I have used Belorussia as shorthand for the lands of White and Black Ruthenia, roughly equivalent to the present boundaries of Belarus, but the Ukraine (Ukraina) then referred only to the palatinates of Kiev and Bracław, and the more southerly of the lands across the Dnieper lost to Russia in 1667. I have kept personal names in the original languages, but have Anglicized those of rulers, where there is a close English equivalent. Thus Catherine, not Yekaterina, and Frederick, not Friedrich (or Frédéric). But what of our hero? Is it to be the Latinate Stanislaus or the Gallic Stanislas? The man himself could not decide. And presumably he must be Stanisław before his election. As no true English version of Stanisław exists, and as 'Stanisław Augustus' hardly rolls off the tongue, he remains Stanisław August.

The very unfamiliarity of the subject to most English-speaking readers has affected the construction of the book. It is not a typical monograph, as my own research is integrated into a much wider picture. Naturally I have tried to follow good academic practice in exploring the fullest implications of my findings. I have also thought it wise to summarize much of the political and cultural history of eighteenth-century Poland–Lithuania. Simply referring readers to the work of other historians (particularly those writing in Polish) would frustrate rather than enlighten them, and render the book disjointed. The resultant mixture of broad and fine brushstrokes may well surprise Polish historians, but a blend of monograph, synthesis, and biography has its own rich potential, which I have tried to exploit.

I am grateful to the following libraries and archives for access to documents and permission to quote from them: the Archiwum Główne Akt Dawnych (AGAD) in Warsaw, the Biblioteka Czartoryskich, Biblioteka Polskiej Akademii Umiejętności, and Biblioteka Jagiellońska in Cracόw, the Ossolineum in Wrocław, the British Library, the Public Record Office, the Royal Society, the Bodleian Library, Newport Borough Library, and the Lewis Walpole Library in Farmington. I extend my thanks to all the archivists and librarians who have helped me, especially those of AGAD, the State Archive in Łόdź, the National Library in Warsaw, and the University Library in Łόdź, for enabling me to read many documents on microfilm in Łόdź, and Anna Malicka of the Lewis Walpole Library for arranging to have a microfilm made. I thank Dr Michael Kitson of the Paul Mellon Centre for British Art for allowing me to peruse his forty-eight volumes of *Horace Walpole's Correspondence*. I am grateful for financial aid from the British Academy, the Polish Government, the British Council, and the Principal and Fellows of Hertford College, who elected me Mary Staruń Senior Scholar, thanks to the endowment of the late Mr L. Staruń.

My academic debts of gratitude are many and profound. My supervisor and sub-editor, Professor Robert Evans, has been an unending source of friendly interest, meticulous and perceptive criticism, and generous hospitality. Professor Zofia Libiszowska has looked after me in Poland, and offered me not only her immense knowledge of the subject, but, together with her husband, her open-hearted friendship as well. Our many hours of discussion have been as pleasurable as they have been instructive. Professor Lucjan Lewitter first suggested this subject to me, oversaw my first steps, and has continued to encourage and advise me. Professor Derek Beales inspired me with an interest in the Enlightenment, and has taken a lively interest in my progress. Dr Gerald Stone has been a supportive and cerebral 'moral tutor' at Hertford, to whom I owe the publication of Chapter 5 in *Oxford Slavonic Papers*. Various drafts of this book, in whole or in part, have also been read (and sometimes reread) by Professor Peter

Dickson, Dr Jerzy Lukowski, Mr Michael Hurst, Dr Hubert Zawadzki, Professor Zofia Zielińska, the late Dr Bożenna Majewska-Maszkowska (my guide to Stanislavian art), Professor Zofia Sinko, Professor Jerzy Michalski, Dr Anna Grześkowiak-Krwawicz, Dr Tim Hochstrasser, Miss Gertrude Seidmann, and Ms Elaine Chalus. To all, my heartfelt thanks. I am also in the debt of Professor Jerzy Grobis and all my former colleagues in Łódź, Professor Mariusz Kulczykowski, Dr Zofia Gołębiowska, Mr George Gömöri, Dr Karin Friedrich, Dr Leslie Mitchell, Dr Grzegorz Chomicki, Dr Magdalena Ślusarska, and Dr Stuart Moore. I shall always regret that I did not have the privilege of meeting Professor Emanuel Rostworowski, who died the very week I arrived in Cracow in 1989. My debt to his publications will be apparent.

I wish to thank my family for all the practical and spiritual help they have given me. My wife accompanied me in my travels, copied out numerous documents in the archives, and helped with the genealogical table, illustrations, and map. Her love and encouragement have kept me going. This book is for her.

CONTENTS

List of Illustrations	xiii
A Note on Pronunciation	xiv
Glossary	xv
Abbreviations	xviii
Genealogical Table	xx
Map	xxi

Introduction		1
1	Sarmatia and England	15
2	The Enlightenment and England	35
3	The Education of an Enlightened Anglophile	65
4	The Influence of Sir Charles Hanbury Williams	86
5	Stanisław's Visit to England in 1754	102
6	The Contacts of Stanisław and his Circle with the English World after 1754	124
7	The English Constitution and the First Efforts to Reform the Commonwealth (1763–1768)	146
8	Stanisław August and English Literature	172
9	Stanisław August and English Art	191
10	*Sapere Aude*	223
11	'Less Showy Means': From the Confederacy of Bar to the Four Year Seym	245
12	The Influence of the English Constitution on the Constitution of 3 May 1791	275
Conclusion		310

Bibliography	321
Index	353

ILLUSTRATIONS

Genealogical table of the Poniatowskis and the Czartoryskis   xx
Map to show the Commonwealth of Poland–Lithuania in 1764   xxi

1. *Frontispiece*: G. B. Lampi the elder, *Stanisław August*, c.1790.   ii
2. A. R. Mengs, *Sir Charles Hanbury Williams*, 1751.   101
3. The Marble Room at the Royal Castle.   201
4. The Library at the Royal Castle.   206
5. The Ballroom at the Royal Castle.   207
6. The Knights' Hall at the Royal Castle.   208
7. The *Chambre de Conférence* at the Royal Castle, showing Gainsborough's *George III*.   209
8. J. C. Kamsetzer, plan for the king's bedchamber and study at the Royal Castle, 1792.   211
9. Stanisław August's plan for Łazienki, 1784.   212
10. The north façade of the palace on the island, Łazienki.   214
11. The Ballroom at Łazienki.   215
12. The stage on the island at Łazienki.   216

Permission to publish the illustrations is gratefully acknowledged: Muzeum Narodowe w Warszawie: 1; Muzeum Łazienki Królewskie: 2, 10–12; Zamek Królewski w Warszawie: 3–7; Gabinet Rycin Biblioteki Uniwersytetu Warszawskiego: 8–9.

A NOTE ON PRONUNCIATION

Polish pronunciation looks frightening (Poles delight in getting foreigners to repeat tongue-twisters like 'Chrząszcz brzmi w trzcinie'—'a cockchafer buzzes in the rushes'), but it is at least regular. The vowels are simple and unvarying, and the stress falls on the penultimate syllable, with very few exceptions. The following notes may help the non-specialist reader to cope with the Polish names and terms in this book.

ą	A nasal sound like the French *on*, roughly equivalent to 'om' or 'on'.
c	A 'ts' as in 'lots'.
ch	Like the 'ch' in the Scottish 'loch', but often shortened to 'h'.
ci, ć	A soft 'ch', as in 'cheese'.
cz	A hard 'ch', as in 'catch'.
dzi, dź, dż	A 'j' as in 'jeans' or 'jam'.
ę	A nasal sound, roughly equivalent to 'em' or 'en'.
i	Like the 'ee' in 'beet'.
j	A 'y' as in 'yes'.
ł	A 'w' as in 'wood'.
ni, ń	A soft 'n' as in 'news'.
ó, u	A short 'oo', as in 'hood'.
rz, ż	A 'zh', or a harsher version of the 'j' in the French 'je'.
si, ś	A soft 'sh', as in 'sheep'.
sz	A harder version of the 'sh' in 'show'.
szcz	A 'shch' together, as in 'fish-chips'.
ści, ść	A softer version of *szcz*.
w	A 'v' as in 'van'.
y	A short 'i', as in 'lit'.
zi, ź	A softer version of *rz, ż*.

A few examples (not for phonetic purists). Softened consonants are indicated by '.

Stanisław August Poniatowski	Sta-*nee*-swav *Ow*-goost Po-n'a-*tov*-skee
Adam Kazimierz Czartoryski	*Ad*-am Ka-*zhee*-miezh Char-to-*ri*-skee
Tadeusz Kościuszko	Ta-*de*-oosh Kosh'-*ch'oosh*-ko
Włodzimierz	Vwo-*jee*-m'ezh
Brześć Litewski	Bzhesh'ch' Lee-*tev*-skee

GLOSSARY

Castellan (*kasztelan*)	Originally the keeper of a royal castle, now a senator.
Chamber of envoys (*izba poselska*)	The lower house of the Seym, composed of envoys elected by the *seymiki*.
Commonwealth (*rzeczpospolita*, *res publica*)	The Polish–Lithuanian state, formed from the kingdom of Poland, the grand duchy of Lithuania, the vassal duchy of Courland, and the remnants of the Polish–Lithuanian condominium of Livonia.
Confederacy (*konfederacja*)	A league of nobles, formed in a national emergency (real or otherwise). A Seym deliberating under the auspices of a confederacy was not subject to the *liberum veto*.
Crown (*korona*)	The kingdom of Poland, as opposed to Lithuania. It comprised Great Poland, incorporating Kujavia, Mazovia, and (more controversially) Polish Prussia; and Little Poland, incorporating Ruthenia, Podolia, Volhynia, and the Ukraine.
Crown estates (*królewszczyzny*)	Leased for life to individual nobles as part of lucrative *starostwa*.
Deputy (*deputat*, pl. *deputaci*)	Judge of a tribunal, elected by the *seymiki*.
Hetman	Military commander. The Crown and Lithuania each had a grand hetman and a field hetman.
Liberum veto	The individual right to refuse consent to resolutions and legislation of the Seym or *seymiki*, invoking the principle of unanimity. Its extreme form was the *liberum rumpo*, the licence to curtail the proceedings at will and wipe out all the legislation agreed to so far.

Magnateria	The magnates, or the wealthy élite of the *szlachta*, but not a legally defined group.
Ministers	The grand marshals, the grand chancellors, the vice-chancellors, the treasurers, and court marshals, joined in the senate in 1768 by the grand and field hetmans, and in 1775 by the court treasurers. Each office was duplicated for the Crown and Lithuania.
Pacta Conventa	Conditions to which the newly elected king had to swear to honour. They included the unchanging 'Henrician Articles', drawn up for Henry Valois in 1573, which set out the duties of the monarch. If the king defaulted, his subjects could refuse obedience.
Palatinate (*województwo*)	An administrative unit within the provinces of Great Poland, Little Poland, and Lithuania, sometimes subdivided into 'lands' (*ziemie, terrae*) and/or districts (*powiaty*).
Palatine (*wojewoda*)	Originally the military governor of a palatinate, now a senior senator.
Primate (*prymas*)	Head of the Church in Poland, archbishop of Gniezno, first senator, and *interrex* or supreme authority during an interregnum.
Sarmatism	Originally the theory that the *szlachta* was descended from ancient Sarmatians. It developed into the distinctive culture and lifestyle of the *szlachta*, and became synonymous with noble republicanism and intolerant Catholicism.
Senate (*Senat*)	The upper house of the Seym, comprising bishops, palatines, castellans, the starosta of Samogitia, and the ministers, chosen by the king for life, generally, but not exclusively, from the *magnateria*.
Senate council (*senatus consilium*)	Called by the king to decide on matters of state between Seyms. Abolished in 1775.

Seym (modern *Sejm*)	Parliament or diet, comprising the king, senate, and chamber of envoys.
Seymik, pl. *seymiki*	Provincial assembly of the *szlachta* in palatinates, 'lands', and/or districts.
Starosta	Originally a royal official, now a holder of Crown estates. A judicial (*grodowy*) starosta had some judicial and administrative responsibilities. A non-judicial (*niegrodowy*) starosta did not, and his *starostwo* was generally more lucrative.
Starostwo, pl. *starostwa*	The office and Crown estate held by a *starosta*.
Szlachta	The legally defined nobility (rather than gentry), encompassing the senators, but loosely used to refer to the 'knighthood' (*rycerstwo, ordo equestris*) or non-senatorial nobility.
Tribunals (*trybunały*)	The supreme courts of the *szlachta*, for the Crown and Lithuania.

ABBREVIATIONS

AGAD	Archiwum Główne Akt Dawnych, Warsaw
AKP	Archiwum Królestwa Polskiego, AGAD
AKsJP	Archiwum Księcia Józefa Poniatowskiego i Marii Teresy Tyszkiewiczowej, AGAD
APH	*Acta Poloniae Historica*
APP	Archiwum Publiczne Potockich, AGAD
ARP	Archiwum Rodzinne Poniatowskich, AGAD
BCzart.	Biblioteka Książąt Czartoryskich, Cracow
BJag.	Biblioteka Jagiellońska, Cracow
BL Add.	British Library Additional Manuscripts
BL Egerton	British Library Egerton Manuscripts
Bodl.	Bodleian Library, Oxford
DNB	*Dictionary of National Biography*
EHR	*English Historical Review*
HJ	*Historical Journal*
Kor.SA	Korespondencja Stanisława Augusta, AGAD
KwH	*Kwartalnik Historyczny*
LWL CHW	Lewis Walpole Library (Yale University), Sir Charles Hanbury Williams Manuscript Collection, Farmington, Connecticut
Mémoires	*Mémoires du roi Stanislas Auguste Poniatowski*, ed. S. Goryainov *et al.* (vol. 1, St Petersburg, 1914; vol. 2, Leningrad, 1924)
MNK	Muzeum Narodowe w Krakowie
Muz. Nar.	Zbiór z Muzeum Narodowego, AGAD
OSP	*Oxford Slavonic Papers*
os	old style (dates)
Oss.	Biblioteka Zakładu Narodowego imienia Ossolińskich (Ossolineum), Wrocław
Pam. Lit.	*Pamiętnik Literacki*
PAU	Biblioteka Polskiej Akademii Umiejętności, Cracow
PH	*Przegląd Historyczny*
PHP	*Pamiętnik Historyczno-Polityczny*
PRO FO	Public Record Office, Foreign Office Papers
PRO SP	Public Record Office, State Papers

PSB	*Polski Słownik Biograficzny*
RS	Royal Society, London
SA	Stanisław August (from 1764)
SEER	*Slavonic and East European Review*
Stan.	Stanisław Antoni Poniatowski (to 1764)
Zb. Gh.	Zbiór Ghigottiego, AGAD
Zb. Pop.	Zbiór Popielów, AGAD
ZNUJ	*Zeszyty Naukowe Uniwersytetu Jagiellońskiego*
ZNUŁ	*Zeszyty Naukowe Uniwersytetu Łódzkiego*
ZPP	*Zabawy Przyjemne i Pożyteczne*

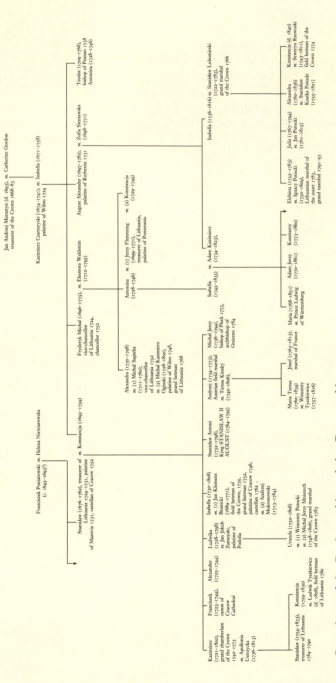

Genealogy of the Poniatowskis and the Czartoryskis

SWEDEN

RUSSIA

● Riga

COURLAND

POLISH
LIVONIA

SAMOGITIA

Dyneburg ●

Dvina

GRAND

Danzig ● ● Königsberg

Wilno
●

Smolensk
●

Elbing

WARMIA

POLISH
PRUSSIA

DUCHY

BELORUSSIA

Grodno ●

Dnieper

Poznán ●

Thorn ●

● Nowogródek

● Łomza

Płock ●

Białystok ●

OF

GREAT
POLAND

C

MAZOVIA
● Warsaw

LITHUANIA

● Wołczyn

Kozienice ●

R

PRUSSIA

Piotrków ●

● Puławy

Radom ●

O

Lublin ●

● Owrucz

Częstochowa

LITTLE

W

● Włodzimierz

● Kiev

Cracow ●

POLAND

Vistula

VOLHYNIA

● Lwów

N

● Kaniów

RUTHENIA

Korsuń ●

UKRAINE

HABSBURG

● Bar

MONARCHY

PODOLIA

● Tulczyn

● Targowica

Kamieniec
Podolski

- - - - - Lands lost in the First Partition of 1772

OTTOMAN EMPIRE

The Commonwealth of Poland–Lithuania in 1764

Introduction

Crowds of Varsovians silently filed past their deceased king, come to pay their respects, to pray for the repose of his soul, or merely to satisfy their curiosity. The primate of Poland presided, attended by dignitaries of Church and State, as King Stanisław August Poniatowski was laid to rest in the Cathedral of St John the Baptist in Warsaw. This was no ordinary royal funeral. The king had been dead for 197 years. It was 14 February 1995. Two centuries earlier, the truncated Commonwealth of Poland–Lithuania finally disappeared from the map of Europe, her lands divided among her neighbours, her king bullied into abdicating. Stanisław August died in St Petersburg on 12 February 1798, part honoured guest, part prisoner of state. He was given his first funeral by Tsar Paul I, the son of his one-time lover and long-time tormentor, Catherine the Great.

A hundred and twenty years on, the realms of the Romanovs, Hohenzollerns, and Habsburgs were no more, swept away by defeat in the First World War. A reborn Poland led by Józef Piłsudski successfully defended her independence from the Bolshevik invaders. By the Treaty of Riga in 1921, Poland recovered many of the cultural and historical treasures plundered during the period of partition. Stanisław August was not among them. He was not wanted. In 1938, the Soviet authorities planned to bulldoze the Church of St Catherine in Leningrad and unilaterally handed back his coffin. The 'colonels' who ruled Poland found themselves in a predicament. Tradition demanded a royal funeral on Wawel Hill in Cracow, but just three years since they had buried Piłsudski there. To their minds, Poniatowski was a morally degenerate coward, if not a traitor. By failing to throw himself on his sword or a Muscovite bayonet when Russia invaded in 1792, and by ignominiously abdicating in 1795, he had forfeited his right to an honourable funeral in Cracow or Warsaw. Stanisław August was quietly put away in the parish church at Wołczyn, where he had been baptized in 1732. When the news leaked out, a public debate ensued on the merits and faults of the last king, and on where to bury him. Before any decision was reached, Nazi Germany and Soviet Russia once more partitioned Poland. Poland emerged from the war shunted west and under Soviet domination. Wołczyn lay a few miles east of the new frontier.

The communist regime had no wish to provoke embarrassing analogies, and the matter was conveniently forgotten. Occasionally it surfaced in the literary press, but every request for intervention was turned down until 1987–8, when, under pressure from writers and historians, the Ministry of Culture appointed a commission to travel to Wołczyn. When it reached the devastated church in December 1988, it found only bits of the coffin. It returned to Warsaw with some fragments of the royal robes found by some Belorussian academics a year before.[1] Six frustrating years of delay and procrastination followed, six years in which Polish life was transformed. Perhaps time was needed for the emotions generated by the collapse of communism and the rancorous break-up of 'Solidarity' to cool. Stanisław August's scanty remains, mixed with earth from Wołczyn, were finally interred in a Poland less absorbed and less divided by the questions of independence and liberty; a Poland not yet at ease with its own history, but no longer preoccupied by it. Nationalist politicians grumbled about the funeral, Primate Glemp almost apologized for it in his sermon, and the press showed little interest, but the last king was finally laid to rest in his capital, with something approaching propriety.[2]

If the king's remains were largely symbolic, so too was his resting-place. St John's Cathedral, the site of his coronation, and where the *Te Deum* was sung after the passing of the Constitution of 3 May 1791, was itself rebuilt after being destroyed along with 90 per cent of Warsaw by the Nazis in 1944, while the Red Army was halted across the Vistula by Stalin's orders.

For all the dissimilarities between Stanisław August's huge, multi-faith, multi-ethnic Commonwealth of the Two Nations, Polish and Lithuanian (to give it its full title) and today's compact Third Polish Republic, religiously and ethnically homogeneous, one analogy is fundamental. Both were perceived at home and abroad as being on the backward peripheries of Europe, as needing to learn from and catch up with more advanced states. It has recently been argued that it was the Enlightenment which created the concept of a backward 'Eastern Europe' beyond

---

[1] See A. Zgorzelska, *Powrót króla* (Warsaw, 1991) and the annexes to M. M. Drozdowski (ed.), *Życie kulturalne i religijność w czasach Stanisława Augusta Poniatowskiego* (Warsaw, 1991).

[2] On 15 Feb. 1995 *Życie Warszawy* and the post-communist *Trybuna* gave the funeral very brief coverage, while *Rzeczpospolita* published the complaints of nationalist politicians, some of whom had appealed to the primate for a purely religious service. Only the liberal *Gazeta Wyborcza* mentioned the sympathy of the Varsovians in attendance for the king. Was St Valentine's Day chosen as a joke in poor taste, or to deflect attention from the funeral? Or did it simply coincide with a gap in President Wałęsa's diary?

the Elbe.[3] Stanisław August and his enlightened compatriots had no clear concept of 'Eastern Europe' (they rather adhered to the traditional divide between South and North), but they were acutely conscious of the distance separating Poland from states and cultures such as France, England, and the Netherlands. If they did not yet think of those countries as 'the West', we can still discern in embryo the post-Communist countries' current preoccupations with their relative backwardness.[4] In Central and Eastern Europe today, foreign models of various types are the subject of intense interest, controversy, and hostility. Foreign fashions have invaded dress, speech, and manners. For every reformer convinced that only the rapid application of foreign expertise can solve his country's problems, there is an impassioned defender of traditional national values, who denounces 'the West' for its amorality and irreligion. Something very similar took place in Stanisław August's Poland.

In the 1990s, Great Britain may pride itself on the 'Know-how Fund' and one or two other initiatives to help Central and Eastern Europe. British privatization of state-owned industries has attracted much interest, but the former 'Peoples' Republics' have not stampeded to adopt constitutional monarchy or first-past-the-post electoral systems. If the English language has scored a worldwide triumph, that must be attributed more to the strength of the American economy than to the legacy of the British Empire. In the eighteenth century, England's contribution to European

---

[3] L. Wolff, *Inventing Eastern Europe: The Map of Civilization on the Mind of the Enlightenment* (Stanford, Calif., 1994). Wolff writes about 'Western' perceptions of 'Eastern Europe', rather than about the identity felt by 'Eastern Europeans'.

[4] Following two centuries of diverse reflections upon the supposed backwardness—economic, racial, or otherwise—of the various lands and peoples of Central and Eastern Europe, 'Eastern Europe' was defined with brutal clarity as the countries under Soviet domination in the wake of Churchill's 'Iron Curtain' speech in 1946. Since 1989, the inadequacies of the term 'Eastern Europe' have become increasingly apparent. It has sometimes been restricted to the former Soviet Union, while the term 'Central Europe' has been revived in the former Habsburg lands. Poles (except those from the former Austrian partition) have traditionally been wary of 'Central Europe', associating it with a German-dominated *Mitteleuropa*, and they tend to prefer 'East-Central Europe' (*Europa środkowo-wschodnia*). Nevertheless, 'Eastern Europe', with its connotations of backwardness, is proving a difficult concept to dispel. Norman Davies has produced a powerful critique of the labels 'East' and 'West', which rightly stresses the differences between, for example, Poland and Bulgaria, or between England and Ireland. However, in his distaste for 'Western' ignorance and contempt for the 'East', he addresses neither the common problems bequeathed (in varying measure) by Soviet domination to the former members of the Warsaw Pact, nor the real civilizational differences in the eighteenth century between England, the Netherlands, and urban France, and vast areas to the east, including Poland–Lithuania, Russia, Hungary, and the Ottoman Empire. 'Cztery strony i serce', *Gazeta Wyborcza*, 2–3 Sept. 1995. See also *Europe: A History* (Oxford, 1996), 19–31 and *passim*.

civilization was incomparably greater. Experimental science and the Lockean *tabula rasa* provided important philosophical foundations for the Enlightenment, especially in France. The English constitution was held up to Europe as a model by Montesquieu and others, and the growing number of critical voices later in the century did not significantly dent faith in its theoretical virtues. English fashions based upon the cult of nature and sensibility swept over Europe in the last third of the century. One of eighteenth-century Europe's most notable Anglophiles was Stanisław August Poniatowski. This book explores the nature of his Anglophilia, and analyses the role it played in his efforts to 'create anew the Polish world',[5] reduced in the first half of the eighteenth century to a near abyss of political anarchy and corruption, intellectual barrenness and insularity, religious prejudice and social oppression.[6]

No one aspect of Stanisław August's activity can be separated properly from the whole. In accordance with the spirit of the Enlightenment, 'good laws' were to create the conditions for the flourishing of the arts and sciences, while the arts and sciences were to re-educate the ruling nobility (the *szlachta*), in order to persuade it of the need to overhaul the constitution. Stanisław August fought on virtually all fronts simultaneously, with energy and determination. However, as king, early experience taught him that his room for political manoeuvre was severely curtailed by Russian hegemony in Poland. He tried to achieve as much as possible in conditions of restricted sovereignty, and in political crises preferred lesser evils, however humiliating, to defiant gestures that he thought pointless or even harmful. When Russia obliged Stanisław August to shelve all major constitutional reform, he concentrated on administrative improvements and education. He sought to edify his compatriots both by didactic use of their own history and traditions and by introducing into Poland the best elements of foreign cultures, where they would be most useful.

The Commonwealth of the Two Nations was a sprawling conglomerate, which had taken shape in the late Middle Ages. The fragmented

---

[5] The phrase was frequently employed by Stanisław August, e.g. in a speech to the Seym on 11 Oct. 1766: 'Nowe to niby mamy przed sobą, albo raczej powtórne świata polskiego tworzenie' (We have before us, as it were, a new, or rather a second creation of the Polish world), quoted after W. Konopczyński, *Geneza i ustanowienie Rady Nieustającej* (Cracow, 1917), 90.

[6] I do not find the attempts to rehabilitate the Saxon period particularly convincing, at least not before *c*.1750. See below, Ch. 3. J. A. Gierowski, one of the earliest to discern positive phenomena, has now, prompted by the politics of post-1989 Poland, warned that the rehabilitation has gone too far. 'Rozkład państwowości szlacheckiej w czasach saskich', in T. Chynczewska-Hennel *et al.* (eds.), *Między wschodem a zachodem: Rzeczpospolita XVI–XVIII w.: Studia ofiarowane Zbigniewowi Wójcikowi . . .* (Warsaw, 1993).

medieval kingdom of Poland had lost ground in the west, but when partly re-united in the fourteenth century, it expanded to the south-east. Under Casimir the Great (1333–70), Poland was one of the best-governed kingdoms in Europe. Casimir established an effective administration, codified the laws, fortified his frontiers, encouraged settlement, and founded a university. His achievement lasted centuries, for it was not renewed. None of his successors enjoyed an indisputable hereditary right to the crown, which, given their persistent penury, enabled the nobility to extract wide-ranging personal and political privileges from them, and to consolidate its hegemony over the towns and peasantry. The Seym (diet or parliament) emerged around 1500 as a bicameral institution, made up of three estates: the king, the senate (which evolved from the royal council), and the chamber of envoys, comprising the representatives of the *szlachta* elected at territorial *seymiki* (dietines). From 1505, the consent of all three estates was required for new legislation. In 1385 Poland had linked herself to the grand duchy of Lithuania, a dynamic if ephemeral power, which had over-run the vast duchies of Kievan Rus'. After nearly two centuries of uneasy personal union, the Polish and Lithuanian nobles agreed to a parliamentary union at Lublin in 1569. Three years later, with the extinction of the Jagiellon dynasty, the throne became elective in fact as well as in theory, and the *szlachta*, which made up about 5 to 7 per cent of the population, cemented its control of the state.[7]

In the sixteenth century, the *szlachta* developed an advanced political culture of far-reaching political and religious liberty. Medieval privileges were embellished with classical republican ideals of civic virtue, which were absorbed from humanist education. Unfortunately, even as this political culture began to mature, it entered phases of stagnation and then decay. The administration left by Casimir and some military reforms in the late sixteenth century sufficed to keep Poland–Lithuania in the first rank of European powers until the mid-seventeenth century. Thereafter, buffeted by war, the political system, which depended to a great degree

---

[7] Two excellent general introductions are R. I. Frost, 'The Nobility of Poland–Lithuania, 1569–1795', in H. M. Scott (ed.), *The European Nobilities in the Seventeenth and Eighteenth Centuries*, vol. 2, *Northern, Central and Eastern Europe* (London, 1995), and H. Roos, 'Ständewesen im parlamentarische Verfassung in Polen 1505–1772', in D. Gerhard (ed.), *Ständische Vertretungen in Europa im 17. und 18. Jahrhundert* (Göttingen, 1969). E. Rostworowski, 'Ilu było w Rzeczypospolitej obywateli szlachty?', *KwH*, 94 (1987), estimates that out of a population of 14 million before the First Partition in 1772, 6–6.5% were noble. This compares with estimates of up to 10%, which have been accepted since the late 19th century. The proportion of nobles in the population is generally thought to have increased in the early modern period.

upon the collective wisdom of the *szlachta*, began to seize up, and the position of the Commonwealth deteriorated sharply. Foreign intervention in Polish politics became normal.

During the Great Northern War (1700–21), Peter the Great transformed Muscovy into one of Europe's great powers. At the same time, the Commonwealth fell from being a crisis-ridden but still weighty second-rank power to a defenceless object of international diplomacy. For a while, the scale of this débâcle was masked by the personal union of Saxony with the Commonwealth, but by the 1730s it could no longer be concealed. The Commonwealth had become a buffer protecting Russia, and at the same time Russia's gateway to Europe.[8] The process was complete by the time Catherine II made Poniatowski King of Poland in 1764. Russian *raison d'état* dictated that Poland should be prevented from ever recovering its position on the European stage. When Russian supremacy was challenged, however, the Commonwealth became perilously exposed to the compensating mechanisms of the international balance of power. The disturbance in the balance of power caused by the revolt of a large part of the *szlachta* against Russian hegemony and Stanisław August (the Confederacy of Bar) and the resulting Russo-Turkish war was ended only by the First Partition in 1772. The renewal of war between Russia and Turkey in 1787 was soon followed by another rebellion against Russia and the king, this time parliamentary rather than military, at the beginning of the Four Year Seym of 1788–92. The outcome of the reconciliation between the king and the opposition was the Constitution of 3 May 1791 and its associated legislation. Russia's reply, after concluding peace with Turkey, was to invade Poland and to suppress the Constitution. Poland's Prussian ally deserted her. Stanisław August bowed to the inevitable and joined the Russian-sponsored Confederacy of Targowica. After a second partition and a hopeless insurrection led by Tadeusz Kościuszko, the remnants of the Commonwealth were finally divided between Russia, Prussia, and Austria in 1795.

Neither contemporaries nor posterity were slow to blame Stanisław August for the catastrophe.[9] For other Polish politicians, it was a matter of political convenience. The Polish romantic tradition found its solace in heroic, martial failures, like that of the king's nephew, Prince Józef

---

[8] Cf. *Mémoires*, vol. 1, 510.

[9] A comprehensive account of historians' and writers' assessments of Stanisław August is provided by A. Zahorski, *Spór o Stanisława Augusta* (Warsaw, 1988). Here I restrict myself to sketching the main phases of the debate.

Poniatowski. Stanisław August was and remains the butt of anti-Russian sentiments. Not until after the failure of the 1863–4 uprising did the political climate favour his rehabilitation. Stanisław August's efforts to reform Poland in conditions of limited sovereignty appealed to the 'positivist' era's slogan of 'organic work'. A Cracovian historian, Walerian Kalinka, censured Stanisław August on moral grounds, but after heroic archival labours concluded that the king's pro-Russian policy was the only sensible one in the circumstances.[10] The Cracovian school's stern message, that the Poles had lost their independence through their own mistakes and vices, especially an immoderate love of liberty, was not likely to be popular. It generated an 'optimist' reaction in Warsaw. Tadeusz Korzon, in the economic sphere, and Władysław Smoleński, in the intellectual one, demonstrated that the reign of Stanisław August was a time of national revival.[11] The king did not reap the credit, however. If Poland had lost her independence because of foreign aggression, then Stanisław August's surrender was treasonable. The condemnation of the last king reached a peak in the work of Szymon Askenazy at the turn of the century. Askenazy tried to prove that the Prussian alliance was viable. Bronisław Dembiński attacked that standpoint, and gave a critical but more balanced assessment of Stanisław August.[12] Poland's greatest interwar historian, Władysław Konopczyński, admitted the political wisdom of Stanisław August and exposed the mistakes of his opponents in the meticulous detail of his works, but he was too involved in nationalist politics to approve of the last king in his overall judgements, and repeatedly condemned his lack of 'character'.[13]

After the Second World War, as Marxist historiography neglected the individual in favour of economic history, the first major work on Stanisław August came from abroad. The French literary historian Jean Fabre explored Poland's place in the European Enlightenment, and drew a subtle portrait of the king. He turned the popular image of the king

---

[10] *Sejm Czteroletni* [1880–7] (4th edn., 2 vols.; Warsaw, 1991).

[11] Korzon, *Wewnętrzne dzieje Polski za Stanisława Augusta 1764–1795: Badania historyczne ze stanowiska ekonomicznego i administracyjnego* (2nd edn., 6 vols.; Cracow, 1897–8). Smoleński, *Przewrót umysłowy w Polsce wieku XVIII: Studia historyczne* [1890] (4th edn., Warsaw, 1979).

[12] Askenazy, *Przymierze polsko-pruskie* (2nd edn., Warsaw, 1901). Dembiński, *Polska na przełomie* (Lwów, 1913).

[13] Especially in *Geneza i ustanowienie Rady Nieustającej, Konfederacja barska* [1936–8] (2nd edn., 2 vols.; Warsaw, 1991) and *Dzieje Polski nowożytnej* [1936] (3rd edn., 2 vols.; Warsaw, 1986).

upside down; for Fabre, Stanisław August was a ruler who subordinated taste and 'philosophy' to the rebuilding of the Polish state.[14] One of Fabre's and Dembiński's insights, that Stanisław August was the primary author of the Constitution of 3 May, was conclusively proved by Emanuel Rostworowski in 1963. Rostworowski went on to write a short but scholarly biography of Stanisław August, in which he reassessed more favourably, although by no means uncritically, the delicately poised political course charted by the king.[15] Rostworowski's arguments were developed by Jerzy Michalski, who presented Stanisław August as a far-sighted and consequential reformer, whose elastic tactics always served either to strengthen the Commonwealth or to rescue as much of it as possible, or in the end to relieve the distress of his compatriots.[16] However, Stanisław August's rehabilitation by specialists was not easily accepted by the Polish nation.

Historians of art began to explore Stanisław August's services to Polish culture in the early twentieth century. Their emphasis on the didactic aims of Stanisław August's patronage has been lost in the popular imagination, alongside the enormously influential picture painted by Stanisław Wasylewski of 'King Stan' (*Król Staś*), as frivolous and refined as a figure in Meissen porcelain, and about as useful in defending the state.[17] Hundreds of guides repeat it to tens of thousands of visitors to Warsaw every year. Jerzy Łojek, an able if unscrupulous historian, reacted violently against Rostworowski and Michalski, and missed no opportunity to condemn Stanisław August's character and pro-Russian policy in his widely read articles and books.[18] The average Pole continues to think that Stanisław August would have made a great minister of education and culture, but was unfit to be king. Adam Zamoyski's attractively written biography,[19] now translated into Polish, should add to the number of the king's admirers.

Stanisław August still awaits a full-length scholarly biography. Because his initiatives touched virtually every area of Polish life, specialist political, literary, or art history cannot hope to represent the king's programme

---

[14] *Stanislas-Auguste Poniatowski et l'Europe des lumières: Étude de cosmopolitanisme* (Paris, 1952). Fabre's criticism of Stanisław August's taste has been rejected by Polish cultural historians.

[15] 'Marzenie dobrego obywatela, czyli królewski projekt konstytucji', in Rostworowski, *Legendy i fakty XVIII wieku* (Warsaw, 1963). *Ostatni król Rzeczypospolitej: Geneza i upadek Konstytucji 3 Maja* (Warsaw, 1966).

[16] In particular, 'Stanisław August Poniatowski', in *Poczet królów i książąt polskich* (2nd edn., Warsaw, 1984).

[17] *Na dworze króla Stasia* (Lwów, 1919).

[18] e.g. *Siedem tajemnic Stanisława Augusta* (Warsaw, 1982).

[19] *The Last King of Poland* (London, 1992).

fully. It seemed to me that a greater step forward than a book dealing with a short period of his life or a single aspect of his activity would be one on a theme running through his entire life and almost every sphere of his activity. One such theme is Stanisław August's Anglophilia, which extended from the English constitution to English art, science, and literature.

Stanisław August's predilection for England is well known to Polish historians. At the beginning of this century, Ludwik Bernacki brought his translation of Shakespeare's *Julius Caesar* to light.[20] Bronisław Dembiński was among the first to call to attention the king's admiration of the English constitution.[21] Władysław Konopczyński, a great admirer of the British Parliament, provided more detail.[22] Jean Fabre, analysing Stanisław August's Anglophilia within the wider context of cosmopolitanism, laid stress on his concern for utility rather than beauty. Fabre's *magnum opus* remains the chief point of departure for the present work. Emanuel Rostworowski considered the influence of the English constitution upon Stanisław August's political aims, and noted the parallels between Polish and Anglo-American republicanism.[23] Zofia Libiszowska has written extensively about Anglo-Polish relations during the reign of Stanisław August in the diplomatic, cultural, scientific, and personal spheres, as well as on the Polish reception of the American Revolution.[24] There have also been a number of studies of the 'English model' in eighteenth-century Polish political thought, and of English literary and artistic influences.[25] Many more monographs and syntheses on eighteenth-century Poland have taken 'English influences' into account.

Studies of Anglophilia have tended to pass over the king himself rather briefly. On the other hand, works on Stanisław August could not devote

[20] 'S. A. Poniatowski tłumaczem Szekspira', *Pam. Lit.*, 2 (1902).

[21] 'The Age of Stanislas Augustus and the National Revival', in *The Cambridge History of Poland*, ed. W. F. Reddaway (vol. 2; Cambridge, 1941), 115, 134–5.

[22] In particular, 'Anglia a Polska w XVIII wieku', *Pamiętnik Biblioteki Kórnickiej*, 4 (1947).

[23] Rostworowski, *Ostatni król*, 212, 217, 221. Idem, 'Republikanizm polski i anglosaski w XVIII wieku', *Miesięcznik Literacki*, 11, nos. 7/8 (1976).

[24] Among others, *Opinia polska wobec rewolucji amerykańskiej w XVIII wieku* (Łódź, 1962), *Misja polska w Londynie w latach 1769–1795* (Łódź, 1966), and *Życie polskie w Londynie w XVIII wieku* (Warsaw, 1972).

[25] e.g. Libiszowska, 'Model angielski w publicystyce polskiego Oświecenia', *Sprawozdania z Czynności i Posiedzeń Łódzkiego Towarzystwa Naukowego*, 23, no. 10 (1969); A. Grześkowiak, 'Publicystyka polska lat 1772–1792 o angielskim systemie rządów', *Przegląd Humanistyczny*, 29, nos. 5–6 (1985); Z. Sinko, *Powieść angielska osiemnastego wieku a powieść polska lat 1764–1830* (Warsaw, 1961); S. Lorentz, 'Stosunki artystyczne polsko-angielskie w dobie Oświecenia' in J. Białostocki and I. Kołoszyńska (eds.), *Polska i Anglia: Stosunki kulturalno-artystyczne: Pamiętnik wystawy sztuki angielskiej* (Warsaw, 1974).

sufficient space to his interest in England. The questions of *which* aspects of England Stanisław August was most interested in, and *why*, have hardly been touched upon. There is a need, therefore, both to put the king back at the heart of the history of English influences on Stanislavian Poland, and to analyse the importance of England to the person and policies of Stanisław August. Such a study is made all the more desirable by the obsolescence of the characterizations of eighteenth-century England in Polish historiography; a situation arising not from wilful neglect, but from the great cost of imported books. The vast expansion of eighteenth-century English historiography during the last two decades has yet to filter through.

Eighteenth-century England had many faces, which were encountered by different Poles and have been highlighted by different historians. Whereas magnates like the Czartoryskis remained firmly in John Cannon's *Aristocratic Century*, humbler travellers like Julian Ursyn Niemcewicz also met the 'middling sort', described by Paul Langford as *A Polite and Commercial People*.[26] Historians such as Jonathan Clark and Eveline Cruickshanks have rescued Jacobites, Tories, Oxford divines, and religious orthodoxy from the near-oblivion to which they were consigned by the Whig tradition,[27] yet the Whig England of hostility to royal power and natural religion existed as well. The term 'Whig' itself comprehends great ideological diversity: from radical interpretations of Lockean contract theory, stressing the right of resistance and the sovereignty of the people, to uncompromising defences of parliamentary and aristocratic supremacy and an extensive royal prerogative. Developments in English historiography open up the prospect of fresh insights from the comparison of eighteenth-century England and Poland. It becomes by the same token essential to identify the sources of Stanisław August's information about England, and the outlook of the circles that he moved in and corresponded with.

The place of England in the Enlightenment and the influence of English thought and civilization on eighteenth-century Europe have recently become live issues among English historians. This reaction to a long tradition of insularity is certainly welcome, but detailed studies of these

[26] Z. Gołębiowska, 'Podróż Izabeli i Adama Czartoryskich do Wielkiej Brytanii (1789–1791)', *Annales Universitatis Marie Curie-Skłodowska*, 28/29, Sect. F (1983/4). J. Cannon, *Aristocratic Century: The Peerage of Eighteenth-Century England* (Cambridge, 1984). J. Niemcewicz, *Pamiętniki czasów moich*, ed. J. Dihm (2 vols.; Warsaw, 1957), vol. 1, 227–33. P. Langford, *A Polite and Commercial People: England 1727–1783* (Oxford, 1989).

[27] J. D. C. Clark, *English Society 1688–1832: Ideology, Social Structure and Political Practice during the Ancien Régime* (Cambridge, 1985). E. Cruikshanks, *Political Untouchables: The Tories and the '45* (London, 1979).

questions remain scarce. A study of Anglophilia in one of eighteenth-century Europe's largest but least known states would seem to be a particularly desirable contribution, needing no further justification. I wish to add weight to the reaction against too discrete a view of 'national Enlightenments' by stressing the importance of the diffusion of ideas from one country to another, often refracted through the prism of a third—usually France. I have generally written England, rather than Britain, despite the appearance throughout the book of a number of Scots. The reasons are twofold. First, then as now, Poles (like most Europeans) rarely distinguished between the two. They saw Ossian as distinctly Scottish, but not Hume, Ferguson, Robertson, or Smith. Second, the Scottish Enlightenment may be viewed partly as a movement of Anglicization. By the end of the eighteenth century, some Scots were using England and Britain as synonyms.[28]

The approach of the present work is as follows: the first aim is to set Stanisław August in the context of Polish and European attitudes to England, the second is to analyse the sources of Stanisław August's Anglophilia, and the third its effects on his activity and on the history of Poland–Lithuania. These aims are reflected in the organization of the chapters, although many of the later chapters, dealing with effects, include sections on sources of information. English influences cannot be examined in a vacuum, but only in comparison with other foreign influences and native Polish traditions. Entire books have been written in an effort to define 'culture'. At its widest, it must include the entire common existence and creative output of a society. I have chosen it as the only term that can adequately comprehend the extent of English influences on Stanislavian Poland (the grander 'civilization' implies the whole of Christian Europe). I have focused in particular on the visual and literary creative arts, religion, learning, and the chief means of their nourishment, education. Within the compass of culture, I have used 'political culture' to refer to the ideas, assumptions, language, and behaviour of those involved in politics. Political culture has particular importance. Stanisław August aimed not merely to reform outdated institutions, but to change the attitudes that sustained them. However, it should be borne in mind that in the age of the Enlightenment, virtually all culture was politicized and didactic; *belles-lettres*, for example, merged seamlessly into political thought. A purely political approach is neither possible nor desirable.

[28] See below, p. 134. F. Oz-Salzberger, *Translating the Enlightenment: Scottish Civic Discourse and the German Enlightenment* (Oxford, 1995), ch. 2. L. Colley, *Britons: Forging the Nation 1707–1837* (New Haven, 1992), 162.

From these pinnacles of ambition, I descended to the problem of how to measure the influence of one country on another. Some research has been done on the presence of English books in eighteenth-century Polish libraries and booksellers' catalogues, noting whether they were in English, or in Polish, French, or German translation. The limitations of this exercise have also been pointed out. It is impossible to determine statistically whether the books in question were read, understood, or agreed with. Such inquiries have some value in the realms of literature and political thought, but very little in determining English influence on efforts at reform.[29] I cannot see a better alternative to an impressionistic approach, using a wide variety of primary and secondary sources, at each stage trying to take account of possible bias. Sometimes a statement in the king's correspondence makes it clear that he was explicitly following an English model in proposing a reform, but just as often English inspiration must be either inferred or discounted. It was not always politic to justify reform by the example of England. At other times, the authority of England was used to buttress a proposal which would have been made anyway. Naturally, the conclusions reached will have varying degrees of probability.

The source materials for this study may be divided up into four main categories. The first is the correspondence of Stanisław August and his circle with Englishmen. The second comprises the opinions of Stanisław August about England, expressed in his *Mémoires*, a few essays, and letters to his diplomats and foreign correspondents. The third is the opinions of English diplomats and travellers about Stanisław August. The fourth is made up of the documents describing the royal library, collections, and residences, which assist in the evaluation of English literary and artistic influences upon him. Of the published sources, the most fruitful have been Stanisław August's *Mémoires*, his correspondence with Madame Geoffrin and Maurice Glayre, the Lee Papers, William Coxe's *Travels*, and the documents of the Royal Library (the efforts made by the Bodleian Library on my behalf to procure a microfilm of the original catalogue in Kiev proved unsuccessful). I have also delved into the extensive political literature and periodicals of eighteenth-century Poland, as well as the works of Montesquieu, Voltaire, Rousseau, and other luminaries of the Enlightenment.

Archival research forms the core of the study. This material is widely scattered, so the reader is referred to the bibliography for full details. The material was not originally intended to document Stanisław August's

---

[29] See below, pp. 174–5.

Anglophilia. Much of it required skim-reading of several volumes, in order to turn up a single revealing comment. Other sources were concentrated blocs of information. Some sources, like the king's enormous domestic correspondence, disappointed. On the other hand, even well-sifted material such as Stanisław August's letters to his envoy in St Petersburg, Augustyn Deboli, yielded unexpected pearls. A quarter of Stanisław August's thousand-volume archive vanished mysteriously in the nineteenth century. Of the rest, the part in the Popiel Collection, held in the central archive in Warsaw (AGAD), is the most valuable, as it includes the king's correspondence with foreigners and Deboli. Another part, the so-called Archive of the Kingdom of Poland, also in Warsaw, contains the official correspondence of the department of foreign affairs with the envoys in London, Franciszek and Tadeusz Bukaty. The greater part of the king's own correspondence with the Bukatys and some letters and other papers from his youth are to be found in the Czartoryski library in Cracow. The interiors of the royal residences can be reconstructed from the inventories in the Archive of Prince Józef Poniatowski, in Warsaw. Drafts of the king's letters to his brother, Primate Michał Poniatowski, during the latter's stay in Italy, France, and England in 1790–1, until now hardly disturbed, are in the Ghigotti Collection in Warsaw. Important fragments of Stanisław August's correspondence with the Bukatys are in the library of the Polish Academy of Learning in Cracow. The British Library holds the Hardwicke Papers, which, apart from some letters from Stanisław, also contain some interesting comments on Stanisław and Poland by members of the Yorke family. I tracked down Stanisław's letters to Sir Charles Hanbury Williams to the Lewis Walpole Library in Farmington, Connecticut. Finally, British diplomatic correspondence provides much background information.

A book on Stanisław August necessarily touches on many aspects of the constitutional, literary, artistic, religious, and intellectual history of Poland, England, and Europe. The subject also demands an orientation in the political and diplomatic history of Poland and Europe in the eighteenth century, which determined the shifting restrictions on Stanisław August's ability to renew the Polish world. The result is that while the secondary literature devoted to the subject is modest in its extent, that potentially relevant to it is huge, exceeding by far the capabilities of any one historian to digest it all. This is particularly the case with regard to the context and effects of Stanisław August's Anglophilia. In consequence, this book takes into account Stanisław August's compatriots, but aims to be comprehensive only with regard to the king himself. It does not cover Anglo-Polish diplomatic and commercial relations, except in so far as they affected the above restrictions, and only briefly touches upon the image of Poland in eighteenth-century England. For reasons of space, I have not attempted to deal with the interesting question of English influence on the system of government envisaged by the legislation of the Grodno Seym of 1793, which was called to ratify the Second Partition. Stanisław August tried to persuade Russia to preserve as many as possible of the reforms of 1791–2. This system never had the chance to function and was almost immediately engulfed by the Kościuszko uprising.[30] For all that, the subject remains a vast one, a challenge to writer and reader alike.

[30] Ł. Kądziela, *Między zdradą a służbą Rzeczypospolitej: Fryderyk Moszyński w latach 1792–1793* (Warsaw, 1993), which contains the best account of the Grodno legislation, does not detect any English influence, but refers briefly to Moszyński's experience in Saxony and Austria, 101–2.

I

Sarmatia and England

In 1744, Stanisław Poniatowski the elder invited his compatriots to cast their eyes over 'other free states and republics in Europe'. England, he wrote, did not differ much in its laws and constitution from Poland, yet it governed itself 'beautifully' and enjoyed general esteem.[1] The comparison seems surprising at first. What could eighteenth-century England, the epitome of political, military, economic, intellectual, and cultural achievement, have in common with the ultimate eighteenth-century failure? At a second glance, the similarities of the two largest exceptions to eighteenth-century absolutism are more apparent. A third look brings home the essential differences. Such was the problem posed by Poniatowski. More than two centuries later, it was addressed by Emanuel Rostworowski.[2] With the aid of recent historiography, let us tackle it again. Only then can we understand the attitude of most Poles in the mid-eighteenth century to England.

I

It goes almost without saying that Polish and English social structure differed vastly. In England, the disappearance of the peasant was virtually complete, and agrarian structure was based on landed proprietors, tenants, and wage-labourers. In Poland, the omnipotent *szlachta* tied the peasants to the soil, and labour dues were the rule. English trade and towns were in a far more advanced condition than Polish ones, and legally defined social estates were non-existent in England, bar the minuscule peerage.[3] Nevertheless, similar social structures to Poland's elsewhere in Central and Eastern Europe did not prevent the emergence of strong polities, and even in England landed proprietors dominated Parliament. It is primarily to the political sphere that we must look for an explanation of the differing fortunes of the two states.

---

[1] Quoted in full below, p. 76.
[2] *Historia powszechna: Wiek XVIII* (3rd edn., Warsaw, 1984), 568–78.
[3] J. T. Lukowski, *Liberty's Folly: The Polish-Lithuanian Commonwealth in the Eighteenth Century* (London, 1991), is not only the most accessible and comprehensive introduction to 18th-century Poland–Lithuania, but also a salutary dose of critical realism in the long-running debate between 'optimists' and 'pessimists'.

Both the United Kingdom of Great Britain and the Commonwealth of Poland–Lithuania had national parliaments, rather than the provincial estates characteristic of most of Europe. Both were unions of formerly separate polities. In both, the ruler of the lesser power had become king of the greater, and before the extinction of the dynasty a parliamentary union was carried through. Over both now reigned electors of the Holy Roman Empire, the rulers of Hanover and Saxony respectively. In Britain, the supreme legislative power was vested in the king in parliament. In Poland, the Seym was made up of three estates, the king, the senate, and the chamber of envoys. Analogies could be found in ideology as well. The fear of an over-mighty Crown, which through prerogative, a standing army, and corruption threatened despotism, was common to many Englishmen and Poles. So too was the conviction that government was safe only in the hands of independent men of public virtue and landed property. Individual rights were similarly jealously guarded. The English habeas corpus was analogous to the much older Polish *Neminem captivabimus nisi iure victum.* In both states, wealthy aristocrats commanded the political and economic heights, and limited the real power of the Crown. Their method of conducting politics has commonly been described as oligarchical. Less attractive common characteristics were propensities for hard drinking, xenophobia, and religious prejudice.

Rostworowski, following Poniatowski and certain other eighteenth-century Polish writers, classified both England and Poland as 'republics', explaining that a crowned head was not inconsistent with the term in the eighteenth century. What was important was whether the state in question was 'free'.[4] Most contemporary European writers, however, insisted that England was a mixed or limited monarchy, in which the sovereign king in parliament represented monarchy, aristocracy, and people. Eighteenth-century Poland, on the other hand, was no longer described as a *monarchia mixta,* as it had been in the early seventeenth century.[5] The *szlachta* was the sole repository of sovereignty, and it expressed its rights dramatically, by electing its king in person, and extracting from him a list of concessions and undertakings—the *pacta conventa.* If the king broke his oath, the *szlachta* possessed, and sometimes exercised, the right *de non praestanda oboedientia.* This was republicanism with a vengeance.

---

[4] See Rostworowski, 'Republikanizm polski i anglosaski', and A. Grześkowiak-Krwawicz, '*Rari avis* czy wolni wśród wolnych?', in Ł. Kądziela *et al.* (eds.), *Trudne stulecia: Studia z dziejów XVII i XVIII wieku ofiarowane Profesorowi Jerzemu Michalskiemu . . .* (Warsaw, 1994).

[5] J. Dzięgielewski, *Izba poselska w systemie władzy Rzeczypospolitej w czasach Władysława IV* (Warsaw, 1992), 136–8.

In England, the right to resistance was generally understood to mean the last resort in the face of insufferable tyranny; certainly not the right of the people, or their elected representatives, to depose their king for misrule. While the Whigs had developed a fairly radical interpretation of the right of resistance before the Glorious Revolution in order to justify their opposition to the Stuarts, after 1688 most Whigs were keen to play it down. This was in part the consequence of Whigs enjoying power, and their interpretation hardened still further after 1714. But it was also the result of the enduring strength of the Tory 'ideology of order'. Polish political culture had absolutely no equivalent to the Tory doctrines of divine indefeasible hereditary right, non-resistance, and passive obedience. These doctrines were all-pervasive in England during the 1680s, and although most of the political nation had to compromise them at the Revolution, they revived in Anne's reign and persisted, like Banquo's ghost, to trouble the consciences of squires and parsons well into the eighteenth century. At least as significant as the survival of actual Tories under the first two Hanoverians was the impact of Tory ideology on the Whigs. If the Whigs were to win the support of the landed gentry, they had to stress the necessity of obedience to authority and a respect for the royal prerogative within the 'balanced constitution'. Mainstream Whigs replaced indefeasible divine hereditary right by providential divine hereditary right, rather than an exclusively parliamentary title to the throne.[6]

The ideological similarities mentioned earlier were nevertheless no fiction. A small minority of the English political nation was committed to a constitution based on the sovereignty of the people and an original contract, which would enshrine the right of resistance, further restrict the royal prerogative, and perhaps even make the throne elective. The ideology of these radical Country Whigs, or 'Commonwealthmen', in the early eighteenth century was certainly comparable to Polish noble republicanism.[7] They had common roots in the agrarian-military ideas of classical republicanism. While both traditions defended the rights of the individual citizen in the face of royal authority, the liberty which they exalted was primarily the 'republican' freedom to participate in government, rather than the 'liberal' freedom from government.[8] While few Englishmen endorsed the

[6] H. T. Dickinson, *Liberty and Property: Political Ideology in Eighteenth-Century Britain* (London, 1977), chs. 1, 2, and 4. Clark, *English Society*, 119–36.

[7] Polish writers often defined Whigs and Tories as republicans and monarchists respectively, e.g. K. J. Skrzetuski, *Historya polityczna dla szlachetney młodzi . . .* (2nd edn., Warsaw, 1777), 141.

[8] See I. Berlin, 'Two Concepts of Liberty', in idem, *Four Essays on Liberty* (Oxford, 1969). A. Walicki follows the Polish cult of the unanimous 'national will' from the 'golden freedom' through to the 1980s in *Trzy patriotyzmy* (Warsaw, 1991), 10–41.

Commonwealthmen's constitutional programme, the language in which Country ideology was expressed was almost the sole form of political discourse. It provided the materials with which to attack the conduct of ministries, and dictated the terms on which ministries were forced to respond. Except perhaps in 1697–1701, when some contemporaries feared Parliament would go the way of the Polish Seym,[9] Country ideology never triumphed. Under Charles II and James II important steps were taken to modernize the State (notably the creation of the excise department in 1683), and the long struggle with Louis XIV consummated the process. War brought about a vast expansion of the apparatus of government, unprecedented taxation, and a standing army which topped 100,000 in wartime and remained at 35,000 afterwards (including the Irish establishment). This coincided, however, with the limiting of the royal prerogative and a tight-fisted financial settlement which made the king dependent on Parliament even in peacetime. At first, the gentry preferred the burdensome land tax, under their own control, to an intrusive expanded excise. The price extracted for the expansion of government was its detailed scrutiny, especially by the Commissions of Public Accounts. Among the results of the tension between Country and Court was a more honest and efficient administration than might otherwise have been the case. John Brewer writes: 'Paradoxically, a strong parliament effectively resisting much that was proposed by government eventually produced a stronger state.'[10]

Country ideology also preserved the independence of Parliament, without making stable government impossible. While 'place bills' never succeeded in excluding all office-holders from the Commons (and thereby introducing a strict separation of the legislature from the executive), the exclusion of certain categories of office-holders checked the rising number of 'placemen' at about 140. The strength of Country ideology inflicted some notable parliamentary defeats on ministries and forced them to retreat on certain issues. By the 1740s, however, it was largely a spent force. Its legacy was a vague concern with royal corruption, which would next be picked up on both sides of the Atlantic in the 1760s. Three main reasons may be identified for its weakness. One was the continuing pull of party loyalty. Another was the campaign waged by Court Whigs to convince the public that the rapid changes wrought by warfare on the English state

---

[9] P. G. M. Dickson, *The Financial Revolution in England: A Study in the Development of Public Credit 1688–1756* (London, 1967, repr. with revisions, 1993), 13.

[10] J. Brewer, *The Sinews of Power: War, Money and the English State 1688–1783* (London, 1989), 30–2, 137–61 and *passim*. See also J. G. A. Pocock, 'The Varieties of Whiggism from Exclusion to Reform', in idem, *Virtue, Commerce, and History* (Cambridge, 1985), 215–53.

and society since 1689 were beneficial, and that the heroic, self-denying public virtue preached by the Country opposition was inappropriate; politeness and philanthropy would cope with the moral problems posed by the growth of commerce. But perhaps the most important was the deep sense of loyalty, nay, obedience to the Crown that pervaded English society. Organized opposition was frowned upon. The average backbencher considered that it was his duty to support the king's ministers, unless he had an overwhelming reason *not* to do so.[11]

In Poland, the conflict *inter maiestatem ac libertatem* produced a debilitating constitutional stalemate. The system of mixed monarchy established in the 1560s was immediately shaken by a succession of disruptive and divisive interregna. No king was able to win the trust of the *szlachta*, which, after a series of crises in the 1580s, 1590s, and 1600s, came to mistrust every royal initiative as a potential assault on its 'golden freedom'. The *szlachta* was more concerned by the fall of the Italian city-states, the advance of absolutism in Bohemia and France, and the arbitrary despotism of Turkey and Muscovy, than by the shortcomings of the Commonwealth. The king was allowed to make policy (he could usually manage the resident senators he was supposed to consult), but was denied the financial and administrative means to do so effectively. The political system depended on the sense of responsibility and independence of the envoys, yet both were gradually eroded after the Union of Lublin. Alongside the authentic representatives of the middling and wealthier *szlachta*, the chamber of envoys now admitted the clients of Lithuanian and Ruthenian princes. The transfer of the virtually unpopulated Ukraine to the Polish Crown (*korona*) from the grand duchy in 1569 allowed its rapid colonization and the rise of some fabulous fortunes. The courts and private armies of the marchland magnates employed poor nobles from across the Commonwealth. The new magnates began to make their influence felt in the original Polish kingdom as well. The waning of the intellectual Renaissance and the waxing of the sensual Baroque, together with the retreat of Protestantism to defensive positions in the face of the Counter-Reformation, contributed to a more conservative and conformist climate. By the 1630s and 1640s, the chamber of envoys was

---

[11] Dickinson, *Liberty and Property*, chs. 3 and 5. Brewer, *Sinews of Power*, 158–9. Cf. G. Holmes and D. Szechi, *The Age of Oligarchy: Pre-Industrial Britain 1722–1783* (London, 1993), 45–6, 282. S. Burtt, *Virtue Transformed: Political Argument in England, 1688–1740* (Cambridge, 1992), is a more nuanced account of the transformation of old-fashioned republican virtue into a privately oriented civic virtue in which private virtues and even enlightened self-interest contribute to the public good, than the classical tragedy proffered by Pocock and others, of the victory of 'liberal' over 'republican' freedom in England.

ceasing to be a forum for achieving consensus in state affairs, and was becoming the passive defender of noble liberties. It expanded its institutional role at the expense of the senate, but it increasingly became the battleground of factions led by senators, who demagogically played fast and loose with the principle of unanimity in order to block decisions against their interests.[12]

The unwritten principle of unanimity in decision-making was in many respects laudable, for it forced conflicting interests to seek consensus. Minorities were frequently persuaded to accept the will of the majority for the good of the kingdom, but determined protests by envoys of standing were respected. However, the suicidal precedents of 1652 and 1669 established not only the *liberum veto*, the right of an envoy to block any measure whatsoever, but also its extreme form, the *liberum rumpo*, or the licence to break up the proceedings of the Seym at will, and thereby wipe out all the legislation passed by it. The moral odium attached to the abuse of the *veto* was such that it was used infrequently for some decades, but by the end of the reign of John III Sobieski (1674–96), the Seym was close to total paralysis, a state it finally attained under Augustus III (1733–63). The *liberum veto* allowed foreign powers to neutralize threats to their interests, and gave ministers *carte blanche* to abuse their positions. The hetmans (military commanders), marshals, chancellors, and treasurers of the Crown and Lithuania, and their deputies were appointed by the king for life, and could be deprived only by the Seym. The effects of the *veto* were worsened by the binding instructions that envoys received from the *seymiki* which elected them. The *seymiki* occasionally instructed their envoys to wreck the Seym if their demands were not met. The upholding and then the catastrophic cult of the *liberum veto* reflected the downfall of political culture. Often viewed as the quintessence of individualist anarchy, the *veto* was in fact a pillar of conformism, a disincentive to novel and controversial proposals, and such were all ideas of serious reform.[13] The *szlachta* became convinced that the king could corrupt the majority of the Seym, and so the *liberum veto* became the hallowed *pupilla libertatis*.[14]

[12] See Dzięgielewski, *Izba poselska*, *passim*; R. I. Frost, *After the Deluge: Poland–Lithuania and the Second Northern War 1655–1660* (Cambridge, 1993); and idem, ' "Liberty without Licence?": The Failure of Polish Democratic Thought in the Seventeenth Century', in M. P. Biskupski and J. S. Pule (eds.), *Polish Democratic Thought from the Renaissance to the Great Emigration* (Boulder, Col., 1990).

[13] Konopczyński's *Dzieje Polski nowożytnej*, vol. 2, 173.

[14] Konopczyński's *Liberum veto* (Cracow, 1918) should be supplemented by W. Czapliński, 'Sejm w latach 1587–1696', and J. Michalski, 'Sejm w czasach saskich', in *Historia sejmu polskiego* (vol. 1, ed. J. Michalski; Warsaw, 1984), 274–83, 338–43; E. Opaliński, 'Między

The crippling of the Seym seemed to offer the monarch the opportunity to bypass it. Successive kings tried to rule through the senate council, which, at least to start with, was reasonably good at crisis management. The problem lay in obtaining the co-operation, not of those senators who attended it, but of those who did not. It never commanded the authority or power to impose political reform, or even enforce the payment of taxes.[15] The main weapon of the king was the distribution of lucrative Crown estates (*Królewszczyzny*)—again for life—to the 'deserving'. In practice, the king was left manoeuvring between the richest families for support. During the seventeenth and early eighteenth centuries, the political and economic role of the magnates certainly increased at the expense of the middling *szlachta*, but the term 'magnate oligarchy', meaning the control of political life by a group of aristocratic families in their own selfish interests, is misleading. The *magnateria* was never legally defined, it exhibited precious little caste solidarity, and its composition was highly fluid. The *raison d'être* for a Radziwiłł was to crush the upstart Sapiehas; for a Potocki it was to humble the impudent Czartoryskis. Magnate dominance of local political life was greater in some areas, such as Lithuania and the Ukraine, than in others, such as Great Poland, where the line between the local *magnateria* and the wealthier *szlachta* was difficult to draw. Magnates could rarely dictate to the *seymiki*.[16] If their demagogic slogans about the 'golden freedom' were insincere, they were still obliged to recite them. The dispersal of most *latifundia* made the pattern of magnate political influence a complicated and shifting mosaic. The Commonwealth never became as fragmented as the German *Reich*, and the plans of the Radziwiłłs, Sapiehas, and Potockis to carve out their own principalities during the Northern wars were exceptional. Oligarchical tendencies were also combated with some success by the king's distribution of patronage. Partible inheritance meant that magnate families needed Crown estates simply to maintain their position. It was magnate rivalry rather than oligarchy that enervated the political system. If a magnate clan and its allies held the office of grand hetman and one of the other ministries, it was formidable indeed, and woe betide the king who gave

"liberum veto" a głosowaniem większościowym: Funkcjonowanie semu w latach 1587–1648', in *Między wschodem a zachodem*; and A. Lityński, *Sejmiki ziemskie 1764–1793: Dzieje reform* (Katowice, 1988), 20–31.

[15] For the senate council, the changes in its make-up, its limited successes and its deeper failures, see Frost, *After the Deluge, passim*; M. Markiewicz, *Rady senatorskie Augusta II (1697–1733)* (Wrocław, 1988); idem, 'Rady Senatu za Augusta III', *Zeszyty Naukowe Uniwersytetu Jagiellońskiego*, 614 (1985).

[16] See below, pp. 84–5.

Crown estates to their rivals or tried to create his own party by preferring nobles of modest fortune. Although such magnates could not dictate policy to the king, they could frustrate royal initiatives with ease.[17]

The concept of 'Whig oligarchy' is more convincing than 'magnate
oligarchy', but requires qualification. It is one thing to demonstrate that
a small number of rich families enjoyed an increasingly disproportionate
share, verging on a monopoly, of high office, and an increasing number
of clients in the House of Commons.[18] It is quite another to suppose that
they ran the state as they pleased. The Whig supremacy was no aristocratic mafia. Party loyalty remained the main axis of politics under the
first two Georges, and all Whigs rallied instinctively to the canon of the
Protestant succession, the mixed and balanced constitution, and some
measure of toleration for Protestant dissenters. The combined strength
of Court and Treasury placemen and aristocratic connections was never
enough in itself to assure a majority in the House of Commons, although
it did ensure that the Tories were consigned to permanent opposition.
Robert Walpole and Henry Pelham devoted the major part of their ener-
gies to explaining policies to independent Whig backbenchers, and persuading them to vote for the ministry. Likewise, classic rotten boroughs
formed but a small part of the electoral system. Many boroughs usually
returned the candidate of the leading local landowner, but only if His
Lordship was assiduous in his attention to local interests and showed his
respect for the local community. The building of electoral empires was
a hugely expensive and time-consuming business.[19]

Another indispensable component of 'Whig oligarchy' was the support
of the Crown. Neither George I nor George II was a cipher, particularly
in foreign and military affairs, but in questions of domestic policy they
could usually be led by their ministers. Neither was equipped by temperament to direct policy as William III had done. George I and George
II were boxed in by their refusal to trust the Tories, and when George

[17] Frost, 'The Nobility of Poland-Lithuania', vol. 2, 199–216. Lukowski, *Liberty's Folly*,
11–18, 23–4, 88–9. J. Staszewski, *August III* (Wrocław, 1989), 207–8. Cf. W. Szczygielski,
'Polska kultura republikańska XVI–XVIII wieku', *Rocznik Łódzki*, 32 (1982), for an exposi-
tion of the argument that successive kings missed opportunities for an alliance with the
middling *szlachta* against the *magnateria*. It may be objected that (i) neither the *magnateria*
nor the middling *szlachta* possessed much coherence as political forces and (ii) the ability
of noble republicanism to accommodate elements of monarchism is highly doubtful, to say
the least, until 1791.
    [18] J. Cannon has done so convincingly: *Aristocratic Century*, ch. 4. But cf. Langford,
Polite and Commercial People, 590–600, 689–91.
    [19] Holmes and Szechi, *Age of Oligarchy*, chs. 2 and 3. F. O'Gorman, *Voters, Patrons, and
Parties: The Unreformed Electorate of Hanoverian England 1734–1832* (Oxford, 1989).

II did try to appoint his own ministers, in 1727 and 1744, he was spectacularly defeated. But once the Jacobite threat had passed, and George
III declared his intention to be 'king of all his people', Tory unity collapsed, and the Whigs followed in their wake. Politics was atomized into
a chaos of aristocratic factions, independents, and placemen, who were
known as the 'king's friends'. The 'old corps' Whigs were reduced to a
rump grouped around the Marquess of Rockingham. George III became
the key player in the formation of ministries, though he was content subsequently to leave political management to Lord North, and later to William
Pitt the younger. His grasp on policy was at its height during the American war. But for the straitjacket of dynastic insecurity combined with
strong party loyalties, there was nothing to prevent the king playing a
leading political role, if he had the ability and inclination to do so.[20]

In the 1680s, both England and Poland were second-ranking powers.
By 1720 England was the equal of France, while Poland had ceased to
play an independent role in European affairs. England and Poland's contrasting experience of warfare offers a promising line of enquiry. England
was isolated from Continental warfare for much of the sixteenth and seventeenth centuries, and the damage caused by the Civil War was trivial
in comparison with the wastelands created in Germany and Bohemia.
When England did re-enter European warfare, she was unburdened by
debt and prosperous. The essentials of the mercantile system were in place
and colonial expansion was well under way. A system of public credit
was made possible by parliamentary approval of government borrowing.
The king in parliament was a more trustworthy debtor than the monarch
alone, and this enabled short-term debts to be converted into long-term
government stock, paying a lower rate of interest, underwritten by specific taxes. The Bank of England (founded in 1694) and other corporations
helped to create a market in government securities which was essential to
the raising of large sums. The rapid enrichment and rise to political influence
of predominantly Whig and dissident financiers naturally provoked a
bitter reaction from Anglican Tory squires, but after 1713 the conflict
between the landed and monied interests diminished markedly. The land
tax became less burdensome to landowners as the role of the excise increased,
while the number of landowners who owned government or company
stock, or whose younger sons enjoyed government office or a military

---

[20] Holmes and Szechi, *Age of Oligarchy*, 29–35, 277–82, 290–1. J. B. Owen, 'George II
reconsidered', in A. Whiteman *et al.* (eds.), *Statesmen, Scholars, and Merchants* (Oxford,
1973). R. Pares, *Limited Monarchy in Great Britain in the Eighteenth Century* (Historical
Association pamphlet, London, 1957).

commission, rose steadily. The landed gentry of the 1740s were on the whole reconciled to a fiscal-military state which their fathers had viewed with horror.[21]

Poland, on the other hand, suffered warfare on her own soil. It is difficult to exaggerate the havoc wreaked by the Cossack revolt, the Swedish 'Deluge', and the wars against Muscovy and Turkey in the quarter of a century after 1648. The population fell by a quarter or more through plague, starvation, and flight; agricultural yields plummeted, the towns were ruined, and grain exports were reduced to a trickle. The shoots of recovery under Sobieski were trampled in the Great Northern War, much of which was fought in the Commonwealth. Whereas England experienced a revolution in finance and government, Poland's ramshackle administration could not cope with the strain. The Polish army, whose morale had already suffered from repeated failures in Sobieski's last years, broke up into factions which could only fight each other successfully. Unpaid Polish soldiers were scarcely less terrible to the population than the Swedes and Russians. With the Seym virtually paralysed, individual *seymiki* tried to make pacts with passing armies, the culmination of a process of decentralization which had been gathering strength for decades. The compromise reached under Russian mediation between Augustus II and his republican opponents in 1716, and enacted in 1717, represented an improvement. The Commonwealth's budget was fixed and the army was henceforth paid regularly from specified taxes. Unfortunately, as Rostworowski commented acerbically, 'the regulation of the military and fiscal affairs would have been a major achievement, had it not been for the establishment of the budget and the numbers of the army at a level appropriate to a second-rank state of the German *Reich* or Italy.' The legislation established 24,000 units of pay, which through an excess of officers reduced the army to a ridiculous 12–14,000. The power of the *seymiki* to levy taxation was curtailed, but the Seym and the central administration (if it can be so dignified) were left virtually untouched.[22] Worse, the settlement of 1716–17 marked the Commonwealth's end as a fully sovereign state. Poland was not yet a Russian satellite, but Peter the Great had become the arbiter of Polish politics and could easily torpedo any attempt to strengthen the state, as he did in 1719. The Russian ambassador's signature on the agreements was of less importance than the factual

---

[21] Brewer, *Sinews of Power, passim*. Dickson, *Financial Revolution*, esp. 1–91.

[22] Z. Wójcik, *Jan Sobieski 1629–1696* (Warsaw, 1983), *passim*. Lukowski, *Liberty's Folly*, 129–51. Rostworowski, 'Czasy saskie i Oświecenie', in J. Tazbir (ed.), *Zarys Historii Polski* (Warsaw, 1980), 300–1.

transformation of the balance of power since Poltava in 1709. After Peter's death, there may have been a fleeting chance to slip the leash, but Russian hegemony was confirmed in 1733–4, when the election of Stanisław Leszczyński was overturned by force.[23]

In both countries, war hardened religious attitudes and strengthened national identity. The Poles' ever more militant Catholicism was matched by the belligerent Protestantism of the British. Faith and liberty were inter-twined. In both countries, belief in Divine Providence was strong, but it was interpreted very differently. Victory in war confirmed the belief of the English that the Glorious Revolution was a miracle, and they resolved to defend it.[24] In Poland, defeat and misfortune were explained as divine punishment for sin, and in particular for tolerating heresy. It was the degradation of the sixteenth century's preference for good men, rather than good institutions. The two major events of 1717 are symbolic in their coincidence—the legislation of the 'Dumb Seym' and the 'corona-tion' of the picture of the Black Madonna of Częstochowa, symbolizing the Virgin's role as 'Queen of Poland'. Belief in Divine Providence was accompanied by passivity, not to say fatalism. The Great Northern War with its accompanying natural disasters seems to have accustomed the *szlachta* to defeat and impotence.[25] Polish noble society turned inwards and sought a pacific pastoral idyll, which was given some reality by eco-nomic recovery from the 1720s. The maxim 'Poland subsists by anarchy' (*Polska nierządem stoi*) was based on a truism; that like the Holy Roman Empire, the Commonwealth's very weakness made it indispensable to the European balance of power. This too was interpreted as divine favour, and few realized that the situation would not last indefinitely.

After the frightening experience of Puritan fanaticism, a group within the Church of England, pejoratively called 'latitude-men', managed to

[23] T. Cegielski and Ł. Kądziela, *Rozbiory Polski: 1772–1793–1795* (Warsaw, 1990), 40–50. Cf. Staszewski, 'Między Wiedniem i Petersburgiem: Uwagi na temat międzynarodowego położenia Rzeczypospolitej w XVII i XVIII w.', in *Między wschodem a zachodem*, which argues that the Commonwealth was dependent on Austria in the later 17th century, and that from 1697 until 1740, Austrian influence rivalled Russian. However, the position of the Common-wealth should be distinguished from that of the king-elector 'between Vienna and St Peters-burg'. L. R. Lewitter, 'Intolerance and foreign intervention in early eighteenth-century Poland–Lithuania', *Harvard Ukrainian Studies*, 5 (1981), shows how Peter was careful not to jeopardize his hegemony in Poland by an attack on the Roman Catholic Church.

[24] Colley, *Britons*, ch. 1.

[25] Z. Kuchowicz, *Człowiek polskiego baroku* (Łódź, 1992), 226–8, 257–63. Staszewski, *August III*, 154. See Lewitter, 'Intolerance', for details of the marked increase in forced conversions and harassment of the Orthodox from the late seventeenth century, and the rising tide of hostility towards Protestants, expressed in discriminatory restrictions, following the Swedish withdrawal in 1710.

come to terms with scientific discoveries, and indeed to use science to defend Christian belief. Clergymen were at the forefront of intellectual life, and forced to remain there by the refusal of the post-Revolution State to silence dissenters and deists. From an eccentricity in the 1660s, 'latitudinarianism' developed into a mainstream position after 1689 and into an orthodoxy after 1714, before losing some ground to a resurgent 'High Church' party after 1760.[26] In Poland, the Catholic Church was hostile to scientific theories which undermined the literal truth of the Bible. The Counter-Reformation was in some ways the victim of its own success. Its intellectual standard, high in the early seventeenth century, fell as the ranks of Protestant *szlachta* were decimated by Jesuit education, the sensuousness and spectacle of Catholic liturgy, poorer prospects of office, and, especially after the Swedish 'Deluge' of 1655–6, the growing hostility of their Catholic neighbours. Without the spur of competition, the education offered by the Jesuits and other orders declined in quality. They taught formulaic Latin, which proved a nobleman's 'learning' by ruining his Polish. By the early eighteenth century, Polish religiosity was provincial, theatrical, and bereft of any real theological content.[27]

Sarmatism had its origins as a racial or genealogical theory in the sixteenth century. The separate ancestors of the nobility, whether Polish, Lithuanian, or Ruthenian, were supposed to be the ancient tribe of Sarmatians, mentioned in Roman accounts, who, rather like the Franks in Gaul (according to Boulainvilliers) founded their nobility on the right of conquest. Sarmatism came to encompass a feeling that 'Sarmatians' were basically different from other Europeans, which found expression in a distinctive Sarmatian culture. The baroque taste for contrast and theatricality assumed a colourful and oriental guise in the dress, rhetoric, manners, and lifestyle of the *szlachta*. The realistic 'Sarmatian portrait', often attached to the subject's coffin, was a notable contribution to European art. Sarmatism gave a lasting cultural unity to the *szlachta* across the Commonwealth, but it proved incapable of adapting to changing circumstances. It became inseparable from the 'golden freedom' and intolerant Catholicism. The cult of agrarian virtue led to deepening insularity.

---

[26] G. Holmes, *The Making of a Great Power: Late Stuart and Early Georgian Britain 1660–1722* (London, 1993), 143–59, 350–87. R. Kroll *et al.* (eds.), *Philosophy, Science and Religion in England 1640–1700* (Cambridge, 1992). J. Gascoigne, *Cambridge in the Age of the Enlightenment: Science, Religion and Politics from the Restoration to the French Revolution* (Cambridge, 1989). Cf. J. Spurr, ' "Latitudinarianism" and the Restoration Church', *HJ*, 31 (1988).

[27] Tazbir, 'Wazowie i barok', in *Zarys Historii Polski*, 281–2, 290. Kuchowicz, *Człowiek polskiego baroku*, 229–30, 236–9.

By the eighteenth century, Sarmatism had rotted into 'a synonym of conservatism, bigotry, backwardness, and ignorance'. Suspicion of all things
foreign was complemented by self-satisfaction and a glorification of the
national past.[28] Of course, eighteenth-century Englishmen were hardly
free of xenophobia and complacency. Those faults did not, however, lead
to the ossification of the State (although early nineteenth-century critics of
'old corruption' might have been of a different opinion). Many eighteenth-
century Englishmen believed that their constitution was incapable of
improvement, but in the quarter of a century after 1688 it had been transformed into a powerful and flexible organism, capable of coping with the
strains of war and representing diverse economic interests.[29]

The faults of the Seym, notably the catastrophic *liberum veto*, have often
been identified as the main cause of Poland's decline. But it is going too
far to argue, as did Rostworowski, that had the Seym functioned properly in the early eighteenth century, an ordered parliamentary oligarchy
would have taken the place of anarchic oligarchy.[30] We must delve
deeper, to the political culture that obstructed reform. The thesis that
the English Parliament was better educated and more 'mature' than the
Polish at the turn of the sixteenth and seventeenth centuries,[31] even if
correct, does not seem to be particularly helpful in explaining the contrasting development of the two polities. Both had time enough to absorb
the harsh tannins of youth, but only the English became a powerful, supple,
complex, and long-lived vintage. One might say that the promising Polish *cru* was spoilt by an excess of oxygen and turned sour. In England, the
oxygen of liberty was balanced by the inert nitrogen of monarchism.

War galvanized England; it petrified Poland. The same quarter of a
century raised England to a great power and eclipsed Poland. This was
not inevitable. It is not altogether inconceivable that Augustus II might
have emerged the victor of the Great Northern War, and transformed
Saxony–Poland–Lithuania into the leading political and economic power
of Central and Eastern Europe. On the other hand, not much saved England
from further constitutional and religious conflict under 'James III' as an
appanage of France. As it turned out, however, the mistakes of James II
and Louis XIV produced such a patent threat to Englishmen's religion,

[28] S. Cynarski, 'The ideology of Sarmatism in Poland', *Polish Western Affairs*, 32 (1992).
Tazbir, 'Stosunek do obcych w dobie baroku' and Michalski, 'Sarmatyzm a europeizacja
Polski w XVIII wieku', both in Z. Stefanowska (ed.), *Swojskość i cudzoziemszczyzna w dziejach kultury polskiej* (Warsaw, 1973). On Sarmatian culture see Kuchowicz, *Człowiek polskiego baroku*, and M. Bogucka, *Staropolskie obyczaje w XVI–XVII wieku* (Warsaw, 1994).
[29] Langford, *Polite and Commercial People*, ch. 14.   [30] *Historia powszechna*, 575.
[31] S. Hołdys, 'Sejm polski i parlament angielski XVI–XVII wieku', *PH*, 71 (1980).

property, and liberty that England's political classes had no choice but to stomach the distasteful creation of a powerful but accountable fiscal-military state. A similar act of realism on the part of the *szlachta*, all the more necessary as Poland was protected by no sea and no navy, was precluded by its inordinate fear of royal power. In England, the heritage of Tory ideology sweetened the pill. Geopolitics had much to do with it, but perhaps the best explanation of the divergent fortunes of England and Poland is to be found in their political cultures. Sharing certain concepts, but greatly differing in emphasis, they conditioned the contrasting responses of the two political nations to international challenge. One can go further and argue that none of Europe's 'republics' survived the eighteenth century and the revolutionary wars that followed, except Sweden, saved by a monarchical *coup d'état* in 1772, and England, protected by the English Channel, which was hardly a republic at all.

II

The broad constitutional similarities between England and Poland, coupled with the evident success of the one and the failure of the other, would seem to have made England an obvious model for the few Polish reformers. Until the 1760s, this was not so. As Chapter 3 will show, they rarely mentioned the English constitution. England had to overcome a particularly deep hostility among the *szlachta*. The Sarmatian image of England cannot be ascribed simply to intellectual rigor mortis and xenophobia. Economic and political factors played their part, although mainly negatively. Anglo-Polish trade reached its peak in the early seventeenth century, and the large colony of British, mainly Scottish, merchants at Danzig acted as a cultural link with the Commonwealth. In the later seventeenth century, however, Polish exports became less important to British trade as a whole.[32] The political situation of England and Poland in the sixteenth and seventeenth centuries never necessitated any sustained or intensive relations—projects for marriage alliances were never concluded and diplomatic incidents never led to war. Such bouts of interest peaked in the early seventeenth century, when Poles like Zygmunt Myszkowski, Jakub Sobieski, and Jerzy Ossoliński visited England. Thereafter the interest fell off.[33]

---

[32] E. A. Mierzwa, *Anglia a Polska w pierwszej połowie XVII wieku* (Warsaw, 1986), ch. 7. Idem, *Anglia a Polska w epoce Jana III Sobieskiego* (Łódź, 1988), part II.

[33] See Mierzwa, *Anglia a Polska w pierwszej połowie XVII wieku*, chs. 1–6, J. Jasnowski, *England and Poland in the XVIth and XVIIth Centuries (Political Relations)* (London, 1948), and R. Przeździecki, *Diplomatic Ventures and Adventures: Some Experiences of British Envoys at the Court of Poland* (London, 1953).

The mutual images of England and Poland were formed mainly by religious conflicts. In the sixteenth century, both states veered between Protestantism and Catholicism, and the opportunities for interchange were extensive. Jan Łaski was active in the English Reformation as 'John a Lasco' before returning to Poland to try to unite the Protestants. Both English Catholics, especially Jesuits, and Protestant sectaries found a haven in the Commonwealth. In this context, Polish Catholics denounced Elizabeth I as a 'popess' (*papieżyca*), whose hands were stained with the blood of Catholic innocents, while Protestants idolized her. Francis Bacon replied to one particularly coarse attack, while the refusal and inability of Sigismund III to stem the onslaught on Elizabeth and James I strained diplomatic relations.[34] Stanisław Krzystanowicz visited England in 1605 and the following year wrote a pamphlet, *Examen catholicum edicti anglicani*, criticizing anti-Catholic legislation, which was widely read in England.[35] The pattern established in the sixteenth century lasted, though declining in intensity, into the eighteenth. The Jesuit Piotr Skarga's *Żywoty świętych* ('Lives of the Saints', 1579) went through countless editions and graphically described the deaths of English martyrs to several generations of Poles. A Scottish Protestant, perhaps a second-generation immigrant, Victorinus Euthanasius, translated *Manchester al mondo*, a devotional tract by Henry Montagu, Earl of Manchester, into Polish in 1648 at the Mohyla Academy in Kiev, and dedicated it to the Orthodox magnate Adam Kysil.[36] Both the Calvinists and the *Unitas Fratrum* or Bohemian Brethren established links with the Church of England. Students travelled in both directions, and the rector of the Bohemians' school at Leszno, Jan Komenský (Comenius) acquired a measure of fame in England. Daniel Ernest Jabłoński, a leading defender of Calvinist rights, made friends with the future Archbishop of Canterbury, William Wake, during his time at Oxford (1680–3). As the Catholic reaction intensified in the later seventeenth and early eighteenth centuries, Polish Protestants sought financial and political support in Britain. In doing so they consolidated the image of Poland as a land afflicted by Catholic fanaticism.[37]

---

[34] N. Davies, *God's Playground: A History of Poland* (2 vols.; Oxford 1981), vol. 1, 189–90. Tazbir, 'Elżbieta I Tudor w opinii staropolskiej', *Odrodzenie i Reformacja w Polsce*, 24 (1989).

[35] G. Gömöri, 'Polish authors in Ben Jonson's Library', *Polish Review*, 38 (1993).

[36] R. Koropeckyj, 'The Kiev Mohyla Collegium and seventeenth-century Polish–English literary contacts: a Polish translation of Henry Montagu's *Manchester al Mondo*', *Harvard Ukrainian Studies*, 8 (1984).

[37] N. Hans, 'Polish Protestants and their connections with England and Holland in the 17th and 18th centuries', *SEER*, 37 (1958–9), 196–205. W. Kriegseisen, *Ewangelicy polscy i litewscy w epoce saskiej (1696–1763): Sytuacja prawna, Organizacja i stosunki: międzywyznaniowe*

However, as late as 1683 a Tory propagandist could credibly indict Poland as a land of anarchic religious liberty by making it the setting for a satirical scheme of toleration for Presbyterian dissenters, and all other enemies of political and ecclesiastical order.[38]

The Socinians, known as the Polish Brethren, quickly caused a stir in Europe with their anti-Trinitarian heresy and their social egalitarianism. Most of their works reached England in Latin, but those of Jan Crell (Crellius) were translated into English. Some of the Brethren visited England in 1618, and contacts increased after the closure of the Raków academy in 1638, especially after the Socinians' banishment in 1658. Some studied at Cambridge, where they met latitudinarian clergymen like John Tillotson and scientists like Newton. In Holland during the 1680s, they exercised a particular influence on Locke and the other Whig exiles, including some of the future deists.[39] The fame of the Socinians should not obscure the wider picture. As England became overwhelmingly Protestant and Poland (that is, the *szlachta*) more firmly Catholic, real contacts ebbed, leaving stereotypes behind.

Ironically, the achievements of Polish science were more appreciated in seventeenth-century England than in Poland. England's élite readily accepted the Copernican solar system, and by the end of the seventeenth century it was being taught to students of navigation. Samuel Hartlib from Elbing studied at Cambridge in the 1620s, and helped lay the foundations for the Royal Society. The astronomer Hevelius frequently sent his observations to the Society and became a Fellow in 1664. Edmond Halley visited him in Danzig in 1679. The works of the alchemist Michał Sędziwoj were extremely popular in English scientific circles, and Newton read them closely. The mathematics of Jan Brożek also made an impact in England. None of these scientists, often Germanophone Lutheran burghers, won due renown in his native land during his lifetime. John III's patronage of science stood out against the *szlachta*'s and *magnateria*'s lack of interest.[40]

(Warsaw, 1996), 129, 139–40, 153–4, 264. *A Short View of the Continual Sufferings and Heavy Oppressions of the Episcopal Reformed Churches, formerly in Bohemia, and now in Great Poland and Polish Prussia* (London, 1716).

[38] *The Saints Liberty of Conscience in the New Kingdom of Poland proposed for the Consolation of the Distressed Brethren* (Warsaw [London], 1683). A number of Whigs, their names appended with *-iski*, were listed as 'Grand Commissioners and Farmers of Liberty of Conscience'.

[39] Hans, 'Polish Protestants', 205–11. Mierzwa, *Anglia a Polska w epoce Jana III*, 126–31. Voltaire, *Lettres Philosophiques*, Lettre VII.

[40] Mierzwa, *Anglia a Polska w epoce Jana III*, 106–13. K. Targosz, *Jan III Sobieski mecenasem nauk i uczonych* (Wrocław, 1991). Idem, *Jan Heweliusz: uczony-artysta* (Wrocław, 1986).

In the realm of political thought, Bishop Wawrzyniec Goślicki's *De optimo senatore*, published in Venice in 1568, appeared in English as *The Counsellor* in 1598. Goślicki (Goslicius) praised mixed governments of monarchy, aristocracy, and democracy, but argued that an educated senate was best equipped to govern. The translator left out Goślicki's preference for elective monarchy and his condemnation of the Reformation.[41] Cromwell was reportedly interested in the Polish constitution as a model in 1653,[42] but there was less interest in the other direction. When Wawrzyniec Chlebowski boasted of the golden Polish freedom, and compared the felicities of various nations, he left out England altogether.[43] The Civil War hardly produced an echo, and Poles greeted the Glorious Revolution with silence. Half a century later, Władysław Łubienski (a future primate) denounced it as a rebellion of heretics against their lawful Catholic king.[44] A fresh translation of Goślicki, titled *The Accomplished Senator*, was made in 1733 by William Oldisworth. The dedication (to Walpole and other leading Whigs) illustrates some of the differences between Polish and English political culture in the first half of the eighteenth century. As 'Advocates for *Arbitrary Power*' had often used Poland's disorders to illustrate the dangers of political liberty, Oldisworth felt obliged to defend Goślicki from the suspicion of republicanism, by insisting that Goślicki's strictures on tyrants could not refer to a limited monarchy. 'What Gozliski [*sic*] hath advanced in *Defence* of *Loyalty* and *Liberty*, and to make these Two Principles compatible, will I hope deserve the Attention of such Patriots, as are alike Zealous for the *Prerogatives* of the *Crown*, and the *Interests* of the *People*.' He added that Poland's constitution had avoided the convulsions suffered by '*Popular States* and *Absolute Monarchies*', he eulogized the bravery of Poles and insisted that Englishmen, who shared their love of liberty, give them a hearing. This rare Polonophile found the sixteenth-century theorist of *monarchia mixta* relevant to the limited monarchy of the Hanoverians.[45] It was not only

---

[41] T. Bałuk-Ulewiczowa, 'The Senator of Wawrzyniec Goślicki and the Elizabethan Counsellor', in S. Fiszman (ed.), *The Polish Renaissance in its European Context* (Bloomington, Ind., 1988).

[42] Jasnowski, *England and Poland*, 52.

[43] *Wolność złota Korony Polskiey nad insze pod słońcem narody . . .* (Cracow, 1611), 7.

[44] Libiszowska, 'Echa burżuazyjnej rewolucji angielskiej w Polsce', *Przegląd Nauk Historycznych i Społecznych*, 3 (1953). Konopczyński, 'Anglia a Polska', 95. W. Łubicński, *Świat we wszystkich swoich częsciach większych i mniejszych . . .* (Breslau, 1740), 456. This work was designed as a kind of gazetteer to the world, and aimed at the wealthier *szlachta*.

[45] *The Accomplished Senator in Two Books, Written Originally in Latin, By Gozliski, Done into English, from the Edition Printed at Venice, in the Year 1568. By Mr. Oldisworth* (London, 1733).

Tory monarchists who used Poland to attack Whig 'republicans'; Daniel
Defoe's savage mockery of the Seym was aimed at the Tories—at their
opposition to religious toleration and the war with France.[46]

Up to the end of the seventeenth century, English and Polish perceptions of each other were moulded by religious acrimony and political
indifference. Contacts were based upon Polish Protestants and British
Catholics. Poland probably had a higher profile in England than England
in Poland; Sobieski's victories, for example, were avidly reported in the
English press, and Bernard O'Connor gave an accurate and detailed account
of the Commonwealth in his *History of Poland* (1698).[47] To the Poles, England was a rather insignificant strife-torn kingdom on the edge of Europe.
Very few magnates visited England after Jan and Marek Sobieski in 1647.
Wacław Rzewuski, the future hetman, was an isolated exception about
1725.[48] By the 1720s, however, England was unquestionably a world power,
and by the 1730s, Poland was established as the laughing-stock of Europe,
dismissed by Englishmen (Oldisworth excepted) in truisms and clichés
about religious fanaticism, social oppression, and political anarchy. England's
image in eighteenth-century Poland was slow to improve.

Those Poles who did take an interest denied that England was truly
free, and saw in Parliament a hopelessly corrupt instrument of royal despotism. Augustus II's frequent use of the *limita* (an agreed prorogation of
the Seym, and its reconvening at a later date without new elections) raised
fears of abuses in the English style. The king would be given time to
soften his adversaries with corruption or threats, and thereby introduce
absolutum dominium. It is doubtful, though, that any of the protesters were
well informed about Charles II's use of prorogation to great effect during the Exclusion Crisis. The *limita* certainly provoked an analogy with
the Septennial Act of 1716, which extended to seven years the maximum
life of a parliament (and so postponed the next general election from 1718
to 1722). The Seym of 1726 outlawed the practice.[49] If the *szlachta* was
inclined to look to any foreign models, its favourite was decrepit Venice,
whose doge was chained even more securely than the King of Poland.
The Swiss cantons also attracted some attention, as a result of their militia system. Some writers fancied a resemblance to the general levy of the
szlachta (*pospolite ruszenie*), which by now was more theory than reality.[50]

---

[46] [Defoe], *The Dyet of Poland, a Satyr, by Anglipoloski* . . . (Danzig [London], 1705).
[47] Mierzwa, *Anglia a Polska w epoce Jana III*, part IV.
[48] Z. Zielińska, 'Rzewuski, Wacław', *PSB*, 34 (1992), 169–80.
[49] Konopczyński, 'Anglia a Polska', 95–6. Lukowski, *Liberty's Folly*, 93, 153.
[50] Rostworowski, 'Republikanizm polski i anglosaski', 96. Grześkowiak-Krwawicz, '*Rara
avis* czy wolni wśród wolnych?', 171.

More potent still than the distrust of the English constitution were traditional religious antagonisms. Old wounds were reopened by the Tumult of Thorn in 1724. After a Protestant riot during a Catholic procession, ten Protestants, including some of the town council, were beheaded. Prussian propaganda found a ready audience and response in England. Pamphlets rolled off the presses, denouncing the barbarity of the Jesuits. The English government seized the opportunity to attack Jacobitism and construct a Protestant coalition by protesting vigorously, to be answered equally forcefully by the Polish recapitulation of the wrongs done to English Catholics. The Poles were saddled irreversibly with a reputation for fanaticism, whereas in Polish eyes the English were confirmed as perfidious and hypocritical heretics, the sworn enemies of the true faith.[51]

In an expressive coda to the traditional pattern of Anglo-Polish contacts, Bunyan's *Pilgrim's Progress* was translated into Polish in 1764—in Königsberg, for Polish-speaking Protestants in Prussia and the Commonwealth.[52] The Sarmatian attitude to England is exemplified by two works published towards the end of the Saxon period. Benedykt Chmielowski's widely read compendium of information and superstition, *Nowe Ateny*, played the familiar tune of grievances and insults in the section entitled

Już nie *Angelica, natio Anglica*: w Anglii Błędów Zaszczepienie, Jest od Katolickiego Kościoła opadnienie. Atlas o zgubney Anglików Schizmie, Przez ktorą Henryk VIII Kościoła zrazu *Defensor*, potym stał się Boga y Religii Katolickiey *Offensor*, y owszem *Catholicismi* w Synu swoim Edowardzie y Corce Elżbiecie formalny *Eversor*.

(No longer Angels, the nation of Angles: the implantation of errors in England is its fall from the Catholic Church. An atlas of the ruinous schism of the English, through which Henry VIII, once the Defender, became the enemy of God and the Catholic Religion, and the destroyer of Catholicism in his son Edward and daughter Elizabeth.)[53]

---

[51] S. Salmonowicz, 'The Toruń Uproar of 1724', *APH*, 47 (1983). G. Król, 'Anglia wobec wydarzeń toruńskich 1724 roku', *Zapiski Historyczne*, 56 (1991).

[52] Sinko, 'Polskie przekłady "The Pilgrim's Progress" Johna Bunyana', *Pam. Lit.*, 68 (1977).

[53] *Nowe Ateny, albo akademia wszelkiey scyencyi pełna na różne tytuły, iak na szkolne classes podzielona* (8 vols.; Lwów, 1756), vol. 4, 83–119. *Nowe Ateny* is often quoted to demonstrate the intellectual barrenness of the 'Saxon night', but the charge is better applied to its readers than to its author, who maintained an ironic distance towards the sensational tales he included. S. Grzybowski, 'Z dziejów popularyzacji nauki w czasach saskich', *Studia i materiały z dziejów nauki polskiej*, seria A, 7 (1965), 111–32. The Jesuit Jan Poszakowski spread the same message in more detail to a narrower readership in his *Historya o początku odszczepieństwa Kościoła Anglikańskiego y weyściu do niego herezyi kalwińskiey . . .* (Warsaw, 1748).

Szymon Majchrowicz's *Trwałość szczęśliwa królestw* ('The Happy Endurance of Kingdoms') contained the ultimate in Sarmatian wishful thinking. Published a year after the end of the Seven Years' War, which had dramatically worsened the Commonwealth's international position, its main thesis was that the supreme felicity of any nation was liberty. God had rewarded *Polonia semper fidelis* with the golden freedom. Free nations which had fallen into heresy were punished with the loss of their freedom. The English were in the process of losing theirs—the only proof offered was high taxes, paid also by the nobility.[54]

At this point we can tie some ends together. In the year of Stanisław August's election, Majchrowicz epitomized the Sarmatian view of England—an abhorrence of Protestant heresy, a conviction of the illusory nature of English freedom, and a total lack of awareness of European realities. The yawning gulf between Poland and England was in large measure the result of the political culture personified by Majchrowicz, which combined rigid conservatism and an inveterate suspicion of kings with an escape from the realities of power into comforting myths and a reliance on Divine Providence. English political culture steeled itself to meet an international threat at the turn of the seventeenth and eighteenth centuries, and compromised some of its dearest tenets. By the time Majchrowicz was writing, a small but increasing number of Poles were ready to confront reality and looked to corrupt, heretical England for a model.

How did this transformation come about? The traditional channels of Anglo-Polish exchange had all but dried up, and were in any case virtually irrelevant to the overwhelming Catholic majority. A new medium was needed. That medium was the European Enlightenment. As the Enlightenment crept cautiously into Poland, attitudes to England slowly began to change.

---

[54] *Trwałość szczęśliwa Krolestw albo ich smutny upadek wolnym narodom przed oczy stawione, na utrzymanie nieoszacowanej szczęśliwości swoiey* (4 vols.; Lwów, 1764), esp. vol. 1, 181–201, vol. 2, 62–70, vol. 3, 64, 110, 150. Rostworowski, 'Theatrum polityczne czasów saskich', in idem, *Popioły i korzenie: Szkice historyczne i rodzinne* (Cracow, 1985), 55–6. See Grzybowski, 'Z dziejów popularyzacji', 133–45.

2

The Enlightenment and England

What is Enlightenment? The emergence of man from 'self-imposed immaturity'; an individual or collective inability, fear, or downright refusal to think for oneself. Free thinking, the essence of the answer given by Immanuel Kant in 1784, remains the best definition of an elusive phenomenon, which has attracted tags as diverse as reason, nature, and utility. The other essential point of Kant's answer was that Enlightenment was a process. Kant did not believe his age was an enlightened one, but he did believe it was an age of Enlightenment.[1]

The Enlightenment was a process in which more and more Europeans came to use their own reason to view, question, and comprehend the world and universe around them. It was marked, in varying degrees, by a doubting of traditional Christianity reliant on revelation, increased toleration of other religious views, and in general by criticism of the religious, political, and social status quo. The doctrine of original sin tended to give way to an optimistic view that man was naturally good and perfectible. Christian theories of natural law, the divinely ordained principles of the natural order, were secularized and became by degrees assertions of the natural rights of man. This contributed to a cult of 'nature', however vaguely defined, which prepared the ground for Romanticism's later rejection of reason in favour of feeling. The increased value put on man gave rise both to a growing humanitarianism and to utilitarianism, which dogmatically pursued the 'general good' and universal happiness. The principles of Enlightenment ultimately pointed to political liberty, increased popular participation in politics, and the breakdown of social orders based mainly on birth, but in the short run, Enlightenment increased the divide between élites and masses, and was often fostered by absolutist monarchies. For Kant and many others, it applied especially, but not exclusively, to questions of religion. Far from being the 'ideology of the rising bourgeoisie', Enlightenment came overwhelmingly from

---

[1] 'An Answer to the Question "What is Enlightenment?"', in *Kant's Political Writings*, ed. H. Reiss (Cambridge, 1971). Taking Kant as his starting-point, Rostworowski emphasizes that free thinking need not mean the aggressively anti-clerical 'freethinking' of the deists. *Historia powszechna*, 174–6.

above, from the most educated sections of society, and self-consciously combated the 'social forces' of ignorance, superstition, and fanaticism.[2] Precisely because its adherents saw Enlightenment as a didactic process and not as abstract speculation, enlightened ideas were communicated in an unprecedentedly accessible manner. Enlightenment was promoted not only in costly tomes in folio or quarto, but also in handy little volumes, in newspapers and magazines; not in impenetrable Latin treatises, but in straightforward prose, epigrammatic couplets, and devastating *bons mots*. Europe's universities often lagged behind provincial academies, scientific societies, reading-rooms, salons, Masonic lodges, and coffee-houses. Never had the leading thinkers of an age reached such a wide audience, and never was an age so preoccupied with the practical impact of ideas.

The Enlightenment was a process which took place over space as well as time. Ideas were transmitted and retransmitted across frontiers, but in the process they were modified. The prevailing westerly winds carried the seeds of the richly variegated flora of the French Enlightenment to diverse soils across Europe, while cross-pollination with local strains produced a multiplicity of new subspecies. However, southerly and easterly breezes provided some variety, and bracing northerlies brought France seeds from England. The former picture of the wider European Enlightenment as a transplant from Paris, dominated by a few great names, has rightly been displaced by an emphasis on national context.[3] However, national and, for that matter, local and regional context ought to mean more than the rediscovery of forgotten figures of merely local significance, of Panglosses in Thundertentronkhs. The Enlightenment cannot be split into discrete mini-Enlightenments, owing little or nothing to one another, and united only by a general disapproval of religious fanaticism. It was self-consciously international, and to be 'enlightened' (*éclairé, aufgeklärt, illuminato, oświecony*) almost by definition meant open to ideas from abroad.

The nature of that openness underwent a significant evolution. The early Enlightenment crystallized in the self-styled 'Republic of Letters'. This loose association of writers and publishers, which flourished from the 1680s to the 1720s, was centred upon Huguenot refugees. Made stateless by religious intolerance, a cosmopolitan identity came easily to them.

---

[2] D. E. D. Beales, 'Social Forces and Enlightened Policies', in H. M. Scott (ed.), *Enlightened Absolutism: Reform and Reformers in Later Eighteenth-Century Europe* (London, 1990).
[3] Most explicitly in R. Porter and M. Teich (eds.), *The Enlightenment in National Context* (Cambridge, 1981).

In the Netherlands in the 1680s, they associated with Polish Socinians, the victims of Sarmatian Catholicism, English Whigs, persecuted for their audacious assault on divine right monarchy, and the Dutch disciples of Spinoza. In such company, and forced to argue for religious toleration, some of the Huguenots made the crossing from Calvinism to freethinking. The most brilliant was Pierre Bayle. Many came to England. A number of them, such as Abel Boyer, Pierre Coste, and Pierre Des Maizeaux, made their living as translators or as correspondents of Francophone periodicals in the Netherlands. At the very moment when the vernacular's displacement of Latin as the language of learning threatened to isolate English thought, the Republic of Letters surmounted the obstacle.[4]

The journals and translations of the Huguenots were the first ways for English thought to reach the Continent. Increasingly, however, influential Europeans came to see for themselves the country which had so startlingly challenged French hegemony in the War of the Spanish Succession, and which scaled vertiginous peaks in the Seven Years' War. While the reception of the *philosophes* in English literary and high society in the 1760s continued the cosmopolitan camaraderie of the Republic of Letters, a continent-wide patriotic spirit of emulation was spreading among less fêted visitors. Fashionable aristocrats, learned professors, and aspiring journalists all took notes on the most diverse subjects, from crop rotations to the provisions for dealing with beggars. The cosmopolitan aspect of the later eighteenth century is epitomized by the Francophone Prince de Ligne, equally at home in Paris, Vienna, and St Petersburg; yet as purely dynastic loyalty began to wane, it was also a time of developing state and national patriotism, out of which sprang the nationalist creeds of the future.[5]

A cosmopolitan outlook naturally facilitates the adoption of foreign ideas on the basis of their universal verity, but a patriotic (as opposed to a xenophobic) one encompasses the adaptation of foreign ideas and models to meet national needs. This relationship between cosmopolitanism and patriotism in the Enlightenment lies at the heart of Franco Venturi's vast

---

[4] See P. Hazard, *The European Mind (1680–1715)* (London, 1953), 68–73, 80–115, and J. Almagor, *Pierre Des Maizeaux (1673–1745), Journalist, and English Correspondent for Franco-Dutch Periodicals, 1700–1720* (Amsterdam, 1989). The as yet unpublished work of Jonathan Israel reveals a vital Dutch and especially Spinozist contribution to the *radical* Early Enlightenment, and (more controversially) downplays the importance of England. 'Who began the European Enlightenment: the English or the Dutch?' (paper delivered in Oxford, 13 Oct. 1995).

[5] P. Hazard, *European Thought in the Eighteenth Century* (Harmondsworth, 1965), 471–93.

synthesis, *Settecento riformatore*.[6] Venturi has also traced some of the inter-actions between national and regional Enlightenments, and sketched out a general chronology and geography of the Enlightenment.[7] Adopting a similar approach, we shall focus here upon the reception of English thought, the English constitution, and English culture in the European Enlightenment.[8] The 'English Enlightenment' is not really relevant, but we may observe in passing that it presents persistent difficulties in defini-tion. Perhaps that is the outcome of trying to project a movement, which became self-conscious elsewhere, back to the country in which it found so many of its sources.[9]

I

Modern science, or natural philosophy, was one of the pillars of the Enlight-enment. The destruction of the certainties of the Aristotelian universe was not, of course, the work of Englishmen. Copernicus, Galileo, Descartes, and others had done that, at least for Europe's tiny intellectual élite. But it was Francis Bacon, an early seventeenth-century scientific patron, who advocated the empirical and inductive investigation of natural phenom-ena, and it was under his influence that two brilliant generations of sci-entists changed for ever the educated men's understanding of the world. Robert Boyle, Robert Hooke, Edmond Halley, and above all, Isaac Newton made it seem as though observation, experiments, and mathematical induction would soon unveil all the remaining secrets of the universe.

The Royal Society and the French Academy of Sciences maintained close links from their inception in the 1660s, and Hans Sloane and the Abbé Bignon even managed to send each other books and papers via diplomatic channels in wartime. Although the impact of the Society's *Philosophical Transactions* was limited by the unfamiliar English language,

[6] See J. Robertson, 'Franco Venturi's Enlightenment', in *Past and Present*, 137 (1992).
[7] F. Venturi, *Utopia and Reform in the Enlightenment* (Cambridge, 1971), 117–36, and *Italy and the Enlightenment: Studies in a Cosmopolitan Century* (London, 1972), 1–32. The extensive chapters on the Enlightenment in Rostworowski's *Historia powszechna*, which dis-cuss the changing 'geography of culture', are regrettably unavailable in a Western language.
[8] See J. S. Bromley, 'Britain and Europe in the eighteenth century', *History*, 66 (1981), for an overview of British borrowings *from* the Continent.
[9] Two broadly similar general interpretations, arguing that the early victory of the Enlightenment made it uncontroversial thereafter, are R. Porter, 'The Enlightenment in England', in Porter and Teich (eds.), *The Enlightenment in National Context*, and A. M. Wilson, 'The Enlightenment came first to England', in S. B. Baxter (ed.), *England's Rise to Greatness 1660–1760* (Berkeley, Calif., 1983). Venturi, *Utopia and Reform* and *Italy and the Enlightenment*, and M. C. Jacob, *The Radical Enlightenment: Pantheists, Freemasons and Repub-licans* (London, 1981) attach greater importance to the English deists and their battles.

they were reviewed by the *Journal des Sçavans* from 1665, and also by the *Acta Eruditorum* of Leipzig. The discoveries of English astronomers were swiftly appreciated in Paris, while the work of Boyle probably attracted most attention. By the end of the seventeenth century, an increasing amount of information about scientific developments in England was available from Dutch-based periodicals, such as the *Histoire des Ouvrages des Sçavans*. They were joined by a growing number of French journals after the Peace of Utrecht in 1713.[10]

The publication of Newton's daunting *Naturalis philosophiae principia mathematica* in 1687 passed virtually unnoticed on the Continent. Indeed, the *Principia* required much explanation by Newton's disciples, notably Richard Bentley, Samuel Clarke, John Keill, and David Gregory, before it was appreciated in England. Willem Jacob 's Gravesande, a professor at Leiden, took up the cause abroad. Apart from writing an *Introductio ad philosophiam Neutonianum* (1720–1), he promoted Newtonianism as an editor of the *Journal Littéraire*, stressing that while Cartesian vortices could not account for observed planetary motion, gravitation did so exactly. The French Cartesians saw in 'attraction' a mutant scholastic animism, and hit back by ridiculing it as a mysterious occult force, although Malebranche and his followers did significantly modify the system of vortices. The controversy reached its height when Louis de Maupertuis became the first academician fully to espouse Newtonianism in 1732. Newton's *Opticks* (1704) made a greater initial impact, as Étienne Geoffroy gave a summary to the Academy. Clarke's Latin translation (1706) and independent verifications of the experiments ensured that Coste's French translation (1720, 1722) was only the final step towards the general acceptance of Newton's theories of light and colour.[11]

Unlike Newton, who was careless about disseminating his ideas, John Locke took pains to see that his philosophy was rapidly diffused on the Continent.[12] He arranged for a detailed '*abrégé*' of his *Essay on Human*

[10] G. Bonno, *La culture et la civilisation britanniques devant l'opinion française de la Paix d'Utrecht aux "Lettres Philosophiques" 1713–1734, Transactions of the American Philosophical Society*, new series, 38 (1948), 123–5.

[11] Bonno, *La culture et la civilisation britanniques*, 125–38, and P. Brunet, *L'introduction des théories de Newton en France au XVIIIe siècle avant 1738* (Paris, 1931), should be corrected by H. Guerlac, *Newton on the Continent* (Ithaca, NY, 1981), chs. 3–5. On 's Gravesande, see Jacob, *Radical Enlightenment*, 185–7, and *passim*. The sheer difficulty of the Mathematics accounted for the still later reception of Newtonianism at French universities than among the academicians. See L. W. B. Brockliss, *French Higher Education in the Seventeenth and Eighteenth Centuries* (Oxford, 1987), 350–77.

[12] Bonno, *La culture et la civilisation britanniques*, 77, 80–6. Idem, *Les Relations Intellectuelles de Locke avec la France* (Berkeley, Calif., 1955), 152–6.

Understanding to be published in Jean Leclerc's *Bibliothèque Universelle* in 1688, two years before the whole work was published in English. He supervised Coste's translation, which appeared in 1700. This translation, re-issued in 1723 and 1729, was read by all the major figures of the European Enlightenment, from Montesquieu to Muratori. Locke's assertion that the human mind was a *tabula rasa*, devoid of innate ideas, challenged the Cartesian system at its most basic premiss. The mind had 'all the materials of Reason and Knowledge . . . from Experience'. Ideas were formed by 'sensations' of external objects and the internal operations of the mind.[13] If experience was all, then pedagogy was of vital importance. Locke's *Some Thoughts Concerning Education* (1693) was translated by Coste in 1695, and was repeatedly reprinted. By 1721, Leclerc could write that it was not less esteemed in France and Holland than in England. Locke, revolted by the brutality and corrupting influence of the public schools, advocated individual instruction, but Charles Rollin, rector of the Sorbonne, adapted his prescriptions to a school environment in his *Traité des Études* (1726). The success of Locke's educational thought aided the progress of his 'sensationist' philosophy. The Cartesian *Journal des Sçavans* found that its policy of silence failed to stem the tide.[14]

Empiricism made far slower progress in Germany, as the systematic approach of the Natural Law philosophers, headed by Christian Wolff, was well entrenched. The Newtonian system was treated as just that, a system. Wolff's rationalism was easily reconciled with revelation, and for that reason he was acceptable to Catholic philosophers dissatisfied with scholasticism. Most common, however, in Catholic Germany, Italy, and Poland, was an eclecticism that taught Wolffianism, Cartesianism, Newtonianism, Lockean sensationism, experimental science, aspects of scholasticism, and other philosophies, judging them all in the light of revelation.[15]

Both Newton and Locke saw themselves as sincere Christians, for all their doubts on the Trinity. They wished to provide a new and secure basis for the defence of Christian belief. Locke essayed to do so by defining the limits of reason; all that lay beyond he left to revelation.[16] The French

[13] *An Essay Concerning Human Understanding*, ed. P. H. Nidditch (Oxford, 1975), 104–5.
[14] Bonno, *La culture et la civilisation britanniques*, 80, 87.
[15] See B. Bianco, 'Wolffianismus und Katholische Aufklärung: Storchenaus' Lehre von Menschen' in H. Klueting (ed.), *Katholische Aufklärung—Aufklärung in katholischen Deutschland* (Studien zum achtzehnten Jahrhundert, 15; Hamburg, 1993); Rostworowski, *Historia powszechna*, 443–5, 632; and see below, pp. 68, 70–3.
[16] See J. Brooke, 'The God of Isaac Newton' and P. Rattansi, 'Newton and the Wisdom of the Ancients' in J. Fauvel *et al.* (eds.), *Let Newton Be!* (Oxford, 1988) and J. Dunn, *Locke* (Past Masters, Oxford, 1984), 60–86.

Jesuits, who had long been suspicious of Descartes's philosophy, gave the denial of innate ideas a guarded welcome in their *Mémoires de Trévoux*. Claude Buffier, a leading Jesuit philosopher respected by Voltaire, agreed with Locke that the truths of revelation were beyond, rather than contrary to reason, although in cases of doubt he transposed the certainties somewhat in favour of revelation. He accepted that simple ideas came from sensations, but remained unconvinced that reflection and reason did likewise.[17] The Newtonian universe lent itself to the demonstration of a Divine 'master-clockmaker'. Surely this wondrous, perfectly calibrated machine must be 'the work of an almighty hand'?[18] Indeed, the early years of Newtonianism are indistinguishable from a concerted campaign of Christian apologetics conducted by a group of latitudinarian clergymen. Their chief platform was the Boyle lectures, founded by the scientist to use the findings of science to defend religion.[19]

However, the empirical method, which refused to accept as proven anything that could not be induced from experiment or observation, could lend support to an alternative, Spinozist explanation of the universe. Newton's proviso that the clock would 'wind down' and would require regular divine recalibration was famously derided (although from an orthodox standpoint) by Leibniz. Locke's border between the knowable and the unknowable, which led him into Socinianism, could be shifted much further in favour of reason. All mystery was knowledge not yet achieved; religious awe was simply superstition, the works of pernicious 'priestcraft'; God was a distant and subsequently irrelevant first cause; Nature, and by extension, civil society, was the only true religion for man. So declared the English deists or pantheists, among them John Toland, Anthony Collins, and Matthew Tindal.[20]

The latitudinarians and deists fought a grand battle over the Newtonian inheritance, a struggle fully reported in the Dutch press, and in a more partisan manner in the French journals. A number of the Huguenot exiles had close links with the latitudinarians, and among their translated works were the sermons of Archbishop John Tillotson and many of the Boyle lectures. The *Journal des Sçavans* eulogized Samuel Clarke: 'On ne saurait

[17] Bonno, *La culture et la civilisation britanniques*, 87–91.

[18] J. Addison, 'The spacious firmament on high', *The New English Hymnal* (Norwich, 1986), no. 267.

[19] See Jacob, *Radical Enlightenment*, 87–93; J. Gascoigne, *Cambridge in the Age of the Enlightenment: Science, Religion and Politics from the Restoration to the French Revolution* (Cambridge, 1989) and Holmes, *Making of a Great Power*, 143–59, 350–87.

[20] See J. A. I. Champion, *The Pillars of Priestcraft Shaken: The Church of England and its Enemies, 1660–1730* (Cambridge, 1992), and Jacob, *Radical Enlightenment, passim*.

trop louer les philosophes anglois de ce qu'ils emploient les mathéma-
tiques et la philosophie pour établir la vérité de la religion.' Perhaps the
most influential latitudinarian abroad was William Derham, whose 1711 and
1712 Boyle lectures, published as *Physico-Theology* in 1713, were a *tour
de force* of the latest scientific discoveries applied to theological ends. He
followed up with *Astro-Theology* in 1715. Both were translated into French
in 1726, and greeted with a concert of praise from all the periodicals.
Astro-Theology was in addition translated into Latin, German, Dutch, and
Italian. The Abbé Pluche borrowed extensively from Derham in his *Spectacle de la Nature* (1732–50), so too did the Genevan Jacques Plantier in
his *Vérités capitales de la religion* (1733), while Paul Dulard was inspired
to exalt *Le Grandeur de Dieu dans les merveilles de la Nature* in verse (1749).[21]

The deists also had their adherents in the Republic of Letters, and a
few of their tracts were translated and published in the Netherlands, and
then smuggled into France. Among them was Collins's seminal *Discourse
of Free Thinking* (1714). Some others were clandestinely circulated as
manuscript copies, notably Toland's *Pantheisticon* (1720).[22] Assisted by
the discreet protection of Prince Eugene of Savoy, the deists' social network reached to various corners of Germany and Italy. One adherent was
Alberto Radicati di Passerano, whose *Philosophical Dissertation upon Death*
(1732), extending the train of Locke's thought, declared death was an
acquired idea like any other, and denounced the excessive fear of death
and an angry, punitive deity as a cruel deception.[23] In 1733 Des Maizeaux
was told by a correspondent in Paris: 'Freethinking is very rife in this
town, and a Northerly wind hath blown down a great spirit of freedom
in this respect.' In such circles, the young Denis Diderot plied his trade
as a translator from English. His 1745 translation of Shaftesbury's *Inquiry
Concerning Virtue and Merit* contained copious footnotes at the most het-
erodox points, especially on the idea that rational morality can be independent of religion. His marginalia became his *Pensées philosophiques*
(1746). As Diderot's beliefs evolved through various shades of deism to
outright materialist atheism, he found Toland a fruitful source of images
and concepts. In *Le Rêve de d'Alembert* (1769) he combined them with
his own theory of evolution.[24] However, historians have concluded that,

[21] Bonno, *La culture et la civilisation britanniques*, 112–22. Almagor, *Des Maizeaux, passim.*
[22] See I. O. Wade, *The Clandestine Organization and Diffusion of Philosophic Ideas in France
from 1700 to 1750* (Princeton, NJ, 1938).
[23] Venturi, *Italy and the Enlightenment*, 63–81. Jacob, *Radical Enlightenment*, chs. 5 and 6.
[24] A. M. Wilson, *Diderot* (London, 1973), 49–60, 559–81. L. Crocker, 'John Toland et
le matérialisme de Diderot', *Revue de l'histoire littéraire de la France*, 53 (1953).

in general, the English deists encouraged rather than directly influenced their French counterparts, among whom the influences of Spinoza and Bayle were paramount. Similarly, French divines who defended Christianity 'par les lumières de la raison' acknowledged the contribution of English latitudinarians, but rarely borrowed their arguments.[25]

The anti-Christian potential of empiricism linked to Spinozist pantheism is apparent from 'Le Philosophe', one of the most important writings of the French Enlightenment. It was probably written by Dumarsais around 1730, and was first published in a collection entitled *Nouvelles libertés de penser*, appropriately dedicated to Collins, in 1743. Diderot reprinted a toned-down version in the *Encyclopédie*, and it was subsequently reworked by Voltaire and Naigéon. It can therefore stand as a manifesto of some of the leading *philosophes*. It declares that 'le peuple' act on maxims without investigating or verifying them. In contrast, 'le philosophe forme ses principes sur une infinité d'observations particulières.' The conclusion reached was shocking; civil society was the only divinity a *philosophe* would recognize on earth.[26]

If the logical corollary of the deists' religious views was political republicanism (not for nothing did they revel in the name of 'Commonwealthmen'), then the benign and providential Newtonian universe implied an ordered, but liberal and commercial society.[27] The gospel of politeness and philanthropy, personified by the merchant 'Sir Andrew Freeport', was preached in Joseph Addison's and Sir Richard Steele's *Spectator* (1711–14), English literature's most successful export in the first half of the century. Of the 635 numbers, 417 were translated by Boyer and published in four volumes in Amsterdam in 1714–18. *Le Spectateur, ou le Socrate moderne* was reviewed with acclaim by numerous gazettes. This translation was expanded and republished frequently throughout the century. The German translation, *Der Zuschauer*, came out in 1739–43, while certain numbers appeared in the Russian *Primiechaniyak viedomostiam* as early as 1728. The French editions of the *Tatler*, the *Guardian*, and the *Freeholder* formed a supporting chorus when they came out in the 1720s. The essay periodicals were swiftly imitated. Justus Van Effen was first

[25] Bonno, *La culture et la civilisation britanniques*, 112, 121–2. Wade, *Clandestine Organization*, 265–9. Israel, 'Who began the European Enlightenment?'

[26] H. Dieckmann, *Le Philosophe: Texts and Interpretation* (St Louis, Mo., 1948), 1–26. A. W. Fairbairn, 'Dumarsais and Le Philosophe', *Studies on Voltaire and the Eighteenth Century*, 87 (1972).

[27] J. G. A. Pocock, 'Clergy and Commerce: The Conservative Enlightenment in England', in R. Ajello *et al.* (eds.), *L'età dei lumi: Studi storici sul settecento europeo in onore di Franco Venturi* (vol. 1; Naples, 1985). Jacob, *Radical Enlightenment*, 87–98.

with his *Misanthrope* (1711–12), and it was followed by many others in French, Dutch, German, Italian, Russian, and, as we shall see, Polish.[28]

The *Spectator* diffused English thought on aesthetics, notably Addison's series on the 'pleasures of the imagination', and often introduced Continental readers to English literature. The references could be unscrambled with the help of Van Effen's 'Dissertation sur la poésie anglaise', printed in the *Journal littéraire* in 1717, and the reports of Des Maizeaux. The list of translations opened with Addison's *Cato* in 1714. As with the *Spectator*, it met with a generally favourable reception. The most classical of English authors was close enough to French taste not to cause offence, but he encouraged the French to relax somewhat their interpretation of the unities. However, Milton's *Paradise Lost*, Defoe's *Robinson Crusoe*, and Swift's *Gulliver's Travels* were thought by their translators too raw for French readers, and were duly 'refined', setting a pattern for the rest of the century. *Robinson* and *Gulliver* appealed to a developing taste for exotica and inspired a genre of mostly mediocre imitations. Pope was first noted as a translator of Homer, but by the 1730s, several of his own poems had been translated. By then, the *terra incognita* of English literature had been mapped in outline, but it was still widely regarded as a wild and uncouth periphery of the literary world.[29]

English literature supposedly reflected the untamed English character, but 'Mr Spectator' enabled Europeans to view the English through English eyes. Naturally, he confirmed some unfavourable stereotypes by his criticisms of boorish and egotistic behaviour, but the idea of a supposedly wild, bizarre, and humourless Englishman promulgating good manners, good conversation, and 'good sense'—in pointed contrast to French 'foppery'—helped bring about a revaluation of the English national character. It was a process abetted by the Swiss Beat Muralt, whose *Lettres sur les Anglois et les François* were published in 1725, and went through several editions. Muralt, despite his protestations of even-handedness, made his comparisons favour the English, whom he had visited back in 1693. The French had *esprit*; the English *bon sens*. Muralt provoked French protests, but the Abbé Prévost went still further in his novels, soon translated into English, German, Italian, Russian, and Danish. In addition to good sense, he depicted Englishmen of benevolence and *sensibilité*. All in

[28] Bonno, *La culture et la civilisation britanniques*, 20–1, 50, 64–7. Z. Sinko, *'Monitor' wobec angielskiego 'Spectatora'* (Wrocław, 1956), 29–36. R. M. Colombo, *Lo Spectator e i giornali veneziani del settecento* (Bari, 1966).

[29] Bonno, *La culture et la civilisation britanniques*, 52–76. Sinko, *Powieść angielska a powieść polska*, 17–57.

all, the famed attachment of the English to their liberty came to seem less ferocious than reasonable and public-spirited.[30] Nevertheless, despite a few signs of change by the late 1720s, the image of England as riven by faction and civil strife remained deeply embedded in France. Bloodthirsty histories of revolutions and conflicts were snapped up by the reading public, while Jacobite exiles regaled their listeners with tales of odious regicides. Even the Huguenots Rapin de Thoyras and Emmanuel de Cizes, who admired the principles of the mixed constitution, were alarmed by the fierce quarrels between Whigs and Tories, and took complaints of corruption at face value. Among some noble critics of absolutism, there was some speculation about the Germanic origins of English liberty, relevant to Boulainvilliers's theory of the Frankish conquest, but political Anglomania was still some way off.[31]

Besides the journals, translations, and the still limited number of visitors, Freemasonry provided a less tangible channel for English influence. At the end of the seventeenth century in England, fraternities of professional builders or masons completed their transition into philosophical 'lodges', which had as their goal the building not of physical temples, but of temples for humanity—a perfect society, based on the equality of man before the law. Masonic lodges soon comprised much of the country's intellectual and social élite. The lodges organized themselves into a hierarchy in 1717, and their principles were printed as the so-called Anderson constitutions in 1723. Masonic virtues bore a striking resemblance to the politeness and philanthropy preached by the latitudinarians, and the lodges soon assumed a Whiggish political aspect. The Reverend Jean Desaguliers, the son of Huguenot refugees and 'the guiding force in British freemasonry',[32] presided over the official establishment of the Dutch lodges in the early 1730s, and the London system of lodges soon reached across northern, Protestant Europe. However, from the scant early sources, Margaret Jacob has argued that less respectable Masonic or quasi-Masonic societies were already active in the Netherlands by the 1710s. Jean Rousset de Missy, the leading light in Dutch Freemasonry, was at the centre of a web of English, Dutch, and French deists. Freemasonry, it would seem, sheltered a radical underworld.

---

[30] Bonno, *La culture et la civilisation britanniques*, 20–31. M. Maurer, *Aufklärung und Anglophilie in Deutschland* (Göttingen and Zürich, 1987), 29–32.

[31] Bonno, *La culture et la civilisation britanniques*, 37–47. Cf. J. Dedieu, *Montesquieu et la tradition politique anglaise en France: Les sources anglaises de 'l'esprit des lois'* (Paris, 1909), ch. 3.

[32] Jacob, *Radical Enlightenment*, 122.

From the start, the lodges offered a forum in which divisions of class and creed could be overcome, although they acquired an increasingly aristocratic profile during the eighteenth century. The Catholic Duke of Norfolk became grand master of the Grand London Lodge in 1729. Many Frenchmen in England, including Montesquieu, were initiated. This tolerance enabled Freemasonry to spread to Catholic countries, where Jacobite émigrés played a significant role. Although started by Englishmen abroad, the lodges swiftly became domesticated. By the 1740s, Freemasonry had established itself all over Europe and among its members was the Holy Roman Emperor, Francis Stephen, the husband of Maria Theresa, whom Walpole had initiated at Houghton Hall in 1731. Papal prohibitions in 1738 and 1752 had the effect of pruning on a vigorous plant. The French lodges soon threw off the tenuous supremacy of London; a revolt which went beyond natural political and institutional rivalry. French Freemasonry tended to be more occultist and less rationalist. It was French rather than English Freemasonry that dominated Central and Eastern Europe, although periodical splits caused some lodges to revert to the London system. The transposition from England to the Continent of Masonic institutions entailed their relative radicalization. Democratic doctrines and practices, which raised few eyebrows in England, sounded dangerous and subversive in the more rigid Continental monarchies. The claim that the lodges were the seed-bed of the democratic political culture of the French Revolution is at least plausible. However, beyond this, Freemasonry does not seem to have played a distinct role in the diffusion of English thought and culture. It was a medium for all Enlightened culture, including its English components.[33]

The example of Freemasonry shows that not all manifestations of English culture in Germany were echoes of developments in France. The Hanseatic cities, particularly Hamburg, had old trading links with England. Many sailors and merchants had some knowledge of English and England, which created the conditions for the establishment and growth of coffee-houses, lodges, and 'Patriotic Societies'. The union of Hanover with the English Crown ensured that it, in turn, became 'an outpost of English civilization', and its University of Göttingen the most receptive in Germany to English influences. Many of the eighteenth-century German

[33] L. Hass, *Wolnomularstwo w Europie środkowo-wschodniej w XVIII i XIX wieku* (Wrocław, 1982), 38–190. Jacob, *Radical Enlightenment, passim*. Eadem, *Living the Enlightenment: Freemasonry and Politics in Eighteenth-Century Europe* (Oxford, 1991). J. Kroupa, *Alchymie štěstí: Pozdní osvícenství a moravská společnost* (Brno, 1987), chs. 3 and 4. On the Rosicrucian contribution to early English Freemasonry see T. Cegielski, '*Ordo ex chao': Wolnomularstwo i światopoglądowe kryzysy XVII i XVIII wieku*, vol. 1, '*Oświecenie Różokrzyżowców' i początki masonerii spekulatywnej 1614–1738* (Warsaw, 1994).

translators of English literature had some connection with Hamburg or Hanover. A professor at Göttingen, Gottfried Achenwall, formed a distinctly German view of the English constitution in his popular *Staatsverfassung der heutigen vornehmsten europäischen Reiche* (1749). He paid less attention to Parliament than to the strong royal prerogative, which was tempered by the freedoms of the people enshrined in law. His essentially legal conception of *Englische Freiheit* reflected German concerns with the actual exercise of princely power.[34] French writers, who had less hope of convincing their ruler, used England's constitutional machinery for a more abstract critique of 'despotism'.

II

England was certainly revealed to Francophone Europe before Voltaire published his *Lettres philosophiques* in 1734. However, Voltaire's synthesis did much to make England fashionable.[35] Despite or perhaps because of being burnt by the public hangman, the *Lettres philosophiques* proved one of the most popular books of the century, with over 20,000 copies printed within five years.[36] After coming to England in 1726 smarting from his thrashing by the lackeys of the Chevalier de Rohan and a sojourn in the Bastille, it was not surprising that he found much to praise in England's political and social relations. Political theory was never a priority for Voltaire, and he did not give the English constitution much space in the *Lettres philosophiques*, but his remarks were unreservedly positive. Above all, England was the land of liberty. He believed that habitual free speaking had embedded freedom in the English language itself.[37] The discords of the seventeenth century had eventually produced, in contrast to ancient Rome, 'ce mélange heureux, . . . ce concert entre les Communes, les Lords et le Roi'. Indeed,

La nation anglaise est la seule de la terre qui soit parvenue à régler le pouvoir des rois en leur résistant, et qui, d'efforts en efforts, ait enfin établi ce gouvernement sage, où le Prince, tout-puissant pour faire du bien, a les mains liées pour

---

[34] Maurer, *Aufklärung und Anglophilie*, 39–65.

[35] I. O. Wade, *The Structure and Form of the French Enlightenment* (2 vols.; Princeton, 1977), vol. 1, 125–48, underlines its significance as the first analysis of a foreign civilization.

[36] R. Pomeau, *D'Arouet à Voltaire 1694–1734* (*Voltaire et son temps*, vol. 1; Oxford, 1985), 330. The English original of the *Lettres philosophiques*, *Letters concerning the English Nation* (1733), has recently been republished by N. Cronk (Oxford, 1994). Because we are interested in European perceptions of England, all citations will be from the French version (Paris, 1964).

[37] J. Barnouw, 'The Contribution of the English—and English—to Voltaire's Enlightenment', to be published in *Studies on Voltaire and the Eighteenth Century* (forthcoming).

faire le mal, où les seigneurs sont grands sans insolence, et où le peuple partage le gouvernement sans confusion.

Voltaire thoroughly approved of the taxation of all Englishmen irrespective of rank, and of the dominance of the Commons in financial affairs. The commercial spirit was the key to England's greatness and liberty; 'le commerce qui a enrichi les citoyens en Angleterre, a contribué a les rendre libres, et cette liberté a étendu le commerce à son tour; de là s'est formée la grandeur de l'état.' German princes would not be able to conceive that the younger son of an English peer could be only a rich and powerful bourgeois. Voltaire contributed powerfully to the myth of the English aristocracy as an open élite, in order to set up an example to France. It is probably true, however, that the contrast between the French and English aristocracies' attitude to commerce was sharper in the 1720s than in the 1780s.[38]

Essential to English liberty and commerce was religious toleration. Voltaire believed that the atmosphere of toleration, and even indifference, was more important than the legal disabilities suffered by the Nonconformists. He viewed those as a simple civil obligation, for the Anglican Church was far from fussy about the doctrinal stance of its members. Voltaire admired the sincerity, humanity, and morality of the Quakers, although he could not take their doctrines seriously, but he was most in sympathy with the Socinians. In the *Lettres philosophiques*, Voltaire sniped at the outworks of Christian orthodoxy rather than at basic Christian belief. Only in the 1760s did he draw upon the biblical criticism of certain English deists, notably Tindal and Peter Annet, as his crusade against 'l'infâme' entered a more aggressive phase.[39]

Among the Socinians, Voltaire was delighted to list Newton, Locke, and Clarke. Clarke befriended him following his arrival in England, and impressed him with his reasoning. Voltaire accepted his arguments in favour of the existence of God and used them in his *Traité de métaphysique* (1734). Not the least of Voltaire's achievements was to resolve the debate on Newtonianism. Four of the *Lettres* served to familiarize a wider public

[38] Lettres VIII–X. P. Gay, *Voltaire's Politics: The Poet as Realist* (2nd edn., New Haven, 1988), 40–65. Cannon, *Aristocratic Century*, 6–7, argues strongly that the contrast has been over-drawn (very few sons of peers entered trade), and that the English aristocracy were *increasingly* exclusive. Also see Cannon, 'The English Nobility 1660–1800', and J. Swann, 'The French Nobility 1715–1789', in H. M. Scott (ed.), *The European Nobilities in the Seventeenth and Eighteenth Centuries*, vol. 1, *Western Europe* (London, 1995).

[39] Lettres I–IX. N. L. Torrey, *Voltaire and the English Deists* (1930, repr. Oxford, 1963). R. Pomeau, '*Écraser l'infâme*' *1759–1770* (*Voltaire et son temps*, vol. 4; Oxford, 1994), 214–29, 246–9. Idem, *On a voulu l'enterrer 1770–1791* (*Voltaire et son temps*, vol. 5; Oxford, 1994), 170–90.

with Newton and the bones of his theories, probably derived from Clarke and Pemberton's *View of Sir Isaac Newton's Philosophy* (1728). In the *Lettres philosophiques*, Voltaire was most concerned with the honour rendered by the English to Newton, and with the a posteriori method. He hailed Bacon as 'le père de la philosophie experimentale', who without yet knowing nature, 'savait et indiquait tous les chemins qui mènent à elle'. Voltaire spent the next few years studying Newtonianism in the company of Madame du Châtelet. Her translation of the *Principia* was posthumously published in 1759. They were visited at Cirey by Francesco Algarotti, who took the diffusion of Newtonianism a step further in his *Il Neutonianismo per le dame* (1737). Voltaire's *Élémens de la philosophie de Neuton* had an enormous impact after publication in 1738. 'Tout Paris retentit de Newton, tout Paris bégaie Newton, tout Paris étudie et apprend Newton,' testified the *Mémoires de Trévoux*.[40] D'Alembert could write confidently of the triumph of Bacon and Newton in his preliminary discourse for the *Encyclopédie*, and elsewhere he defined 'philosophie expérimentale' as 'celle qui se sert des expériences pour découvrir les lois de nature'.[41]

Voltaire dampened the flames of controversy over Newton, but over Locke he fanned them. Locke had been accused by Bishop Edward Stillingfleet of Spinozist materialism for allowing the possibility that, if God willed it, matter might think. In its time, the dispute had been reported in the Francophone journals. The 1729 edition of Coste's translation contained extensive annotations detailing the controversy. Voltaire disingenuously used Locke's replies to Stillingfleet to cast doubt upon the immortality of the soul, and pointedly contrasted the certainties of reason with those of revelation. He gave a twist to Locke's arguments and some of Voltaire's critics did not hesitate to tell him so. However, others weighed in against 'thinking matter', while a few defended it. Voltaire himself found it difficult to accept the cold, materialistic implications, and was drawn towards Shaftesbury's optimistic and lyrical deism, which retained an innate sense of justice. Voltaire never fully resolved his dilemma, but with 'thinking matter' restored to the philosophical agenda, La Mettrie and Baron d'Holbach drew the logical conclusions from the idea in constructing their utterly materialist and determinist systems. Condillac, Locke's greatest

---

[40] Lettres XII, XIV–XVII. R. Vaillot, *Avec Madame du Châtelet 1734–1749* (*Voltaire et son temps*, vol. 2; Oxford, 1988), 27, 33, 63–91. See W. H. Barber, 'Voltaire and Samuel Clarke', in *Voltaire and the English, Studies on Voltaire and the Eighteenth Century*, 179 (1979).
[41] 'Discours préliminaire', in *Encyclopédie, ou dictionnaire raisonné des sciences, des arts et des métiers*, vol. 1 (Paris, 1751), pp. xxliv–v. 'Expérimental', ibid., vol. 6 (1756), 298–301. 'Newtonianisme' also has a self-assured tone. Ibid., vol. 11 (Neuchâtel, 1765), 122–5.

disciple, who analysed language as the link between sensations and under-standing, was careful not to commit himself to materialism, but some of his numerous followers did just that. D'Holbach's coterie was a strong-hold of sensationist, materialist, and violently anti-Christian atheism.[42] Just as corrosive of religious orthodoxy was the moral relativism implicit in Locke's philosophy. Experience must vary according to the senses, and Diderot explored the subversive possibilities for the blind, and the deaf and dumb. Experience must also vary according to historical and climatic circumstances—a theme taken up by Montesquieu. Such relativism was relevant in the eighteenth century's discussion of the mores of the Tahi-tians.[43] Rousseau was forced into asserting innate pity, and Kant into an innate standard of *Recht*.[44]

The polemics of Voltaire and the *Encyclopédie* give the impression of a well-defined antithesis between the empiricism of Newton and Locke and the a priori reasoning of Descartes, Leibniz, and others. Reality was more complicated. Not everyone saw a necessary conflict between the two approaches, and Locke's political treatises were based on deductive reasoning. Leibniz liked experimentation and wrote against Descartes. Nevertheless, both the Newtonian explanation of the universe and the Lockean explanation of man represented a distinctive English and empir-ical contribution to the Enlightenment.

The publication of *De l'esprit des lois* in 1748 launched political Anglomania. Montesquieu had stayed in England for eighteen months in 1729–31. He arrived in the company of Lord Chesterfield and frequented the company of the leaders of the opposition: Carteret, Pulteney, Bol-ingbroke, and Townshend. Montesquieu had already met Bolingbroke in France, and the *Craftsman* greatly influenced his understanding of English politics. Montesquieu neglected the Whig–Tory polarity and stressed Bolingbroke's concept of a Court–Country divide. This had a critical bearing on Montesquieu's development of the doctrine of the separation of powers. The Court apologists defended the influence of the Crown (and to a lesser extent of the peers) over the House of Commons. Their ideal was the 'mixed and balanced constitution', their classical authority Polybius. The presence of ministers and placemen in the Commons was

---

[42] Lettre XII. Bonno, *La culture et la civilisation britanniques*, 92–6. J. W. Yolton, *Locke and French Materialism* (Oxford, 1991). U. Ricken, *Linguistics, Anthropology and Philosophy in the French Enlightenment: Language Theory and Ideology* (London, 1994), ch. 8. Rostworowski, *Historia powszechna*, 592–5. D. B. Schlegel, *Shaftesbury and the French Deists* (Chapel Hill, NC, 1956), is marred by an uncritical assumption of its subject's all-pervading influence.
[43] Wilson, *Diderot*, 67–8, 96–100, 121–2, 588–93. Montesquieu, *Esprit des lois*, Book XIV.
[44] H. Reiss, Introduction to *Kant's Political Writings* (Cambridge, 1971).

necessary both to reduce friction and to keep the Commons from endangering the prerogative of the Crown. They held the legislature supreme over the executive and the judiciary, so the legislative power was shared among the king, Lords, and Commons, who respectively represented the monarchy, aristocracy, and people. Unless mutually checked, they would descend into tyranny, oligarchy, and anarchy. The Country opposition strove instead for the rigid separation of the executive and legislative powers, often represented by the Crown and the Commons respectively, with the nobility, separately represented in the legislature, playing a mediating role. As the *Craftsman* put it on 27 March 1730 (OS), 'the safety of the whole depends on the balance of the parts, and the balance of the parts on their mutual independency of each other.' Patronage was simply royal corruption, and the Commons must strive to keep incipient royal despotism at bay. Montesquieu copied out the *Craftsman* of 13 June 1730 (OS) in his *Spicilège*: 'The love of power is natural. It is insatiable almost constantly whetted never cloyed by possession.'[45]

The ideological contest over the English constitution was therefore between harmony and friction as the surest means to political liberty. Montesquieu plumped decisively for the latter, adopted Bolingbroke's slogan of the separation of powers, and abstracted it into a powerful political theory. He failed to understand the role of ministers, overestimated the efficacy of the royal veto, and condemned patronage; noting that 'les Anglais ne sont plus dignes de leur liberté. Ils la vendent au roi; et si le roi la leur redonnait, ils la lui vendraient encore.'[46] There was a danger, in fact, in the absence of natural intermediary powers such as the privileges of the French nobility and the *parlements*. The consequence of the total corruption of Parliament by the executive would be an irresistible despotism.[47] Montesquieu simplified and democratized the English constitution. He passed over Justices of the Peace sitting in the Commons (that is, the confluence of the legislative and judicial powers), rotten and pocket boroughs, and the variations in the franchise (all should be electors but the most indigent, who are 'esteemed to have no will of their own').[48]

---

[45] R. Shackleton, *Montesquieu: A Critical Biography* (Oxford, 1961), 117–45, 54–5, 292–301. Montesquieu, *Oeuvres complètes* (Paris, 1963), 409. Dickinson, *Liberty and Property*, chs. 4 and 5. Cannon, *Aristocratic Century*, chs. 4 and 6.

[46] 'Notes sur l'Angleterre', *Oeuvres complètes*, 333.

[47] *Esprit des lois*, Book II, ch. 4. S. Mason, 'Montesquieu on English constitutionalism revisited: a government of potentiality and paradoxes', *Studies on Voltaire and the Eighteenth Century*, 278 (1990), 109, 120.

[48] As quoted by Blackstone, *Commentaries on the Laws of England* (5th edn., Oxford, 1773), vol. 1, 171.

Montesquieu's view nevertheless had enormous influence, even in England. It was a view of England as she could and should be; an example to France, and the best alternative to Spanish-style despotism.[49]

The benefits of the English constitution were felt by every citizen, for Montesquieu defined liberty (which he rather confusingly called political liberty) as the security and tranquillity of spirit provided by the law: 'La liberté est le droit de faire tout ce que les lois permettent; et si un citoyen pouvait faire ce qu'elles défendent, il n'aurait plus de liberté, parce que les autres auraient tout de même ce pouvoir.' Such security depended above all on the judicial power,[50] and this potentially terrible power was tamed in England by the jury and assize systems, habeas corpus, and the many humane aspects of English law. The judicial power was protected from the encroachment of the legislature and executive by the system of checks and balances between the king (controlling the executive), the Lords, and Commons within the legislature. In this sense, England had 'pour objet direct de sa constitution la liberté politique'. It was the ideal 'gouvernement modéré'. In contrast, 'l'indépendance de chaque particulier est l'objet des lois de Pologne; et ce qui en résulte, l'oppression de tous.'[51]

Voltaire raised the profile of the English constitution; Montesquieu made a political theory of it. Between them, they transformed it from a curiosity into a damning indictment of despotism, eagerly taken up by liberal critics of absolute monarchy. In the *Encyclopédie*, Jaucourt wrote of 'monarchie limitée': 'Sorte de monarchie ou les trois pouvoirs sont tellement fondus ensemble, qu'ils se servent l'un à l'autre de balance et de contrepoids. La monarchie limitée héréditaire paroît être la meilleure forme de monarchie . . . Tel est le gouvernement d'Angleterre.'[52] Conservative defenders of the old order continued to exult in the fidelity of the French to their kings. They pointed to demagogues like Wilkes to justify censorship. But they also began to wield a powerful new weapon, one that

---

[49] Shackleton, *Montesquieu*, 287–8. J. Shklar, *Montesquieu* (Past Masters, Oxford 1987), 86, 88. Mason, 'Montesquieu', 114–15, 122. For a radical 'anti-feudal' interpretation see M. Hulliung, *Montesquieu and the Old Regime* (Berkeley, Calif., 1976), esp. 46–53. In contrast, J. J. Granpré Molière, *La Théorie de la constitution anglaise chez Montesquieu* (Leiden, 1972), briskly denies any real influence on Montesquieu of English thinkers, and sees Book XI, ch. 6 merely as a step along the road from the 'republican' *Lettres persanes* to a programme for a moderate, noble-led French monarchy in most of *De l'esprit des lois*. This view underestimates the importance of the English constitution as an ideal.

[50] Called variously 'la puissance exécutrice [des choses] qui dépendent du droit civil', 'la puissance de juger', and 'la puissance exécutrice de l'État'.

[51] *Esprit des lois*, Book XI, chs. 1–6, XIX, ch. 27. Shklar, *Montesquieu*, 81, 85–9. Mason, 'Montesquieu'.

[52] *Encyclopédie*, vol. 10 (1765), 636–8.

could and eventually did transcend the social structure of the *ancien régime*:
patriotism. During and following the patriotic upsurge produced by the
Seven Years' War, they denounced the *philosophes* for their avowed cosmopolitanism, and for preferring anything English to everything French.
Jaucourt riposted by defining 'le *patriotisme* le plus parfait' as a regard
for the rights of all the peoples in the world. Montesquieu was an exem-
plar of this 'patriotisme universel'; indeed, he had found these rights established 'dans une île voisine'. However, his definition of a patriot as a
zealous citizen of a *free* country sounded a different note. Cosmopolitanism was becoming harder to sustain.[53]

The ire of the conservatives was provoked as much by fashionable
Anglomania as by philosophic Anglophilia. As early as the 1750s (as
Chesterfield would later inform the young Stanisław Poniatowski),[54] an
Anglomane aped the English in his dress, speech, and manners. Promoted
from the heights of French society by the Duke of Chartres (later
Philippe-Égalité), the Count of Artois, and Queen Marie-Antoinette, the
vogue spread throughout the following three decades. He would wear a
frac (frock coat) or a *redingotte* (caped riding coat), would drive around
in his *wiski* (a two-wheeled carriage), and would appear morose and philosophical, only to break into fits of enthusiasm over his English horses and
English jockeys, on which he would gamble away his fortune. She would
pose for her portrait *deshabillée*, in a loose muslin dress and a wide-brimmed
hat, often against the backdrop of a sentimental windswept landscape—
her own or an imaginary *jardin anglois*.[55]

Neither Montesquieu's theory of the English constitution nor Voltaire's glorification of Newton adequately explain this extraordinary popularity. However, while deductive reasoning implied imposing a system on
nature, inductive reasoning entailed drawing conclusions from nature, letting nature, as it were, speak for itself. Thus the campaign against 'l'esprit
de système' in philosophy was linked to a more widespread rejection of
artifice in art and literature, as demanded by the English theorists, Addison and Shaftesbury. With the cult of nature came the cult of man's natural sensibility. Prévost was a precursor. Beginning with *Pamela* in 1741,

[53] F. Acomb, *Anglophobia in France 1763–1789: An Essay in the History of Constitutionalism and Nationalism* (Durham, NC, 1950), chs. 2 and 4. J. Grieder, *Anglomania
in France 1740–1789: Fact, Fiction and Political Discourse* (Geneva, 1985), ch. 4. Wilson,
Diderot, 285, 393–4. 'Patriote', and 'Patriotisme', in *Encyclopédie*, vol. 12 (1765), 181.

[54] See below, pp. 108–9.

[55] L.-C. Fougeret de Montbron seems to have coined the term in his *Preservatif contre
l'anglomanie* (1757). See Grieder, *Anglomania*, ch. 2, S. Schama, *Citizens: A Chronicle of
the French Revolution* (London, 1989), 217–22.

the sentimental novels of Samuel Richardson and his successors enjoyed immediate success in France, and inspired a genre of pseudo-English sentimental *romans*, which in turn were often translated into English. The 'Gothic' novel, inaugurated in 1764 by Horace Walpole's *Castle of Otranto*, won almost equal popularity. The most spectacularly successful French novel was Rousseau's *Julie, ou la nouvelle Héloïse* (1761), which described and extolled a 'natural' garden.[56] Within a few years, the *jardin anglois* or *anglo-chinois* had become all the rage in France. They were more contrived and on a smaller scale than Lancelot Brown's rolling pastoral landscapes, and tended to be crowded with exotic attractions, arranged on a winding circuit through trees and bushes, with less concern for distant vistas. However, they were more 'natural' than Voltaire's garden at Ferney, which he described as 'English' to the bemusement of his visitors. His taste had stopped at Chiswick in the 1720s. Rousseau's recommendation of *Robinson Crusoe* in *Émile* (1762) resulted not only in the swift appearance of a new French translation in 1766, but also in the proliferation of 'Robinson's huts' in fashionable gardens. The Marquis of Girardin provided first a haven and then a tomb for Rousseau in his park at Ermenonville. It soon became a shrine to the prophet of *sensibilité*, and Marie-Antoinette led the worshippers.[57]

The revolt against formality and the cult of sensibility were also reflected in the growing popularity of Shakespeare. Voltaire had been shocked but fascinated during his stay in England, and wrote a sanitized version of *Julius Caesar*, *Le Mort de César* (1731). In the *Lettres philosophiques*, he grandly declared that Shakespeare 'avait un génie plein de force et fécondité, de naturel et de sublime, sans la moindre étincelle de bon goût et sans la moindre connaissance des règles'. Voltaire intended to encourage richness of expression, but started a revolution. When the *Journal encyclopédique* dared prefer Shakespeare to Corneille in 1760, he responded with a declaration of war against such 'barbarie'. The ease with which Le Tourneur's translation attracted subscribers in 1776 provoked him to new flights of venom. All in vain; the cause was lost. The *Journal des Sçavans* printed 56 pages of extracts.[58] Mainstream publications such

[56] Grieder, *Anglomania*, ch. 3. Sinko, *Powieść angielska . . . a powieść polska*, 17–57.

[57] Grieder, *Anglomania*, 13–16. Schama, *Citizens*, 147–62. C. Thacker, 'Voltaire and Rousseau: eighteenth-century gardeners', *Studies on Voltaire and the Eighteenth Century*, 90 (1972). B. Majewska-Maszkowska, *Mecenat artystyczny Izabelli z Czartoryskich Lubomirskiej 1736–1816* (Warsaw, 1976), 176–9. D. Jacobson, *Chinoiserie* (London, 1993), ch. 6. C. Quest-Ritson, *The English Garden Abroad* (London, 1992), 100–4, 194–8.

[58] Lettre XVIII. Pomeau, *D'Arouet à Voltaire*, 223, 276–80. Idem, *'Écraser l'infâme'*, 100. Idem, *On a voulu l'interrer*, 156, 191–204. J. de la Harpe, *Le Journal des Savants et l'Angleterre 1702–1789* (Berkeley, Calif., 1941), 460.

as the *Journal des Sçavans* and the *Mémoires de Trévoux* not only reported the triumph of English literature, English gardens, inoculation against smallpox, and every other manifestation of Anglomania; they contributed to it.[59]

Anglomania in other countries in many ways echoed that in France, and was part of the French cultural hegemony. Fashionable European aristocrats read their English novels in French, drank their *thé à l'angloise*, and practised their *mélancolie angloise* while taking a turn around their English gardens. Prince Leopold of Anhalt-Dessau laid out the first English garden in Germany at Wörlitz in 1766.[60] However, fashion imbibed from France could sometimes lead to a genuine appreciation of English culture. Interior decoration was one of the first spheres to be affected. Flock wallpaper, often in 'Chinese' patterns, fitted carpets of Wilton moquette, and mahogany furniture were all fashionable in several countries by the 1740s. By the 1770s, Wedgwood and others were exporting porcelain to Europe on a massive scale.[61] Catherine the Great famously commissioned a vast service from Wedgwood decorated with views of English houses and gardens. 'J'aime à la folie présentement les jardins à l'anglaise, les lignes courbes, les pentes douces, les étangs en forme des lacs, les archipels en terre ferme, et j'ai un profond mépris pour les lignes droites, les allées jumelles. Je hais les fontaines qui donnent la torture à l'eau . . . en un mot, l'anglomanie domine ma plantomanie,' she gushed to Voltaire. She even sent her gardener Vasilii Neelov to England in 1771, and engaged a Scottish architect, Charles Cameron, in 1779. The gardens and buildings at Tsarskoe Selo, especially the near-copy of the Wilton Palladian bridge, were the upshot. Other patrons followed her lead. William Coxe noted that 'most of the Russian nobles have gardeners of our nation, and resign themselves implicitly to their direction.' Cameron prospered in Russia until his death in 1812 and left a number of pupils. Catherine also sponsored Russian translations of a number of English novels (alongside many more French ones) and patronized periodicals modelled upon the *Spectator*. She was an avid reader of Shakespeare (in French translation), and even wrote a 'Life of Rurik' in imitation, freed from the unities.

---

[59] De la Harpe, *Le Journal des Savants*, 372–468. C. B. O'Keefe, *Contemporary Reactions to the Enlightenment (1728–1762)* (Paris, 1974), 100–1.

[60] Maurer, *Aufklärung und Anglophilie*, 28, 81–4, 178. A. Graf, *L'Anglomania et l'influsso inglese in Italia nel XVIII secolo* (Turin, 1911), ch. 14. Kroupa, *Alchymie štestí*, 112–13, 118, 170. L. Országh, '"Anglomania" in Hungary, 1780–1900', *New Hungarian Quarterly*, 22 (1981), 170–1. See below, ch. 9, section I.

[61] P. Thornton, *Authentic Decor: The Domestic Interior 1620–1920* (New York, 1984), 99–101, 140. R. Reilly, *Josiah Wedgwood 1730–1795* (London, 1992).

Shakespeare was first performed in Russia by an English troupe in 1771, but no Russian translation of his works appeared in the eighteenth century.[62]

For the aristocracies of Central and Eastern Europe, Anglomania and Gallomania were complementary; but for Italian, and especially for German intellectuals, England became a weapon in a struggle between Gallomania and Gallophobia.[63] Lessing's famous 'Literaturenbrief' of 1759, which knocked French classicism from its pedestal, should be understood in the context of the Seven Years' War. England, Prussia, and many of the smaller Protestant states were ranged against France. The victory of Rossbach in 1757 stirred reflections on the need for a similar cultural emancipation. Ancient kinship made the 'natural' qualities of English literature seem far more suitable for Germans than the wit and art of the French. The English language had been taught at Protestant universities from the early eighteenth century. In mid-century, they were joined by higher schools which taught it on an equal basis to French, while private tuition became highly fashionable; Goethe was taught by an Englishman in 1762. Catholic Germany took longer to follow suit. Maria Theresa feared the effect of English on religion and morals, and was keen to prevent Joseph II from travelling to England. Yet in the end even she caved in; a chair of English was founded at Vienna in 1778.[64] Translations of English periodicals and literature, increasingly done from the original rather than French, mushroomed from the 1740s. They included 320 novels between 1740 and 1799. Of the poets, Edward Young and Thomas Gray made a particular impact, with their melancholy and sensibility, while James MacPherson's fraudulent Ossian caused a rare sensation. Milton's *Paradise Lost*, translated back in the 1720s, struck a deeper chord in Germany than in France. Above all, Shakespeare became the talisman of the Gallophobes. Some of his dramas had long been performed in Germany,[65] but Lessing's intervention heralded two large-scale translations, by Wieland (1762–6),

---

[62] A. G. Cross, *'By the Banks of the Thames': Russians in Eighteenth-Century Britain* (Newtonville, Mass., 1980), esp. 219–22, 231–2, 247–8, 270–1. I. de Madariaga, *Russia in the Age of Catherine the Great* (1981, repr. New Haven, 1990), 330–1. W. Serczyk, *Kultura rosyjska XVIII wieku* (Wrocław, 1984), 208–9, 214, 230, 241. D. Shvidkovsky, *The Empress and the Architect: British Architecture and Gardens at the Court of Catherine the Great* (New Haven and London, 1996).

[63] See Graf, *L'Anglomania*, ch. 1; Maurer, *Aufklärung und Anglophilie*, 16, 21–2, 49–58, 76–80, 292–313, 330–69, 419; and Oz-Salzberger, *Translating the Enlightenment*, ch. 2.

[64] R. J. W. Evans, 'Über die Ursprünge der Aufklärung', in *Das achtzehnte Jahrhundert und Österreich, Jahrbuch der österreichischen Gesellschaft zur Erforschung des achtzehnten Jahrhunderts* (vol. 2; Vienna, 1985), 13–14. Beales, *Joseph II*, vol. 1, *In the Shadow of Maria Theresa* (Cambridge, 1987), 253–4.

[65] See below, p. 181.

and Eschenburg (1775–7). Shakespeare had an immense influence on German drama, much to the disgust of Frederick the Great:

To see just how bad contemporary taste in Germany is, just visit any theatre. There you will see the abominable plays of Shakespeare being performed in German translations and the audiences deriving great pleasure from these ridiculous farces which merit only to be performed in front of savages in Canada . . . Shakespeare can be forgiven because he lived at a time when English culture had developed but little. However, there is no excuse for our contemporaries making the same mistakes—as has been done, for example, in Goethe's *Götz von Berlichingen*, an abominable imitation of those bad English plays. Yet the public warmly applauds this rubbish and demands that it be repeated.[66]

Through Shakespeare and Ossian, Herder searched for the *Volkspoesie* of a common 'Nordic' past.[67] His generation was electrified by Montesquieu's surmises on the origins of English liberties in the forests of Germany. In England, the ancient Germanic freedoms had endured. Why should not Germans enjoy them again? To some, part of the answer seemed to lie in the long hegemony of the nobility over the *Bürgerstand*. Perhaps the traditional Hanseatic links with England help to explain the differences between Gallophobic, *bürgerlich* Anglophilia and the Francophone Anglomania of the aristocracy. At any rate, by the 1780s, many a German burgher knew English and sent his son to study in England. *Bürgerlich* Anglophilia may have been, but German intellectuals found the concerns of enlightened Scottish thinkers with the roles of virtue and commerce in modern society untranslatable. They admired England for its open 'public sphere' of free reasoning about and wide participation in the polity, but they themselves were only beginning to emerge from their own 'private spheres';[68] hence the deeper literary and philosophical, rather than political impact of Anglophilia. The main thrust of comment on English liberty was directed at illiberal princely rule, and the lack of individual English rights, such as press freedom, habeas corpus, and trial by jury. Parliament weighed in lower down the scale. The English constitution was not without its critics (among them Frederick II), who were appalled

---

[66] *Sur la littérature allemande* (1780), quoted after the translation by T. C. W. Blanning, in 'Frederick the Great and German Culture', in R. Oresko *et al.* (eds.), *Royal and Republican Sovereignty in Early Modern Europe: Essays in Memory of Ragnhild Hatton* (Cambridge, 1997), 534. I am grateful to Prof. Blanning for a typescript.

[67] A. Gillies, 'Herder's Essay on Shakespeare: "Das Herz der Untersuchen"', *Modern Language Review*, 32 (1937). Maurer, *Aufklärung und Anglophilie*, 352–6.

[68] Oz-Salzberger, *Translating the Enlightenment*. The classic account of the growing 'public sphere' is J. Habermas, *The Structural Transformation of the Public Sphere* (Cambridge, 1989). Cf. Blanning, 'Frederick the Great and German Culture'.

by corruption and disturbed by events in America. The American Revolution fired a number of enthusiasts for the cause of liberty, but did not stimulate a deeper interest in constitutional problems. Even these difficulties seemed over by the mid-1780s, when Anglophilia reached its height. Numerous periodicals reported on the 'happy isle', and the leading Anglophile publicist of the time, J. W. von Archenholtz, presented a straightforward dialectic of progress and regress in his *England und Italien* (1785), swiftly translated into English, Dutch, Swedish, Russian, and, in parts, into Polish.[69]

Italians tended to be more dependent upon the French for their views of England, but direct links existed as well. Vicenzio Martinelli arrived in 1748, aged 46, and stayed twenty-six years. Following in the footsteps of Montesquieu, he became acquainted with the former opposition to Walpole. Martinelli contrasted English liberty, especially the freedom of the press and the restrictions placed on the prince, with continental absolutism. He communicated his thoughts in his *Istoria critica della vita civile*, which went through repeated editions, and in his Whiggish, anti-feudal *Istoria d'Inghilterra*. If the strife of the 1760s made some observers, such as the Abbé Galiani, forecast England's imminent decline, the very ferocity with which liberty was defended convinced others that all was well. Alessandro Verri found liberty a part of daily life; an exhilarating experience. Italian gazettes and journals followed the Wilkesite troubles with growing interest, and marvelled at such displays of liberty as banquets in prisons. The Florentine *Notizie del Mondo* sought to explain the constitution to its readers in line with the political principles of John Locke, with a prominent right of resistance.[70] Similarly, for the Genevan Jean de Lolme, through the freedom and wide circulation of the press, the nation formed an 'irritable whole', always ready to exercise that right of resistance. For this reason, liberty had found an unassailable refuge from creeping despotism in England. De Lolme's vision was wholeheartedly

[69] Maurer, *Aufklärung und Anglophilie*, 65–7, 71, 120–1, 185–205, 225–38, 409–16, 423–9. S. Haikala, *'Britische Freiheit' und das Englandbild in der öffentlichen deutschen Diskussion in ausgehenden 18. Jahrhundert* (Studia Historica Jyväskyläensia, 32; Jyväskyla 1985). Frederick II, 'Essai sur les formes de gouvernement et sur les devoirs des souverains' (1777), in *Oeuvres de Frédéric le Grand*, ed. J. D. E. Preuss (31 vols.; Berlin, 1846–57), vol. 9, 198. H. Dippel, *Germany and the American Revolution, 1770–1800: A Sociohistorical Investigation of Late Eighteenth-Century Political Thinking* (Wiesbaden, 1978). See below, ch. 8, nn. 58, 65.

[70] F. Venturi, *The End of the Old Regime in Europe, 1768–1776: The First Crisis* (Princeton, NJ, 1989), 384–404. K. Żaboklicki, *Ferdynand Galiani (1728–1787): Życie i Twórczość* (Wrocław, 1966), 51–2, 174–5.

apologetic. The early French editions of *De la constitution d'Angleterre* (1771) proposed the elimination of rotten boroughs like Old Sarum, but even that disappeared with the first English edition in 1775. Unsurprisingly, it went through eight more by 1800.[71]

Continental absolutists could feel threatened by English liberty, but were usually more than happy to learn from England in fields such as agriculture, industry, finance, and administration. Taking their lead from the Elector of Hanover ('Farmer George') after 1760, they patronized translations of agricultural literature, and the foundation of 'oeconomical societies'. Frederick II and Catherine II differed on Shakespeare, but both sent young men to England to study. Catherine, as might be expected, was more lavish. Where Frederick sent four 'apprentices' to study agriculture,[72] she, following in the footsteps of Peter the Great, despatched hundreds to study a multitude of subjects. S. E. Desnitsky attended Glasgow University in 1761-7 and listened to the lectures of Adam Smith. On his return to Russia, he set a detailed plan for legal and political reform before the tsaritsa, strongly influenced by Smith. She in turn adopted some of Desnitsky's ideas in chapter 22 of her *Nakaz*. The indebtedness of the *Nakaz* to Montesquieu is well-known. It included some favourable references to the English judicial system, but did not countenance any serious rights for an independent legislature. James Harris admitted that Catherine was 'perfectly mistress of our laws and Constitution', although she could not understand opposition and resignation. She made extensive and detailed use of William Blackstone's *Commentaries on the Laws of England* (which were later partly translated into Russian by Desnitsky in 1780-2) when reforming local government and in her projects for judicial reform in the 1770s. She exclaimed to Grimm: 'oh, ses commentaires et moi, nous sommes inséparables.' The 'Autocratrix' was interested in specific aspects of English jurisprudence, not to promote political liberty, but to strengthen and modernize her state.[73] Diderot's famous complaint,

---

[71] Cannon, Aristocratic Century, 156. Venturi, *The End of the Old Regime in Europe, 1776-1789*, vol. 1, *The Great States of the West* (Princeton, NJ, 1991), 147-54. R. R. Palmer, *The Age of the Democratic Revolution* (2 vols.; Princeton, NJ, 1959-63), vol. 1, 145-8.

[72] Maurer, *Aufklärung und Anglophilie*, 85-95.

[73] Cross, '*By the Banks of the Thames*', esp. 264-7. M. S. Anderson, 'Some British influences on Russian intellectual life and society in the 18th century', *SEER*, 39 (1960). M. Raeff, 'The Empress and the Vinerian Professor: Catherine II's Projects of Government Reforms and Blackstone's *Commentaries*', *OSP*, new series, 7 (1974). A. H. Brown, 'S. E. Desnitsky, Adam Smith, and the *Nakaz* of Catherine II', *OSP*, new series, 7 (1974). Madariaga, *Russia in the Age of Catherine*, 151-63.

that she had taken Montesquieu's description of despotism and called it monarchy, is testimony to the effect of national context on enlightened ideas.[74]

Few French conservatives were prepared to deny England's superiority in areas such as agriculture and machinery. However, by the 1780s a striking realignment had taken place concerning the English constitution. The first signs of disquiet appeared among the *philosophes* in the 1760s. John Wilkes helped convince his friend d'Holbach that English liberty was in danger, and electoral corruption shocked the baron when he visited England in 1765. In his article 'Représentans' for the *Encyclopédie*, he criticized the infrequent elections and the lack of binding instructions upon members. As indigence tended to produce corruption, the franchise property qualification ought to be raised.[75] Diderot reported d'Holbach's impressions, with apparent approval, to Sophie Volland. Elsewhere the Court commanded and did as it pleased, but in England it corrupted and did as it pleased, and the corruption of its subjects was perhaps worse, in the long run, than tyranny.[76] Accompanied by Hume, Rousseau also visited England in 1765, but was not impressed. He gave vent to his criticism in his *Considérations sur le gouvernement de Pologne*, published in 1781 in French and 1789 in Polish. Although England had a continuous legislature, the English had lost their freedom for the same reasons as were identified by d'Holbach. In consequence, the Court could afford to buy Parliament every seven years. Rousseau was alarmed at the refusal of admission to Wilkes. Hereditary monarchy was clearly leading England down the same road to despotism as in Denmark, and imminently in Sweden. A hereditary throne and a free nation were incompatible. The English judicial system was too complicated, which resulted in swarms of lawyers and interminable lawsuits. The root of the decline lay in the corruption of the English nation, like virtually every other in Europe, by luxury and French fashions.[77] The Abbé Mably was a long-standing critic of the

---

[74] *Observations sur l'Instruction de Sa Majesté Imperiale*, In Diderot, *Oeuvres complètes*, ed. R. Lewinter (15 vols.; Paris, 1969–75), vol. 11, 316.

[75] *Encyclopédie*, vol. 14 (1765), 143–6. Venturi, *The End of the Old Regime in Europe 1768–1776: The First Crisis* (Princeton, NJ, 1989), 396.

[76] Diderot to S. Volland, 6 Oct. 1765, in *Oeuvres complètes*, vol. 5, 943–9. Also 20 Sept. 1765, vol. 5, 938, and 12 Nov. 1765, vol. 6, 351–6.

[77] *Considérations sur la gouvernement de Pologne et sur sa réformation projetée*, ed. J. Fabre, in J.-J. Rousseau, *Oeuvres complètes*, ed. B. Gagnebin and M. Raymond (3 vols.; Paris, 1959–64), vol. 3, 954, 960, 966, 975, 978–80, 991–2, 1000. *Uwagi nad rządem polskim oraz nad odmianą, czyli reformą onego projektowaną*, trans. M. F. Karp (Warsaw, 1789).

powers of the English Crown. Only English jurisprudence preserved the vestiges of liberty, which were daily being eaten away by cupidity.[78]

The *philosophes* did not all revolt. After spending most of 1764 in England, Helvétius wrote that 'par la forme de l'État, tout jusqu'aux vices est avantageux à l'Angleterre.'[79] Diderot recommended the English constitution to Catherine II, and quoted Voltaire's aphorism that the King of England was free to do good, but kept from doing evil.[80] Voltaire equivocated. At various times he supported a *thèse royale*, and flattered Frederick II and Catherine II. Like Beccaria, he opposed intermediary bodies as resisters of Enlightenment. Yet he had more sympathy for the Genevan plebeians than Rousseau. In *L'ABC* (1768), which contains perhaps his most systematic political thought, 'B' presents a more democratic standpoint than either England (represented by 'A') or aristocratic republics like Venice (represented by 'C').[81]

The outbreak of war in America and the unrest in Ireland confirmed the existence of a malady in the Britannic world. No longer could its discontents be shrugged off as signs of health. The *Notizie del mondo* concluded that, as in ancient Rome, the liberty of the centre was the oppression of the provinces.[82] Raynal's *Histoire philosophique*, written with considerable assistance from Diderot, encouraged comparisons of England with Carthage, wrecked on the rocks of avarice. Yet while it applauded the American rebels, it still endorsed 'le gouvernement mixte des Anglais', which 'saisissant les avantages de ces trois pouvoirs, qui s'observent, se tempèrent, s'entr'aident et se répriment, va de lui-même au bien national'.[83] Some Anglophiles such as the Abbé Morellet feared that American independence would weaken England's standing in Europe, and so damage the cause of freedom. Few in number were the Brissots and Mirabeaus who wished to intervene in America as part of a general crusade for liberty. A few conservatives did bridle at aiding rebellion against

[78] Acomb, *Anglophobia*, 36–40, 98–9.

[79] Helvétius to J. Servan, 19 Oct. 1764, *Correspondance générale d'Helvétius* (vol. 3; Toronto and Oxford, 1991), 150.

[80] *Mémoires pour Cathérine II*, in *Oeuvres complètes*, vol. 10, 648. *Observations sur l'Instruction*, ibid., vol. 11, 209, 218.

[81] Voltaire, *Oeuvres complètes* (vol. 27; Paris, 1879), 311–400. Cf Gay, *Voltaire's Politics*, 235–7, and Venturi, *Utopia and Reform*, 86–8, with Pomeau, '*Écraser l'infâme*', 376–8.

[82] Venturi, *End of the Old Regime 1776–1789*, vol. 1, 154–65. An opinion recently ventured by L. Colley, *Britons*, ch. 2.

[83] Venturi, *End of the Old Regime*, vol. 1, *1776–1789*, 4–19, 155–6. G. T. Raynal, *Histoire philosophique et politique des établissemens et de commerce des Européens dans les deux Indes* [1781] (10 vols.; Paris, 1820), vol. 10, 72, 71–89, vol. 7, 297–8, vol. 9, 225–35.

legitimate authority, but far stronger was the urge among traditional Anglophobes for revenge. However, American political ideas, diffused in Paris by the generally venerated Franklin, did contribute to a radicalization among the surviving *philosophes*.[84]

Foremost among them was Condorcet, for whom the American Revolution was a sublime vindication of the rights of man. It would lead to the victory of liberty in Europe, and would save it in England. England's liberty endured in spite of its mixed constitution. The physiocrats had traditionally rejected 'counterforces' as contrary to the *évidence* on which wise policy should be based. Condorcet now believed that an élite of virtue and intelligence could guide a representative democracy, constructed according to the light of reason.[85] Likewise, Gaetano Filangieri depicted the American Revolution as an international struggle of democracy and liberty against the tyranny of mercantilist empires in *La scienza della legislazione* (1780–3). He devoted a chapter to refuting Montesquieu and mixed government. Blackstone's *Commentaries* convinced him that the royal prerogative was dangerously great and undefined, and that Parliament needed reforming and strengthening. The reign of Henry VIII showed how Parliament might be manipulated.[86]

De Lolme had also emphasized the strength of the royal prerogative. He was proved right by the events of 1783–4, when George III prevailed upon the House of Lords to reject Fox's India Bill, dismissed the Fox–North ministry, and maintained Pitt in office despite a hostile Commons majority. Pitt and the king then triumphed in the election of 1784.[87] As the Americans wrestled with the problems of constructing a new state,[88] Britain settled into an unruffled prosperity. Monarchist and aristocratic French critics of England, who had hitherto regarded the king and the Lords as nonentities, were impressed. The English constitution was evidently less republican, and the English people less insolent towards their king, than they had assumed. In the later 1780s, as the French monarchy slid into its terminal crisis, many writers of a conservative disposition

---

[84] Acomb, *Anglophobia*, ch. 5, 96–101. See the discussion in Palmer, *Age of the Democratic Revolution*, vol. 1, 239–63.

[85] Acomb, *Anglophobia*, 101–4. Venturi, *End of the Old Regime*, vol. 1, *1776–1789*, 100–4.

[86] Venturi, *End of the Old Regime*, vol. 1, *1776–1789*, 19–25. D. Carpanetto and G. Ricuperati, *Italy in the Age of Reason 1685–1789* (London, 1987), 289–96.

[87] See J. Cannon, *The Fox–North Coalition: Crisis of the Constitution 1782–4* (Cambridge, 1969).

[88] The difficulties and opportunities of the states were discussed in Paris and reported in Italian gazettes. Venturi, *End of the Old Regime*, vol. 1, *1776–1789*, 63–81, 95, 104–43. Palmer, *Age of the Democratic Revolution*, vol. 1, 264–82.

called for the establishment of a constitutional monarchy, such as that described by Montesquieu in England. These demands were echoed in most of the noble and bourgeois *cahiers de doléances* to the Estates-General in 1789.[89]

The triumph of Anglophilia and Anglomania across Europe was the triumph of Enlightenment. From subversion, heresy, and barbarity had come the political, philosophical, and cultural orthodoxy of the establishment. In the fevered Anglo-Dutch world of the turn of the eighteenth century, the freethinking Enlightenment had crystallized around Huguenot refugees. The developments in English science and philosophy of the same period thus first found their way onto the Continent, to be popularized in the 1730s by Voltaire on a far wider scale. By then, the ferment in England had subsided, as a result of political and religious moderation, and passed to France, where, at first repressed, it burst forth in the late 1740s. The *philosophes* looked to England as a model for France to follow. Their view of England was filtered by their contacts with the opposition to Walpole, mostly Whig aristocrats, who by the 1750s were increasingly content with the status quo. It was at just this time that the young and impressionable Stanisław Poniatowski visited England. The influence of the *philosophes*, supplemented by that of other foreign visitors, diffused the exemplary image of England across Europe. Montesquieu's interpretation of the English constitution was particularly pervasive. It was complex enough to inspire diverse reactions in France, Germany, Russia, and elsewhere. In the 1760s, England's political conflicts contributed to a reappraisal. It is surely no coincidence that the same Whigs and their heirs, whose opinions, if not representative, were extremely vocal, were now far from content. The American Revolution, reported in gazettes on a European scale, amplified the doubts. However, nothing could halt the runaway popularity of English literature and gardens, based on the cult of nature and sensibility. Anglomania overran the Continent. As the number of Europeans learning English and visiting England grew relentlessly, English culture began to establish its independence from French patronage and mediation. Particularly in Germany, it was vital to the destruction of French cultural hegemony. Declarations of 'a century of philosophy' notwithstanding, as an academic discipline, philosophy was often reduced to experimental science and the sensationist psychology of Locke and his disciple,

---

[89] Acomb, *Anglophobia*, 19–29, 104–7. Also see Grieder, *Anglomania*, 141–4, and G. Chaussinand-Nogaret, *The French Nobility in the Eighteenth Century: From Feudalism to Enlightenment* (Cambridge, 1985), ch. 8.

Condillac. In the 1780s, even the doubts on the English constitution were subdued. France seemed poised to follow its example.

However, the critics suddenly vanquished the Anglophiles in the early stages of the French Revolution. France scorned English experience; she would trust to her own reason. It marked the parting of the ways for cosmopolitanism and Enlightenment, and Enlightened Europeans applauded. As the English government allied with absolute monarchies and repressed its domestic critics, liberty seemed to many former Anglophiles to be lost in England. However, as the Revolution descended into the Terror, and as the French crusade for liberty became a war of conquest and plunder, England's stock recovered. England entered the post-war era no longer the icon of liberty, but a model of moderate liberalism. Some commentators had preferred absolutism all along. English ascendancy in culture and philosophy passed away quietly. For all the popularity of Byron, England did not lead romanticism as she had sensibility. The philosophy of Locke bowed to that of Kant, while experimental science slowly lost its association with Englishness. The First Industrial Nation long continued to be admired, yet Britannia's complacent assumption of her superiority became ever more questionable.

3
The Education of an Enlightened Anglophile

Enlightenment and Anglophilia were not brought to Poland by Stanisław August Poniatowski. Poland's last king grew up in an environment already affected by both. In order to assess the extent of English influence, we must cast an eye over the whole of the early Enlightenment in Poland. The 'early Enlightenment' remains controversial among Polish historians. The traditional image of the 'Saxon night' was the result of an uncritical acceptance of the polemics of enlightened reformers under Stanisław August against the previous reign. After the Second World War, the Marxist insistence upon 1764 as a watershed in the replacement of a 'feudal' economy by a 'capitalist' one, and a generally critical attitude to the values of the old Commonwealth, only served to reinforce the traditional interpretation.[1] In the last thirty years or so, however, the Saxon era, and in particular the reign of Augustus III, has made a comeback. Historians of literature were the first to push back the beginning of the Polish Enlightenment to 1730 or 1740. Instead of 'pioneers' or 'precursors' of the Enlightenment, mid-century educational reformers, *literati*, and the leading political publicists are now commonly described as representatives of the 'early Enlightenment'.[2] Jacek Staszewski has perhaps done most to focus attention on projects for political reform and cultural achievement alike during the reigns of both Wettins. However, a general rehabilitation of the Saxon period has not won universal acceptance. By 1978, Emanuel Rostworowski was already sounding a note of caution.[3] No doubt the argument will continue to run, but it seems valid to use the term 'early Enlightenment', provided that, in accordance with our

---

[1] A convenient summary of the Marxist interpretation of the Polish Enlightenment is *Kołłątaj i wiek Oświecenia* (*PH*, Warsaw, 1951).

[2] e.g. M. Klimowicz, *Oświecenie* (1972, 4th edn., Warsaw, 1980), 5–75.

[3] See in particular two overviews; 'Reformowanie Rzeczypospolitej przed Sejmem Wielkim', in A. Grześkowiak-Krwawicz, *Konstytucja 3 Maja: Prawo—Polityka—Symbol* (Warsaw, 1992), and 'La Culture polonaise durant la crise du XVIIIe siècle', *APH*, 55 (1987). Cf. the discussion of Staszewski's paper in *Konstytucja 3 Maja; Prawo—Polityka—Symbol*, 113–14, and Rostworowski, 'Theatrum polityczne', in *Popioły i korzenie*.

Kantian definition, we mean not an enlightened age, but an age of Enlightenment, however slow and limited the process was at first.

I

The first half of the eighteenth century was by no means barren of plans to reform the Commonwealth. Augustus II and his entourage, notably Field-Marshal Jacob Heinrich Flemming, drew up a number of plans in the first half of his reign to transform Poland into a state powerful militarily, flourishing economically through typically mercantilist measures, and governed in a more or less absolute manner. Bishop Konstanty Szaniawski, a supporter of the Court, proposed reforms in the execution of justice and the army, a policy to encourage the recovery of urban life, and the creation of an executive council of residents, without diminishing or extending the royal prerogative. In contrast, Stanisław Dunin Karwicki, the chamberlain (*podkomorzy*) of Sandomierz, expressed the republican convictions of the middling and wealthier *szlachta*. In his *De ordinanda republica* (which was written in 1704–10 and circulated in manuscript), Karwicki proposed annual Seyms which could reconvene themselves whenever necessary. He wished to restrict the *liberum veto* to the protest of all the envoys of a palatinate, and abolish the *liberum rumpo*. The Seym would take over the royal distributive and nominative powers, as well as the executive. To this end it would divide itself into three chambers comprising both senators and envoys, for internal, foreign, and treasury affairs. Karwicki's project was also aimed at the *magnateria*, for he proposed elected senators and ministers—who would be strictly responsible to the Seym and hold office for limited periods.[4]

In 1732, Antoni Dembowski dared to attack the dogmas of the *liberum veto*, binding instructions, and free royal elections, and challenged Sarmatian megalomania, through the device of a Frenchman's conversation with a Pole.[5] The election of Stanisław Leszczyński in 1733, swiftly followed by the imposition of Augustus III, gave a further impetus to political thought. The worsening of the Commonwealth's international position was no longer open to doubt. In the following years, the call to

[4] *De ordinanda republica*, in Karwicki, *Dzieła polityczne z początku XVIII wieku*, ed. A. and K. Przyboś (Wrocław, 1992). Staszewski, 'Pomysły reformatorskie czasów Augusta II', *KwH*, 82 (1975). Konopczyński, *Polscy pisarze polityczni XVIII wieku* (Warsaw, 1966), 32–51.

[5] A. Rosner, 'Wolność polska rozmową Francuza z Polakiem roztrząsana', in A. Mączak *et al.* (eds.), *Francja-Polska XVIII–XIX w.: Studia z dziejów kultury i polityki poświęcone Profesorowi Andrzejowi Zahorskiemu . . .* (Warsaw, 1983).

increase the army was a popular one among the *szlachta*. Unfortunately, there was no agreement on the means of financing the new troops, or on who should control them.[6] Stanisław Leszczyński (as Duke of Lorraine and titular King of Poland) published *Głos wolny wolność ubespieczaiący* ('A free voice securing freedom') about 1743. Bold in his criticism of serfdom and proposals for elected ministerial and provincial councils, the author of *Głos wolny* insisted that he wished to conserve the *liberum veto* 'in omne authoritate', despite its abuse by 'malevoli'.[7] In general, reformers treated the *veto* with kid gloves, until at the end of the Saxon era, Stanisław Konarski demolished it intellectually and demonstrated to the *szlachta* how the dreaded majority voting could be reconciled with freedom.[8]

The *szlachta* began to realize the importance of trade, towns, and manufactures in the late 1730s and 1740s, if only to pay for the augmented army it desired, and *seymiki* instructions from these years contain many ideas for their revival. *Głos wolny* and Stanisław Poniatowski's *List ziemianina*[9] devoted much space to economic matters, while Antoni Potocki even proposed that representatives of the towns take part in the Seym's deliberations on urban affairs. The long stays in Dresden required of his Polish ministers and officials by Augustus III acquainted them with modern administrative practices and cameralist economic thought. Stefan Garczyński, in his *Anatomia Rzeczypospolitey*, begun in the 1730s but published in 1751, demanded the limitation of peasant labour services and preached the work ethic to the *szlachta*. He criticized clerical affluence and proposed the abolition of celibacy to increase the population. Garczyński was the first Polish writer to note the 'agricultural revolution' in the East Anglian fens.[10]

Before 1760, England scarcely figured in reformers' arguments at all. Karwicki referred to Venice, Holland, and Switzerland as *respublicae*, and made no mention of England. Konarski, in a manuscript of 1734 and Leszczyński, in one version of *Głos Wolny*, referred to England as a

---

[6] Z. Zielińska, *Walka 'Familii' o reformę Rzeczypospolitej 1743–1752* (Warsaw, 1983), 19–216.

[7] *Głos wolny wolność ubespieczaiący* (Nancy, 1733 [1743]), esp. 41–4, 48–53, 70–2, 83–5, 100–4. Konopczyński, *Polscy pisarze polityczni*, 94–129. E. Cieślak, *Stanisław Leszczyński* (Wrocław, 1994), 19, 205–13. Cf. J. Feldman, *Stanisław Leszczyński* (3rd edn., Warsaw, 1984), ch. 9, with Fabre, *Stanislas-Auguste Poniatowski*, 86–8. Rostworowski, *Legendy i fakty*, 68–144, argued that Leszczyński only sponsored *Głos wolny*, and that the real author was his supporter, Mateusz Białłozor, but the matter remains contentious.

[8] See below, Ch. 7, section I.   [9] See below, pp. 75–6.

[10] Garczyński, *Anatomia Rzeczypospolitey Polskiey* ... (Warsaw, 1751), esp. 22–39, 45, 175–80, 270–1. Konopczyński, *Polscy pisarze polityczni*, 143–51. Staszewski, *August III*, 206, 284.

free country.[11] Even Stanisław Poniatowski only made a single favourable reference to England, and he stopped just short of using the English example to argue that Poland might introduce majority voting without endangering liberty. No one dared advance a similar argument for a hereditary throne. Moreover, it is difficult to count programmes of reform like Karwicki's at one extreme or Augustus II's at the other as part of the European Enlightenment. The one was a new formulation of traditional noble republican doctrine by a man born in 1640. The other could have been approved by any European ruler of the early eighteenth century. The denunciations of the oppression of the peasants and the wealth of the clergy in *Głos wolny* and *Anatomia Rzeczypospolitej* bear a more enlightened stamp, but they also breathe the concepts and rhetoric of Sarmatia. We should remember that the French Enlightenment produced very little political thought before 1748, the year of *De l'esprit des lois*. In Polish political thought, it is more relevant to talk of reform than Enlightenment, at least until later in the century.

It is less problematical to speak of the Enlightenment, and within it English influences, in the realms of philosophy, science, education, and literature. The bracing disputes between Pietism and Orthodoxy affected Lutherans in the Commonwealth as much as in the *Reich*, and the *Gymnasien* of Thorn and Danzig were soon affected by trends from Halle, notably the philosophy of Christian Wolff. Wolffian philosophy was also dominant at the University of Leipzig, and among his Polish adherents were men like the Załuski brothers, closely connected with the Saxon Court. Wolff's philosophy won acceptance in some Italian Catholic circles in the second quarter of the century, and the studies of some leading monastic and secular clergymen in Italy helped the ideas of a moderate Catholic Enlightenment filter into Poland. The Arcadian Academy in Rome, a prestigious literary society with branches across Italy, counted thirty Polish clerical and lay members by 1764.[12] Contacts with France, through the voyages of the lay and clerical élites to Paris, remained lively throughout the first half of the century. French influences were particularly strong in architecture and interior decoration; the classic example is Jan Klemens Branicki's palace at Białystok, the 'Podlasian Versailles'. French was widely spoken among the *magnateria*, French governors were popular, and Warsaw booksellers sold a wide variety of French books by the

---

[11] Grześkowiak Krwawicz, '*Rara avis* czy wolni wśród wolnych?', 173. Michalski, 'Sarmatyzm a europeizacja', 131.
[12] W. Roszkowska, 'Polacy w rzymskiej "Arkadii" (1699–1766)', *Pam. Lit.*, 56 (1965).

early 1760s. Fashion helped to prepare the way for enlightened thought. From the 1740s, an increasing number of French works were translated into Polish, including some plays by Voltaire.[13]

Another channel for new ideas was Freemasonry. The first ephemeral lodges in Poland were set up as early as 1720 by Polish aristocrats initiated abroad, in Franco-Jacobite lodges, neither subject to London nor much influenced by English rules. The lodge in Protestant Danzig, which numbered British merchants among its members, was an exception. Augustus II's natural son Count Rutowski established the first lodge in Saxony in 1738, and from then on, quietly encouraged by the Court despite papal strictures, Freemasonry served to unite Polish and Saxon élites. It would be wrong to attribute to Polish Masons any sort of coherent programme, whether philosophical or political. The Poles had no need of lodges to introduce them to the principles and practice of elective and representative government. At most, Freemasonry provided a private forum, where novelties could be discussed, without fear of the reaction of the Catholic *szlachta*.[14]

The role of Dresden, one of the cultural centres of Europe, in promoting new artistic ideas should not be underestimated. Many Poles spent long periods at the Saxon Court, as ministers, officials, courtiers, or pages. When the Court settled in Warsaw during the Seven Years' War, music, painting, and architecture received a fillip from the patronage of the Court and the Polish magnates who congregated there for the 'season'. About 1760, neo-classical architecture made its first appearance in Poland. The presence of the Court also contributed to the increased popularity of the French language, dress, and manners, and the corresponding decline of Sarmatism among the élite.[15]

We should not, however, restrict the early Enlightenment in Poland to foreign influences. Konarski and the Jesuit Franciszek Bohomolec campaigned for the purification of the Polish language from Latin incrustations. The translation of foreign books promoted by Józef Andrzej

[13] J. A. Gierowski, 'U źródeł polskiego Oświecenia', in A. Zahorski (ed.), *Wiek XVIII: Polska i świat: Księga poświecona Bogusławowi Leśnodorskiemu* (Warsaw, 1974), 47–9. Klimowicz, *Oświecenie*, 14–16, 25–8, 62, 70. Sinko, 'Kontakty literackie z zagranicą', in T. Kostkiewiczowa (ed.), *Słownik literatury polskiego Oświecenia* (2nd edn., Wrocław, 1991), 244–53. J. Kurkowski, *Warszawskie czasopisma doby Augusta III* (Warsaw, 1994). On Branicki's residences, see E. Kowecka, *Dwór 'najrządniejszego w Polszcze magnata'* (Warsaw, 1991).

[14] Hass, *Wolnomularstwo*, 62–5, 74–81. Staszewski, *Polacy w osiemnastowiecznym Dreźnie* (Wrocław, 1986), 112–28. Idem, *August III*, 182, 244. Smoleński, *Przewrót umysłowy*, 199–203.

[15] Staszewski, *August III*, 175–91, 237–45. Idem, *Polacy w osiemnastowiecznym Dreźnie*, 86–146. S. Lorentz and A. Rottermund, *Klasycyzm w Polsce* (2nd edn., Warsaw, 1984), 11–12, 42, 76–7.

Załuski, and the huge public library he opened in 1747 with his brother, Andrzej Stanisław, were intended to raise the level of Polish literature and learning. Józef Załuski and Konarski began to publish a monumental compendium of Poland's laws, the *Volumina Legum*, in 1732, while in Danzig, Gottfried Lengnich wrote the first scholarly legal history of Poland.[16]

The Italian Theatine order established small schools in Warsaw, Wilno, and Płock in 1737. They were the first Catholic schools in which one of the main languages of instruction was Polish. From 1740, the principal of the Warsaw school was Antonio Mario Portalupi, who was a follower of Wolff, as well as a notorious philanderer. The Theatines laid emphasis on good manners, theatrical productions, modern languages, history, mathematics, and science, but their curriculum was not based on any consequential system of education.[17] The Theatines' Warsaw school probably stung the Piarist order into establishing a Collegium Nobilium in Warsaw in 1740–1, the direction of which was entrusted to Stanisław Konarski.

Konarski took as his model the Piarists' own Collegium Nazarenum in Rome, where he had studied in 1725–9. There he was exposed to elements of the 'newer philosophy' (*philosophia recentiorum*), modern mathematics and science, and the Latin literature of the golden age. In Paris he deepened his knowledge of philosophy, and studied the educational thought of Locke (in French translation). In addition, he saw productions of Molière and Corneille and read Voltaire's *Histoire de Charles XII*. Konarski's programme was more systematic than that of the Theatines. His aim was to educate a new generation of virtuous patriots, who would reform the ailing Commonwealth. From the start, the Collegium Nobilium was an élitist school for the *magnateria*. From Locke, Konarski took an emphasis on the moral upbringing of the nation's natural leaders, based on honour and the principles of the Christian religion, the reduction of corporal punishment to a minimum, the teaching of geography with the aid of a globe, and the teaching of Latin and other languages, not as an aim in itself, but to enable pupils to read literature. Konarski placed less stress than Locke on physical education, but more on aesthetics and science. Although he followed Locke in attaching weight to the native language, in general Latin lost ground to French rather than Polish. The

---

[16] Klimowicz, *Oświecenie*, 16–21, 34–8. On Lengnich, see K. Friedrich, 'Gottfried Lengnich (1689–1774) und die Aufklärung in Preußen königlich-polnischen Anteils', in H. Schmidt-Glinzer (ed.), *Förden und Bewahren: Studien zur europäischen Kulturgeschichte der frühen Neuzeit* (Wiesbaden, 1996).

[17] *Mémoires*, vol. 2, 207. Konopczyński, *Stanisław Konarski* (Warsaw, 1926), 99.

biggest difference was that Locke was a supporter of education at home. For adapting Locke's theories to a school environment, Rollin's *Essai sur les études* was essential. Public disputes and moralizing theatrical productions formed an integral part of the curriculum. In 1754, with the assistance of Cypryan Komorowski, named visitor to the Polish Piarists by Pope Benedict XIV at Konarski's request, Konarski was able to reform the other twenty Piarist schools. The model was the Collegium Nobilium, but the curriculum was necessarily less ambitious and the intake less aristocratic.[18]

The Piarists' introduction of *philosophia recentiorum* into their schools was marked by a deliberate eclecticism that distinguishes their programme from the more systematic approach of Wolff. On the one hand, they retained scholastic ontology and insisted on revelation, as both a complementary source of truth and a standard for choosing between philosophical systems. On the other hand, they established experimental physics as the basis of natural philosophy and laid far greater stress than Wolff on the a posteriori. Thus Konarski recommended that Piarist libraries contain the works of Galileo, Leibniz, Gassendi, Newton, Wolff, Descartes, Locke, Genovesi, Bacon, Voltaire, and others. With time, the emphasis became more empiricist, and physics pushed out metaphysics completely.[19] Father Antoni Wiśniewski, a teacher at the Collegium Nobilium, provoked criticism from the Jesuits and the Dominicans in 1746, when he organized a public dispute in Andrzej Załuski's palace among his pupils on the 'newer philosophy', including Descartes, Wolff, and Newton. Konarski enabled Wiśniewski to study abroad in Rome, Turin, Paris, London, Halle (where he met Wolff), and Leipzig. He returned to the Collegium Nobilium with a number of instruments and taught experimental physics, incurring the renewed wrath of the scholastics. He was one of the first Poles unequivocally to defend the Copernican solar system in print.[20] Father Samuel Chróścikowski indicated his preference for the Newtonian theory of matter over those of Descartes and Leibniz in his *Fizyka, doświadczeniami potwierdzona* ('Physics, verified by experiments') of 1764. In that book,

---

[18] See J. Nowak-Dłużewski, *Stanisław Konarski* (1951, 2nd edn., Warsaw, 1989), 27–32, 46–73, 183–215; Konopczyński, *Konarski*, chs. 1, 4, 5, 6; W. J. Rose, *Stanislas Konarski, Reformer of Education in XVIIIth Century Poland* (London, 1929), part III; and K. Haupt, 'Recepcja poglądów Johna Locke'a przez Stanisława Konarskiego' (unpublished MA thesis, Łódź, 1964).

[19] S. Janeczek, *Oświecenie chrześcijańskie: Z dziejów polskiej kultury filozoficznej* (Lublin, 1994), overturns the received idea of the dependence of the early Polish Enlightenment upon Wolff, and argues that the Polish Piarists were in the vanguard of the European Catholic Enlightenment.

[20] Smoleński, *Przewrót umysłowy*, 67–70, 138.

intended for the pupils of the Collegium Nobilium, he expounded the Newtonian theory of gravity without explicitly endorsing it, but two years later, he wrote that Newtonian 'attraction' seemed more probable than the unspecified material 'invented' (*wymyślona*) by Descartes. Attacking the deists, 'the wiseacres of the present age', he used Newton's Laws of Motion to demonstrate the necessary existence of a Creator-God.[21]

Spurred on by the Piarist competition, the Jesuits reformed their own schools along similar lines in the 1750s, and, in Stanisław August's opinion, even surpassed the less intellectual Piarists in the quality of education they provided.[22] The Jesuits certainly showed most enthusiasm for experimental science and astronomy. The Wilno observatory was built in 1753 and equipped with instruments from England and elsewhere, thanks to the patronage of Elżbieta Puzyna, Hetman Michał Radziwiłł, and Bishop Józef Sapieha. Jesuit astronomers also observed the heavens in Warsaw, Lwów, and Poznań. The Jesuits demonstrated experiments in physics during the Lithuanian tribunal of 1753, and at Nowogródek in 1760 they displayed an English microscope and used prisms from London and Paris to show that Newton's theory of colours was 'closer to the truth' than Descartes's. Their college in Wilno opened a museum containing mathematical and physical instruments, bought in Paris, in 1761. Among the Jesuits expelled from France was Jean Flernet, who became professor of experimental physics at Wilno in 1762. Józef Rogaliński, who lectured in experimental physics and astronomy at Poznań, supported Newton's criticism of Leibniz's and Wolff's monads.[23]

Philosophia recentiorum met with a less hospitable reception at the venerable Jagiellonian University. As Bishop of Cracow from 1746 to 1755, Andrzej Załuski was the university's chancellor. He wished to replace scholasticism with the philosophy of Wolff, whom he knew and admired. Załuski sent young Marcin Świątkowski to Halle to study, and from 1749 Świątkowski lectured on mathematics and astronomy. Załuski described experimental physics as the 'mother of the most beautiful discoveries', but was unable to introduce it. His efforts to impose reform from above ran into a wall of opposition from the professors. *Philosophia recentiorum*

---

[21] Chróścikowski, *Fizyka, doświadczeniami potwierdzona* . . . (Warsaw, 1764), 20–5, 47–53, 63–80, 115–16, 140–5. Idem, *Filozofia chrześciańska o początkach praw naturalnych przeciwko deistom czyli teraźnieyszego wieku mędrkom* . . . (Warsaw, 1766), 210, 237–8, 310–11.

[22] *Mémoires*, vol. 2, 207–9. The Danish minister Saint Saphorin to Count Bernstorff (reporting a conversation with the king), 12 Mar. 1766, repr. in Konopczyński, *Konarski*, 451–2.

[23] Smoleński, *Przewrót umysłowy*, 83–90, 92, 120–32.

slowly gained ground, but until the 1770s it coexisted with scholasticism, while experimental science was non-existent.[24]

English influence on the early Polish Enlightenment was centred on Konarski's use of Locke's *Thoughts Concerning Education*. However, as *philosophia recentiorum* established itself, experimental physics began to assume a leading role, and the Newtonian contribution to both Piarist and Jesuit teaching increased. The main channels of Enlightenment were the Saxon Court, the contacts of some of the monastic orders with Rome, and the journeys of the lay and clerical élite to Paris. The English component was chiefly imported from France. If English science and philosophy generally reached Poland at second or even third hand, the English constitution scarcely figured at all in projects for political reform. England played a minor part in a movement whose impact should not be exaggerated. Until around 1760, the Enlightenment produced only a few gentle ripples across the surface of the murky and stagnant pond that was the world of the *szlachta*.

II

No one could accuse Stanisław Poniatowski (1676–1762) of Sarmatian insularity. Born into a *szlachta* family of no great antiquity, wealth, or renown, this extraordinary man ended his life as castellan of Cracow, the first lay senator of the Commonwealth. Having served under Michał Sapieha in the Imperial army against the Turks, Poniatowski was recruited by Charles XII when the Swedish king invaded Lithuania at the start of the Great Northern War. Poniatowski was responsible for the king's escape at Poltava in 1709. His knowledge of Turkish subsequently made his diplomatic services indispensable, and he later acted as governor of Charles's German territory of Zweibrücken. Poniatowski made his peace with Augustus II in 1719. He swiftly won the king's trust and was employed on a number of diplomatic missions. In 1720 he married Konstancja Czartoryska (1695–1759), the daughter of the Lithuanian vice-chancellor Kazimierz Czartoryski, who, by his skill in picking political winners and his marriage to Izabella Morsztyn had managed to reburnish the faded lustre of his ancient princely house.[25]

[24] M. Chamcówna, *Uniwersytet Jagielloński w dobie Komisji Edukacji Narodowej: Szkoła Główna Koronna w okresie wizyty i rektoratu Hugona Kołłątaja 1777–1786* (Wrocław, 1957), 18–50.

[25] A. Link-Lenczowski, 'Poniatowski, Stanisław', *PSB*, 27 (1983) 471–81. K. Kantecki, *Stanisław Poniatowski, kasztelan krakowski, ojciec Stanisława Augusta* (2 vols.; Poznań, 1880).

Izabella Morsztyn was the daughter of the poet Jan Andrzej Morsztyn, treasurer of the Crown under Sobieski, and Lady Catherine Gordon, the daughter of the Catholic Marquis of Huntly, who had emigrated to Poland in 1649. Lady Catherine married Morsztyn in 1659. Izabella was 12 when the family fled to France after Morsztyn was impeached for treason in 1683, and she grew up in Paris. After her marriage to Kazimierz Czartoryski in 1693, she created Poland's first salon. Her four children were brought up in an atmosphere dominated by French culture. Between themselves, they preferred to write in French. Izabella passed on to them her driving ambition, and also exerted an influence on the upbringing of her grandchildren.[26]

Konstancja's eldest brothers, Michał (1696–1775) and August (1697–1782), were young and ambitious. In Poniatowski, the Czartoryskis found a leader of unmatched military, diplomatic, and political experience and talent, who brought them closer to the Court. Poniatowski became treasurer of Lithuania in 1722, and Michał Czartoryski succeeded his father as Lithuanian vice-chancellor in 1724. By the late 1720s, the *Familia*, as they began to be called, was a force to be reckoned with. Augustus II wished to make Poniatowski grand hetman of the Crown, but the Potockis prevented the nomination by breaking up successive seyms before the election of the marshal. Poniatowski exercised command over the army as its acting commander (*regimentarz*) instead.[27] August Czartoryski emerged from his brother's shadow in 1731 when he married Zofia, the daughter and heiress of Adam Sieniawski and the widow of Stanisław Denhoff. Her enormous fortune gave the *Familia* the financial muscle it had hitherto lacked. In the same year, August Czartoryski became palatine of Ruthenia and Poniatowski palatine of Mazovia. At the Seym of 1733, the *Familia* managed to break the Potockis' resistance and elect a client as marshal, but Augustus II was on his deathbed, and expired with the hetmanships still vacant.[28]

---

[26] A. Przyboś, 'Gordon de Huntlej, Henryk', *PSB*, 8 (1959–60), 302. S. Sidorowicz, 'Czartoryska, Izabella z Morsztynów', *PSB*, 4 (1938), 241. Konopczyński, *Dzieje Polski nowożytnej*, vol. 2, 66–7. M. Dernałowicz, *Portret Familii* (Warsaw, 1974), draws a vivid portrait of Izabella Morsztyn. Her political importance within the *Familia* well into the 1750s emerges from the many letters of Konstancja Poniatowska to her husband, preserved in ARP 373, vol. 1, e.g. 22 May 1755. J. M. Bulloch, 'The Gordons in Poland', *Scottish Notes and Queries*, 12 (1898), and 'Polish alliances with the Gordons', *Scottish Notes and Queries*, 2nd series, 4 (1902–3) are full of errors.

[27] Since 1717, the hetmanships could only be granted at a Seym after the election of a marshal.

[28] Lukowski, *Liberty's Folly*, 153–6. On the Czartoryskis, see the biograms by Konopczyński in *PSB*, 4 (1938), 272–5, 288–94.

The *Familia* backed Stanisław Leszczyński in 1733. It proved to be a mistake. Poniatowski was quick to recognize Augustus III, but he had resigned his claims to the hetmanship to Józef Potocki for the sake of a common front in support of Leszczyński, and Potocki's appointment was confirmed in 1736. Despite Poniatowski's efforts at reconciliation, and the favour of Russia, the *Familia* remained out of grace. The Court only turned to it in 1743, after its efforts to increase the army and pass new taxes in co-operation with the Potockis had ended in a complete fiasco. The Potockis were interested in an increased army only in so far as it served their private interests.[29] Poniatowski was keenly aware of the danger posed by Prussia and knew that Poland would have to strengthen itself militarily, if it were ever to recover its importance on the European stage. His brothers-in-law, although not possessed of his strategic vision, also appreciated the need for a thorough overhaul of the Commonwealth. Michał Czartoryski's maxim was *extremis malis, extrema remedia*. Whether the Czartoryski brothers wished rather to reform the state to enjoy power, or to seize power to reform the state, during their periods of favour, those objectives coalesced.

Stanisław Poniatowski's pamphlet, *List ziemianina do pewnego przyjaciela z inszego województwa* ('Letter of a landowner to a certain friend in another palatinate'), published in the run up to the 1744 Seym, rose above the usual run of demagogic slogans employed by the *Familia* and its opponents alike. In order to revive the towns by immigration, he proposed greater religious freedom. He reassured his readers that his motive was not to introduce heresy, for the clergy would convert more heretics by preaching and godliness than by violence and persecution. (Poniatowski built a church for Protestant craftsmen on his own estates.) The main difficulty for Poniatowski was not in convincing the *szlachta* of the need to augment the army, but in persuading it to find sufficient money. Poniatowski dared not challenge the *liberum veto* outright, but argued that it should be suspended in order to increase the army and pass the necessary taxes. The palatine of Mazovia showed his true colours in writing that Poland might have something to learn from abroad:

Having accounts of certain customs in various countries, I wish that we would imitate them. Among other things I think that the greatest and most difficult matters are happily settled by majority vote.

Delicate matters, like elections at *seymiki*, might be resolved by secret ballot. Poniatowski concluded his appeal thus:

[29] See Staszewski, *August III*, 203–9 and Zielińska, *Walka 'Familii'*, 19–46.

In short, if we only wanted to use all the means towards good government which we find at home, we should be completely happy. Let us look at other free estates and republics in Europe. England differs little from us in her laws and domestic constitution, and how beautifully she governs herself, and maintains her fame! Holland, Venice, and Switzerland keep up their pride and consideration. Let us also have strength, let us have order, we will have everything, we will prosper in everything, more than one power will seek our friendship and affinity, and we will win ourselves certain and undisputed fame in neighbouring nations.[30]

Poniatowski did not explicitly hold up England as a model, although he justified the suspension of the *liberum veto* by the example of other countries. The Poles had all they required to repair their state within their own political tradition. He cited England and other 'free states and republics' ostensibly to show that liberty was not incompatible with good government and international respect. He played upon the *szlachta*'s national pride. All the same, Poniatowski was probably the first Pole in the eighteenth century to proclaim in print his admiration for the English constitution. What is more, he rated it above the Dutch, Venetian, and Swiss. He breached the ramparts of Sarmatian suspicion, though few were prepared to follow. Among those willing were his brothers-in-law. When, during the Seven Years' War, Count Heinrich Brühl, Augustus III's first minister and the Austrian and Russian ministers objected to August Czartoryski's sending his son Adam Kazimierz to England, the Palatine of Ruthenia is reported to have answered that he 'was at full liberty to direct His Son's Education, as He pleased; and that He sent him to England, as thinking it the Country in the world, where there was most to be learned'.[31]

Unfortunately, every effort at military, fiscal, or judicial reform failed, victims either of filibusters or the *liberum veto*. The *Familia* blamed all setbacks on the Court's apparent lack of enthusiasm for reform, and the king's supposed sloth. Augustus III and Brühl, for their part, failed to see the point of distributing patronage according to the *diktat* of the *Familia* and tying themselves to one faction, if the Seyms failed to achieve anything anyway. Personal factors also played a role. Michał Czartoryski would not spare Brühl his sardonic wit, and Poniatowski's eldest son Kazimierz refused to marry Brühl's daughter. Perhaps most important, the Czartoryskis were reluctant to help secure the succession for the Wettins.[32]

---

[30] *List ziemianina*, repr. in Kantecki, *Poniatowski*, vol. 2, pp. lxxxix–civ. Ibid., vol. 1 136–7. See Konopczyński, *Polscy pisarze polityczni*, 135–9.

[31] Stormont to Holderness, 22 June 1757, PRO SP 88/81.

[32] Zielińska, *Walka 'Familii'*, restates Konopczyński's endorsement of the *Familia* as the only serious group of reformers, while Staszewski, *August III*, takes a more sympathetic view of the Saxon Court.

The greatest obstacle was not, however, the tension between the Court and the *Familia*, but the ability of foreign powers to torpedo any measure that might strengthen the Commonwealth, through the use or threat of the *liberum veto*. The sad truth was that Russia as well as Prussia was determined to keep Poland in political anarchy. Even the Grodno Seym of 1744, traditionally seen as the one occasion when fiscal and military reform might have succeeded, did not stand a chance. Austria and Britain offered only good wishes, while Russia feared a rejuvenated Poland under the hereditary rule of the Wettins even more than Prussian expansionism. Tsaritsa Elizabeth reassured Frederick II that if he did not manage to wreck the Seym, she would. Faced with the certain failure of the *Sejm*, the *Familia* managed to cover the Prussian party in odium when a *Familia* supporter threw down a bag of ducats in the chamber, claiming he had refused a bribe to use the *veto*. The Seym fell victim to filibusters organized by Frederick's henchman Antoni Potocki. This leads to the sobering conclusion that the Poles' only hope of carrying through any major reform lay in an international conjunction which would prevent both Russia and Prussia from intervening.[33] The *Familia*, however, continued to believe that Russia could be persuaded to support reform.

The *Familia* also tried to interest England in its plans. The first contacts were not auspicious. In 1717 Poniatowski was arrested on the orders of George I, as he was in touch with agents of the Old Pretender. Michał Czartoryski delivered an indignant lecture on the situation of English Catholics to envoy Finch, when the latter protested about the sentences handed out to the Protestants of Thorn in 1724.[34] However, Finch's successor George Woodward found himself treated with 'great civility', stayed with Poniatowski at his country residence of Wołczyn, and wrote of August Czartoryski as 'my friend'.[35] At first Woodward and Sir Luke Schaub (who arrived on a special mission in 1730–1) were, like the *Familia*, secretly working with the French in support of Leszczyński. That changed in February 1732, but Woodward did not break with the *Familia*. The families of Czartoryski and Poniatowski were 'indisputably the most polite and the most reasonable and the most sensible that I know

[33] Zielińska, *Walka 'Familii'*, esp. 55–162. J. Staszewski, 'Co się wydarzyło na sejmie w Grodnie w 1744 roku?', in K. Iwanicka *et al.* (eds.), *Parlament, Prawo, Ludzie: Studia Ofiaroware Profesorowi Juliuszowi Bardachowi . . .* (Warsaw, 1996), 273–8. M. G. Müller, *Polen zwischen Preussen und Russland: Souveränitätskrise und Reformpolitik 1736–1752* (Berlin, 1983). Cegielski and Kądziela, *Rozbiory*, 60–74.
[34] Konopczyński, 'Anglia a Polska', 98. Przeździecki, *Diplomatic Ventures and Adventures*, 173–8.
[35] Woodward to Tilson, 30 July 1729, 6 Aug. 1729, BCzart. 1983, ff. 9, 17.

in the country. I am not ashamed to own, that I have ever since my being here much more frequented them than any other; but I am very ignorant of that being in the French interest,' he wrote in self-justification to his colleague at Vienna.[36] The *Familia*'s espousal of Leszczyński led to a hiatus in this intimacy, which was only gradually resumed during the mission of Woodward's successor, Thomas Villiers. In 1740, Lord Harrington cautioned Villiers against Poniatowski, 'an artful and intriguing person, and one wholly in the interest of France'.[37] Poniatowski did his best to win Villiers's trust: 'He almost cried to me when he described the contempts & mepris his country was exposed to from this anarchy.'[38] By 1743, the interests of the *Familia* and Britain coincided in an anti-French, pro-Russian stance. Political considerations no longer obstructed personal friendship,[39] which bloomed into full flower during the missions of Sir Charles Hanbury Williams and Lord Stormont.

Besides the political motives, these friendships were more an effect of the *Familia*'s admiration of England than its cause. Poniatowski and the Czartoryskis were cosmopolitans in an age of insularity. Poniatowski had his eyes opened to the world in the course of his travels, which included Paris in 1717 and again in 1740–1, and the Czartoryskis also traversed Europe in their youth. August Czartoryski met Montesquieu in Vienna in 1728. Both Czartoryskis were members of the first Masonic lodge in Poland.[40] Moreover, they grew up in a household whose tone was set by their dazzling mother. As a result, all three were free from Sarmatian illusions and open to foreign ideas, which they might adapt to the needs of their country.

III

Stanisław Antoni Poniatowski was born at Wołczyn on 17 January 1732. He was the sixth surviving child and the fourth son of Stanisław and Konstancja Poniatowski. He was joined by two more brothers within four years. This large number of sons had important consequences. Although Stanisław Poniatowski had enriched himself over the years, and had made

---

[36] Instructions to Woodward, 22 Oct. 1728 (os), and 29 Feb. 1732 (os). Woodward to Robinson, 24 Mar. 1733, BCzart. 1983, ff. 5, 29, 35–6.

[37] Harrington to Villiers, 25 Mar. 1740 (os). Villiers to Harrington, Dresden, 17 Apr. 1740, BCzart. 1983, ff. 165, 167.

[38] Villiers to Harrington, Dresden, 21 Aug. 1740, BCzart. 1983, f. 175.

[39] When Villiers arrived in Warsaw in 1744, he spent his very first evening at Izabella Czartoryska's. K. Poniatowska to S. Poniatowski, 16 Nov. 1744, ARP 373, vol. 1.

[40] Hass, *Wolnomularstwo*, 63. Smoleński, *Monteskjusz w Polsce wieku XVIII* (Warsaw, 1927), 49.

his way into the lower ranks of the *magnateria*, he was no Croesus. If the Poniatowskis were not to return to the middling *szlachta* as swiftly as they had emerged from it, only the eldest son, Kazimierz, could expect to receive much of an inheritance. The others had to make careers for themselves. The second son, Franciszek, became a canon of Cracow Cathedral. The third, Alexander, became an officer in the French army. After Alexander was killed in battle in 1744, and the epileptic Franciszek died in 1749, the two youngest sons, Andrzej and Michał Jerzy, followed in their footsteps. Stanisław was destined for diplomacy.[41]

For someone as ambitious for her children as Konstancja Poniatowska, who was almost twisted by her anxiety that they should be not treated by their uncles as poor relations, their education was an unusually pressing matter.[42] In particular, she doted on Stanisław, who was kidnapped in infancy by Józef Potocki and held for several months, and whose health gave her frequent alarms. Her husband, already 55 at the time of Stanisław's birth, took less interest in his younger sons than in the elder three. Most of Stanisław's early years were spent in Danzig, and from the age of 3, his mother 'commenca des hors à s'occuper de mon éducation avec cette intelligence supérieure qui lui faisait déjà une réputation célèbre par l'éducation de mes ainés, mais avec une attention encore plus soignée'. She was determined that Stanisław should be a good Pole and a good Catholic, and made him wear Sarmatian costume. His father, for his part, thought it 'honteux d'ignorer sa langue maternelle', and Stanisław could write correct Polish at the age of 7. However, Konstancja isolated him from other children, fearing their corrupting influence, and instilled in Stanisław a contempt for the ignorance and falsity that characterized many of his contemporaries. Looking back, Stanisław August regretted that he had not been allowed to enjoy his childhood; 'c'est comme si l'on ôtait le mois d'avril de l'année.' He found it easier to talk to adults than children his own age, and became a proud, prudish, awkward, and morose youth. 'Stanislas croit estre un grand homme, il l'est a proportion de son age, mais je n'ecris pas qu'il se l'imagine, nous n'avons d'autres sujets de querelles en semble,' wrote Konstancja.[43] She had to reassure

---

[41] J. Nieć, *Młodość ostatniego elekta: St. A. Poniatowski 1732–1764* (Cracow, 1935), 5. Fabre, *Stanislas-Auguste Poniatowski*, 150–5. Zamoyski, *Last King*, 13, 18–20.

[42] See *Mémoires*, vol. 1, 8–10; Fabre, *Stanislas-Auguste Poniatowski*, 134, 159–62, 600 n. 35; Nieć, *Młodość ostatniego elekta*, 7–13; and Link-Lenczowski, 'Poniatowska, Konstancja', *PSB*, 27 (1983), 409–11.

[43] K. Poniatowska to Kaz. Poniatowski, undated [Nov. 1741?], AKsJP 5, f. 21. Also K. Poniatowska to S. Poniatowski, 11 Nov. 1741, ARP 373, vol. 1.

her husband in 1741: 'Soiez tranquil sur le chapitre de Stasiu, son temperament est melieur que celui d'etant les freres, quand à ses estudes il
n'est nulement surchargé, il seroit dangereux de mettre trop de choses à la
fois dans une teste [*sic*: tete] dont l'imagination est si extraordinairement
vive.'[44] Unfortunately, she did not follow her own advice. Konstancja was
a devout Catholic, but her quietist religiosity was very different from
the demonstrative piety of the baroque. She crammed her son's head full
of metaphysics, to the extent that he had a nervous breakdown at the age
of 12, contemplating free will and predestination, and the uncertainty of
knowledge. The family confessor, Father Piotr Śliwicki, calmed him with
an assurance that God would not suffer him to continue in such agonies
of doubt, not a declaration of the efficacy of free will. Stanisław's belief
in destiny was to remain with him for the rest of his life. In some ways,
he inherited the Sarmatian passivity in the face of Divine Providence.[45]

Konstancja was not the only influence on Stanisław. The jurist Gott-
fried Lengnich taught the elder Poniatowski boys law and Polish history in
Danzig, and although Stanisław was not yet 8 when they moved to Warsaw in December 1739, he learned much of his history from Lengnich's
Historia Polona a Lecho (1740), dedicated to the young Poniatowskis.
Lengnich's work was traditionally conceived in terms of mythological origins and time-honoured privileges, but cast the monarchy as the ally of
Danzig against the *szlachta*. In Warsaw, Stanisław exchanged Sarmatian
for French-style dress. 1744 took him to the Theatines' Warsaw school,
which, as we have seen, was one of the most progressive establishments in
Poland. At about the same time, the Russian ambassador Hermann Keyserling began to tutor him in logic and philosophy. The hundreds of defini-
tions which Stanisław wrote down in German and Latin reveal more pedantry
and syllogism than anything else. Keyserling was a disciple of Leibniz,
as well as a religious sceptic. Stanisław certainly did not learn the English
scientific method from him. 'Die Physic ist eine wissenschaft dessen, was
durch Cörperliche dinge möglich ist,' ran definition number eight.[46]

A year later, the Abbé Jacques Allaire returned from accompanying
the elder Poniatowskis abroad to take charge of Stanisław. Allaire was a
broad-minded humanist. He taught Stanisław Ciceronian rhetoric and
ancient and modern history. In keeping with the demands of a diplomatic career, more emphasis than hitherto was put on languages. Allaire

---

[44] K. Poniatowska to S. Poniatowski, 16 Dec. 1741, ARP 373, vol. 1.

[45] See below, Ch. 10, section I.

[46] 'Zabawy szkolne Stanisława Augusta', BCzart. 911, ff. 123–93. Nieć, *Młodość ostatniego
elekta*, 13, 16–17. Fabre, *Stanislas-Auguste Poniatowski*, 166–8. Friedrich, 'Lengnich', 114.

perfected Stanisław's French and Latin, and probably also taught him Italian. Before his journey to St Petersburg in 1755, Stanisław would also learn some Russian. It is likely that Allaire first instructed Stanisław in English. Among Stanisław's exercises was an 'Essay de traduction du César de Shakespeare', comprising the first four scenes of *Julius Caesar*. Ludwik Bernacki, who first brought this text to light and published it, judged that it dated from Stanisław's stay in England in 1754, and was undertaken under the supervision of the Mr Hastings, whom Stanisław August mentions in his *Mémoires* as his tutor in England.[47] Jean Fabre noted that Stanisław August also wrote that he had already read Shakespeare before arriving in England, and judged from the translation that Stanisław's tutor could not have been an Englishman, and was most probably Allaire. The translation was therefore undertaken earlier, perhaps in the late 1740s.[48] This view seems correct. Stanisław later corrected the translation after he had improved his English. He may have done so in St Petersburg, when under the guidance of Sir Charles Hanbury Williams, Stanisław applied himself to English literature. 'J'adore Shakespear, et soutiendrai toutte ma Vie qu'il y a plus d'interet dans son Jules Cesar que dans tout ce que la Regularité Françoise ou la Fertilité Greque a jamais produit dans le Genre Dramatique,' he wrote at that time.[49] However, as he was still unable to unravel all of the 'jeux de mots,' it is also possible that he corrected the translation in Poland in the later 1750s.[50] Of all Shakespeare's plays, *Julius Caesar* best complemented Stanisław's exercises in rhetoric, and was the most relevant to the concerns of the Commonwealth, dealing as it did with the dilemmas of republicans confronted with the threat of personal dictatorship. Józef Załuski and Józef Minasowicz translated Voltaire's *Mort de César* into Polish and staged it at about the same time.[51] Nevertheless, the fact that Stanisław translated Shakespeare at all is remarkable. It was certainly the first such translation made by a Pole, and preceded by a quarter of a century the general European vogue for Shakespeare.[52]

[47] BCzart. 911, ff. 79–95. Bernacki, 'S. A. Poniatowski tłumaczem Szekspira', *Pam. Lit.*, 2 (1902). Idem, *Shakespeare w Polsce do końca XVIII wieku* (Cracow, 1914), 24–6. The text is reproduced in idem, *Teatr, dramat i muzyka za Stanisława Augusta* (2 vols.; Lwów, 1925), vol. 2, 183–9. *Mémoires*, vol. 1, 110.

[48] Fabre, *Stanislas-Auguste Poniatowski*, 164, 605 n. 26. *Mémoires*, vol. 1, 107. Nieć came to the same conclusion. *Młodość ostatniego elekta*, 19.

[49] Stan. to Charles Yorke, St. Petersburg, 17 Dec. 1755, BL Add. 35634, f. 292.

[50] In a number of places Stanisław inserted the sign # and either confessed his ignorance or explained the correct rendering. BCzart. 911, ff. 84, 85, 95. See below, pp. 97–8.

[51] Nieć, *Młodość ostatniego elekta*, 19. See Klimowicz, *Oświecenie*, 62.

[52] See above, pp. 54–7.

Another exercise was an unidentified 'Allegorie traduit de l'Anglois', about a dispute between two children of Apollo, *l'Esprit* and *le Savoir*. It ends in a reconciliation: 'L'Esprit persuada au Savoir de converser avec les Graces. Le Savoir s'engagea l'esprit au Service des Vertus. . . . Mariés peu apres par Ordre de Jupiter ils eurent une Lignée nombreuse d'Arts et de Sciences.'[53] It might have been an allegory of Stanisław August's aims as King of Poland.

Stanisław compiled a table of events in Europe during the reign of Louis XIII, which included much information about England under James I.[54] It was not his only foray into English history. Another two volumes of his archive, titled 'Miscellanea Anglica', contain a few translations or essays in Stanisław's hand, on matters such as the claims of Edward III to the throne of France and Henry VII to that of England.[55] The most interesting is probably the 'Histoire abregée de la Succession au Throne de la Grande Bretagne', which in general sought to demonstrate Parliament's right to choose or at least confirm the king, polemicized with divine hereditary right, and argued that government came from God, but its form depended upon men. As there is no mention of the Civil War, the Glorious Revolution, or the Act of Settlement, and the last king mentioned is James I, it would appear that Stanisław translated (or copied a French translation of) a pamphlet from the early seventeenth century.[56] Stanisław translated into Polish an instruction from the citizens of London to their newly elected MPs in 1741. It included the sentence 'the keeping of an army has always been held burdensome to subjects, and dangerous to their liberties.'[57] The mass of pamphlets and gazettes concerning the War of Jenkins' Ear in the two volumes, and the absence of any newspapers from between 1744 and 1763, suggest that Stanisław studied English history and politics in depth with Allaire in the 1740s. The choice of material, as with *Julius Caesar*, indicates republican concerns. Stanisław was not, on balance, brought up as a monarchist.

In 1748, the Palatine of Mazovia decided that Stanisław should, like Kazimierz and Alexander before him, go on campaign. However, no sooner had the preparations for the journey been made than news of the peace preliminaries of Aix-la-Chapelle arrived. Poniatowski decided to send his

---

[53] BCzart. 911, ff. 331–9. The source was not the *Spectator, Guardian, Tatler*, or *Freeholder*.

[54] BCzart. 911, ff. 5–56.   [55] Zb. Pop. 215, ff. 1–5, 32–7.

[56] Zb. Pop. 215, ff. 6–24.

[57] 'Trzymanie Woyska zawsze było miane za ciężkie poddanym, y niebespieczne Wolnosciom Ich.' Zb. Pop. 216, ff. 18–19.

son anyway, for if he did not see war, he would at least see armies. Off went Stanisław to the Low Countries. In his *Mémoires*, Stanisław August wrote regretfully that instead of acquiring a taste for soldiering, he was captivated by the paintings of Rubens and Van Dyck, and bought his first small canvas. This was something of an exaggeration, for Stanisław did conscientiously study military architecture. The real significance of the visit lay, however, in neither art nor warfare. Stanisław was impressed by the Dutch shipyards, warehouses, manufactories, and banks. In the journal he kept, he devoted much space to economic matters, and the contrast with conditions in Poland must have been very apparent.[58]

Stanisław returned to Poland, where the Seym once again achieved nothing, although the co-operation between the *Familia* and the Court reached its height. By this time he was capable of informing his parents of the political news in Warsaw.[59] Afterwards, he went to stay with his uncle Michał for a year to learn the business of politics, but he felt starved of real attention.[60] In October 1749, Stanisław attended the opening (*reassumpcya*) of the Tribunal of the Crown at Piotrków. The stakes were high, for the Potockis wished to invalidate the fraudulent grant of Polish nobility (*indygenat*) awarded to Brühl the previous year when the *Familia* controlled the Tribunal, and to re-try Kazimierz Poniatowski for his killing of Adam Tarło in a duel in 1744. About a thousand of the *Familia*'s retainers were outnumbered by the army of the Crown under Hetman Józef Potocki, and carnage was only narrowly avoided. The outcome was that the usual bargaining over the legality of the elections came to naught, and only five deputies were legally elected.[61] This was two short of the quorum of seven, and so the Tribunal could not be 'constituted' for the first time in its history. Poland's anarchy had plumbed a new depth.[62]

The break-up of the Tribunal made a far greater impact on public opinion than the routine failures of the Seym. An extraordinary Seym

---

[58] *Mémoires*, vol. i, 10–16. S. Poniatowski to Ludwika Zamoyska, 23 May, 10 Oct. 1748, BCzart. 3972, ff. 53, 57. BCzart. 911, ff. 195–240, 449–84. Nieć, *Młodość ostatniego elekta*, 15, 21–5. Zamoyski, *Last King*, 23–4. Fabre, *Stanislas-Auguste Poniatowski*, 176–81, in line with his general argument, doubted the depth of Stanisław's captivation by art.

[59] Stan. to S. Poniatowski, 12 Dec. 1748, ARP 373, vol. i. See Zielińska, *Walka 'Familii'*, 244–68.

[60] *Mémoires*, vol. i, 16–19, 25–6. He kept his parents informed of developments in Lithuania, such as the results of the February 1750 *seymiki*. Stan. to K. Poniatowska, Wołczyn, 1 Mar. 1750, ARP 373, vol. 2.

[61] Deputies had to be unanimously elected at the *seymiki*, and the manoeuvring between the parties at the Tribunal centred on placing protests and counter-protests from the *seymiki* on the judges' table.

[62] *Mémoires*, vol. i, 26–33. See Zielińska, *Walka 'Familii'*, 288–90.

was summoned earlier than usual in 1750 with the aim of strengthening the judicial system, and Stanisław was elected one of the Mazovian envoys at Zakroczym, near Warsaw. However, a partisan of the Potockis wrecked the Seym with the *liberum veto*. The Court felt unable to agree to the *Familia*'s demands for the calling of an extraordinary confederated Seym in the face of Frederick II's threats of intervention, the opposition of Russia, and England's inability to offer more than good wishes. Reform had clearly run into an impasse. Henceforth the Court concentrated on securing the succession *vivente rege* for one or other of the electoral princes.[63]

Two years later, Stanisław was elected envoy by the *seymik* of Łomża. He recalled his experiences in his *Mémoires*. The Commonwealth, with the possible exception of its northern and south-eastern borderlands, had no equivalent to English pocket boroughs. As in most boroughs and in the counties in England, aristocratic families had to work hard to get their candidates elected. Stanisław was shown the ropes by one of his father's clients, Antoni Glinka. For eight days before the opening of the *seymik*, it was necessary to visit the landed noblemen of the district. Half were illiterate, and most of the rest were clients of the same grandees who sought their votes every two years.

Il fallait . . . admirer leur bavardage, paraître enchanté de leurs mauvais bons mots et de plus embrasser continuellement leurs sales et pouilleuses personnes. Pour refraichissement il fallait, dix ou douze fois par jour, aller conférer avec les gros bonnets du canton, c'est à écouter sous l'appareil du plus grand secret, les détails de leurs petites querelles domestiques, ménager leurs jalousies réciproques, s'entremettre pour leurs promotions aux charges du district, concerter avec eux, combien et à qui il fallait donner l'argent comptant aux très nobles électeurs et puis déjeuner, diner, goûter, souper avec eux, à des tables aussi malpropres que mal servies.

Stanisław August added in the margin: 'il n'y avait pas à nos diétines le serment préchable aux elections anglaises, *de non accipienda pecunia*.' Moreover, several days' hard work could be wasted in a moment of pique or petty jealousy against a local dignitary. Stanisław lasted the course and was elected unanimously as one of the two envoys. Worse was in store for him when he and Glinka went to celebrate his victory at the house of the old starosta of Maków, 'qui n'existait que pour boire'. Stanisław was forced to dance a quadrille with Glinka, the starosta's wife, and Glinka's 18-year-old daughter, 'grosse, blanche, une vraie Cunégonde', from six

---

[63] Zielińska, *Walka 'Familii'*, 293–327.

in the evening until six in the morning, before he was finally allowed to rest.[64] The Seym of 1752 fell victim to the *liberum veto*.

Showing through the burlesque is Stanisław's deeply felt distaste for Sarmatia. Brought up to despise ignorance, stupidity, boorishness, and drunkenness, in a cosmopolitan family priding itself on its *lumières*, and having experienced a different world abroad, it was natural that Stanisław should have reacted so critically to the provincial *szlachta* who possessed these vices in abundance. Moreover, his political début coincided not with the hopes of 1744, but with the Commonwealth's slide into an anarchic mire, which would last until the end of the reign. Quite palpably, Sarmatia could not reform itself. Stanisław had been brought up within a reformist yet still republican political tradition, but it is quite likely that the timing and manner of his entry into political life, combined with the contempt for folly imbibed in his childhood, sowed the seeds of his later embrace of more monarchical attitudes. Stanisław Poniatowski the elder saw in England another 'republic'. His son would draw different conclusions.

[64] *Mémoires*, vol. 1, 58–62.

4

The Influence of
Sir Charles Hanbury Williams

Sir Charles Hanbury Williams (1708–59), satirist and diplomat, owes his historical renown to an introduction. In June 1755, the then British Ambassador to St Petersburg presented his secretary, the 23-year-old Count[1] Stanisław Poniatowski, to the 26-year-old Grand Duchess Catherine, the wife of the heir to the throne of Russia. The consequences are well known. In the most fundamental way, the efforts of Stanisław August to 'create anew the Polish world' were made possible by Sir Charles Hanbury Williams.

The whiff of scandal that hangs over the remarkable friendship between Williams and Poniatowski was diffused mainly by Claude Rulhière, who collected gossip smearing Stanisław August from the agents of the Confederacy of Bar.[2] Jerzy Łojek interpreted the friendship as frustrated homosexual love on Williams's side and cynical exploitation on Poniatowski's. His widely read essay is flawed by a complete lack of references and several errors of fact.[3] Other historians have made more serious contributions to knowledge.[4] The present chapter is the first study to use both halves of the correspondence between Stanisław and Sir Charles. This correspondence testifies to a tender but didactic father–son relationship, with no hint of eroticism. Certainly, Stanisław's alert and strait-laced mother, who was disturbed by his affair with Catherine, had no qualms about Williams; 'il aime tendrement Przemyski [Stanisław was the starosta of Przemyśl] et

---

[1] The title was a polite fiction, used by the Poniatowskis when travelling abroad.

[2] 'Le comte Poniatowski avait prit en Pologne des intimes liaisons avec cet ambassadeur, si intimes mêmes, que l'un étant fort beau, l'autre fort dépravé, on en avait médit'. *Histoire de l'anarchie de Pologne et du démembrement de cette république . . . suivie des anecdotes sur la révolution de Russie, en 1762* (4 vols.; Paris, 1807), vol. 4, 292.

[3] 'Przyjaciel Williamsa', in Łojek, *Siedem tajemnic Stanisława Augusta* (Warsaw, 1982), esp. 32–3.

[4] Fabre, *Stanislas-Auguste Poniatowski*, 170–4. Nieć, *Młodość ostatniego elekta, passim*. The Earl of Ilchester and Mrs Langford-Brooke, *The Life of Sir Charles Hanbury Williams, Poet, Wit and Diplomatist* (London, 1929). Zamoyski, *Last King*, 29–72. I have corrected several dates given by Nieć and Zamoyski on the basis of the source materials, but I have not burdened the footnotes by listing each change.

l'estime,' she told her husband with satisfaction.[5] This is not the place for a detailed reconstruction of their friendship. Indispensable, however, to a study of the last king of Poland's attempts to reform the Polish world *à l'anglaise* is an analysis of the role of Sir Charles in preparing Stanisław for public life and in forming his character, tastes, and outlook. Nor is this a study of Williams's political relations with the *Familia*, but a little background may be of use.

I

When on 9 July 1750 the young Stanisław Antoni Poniatowski, sent to Berlin for the sake of his health, caught the eye of the British Minister there, Sir Charles Hanbury Williams,[6] there were good political reasons for the Englishman to pay special attention to the young Pole. Besides his mission in Berlin (1750–1), Williams had since 1747 been the British envoy to Saxony and Poland, with instructions to oppose French influence and support the pro-Russian Czartoryskis. Williams had met the leaders of the *Familia*, notably Stanisław Poniatowski, but as he had not attended the Seym of 1748, he did not yet know Polish affairs as well as he might.[7] The British diplomat was now presented with an opportunity to strike up closer relations with a scion of the *Familia*. Neither would Stanisław for his part have passed over the chance to get to know the envoy and secure his more active backing for his family's cause. Whatever the political incentives, Williams was 'sorry to part with young Poniatowski' a fortnight later.[8]

Williams arrived in Warsaw on 6 August 1750, in time to see the Seym broken by the *liberum veto*. He worked closely with Keyserling and the *Familia*, and encouraged the Court to distribute patronage according to their recommendations. During his stay, his friendship with Stanisław, who had been elected to the Seym for the first time, deepened, 'et servit beaucoup à me donner dans le grand monde une grande considération et

[5] K. Poniatowska to S. Poniatowski, 27 May 1755, ARP 373, vol. 1. Besides Rulhière's innuendo, I am not aware of any evidence of Williams's homosexuality or bisexuality, while his *Works* (3 vols.; London 1822) and papers contain heterosexual erotica of a very earthy kind. A selection is quoted by J. Black, *The British Abroad: The Grand Tour in the Eighteenth Century* (Stroud, 1992), ch. 9.

[6] Ilchester, *Williams*, 187–8. Zamoyski, *Last King*, 29–30. *Mémoires*, vol. 1, 36, 39. 'Journal begun at Berlin in July 1750', Newport Central Library (Gwent), Williams papers, qM 411 012, ff. 4–6.

[7] D. B. Horn, *Sir Charles Hanbury Williams and European Diplomacy 1747–58* (London, 1930), 34–54. PRO SP 88/69–70, *passim*.

[8] 'Journal begun at Berlin', f. 50.

un air d'un homme fait que mon âge ne m'accordait encore'.[9] Sir Charles proposed the establishment of a correspondence, in which Stanisław would inform him of developments in Poland. Both Williams and the *Familia* profited from the liaison.[10]

Sir Charles was deeply impressed by Stanisław's qualities. He saw himself as the man to complete young Poniatowski's education, and to prepare him for the illustrious public career that he envisaged for him.[11] Williams suggested to Stanisław that he come to Saxony and spend some time under his wing. After some hesitation, Stanisław and Konstancja Poniatowski agreed to their son's repeated requests, 'parce que dit'on j'y trouverai quelqu'un qui aura la Charité de m'avertir des sottises que je ferai'. Stanisław added: 'j'ose me flatter qu'un homme qui a eu la bonté de m'offrir son coeur et sa maison ne me refusera de me gouverner despotiquement.'[12] Williams introduced Count Poniatowski to Court society in the convivial surroundings of Hubertusburg, where Augustus III was in the best of spirits. A day's hunting would be followed by a concert or ballet and supper. After the king had retired, the evening was spent *chez* the Crown Princess Marie-Antoine or the Countess Brühl, who treated Stanisław as the 'enfant de la maison'. About midnight, Stanisław, Sir Charles, the Dutch envoy Kalkoen, the Piedmontese Count Salmour, and, one supposes, Williams's young secretary Harry Digby, would leave 'pour passer chez l'un d'eux encore une heure et davantage, à récapituler en riant tous les faits et gestes de la journée'. After six weeks, 'cette joyeuse

[9] Journal begun at Berlin, ff. 68–158. *Mémoires*, vol. 1, 42. Williams to Newcastle, PRO SP 88/71, esp. 23 Sept. 1750. Zielińska, *Walka 'Familii'*, 313, 319.

[10] *Pace* Łojek, *Siedem tajemnic Stanisława Augusta*, 13, who argues that Williams was exploited by Michał Czartoryski. Łojek follows Nieć, *Młodość ostatniego elekta*, 47, who cites a letter of 2 June 1751 from Michał Czartoryski to Jacek Ogrodzki in Dresden as evidence. This might be a misprint, as no letter of that date survives. Neither the letter of 2 May nor that of 26 June contains anything more than a request to pass on greetings to Williams, and ask him to obtain a book, recently published in England, on teaching elementary Latin. BCzart. 3429, ff. 261–2, 272. On other occasions, Czartoryski asked Williams to pursue in Vienna some long-overdue interest payments on his behalf, and once, to use his influence to obtain royal graces. Ditto, 22 Jan., 13 Mar., 6 Apr. 1751, BCzart. 3429, ff. 240, 247, 256. M. Czartoryski to Williams, 22 Jan. 1751, LWL CHW 50–10918, ff. 387–90, 14 Nov. 1752, LWL CHW 55–10877, ff. 111–12.

[11] Depicting 'the present state of Poland' to the Duke of Newcastle on 27 June 1752, Williams lauded the young Poniatowskis. The elder sons 'are both young men of great merit. The youngest has certainly very superior talents and will one day make a great figure in Poland'. PRO SP 88/75. Stanisław had then one elder brother and two younger brothers living, but seems a more likely candidate to be 'the youngest' than either Michał or Andrzej, with whom Williams was far less intimate than with Stanisław or Kazimierz.

[12] Stan. to Williams, 11 Sept. 1751, LWL CHW 54–10910, ff. 27–8.

vie' was interrupted by an instruction from Stanisław's parents for him to proceed to Vienna.[13]

Williams gave his young friend letters of introduction to the British envoy, Sir Robert Keith, and to the Countess Rosa Harrach, popularly called 'la reine des anglais' on account of her partiality for them. Sir Charles carefully monitored his friend's progress from Dresden, and sent him several letters of advice (beginning as usual with 'Mon cher Palatinello'). He strongly recommended the society of Keith and Count Firmian, whose Anglophilia was extraordinarily wide-ranging. Firmian was a true connoisseur of English art, literature, and science, and a master of the English language.[14] He risked catching cold to show Stanisław some Sarmatian portraits in the freezing imperial library, and paid homage to 'la fécondité du Génie des Poètes Anglais'. Keith seemed to exhibit some reserve at first, but invited the Pole for tea, not knowing that Stanisław hated the drink—one aspect of English civilization to which he did not take.[15] At Williams's request, Stanisław wrote some vignettes of the foreign ministers in Vienna.[16] Stanisław was glad of the presence of Harry Digby and of Williams's future son-in-law Lord Essex, and he went about a good deal with them. Digby's early return to Dresden deprived Stanisław of his best friend in the Austrian capital.[17]

When Stanisław wrote to Sir Charles that he was sorry that Digby had not met one Commander Zinzendorf,[18] Williams reacted with alarm: 'je le connois fort bien, mais je ne recommanderois jamais sa connoissance à mes jeunes amis.' Zinzendorf possessed 'l'Esprit, et selon moi, c'est son unique mérite'. Having turned his friends into enemies by *bons mots*, he was now 'condamné à se réflechir sur une jeunesse mal passée'. Sir Charles warned Stanisław lest his admiration become imitation, and counselled:

---

[13] *Mémoires*, vol. 1, 42–4. Nieć, *Młodość ostatniego elekta*, 47–50. Princess Marie-Antoine to S. Poniatowski, Dresden, 17 Dec. 1751, BCzart. 937, f. 521.

[14] Williams to Keith, 29 Nov. 1751, BL Add. 35472, f. 55. Quoted by Fabre, *Stanislas-Auguste Poniatowski*, 172, and Zamoyski, *Last King*, 32. *Mémoires*, vol. 1, 45–6. Nieć, *Młodość ostatniego elekta*, 50–3. Williams to Stan., 9 Jan. 1752, Zb. Pop. 318, f. 187. Firmian later governed Lombardy. On his Anglophilia, see E. Garms-Cornides, 'Un trentino tra Impero, antichi stati italiani e Gran Bretagna: l'anglomane Carlo Firmian' in C. Mozzarelli and G. Olmi (eds.), *Il Trentino nel settecento fra Sacro Romano Impero e antichi stati italiani* (Bologna, 1985).

[15] Stan. to Williams, 1 Jan. 1752, LWL CHW 54–10910, ff. 210–11.

[16] Williams to Stan., 21 Jan. 1752, Zb. Pop. 318, ff. 189–91. Stan. to Williams, 29 Jan. 1752, LWL CHW 54–10910, ff. 260–2.

[17] Digby to Williams, 25 Dec. 1751, BL Add. 51393, ff. 73–8. Stan. to Williams, 29 Jan. 1752, LWL CHW 54–10910, ff. 214–15.

[18] 29 Jan. 1752, loc. cit. Count Ludwig Friedrich Julius Zinzendorf/-ff (1721–80). *Allgemeine Deutsche Biographie* (vol. 45; Leipzig, 1900), 353–6.

Ce n'est pas l'Esprit qui Vous manque. Vous en avez déja suffisament et comme l'Esprit est la seule Marchandise qui se vend à la Boutique du Chevalier je Vous conseille de dépenser le Reste de Votre tems en achetant du bon sens, du Jugement et de l'Expérience chez Keith et Firmian.

Enfin mon cher Stanislaus, cessez de frequenter, ou pour le moins d'admirer Le Chevalier en Question. Souvenez Vous que c'est l'amitié qui Vous a dit.

Williams signed the letter 'Votre fidel Conseiller, Ami et Serviteur', which brought an immediate response from Stanisław to 'Mon cher Conseiller et Ami', in which, although he assured Sir Charles that he preferred the good sense of Keith and Firmian, Stanisław defended Zinzendorf. He met him again in St Petersburg in 1755. 'Son Amitié est aussi instructive qu'agréable,' he told his mother. In his *Mémoires*, Stanisław August seems more guarded; he compared him to 'un vieux libertin français', agreeable and well read, but with some remarkable stains on his reputation.[19]

The episode shows Williams's concern that Stanisław should frequent only the best company, and some worry that his young friend attached too much weight to *esprit* (which can be translated only incompletely as 'spirit') and too little to good sense. Williams had earlier advised Stanisław that 'Vous êtes trop jeune pour primer, et ceux qui priment à dix-neuf ans font ordinairement une très mauvaise figure à trente.'[20] Here again, one senses Williams's anxiety that social success achieved too early might go to Stanisław's head. This concern is once more evident in May 1752, when Sir Charles wrote to Stanisław that it would be good for him to spend two years away from Poland. He would then avoid the flattery of the partisans of the Palatine of Mazovia.[21] On 1 June, Williams proposed that Stanisław come to Dresden and Hanover with him.[22] The newly appointed Castellan of Cracow and his wife refused, however, as

[19] Williams to Stan., 18 Feb. 1752, Zb. Pop. 318, ff. 192–4. Stan. to Williams, 23 Feb. 1752, LWL CHW 55–10877, ff. 89–90. Stan. to K. Poniatowska, 24 June 1755, ARP 373, vol. 1. Zinzendorf was the bearer of Austrian congratulations on the birth of the Grand Duke Paul. *Mémoires*, vol. 1, 46.

[20] 21 Jan. 1752, loc. cit. (n. 16). Łojek, *Siedem tajemnic Stanisława Augusta*, 14–15, wrongly alleges that Williams was also in Vienna, and that, jealous of Stanisław's romance with Countess Angelika Kotulinský, he arranged for Stanisław's recall to Poland. The only foundation of this might be that Stanisław did not write about her to Williams, but Łojek did not make use of Stanisław's side of the correspondence anyway. In his *Mémoires*, vol. 1, 48, Stanisław August states that the papal nuncio *falsely* informed Stanisław's parents that their son had proposed marriage to her, and that his father then wrote him 'une lettre foudroyante', forbidding him to see the Countess if this were so. Stanisław then decided to return home in any case.

[21] 8 May 1752, Zb. Pop. 318, ff. 196–7.   [22] Zb. Pop. 318, ff. 198–200.

Stanisław was serving on the treasury commission at Radom. Williams lamented: 'Vous seriez allé à Hanovre dans mon [*sic*] Carosse, Vous auriez été bien reçu par mon Maitre [George II] et son Ministre [Newcastle], et vous auriez fait des connoissances qui Vous auroient été utile pour le reste de Vos Jours.'[23]

The two friends had to wait to see each other until Williams's arrival in Warsaw on 31 August 1752 in the lead-up to the Seym, which was to be held in Grodno. Williams had conceived, or at least supported, a plan for an election *vivente rege*, and worked closely with the *Familia*.[24] Stanisław had again been elected envoy, and the two friends journeyed together via the magnificent, if grotesque, junketings at Hetman Branicki's Białystok to Grodno, where they lodged in Count Flemming's house. The Seym, as expected, fell victim to the *liberum veto*, but there were diversions. One day, Poniatowski, Williams, and Flemming went to laugh at Hetman Michał Radziwiłł's bad taste in arranging his house (one of only two built of brick in the town), and went on to a ball. Despite the rats at Flemming's house, Stanisław enjoyed the Seym, and shared with Williams the amusement presented by provincial Sarmatia.[25]

Soon afterwards, Stanisław was sent on a long voyage.[26] In April 1753 he arrived in Vienna. Williams, who had been sent there to try to reinvigorate the Anglo-Austrian alliance, was waiting for him. Sir Charles soon fell dangerously ill, and Stanisław nursed him, until he was sent on to Saxony by his parents. Sir Charles felt a deep debt of gratitude to his young friend.[27] He suffered a further relapse in Dresden in June, so that it was only on 24 July that they left. In Hanover, Sir Charles gave his young friend a valuable lesson in the politics of 'the back stairs' by assiduously renewing 'connaissance avec toutes les personnes des deux sexes et de tout age qui avaient quelque connexion avec mylady Yarmouth [George II's mistress]'. Stanisław told his mother that Williams 'm'y a presenté, et fait faire connoissance avec ce qu'il y a de mieux, d'un façon que je ne trouverai nullement ambarassé si jamais j'y retourne.' On 27 July they reached The Hague, where in the course of a week Sir

[23] 5 Aug. 1752, Zb. Pop. 318, ff. 202–3.
[24] Horn, *Williams*, 128–38. PRO SP 88/73, 75 ('Account of the Present State of Poland', n. 11). Zielińska, *Walka 'Familii'*, 338–9.
[25] *Mémoires*, vol. 1, 62–8. Nieć, *Młodość ostatniego elekta*, 60–4. Zamoyski, *Last King*, 35–8.
[26] See below, p. 103.
[27] *Mémoires*, vol. 1, 70–1. Williams to Stan., Vienna, 26 May 1753, 30 May 1753, Zb. Pop. 318, ff. 208–9.

Charles introduced Poniatowski to all the most important personages before departing for England.[28] Stanisław stayed on at Williams's suggestion, and kept him well informed of Saxon intrigues in Holland, and of his own studious activities: 'Pour vous prouver que je voyage avec profit, Je Vous ferai part des recherches Historiques et Naturelles que j'ai fait dans ce Pays.' Williams was treated to a partly mythological, partly economic account of the windmills of North Holland.[29] Poniatowski also wrote to his friend of his experiences in Paris, and looked forward to seeing him in England, where Stanisław expected that Williams would 'diriger' his visit.[30] In fact, they saw very little of each other in England, probably due to Sir Charles's pressing political business. There is no evidence to suggest any rift between them.[31]

Poniatowski and Williams were reunited in the autumn at the Seym of 1754. The Englishman's ardent espousal of the Czartoryski cause in the Ostróg affair led to his open rupture with Brühl. To his chagrin, Stanisław was ordered to remain on the sidelines by his parents,[32] but the approval of his behaviour by Williams may have offered some consolation: 'Go on, my dear Stanislaus in the same conduct, and in the same road you went in during the last Diet and you will gain the Confidence and Friendship of all worthy Persons.' Sir Charles warned him, however, to 'take care to correct those few strokes of what the French call Humeur that you still have about you, and which tho' trifles will often make your friends sorry and your enemies glad.'[33]

Williams was shortly afterwards named Ambassador to Russia and asked that Stanisław should accompany him as his secretary. The *Familia* gratefully seized the opportunity to send its own private mission to St Petersburg, and for Stanisław to receive a thorough training in diplomacy. Williams went on ahead, and Konstancja busied herself with the arrangements for Stanisław's journey, so that he could join Sir Charles

---

[28] *Mémoires*, vol. 1, 73–6. Williams to H. Fox, 6 Apr.–31 July, BL Add. 51393, ff. 139–59. Williams to Newcastle, 31 Mar.–27 July 1753, PRO SP 88/75. Stan. to S. Poniatowski, Dresden, 23 June 1753, ARP 373, vol. 1. Stan. to K. Poniatowska, The Hague, 28 July 1753, ARP 373, vol. 2.

[29] 21 Aug. 1753, 11 Sept. 1753, LWL CHW 57–10904, ff. 50–1, 89–92.

[30] 2 Nov. 1753, 3 Jan. 1754, LWL CHW 57–10904, ff. 159–61, 58–10907, f. 5.

[31] See below, p. 110. Pace Łojek, *Siedem tajemnic Stanisława Augusta*, 18–19.

[32] Horn, *Williams*, 164–71. PRO SP 88/76, *passim*. The Ostróg affair was about the sale and break-up of the Ostróg entail by Janusz Sanguszko to a clique of magnates headed by August Czartoryski, which was vociferously opposed by Hetman Branicki. See below, p. 121.

[33] 8 Jan. 1755, Zb. Pop. 318, ff. 220–1.

as early as possible.[34] Williams employed him to cipher and decipher the most confidential despatches.[35] The months of living together brought the two men still closer. Sir Charles encouraged Stanisław's burgeoning romance with Catherine. In December 1755, Stanislaw wrote of him to Charles Yorke:

L'amitié dont il m'honore, ses Lumieres dont je daigne me faire part pour me former, me font en quelque façon participer au Role distingué qu'Il joue dans le Pays. Je dois des obligations si particulieres au Chevalier Williams qu'il n'y a qu'une reconnoissance aussi longue que ma Vie qui puisse m'acquitter envers Lui. Je regards cela comme un devoir qu'il me sera aussi agréable qu'indispensable de remplir.[36]

This touching and sincere appreciation comprehensively refutes Łojek's charge of cynicism. The Yorkes were, as Stanisław knew, the political opponents of Williams and his friend Henry Fox.[37]

Stanisław shared Williams's joy at the signing of the Anglo-Russian treaty. The *Familia* had desired such an alliance for years. Stanisław also shared his friend's frustration when the British ministry made a fuss about precedence, and his despondency after news broke of the Anglo-Prussian Convention of Westminster, which broke the back of Williams's cherished treaty.[38] On the evening of 1 April 1756, the strain on Williams finally told. During a discussion on predestination, Sir Charles argued that there was no failure or success of any individual which could not be ascribed to their own fault or merit. Stanisław disagreed persistently, and Sir Charles exploded with rage. He told Poniatowski to get out, and that he wished never to see him again. Stanisław was debating whether or not to leap from the balcony, when he was stopped by Williams. 'Tuez moi plutôt que de me dire que vous ne voulez plus me voir,' cried Stanisław. Sir Charles tearfully put his arms round his friend.[39] Williams's deep depression over the failure of his mission and the intensity of the two men's friendship are evident.

[34] K. Poniatowska to S. Poniatowski, 8 May, 15 May, 22 May, 27 May, 5 June, 8 June 1755, ARP 373, vol. 1. Izabella Branicka to K. Poniatowska, 22 May 1755, ARP 373, vol. 2. K. Poniatowska to Williams, 7 June 1755, LWL CHW 62–10895, ff. 222–3. *Mémoires*, vol. 1, 145–6.

[35] *Mémoires*, vol. 1, 149. Ilchester, *Williams*, 334.

[36] 17 Dec. 1755, BL Add. 35364, ff. 291–4.   [37] See below, p. 116.

[38] *Mémoires*, vol. 1, 149–51. Horn, *Williams*, 190–2, 228–50. Ilchester, *Williams*, 339–42. W. Coxe, *An Historical Tour in Monmouthshire* (2 vols.; London, 1801), vol. 2, 270.

[39] *Mémoires*, vol. 1, 152–4.

When Poniatowski was recalled to Poland by his parents, who wanted him to stand for the 1756 Seym, he, Sir Charles, and Catherine did all they could to arrange his return to St Petersburg as a Saxon envoy. Williams even expressed the hope that Catherine and the King of Prussia would one day make Stanisław King of Poland.[40] Both men felt the separation keenly. After their year together, the correspondence on both sides rose to new emotional peaks. Williams wrote to his 'Dear adopted son' on 21 August 1756:

No wishes you can make for yourself my dear Stanislaus are more sincere for Yr Greatness and Prosperity than mine. You are my Eleve; & no school Master ever had a finer scholar. I could wish you were my son, tho' I cannot wish to deprive Yr Parents of so great a Happiness. All that I now say would look like Flattery if it came from anybody else. But you know by long experience, that I neither can nor will flatter, and that I love truth.[41]

Stanisław replied: 'Mon cher et respectable ami! Mon second Pere! O dulce decus meum!'; 'Adieu mon cher et digne ami; mon Pere adoptif, Apres Collette [Catherine], Je n'aime rien tant que Vous.'[42] Williams wrote to the Castellan of Cracow, hoping that he and his wife would find their son improved; more prudent, able to keep secrets and to be trusted with the most sensitive diplomatic work.[43] They, along with August Czartoryski, sent their thanks and agreed that Stanisław merited the praise.[44]

Unfortunately, when Stanisław did reappear in St Petersburg at the beginning of 1757, as the extraordinary envoy of the Elector of Saxony, Williams was miserably cast in the unlikely role of a 'Prussian spy'. Prussia had invaded Saxony, and *tête-à-tête* meetings were out of the question. The ambassador told Catherine how he longed to see him:

Je le recevrai comme mon fils. Je ne lui parlerai pas un mot de politique. Notre discourse roulera sur vous, lui et sa famille. Je sais par avance que les larmes me viendront aux yeux en l'embrassant. Il n'a qu'à faire, qu'à dire tout ce qu'il voudra. Je suis persuadé qu'il m'aime, et cela me suffit.[45]

[40] Williams to Catherine, 26 Nov. 1756 (OS), *Correspondance de Catherine Alexéievna grande duchesse de Russie et de Sir Charles H. Williams, ambassadeur de l'Angleterre, 1756 et 1757*, ed. S. Goryainov (Moscow, 1909), 287–8, and *passim*. Horn, *Williams*, 270–1. Ilchester, *Williams*, 358–401. Nieć, *Młodość ostatniego elekta*, 144–52. Zamoyski, *Last King*, 61–3. Williams to Stan., 28 Sept. 1756, Zb. Pop. 318, ff. 247–9.

[41] Zb. Pop. 318, ff. 244–6.

[42] 26 Sept. 1756, 17 Oct. 1756, LWL CHW 61–10913, ff. 82–7, 90–4.

[43] 4 Aug. 1756, AksJP 5, ff. 58–60. 11 Nov. 1756, Zb. Pop. 318, f. 251. See also Williams to Stan., 21 Aug. 1756, Zb. Pop. 318, ff. 244–6.

[44] K. Poniatowska to Williams, 26? Sept. 1756, S. Poniatowski to Williams, 26 Sept. 1756, Aug. Czartoryski to Williams, 26 Sept. 1756, LWL CHW 61–10913, ff. 74, 75, 88–9.

[45] 31 Dec. 1756 (OS), *Correspondance de Catherine Alexéievna . . .* , 310–11.

Williams's health, never robust, deteriorated along with the point of his mission, and he finally left in October, several months before Poniatow-ski. On his way home, Williams's health and mind gave way completely, and he died, perhaps by his own hand, in November 1759.[46] Stanisław lamented that most painful of all had been having to work against him.[47]

II

Sir Charles Hanbury Williams's influence on Stanisław's character was profound. He tempered his impetuosity, introduced him to some of the best company in Europe, and above all gave him belief in himself by prophesying a great future for him. Williams's belief in his own prophecy no doubt strengthened Stanisław's belief in his own unchangeable des-tiny, which he retained to the end of his life.[48] Not every aspect of Williams's influence upon Stanisław can be derived from their correspondence or from Stanisław August's *Mémoires*. It was during their long conversations that Sir Charles had the chance to form the outlook and tastes of his young friend. It would be beneficial therefore to search Williams's *Works* and his correspondence with Henry Fox for his opinions and standpoints on politics, religion, literature, and manners, which he would probably have communicated to Stanisław.

Charles Hanbury Williams began his political career as a partisan of Sir Robert Walpole,[49] and served him and his successors in government, the brothers Pelham, as a satirist. William Pulteney, who became Earl of Bath, was lampooned by Williams in twenty-four odes and squibs for having abandoned the principles on which he fought Walpole.[50] Never-theless, Walpole himself did not escape the lash:

> For Walpole still rul'd
> With Corruption and Gold,
> The Monarch he bought,
> The Nation he sold.[51]

Williams's tales may well have found a later reflection in Stanisław August's severe assessment of English political morality.[52]

'You know how good a Whig I am,' wrote Williams to Fox.[53] Sir Charles approved of the Glorious Revolution and thoroughly detested the house

---

[46] Horn, *Williams*, 270–90. Ilchester, *Williams*, 399–428. *Mémoires*, vol. 1, 191, 220–1.

[47] Stan. to C. Yorke, 17 Nov. 1760, BL Add. 35365, ff. 461–4.

[48] For Stanisław August's belief in destiny and Divine Providence, see below, Ch. 10, Section I.

[49] Ilchester, *Williams*, 37–40.   [50] Ibid., 117.   [51] *Works*, vol. 3, 18–22.

[52] See below, Ch. 5, Section III.   [53] 24 Dec. 1752, BL Add. 51393, f. 127.

of Stuart. In supervising Harry Digby's historical reading, he noted with approval his charge's antipathy to the exiled former ruling dynasty.[54] Williams was bitterly hostile to the Scots, whom he regarded as Jacobites and spongers. To 'Butcher' Cumberland (who had brutally put down the 'Forty-five) England owed her liberty.[55] Perhaps Sir Charles spared Stanisław those last comments, on account of his Scottish ancestry. Despite his support for the Hanoverian succession, Williams's opinion of the house of Hanover was extremely critical, and might have influenced Stanisław August's later criticism of George II in his *Mémoires*.[56]

In general, Williams was highly satisfied with the English constitution. Even Jacobites, he wrote, 'will own that England is in a blest Situation'.[57] Sir Charles's most interesting thoughts were provoked by his stay in Poland:

I am, upon reflection, persuaded that a King of England at present has not too much Power, and that the wings of the prerogative are sufficiently clipped: a journey into Poland will convince anyone that nothing is more noxious to Society than Liberty that is degenerated into Licentiousness and where under the name of Freedom, there are more miserable slaves than in any country in the world.[58]

Sir Charles, who backed the *Familia*'s plans to reform the Commonwealth, certainly conversed with Stanisław on such subjects. He wrote to him early in 1751 that if the Saxon court continued to be guided in the distribution of offices by the *Familia*, 'tout ira aussi bien en Pologne qu'en Angleterre.'[59] Although it is impossible to determine the extent of Williams's influence on Stanisław's view of the English constitution, Sir Charles's orthodox, fairly conservative brand of mid-century Whiggery did not meet with any resistance in Poniatowski.

Williams's personal politics seem not to have made much impact upon Stanisław. Williams informed him of Fox's successes in 1755, but in England Stanisław had associated, not with Fox, but with his enemies the Yorkes.[60] In Stanisław's outlook on international politics, however, Williams's influence, coupled with that of his father, may have been profound. Stanisław was exposed on the one hand to a violent hatred of Frederick II ('the compleatest Tyrant that God ever sent for a scourge

---

[54] To Fox, 22 Mar. 1752, 24 May 1752, BL Add. 51393, ff. 85–6, 99–100.

[55] To Fox, 23 Jan. 1753, BL Add. 51393, ff. 130–3.

[56] See below, p. 118. E.g., a parody of the *Te Deum*: 'O King, spare thy people of England: And now squeeze thy people of Hanover', *Works*, vol. 3, 40–2.

[57] *Works*, vol. 2, 63.   [58] To Fox, 24 Dec. 1752, loc. cit. (n. 53).

[59] Undated, Zb. Pop. 318, ff. 214–15.

[60] Williams to Stan., 18 Jan. 1755, 8 Mar. 1755, Zb. Pop. 318, ff. 222–3, 229–30. See below, pp. 116–17.

to an offending people . . . he hates in general to see people happy'),[61] and on the other to efforts to secure the support of Russia. In Williams's plans, Russia would, in alliance with England and Austria, support the renewal of Poland by the *Familia*.[62] If Williams was destroyed by the Diplomatic Revolution, Stanisław August never escaped its shadow. He had placed his early hopes in Anglo-Russian co-operation against Prussia, and never ceased to dream of the return of that diplomatic constellation to the ascendant, but it never recovered from the Convention of Westminster.

According to Rulhière, Williams was a notorious deist. The charge of deism against Stanisław August was common among the Confederates of Bar, from whom Rulhière gathered his information, and the connection with Williams was easy enough to suppose.[63] The best answer to this charge is the advice given by Williams to Lord Essex at the turn of 1750 and 1751. Regarding the works of Tillotson, he wrote:

the most universal charity (which is the true characteristic of a Christian) reigns thro the whole . . . I am convinced that there is nothing [that] can [better] purify the mind & open the way to happiness than the faith and practice of Christianity. With shame I confess to you that I did not always think so: nay, I laughed at such things. But then I freely own to you that at that time I had very little knowledge of them. But now I have the necessary knowledge, and the more I know, the more I am satisfy'd.[64]

However little attention Williams may have paid to religion in his youth, by the time he met Stanisław, he would have counselled the same undogmatic Christianity he recommended to Essex.

Even if, as seems likely, Stanisław knew some English before meeting Williams, Sir Charles would certainly have improved Stanisław's command of the language. It is striking, however, that only from 1755, after Poniatowski's return from England, did Williams begin to write in English rather than in French. Likewise, only after Stanisław's stay in England do English expressions begin to appear in his letters, which were still written in French. Again, it is only during their stay in St Petersburg that there is any direct evidence of Williams's encouraging Stanisław's reading of English literature. 'C'est encor avec lui [Williams],' Stanisław

[61] Ilchester, *Williams*, 215–17, 169–217, *passim*. Horn, *Williams*, 46–67, *passim*.

[62] This is most clearly stated in 'Account of the present state of Poland' (n. 11). The illusory nature of such 'support' from Russia is one of the main themes of Zielińska, *Walka 'Familii'*.

[63] Rulhière, *Histoire de l'anarchie de Pologne*, vol. 1, 207. See below, p. 225.

[64] Ilchester, *Williams*, 234–5.

told Charles Yorke, 'que je mets journellement en usage le Gout que vous m'avez inspiré pour la Littérature Angloise.' Shakespeare had caused Stanisław to respect Brutus, despite his assassination of Caesar, but Middleton's account of Cicero ('un Livre charmant') had disabused him. Stanisław also wrote: 'De mes Jours rien ne m'a tant amusé, hors l'Histoire de Mylord Clarendon (excepté le second volume)' (that is, Clarendon's *History of the Rebellion*).[65] Under Williams's supervision, it is worth noting, Digby had compared the histories of Clarendon and Rapin.[66] To Lord Essex, Williams recommended as reading material his old friend Fielding, Swift, Addison's *Spectators*, and the divines Atterbury and Tillotson,[67] recommendations which he probably passed on to Stanisław. Russia, wrote Poniatowski to Charles Yorke, was similar 'par son immensité à l'Empire de Brobdignac'.[68] Williams was a great admirer of Pope,[69] yet when Stanisław August wrote of Pope in his *Mémoires*, he connected him with the friends of Charles Yorke—William Warburton and Sir Ralph Allen—rather than with Williams.[70] As far as the English language and English literature were concerned, the turning-point seems to have been Stanisław's stay in England in 1754. Sir Charles helped, but his role was not decisive.

It was a different story with Latin. Williams's true literary passion was the poetry of Horace, Virgil, and Ovid.[71] On both sides the correspondence from start to finish is studded with Latin quotations. The only reference to an English poet, Milton, is in the form of some Latin verses, composed for the poet's burial in Westminster Abbey. (Williams also informed Poniatowski that Milton had been [Latin] secretary to Cromwell and had defended the execution of Charles I in print.)[72] Williams's tastes were cosmopolitan. He had met Voltaire in Berlin, and while on a personal level Williams dismissed the *philosophe* as 'that vain, talkative Frenchman',[73] he eagerly read his works and certainly discussed them with Stanisław. In St Petersburg, when Sir Charles was suffering from

[65] 17 Dec. 1755, BL Add. 35634, ff. 292–3. See above, p. 181.

[66] To Fox, 24 May 1752, loc. cit. (n. 54).

[67] Ilchester, *Williams*, 233–5. Tillotson's restrained and unspectacular prose met with general acclaim in the eighteenth century. A. Humphreys, 'The Literary Scene', in B. Ford (ed.), *From Dryden to Johnson* (New Pelican History of English Literature, vol. 4; Harmondsworth, 1991), 71–2.

[68] 17 Dec. 1755, loc. cit. (n. 65), f. 291.

[69] 'O Pope, whom every muse inspires', 'Ode to Pope', *Works*, vol. 2, 76.

[70] See below, p. 113.   [71] Ilchester, *Williams*, 115.

[72] Williams to Stan., 12 Mar. 1755, Zb. Pop. 318, ff. 231–2. Stan. to Williams, 22 Mar. 1755, LWL CHW 60–10903, ff. 210–11.

[73] 'Journal begun at Berlin', f. 162. Ilchester, *Williams*, 202.

depression, he could hardly contain his joy when Voltaire's *Pucelle d'Orléans* arrived, sent to Stanisław by his father. Stanisław was no less enthusiastic.[74] It is probable that Williams played an important role in the development of Stanisław's taste for Voltaire. The question of when Poniatowski first read the *Lettres philosophiques* remains a mystery.

We have seen that Williams's main effort in 'finishing' Stanisław was to insist upon his frequenting good company and to curb his *esprit*, which bubbled a little high at times. It remains to say a word or two on a subject fundamental to both English and Polish culture in the eighteenth century—the progressive polishing of manners, which should be easy yet respectful, neither rough nor affected. Jane Austen's novels are proof of how far the process had gone by the end of the century,[75] but, even after allowing for the personalities of the authors, the mid-century world of Fielding's *Tom Jones* was considerably coarser. Sir Charles Hanbury Williams was among those who criticized the manners of English youth and sought to improve them in his charges. Good manners and pleasing carriage were an essential part of training for public life *chez* Williams. Sir Charles's letters to Fox tell the story of Williams's untiring and not unsuccessful efforts to turn Harry Digby from a sloppy schoolboy into a polite and pleasing young diplomat. Harry was good-natured, but Sir Charles had cause to lament:

He makes such Bows. Eats his victuals awkwardly. Puts on his hat like a fool. Never speaks to anybody . . . Why shoud I mention his picking his teeth, his nose and his ear with the same finger. Or his coming into a room full of company without knowing or seeming to know that the room is not empty. All this, tho' trifling in itself, becomes essential & gives strangers prejudices and sometimes aversions . . . I have persuaded him to take a dancing master. And he has begun to learn German. Pray help me in all of this. & write to him on the chapter of inattention in company & personal awkwardness.[76]

Williams also complained (with justice) that 'he writes a vile hand, which must be mended.'[77] Sir Charles persevered, and found Harry much improved by his trip to Vienna—in the company of young Stanisław Poniatowski. Soon afterwards, Williams pronounced Digby fit for a minor post in a diplomatic legation.[78] Neither the manners nor the handwriting

---

[74] *Mémoires*, vol. 1, 178–9.

[75] In *Northanger Abbey* (1803), ch. 5, she condemned the language of the *Spectator* (which led the campaign for politeness at the beginning of the 18th century) as 'frequently so coarse as to give no very favourable idea of the age that could endure it' (Harmondsworth, 1972, p. 59).

[76] 3 Oct. 1750, BL Add. 51392, f. 149.   [77] 6 June 1750, BL Add. 51392, f. 96.

[78] See esp. 1 Jan. 1752 and 8 Mar. 1752, BL Add. 51393, ff. 71, 83.

of Count Poniatowski required anything like as much attention. Sir Charles may well have seen in Stanisław a model for Harry to follow, but it is very doubtful that from the beginning Stanisław was spared Williams's advice altogether. Under Williams's wing, the introverted youth became a charming young gentleman. Count Poniatowski's manners won acclaim on his voyages, and the pleasantness of the king's company was remembered by both political opponents and foreign travellers alike.[79]

Sir Charles Hanbury Williams's influence upon Stanisław was powerful indeed. Between the ages of 18 and 25, it was largely Sir Charles who introduced Stanisław into the world and prepared him for a political career. 'Il m'a servi comme de gouverneur, de précepteur, de tuteur. Mes parents m'ont confié à lui, il m'a longtemps si tendrement aimé,' wrote Stanisław August in his *Mémoires*, recalling his thoughts on the balcony in St Petersburg.[80] The impact of the cosmopolitan Englishman upon Stanisław's character, outlook, and tastes was, as Fabre and Zamoyski conclude, decisive in many ways. Through the agency of Williams, destiny brought Poniatowski the crown of Poland. Certainly, Williams had helped to make Stanisław an Anglophile. 'Heureux est le Pays, auquel on peut appliquer avec verité les Vers de l'Epitaphe de Milton. Ils sont magnifiques,' Stanisław told him in 1755.[81] Above all, however, it was the memory of their friendship that Stanisław August kept in his heart until the end. Stanisław August made great efforts to acquire the portrait of Williams painted by Mengs in Dresden, explaining to his minister in London, 'as I was a great friend of the said Williams'. It still hangs proudly at Łazienki as testimony (Fig. 2).[82]

---

[79] Niemcewicz, *Pamiętniki czasów moich*, vol. 2, 17. See below, p. 135.

[80] *Mémoires*, vol. 1, 153.   [81] 22 Mar. 1755, LWL CHW 60–10903, f. 211.

[82] 'Gdyż byłem wielkim tegoż Williamsa Przyjacielem.' Stanisław August instructed Bukaty to try to obtain the portrait in 1781, and Richard Rigby, who had met Stanisław at Stowe in 1754, sent it to him, receiving in exchange a portrait of Stanisław August and some Tokay. SA to Bukaty, [Sept. 1781], BCzart. 849, f. 12. Bukaty to cabinet, 12 Oct. 1781, 27 Oct. 1781, 7 Dec. 1781, 14 Dec. 1781, 22 Jan. 1782, 1 Mar. 1782, 7 June 1782, Bukaty to SA, 16 Oct. 1781, 27 Nov. 1781, BCzart. 3998, ff. 38–60, 273–4. Rigby to SA, London, 16 Oct. 1782, Zb. Pop. 222, ff. 36–7. T. Mańkowski, *Galerja Stanisława Augusta* (Lwów, 1932), 299.

F IG. 2   A. R. Mengs, *Sir Charles Hanbury Williams*, 1751

5

Stanisław's Visit to England in 1754

Stanisław's education and his friendship with Williams prepared the ground, but it was his stay in England that made him a confirmed Anglophile.[1] A number of historians have presented the rich tapestry of Stanisław's experience of English life from Shakespeare to cock-fights, and related the visit to his later political aims.[2] No one, however, has yet fully explored Stanisław's comments on English politics in his *Mémoires*, which reveal a very different approach to that of most foreign commentators. Stanisław neither marvelled at English religious toleration nor rhapsodized over English liberty. Here is no formal analysis of the checks and balances of the constitution, but a review of contemporary political history, and from that, an attempt to trace the sources of the political culture of the governing élite to its education and manners. The style is light-hearted and anecdotal, which perhaps explains why these passages have not been given the seriousness they merit.[3] They were written in 1775, with added comments on events occurring in the intervening period, and their implications at that time will be dealt with later. Nevertheless, Stanisław August must have drawn upon his own notes and correspondence from 1754.[4] Apart from the *Mémoires*,[5] the main source materials are a few surviving letters that Stanisław and his acquaintances wrote during his visit, and later correspondence in which the visit is referred to. Unfortunately, Stanisław August tells in his *Mémoires* of how, in a fit of grief after her death, he burnt his letters to his mother, in which he had recorded 'tout ce que j'avais fait, dit et pensé pendant mes voyages'.[6] In fact, a few have

---

[1] Because of the pressure of space, I have left out some details already printed in my article 'The visit to England in 1754 of Stanisław August Poniatowski', *OSP*, new series, 25 (1992), but I have included some new material here.

[2] Fabre, *Stanislas-Auguste Poniatowski*, 196–204. Nieć, *Młodość ostatniego elekta*, 93–101. Libiszowska, *Życie polskie*, 37–42. Zamoyski, *Last King*, 46–9.

[3] W. Lipoński, 'The influence of Britain on Prince Adam Jerzy Czartoryski's education and political activity', *Polish–Anglo-Saxon Studies*, 1 (1987), 38, claims that Stanisław's study of English politics in 1754 was marked by its superficiality. I shall be contesting this view.

[4] Nieć has shown how he did so when describing Paris. *Młodość ostatniego elekta*, 76.

[5] *Mémoires*, vol. 1, 105–31.   [6] Ibid., vol. 1, 358–9.

survived, but none from France or England. It is reasonable to conclude that Stanisław's initial reaction to England was more favourable than the account in his *Mémoires* would suggest.[7] By 1775, the middle-aged king had seen his early hopes dashed. England had not resisted the Partition, and seemed to be heading for disaster in America.

I

There were a number of reasons for Stanisław's voyage to France and England. From his *Mémoires*, it transpires that his uncle, the Palatine of Ruthenia, had become alarmed at the attachment that had arisen between his daughter Izabella and Stanisław, and had therefore requested his brother-in-law to send his son abroad.[8] Stanisław could also represent the political interests of the *Familia*. The idea accorded with the Castellan of Cracow's plans for his son. Poniatowski's elder sons had already journeyed to France and, in his *List ziemianina*, he had recommended voyages abroad for young noblemen,

so that, in gathering experience of the world, they might also inform themselves about the means of government, about the economy, about the position, the power, strengths, and interests of different states, and so that from this might then choose, what might be proper and useful in the Commonwealth.[9]

This was written at a time when the overwhelming majority of the *szlachta* were convinced that it had nothing at all to learn from abroad. To send a young man to heretical, corrupt England for educational purposes was deeply suspect.

Stanisław travelled with Williams to The Hague, from where Sir Charles went on to England, leaving Stanisław with the British envoy, Joseph Yorke, the former secretary to the Paris embassy, 'un des hommes les plus agréables, comme les plus solides qu'on puisse connaître'. Stanisław also met Joseph's elder brother Charles, and the brothers recommended Count Poniatowski to their father, Lord Chancellor Hardwicke.[10]

---

[7] Fabre, *Stanislas-Auguste Poniatowski*, 186, makes a similar point about his reaction to Paris.

[8] *Mémoires*, vol. 1, 69–70.

[9] Reprinted in Kantecki, *Poniatowski*, vol. 2, pp. cii–ciii.

[10] *Mémoires*, vol. 1, 70–7. Stan. to Williams, The Hague, 21 Aug. and 11 Sept. 1753, LWL CHW 57–10904, ff. 51, 89–92. Stan. to K. Poniatowska, 28 July 1753, ARP 373, vol. 2. P. C. Yorke, *The Life and Correspondence of Philip Yorke, Earl of Hardwicke, Lord High Chancellor of Great Britain* (3 vols.; Cambridge, 1913), vol. 2, 148–54. C. Yorke's visit to The Hague is mentioned by J. Yorke to Hardwicke, 28 Aug. 1753, BL Add. 35356, f. 175.

Stanisław arrived in Paris on 24 September 1753.[11] His father had gained him entry into some of the best houses in Paris, notably the salon of Madame Geoffrin, who became his dear 'maman'. He met Montesquieu there, but instead of uttering profundities, the great man recited a trivial song.[12] Williams had written to the British Ambassador, Lord Albemarle. His house became for Stanisław 'une société anglaise, que j'allais voir . . . avec beaucoup de plaisir, mais qui ne me donna aucune liaison française'.[13] Stanisław met the young Lord North and Lord Dartmouth, with whom he visited Versailles. Stanisław found maintaining his good début in society difficult. In his *Mémoires* he claimed that he was frustrated by the frivolity of the conversation, which centred on the controversy over Italian opera and not the exile of the *parlements*, but at the time he wrote to Williams about the opera without complaining. In any case, the longer he stayed, the more accustomed good company became to him, and the more he was able to benefit from the company of 'hommes profonds dans les sciences et supérieurs dans les arts'. Moreover, 'les femmes en général valent beaucoup mieux que les hommes.'[14] Madame de Brancas testified to the impression made by Count Poniatowski in a letter to Countess Brühl, which Stanisław August proudly inserted in his *Mémoires*:

sa conversation est agréable et bien au-dessus de celle de la plupart de nos Français. Il cherche à s'instruire de tout . . . il est également de bonne compagnie pour un ministre, pour un général, pour un académicien, pour une vieille dame d'honneur, et j'entends dire que nos jeunes et belles dames croient qu'il ne sait que plaire et qu'il y est généralement parvenu.[15]

Around the new year, Stanisław received orders from his father to travel to England. Stanisław regretted his impending departure. France had conquered him:

---

[11] Stan. to Williams, Fontainebleau, 2 Nov. 1753, LWL CHW 57–10904, ff. 159–61. On Stanisław's stay in Paris, see Fabre, *Stanislas-Auguste Poniatowski*, 186–96; Nieć, *Młodość ostatniego elekta*, 70–90; Zamoyski, *Last King*, 42–6; A. Gawerski, 'Stanisław August Poniatowski w Paryżu', in *Francja-Polska XVIII–XIX w.*

[12] *Mémoires*, vol. 1, 86–9.

[13] Ibid., vol. 1, 79–81. Stanisław had great trouble in gaining entry to Albemarle's residence, going to the door ten times in vain before finally encountering Lord Albemarle. Stan. to Williams, Fontainebleau, 2 Nov. 1753, loc. cit. (n. 11).

[14] *Mémoires*, vol. 1, 90, 99–100. Stan. to Williams, Fontainebleau, 2 Nov. 1753, loc. cit. Stan. probably to August Sułkowski, Fontainebleau, 6 Nov. 1753, BCzart. 798, ff. 52–5. Ditto, Paris, 4 Jan. 1754, BCzart. 798, ff. 43–5.

[15] *Mémoires*, vol. 1, 82–3.

Il n'est guère possible de se soustraire au charme magique qui, peu à peu, façonne l'âme la plus austère et fait désirer de vivre au milieu d'une nation quelquefois affectueuse et presque toujours facile et gaie, dont le peuple est vraiment bon, dont la bourgeoisie est généralement fort industrieuse, dont la qualité enfin, telle volage et superficielle qu'on veuille la supposer, fournit pourtant mille exemples respectables de tout genre.

The French language itself, learned by every educated young man across Europe, inspired a certain feeling of French superiority.[16] Stanisław thus came to England, polished by and disposed towards Parisian society and manners, and this was to affect his reactions to England. On the other hand, he sympathized with the *parlements* in their struggle with Louis XV.[17] Before leaving, he confessed his apprehension of the reputed singularity of the English: 'Je ne scais pas comment j'y serai reçu . . . car j'ai une idée peutêtre fausse que communément dans un Anglois il y a assez bonnes ou de mauvaises choses, pour en faire trois François, et par conséquent, qu'il faut trois fois plus de tems pour connoitre les Anglois que les François.'[18] At the end of February, in the company of a Captain Stanhope, he left Paris for Calais.[19]

II

The passage to Dover was very rough and lasted nine hours, giving Stanisław sea sickness. He was afficted for some hours even after setting foot on land, but good water, which he had not enjoyed in Paris,[20] and the joy of arriving in England soon revived him. At the inn at Canterbury, Stanisław heard a servant disputing with a postilion about his nationality. Because the visitor held his fork in his left hand, like an Englishman, he could not be a Frenchman, and was certainly better than one. Stanisław made a mental note never to hold a fork in his right hand whilst in England.[21] On to London, where he lodged with a Mr Coppenhole in Suffolk street.[22]

The Castellan of Cracow procured for his son a warm welcome from his old friend, Sir Luke Schaub, and his wife. The venerable former

---

[16] Ibid., vol. 1, 100–1.
[17] Ibid., vol. 1, 90–1. Two decades later, after another clash between king and *parlements*, Stanisław August undoubtedly felt more strongly than as a youth of 21, but there is no reason to suppose that he was unconcerned or unsympathetic in 1753–4.
[18] Paris, 4 Jan. 1754, loc. cit. (n. 14). [19] *Mémoires*, vol. 1, 104.
[20] On Parisian water, J. McManners, *Death and the Enlightenment* (Oxford, 1981), 20–1.
[21] *Mémoires*, vol. 1, 105–6.
[22] So Mme de Broglie addressed her letters to Stanisław from Paris. Zb. Pop. 318, ff. 262–3.

diplomat was now, it seemed, reduced to near-senility; 'il sortait peu, et dans sa conversation je ne vis qu'un vieillard tres affectueux.' At midnight though, he came alive, and his conversation on all manner of subjects sparkled with precision and an exact memory. The next day, Sir Luke was as old in his spirits and opinions as ever, but a few nights later he was again 'aussi lumineux que la première fois'. Perhaps, thought Stanisław, the calm of night allowed his spirit a liberty which the noise and bustle of the immense city denied him during the day.[23] The Schaubs were enchanted by Stanisław, and approved of the serious way in which he sought out that which might be of value in England. Sir Luke sent a glowing testimonial back to Stanisław's parents:

Sage et reglé dans ses moeurs, aisé, posé, modeste et décent dans ses manieres, judicieux dans ses observations, discret et considéré dans ses propos, il fait également honneur aux soins éclairés qui l'ont formé, et aux exemples de Sa Famille, sur lesquels il avoit à se mouler. Jamais aussi jeune voyageur ne s'est fait distinguer et rechercher comme Luy de tout ce qu'il y a de meilleur dans cette nation.[24]

The day after his arrival, Lady Schaub presented Count Poniatowski at Lady Caroline Petersham's, and there Hans Stanley, a somewhat eccentric politician and Gallophile,[25] introduced himself, having received a letter recommending Stanisław from Madame Geoffrin. Stanley invited the count to dinner on the next day, when Stanisław met, among others, Lord Barrington, Lord Strange, and George Bubb Dodington.[26] The last named, then over 60, was 'un des plus agréables vieux débauchés qu'on peut rencontrer', who liked to play the part of a father figure to young men.[27] Enormously rich, 'Papa' Dodington dressed in gold braid. His carriages, books, and marbled gallery at his St James Street house matched this magnificence, yet he claimed his dress showed his economy, for, having been on missions abroad, he found on his return that gold braid covered his nudity as well as a frock coat. His attire was as well known at the racecourse and the cockpit as at Court.[28] Dodington opened his house to Poniatowski, and Stanisław dined there four times. On the first

[23] *Mémoires*, vol. 1, 106–7.   [24] 20 May 1754. BCzart. 798, ff. 55–7.
[25] *DNB*, 18 (1889), 955–6.   [26] *Mémoires*, vol. 1, 110.
[27] For an example, see the letters of advice written to a Mr East in 1755, *Historical Manuscripts Commission: Reports on Manuscripts in Various Collections*, 6 (1909).
[28] *Mémoires*, vol. 1, 110–11. Horace Walpole noted that Dodington 'made more display at less cost than anyone in the kingdom but himself could have done'. Williams, *Works*, vol. 2, 48–51.

occasion, Lords Bolingbroke, Strange, Hobart, Stormont, and Barrington, and Messrs Stanley and Cambridge made up the company.[29] Stanisław makes no comment in his *Mémoires* about Dodington's dubious political reputation as a shameless place seeker, which perhaps shows Stanisław's affection for him.

Lord Strange, heir to the earldom of Derby, who in contrast to Dodington dressed simply in a Quaker's black, was also an *habitué* of the cockpit. He took Stanisław to see a cock fight, and in doing so gave him an insight into the English national character.[30] Three or four hundred people of all ranks, from the hugely popular symbol of English beef and pudding, the Duke of Cumberland,[31] to sedan-chair porters, were squeezed into a small room. They engaged in a thousand different ways of betting upon the outcome, and made a terrible noise until one of the cocks expired. Yet with the victim's last gasp a perfect silence descended upon the throng. Unbroken silence and 'clameurs atroces' alternated all evening; 'leur passions semblent être à leurs ordres, ou leur durée dépendre d'un ressort mécanique.' Stanisław contrasted such ritualized behaviour with the usual tendency of crowds to remain agitated for some time after the storm had passed, like the waves of the sea.

Stanisław discerned a parallel in the behaviour of English mobs. A crowd of 50,000, which might seem to menace throne and state, could be peacefully dispersed by the reading of the Riot Act by a single Justice of the Peace and one constable. The mob seemed to wait only for this formality before, with its glory secured, going home to show its respect for the law.[32] In 1764 the *Gazetteer and New Daily Advertiser* informed its readers that the new King of Poland 'was fond of the persons in genteel life with whom he conversed; but considered the lower classes in a very unfavourable light, on account of some mobs which he chanced to be a spectator of.'[33] Count Poniatowski remained an aristocrat, and evidently

---

[29] *The Political Diary of George Bubb Dodington*, eds. J. Carswell and L. A. Dralle (Oxford, 1965), 262 (31 Mar. 1754), 270 (3 May 1754, 16 May 1754), 283 (26 June 1754). Stanisław met the second Viscount Bolingbroke, not his famous father, who had died in 1751.

[30] *Mémoires*, vol. 1, 111–12.

[31] Cumberland was hugely popular, not only for his victory at Culloden, and for his devotion to George II (*Mémoires*, vol. 1, 115), but also because his gargantuan frame personified the virtues of 'roast and boiled' in contrast to French 'soupe maigre'. See a pair of prints by Hogarth, reproduced in *The English Satirical Print* (7 vols.; Cambridge, 1986), vol. 3, *The Englishman and the Foreigner*, ed. M. Duffy, 172–5.

[32] *Mémoires*, vol. 1, 112.

[33] Copy in Zb. Pop. 215, f. 269. The newspaper would probably have got its information from one of Stanisław's English friends, who then presumably sent the copy to the new monarch.

reacted as had many travellers before him. The figure of 50,000 was, however, wildly exaggerated.[34]

The English sailors fascinated Stanisław. They resembled apes for their adroitness and gaiety, but could speak and lacked their malice. When on shore, they immediately spent all their pay on women in houses protected by the government, thus fulfilling the only necessity of life which maritime service did not afford them. Of religion they knew little; in sum, 'on dirait, à les voir, qu'en les formant, on a voulu essayer quel était le plus petit nombre d'idées et de notions, avec lesquelles il serait possible de faire exister et agir des créatures humaines.' Their bravery was legendary, for fear of severe corporal punishment, not of death, ruled their lives. English liberty was limited to the land; 'il n'y a point de commandement plus despotique, point de sujétion plus obéissante que celle que l'on voit sur leurs vaisseaux de guerre.'[35]

Lord Strange also took Stanisław to see his first play by Shakespeare. Young Count Poniatowski carried with him the memory of the rules of the three unities, the observing of which gave French dramatists cause to consider themselves superior to the English. Yet the more Shakespeare Stanisław saw, the more he felt himself a heretic on that point, and greatly appreciated Shakespeare's and others' free handling of time and space, and their use of illusion.[36]

In contrast to Lord Strange, who felt himself dishonoured by uttering a word of French, and Lord Granville, who had a passion for Spanish, Philip Dormer Stanhope, the fourth Earl of Chesterfield, was a Gallomaniac, who spoke better French than any Englishman Stanisław had yet met. He even paid a correspondent in Paris to send him the latest expressions of the moment; thus Stanisław learned that a *poilou* (*sic*) was a man of obscure origins or of no distinction, whereas *un homme comme il faut* in Paris was one who had adopted the English custom of taking a morning stroll *en habit des coquins*, 'et c'est la connaissance de cette importante vérité'. Chesterfield was also a connoisseur of manners. In his *Letters to His Son* (published posthumously) he set out to make his son 'shine, equally in the learned and polite world'. Learning and virtue, if unadorned with 'les manières nobles et aisées, la tournure d'un homme de condition, le ton de la bonne compagnie, les Grâces, le je ne sçais quoi qui plaît,' were as a rough diamond is to a polished one; 'for ever a dirty rough mineral,

---

[34] Such a figure was quite unprecedented until the Gordon riots in 1780, which were dispersed far from peacefully. See J. Stevenson, *Popular Disturbances in England 1700–1870* (London, 1979), 59–90.

[35] *Mémoires*, vol. I, 126–8.   [36] Ibid., vol. I, 112–13. See below, p. 178.

in the cabinets of some few curious collectors'. He was an unrelenting critic of awkwardness, uncleanliness, inattention, pedantry, inelegant and incorrect language, mumbling, and loud laughter, and the first targets of his criticism were his own countrymen. Williams, as we have seen, was similarly disposed, and informed Chesterfield of young Philip Stanhope's inattention and awkwardness whilst at Dresden.[37] Many of Stanisław's criticisms of English youth, at school, at university, and on the Grand Tour, can also be found in Chesterfield's and Williams's letters. Stanisław found Chesterfield's language a little affected, but nevertheless enjoyed his conversation. Chesterfield, in his turn, considered Count Poniatowski as a model young gentleman; pleasing in his manners and desirous to instruct himself while on his tour.[38]

Beneath Chesterfield's Gallomania, the two shared a love of French culture, and similar attitudes on the necessity of more polished manners. In Poland, the contrast between the dirty, drunken, xenophobic mass of the *szlachta* and the cultured, polite, Gallophile part of the élite, between *wąsy* and *peruka* (whiskers and wig), was far greater than anything comparable in England, yet the comic figure of Fielding's Squire Western was one Stanisław could recognize. Likewise, after French ladies, who 'malgré la première apparence de leur extreme futilité', and their sublime, unintelligible jargon turned out to be well educated, spirited, and possessed even of a tincture of *philosophie* (perhaps only the effect of their *libertinage*),[39] Stanisław found English gentlewomen rather less refined. They commonly went out without rouge and powder, they did not take care of their teeth, and hardly one in forty spoke French; 'leur habillement et leurs manières étaient en tout l'opposé des Françaises.'[40] Chesterfield later told Stanisław that he had left several ladies disappointed, not to have been more intimately acquainted with him.[41] In women, Stanisław's tastes remained decidedly Gallophile.

One lady, whose heart Stanisław caused to flutter, was Katherine, dowager Duchess of Gordon. Horace Walpole recounted the following story to John Chute of

---

[37] *Letters to His Son and Others*, ed. R. K. Root (London, 1929, repr. 1986), 22 Sept. 1749 (OS), 117–18, 27 Sept. 1749 (OS), 123, 6 July 1749 (OS), 128. See the life in *Letters of Philip Dormer Stanhope, 4th Earl of Chesterfield*, ed. B. Dobrée (6 vols.; London, 1932), vol. I, 11–221.

[38] *Mémoires*, vol. I, 129–30. Chesterfield to Stan., 25 Sept. 1754, Zb. Pop. 173, ff. 300–1.

[39] Fontainebleau, 6 Nov. 1753, Paris, 4 Jan. 1754. BCzart. 798, ff. 52–5, 43–5; *Mémoires*, vol. I, 100.

[40] *Mémoires*, vol. I, 126.   [41] 25 Sept. 1754, Zb. Pop. 173, ff. 300–1.

the most extraordinary declaration of love that was ever made. Have you seen young Poniatowski? He is very handsome. You have seen the Duchess of G[ordon] who looks like a raw-boned Scotch metaphysician that has got a red face by drinking water. One day at the Drawing Room, never having spoken to him, she sent one of the foreign ministers to invite Poniatowski to dinner with her the next day. He bowed, and went. The moment the door opened, her little sons attired like Cupids with bows and arrows, shot at him, and one of them literally hit his hair, and was very near putting his eyes out, and hindered his casting it to the couch

where she, another sea born Venus lay.

The only company besides this Highland Goddess were two Scotchmen who could not speak a word of any language but their own Erse; and to complete his astonishment at this allegorical entertainment, with the dessert, there entered a little horse, and galloped round the table, a hieroglyphic I cannot solve. Poniatowski accounts for this profusion of kindness by his great grandmother being a Gordon, but I believe it is accounted for by ****.[42]

But it is clear from her letters to Stanisław that the duchess bore him a great deal of affection.[43]

Sir Charles Hanbury Williams was at first kept in the country by the need to assure his election to Parliament as member for Leominster. Stanisław saw very little of him. Neither Stanisław's *Mémoires* nor Williams's biography mention any meeting, but Sir Charles wrote in 1755 that they had been together in England, and Stanisław's first letter to Williams after leaving England contains no impressions of his visit, which seems to indicate that they met before his departure.[44] Stanisław did visit Sir Charles's future son-in-law, Lord Essex, at Cassiobury, and became a great favourite with Williams's wife—'for he has none of the English brutality about him'—and his daughters Frances and Charlotte. He declined to go with them to a performance of Handel's *Messiah*, but Charlotte wrote to her father that Stanisław had confessed that, had Sir Charles been present, he would not have dared refuse.[45]

In Williams's absence, Count Poniatowski was presented at Court by one of the lords-in-waiting. Sir Charles had prepared the way by telling George II that Stanisław had first gone to Paris in order to improve his

---

[42] 14 May 1754, *Horace Walpole's Correspondence*, ed. W. S. Lewis *et al.* (48 vols.; New Haven, 1937–83), vol. 35, 81–2. The ending was thus printed in Walpole's *Works*, 1793. Also see Walpole to Mann, 13 Sept. 1764, *Horace Walpole's Correspondence*, vol. 22, 253.

[43] 14 Aug. 1754, Zb. Pop. 318, f. 58. 22 Dec. 1764, Zb. Pop. 176, ff. 166–8.

[44] *Mémoires*, vol. 1, 113. Ilchester, *Williams*, 109, 287. Nieć, *Młodość ostatniego elekta*, 100. Stan. to Williams, The Hague, 18 July 1754, LWL CHW 59–10908, ff. 164–5.

[45] Lady Frances Essex to Stan., 20 Dec. 1754, Zb. Pop. 174, f. 21. Ilchester, *Williams*, 287.

English. The septuagenarian monarch extended to Stanisław an 'infini-ment gracieux' welcome, as well he might, when Williams's instructions were to cultivate the Czartoryskis and keep French influence in Poland at bay. The king questioned Count Poniatowski in detail about the Ostróg affair. Stanisław's impression was of 'un homme de sens fort droit, et qui donnait aux affaires une application autant suivie qu'il le fallait, sans pré-tendre au brillant de ceux qui veulent avoir tout fait et tout imaginé par eux-mêmes. Il avait de la valeur comme tous les Brunswick et aimait à parler guerre.'[46]

Soon after his arrival, Sir Luke Schaub mentioned to Stanisław that the current session of Parliament was due to finish on the next day. Entry was procured to the House of Lords, which Stanisław had thought would look more impressive than it actually did. To his distress, he found that his command of English did not allow him to follow the course of the debate easily, due to the pronunciation. He resolved to improve quickly.[47] Lord Chancellor Hardwicke distinguished Stanisław by saluting him as he entered the visitors' gallery, and sent Count Poniatowski a message inviting him to his residence, Powis House in Bloomsbury.[48] Stanisław greatly admired the Yorkes, united in purpose, and gathered around their distinguished and celebrated patriarch, 'a powerfull good being, much above us . . . je retiendrai toutte ma vie l'impression que m'ont laissés ce Pere et ces enfants, réciproquement si heureux.'[49] He marvelled at their array of talents:

il n'y avait pas de science que l'on ne put apprendre, guerre, politique, marine, jurisprudence, économie publique, littérature de tout genre, tout s'y trouvait par état ou par goût; et leur union intérieure et leur bienveillance pour moi m'a fait regarder cette maison comme une source d'instruction et comme un répertoire d'exemples.[50]

Philip Yorke, Lord Royston, was learned and reputed to be extremely capable, and his modesty alone, writes Stanisław August, kept him from considerable employment. Stanisław wished he could study under him.[51] Admiral Anson was Hardwicke's son-in-law. He was 'le plus doux, le

---

[46] *Mémoires*, vol. 1, 113.   [47] Ibid., vol. 1, 107.

[48] Ibid. Stan. to C. Yorke, Warsaw, 7 Jan. 1755, BL Add. 35634, ff. 109–10.

[49] Stan. to C. Yorke, Warsaw, 17 Nov. 1760, BL Add. 35635, f. 461. On the familial happiness of the Yorkes in the 1750s, see Yorke, *Hardwicke*, vol. 2, 139, 565–6, 579.

[50] *Mémoires*, vol. 1, 107–9.

[51] Stan. to C. Yorke, Warsaw, 7 Jan. 1755, BL Add. 35634, f. 110. On Royston, see Yorke, *Hardwicke*, vol. 1, 212–13, vol. 2, 147–8.

plus sociable des hommes', whose sole fault was that he talked but reluctantly of his adventures.[52]

It was, however, the second son, Charles Yorke, then 32 years old, who possessed 'une aménité de caractère toute particulière', and who became Stanisław's 'ami de coeur'.[53] Charles's sensibility made him notably beloved of his friends. He was his father's intellectual equal, but lacked his confidence and tended to introspection. In the place of his elder brother, who preferred private life, Charles assumed, not without regret, his father's political and legal mantle. He was Member of Parliament for Reigate and, during Stanisław's stay, Charles was appointed Solicitor-General to the Prince of Wales, viewed as the first step of a seemingly inevitable ascent to the Lord Chancellorship. He was already a jurist of note, having in 1744 published the acclaimed *Considerations on the Law of Forfeiture for High Treason*. Charles was temperamentally inclined more to literary pursuits than to the law. He possessed an extensive library richly adorned with the classics ancient and modern, and some of the latest works of the French Enlightenment, especially bought for him in Paris. He was a Fellow of the Royal Society, and prominent in English Freemasonry, into which he may have initiated Stanisław.[54] Above all he was the 'très cher et illustre ami' of Montesquieu. Charles often travelled to France to see the great man, and debated the English constitution with him, arguing that in a limited monarchy, feudal rights against the Crown, far from being 'intermediary powers' as in France, infringed upon the liberties of all. Charles Yorke was, in sum, the English equivalent of a *philosophe*.[55]

Charles Yorke enabled Poniatowski to appreciate the beauties of the English landscape by taking him walking in the country, about which Stanisław wrote his first 'billet' in English:

[52] *Mémoires*, vol. 1, 107–9. Williams quipped that Anson had 'been round it [the world] but never in it'. Williams, *Works*, vol. 2, 271.

[53] *Mémoires*, vol. 1, 107–9.

[54] J. D. Ochocki related rumours that Poniatowski had been initiated in London. *Pamiętniki* (vol. 3; Wilno, 1857), 240, cited after Hass, *Wolnomularstwo*, 101. In 1768 Count Beaujeu, of Lyons, claimed Stanisław August as a fellow Mason, or at least as a sympathizer, when recommending Dussert de Bourgogne as a professor for the king's cadet school. Fabre, *Stanislas-Auguste Poniatowski*, 203, 612 n. 89.

[55] Yorke, *Hardwicke*, vol. 1, 207–8, vol. 2, 140–5, 172 (a letter from C. Yorke to his father reporting his conversation with Montesquieu). *DNB*, 21 (1890), 1252–5. Fabre, *Stanislas-Auguste Poniatowski*, 201–3. Shackleton, *Montesquieu*, 383–4. Letters to C. Yorke regarding books and Montesquieu from Dr J. Jeffreys in Paris, BL Add. 35633, ff. 156, 185–6, 234, 313–14, 386, BL Add. 35634, ff. 16, 24, 36–7. 'Mémoire de Livres fournis' (costing 2393 l.), MS 35633, ff. 271–2. Letters from Montesquieu to C. Yorke, BL Add. 35350, ff. 3–8. C. Yorke to Stan., 9 May 1758, Zb. Pop. 318, f. 59.

Dear Friend

Saturday and Sunday in the next week, I will expect your ordres. I think our walking in the country about seven night, shall succeed yet better, fancying the wetter will in this time correct and fine themselve. And the Sun is indeed a very necessary ornament to a landskip. It is the first Englisch Billet that I have yet writ in my Life.

Therefore excuse me Sir, if I explain not so strongly as I feel it, the Friendship and respect with which

I am

> Dear Sir, your most humble Serveur,
>
> > Poniatowski.[56]

Charles Yorke also took Count Poniatowski on a voyage, in the company of a friend, Richard Owen Cambridge, a would-be poet.[57] Leaving London on 1 June, they reached Salisbury by the evening. On the Sunday, they saw the cathedral, Old Sarum, and Wilton. Stanisław later fondly reminisced to Charles Yorke; 'Plaines de Salisbury! Si vous les renvoyez, saluez les de ma part. Ménez Cambridge à Stone Hinge. Faites le asseoir sur une de ces grandes pierres et qu'il fasse une Poème. Qu'il se souvienne que des soldats Romains sont les fondateurs de la Colline d'Old Sarum!'[58] On the following day they saw Bath, then only beginning its spectacular growth, and were received by Sir George Lyttelton. Lyttelton was the author of the *Letters on the Troglodytes*, which plagiarized the *Lettres persanes* and extolled the English constitution. Stanisław had already met him in London, and greatly admired his learning.[59]

At Prior Park, near Bath, Charles and Stanisław called on Sir Ralph Allen and his niece's husband, Dr William Warburton. Sir Ralph had been an intimate of Pope and talked vividly about the poet, who had frequently graced the house and, no doubt, the famous garden as well.[60] Charles's friend Warburton, who had been Pope's literary agent and was to become Bishop of Gloucester, had made a great impression on Stanisław in London. Charles Yorke wrote to him from Salisbury that Stanisław valued his 'friendly communicativeness', and 'receivd so much satisfaction from his former conversation with you that he is preparing

---

[56] May 1754? BL Add. 35639, f. 200. Also printed (somewhat inaccurately) in Fabre, *Stanislas-Auguste Poniatowski*, 611 n. 84.

[57] Some of Cambridge's letters to C. Yorke are in BL Add. 35639.

[58] C. Yorke to Warburton, Salisbury, 1 June 1754, BL Add. 35404, f. 143. Stan. to C. Yorke, St Petersburg, 17 Dec. 1755, BL Add. 35634, f. 293.

[59] Stan. to Lyttelton, ? Nov. 1764 (draft), Zb. Pop. 177, f. 154. *Mémoires*, vol. 1, 119.

[60] *Mémoires*, vol. 1, 119.

many questions in hopes of your answers, which he regards as oracles'.[61] Besides being a controversial Shakespearean scholar, Warburton was the author of *The Divine Legation of Moses* and *The Alliance Between Church and State*, which argued on latitudinarian and Whig principles for orthodox Anglican Christianity, and for an established Church, not challenging the State, but in return protected by it. Those governing the State were to be members of the Church, but the Church acknowledged the right of individuals to freedom of religious persuasion.[62] Montesquieu was greatly impressed and, via Charles Yorke, sent 'l'illustre docteur' *'une pièce de son vin*, which [he says] is that part of his works he most values'.[63] Charles Yorke made Stanisław a leaving present of all Warburton's works, 'a gratification I could not deny him'. Stanisław wrote to Charles a few months later: 'J'embrasse le vénérable Docteur Warburton. Je suis fâché pour mon ami qu'il soit Hérétique avec tant de piété et de science.' Stanisław had learned to treat with irony the claim of each Church to provide the sole route to salvation.[64]

Stanisław and Charles returned to London via Oxford and Stowe, where they met Richard Grenville, Lord Temple, and his brothers, one of whom was the future First Lord of the Treasury. The famous gardens, full of Whig iconography, drew Stanisław's attention. Undoubtedly, Count Poniatowski had already engaged in conversation about gardening with the Yorkes. Lord Royston and his wife, the Marchioness Grey, were enthusiasts for *chinoiserie*, and in the 1740s and 1750s undertook a series of tours to study many gardens, including Stowe, prior to their employing Lancelot 'Capability' Brown to improve their gardens at Wrest Park.[65] Stowe was venerated as the cradle of the new fashion, which attempted to recreate the Claudean Roman *campagna* in England. However, in decrying symmetry, yews, and all the trinkets which William III had introduced from Holland, the new taste had assumed all the intolerance of a religious sect.[66] When Stanisław hazarded a word or two of regret at the total exclusion of alignment in the laying out of water and paths, he saw

    [61] BL Add. 35404, f. 143.
    [62] A. W. Evans, *Warburton and the Warburtonians: A Study in some Eighteenth Century Controversies* (London, 1932). N. Sykes, *Church and State in England in the XVIIIth Century* (Cambridge, 1934), 284, 316–26. Clark, *English Society*, 139–41. *DNB*, 20 (1889), 758–65.
    [63] Montesquieu to C. Yorke, 4 Dec. 1753, BL Add. 35350, f. 7. C. Yorke to Warburton, 22 Dec. 1753, BL Add. 35404, f. 59.
    [64] C. Yorke to Warburton, 1 Aug. 1754, BL Add. 35404, f. 92. Stan. to C. Yorke, Warsaw, 7 Jan. 1755, BL Add. 35634, f. 110. See below, pp. 226–8.
    [65] M. Batey and D. Lambert, *The English Garden Tour* (London, 1990), 111, 207.
    [66] Addison's criticisms in the *Spectator*, no. 414, 25 June 1712, were particularly influential and often quoted in guide books. Batey and Lambert, *English Garden Tour*, 143.

that he risked falling from favour.[67] Although Stanisław had come to appreciate the English disregard of the unities in drama, in the landscape garden he found an excess of uncontrolled nature.

Stanisław had experienced an England of contrasts; between the formal and the informal, between the Gallophile and the Gallophobe, between the refined and the coarse, and between the exclusive and the egalitarian. His social world, for all its internal contrasts and political disagreements, was overwhelmingly aristocratic, high Whig in its politics and connexions, and latitudinarian in its religion, deeply suspecting enthusiasm. This moderation allowed little room for aggressive 'freethinking' on social, political, or religious questions. It was also a world which was contemptuous of Tory country squires (except when canvassing at election time) and Oxford divines. It was open to enlightened influences, even if, for some, this was more a matter of fashion than of conviction.[68] Stanisław's experiences and his contacts with those in the highest political circles were reflected in his study of politics.

III

On 6 March 1754, Henry Pelham died suddenly. Stanisław had arrived at a most interesting moment, and he studied politics and recent political history with care. For two years, he wrote, since the Duke of Bedford's dismissal, Pelham and his elder brother, the Duke of Newcastle, had been absolute masters of England. 'L'opposition étoit devenu presque honteuse. Il n'y avoit pour ainsi dire plus de débat dans les deux chambres,' while the finances had been put onto 'le chemin de perfection' by Pelham.[69] On the surface all remained calm. Stanisław witnessed none of the stormy scenes that at other times provided such a curious

[67] *Mémoires*, vol. 1, 120. Stanisław, from the perspective of 1775, was writing more about the taste in general than about Stowe in particular. In 1754, although Brown's work had been completed, Lord Temple had not yet made irregular the lakes and avenues. Batey and Lambert, *English Garden Tour*, 122.

[68] Cannon, *Aristocratic Century*, 59–60. The political and religious outlook of Stanisław's circle can best be illustrated by the pungent sarcasm of Warburton, writing to Charles Yorke: 'Oxford that Athens of loyalty and learning. It is hard to say if Church or State be at present more benefitted by it. For I think the fashionable divinity of Hutchinson is well matched by the fashionable politics of Filmar [*sic*]. It is hard to say which has least sense, or more properly the most nonsense. But it is certain Wiggs [*sic*] and rational divines are at present the horror of that renowned university.' 24 Aug. 1754, BL Egerton 1952, f. 35. John Hutchinson (1674–1737) was an opponent of Newtonian physics and defended revelation from natural religion. Clark, *English Society*, 218–19. Sir Robert Filmer (d. 1653) was a defender of absolute divine right monarchy and indefeasible hereditary succession. Dickinson, *Liberty and Property*, 14, 22–4.

[69] Stan. probably to August Sułkowski, London, 12 Apr. 1754, BCzart. 798, ff. 47–50.

spectacle for foreigners and embarrassed the government. He even witnessed the Westminster election without inconvenience, despite being unaccompanied; an oyster-seller explained the proceedings to him—a novel experience for a Polish aristocrat.[70]

Yet Stanisław could discern, imperfectly, deeper political machinations, in which his friends, Charles Yorke and Charles Hanbury Williams, were intimately involved on opposing sides. Williams's close friend Henry Fox expected to succeed, at best to Pelham's dominant position, or at least to the leadership of the Commons, with a share in election management and the disposal of patronage. Lord Hardwicke and Fox were bitter rivals. They had clashed over Hardwicke's Clandestine Marriage Act, which came into force during Stanisław's stay, on 25 March 1754. Fox had attacked the bill and the Chancellor 'aussi personellement qu'il est possible sans [le] nommer'. Hardwicke 'repondit encorplus vivement . . . Vous jugez que cette affaire laisse une pointe dans l'esprit de Mr Fox contre le Chancelier et même contre les freres.' It did not escape Stanisław that Fox 'par hazard est marié par un mariage clandestine'. Sir Charles Hanbury Williams, in fact, had arranged it.[71] After the death of Pelham, Hardwicke and Newcastle were determined to keep Fox from playing a dominant role, and offered him the post of Secretary of State, which Fox accepted in the apparent belief that he would have information on the secret service money (used for bribery) and would be able to dispose of some places in order to lead the Commons, but Newcastle denied this. Fox had second thoughts, especially after a letter from Williams advising him not to accept, and on 14 March declared that he would prefer to remain Secretary-at-War. 'On le prend au mot,' wrote Stanisław.[72]

Stanisław was also connected with, but could only glimpse, the long-running negotiations between Hardwicke and William Pitt and his allies. Charles Yorke was sent to negotiate with Pitt. Stanisław observed Pitt's tall, slender figure and his aquiline nose, but did not meet him, and did not then foresee his greatness. Negotiations were also conducted with Lyttelton and the Grenvilles. Hardwicke and the Pelhams had long

[70] *Mémoires*, vol. 1, 117–18.

[71] London, 12 Apr. 1754, loc. cit. (n. 69). Ilchester, *Williams*, 80–2. J. C. D. Clark, *The Dynamics of Change: The Crisis of the 1750s and English Party Systems* (Cambridge, 1982), 39, 41, 47. Yorke, *Hardwicke*, vol. 2, 59–71. When Williams arrived in The Hague in 1753, Joseph Yorke believed that Williams's primary purpose was to look for evidence to discredit him, and thus damage Hardwicke in order to benefit Fox. J. Yorke to Hardwicke, 13, 17, 24, 31 July, 7 Aug., 4 Sept. 1753, BL Add. 35356, ff. 159–77.

[72] London, 12 Apr. 1754, loc. cit. (n. 69). Williams to Fox, BL Add. 51393, ff. 168–9. Clark, *Dynamics*, 59–62. Ilchester, *Williams*, 284–6.

valued Pitt as an ally and tried to gain his support, without trying to force him as Secretary of State on George II, who detested him. Thus the trip to Bath and Stowe served a very political purpose.[73]

The Duke of Newcastle was truly curious; 'les gestes, l'allure, le langage, toute la manière d'être . . . était l'image d'inquiétude et de l'empressement; on disait de lui qu'habituellement il courait toute la journée après la chose qu'il avait oubliée le matin.' His speech was confused and fast, but his letters were models of justice and brevity. He suffered many severe and often unjust criticisms, 'auxquelles tout ministre anglais semble assujéti par état', and he greatly feared for his credit with the nation and the king, but he ran his ministry as sovereignly as Walpole had his.[74] Walpole held a particular fascination for Stanisław. It seemed to him that the nation had become 'si généralement éclairée et instruite par l'Étude et par les Exemples du Chevalier Walpole', that despite all the changes of personnel since his fall, England was wedded to the same Continental liaisons, and the altercations taking place in North America between French and English settlers were then generally dismissed as petty incidents inevitable on distant frontiers. Only a few (among them Anson perhaps?) complained of the neglect of the armed services, and no one foresaw the Diplomatic Revolution.[75] Stanisław August uncritically repeats a good deal of the opposition's criticism of Walpole (perhaps he consulted the volumes of the *Craftsman* in the Royal Library), but is far from flattering about the opposition. Walpole, in saying that every man has his price, had proved that he had made, 'sans déguisement, de la corruption le principal et presque unique ressort de son administration'. Having been born in a mediocre estate, he left a peerage and a huge fortune to his children.[76]

Carteret, Pulteney, Cobham, and Chesterfield had led the opposition to Walpole, and honoured Pope, whom the king hated. Stanisław considered that Pope had substantially reduced George II's popularity with his subjects. They had gathered around the Prince of Wales (a sort of retribution for George II's own behaviour before 1727), and Lord Cobham had placed the prince's bust in the middle of his Temple of Friendship at Stowe, surrounded by leaders of the opposition. However,

[73] *Mémoires*, vol. 1, 118–19. Clark, *Dynamics of Change*, 74–5. See also P. Lawson, *George Grenville: A Political Life* (Oxford, 1984), 74–5. Yorke, *Hardwicke*, vol. 2, 187–94, 213.
[74] *Mémoires*, vol. 1, 116–17.
[75] London, 12 Apr. 1754, loc. cit. (n. 69). *Mémoires*, vol. 1, 118.
[76] *Mémoires*, vol. 1, 116. 'Catologus Bibliothecae . . . 1783', AKsJP 268, f. 122. Stanisław August may not have been aware that Walpole's estate was heavily encumbered by debt.

Pope had died, and almost all of the prince's partisans, dividing the spoils of Walpole, had deserted him. Cobham did so too, and a visitor to Stowe, on seeing the temple, asked him to whom he was giving its key, to guard this poor, abandoned prince.[77] Carteret was highly favoured by George II, but despite his acknowledged capacity, he did not enjoy the confidence of his fellow Whigs. The king was always seeking to assist Hanover, and this predilection 'a determiné quelquefois ses résolutions politiques d'une manière dont les Anglais croient avec raison de se plaindre'.[78] Stanisław could hardly have failed to make the obvious analogy with Augustus III. Because of Carteret's willingness to favour Hanover, George II more than once had tried to place him at the head of the ministry, but could never maintain him there long. In February 1746, the replacement of Newcastle by Granville (as Carteret had now become) had provoked the resignation of more than 140 persons[79] who occupied all the most important jobs. Faced with a hostile majority in the Commons, Granville had been forced to go almost immediately, and the Pelhams had been recalled. A satirical *History of Lord Granville's Ministry* had been produced, with more than 200 blank pages and containing only newspaper announcements of his elevation and dismissal.[80]

Stanisław's recounting of these events is highly significant. The falls of Walpole and Granville demonstrate that in order to govern, the king required a ministry that could command a majority in the House of Commons, which could determine whom the king should not employ, and that a coherent party, in this case the Pelhamite Whigs, could severely limit his options.[81] The king was not able to govern as he pleased and, while possessing extensive prerogatives, was therefore no despot. It is likely that this study of English politics reinforced Stanisław's conviction that the English constitution provided good government (especially in financial matters), while preventing despotism, and that elements of its principles might profitably be introduced into Poland. Yet there is no attempt in the *Mémoires* or in any surviving letter at formal analysis of the constitution. Stanisław August sticks to his light-hearted, anecdotal tone, and does not at this point in his *Mémoires* make explicit any English inspiration for his political aims or tactics. He certainly learnt much at Stowe, but Nieć exaggerated the impact of the political tactics of the Grenville

---

[77] *Mémoires*, vol. 1, 115, 119–20, 130.   [78] Ibid., vol. 1, 114.
[79] J. B. Owen, *The Rise of the Pelhams* (London, 1957), 295–7, quotes an estimate of about forty-five actual or intended resignations.
[80] *Mémoires*, vol. 1, 130–1, 117.
[81] Clark, *Dynamics of Change*, 453. Owen, *Rise of the Pelhams*, 34–40.

faction upon Stanisław as a model for the *Familia* to follow. The account in the *Mémoires* does not warrant such a supposition, and the political fortunes of the Cobhamites since 1733 were in fact hardly an advertisement for their political tactics, which all too often degenerated into knee-jerk opposition.[82] Stanisław also found much to criticize in English political culture, especially the prevalent tone of egoism.

IV

Stanisław saw the roots of 'cet égoisme assez général' in the education of young English gentlemen,[83] which was, he wrote later, 'une des choses qui me frappa le plus'. No nation, he admitted, rivalled the English in their knowledge of Latin and Greek classics, but at English boarding schools the pupils were taught no manners or civility whatsoever. 'C'est le fouet, et le fouet seul tres libéralement employé, qui semble y faire tout.' When the day's lessons were over, the boys were abandoned entirely to themselves. A schoolboy neither greeted nor stood up for anyone. In their parents' houses, it was common to see them at 10 or 12 years old, sprawling on couches and tables in the presence of company, even resting their feet on the knees of strangers, and not deigning to reply when spoken to. Their parents would say indulgently; "Tis a true rough schoolboy.' At about 15 years of age, the young ruffians were sent to Oxford or Cambridge, to study history, law, mathematics, philosophy, 'et même la théologie', but despite 'le mérite tres réel des instituteurs, à peine dix sur cent de ces écoliers y apprennent quelque chose, tant la liberté des étudiants est grande'.

At 18, it was accepted that young gentlemen should make the Grand Tour. They were placed in the care of a mentor, and departed convinced of the superiority of all things English. They were strongly surprised therefore, to find themselves regarded on arrival in France as savages, who knew not how to greet, nor how to enter or leave a room. Through boredom they frequently fell into the most crapulous debauchery. Tiring of this and ashamed of their début, they began to attend to learning French, reading, though often in bizarrely specialized subjects, and even improving their manners, sometimes to the point of fatuity. 'Quand une fois ils prennent ce penchant, ils surpassent les modèles mêmes des autres nations, les plus décriées dans la leur; car en cela encore la fierté anglaise prétend au mérite de la primauté.' Stanisław picks out here an important division

---

[82] Nieć, *Młodość ostatniego elekta*, 101. Lawson, *Grenville*, 1–77.
[83] *Mémoires*, vol. 1, 120–4. To assess the pertinency of Stanisław's comments, cf. Cannon, *Aristocratic Century*, 34–59, and Black, *The British Abroad*.

in the ranks of high society, between those who had exaggerated French manners, such as Chesterfield, and those to whom all things French were deeply suspect.[84] After a year which had taken them to Italy or Vienna, their assurance and charm were striking, and their knowledge greatly augmented. They returned from their tours 'confirmés dans la commode habitude d'être non pas comme tout le monde, mais chacun à son guise'.

These young men then entered the political arena, flushed with the spirit of liberty. They frequently engaged in opposition to the Court, and so won themselves a popular reputation as 'patriots' which was very flattering for their self-esteem, but which was only the prelude to acceptance of a place or pension from the Court. Stanisław summarizes the political morality produced by this education:

La république est une belle chose, mais j'entends néanmoins qu'avant tout mon individu y soit placé de la manière dont il me convient; mon originalité dont je ne prétends pas me départir m'a donné des goûts bizarres et couteux; il me faut des moyens d'y subvenir, embrassons ceux qui se présentent, la faveur populaire me rendra considérable et nécéssaire à la cour; après que j'en aurai bien médit à tort et à travers, elle finira par m'acheter, et je me moquerai alors de l'idôle populaire que j'aurai paru avoir d'abord encensée; car je ne suis pas assez simple, j'ai trop appris à penser d'après moi-même; j'ai trop secoué des préjugés, pour me croire ridiculement asservi aux lieux communs appelés devoirs dans les vieux livres: *Primo mihi*, voilà notre dévise.[85]

This was written in 1775, at a moment when, on the eve of the American war, Stanisław August was convinced that England had already passed its peak of greatness. He sought the roots of that decline in a decadent political morality;[86] he asks those who had been in England twenty years later than himself if they had not heard the same maxims openly expressed. Nevertheless, when due allowance has been made, the following is clear: that Stanisław arrived in England fully polished by Paris, that he found the ill-mannered behaviour of English youth shocking, and that he intently studied English politics and recent political history, and conversed with those engaged in it. It would seem likely that in 1754 he made the connection between upbringing and political behaviour, and that in 1775 he added the notion of decline, in order to weld his thoughts into a coherent exposé of English political culture.

---

[84] For illustration of the contrast between Gallophilia and Gallophobia see *The English Satirical Print*, vol. 3, 36–7, 180–1, 204–5.

[85] *Mémoires*, vol. 1, 124.   [86] See below, pp. 250–1.

In June, Stanisław received orders from his father to return home. He wished to delay his journey so as to travel in the company of Joseph Yorke, but after reiterated instructions from his father, Stanisław could put off his departure no longer. Lady Petersham invited him to a farewell *soirée*.[87] Having to return alone, Stanisław told Charles Yorke on 11 July, 'augmenterait du double la peine que j'ai de m'arracher d'ici'.[88] Very soon afterwards, he reluctantly left for Harwich. When he reached home, he was received tenderly and graciously by his parents, but they soon began to criticize his lack of care in his domestic affairs. Stanisław August writes that the next three months were some of 'les plus tristes de ma vie'. He regretted that his parents had not allowed him enough time in France and England, where 'je n'avais pas vu le quart des choses, que j'aurais désiré d'y voir et y étudier.' A friend told him after receiving an account of his discontents: 'Vous apellez cela Spleen, parce que Vous avez eté en Angleterre, mais moi qui ne connoit point ce Pays, j'hazarde de le nommer Ennui.'[89] Moreover, he had returned believing that he would be elected as an envoy to the forthcoming Seym, and had been looking forward to distinguishing himself. Instead of taking up his uncles' cause in the Ostróg affair as he wished, Stanisław was forbidden by his father to be a candidate, so as not to antagonize either his uncles or his elderly brother-in-law, Hetman Branicki, and the Court. Stanisław envied the orators of the Czartoryski party; 'on se figure aisément, combien il était tentant pour un jeune homme, qui revenait d'Angleterre, de pouvoir figurer dans un rôle qui paraissait non seulement courageux, mais juste.'[90] In his first letter to Charles Yorke, Stanisław wrote sadly that 'j'ai été obligé de réformer les idées et les esperances que vous m'avez vu en Angleterre.'[91]

Historians have stressed the significance of this visit for Stanisław August's future political aims and cultural activity. The king's opponents were inclined to agree. In a 'dialogue of the dead' between Augustus II, Augustus III, and Stanisław Leszczyński, printed during the Confederacy of Bar, 'Augustus III' says:

when he returned from England, he boasted in front of women of little worth, who today are the most famous in Warsaw and take a lead in godlessness, that he would not die, until he had seen England made from Poland.[92]

[87] Zb. Pop. 178, f. 312.   [88] London, 11 July 1754, BL Add. 35635, f. 271.
[89] Aug. Sułkowski to Stan., Vienna, 5 Feb. 1755, BCzart. 712, f. 35.
[90] *Mémoires*, vol. 1, 131–3.   [91] 7 Jan. 1755, BL Add. 35634, f. 109.
[92] Quoted by Z. Sinko, *Oświeceni na polach elizejskich: Rozmowy zmarłych: Recepcja-twórczość oryginalna* (Wrocław, 1976), 176–7.

This was a little wide of the mark. Stanisław August writes of 'la disposition sincère où j'étais à révérer et à aimer les Anglais et presque tous leur goûts et leur manière d'être, disposition qui ne m'empêchait pas de remarquer cependant bien des choses en leur façon de voir et de sentir qui ne se rencontraient pas avec la mienne'.[93]

The word *sentir* is important. In England, Stanisław had encountered a world which, within certain bounds, had begun to exult sensibility and nature over formality and symmetry. At the same time, it was a world in which the rough native singularities had not yet been smoothed by French social conventions. Some of the uncontrolled nature Stanisław took in, some he did not. He admired the freedom of English drama, he enjoyed his country walks and Stonehenge, he was fascinated by English peculiarities such as the sailors and cock fights. Yet he thought the education of the English too often produced not healthy individualism, but egoism and political corruption. He had mixed feelings about the landscape garden. English ladies were insufficiently polished. The balance, however, remains overwhelmingly positive. Although Stanisław did not systematically analyse the system of government, it is quite clear, despite Walpole's corruption, that he approved of it and studied it intently. Above all, Stanisław had met Charles Yorke, who made a profound impact upon him. The two shared what may be called an enlightened and cosmopolitan patriotism. They exchanged their hopes and ideals. They spoke the language of 'le bien général du Pays', 'véritablement bons citoyens et bons humains', and 'the general cause of liberty'.[94] A year and a half after his departure, Stanisław wrote to Charles:

Vous m'avez assez bien connu pour scavoir que le redressement de l'état Politique de ma Patrie, et le développement du Génie de ma Nation sont les principaux buts de mon ambition. Ceci vous dit combien je désire de revoir une fois l'Angleterre.[95]

It was as his father would have wished. Stanisław could best serve his country by absorbing the best of what England had to offer, and passing it on to his compatriots.[96] Charles Yorke wrote to Warburton soon after Stanisław's departure:

---

[93] *Mémoires*, vol. 1, 120.

[94] BL Add. 35634, f. 109, BL Add. 35635, f. 462, Zb. Pop. 179, f. 267.

[95] St Petersburg, 17 Dec. 1755, BL Add. 35634, f. 293.

[96] This was the opinion of Joseph Yorke, expressed in a letter of 12 June 1764 to his brother Royston, now the second Earl of Hardwicke, noting the reforms of the Convocation Seym: 'One cannot but approve the Patriot Views of Czartorinsky [*sic*] and Poniatowski, who in their Travels have acquired a freedom of sentiment, have carried it home, & would

I can assure you, both of what I see, both of his judgement and his virtue, there is matter in him capable of catching light and flame. One is sorry at the same time to see a man of his quality and parts, without a theatre to act upon. For Poland is a country, where the unity of the Commonwealth is distracted, or its power annihilated, by the privileges of private men.[97]

Charles Yorke greatly fortified the streak of idealism in Stanisław. The pleasing and polished young gentleman had acquired a purpose, and a motto, 'Patience et Courage', carved upon his buckler.[98] Years later, he wrote to Madame Geoffrin, 'j'ai connu les Anglais et ils me roidirent le caractère.'[99]

willingly communicate its salutary effects to their Country.' BL Add. 35367, ff. 100–1. Adam Kazimierz Czartoryski visited England in 1757–8.

[97] 1 Aug. 1754, BL Add. 35404, ff. 92–3.
[98] Stan. to C. Yorke, Warsaw, 17 Nov. 1760, BL Add. 35635, ff. 461–4.
[99] 8 Jan. 1772, *Correspondance inédite du roi S. A. Poniatowski et de Madame Geoffrin 1764–1777*, ed. C. de Mouy (Paris, 1875), 427.

6

The Contacts of Stanisław and his Circle with the English World after 1754

After returning from England, and throughout his reign, Stanisław maintained his contact with the English world in a number of ways: through correspondence with Englishmen, through friendship with English diplomats and travellers to Poland, through the visits of his family and friends to England, and through his long-serving envoy to the Court of St James, Franciszek Bukaty. Although this book is not intended as a study of Anglo-Polish contacts *per se*, we should not ignore this human dimension. Friendships led to correspondence and careers, and helped smooth the way for diplomatic missions. Such interactions suggest a broadly chronological approach, which has the merits of providing a framework and introducing the cast for the following chapters. Scientific and artistic contacts will be discussed in due course.

I

Six months after his departure from England, Stanisław penned his first letter to Charles Yorke,[1] to which Charles replied in August. In his next, started in St Petersburg in December, but not sent until February, Stanisław admitted that the joy of corresponding was diminished by the surveillance of his letters.[2] The visit to England in 1757–8 of Stanisław's cousin, Adam Kazimierz Czartoryski, presented an opportunity to exchange letters.[3] In November 1760 Stanisław wrote for the last time before his election. Their correspondence was infrequent, but laced with emotion and nostalgia. Charles expressed the hope that Count Poniatowski would be nominated envoy to Great Britain, but Stanisław explained that the *Familia*'s conflict with the Court ruled that out. Stanisław berated English foreign policy for its indifference to anything which did not directly concern it, and warned against trusting the King of Prussia. He confided to

---

[1] Warsaw, 7 Jan. 1755, BL Add. 35634, ff. 109–10.
[2] 17 Dec. 1755, BL Add. 35634, ff. 291–4. I have not found Charles's letter of 28 Aug. 1755.
[3] C. Yorke to Stan., 9 May 1758, Zb. Pop. 318, ff. 59–62. I have not found Stanisław's letter.

Charles his deep pessimism about the chances of reform in Poland, writing 'quand je réflechis à l'état de ma Patrie après avoir pensé à l'Angleterre, je tombe de si haut, que je dis presque; *that place, where hope, that comes to all, comes never.*' He steeled himself: 'Patience and Courage has been my motto long since, but it is terribly worn out by time and adversity. I must write it anew upon my buckler.'[4] For Stanisław, such letters were a rare relief from the sordid realities of Polish politics.

Stanisław possessed a soul mate of sorts in his cousin, Adam Kazimierz Czartoryski (1734–1823), who from birth was destined for the throne by his ambitious father, August. During his stay in England, Prince Adam studied the English constitution and English politics thoroughly. Charles Yorke told Stanisław that Czartoryski better understood 'the principles of the English constitution than nine parts in ten' of the House of Commons.[5] Adam Kazimierz became a convinced Anglophile, possessed of a deep knowledge and appreciation of English literature, and even engaging with British scholars in erudite queries about oriental languages. He returned to England in 1769–70 with his wife Izabella. One of his best friends was the British envoy in Vienna, Sir Robert Murray Keith. Czartoryski drew up a detailed plan of study of England's constitution, economy, society, and science for his son Adam Jerzy, prior to the latter's visit to England in 1790–1.[6] Adam Kazimierz's ambition and application did not match his intelligence, and in 1763 he declared that he would flee the country rather than be elected king.[7] For a few years, he was a close associate of Stanisław August, but after the outbreak of the Confederacy of Bar he went abroad, and his relations with the king deteriorated. He became caught up in the intrigues of the magnate opposition, and broke with Stanisław August entirely in the mid-1780s over the ill-starred 'Dogrumowa affair', in which he tried to involve the British government.[8] Their reconciliation in 1791–2 did not run deep.

---

[4] 17 Nov. 1760, BL Add. 35635, ff. 461–4. J. Yorke to C. Yorke, 9 Jan. 1761, BL Add. 35385, f. 160.

[5] 9 May 1758, Zb. Pop. 318, f. 60.

[6] See some letters of Czartoryski to Keith in BL Add. 35526 and 35536, and BL Egerton 3501, and in general, Z. Gołębiowska, 'W pływy angielskie w Puławach na przełomie XVIII i XIX wieku' (unpublished doctoral thesis, Marie Curie-Skłodowska University, Lublin, 1982); eadem, 'Anglia w planach wychowawczych Adama Kazimierza Czartoryskiego w świetle instrukcji dla syna z roku 1789', *Rocznik Lubelski*, 21 (1979); eadem, 'Podróż Izabeli i Adama Jerzego Czartoryskich'.

[7] Wroughton to Grenville, 2 Feb. 1763, Wroughton to Sandwich, 13 Oct. 1763, PRO SP 88/87.

[8] In January 1785 an adventuress, Marie-Thérèse Ogrumov, having failed to persuade the king that Czartoryski and others were plotting against his life, tricked Czartoryski into believing that the king's chamberlain, Franciszek Ryx, and General Jan Komarzewski were plotting to kill him. The case was exposed in court, but Czartoryski left for Vienna in

Both Czartoryski and Poniatowski made friends with Williams's successor at the Court of Augustus III, Lord Stormont. On arrival in Dresden in 1756, Stormont was critical of the Czartoryskis' intransigent opposition, but he was instructed to cultivate them.[9] When he moved to Warsaw with the Court, he received the 'Greatest civilities' and 'lived much' with August Czartoryski and old Stanisław Poniatowski. He soon made friends with Adam Kazimierz Czartoryski,[10] and recommended him to his uncle, Lord Mansfield, the illustrious judge, when Czartoryski set out for England. Stormont had to wait until the summer of 1758 to meet Stanisław. Poniatowski seems to have become even closer than his cousin to Stormont, for it was to Stanisław that the *Familia* entrusted a delicate matter in November 1759. It offered to counteract French activity in Poland in return for an annual subsidy of £20,000. Stormont, realizing the inevitability of a negative answer, did not comment on the proposition in passing it on to London, but assured his superiors of the *Familia*'s integrity and capability.[11] Stanisław asked Charles Yorke to tell Mansfield that 'j'aime Mylord Stormont presqu'autant que mon frere, et que je n'estime peutetre personne davantage que lui.'[12] After the Seym of 1761, Stormont left for the Imperial Diet (*Reichstag*) at Regensburg and then returned to London. From there he wrote to Stanisław that 'I shall never love you a bitt the better whether your Merit is rewarded as it ought to be or not however ardently I desire it'—probably an allusion to Poniatowski's hopes of the crown.[13] He continued to correspond with Stanisław when he moved back to Dresden, and then on to Vienna, whence he sent him information on the international situation in 1763 and 1764.[14] In 1765 Stanisław August wished to marry a Habsburg archduchess, strengthen the Polish Crown, and in doing so bring Russia closer to Austria. Stormont was a supporter of the traditional concept of an Anglo-Russian-Austrian

dudgeon. He denounced the verdict to Keith, and asked for British intervention on behalf of 'Dogrumowa's' accomplice, an English merchant, William Taylor. Keith did so, but the matter went no further. Czartoryski to Keith, Vienna, 10 May 1785, Keith to Camarthen, 10 May 1785, BL Egerton 3501, ff. 84–7. See Zamoyski, *Last King*, 284–6.

[9] Stormont to Holderness, 27 July 1756, PRO SP 88/78. Holderness to Stormont, 26 Nov. 1756, PRO SP 88/79.

[10] Stormont to Holderness, 1 Jan. 1757, 2 Feb. 1757, PRO SP 88/80, 9 June 1757, BL Egerton 3419, ff. 203–4 (recommending Czartoryski in a private character while in England).

[11] Stormont to Holderness, 29 Nov. 1759, PRO SP 88/83.

[12] 17 Nov. 1760, BL Add. 35635, f. 464.

[13] Stormont to Stan., Regensburg, 8 July 1761, Zb. Pop. 178, ff. 320–1. London, 12 Feb. 1762, 4 May 1762, Zb. Pop. 318, ff. 64–7.

[14] Several letters from Stormont from this period are in Zb. Pop. 178, ff. 301–25. I am advised by Dr Hamish Scott that Stanisław's letters seem not to have survived.

bloc, and strongly backed Stanisław August's attempt. He could not, however, endorse Stanisław August's appeal to Austria for help *against* Russia in 1766. Stormont was equally powerless to prevent the First Partition of Poland, despite his efforts to persuade Maria Theresa to resist.[15]

Stanisław's election as King of Poland brought him letters of congratulation from some of his English friends. Stanisław August replied in the warmest terms, and his correspondents sent their thanks for his monarchical condescension. The election of a young and enlightened king aroused extravagant hopes. Lord Lyttelton wrote:

le legislateur des Troglodites aura le Plaisir de voir, que ses idées d'une République imaginaire n'egalent pas le Bonheur d'un peuple soumis à un Roy Philosophe, qui en voyageant a recueilli pour le Bien de sa Patrie tout ce que son esprit penetrant a trouvé de meilleur dans les differens Gouvernemens, et tout ce que la Connoissance la plus exacte de la Nature humaine peut ajouter aux Reflexions les plus profondes sur la Theorie politique.[16]

Charles Yorke poured forth his Masonic ideals:

The civil constitution will receive its proper energy; the nation will feel its natural resources, its weight in foreign countries; and having understood in every age, how to value and preserve its own liberty, it may perhaps be called forth in some future day to support the general cause of liberty, with other wise and well-intentioned powers, against those confederacies which are in the world. Such are the ideas and prospects, which fill my mind in these visionary moments of joy.[17]

Jean Fabre commented: 'Pour lui [Stanisław August], la philosophie devait servir d'abord à reconstruire la Pologne; pour eux, la Pologne, recrue nouvelle, devait se mettre instantément au service de la philosophie.' This was to lead to a lack of understanding of the difficulties in improving the situation of the dissidents. It was all Stanisław August could do to try to dampen such expectations.[18]

Sir Joseph Yorke followed events in Poland in 1764 from The Hague with an eye to Poniatowski's chances, and related them to his brother, the second Earl of Hardwicke. On hearing of Stanisław's election, he

---

[15] See Rostworowski, 'Edukacja ostatniego króla', in *Popioły i korzenie*. Stormont to SA, dated 1765, Zb. Pop. 178, f. 328. Ditto, 7 Mar. 1772, Baden, 11 June 1772, Zb. Pop. 178, ff. 326–7.

[16] Lyttelton to SA, 15 Oct. 1764, 17 Dec. 1764, SA to Lyttelton, undated (Nov. 1764?), Zb. Pop. 177, ff. 149–54. Archibald Gibson (consul in Danzig since the 1730s) to SA, 12 Sept. 1764, 13 Oct. 1764, SA to Gibson, 19 Sept. 1764, Zb. Pop. 176, ff. 142–4. Duchess and Duke of Gordon to SA, 22 Dec. 1764, ff. 166–7.

[17] C. Yorke to SA, 10 Oct. 1764, Zb. Pop. 179, ff. 272–4.

[18] *Stanislas-Auguste Poniatowski*, 266. See below, p. 162.

despatched a letter of congratulation which he described as 'a little bom-
bast, but I hope it will pass in a Country where Sound still has as much
effect as Sense'. Joseph was less sentimental than Charles, although he
undoubtedly wished Stanisław well.[19] When Charles asked the king for
his old buckler, on the grounds that it was now useless, Joseph warned
his brother that Stanisław would need it for some time yet.[20] Stanisław
August replied to Yorke's letter with more sincerity. In a part destined
for Charles he wrote 'Venez m'aider,' as he had heard that Charles was
without employment, and repeated the invitation in his reply to Charles.[21]
Joseph Yorke was surprised, but thought the letter deserved the attention of Charles, 'for whom Stanislaus II has such a Consummate Respect,
that I am persuaded he would make him his Prime Minister on arrival'.
Charles declined the invitation, and Joseph asked the British envoy
Wroughton to explain to the king that Charles had too much private business to travel, although if Poland were as close as Paris, he would certainly pay him a visit.[22]

Stanisław had met Thomas Wroughton in St Petersburg, where he was
secretary to the embassy until he was sent to Poland to replace Stormont
in 1762. Wroughton's friendship with Stanisław did not prevent him from
being, on occasion, extremely critical of him, both before and after his
election. In February 1763, he wrote that Poniatowski was 'disliked on
account of a haughty behaviour,—which has been of infinite Disservice,
and deprived him of that affection, which his Honesty, and Patriotism
had reason to demand'.[23] During the second half of 1764, however, Stanisław won the envoy's enthusiastic admiration.[24] Through Wroughton and
his brother, Lord Edward Montagu, Stanisław August arranged various
purchases and commissions in England.[25] Wroughton also sent some of
the king's letters to Englishmen. The British minister soon disapproved,
however, of the influence of the king's brothers, and the extravagance of
Court entertainments. Stanisław August ignored Wroughton's advice not
to offend Catherine II in 1766.[26] As Britain's own relations with Russia

[19] J. Yorke to Hardwicke, 21 Sept., 25 Sept. 1764, BL Add. 35367, ff. 155–7. J. Yorke
to SA, 21 Sept. 1764, Zb. Pop. 179, ff. 268–9.
[20] J. Yorke to C. Yorke, 23 Oct. 1764, 35385, f. 176.
[21] SA to J. Yorke, 6 Oct. 1764, BL Add. 35433, ff. 74–5, BL Add. 35367, f. 162. SA to
C. Yorke, 28 Nov. 1764, BL Add. 35349, f. 67.
[22] J. Yorke to Hardwicke, 19 Oct. 1764, BL Add. 35367, ff. 173–4. J. Yorke to C. Yorke,
23 Oct. 1764, loc. cit. (n. 20).
[23] Wroughton to Grenville, 2 Feb. 1763, PRO SP 88/87.
[24] See PRO SP 88/89 and below, pp. 161–2.   [25] See below, p. 221.
[26] Wroughton to Conway, 25 Oct. 1766, PRO SP 88/92. N. W. Wraxall, *Memoirs of the
Courts of Berlin, Dresden, Warsaw and Vienna in the Years 1777, 1778 and 1779* (2 vols.;
London, 1806), vol. 2, 55.

deteriorated, Wroughton drew closer again to the Czartoryskis during the Confederacy of Bar. After the Partition, Wroughton did not believe the Commonwealth could subsist much longer. At the end of the Seym of 1773–5, he was 'sorry to say . . . that His Majesty's Conduct, during this Diet particularly, has been such as to render him the object of General Detestment'. Wroughton's opinion was accepted in London: 'The Account you give of the low Estimation into which His Polish Majesty is fallen in the Republick I fear is but too true, & too much merited,' wrote Lord Suffolk.[27] Confidential criticism did not impede friendship. It was when Wroughton refused to retract some intemperate language that Stanisław August finally complained and sought his transfer. He regretted too late, wrote Stanisław August in his *Mémoires*. Wroughton related his final audience before departing for Sweden in 1778:

I have lived with him for many years in the strictest friendship & Intimacy as a private Gentleman before His coming to the Throne, & since His Elevation, His regard and Confidence in me has been *almost uninterrupted*; Our Separation was . . . one of the most extraordinary that ever passed between a Crowned Head, & a Foreign Minister.[28]

On his arrival in Stockholm, Wroughton wrote Stanisław August some letters about Swedish affairs.[29]

Wroughton presented a number of English travellers to Stanisław August during his long tenure of the Warsaw mission. The first was Colonel Charles Lee, who brought a letter of recommendation from Charles

[27] Wroughton to Suffolk, 15 Apr., 25 Oct. 1775, Suffolk to Wroughton, 14 Nov. 1775, PRO SP 88/110.

[28] Stanisław August's version in his *Mémoires*, vol. 2, 547, that early in 1778 Wroughton was angry at the king's inability to grant a small grace for an acquaintance, is supported by Suffolk's informing Wroughton of his transfer on 11 Mar. 1778, and by Wroughton's regretful despatches of 1 Apr., 20 May, 25 July and 12 Aug. 1778 (quotation), all in PRO SP 88/114. However, in 1775 Wroughton had taken up the case of the English merchant Taylor (the same as in n. 8 above) against his Warsaw partner, and wrote a letter, describing the Poles as 'the most vicious and the most depraved Nation on earth', which Taylor showed freely in England, and which provoked Polish diplomatic intervention. In September 1776, on the death of the British envoy to Sweden, John Lind asked for Wroughton to be sent there. Department of Foreign Affairs to Bukaty, 27 July, 18 Sept., 19 Oct., 15 Nov., 13 Dec., 28 Dec. 1775, Bukaty to dept., 13 June, 25 Aug., 17 Nov. 1775, 16 Jan. 1776, 27 Sept., 25 Oct. 1776, AKP 78, ff. 17–21, 58, 65, 79, 95, 140, 144. Suffolk to Wroughton, 9 June, 30 Aug. 1775, Wroughton to Suffolk, 1 July, 15 July, 20 Dec. 1775, PRO SP 88/110. Libiszowska, *Misja polska*, 48, 70–1, sees this as the cause of Wroughton's transfer. But on 21 Oct. 1776, the department informed Bukaty that the king wished to *prevent* Wroughton's transfer to Stockholm. AKP 78, f. 27. Either the decision took 18 months, and Stanisław August's account is misleading, or (more probably) Wroughton tried the king's patience not once but twice.

[29] Wroughton to SA, 25 Sept., 6 Oct., 3 Nov., 17 Nov. 1778, SA to Wroughton, 21 Oct., 10 Dec. 1778, Zb. Pop. 179, ff. 211–27.

Yorke.[30] The king was unable to provide for Lee in the army, but made him his aide-de-camp at Court. Lee was enchanted with the king. At length, Stanisław August sent Lee on a trip to Constantinople. Lee returned to England in December 1766, but Stanisław August's recommendation could not obtain for him a resumption of his career in the British army. As an unofficial agent of the King of Poland, Lee also failed to achieve anything, and by the spring of 1769 he was back in Poland. He fought for Russia against the Turks, before returning once more to England and emigrating to America, where he betrayed the revolutionary cause. In his politics, Lee was a radical Whig, a violent foe of crowned heads in general, and George III in particular. It was to Lee that Stanisław August expressed some arresting views on British affairs.[31]

John Lind was chaplain to the British embassy in Constantinople when Charles Lee suggested that he enter the Polish service. In 1767, Stanisław August made Lind director of his cadet school and governor to his nephew, Prince Stanisław. Lind acquired Polish nobility and became a member of a Warsaw Masonic lodge. In 1771, he accompanied Prince Stanisław to England.[32] James Harris arrived in Poland on his Grand Tour in October 1767, also recommended by the Yorkes. The king made the young Englishman a confidant of his distress at the situation of the Commonwealth, and advised him not to pursue grand employments. Harris admired the king's efforts to reform Poland, but privately deplored the influence of the king's brothers and Xawery Branicki over him. When Harris left in March 1768, he carried several letters with him. In the most remarkable, written to Sir Joseph Yorke, Stanisław August wondered if the misfortunes of his nation might not in the long term serve to reform it. Such was his struggle to find in destiny a glimmer of light amid the political gloom, that 'je ne scai si j'écris une Lettre ou un testament.'[33]

At the same time as these Englishmen visited Poland, more Poles began to travel to England. Stanisław August sent Barnaba Zawisza to the United Provinces as his resident. There he was befriended by Sir Joseph

[30] C. Yorke to SA, 3 Dec. 1764, Zb. Pop. 179, ff. 276–7. J. Yorke to Hardwicke, 18 Dec. 1764, BL Add. 35367, f. 212.

[31] *The Lee Papers, Collections of the New York Historical Society*, 1871–4 (4 vols., 1872–5). Libiszowska, 'Lee, Karol', *PSB*, 16 (1970), 638–9.

[32] Wroughton to Lee, Warsaw, 29 Apr. 1767, *Lee Papers*, vol. 1, 54. Libiszowska, 'Lind, John', *PSB*, 17 (1972), 349–50.

[33] *Diaries and Correspondence of James Harris, First Earl of Malmesbury* (vol. 1; London, 1844), 10–30. C. Yorke to SA, 4 May 1767, J. Yorke to SA, 26 May 1767, Zb. Pop. 179, ff. 283–6. SA to J. Yorke, 20 Mar. 1768, BL Add. 35433, ff. 93–4, SA to C. Yorke, 20 Mar. 1768, BL Add. 35349, f. 64.

Yorke. During his time in The Hague, Zawisza visited England, and compiled his 'Observations générales sur l'Angleterre', which extolled England's legal system, public spirit, and advanced agriculture. It is probable that Zawisza sent the king his comments.[34] Michał Jerzy Mniszech, on the other hand, was not from the royal circle. It was his relative, the Saxon minister Moritz Brühl, who introduced him to London society in 1766. Mniszech wrote a detailed 400-page account of his travels, systematically describing not only the major tourist attractions of London and the country seats of the aristocracy, but also hospitals, poorhouses, scientific experiments, inventions, the mint, and the political situation. Mniszech later became Grand Marshal of the Crown, and married the king's niece Urszula. He drew on his experiences in England in his future political and educational activity.[35] The king's sister Ludwika came to England in 1767, when she saw the Duke and Duchess of Newcastle, and visited Oxford.[36]

In June 1768, the Castellan of Smolensk, Tadeusz Burzyński, informed Stanisław August of his wish to visit England. The king was delighted, advised him to learn English, and recommended him to the Yorkes, Montagu, and Mansfield. Burzyński made an excellent impression, and applied himself to the study of English institutions and science.[37] He was followed to England in 1769 by the scribe (*pisarz*) of Lithuania, Joachim Chreptowicz, and Michał Przeździecki, whom Stanisław August similarly recommended to the Yorkes and Mansfield. They were travelling, he wrote, with the same laudable aims as Burzyński. Chreptowicz became one of the king's most trusted lieutenants in politics and education.[38]

II

Until this point, Stanisław August had no resident diplomat in England, but relied on his English friends and agents like Lee. Given Poland's critical international situation in 1769, and wishing to engage England in a

[34] Libiszowska, *Życie polskie*, 52–3. J. Yorke to SA, 26 May 1767, 17 July 1767, Zb. Pop. 179, ff. 285–7.

[35] Libiszowska, *Życie polskie*, 11–35, 47–52. A. Rosner, 'Mniszech, Michał Jerzy', *PSB*, 21 (1972), 480–2.

[36] L. Poniatowska (Zamoyska) to Newcastle, 9 Aug. 1767, BL. 32984, f. 231. Bulloch, 'Polish alliances with the Gordons', 49–51.

[37] The correspondence between the king and Burzyński is in Zb. Pop. 216. SA to C. and J. Yorke, 6 July 1768, BL Add. 35349, f. 66. J. Yorke to C. Yorke, 15 Sept. 1769, BL Add. 35385, f. 222. C. Yorke to SA, 16 Mar. 1769, Zb. Pop. 179, ff. 290–1. Libiszowska, *Życie polskie*, 53–6.

[38] SA to Mansfield, J. Yorke, and C. Yorke, 1769, Zb. Pop. 216, ff. 80–1. Libiszowska, *Życie polskie*, 191–2. J. Iwaszkiewicz, 'Chreptowicz, Joachim', *PSB*, 3 (1937), 441–3.

general pacification of the Commonwealth, the senate council decided to send an extraordinary envoy to England, leaving the choice to the king. There could be only one candidate. Burzyński arrived at the end of 1769, again recommended to the Yorkes, Mansfield, and Shelburne. However, Burzyński's health declined and in December 1771 he left for the southern sunshine. He died in Florence in 1773. Although Burzyński was unable to convince the British government to intervene on behalf of Poland, his activity clearly worried the Russian ambassador Chernyshev, who threatened sequestrations and worse if he refused to depart. Nevertheless, his extraordinary mission grew into a permanent one. As Zofia Libiszowska has shown, the Polish mission became a base for Poles in England and a link in cultural contacts.[39] Stanisław August thus became less dependent on his English friends. The change was hastened by the tragic death of Charles Yorke in 1770. Yorke had accepted the Lord Chancellorship, which he had long coveted, from George III, but his brother Hardwicke threatened to repudiate him for his betrayal of his party, the Rockingham Whigs. Charles died in an agony of indecision. The family's denial that Charles had committed suicide did not convince Stanisław August. 'Cet événement funeste . . . m'affecte bien douloureusement,' wrote the king five years later. 'Il est affreux de penser qu'un des meilleurs humains possibles soit devenu par ses propres mains la victime sanglante d'un excès de sentiment.'[40] The king broke off contact with the Yorkes, and it was twenty years before he could bring himself to request his brother Michał to pass on greetings to the elderly Joseph, by then Lord Dover.[41]

After Burzyński's departure, the unofficial direction of the Polish mission was entrusted to John Lind, who had valuable contacts with Lord North. Lind served Poland well as a publicist, demonstrating the illegality of the Partition in a number of widely read books and pamphlets. After Lind died in 1781, Stanisław August continued to send his widow a pension (although not always on time) until the fall of the Commonwealth.[42]

---

[39] A résumé of Burzyński's diplomatic correspondence is in Zb. Pop. 93, and an index in BCzart. 847. Mansfield to SA, 14 Mar. 1769, Zb. Pop. 177, f. 164. SA to Mansfield, 18 Oct. 1769, Zb. Pop. 216, f. 91. SA to C. Yorke, 19 Oct. 1769, BL Add. 35639, f. 140. J. Yorke to SA, 19 Dec. 1769, Zb. Pop. 216, f. 95. Libiszowska, *Życie polskie*, 56–70. Eadem, *Misja polska*, ch. 1.

[40] *Mémoires*, vol. 1, 109. Cf. *DNB*, 21 (1890), 1252–3.

[41] SA to M. Poniatowski, 22 Dec. 1790, Zb. Gh. 801b, f. 112.

[42] Walpole to Mann, 23 Feb. 1774, Mann to Walpole, 10 Aug. 1773, 29 Mar. 1774, *Horace Walpole's Correspondence*, vol. 23, 502–3, 556, 564–5. D. B. Horn, *British Public Opinion and the First Partition of Poland* (Edinburgh, 1945), 20–32. Libiszowska, *Misja polska*, ch. 2. For the muted official reaction, see H. M. Scott, *British Foreign Policy in the Age of the American Revolution* (Oxford, 1990), 177–83. Mary Lind to SA, 25 Jan. 1781, SA

Nevertheless, an Englishman could not represent Poland in England, and so the nominal successor as chargé d'affaires became Burzyński's secretary, Franciszek Bukaty, a minor Lithuanian nobleman.[43] At first Bukaty seems to have been overshadowed by Lind, and was treated as a nobody in both London and Warsaw. From the start he was handicapped by the inadequacy of his pay. He lacked the resources and the social cachet necessary to maintain Burzyński's impact in high political circles. As he gained in experience, however, he progressed slowly up the diplomatic ladder, helped by the good impression he made on Stanisław August in Warsaw in 1779 and 1784. Among Bukaty's tasks was the compiling of detailed reports on various English institutions. He was also given innumerable commissions by the king and others to acquire books, medals, scientific equipment, and suchlike. A true *honnête homme*, Bukaty helped Poles in London as best he could, even rescuing them from debtors' prison on occasion. During his absences from England his duties were taken over by his cousin, Tadeusz Bukaty, as chargé d'affaires. As the years went by, Bukaty became 'completely transformed from a Lithuanian into an Englishman; he adopted their habits and lifestyle.'[44] He acquired a taste for roast beef and porter, and even joined the élite Whig Beefsteak Club, drinking the toast to 'Beef and Liberty' with gusto.[45]

In a modest way, Bukaty and Stanisław August tried to ameliorate the condition of British Catholics. Bukaty tried to build a chapel in his house, but the enterprise failed because of the lack of enthusiasm of the Catholic priesthood in London for any subscription.[46] Bukaty was absent during the Gordon riots, but he referred to them subsequently with horror, and reported the eccentric activities of Lord George Gordon (one of the two 'Cupids' in 1754), which culminated in his conversion to Judaism and his admonishment of his royal cousin for failing to improve the condition of Polish Jews in the Constitution of 3 May.[47] The Polish Court and

to M. Lind, 21 Feb. 1781, Zb. Pop. 181, ff. 102–3. M. Lind to SA, 28 July 1788, SA to M. Lind, 3 Sept. 1788, Zb. Pop. 184, ff. 95–7. SA to Bukaty, 5 Nov. 1791, PAN 1658, f. 85. Libiszowska, *Życie polskie*, 71–3, 140.

[43] See Libiszowska, *Misja polska*, *passim*, and *Życie polskie*, *passim*. Details of Bukaty's correspondence are given in the bibliography.

[44] Niemcewicz, *Pamiętniki*, vol. 1, 231.

[45] Bukaty to O. Prozor, 15 May 1789, 29 Sept. 1792, BJag. 5992, ff. 32–3, 92–3. Komarzewski to SA, 4 Dec. 1789, BJag. 3510 (not paginated).

[46] Bukaty to dept., 22 Feb., 12 Mar. 1782, Muz. Nar. 76, ff. 61, 77, AKP 80, ff. 226–7. Libiszowska, *Misja polska*, 73.

[47] Lind to SA, 16 June 1780, Zb. Pop. 216, f. 245. Bukaty to dept., 30 Jan., 6 Feb., 6 Mar., 7 Sept. 1781, 19 Nov. 1784, AKP 79, ff. 73–4, 76, 79–80, 114–15, AKP 81, f. 109. T. Bukaty to dept., 10 Nov. 1786, 14 Dec. 1787, 1 Feb. 1788, AKP 82, ff. 125, 229–30,

minister also intervened in defence of the 'natural rights' of Colonel Fabian Gordon, one of Stanisław August's Polish cousins, who in 1776 inherited the estate of Coldwell in Scotland, but was prevented from reclaiming possession of it from his Scottish relatives by the anti-Catholic oath required in court. Lind and Bukaty consulted Stormont, known for his tolerant attitude towards Catholics. A compromise was eventually reached in 1783.[48] Stanisław August was pestered by his Polish Gordon relatives for assistance after the Third Partition.[49] These contacts, however unsatisfactory, reminded Stanisław August of his ancestry. He asked his Italian secretary, Gaetano Ghigotti, to tell Lord Morton 'combien j'aime les Anglois, et que je sent tres bien, que j'ai du sang Ecossais, dans les veines, par ma bisayeule'. Despite this, the king seems to have had little awareness of Scottish nationhood, unlike his cousin Izabella Czartoryska.[50]

Among the increasingly numerous Polish visitors to England in the 1770s and 1780s were such wealthy aristocrats as Adam Poniński, August Sułkowski, Stanisław Kostka Potocki, Seweryn and Jan Potocki with their wives, Izabella Lubomirska, Michał Kazimierz Ogiński, Michał Radziwiłł, and of course, the Czartoryskis. Many of them were hostile to the king, and the Bukatys were sometimes recommended to keep a close eye on them.[51] Stanisław August encouraged his compatriots to cross the Channel and improve themselves. He informed Bukaty in 1788 that Chreptowicz's son 'travels to England at his father's command to acquire polish and the knowledge proper to his birth and estate'.[52] Stanisław August's niece, Maria Teresa Tyszkiewicz, evidently shone in society. 'Il n'y avoit une voix sur son compte, sa Grace, Son Esprit, ses manieres, l'Interet qu'elle inspire des le premier abord, ont frappés tout le monde,' enthused Stormont.[53] When Stanisław August learned of his brother

---

239–40. G. Gordon to SA, Newgate Prison, 6 Aug. 1792, enclosing the *Public Advertiser*, containing a report on the meeting to organize a subscription in aid of Poland (see below, p. 142). Gordon sent a letter of opposition. Zb. Pop. 221, ff. 314–15. Another would-be Jewish reformer was W. Johnson. Johnson to SA, Warsaw, 27 July 1781, Zb. Pop. 165, f. 110.

[48] An extensive correspondence flowed between Warsaw and London on the subject between 1780 and 1784. AKP 79, 80, *passim*. Zb. Pop. 216, *passim*. F. Gordon to SA, 30 Apr. 1783, AKP 80, f. 71.

[49] Kor. SA 3a, ff. 422–51.

[50] SA to Ghigotti, 17 Apr. 1782, Zb. Gh. 514, f. 138. See Gołębiowska, 'Podróż Izabelli i Adama Jerzego Czartoryskich', 139–41.

[51] See Libiszowska, *Życie polskie*, ch. 7. More information may be found in *Horace Walpole's Correspondence*, vol. 12, 224–33, vol. 32, 96, 110, vol. 33, 279–80, 565–6, vol. 39, 447, vol. 42, 196–7.

[52] 28 Apr. 1788, Muz. Nar. 79, quoted after Libiszowska, *Życie polskie*, 223.

[53] Stormont to SA, 1 Nov. 1785, Zb. Pop. 182, ff. 532–3.

Michał's plan to visit England, he wrote that 'il s'est rejoici pour Vous, mais il s'est affligé pour Lui meme de ne pouvoir vous servir de compagnon de voyage et d'Interpreter.' Stanisław August corresponded frequently with the primate during the latter's stay in 1790–1, which vivified the king's contacts with English artistic and scientific circles.[54]

The number of English travellers to Poland also rose after the Partition, although Poland continued to be a rare destination.[55] Stanisław August received them enthusiastically, and took the opportunity to converse with them as much as possible, paying all manner of compliments to the English nation, and he often invited the visitors to private dinners. The intrepid merchant Joseph Marshall claimed to be one of the first, in 1770, but if he did visit Warsaw, he was not singled out for attention by the hard-pressed monarch.[56] Sir Nathaniel Wraxall arrived in June 1778. Wraxall acknowledged that Stanisław August's manners were 'captivating' but was extremely critical of him as a statesman, and amplified all the criticisms of his friend Wroughton.[57] Almost immediately afterwards, Lord Herbert followed with his mentor, William Coxe. Coxe was a scrupulous historian, and went to much trouble to collect information on Poland's history and government. His *Travels*, published in 1784, were for the English reader the most detailed and accurate account available of Stanislavian Poland. Coxe's impressions of Poland did not differ from his predecessors' in their gloominess, and he routinely lacerated backwardness, oppression, and fanaticism, but unlike Wraxall, he described and commended Stanisław August's efforts to renew Poland. Stanisław August naturally followed George III on the list of subscribers, and received a third volume from Coxe in 1791. To Coxe, Stanisław August exclaimed: 'Happy Englishman, your house is raised, and mine is yet to build.'[58]

---

[54] SA to M. Poniatowski, 23 Oct. 1790, Zb. Gh. 801b, f. 90. It is unfortunate that the primate's letters have not survived. The king's letters throw no light on the story recounted by Walpole to M. Berry on 10 Apr. 1791, that the primate was briefly arrested for debt. *Horace Walpole's Correspondence*, vol. 11, 242–3.

[55] Black, *The British Abroad*, 75–6.

[56] Marshall, *Travels through Holland, Flanders, Germany, Denmark, Sweden, Lapland, Russia, the Ukraine and Poland in the Years 1768, 1769 and 1770* (3 vols.; London, 1772), vol. 3, 137–271. John Parkinson, who travelled to Russia in the 1790s, alleged that Marshall had never even crossed the English Channel. Wolff, *Inventing Eastern Europe*, 81.

[57] Wraxall, *Memoirs* (n. 26), vol. 1, 395–418, vol. 2, 1–152.

[58] Coxe, *Travels into Poland, Russia, Sweden and Denmark* (2 vols.; London, 1784), vol. 1, 1–236, esp. 171–84. 'Papers relating to Poland', BL Add. 9261. *Catalogue of the Valuable Library of the late Rev. Archdeacon Coxe* (Salisbury, 1828). Coxe to SA, 3 Feb. 1791, SA to Coxe, 25 May 1791, Zb. Pop. 186, ff. 70–1. See also Wolff, *Inventing Eastern Europe*, 25–31.

The Earl of Morton came to Poland in August 1782,[59] while Lady Elizabeth Craven spent part of January 1786 in Warsaw on her way to Constantinople. Apart from the king, she was impressed by the Polish ladies, who 'seem to have much taste—magnificence—spirit and gaiety —they are polite and lively—excessively accomplished—partial to the English.' Stanisław August asked Lady Craven after Horace Walpole, and when she showed him a letter of Walpole's, the king borrowed it in order to translate it into French for his sister, Izabella Branicka. Walpole was more embarrassed than flattered when the 'strolling Roxana' informed him of the episode.[60] Soon afterwards, through Wincenty Potocki, Stanisław August asked Walpole for the fourth volume of his *Anecdotes of Painting*. Walpole was distressed, 'as they were out of print—and I had only my own set. I was reduced to buy a second hand set'—at three times the original price.[61] The Marquess of Lansdowne, the former Shelburne, recommended his son Lord Wycombe to Stanisław August in 1786. Wycombe also visited the Czartoryskis at Puławy. Stanisław August signified his approval of Wycombe and his mentor, Major Greene, in a reply to Lansdowne, and also in thanking Wycombe for a book on Mogul India.[62] The economist Sir John Sinclair, MP, passed through Warsaw in October 1786, and later sent Stanisław August some of his works.[63] Sir Ralph and Lady Payne were at Warsaw no later than 1787,[64] followed early in 1788 by the Marquess of Titchfield and the Earl of Darnley, recommended to Stanisław August by Sir James Harris as his 'political children'.[65]

Freemasonry offered additional opportunities for contact, although too much can be read into its 'Englishness'. Among the Warsaw Masons were resident Englishmen such as Wroughton and Lind, and many of

[59] Black, *The British Abroad*, 296. A. K. Czartoryski to R. M. Keith, 11 Oct. 1782, BL Add. 35526, f. 241.

[60] *A Journey through the Crimea to Constantinople in a Series of Letters From . . . Elizabeth Lady Craven to . . . The Margrave of Brandebourg, Anspach and Bareith* (London, 1789), 115–22. Walpole to Mann, 16 Mar. 1786, *Horace Walpole's Correspondence*, vol. 25, 632–3.

[61] M. Buller to Walpole, 6 Apr. 1786, Walpole to T. Walpole, 8 Apr. 1786, 26 June 1792, Walpole to SA, 7 Apr. 1786, 20 July 1786, SA to Walpole, 6/7 June 1786, *Horace Walpole's Correspondence*, vol. 36, 238, 280–1, vol. 42, 161–4, Zb. Pop. 183, ff. 631–3. See below, p. 213.

[62] Lansdowne to SA, 17 Apr. 1786, 4 July 1786, SA to Lansdowne, 7 June 1786 (printed below, p. 174), Zb. Pop. 182, ff. 338–42. Wycombe to SA, 30 Jan. 1787, SA to Wycombe, 21/23 Feb. 1787, Zb. Pop. 183, ff. 644–7. A. K. Czartoryski to R. M. Keith, 3 Apr. 1786, BL Add. 35536, f. 195. Gołębiowska, 'Anglia w planach wychowawczych . . .', 95.

[63] Sinclair to SA, 11 Dec. 1787, 18 May 1792, SA to Sinclair, 19 Jan. 1788, Zb. Pop. 222, ff. 227–32. Black, *The British Abroad*, 120.

[64] R. Payne to SA, Lady Payne to SA, The Hague, 17 Sept. 1787, Zb. Pop. 183, ff. 549–50.

[65] Harris to SA, 31 Dec. 1787, SA to Harris, 29 Mar. 1788.

Stanisław August's closest aides, such as Maurice Glayre, held high rank. However, the king declined closer involvement in the squabbles that affected Polish Freemasonry in the 1760s and 1770s. In 1777, as secretly as possible, he finally joined the Warsaw lodge of the somewhat occultist Germanophone Masonic network known as the 'Strict Observance'. The last traces of Stanisław August's Masonic activity date from 1780. The following year, the rival Masonic lodge, which had a more rationalist aspect, and which gathered most of the king's supporters, reconstituted itself as the 'Grand Orient'. It was legalized by the London 'Grand Orient', and its statutes were based upon Anderson's *Constitutions*. In 1784, the Polish 'Grand Orient' proclaimed its autonomy from London, while retaining its ideological link. Its subordinate lodges included one comprising the most fashionable aristocratic ladies. The 'Strict Observance' obedience swiftly collapsed. Did these events contribute in some way to the spread of Anglophilia and Anglomania among the élite? This surmise is plausible, but it is just as incapable of proof as Fabre's theory that it was Stanisław August who brought order to the Masonic chaos. The political trends in Polish Freemasonry generally reflected those in the élite as a whole; Russophile in the mid-1780s, the lodges were caught up in 'patriotic' enthusiasm during the Four Year Seym. Masonic fraternity proved of no use whatsoever in international politics.[66]

After the Partition, Stanisław August did not entirely give up the attempt to use his friends to influence British policy. Stormont became ambassador to France in 1772, and Stanisław August recommended his agents, Jakub Psarski and Maurice Glayre, to him there. As Secretary of State in 1780–2, Stormont treated Bukaty with courtesy, but his only real concession to Polish interests was to send Lord Dalrymple to succeed Wroughton in Warsaw—in 1782, after a gap of four years![67] Stanisław August now placed more hopes in Harris, who was appointed envoy to Berlin in 1772, and who had offered his services. Harris moved to St Petersburg in 1777 and to The Hague in 1783, and was able to visit Stanisław August with his wife and sister on at least one occasion. Lady Harris became friends with Urszula Mniszech. Harris presented Polish concerns to George III and his ministers, and secured, apart from kind

[66] See Hass, *Wolnomularstwo*, 101–8, 127–36, 168–79, 207–12, and Fabre, *Stanislas-Auguste Poniatowski*, 496–501. The London Grand Orient's legalization of the Polish Grand Orient is in AGAD, Archiwum Masońskie, Box 3, 2/1.

[67] SA to Stormont, 12 Aug. 1774, Stormont to SA, 27 Nov. 1774, 22 June 1777, Zb. Pop. 178, ff. 334–6. SA to Stormont, 13 June 1780, Stormont to SA, 21 Aug. 1780, Zb. Pop. 216, ff. 236–8. SA to Stormont, 18 May 1783, Zb. Pop. 181, f. 349. Bukaty to SA, 22 Sept. 1780, BCzart. 3998, f. 4.

words, an assurance that Stanisław August would never be without an English minister, and that in the choice of a successor to Dalrymple, 'great attention will be paid to find a person agreeable to Yr majesty & qualified for the post he is to fill.' In 1783, Harris was happy enough to brief Stanisław August about Potemkin's speculative and abortive proposal of a further partition to Frederick II back in 1779, but he failed to persuade London to promote a Polish-Russian alliance. Later, Harris even evaded his undertaking to inform Stanisław August about British policy by pleading the confusion of affairs.[68]

Once Danzig had been saved from Frederick II, British policy towards Poland after the First Partition was practically non-existent. Dalrymple's successor Charles Whitworth was told that his mission was basically one of gathering intelligence, if a new partition of Poland or Turkey was likely. Nevertheless, London showed an interest in Stanisław August's meeting with Catherine II at Kaniów in 1787, hoping unrealistically that the King of Poland might soften Catherine's disposition towards England.[69] Stanisław August was on friendly terms with both Dalrymple and Whitworth,[70] but neither could offer Poland any real help. The king hoped that Whitworth would repay his debt of friendship by defending the Constitution of 3 May as ambassador to Russia, but Whitworth seems to have equivocated.[71] He later repaid it, at no political cost, by his faithful attention to the former monarch in 1797–8.[72]

When Great Britain did become seriously interested in closer political and trading relations with Poland during the Four Year Seym, it was as the ally of Prussia. Stanisław August was deeply sceptical about a Polish–Prussian alliance, and was proved right by events. At the beginning of 1791, Pitt's cabinet decided on an armed demonstration against Russia (the Ochakov crisis), but had to retreat in the face of Catherine

---

[68] *DNB*, 25 (1891), 8–9. Harris to SA, Berlin, 17 Mar. 1772, SA to Harris, 29 Mar. 1772, Zb. Pop. 176, ff. 249–51. Harris to SA, St Petersburg, 3 Sept. 1781, Cracow, 7 Oct. 1783, SA to Harris, 15 Oct. 1783, Zb. Pop. 165, ff. 29–32, Harris to SA, 12 Aug. 1784, 27 Apr. 1786, SA to Harris, 26 Nov. 1784, 5 June 1786, Lady Harris to SA, 27 Apr. 1786, Zb. Pop. 182, ff. 249–59. Michalski, 'Fryderyk Wielki i Grzegorz Potemkin w latach kryzysu przymierza prusko-rosyjskiego', in *Między wschodem a zachodem*, 223–4. Idem, 'Sprawa przymierza polsko-rosyjskiego w dobie aneksji Krymu', in Z. Wójcik *et al.* (eds.), *Z dziejów polityki i dyplomacji polskiej: Studia poświęcone pamięci Edwarda hr. Raczyńskiego . . .* (Warsaw, 1994), 81–2.

[69] Camarthen to Whitworth, 1785/6, Apr. 1787, PRO FO 62/2, ff. 23–7, 103–4. On the diplomatic efforts to protect Danzig, see Scott, *British Foreign Policy*, 197–202.

[70] SA to Harris, 5 June 1786, Zb. Pop. 182, ff. 255–6. Dalrymple to SA, Paris, 29 June 1785, SA to Dalrymple, 3 Aug. 1785, Zb. Pop. 206, ff. 154–6.

[71] SA to Deboli, 4 June, 8 June 1791, 28 Mar., 4 Apr. 1792, Zb. Pop. 413, ff. 114, 117, 340, 347.

[72] E. Vigée-Lebrun, *Souvenirs*, ed. C. Herrmann (2 vols.; Paris, 1984), vol. 2, 44–5.

II's determination and English public opinion, which was unwilling to countenance war. From then on, England abandoned Poland to her fate.[73] It was especially unfortunate that the British minister, Daniel Hailes, did not disguise his low opinion of the king. Stanisław August complained to Bukaty that Hailes 'not only displays indifference to me personally' but put himself at the service of the Prussians by mounting a campaign to persuade the Poles to cede Danzig and Thorn. The king even had Bukaty intervene to bring about a change in Hailes's behaviour.[74]

Bukaty intervened with his friend, the under-secretary of state at the Foreign Office, James Bland Burges, but the 'strongest hints' to Hailes did not always suffice.[75] Burges owed his appointment at the Foreign Office to the desire of Bristol and Liverpool merchants to silence his once vocal opposition to slavery. He became a firm Pittite. It was to this campaigner, his old colleague at Cambridge, that Prince Stanisław Poniatowski turned in 1783 to seek advice on how best to abolish personal servitude on his estates. Burges recounted the gradual evolution of English villeins into copyholders, and stressed that to be truly free, the peasants must first be made prosperous and independent. They should be given a good example by foreign settlers and a fair system of justice.[76] As under-secretary, Burges gave his friend Bukaty secret information, and was a great admirer of Stanisław August, whom he reputedly dubbed the 'King very Gentleman'. The king in turn was pleased to consider Burges his personal friend, and Burges figured as 'friend' (*przyjaciel*) in the king's correspondence with Bukaty. Burges also met the primate in 1790–1. Burges supported Pitt's bellicosity during the Ochakov crisis, but thereafter he shared the government's preoccupation with France, and could only apologize privately and in print for the inability of the British government to assist the Poles.[77]

[73] On British policy, see J. Ehrman, *The Younger Pitt*, vol. 2, *The Reluctant Transition* (London, 1983), ch. 1; Libiszowska, *Życie polskie*, ch. 4; eadem, *Misja polska*, ch. 5; eadem, 'Misja Ogińskiego w Londynie', in *Wiek XVIII: Polska i świat*; and J. Black, *British Foreign Policy in an Age of Revolution 1783–1793* (Cambridge, 1993), ch. 6. I am grateful to Prof. Black for a draft copy.

[74] 'Dla mnie osobiście nie tylko indyferentyzm się stawia'. SA to Bukaty, 23 May, 13 June, 18 July, 23 Sept., 14 Nov. 1789, BCzart. 849, ff. 81, 97, 107, 113, 117. SA to Deboli, 25 Apr. 1789, Zb. Pop. 414, f. 201. Hailes to Leeds, 8 May 1791, PRO FO 62/4, ff. 123–7.

[75] Burges to W. Gardiner, 3 Jan. 1792, Bodl., Bland Burges Papers 47, ff. 353–4. Bukaty to SA, 24 May 1791, BCzart. 3998, ff. 130–1.

[76] Burges to Bukaty, 17 May 1783, Bodl., Bland Burges Papers 32, ff. 28–40. Published by S. W. Jackman as 'Angielskie świadectwo pomysłów reformatorskich Stanisława Augusta (*sic*). List J. B. Burgesa do W. (*sic*) Bukatego' in *KwH*, 73 (1966).

[77] Libiszowska, 'Prasa i publicystyka angielska wobec drugiego rozbioru Polski', *Rocznik Historii Czasopiśmiennictwa Polskiego*, 12 (1973), 316–24. T. Mostowski to a friend, 1789?, PAU 8, ff. 172–3. M. Poniatowski to Burges, 5 Nov. 1792, Bodl., Bland Burges Papers 45, ff. 133–4.

Another friend of Poland was James Durno, the British consul in Prussian Memel. Durno came to Warsaw in a semi-official capacity as a prospective consul in 1790, and remained through 1791. He tried to convince London of the benefits of increased trading links with Poland. Unlike Hailes, Durno opposed the cession of Danzig. He enthusiastically praised the Constitution of 3 May, and even asked his superiors in London to publish his account of it in one of the newspapers. Durno's relations with Stanisław August were excellent.[78] Kenelm Digby, a cousin of Harry, spent several weeks in Warsaw in the autumn of 1791. 'He liked us greatly, and we him,' Stanisław August told Bukaty. Digby aspired to succeed Hailes as minister, and corresponded with Burges, but the choice fell upon Burges's friend William Gardiner.[79]

Lewis Littlepage and Filippo Mazzei brought Stanisław August contact with newly independent America. Littlepage had fought in the War of Independence before being taken on a diplomatic mission to Madrid in 1780, aged 18. He later accompanied the Prince of Nassau-Siegen to Vienna, Constantinople, and Poland, where he arrived in 1784. Stanisław August offered the young American service as a translator and secretary. In August 1787, the king sent him to Paris on an unofficial diplomatic mission, but Littlepage also visited England and made contact with high-ranking politicians and John Adams. Littlepage spent the next few years in and out of Poland, unable to decide whether or not to go back to America (Stanisław August wrote three separate letters of recommendation to George Washington), and later trying to secure his back-pay from the Russians before finally returning home in 1801. Littlepage gained the friendship of the king, who created him a *szambelan* (gentleman of the bedchamber), and a knight of the order of St Stanisław, but he acquired a bad reputation for inconstancy and intrigue.[80]

The Tuscan Filippo Mazzei spent much of his early manhood in England. He admired the legal system but deplored political corruption, and was alarmed by the implications of the Wilkes affair. At the instigation of

[78] Libiszowska, 'James Durno i jego misja w Polsce', *PH*, 44 (1973). Durno to Grenville, 11 May 1791, 'Extract of a Letter dated Warsaw 4th May 1791. From a Polish Gentleman to his friend in London', PRO FO 62/4, ff. 132–47. Durno to SA, 7 Sept. 1791, Zb. Pop. 186, f. 252.

[79] 'Wiele się w Nas pokochał y my w nim'. SA to Bukaty, 12 Oct. 1791, PAU 1658, f. 83. Digby to Burges, Warsaw, 4 Oct., 8 Oct. 1791, Bodl., Bland Burges Papers, 45, ff. 83–5.

[80] Libiszowska, 'Littlepage, Lewis', *PSB*, 17 (1972), 486–7. SA to Mazzei, 18 Feb. 1789, *Lettres de Philippe Mazzei et du roi Stanislas-Auguste de Pologne*, ed. J. Michalski *et al.* (vol. 1; Rome, 1982), 178.

Benjamin Franklin, Mazzei emigrated to Virginia in 1773, and there found the vigorous and egalitarian society he had sought in vain in England. Through the influence of his friend and neighbour Thomas Jefferson, Mazzei returned to Europe as the representative of Virginia in 1780. After another brief stay in Virginia, he came back to Paris in 1785 to assist Jefferson and write his *Recherches historiques et politiques sur les États-Unis de l'Amérique*, 'a kind of encyclopedia of the American Revolution', which appeared in four volumes between 1786 and 1788.[81] In May 1788, Maurice Glayre, Stanisław August's trusted Swiss counsellor and temporary chargé d'affaires in Paris, proposed that Mazzei become his successor. The king was suspicious, but in the end agreed. Stanisław August did not share Mazzei's revolutionary enthusiasm, and conducted a kind of ideological debate with him. In time, Mazzei became the recipient of some of Stanisław August's most interesting opinions on France, America, and England.[82]

Joel Barlow met Kościuszko in America and Littlepage in Paris. Barlow gave Littlepage a copy of his epic poem, *The Vision of Columbus*, and a letter to pass on to Stanisław August. The king replied that he was 'delighted, both with the subject and beauty of the poem', that he was himself 'taken up with much the same objects' in Poland, and that he would endeavour to have it translated into Polish. Barlow gratefully answered with a long letter, asking for the translation to be made from the forthcoming second edition, and enclosing a pamphlet, *Advice to the Privileged Orders in the Several States of Europe*. The American confided to the monarch his optimistic republican creed. 'How far I go beyond your Majesty's real Sentiments in my ideas of the advantages of a representative republic, & in my detestations of monarchy, I am unable to say, but certain I am that we agree in one point,—in an ardent wish to promote the happiness of the human race.' Barlow offered his congratulations on the constitution: 'as a System framed for one of the inveterate Aristocracies of Europe, I find in it much to admire. You have acted like Solon, & given your country, if not the best law that you could frame, at least the best that circumstances would admit.' This time the king was either unwilling or too busy to answer.[83]

[81] Venturi, *End of the Old Regime 1776–1789*, vol. 1, 82–143.

[82] Glayre to SA, 26 May–18 Oct. 1788, SA to Glayre, 11 Oct. 1788, Zb. Pop. 221, ff. 97–160, 215. 'Mémoire sur Mazzei', Zb. Pop. 165, ff. 296–7. SA, Mazzei, *Lettres*.

[83] Barlow to SA, Paris, 22 Mar. 1791, London, 20 Feb. 1792, Zb. Pop. 186, f. 68, Zb. Pop. 207, ff. 101–4. SA to Barlow, 25 May 1791, Zb. Pop. 186, f. 71. See Libiszowska, 'Joel Barlow wobec rewolucji francuskiej i polskiej reformy', *Wiek Oświecenia*, 11 (1993).

The Four Year Seym, and in particular the Constitution of 3 May and the Law on Towns of 18 April 1791, revolutionized the image of Poland in English public opinion. Horace Walpole, who had long amused himself by cracking Polish jokes, now became an ardent admirer.[84] Representatives of the mainstream of public opinion, like Walpole and Edmund Burke, praised the Poles for emerging from anarchy and above all for avoiding bloodshed—in contrast to France. Radicals sympathizing with the French Revolution were delighted because Poland appeared to be taking part in a general European revolution against prejudice and aristocratic privilege. Both sides eulogized Stanisław August as a wise and enlightened monarch. Bukaty built up a network of press contacts, and the king rewarded the editors of pro-Polish newspapers with medals, bearing the inscription *Merentibus*, but the attention from the radicals embarrassed Stanisław August, who was sensitive to charges of 'Jacobinism'. Bukaty excused himself from a meeting to organize a subscription in aid of Poland on 2 August 1792, on the advice of Burges that it could damage the Polish cause.[85]

In the spring of 1790, a Scot in Paris, Thomas Christie, asked Mazzei if he might become the literary correspondent of Stanisław August. Not trusting in Mazzei's judgement, Stanisław August asked Bukaty to find out more about him. Bukaty confirmed that Christie was suitable after he had met him in January 1791, and the king gave the go-ahead.[86] Stanisław August duly received a twenty-two-page epistle about recent publications—theological, scientific, economic, literary, and political. Christie dwelt upon the controversies engendered by Burke's *Reflections on the Revolution in France*. Among the replies listed were those of Macaulay Graham, Mary Wollstonecraft, Joseph Priestley, James MacKintosh, and Christie himself, who sent the king his *Letters on the French Revolution*. Paine's *Rights of Man* 'notwithstanding the excessive democracy of its principles', was

---

[84] Cf., for example, Walpole to Lady Ossory, 4 July 1781 with ditto, 4 Sept. 1792, *Horace Walpole's Correspondence*, vol. 33, 279–80, vol. 34, 158–9. See R. J. Butterwick, 'Od kpiarza do wielbiciela: Horace Walpole wobec Polski w dobie rozbiorów', in J. Grobis and Z. Anusik (eds.), *Oświeceni wobec rozbiorów Polski* (proceedings of a conference in Łódź, 8–9 Nov. 1995 (forthcoming)).

[85] Zofia Libiszowska has made this subject her own. See 'Polska reforma w opinii angielskiej', in J. Kowecki (ed.), *Sejm Czteroletni i jego tradycje* (Warsaw, 1991), 68–71, 'Odgłosy Konstytucji 3 Maja na Zachodzie', in A. Barszczewska-Krupa (ed.), *Konstytucja 3 Maja w tradycji i kulturze polskiej* (Łódź, 1991), 76–9, *Życie polskie*, ch. 5, and below, p. 303. *Merentibus* medals were received by James Perry (the *Morning Chronicle*), John Heriot (the *Sun* and the *London Gazette*), and the publisher Edward Johnson. 'Polska reforma', n. 7. Here I concentrate on Stanisław August's contacts with men of letters.

[86] SA to Bukaty, 12 May 1790, BCzart. 849, f. 141. Bukaty to SA, 11 June 1790, PAU 1658, f. 15, 11 Jan. 1790, 31 May 1791, BCzart. 3998, ff. 113, 132.

'a master piece of sound logic and manly understanding'. Paine and his friend Mazzei were

more republicans in their sentiments than me. I think monarchical government has many advantages if the prerogative of the Prince be properly limited and though I frankly own that I should wish to diminish the power of most of the Kings in Europe, I certainly at the same time would add if I could, to that which your Majesty possesses in Poland.

Stanisław August asked Bukaty to obtain a number of the books recommended to him, including Dr Hartley's *Observations on Man* as abridged and defended by Priestley, Richard Price's *Four Dissertations on Providence, on Prayer, on . . . a Future State, and on Miracles*, and some poems published under the pseudonym of Peter Pindar and ridiculing George III. The king did not order Adam Smith's *Wealth of Nations*, described by Christie as 'the greatest work on political oeconomy ever published', which probably indicates that Stanisław August already had the book.[87] The king was certainly in possession of Burke's *Reflections*.[88] For once, Stanisław August's manners failed him. He did not reply to Christie, who wrote a year later to ask if his letter and book had reached Warsaw.[89]

On the other hand, Edmund Burke's paeans upon the Polish Revolution in *An Appeal from the New to the Old Whigs* were most welcome.[90] Stanisław August immediately charged Bukaty to thank Burke, and thought to give him a medal or some other present. The envoy passed on the king's thanks, and Burke promised to send Stanisław August the second edition of the *Appeal*, and thanked the king in a letter to Bukaty. Bukaty warned, however, that Burke might be embarrassed by any public reward. Stanisław August decided on a *Merentibus* medal, and left to his envoy the decision on when and how to give it to Burke.[91] Bukaty waited until the new year, whereupon Burke wrote a magnificent letter of thanks to the king, expressing his admiration of the Polish monarch and his achievement. The delighted king had the letter translated into

---

[87] Christie to SA, Paris, 22 May 1791, BCzart. 938, ff. 633–55. 'Livres demandées à M. Bukaty', BCzart. 938, f. 503. Fabre, *Stanislas-Auguste Poniatowski*, 530–1, 679–80, n. 128.

[88] SA to M. Poniatowski, 12 Jan. 1791, Zb. Gh. 801b, f. 116.

[89] Christie to SA, London, 3 Aug. 1792, Zb. Pop. 206, ff. 77–9.

[90] Libiszowska, 'Edmund Burke a Polska', *KwH*, 77 (1970). *An Appeal from the New to the Old Whigs . . .* (London, 1791), 102–4, repr. in N. Davies, '"The Languor of so Remote an Interest": British attitudes to Poland 1772–1832', *OSP*, new series, 16 (1983), 90. See below, pp. 303–4.

[91] SA to Bukaty, 31 Aug.–28 Nov. 1791, PAU 1658, ff. 79–91, *passim*. Bukaty to SA, 20 Sept. 1791, 4 Nov. 1791, BCzart. 3998, ff. 146, 150. Burke to Bukaty, 6 Oct. 1791, PAU 1660, ff. 95–6, *The Correspondence of Edmund Burke*, eds. L. Sutherland *et al.* (10 vols.; Cambridge, 1957–78), vol. 6, 426–8.

Polish and circulated to try to disprove the charge of Polish Jacobinism.[92] It was of no use. When Stanisław August next wrote to Burke, in June 1793, anticipating the arrival of some of Burke's works, he could only console himself that as literature embellishes prosperity, so it also softens adversity.[93]

Colonel William Gardiner, the last envoy of Great Britain to the Commonwealth, had the misfortune to arrive in October 1792, when the constitution had already been overthrown. Gardiner's heart went out to Stanisław August, and the sympathy of the British minister was a consolation for the king. He defended Stanisław August when Warsaw rose against Russia in 1794. Gardiner's was indeed a melancholy mission, as the powerless witness of the murder of the Polish state. He even had to stay in Warsaw until the end of 1797, in order to pay his debts. Stanisław August himself contributed to the easing of the envoy's difficulties. In his last official letter, Stanisław August repeated: 'Toujours il restera vrai que j'aime et j'honore votre roi et votre nation, et vous le leur direz.'[94]

With regard to the English nation at least, this was no mere compliment. It never had been, although it was often pronounced in a political context. Despite successive disillusionments in the English government, Stanisław August was always predisposed in favour of Englishmen (slightly less so, perhaps, in favour of Englishwomen) and strove to win their approbation and friendship. As king, his contacts could never be on as equal a basis as those of other Polish aristocrats, for all his efforts to break down the barriers of etiquette. His position as king made another trip to England impossible, and there could be no question of Catherine or even Paul permitting him to go there after 1795. It remains an open question why Stanisław August did not find in any Englishman a correspondent such as Madame Geoffrin. After the death of Williams, the most likely candidate was Charles Yorke. Perhaps Stanisław August was upset at Yorke's

[92] Burke to SA, 28 Feb. 1792, Zb. Pop. 186, ff. 180–2, Burke, *Correspondence*, vol. 7, 76–9, Zb. Pop. 207, ff. 296–7 (Polish translation). SA to Bukaty, 21 Mar. 1792, BCzart. 849, f. 587.

[93] SA to Burke, 12 June 1793, Burke, *Correspondence*, vol. 7, 374–5.

[94] See Dembiński, 'William Gardiner, ostatni minister Wielkiej Brytanii na dworze Stanisława Augusta', in *Księga pamiątkowa ku czci L. Pinińskiego* (Lwów, 1936) and Libiszowska, 'Insurekcja kościuszkowska widziana z Anglii', in H. Kocój (ed.), *200 rocznica powstania kościuszkowskiego* (Katowice, 1994). Apart from his despatches in PRO 62/5–9, Gardiner described his relations with the king and the primate in his letters to Burges. Bodl., Bland Burges Papers 35. SA to Gardiner, Moscow, 18 May 1797, Gardiner to SA, 27 Sept. 1797, Kor. SA 3a, ff. 500–3. SA to Gardiner, 18 Jan. 1795, PRO FO 62/9, quoted by Davies, *God's Playground*, vol. 1, 545.

refusal to come to Poland. Perhaps Yorke had not time enough to run the errands that were consigned instead to Montagu, nor the wish to engage in diplomatic intrigues. Stormont, the only other authority from his youth, was in a delicate political position in Vienna, and later in Paris.

Stanisław August's friends, visitors, and correspondents represented most shades of the political spectrum, from Burke to Barlow. It is difficult, however, to identify anyone of authoritarian or intolerant views. Most were reformers of one stamp or another. Among English statesmen, Stanisław August most admired Shelburne, for his international vision. If much of Stanisław August's information was filtered through Rockingham Whig circles in the 1760s, it became more objective and comprehensive after the establishment of a permanent diplomatic mission in London. Stanisław August did not support any one political grouping against another. He sought support where it could be found, but when Whig sympathizers with the French Revolution organized a subscription in aid of Poland, it was already too late to make any difference, and the king felt it wiser to distance himself from those tainted with 'Jacobinism'. Stanisław August did not obtain much more than good wishes from his English contacts, but his image as a wise, enlightened, and gracious prince was enduring, and was not tarnished by his accession to the confederacy of Targowica and abdication.[95]

[95] Libiszowska, 'Insurekcja kościuszkowska', 28–31.

7

The English Constitution and the First Efforts to Reform the Commonwealth (1763–1768)

Stanisław August tried to introduce the 'English Government' into Poland. Even before his election, in 1763, he wrote down his own constitutional programme, modelled on the English, which he henceforth tried steadfastly to realize, as far as was possible.[1]

Thus Emanuel Rostworowski unequivocally assessed Stanisław August's constitutional programme and subsequent policies. Stanisław's 'Anecdote Historique sur le Regne de Vladislas IV' summarized his constitutional thought and its importance has been realized by a number of historians.[2] It was not the only programme of reform drawn up at the end of the reign of Augustus III. Stanisław Konarski published his demolition of the *liberum veto*, *O skutecznym rad sposobie* ('On the means of effective counsels'), in four volumes between 1760 and 1763. Konarski had written the first two volumes back in the 1740s, but he had then judged that the time was not yet ripe for publication. The third and fourth volumes were written with the co-operation of Adam Kazimierz Czartoryski, who supplied information and publications on the English constitution. It is possible that Stanisław also advised Konarski.[3] Although Konarski drew closer to the *Familia* at this time, the Czartoryskis had their own distinct plans for reform.[4] Poniatowski, the Czartoryskis, and Konarski all referred

[1] Rostworowski, 'Republikanizm polski i anglosaski', 96.
[2] Including Leśnodorski, Michalski, Zahorski, Zielińska, and Czaja. There is no point in listing every mention. Analyses by Nieć, 'Stanisława A. Poniatowskiego plan reformy Rzeczypospolitej', *Historja*, 3 (1933); idem, *Młodość ostatniego elekta*, 234–6; and Rostworowski, *Ostatni król*, 33–4, 38–42, 214–15.
[3] Konarski, *O skutecznym rad sposobie, albo o utrzymaniu ordynaryinych seymów* (4 vols.; repr. Warsaw, 1923), vol. 4, 36–60. There is no evidence for Nieć's view that Stanisław also helped, *Młodość ostatniego elekta*, 228, but it is logical enough. Konarski may not have wished to cite the proud parvenu Poniatowski as his source.
[4] Konopczyński, *Konarski*, 202–52. Idem, *Polscy pisarze polityczni*, 171–98. Nowak-Dłużewski, *Konarski*, 115–31. G. Chomicki, 'Wpływy angielskie w publicystyce politycznej obozu reform w Rzeczypospolitej od wydania "O skutecznym rad sposobie" do upadku Kodeksu Zamoyskiego (1761–1780)' (unpublished MA thesis, Cracow, 1984), 22–58. Michalski, 'Plan Czartoryskich naprawy Rzeczypospolitej', *KwH*, 63 (1956).

to the English constitution as both a justification for their plans and a source of ideas. They all interpreted the English constitution differently. It would therefore be worthwhile to compare Stanisław's plan both with the others and with the actual mid-century English constitution. Having analysed the role of English models in the plans, we may then follow the fortunes of the attempts of the Czartoryskis and Stanisław August to put English-influenced ideas into practice. We shall first set these programmes in their political context, and outline the rest of Stanisław's political education after his return from Russia.

I

Stanisław returned from St Petersburg in 1758 fired by the hope of marrying Catherine and reforming his country, perhaps even as King of Poland. His hopes of a new mission to Russia soon evaporated, however, and he was forced to wait on events. Stanisław occupied himself with family affairs, his *starostwo* of Przemyśl, and politics. He and his cousin Adam spent the long winter of 1759/60 at Puławy, poring over interminable old histories, and no doubt discussing their experiences in England and Russia, and the steps necessary to revitalize the Commonwealth. Poniatowski was an envoy at the Seyms of 1758, 1760, 1761, and 1762, but he played the inglorious role of saboteur. The *Familia* was no longer the party of reform. Having been cut off by the rapacious marshal of the Court, Jerzy Mniszech, from the fruits of royal patronage, the Czartoryskis were now in open opposition. Stanisław himself, at the head of forty-two partisans of the *Familia*, broke up the extraordinary Seym of 1761, called to deal with the monetary chaos caused by Frederick II's falsification of Polish coins. Although Stanisław found plenty of excuses for his conduct, it troubled his conscience when he came to write his *Mémoires*. With the death of Tsaritsa Elizabeth and the accession of Peter III, hopes of a partition of Prussia vanished, and the chances of a Saxon succession in Poland greatly diminished. The *Familia* felt able to reject the Court's offers of reconciliation. August Czartoryski was aiming at the throne, either for himself or his son. The 1762 Seym broke up in tumult after Stanisław cynically challenged Brühl's Polish nobility, even though the *Familia* had forced it through the Crown tribunal of 1748.[5]

The news of Catherine II's *coup d'état* arrived in July 1762. The new tsaritsa promptly wrote to Stanisław that she was sending Keyserling

[5] Nieć, *Młodość ostatniego elekta*, 184–204, 216–20. *Mémoires*, vol. I, 359, 367–9, 399–418. The best account of the end of Augustus III's reign is Staszewski, *August III*, 249–77.

to Poland to make him or Prince Adam king. But although Stanisław bombarded her with letters, she gave him no encouragement to expect her hand in marriage. At the end of 1762, the Czartoryskis decided upon an armed confederacy against Augustus III and Brühl. Promised support by Keyserling, they began recruiting troops and drawing up plans for reform. Up to now demagogy had sufficed, but as they prepared to assume power, they needed to offer something more positive. Preparations were well advanced when in August 1763 Catherine called a sudden halt. Even she shrank from an open challenge to a fellow monarch. She ordered the *Familia* to await the death of Augustus III.[6]

In June 1763 Stanisław gave his own plan, the 'Anecdote Historique' to the Danish diplomat Osten, to take to Catherine. For some reason she seems not to have received it.[7] What remains is an unfinished draft in Stanisław's own hand, running to seven pages.[8] Stanisław presented his ideas in a literary essay. He recalled the wish of Władysław IV[9] to marry the Protestant daughter of the Elector Palatine, which was frustrated by his subjects. Władysław was made to lament his father Sigismund III's refusal to allow him to marry his beloved during Sigismund's lifetime. Władysław was forced by the Seym to marry a French princess and died an unhappy man. The point was that the Seym would not permit Stanisław as king to wed the Orthodox tsaritsa, so Catherine had better marry him before he was elected. Władysław supposedly asked, when the French marriage was proposed, 'à quoi vous sert, que je me marie, puisque mes Enfans ne vous garantiront pas apres ma mort, des troubles d'un Interregne, et des malheurs attachés à ce precieux droit d'election?'[10] Stanisław was one of the first Poles to challenge this pillar of liberty in the eighteenth century. The chaos and danger of interregna were henceforth to be the standard arguments advanced in favour of a hereditary throne.[11] The Czartoryskis for the moment passed over the subject. Konarski expressed the opinion that the King of England 'has greater prerogatives and power than the Dutch staadhouder, and the English royal house is also the hereditary possessor of the throne, and yet Parliament is a parliament, and the

[6] Nieć, *Młodość ostatniego elekta*, 209–39. Michalski, 'Plan Czartoryskich', 29–31. Zamoyski, *Last King*, 79–83. Staszewski, *August III*, 282, 287.

[7] Nieć, *Młodość ostatniego elekta*, 234–6. Rostworowski, *Ostatni król*, 33–4.

[8] BCzart. 798, ff. 135–42.

[9] King of Poland 1632–48. His reign was regarded as the Indian summer of the Commonwealth, before the disasters that overtook the reign of his brother John Casimir.

[10] BCzart. 798, ff. 135–6.

[11] Z. Zielińska, *'O sukcesyi tronu w Polszcze' 1787–1790* (Warsaw, 1991), 13 and *passim*.

English republic is a free and perfect republic,' but left the question of succession or election unresolved in his plan of reform.[12]

Poniatowski put into King Władysław's mouth a deathbed lament:

à force de circonscrire leurs Roys, les Polonois en ont fait les Esclaves couronnés, et cependant leur Constitution presente est telle, qu'un Roy mauvais ou seulement paraisseux, peut nuire beaucoup au Public, et aux Particuliers, et le Roy le plus habil et le mieux intentionné, ne scavoit faire le vrai bien de l'État.[13]

Here Stanisław neatly reversed Voltaire's aphorism that the King of England was allowed to do good by the constitution, but prevented from doing evil.[14] The saying was also current in Poland, but given the addressee, it is probable that Stanisław consciously alluded to Voltaire. Augustus III was the obvious butt of *paraisseux*. Stanisław then proceeded to a précis of a plan for the reform of the constitution, which had supposedly been found in Władysław's papers. It opened: 'Il faut qu'un Roy de Pologne aye des bornes plus etroites qu'un Roy d'Angleterre pour que la Pologne reste libre, mais il faut qu'il aye plus de pouvoir que ceux d'aujourd'hui.' Stanisław next introduced the theme of mutual dependence; 'il faut que tous les sujets ayent continuellement besoin du Roy et le Roy continuellement besoin de tous ses sujets.'[15]

Unlike the King of England, the King of Poland should not be able to declare war by himself. That was to be left to the Seym. The king alone, however, was to nominate to all offices and dignities (as was generally the case in England). However, each nobleman would have the right at the annual *seymiki* (which would elect both envoys to the Seym and deputies to the tribunals) to propose a vote of no confidence in an official or dignitary of the palatinate without giving a reason. This presumably included the palatine and castellan. If at three successive *seymiki* the official lost such a vote, the king would be obliged to nominate another. Stanisław justified his proposal as contributing to the mutual dependence of king and nation. The king would have to choose his servants well in order to keep the confidence of the nation. If the *seymiki* were able to vote out royal nominees immediately, many able men would fall victim to 'la Cabale des familles riches', before they had the chance to win the affection of the local nobility. Stanisław called this mechanism his 'Censure

[12] 'Większe ma prerogatywy i moc niż Gubernator Hollenderski, y tak że Dom Angielski iest Tronu Dziedzicem, a Parlament iest parlamentem, Rzplitą Angielską wolną y doskonałą Rzplitą.' *O skutecznym rad sposobie*, vol. 4, 129. This is a judgement on the republican nature of the English state; hence the translation 'republic'.

[13] BCzart. 798, f. 136.   [14] See above, pp. 47–8.   [15] BCzart. 798, ff. 136–7.

Publique', one of four restrictions he proposed on royal power. It was a complicated and limited form of political responsibility. Rostworowski observed that an influential monarch might be able to rid himself of rebellious officials in this way.[16]

It is not clear if the Seym was to be able to dismiss the dignitaries of the Commonwealth on a similar basis. The king could not; 'Je ne veux pas que le Roy de Pologne aye le Pouvoir d'ôter les charges comme en Angleterre, afin que la liberté par la meme courre moins de risques.'[17] In England, political responsibility rested not on the ability of Parliament to dismiss ministers (it could not—save by impeachment), but on the fact that no minister who had not the confidence of both the king and the House of Commons could conduct the nation's business adequately. It was not yet established if ministers were responsible collectively or individually to the king.[18] It was a situation that had arisen out of long evolution and which still produced political crises throughout the eighteenth century. It could not be imposed in Poland at a stroke, and Stanisław sought other solutions.

The ministers, wrote Poniatowski, had grown 'trop absolus dans leur departemens'. In particular, the grand hetman could, 'touttes les fois qu'il aura autant de genie que d'ambition troubler tout l'ordre de l'Etat et de venir egalement terrible au Roy et à la liberté.' The grand marshals and treasurers also abused their powers and the grand chancellors were overworked. They were therefore to be given four adjutants (presumably appointed by the king, possibly at his pleasure) and in each department, decisions were to be taken by majority vote. The king was to appoint two secretaries, one for foreign and the other for home affairs, equal in dignity to the other ministers but holding office at royal pleasure, because the king was best able to judge their fidelity, discretion, and intelligence. The king, the two secretaries, four ministers, and sixteen adjutants would constitute a 'conseil privé', which would give local regulations passed by the *seymiki* the force of law.[19] It seems that Stanisław envisaged ending Polish-Lithuanian duality in offices, as he made provision for only four ministers rather than eight. Despite his claim not to want the power of the King of England to dismiss his ministers at will, Stanisław proposed an effective central government in which the ministers were effectively neutralized by royal appointees. Foreign affairs were placed under the sole control of the king. The king would be his own first minister,

---

[16] BCzart. 798, ff. 138–9, 140. Rostworowski, *Ostatni król*, 40–1.
[17] BCzart. 798, f. 140.   [18] Clark, *Dynamics of Change*, 452–3.
[19] BCzart. 798, ff. 140–2.

although it is possible that he might choose to delegate the role. The 'conseil privé' was in some ways similar to the English cabinet, but the strong principle of collegiality at departmental level indicates Sweden, Russia, Prussia, and Saxony as possible models.[20]

The central governments proposed by Konarski and the Czartoryskis were weaker affairs. Konarski's unwieldy 'council of residents' was to be firmly subordinated to the Seym, although its projects were to enjoy priority in the Seym's deliberations. The council was to be composed of 45 members. The primate and eight ministers (the hetmans were replaced by ministers of war) were to sit *ex officio*, the king was to nominate twelve senators, and the chamber of envoys was to elect twenty-four councillors, as far as possible from its own ranks. After the first set had been elected for one year, a further thirty-six senators and envoys were to be selected for a second, and then forty-five reserves. The council was to be divided into military, treasury, police, and justice departments. An interdepartmental delegation for foreign affairs of four senators and four representatives of the *szlachta* was to be chosen by the king. All decisions, both in the departments and in plenary session, were to be taken by majority vote. Detailed reports were to be laid before commissions appointed by the Seym, and punishments were envisaged for neglect of duties, but there was no clear system of political responsibility. Konarski referred to both England and Sweden, but looked rather to the Swedish colleges for his model.[21]

The Czartoryskis also made use of collegiality in the executive power and paid no real attention to the English example. Their chamber of envoys was to elect eighteen councillors to each of the four ministerial councils. The hetmans were to be doubled in number to eight and reduced in importance to divisional commanders, who might be chosen by the king to chair the military council. Higher promotions were to be left to the king, lower ones to unit commanders. The Czartoryskis left open the question of separate councils for Lithuania. A 'consilium secretum', probably borrowed from Saxon practice and comprising the king, the primate, the two grand chancellors, and a number of senators and elected envoys, was to co-ordinate policy.[22]

Stanisław, like Konarski and the Czartoryskis, wished to abolish the *liberum veto*: 'Ainsi que dans toutes les autres assemblées nationales,

---

[20] On collegiality in 18th-century Europe, see Konopczyński, *Geneza i ustanowienie Rady Nieustającej*, 10–38.
[21] *O skutecznym rad sposobie*, vol. 4, 163–93.
[22] Michalski, 'Plan Czartoryskich', 36–8.

grandes et petites, la Pluralité decidera.' The Seym, 'toujours subsistante comme le Parlement d'Angleterre', was to be elected annually at the *seymiki*.[23] Here Stanisław was even more radical than Konarski, who, criticizing the corruptibility of the English Parliament elected for seven years (if the king did not dissolve it earlier), and noting the demands of the 'English republicans' for triennial Parliaments, resolved to keep the term of the Seym at two years, but '*zawsze trwaiący*' (in this case—'always sitting or ready to reconvene'). Konarski's Seym was to decide itself on the prorogation of its sessions. The Czartoryskis did not propose any change in the duration of the Seym, but as in England, the king was to be able to prorogue and call sessions as necessary. Stanisław proposed to treble or even quadruple the number of envoys as a safeguard against royal corruption. The Czartoryskis likewise; the number was to be roughly trebled to 581. Konarski set the number of envoys at 600, but elected in equal electoral districts, whereas the Czartoryskis' increases seem to show no particular pattern. Konarski divided the envoys into two groups of 300, each to sit for a year. The Czartoryskis, confident of mobilizing their own supporters, set a low quorum of fifty. The House of Commons numbered 551 and its quorum was forty. Stanisław passed over the workings of the Seym, but both Konarski and the Czartoryskis proposed the adoption of procedure based on that of the English Parliament and the election of envoys at *seymiki* by open voting by name, as at English county elections. Only *possessionati* (those noblemen holding land in the palatinate) were to vote at the *seymiki*, a measure aimed against the manipulation of the landless *gołota* ('naked' *szlachta*) by magnates.[24]

Stanisław did not refer to the senate, and the Czartoryskis opted for an upper house equal in voting rights to the lower. Senatorial projects were to be discussed after those from the throne, but before those from the chamber of envoys. Konarski, however, drastically weighted the balance of power in favour of the chamber of envoys by stipulating that only a majority of nine-tenths of the senate could reject a bill passed by the envoys. In Konarski's project, senators were to be elected for life by the *seymiki*. The Czartoryskis would have senators elected by the Seym.

[23] BCzart. 798, ff. 137, 140. In 1788, Stanisław August distinguished a reconvenable Seym (*gotowy*) from one in permanent session (*trwały*), and associated the latter with the English model. See below, Ch. 12, n. 26. In 1763, he may have genuinely wanted a virtually permanent Seym (which would have severely cramped the executive); he may have been insincere or he may have been unsure of his facts. The annual sessions of the British Parliament averaged about five months in the later 18th century.

[24] BCzart. 798, f. 137. *O skutecznym rad sposobie*, vol. 3, 253–78, vol. 4, 145–54, 160–1, 200–26, 266–83. Michalski, 'Plan Czartoryskich', 33–6.

The British House of Lords was equal in rights to the Commons, with the vital exception of money bills, which could not be initiated or amended by the upper house.[25]

As a further safeguard against royal corruption, Poniatowski proposed the abolition of the *starostwa*. At present they were at best the means for the gratuitous enrichment of favourites. Stanisław wanted the spirit of the new government to be 'Point de travail sans recompense, mais point de bienfaits sans travail.' If the Crown estates that went with the *starostwa* at present were to be held as hereditary possessions, agriculture would prosper, because the holders would have an incentive to improve the land for the benefit of their children. This 'esprit agriculteur' 'est generalement le plus analogue aux moeurs vertueuses et sentimens Patriotiques'. The *kwarta* (the contribution levied on Crown estates for the army) would then yield more and be paid more regularly.[26] Stanisław seems not to have been proposing a one-off sale of Crown estates, but rather their transformation into hereditary leases, which would ensure a regular income from them. Konarski proposed a sale, with the proceeds going to found a national bank, as in England, Holland, Sweden, and Genoa. The Czartoryskis inclined towards competitive bidding for long-term leases.[27] There was no analogy with England here. Most of the estates of the English Crown had long ago been given away by the king, and he was forbidden to grant any more. They were analogous to the table lands (*dobra stołowe*)—the direct domain lands of the King of Poland. George II was guaranteed a minimum of £800,000 by Parliament in the event of the estates together with other 'hereditary revenues' producing less, but George III agreed on his accession to surrender the 'hereditary revenues' and accept in return a fixed civil list of £800,000. However, the concept of a civil list would recur in various proposals for reform in the future.[28]

Stanisław also proposed an army of 50,000 infantry (the Polish army had a disproportionate amount of cavalry). Such an army would present no threat to Poland's neighbours, but would suffice for defence. To counter

[25] *O skutecznym rad sposobie*, vol. 4, 148–9, 237–45. Michalski, 'Plan Czartoryskich', 35–6. Konopczyński, *Polscy pisarze polityczni*, 191–2, argued that the only real power of the senate up to then lay in the *liberum veto* (which senators never used personally in any case), and that it was unable in practice to reject projects passed by the envoys, when the houses 'joined' to hear them read out at the end of the Seym.

[26] BCzart. 798, ff. 137–8.

[27] A. Stroynowski, 'Sprawa reform królewszczyn w kulturze polskiego Oświecenia', *Acta Universitatis Lodziensis: ZNUŁ*, Seria 1, 8 (1978), 6–7. *O skutecznym rad sposobie*, vol. 4, 301–2.

[28] J. Brooke, *George III* (London, 1972), 202–4. See below, pp. 257, 265–6.

the danger of a royal attempt to impose despotism, he suggested the renewal of the general levy in the form of compulsory musters of the *szlachta* on horseback after the annual *seymiki*. The palatines would command. The idea, or perhaps rather the myth, of the general levy was very popular with the *szlachta* (such musters were regularly demanded by *seymiki* but never took place). It had long been utterly anachronistic as a fighting force. However, the proposal that the towns send detachments of infantry would have undermined the *szlachta*'s claim to be a warrior caste, and, on the principle of *divide et impera*, might have reduced the danger of the musters turning into rebellious confederacies.[29] It is just possible that Stanisław may have been thinking of the English militia, which had been re-established in 1757. He was later to show considerable interest in the idea.[30]

Poniatowski, the Czartoryskis, and Konarski were writing for different purposes, and that explains some of the differences in emphasis. Konarski in a long published treatise aimed to convince the *szlachta* of the need to abolish the *liberum veto*, and so he concentrated upon the functioning of the legislature and its relations with the executive. The Czartoryskis drew up their plans in secret. Only in their implementation would they have to worry about public opinion. Their opposition to Augustus III and, perhaps, their suspicions of their nephew explain some of the restrictions placed on the monarch. As the tribunals had replaced the Seym as the main battleground of politics, they paid much attention to the reform of the courts.[31] Stanisław, the candidate for the throne, was trying in a short essay to convince the tsaritsa of the need to strengthen the monarchy in Poland. He thus concentrated on the executive power and tried to answer fears of the monarchy getting out of control by adopting a 'republican' tone and proposing various safeguards against despotism, so long as he could retain the power of nomination.[32]

Despite the different contexts, basic ideological differences are visible between the three concepts.[33] Konarski modernized noble republicanism. He would resolve the conflict *inter maiestatem ac libertatem* decisively in favour of liberty. The Seym, restored to health by the abolition of the *veto* and of mandatory instructions, with power firmly in the hands of

---

[29] Rostworowski, *Sprawa aukcji wojska na tle sytuacji politycznej przed Sejmem Czteroletnim* (Warsaw, 1957), 34–9, 87. Lukowski, *Liberty's Folly*, 114.

[30] See below, pp. 264–5.   [31] Michalski, 'Plan Czartoryskich', 38–9.

[32] Rostworowski, *Ostatni król*, 39, 40.

[33] Rostworowski, *Ostatni król*, 42, classifies them respectively as noble republicanism, senatorial republicanism, and constitutional monarchy, but stresses the common features: an end to the *veto* and the restriction of the ministers by collegiate organs of government.

the chamber of envoys, would be the source of both the legislative and executive power. The king would be stripped of most of his powers and allowed real influence only in foreign policy. Konarski interpreted the English constitution similarly to the Country opposition in England. Like them he feared royal corruption of the majority of Parliament. He saw English ministers as Court favourites on the lines of Brühl, not as 'the representatives of the Commons with the king and the king with the Commons'.[34] The Czartoryskis' ideas had a senatorial flavour. The king would be similarly tied by collegiate organs elected by the Seym, but the role played by the senate was greater. The Czartoryskis were clearly confident of winning a majority in the Seym, distributing patronage according to their wishes and effectively governing through a network of party connections. Rostworowski compared their programme to the England of the 'Whig oligarchy', with power (= patronage) actually in the hands of a narrow aristocratic clique.[35] This picture has since been shown to be an inadequate one, but the Czartoryskis may have entertained such a vision.

A deeper fissure divided Poniatowski's plan from the other two. Stanisław wanted a hereditary throne, majority voting in the Seym, extensive powers of patronage for the king, and an effective central government. He would replace the conflict *inter maiestatem ac libertatem* with the mutual dependence of king and nation. From his study of English politics he drew the lessons of a healthy Parliament and an extensive royal prerogative, which allowed the king to direct policy personally, if he and his ministers could gain the confidence of the nation. At the same time Stanisław displayed his aversion to blatant Walpolean corruption.[36]

II

Augustus III died on 5 October 1763. The time had come to try to put plans into practice. The arbiter was to be Catherine II. She did not anticipate, though, that her triumph in Poland would be as easy as it proved. France did not give up her traditional opposition to Russia, but after her crushing defeat in the Seven Years' War, she was determined on revenge against England, and had neither the means nor the desire for a war over Poland. Austria supported Frederick Christian, the new Elector of Saxony, but was exhausted, and could do nothing without French support. In any case, Frederick Christian died within a few weeks of his father,

---

[34] Chomicki, 'Wpływy angielskie', 49.
[35] Rostworowski, 'Republikanizm polski i anglosaski', 96–9.
[36] Ibid., 97–9. Idem, *Ostatni król*, 217–18.

leaving the Saxon party without a credible candidate. England was eager to conclude an alliance with Russia, and although she baulked at financing and guaranteeing Poniatowski's election, Wroughton received instructions to co-operate with Keyserling. Frederick II was still more anxious for a Russian alliance, and eventually managed to induce Catherine to admit him as co-guarantor of the Polish constitution.[37]

The Convocation Seym[38] opened on 7 May 1764. The opposition grouped around Karol Radziwiłł and Jan Klemens Branicki walked out, and Radziwiłł's soldiers were soon routed by the Czartoryski militia and Russian troops. On 16 May, the future chancellor of the Crown, Andrzej Zamoyski, set out the *Familia*'s programme. Montesquieu's theory of the separation of powers made its first appearance at the Seym as Zamoyski argued that the legislature, executive, and courts constituted both the nature of government and the basis of landowners' security. Zamoyski called for a 'permanent council of residents', made up of senators and envoys, to supervise collegiate ministries. Here he was closer to Konarski than to the Czartoryskis.[39] Among his proposals were a national system of education and codification of the laws. The strongest emphasis was on economics. The might and happiness of countries depended on their wealth, and apart from the need to revive the towns and trade, he blamed serfdom for the poor condition of Polish agriculture.[40]

Zamoyski's speech was in fact a watered-down version of his first draft. In order not to offend the conservatism of the *szlachta*, he crossed out passages criticizing the *liberum veto* and proposing a tribunal to judge those who abused it. Particularly interesting for us are Zamoyski's appeals to English examples, and the fact that he dared not pronounce them publicly. He wrote that the best procedure for the Seym would be that of the English Parliament, adding that 'in any case, that kingdom is graced with a freedom, which if not greater than our own, is at least equal to it.' According to Zamoyski, economics was the moving spirit of the present century, and England was the proof. In foreign countries, religious freedom encouraged craftsmen to settle, and the lifting of serfdom caused empty fields to be cultivated. The export bounties on wheat paid by the

---

[37] H. M. Scott, 'France and the Polish throne 1763–1764', *SEER*, 53 (1975). Idem, 'Great Britain, Poland and the Russian alliance 1763–1767', *HJ*, 19 (1976). Madariaga, *Russia in the Age of Catherine*, 188–92.

[38] Called by the primate to make arrangements for the royal election and prepare the *pacta conventa*. It was automatically confederated.

[39] B. Leśnodorski, 'Mowa Andrzeja Zamoyskiego na konwokacji 1764 r.', in *Księga pamiątkowa 150-lecia Archiwum Głównego Akt Dawnych w Warszawie* (Warsaw, 1958), 385–7.

[40] Repr. in *Historia Polski 1764–1795: Wybór tekstów*, ed. J. Michalski (Warsaw, 1954).

English treasury brought enormous riches to the country. It was all too radical to be risked in the ears of the *szlachta*.[41]

The Seym nevertheless passed a series of important reforms.[42] Catherine wanted a useful ally against Turkey, and so she enabled the reforms to take place. She also wanted to keep that ally dependent, and so she set their limits.[43] Nevertheless, her nervousness over the election allowed the Czartoryskis a somewhat freer rein than might otherwise have been the case. Treasury commissions were set up for the Crown and Lithuania, which took over the powers of the grand treasurers, who were reduced to the role of chairmen. The commissions took decisions by majority vote and their competence included a wide range of economic matters. A Crown military commission assumed the powers of Hetman Branicki. The need to keep the support of Hetman Michał Massalski delayed the establishment of a similar Lithuanian commission until the Coronation Seym later in the year. The chancellors' assessory courts were also to take decisions by majority vote. Wroughton thought these changes 'an augmentation of power to the King extreamly great . . . which circumstances and a wise king may carry much further than strikes the attention at first view'.[44] Stanisław, giving an account of his conduct to the *seymik relationis*[45] of Warsaw, endeavoured to allay the fears of the *szlachta* on this point with republican rhetoric:

Poznała to Rzplta, że w wolnym, w rządnym narodzie ieden Człowiek tak mocny bydz niepowinien. Poczuła y to z doświadczenia, że byle Król dobrał sobie Hetmanów, Podskarbich, Kanclerzow do upodobania swego y sobie iedynie wiernych, może pod Ich Imieniem absolutycznie y despotycznie rządzić, gnębić, krzywdzić cały narod Polski. Więc podzieliła Rzplta moc tych ministeryów między kilkanaście osób. Boż trudniey Królowi kilkanaście niż iednego uiąc.

(The Commonwealth has come to realize that in a free and orderly nation, one man should not be so powerful. It has perceived from experience, that if the king chooses hetmans, treasurers, and chancellors faithful only unto himself, according to his fancy, he can in their name absolutely and despotically rule, oppress, and wrong the entire Polish nation. Therefore the Commonwealth divided the

---

[41] Leśnodorski, 'Mowa Zamoyskiego', 390–6.

[42] Michalski, 'Sejm w czasach Stanisława Augusta', in *Historia Sejmu Polskiego*, vol. 1, 350–6. Czaja, *Lata wielkich nadziei*, 74–81. Konopczyński, *Liberum Veto*, 410–12. Lityński, *Sejmiki ziemskie*, 144–6.

[43] Michalski, 'Problematyka aliansu polsko-rosyjskiego w czasach Stanisława Augusta: Lata 1764–1766', *PH*, 75 (1984), 695–6.

[44] Wroughton to Sandwich, 16 June 1764, PRO SP 88/88.

[45] A *seymik relationis* met after the Seym and cross-examined its envoys.

power of these ministries between about a dozen persons. For it is more difficult for the king to gain a dozen persons than one.)[46]

A new law on procedure in the Seym gave priority to projects from the throne and relegated private and local matters to the end. Laws came into force immediately upon their being passed, thus avoiding the worst consequences of the *liberum rumpo*. The Seym was to treat proposals from the treasury commissions in economic matters as it would judicial matters, which meant they would be decided by majority vote. Thanks to this manoeuvre, the ailing Keyserling's young assistant, Nikolai Repnin, did not spot this first limitation of the *liberum veto*. An attempt was made to remove the mandatory force of envoys' instructions from the *seymiki* by forbidding the envoys to swear to obey them. In practice, however, instructions were still generally considered to be mandatory and the new law had a negligible effect. The Seym also ordained a survey of Crown estates to improve the revenues from the *kwarta* and a range of other financial and judicial improvements. Internal customs were abolished and work was begun on a general customs system, from which the *szlachta* would not be exempt. Unable to abolish the *liberum veto* altogether, the Czartoryskis bypassed it by prolonging the General Confederacy at the end of the Seym for an indefinite period. Through it they were able to run the country for thirty months.

The Commonwealth obtained its first modern collegiate organs of government, and its judicial machinery was jerked back into life. The thorough reform of the Seym and an effective central government were definitely out of bounds, however. Catherine, confident of the loyalty of her ex-lover, preferred to uphold the nominative powers of the king. The English example did not play an important role in what the *Familia* was able to enact, but it was central to its further aims. Unfortunately, Catherine was not disposed to let reform go any further until the Czartoryskis had paid their political debts, by making at least some improvement in the situation of religious dissidents. Frederick II was determined to destroy everything that had been done so far. If the *Familia* thought that it could send the Russians home as easily as it had called them in, it was deluding itself.

III

With detachments of the Russian army a few miles away, Stanisław Antoni Poniatowski was unanimously elected King of Poland and Grand

[46] BCzart. 940a, ff. 331–6.

Duke of Lithuania by 5,584 noblemen (a low turnout) outside Warsaw on 7 September 1764. He decided to rule as Stanisław August, which was both a gesture of reconciliation towards the Saxon party and a statement of his intention to renew the Polish world, as Augustus had the Roman. It was the first example of the new king's attempt to raise the prestige of the monarchy by the use of monarchical and imperial symbols. Virtually all of the 'iconography of power' of the early years of his reign, from medals, portraits, and literary panegyrics to triumphal arches and the plans to rebuild the Royal Castle underlined 'majesty'. Although Minerva (for wisdom) and enlightened themes such as the flourishing of arts and sciences took precedence over Mars, Stanisław August was glorified mainly in concepts of traditional kingly virtues.[47] The vital question is how far Stanisław August's visual assertion of his monarchical dignity reflected his actual political aims. Was it the case that, intoxicated by the aura of royalty, he forgot the 'Anecdote Historique', and extended his ambitions beyond the limits of the English constitution to enlightened absolutism?[48]

The idea is not as preposterous as it may appear. Recent historiography has made it possible to consider enlightened absolutism as a new approach of rulers and their ministers to the problems of government, strongly influenced by the thought of the wider European Enlightenment.[49] With the emphasis placed firmly on reforms, rather than on the somewhat unlikely attempt to reconcile the thought of the French *philosophes* with royal absolutism or despotism, Poland need not automatically be excluded from the concept. No enlightened absolutist was in fact completely absolute. Many of them had their power limited by representative bodies to some degree. Leopold II extended the constitutional restraints upon the Grand Duke of Tuscany, and Gustavus III's famous *coup d'état* did not restore the legally untrammelled absolutism of Charles XI and Charles XII. Why should Stanisław August, who wished to create an effective executive power and strengthen the monarchy in order to enlighten his country, be discounted? Of course, Poland's system of government was the negation of absolute monarchy, and her neighbours were determined to keep it that way. Whatever he might wish, Stanisław August stood no chance of achieving as much power as a Leopold or a

---

[47] J. Pokora, *Obraz Najjaśniejszego Pana Stanisława Augusta (1764–1770): Studium z ikonografii władzy* (Warsaw, 1993). A. Rottermund, *Zamek warszawski w epoce Oświecenia: Rezydencja monarsza: Funckcje i treści* (Warsaw, 1989), 74–5. See below, p. 201.

[48] This is the argument of M. Rymszyna, *Gabinet Stanisława Augusta* (Warsaw, 1962), 14, 34–8.

[49] H. M. Scott (ed.), *Enlightened Absolutism: Reform and Reformers in Later Eighteenth-Century Europe* (London, 1990). The subtitle is important. See esp. p. 20.

Gustavus, let alone a Catherine or a Frederick. The question hinges on the extent of Stanisław August's ambitions.

The hostile testimony of Stanisław Lubomirski certainly makes Stanisław August sound like Joseph II:

> more than once he lamented the unhappiness of the King of Poland, that nothing could be done in Poland, that coercion was absolutely necessary, that good must be done by force, that the king has no power to do anything, or force anyone to do anything.[50]

In Lubomirski's opinion, Stanisław August tried to increase royal power by any means and showed scant regard for the law in his tussle with the mint and treasury commissions in 1765–6.[51]

Stanisław August found the restrictions placed on him irksome. He sought to evade them by immediately establishing an organ to use effectively what power and influence he did have: the cabinet (*gabinet*). Maria Rymszyna has argued that the cabinet was the instrument of Stanisław August's attempts to establish personal rule, and that the closest model was probably the *conseil du cabinet* created by Augustus II in Saxony. This, however, played more of a policy advisory role than Stanisław August's.[52] The cabinet did not resemble its English namesake. Of necessity, it appeared from the outside to be no more than the king's private office, handling his personal affairs, but in practice it was through the cabinet that the king conducted foreign policy and organized his own political party within the Commonwealth. After the creation of the department of foreign affairs of the Permanent Council, Polish diplomats wrote separate despatches to the cabinet on particularly sensitive matters. When the Four Year Seym created the commission of foreign affairs, which unlike the department was not controlled by the king, diplomats wrote fuller despatches to Stanisław August than to the commission. The king would frequently draft letters to his diplomats himself and then amend his secretaries' copies. Although some of the functionaries of the cabinet, notably Maurice Glayre and Pius Kiciński, became trusted advisers, their influence was always unofficial. Recruited from the middling *szlachta* or abroad, they were totally dependent on the king's pleasure.[53]

---

[50] Lubomirski, *Pod władzą księcia Repnina: Ułamki pamiętników i dzienników historycznych (1764–1768)*, ed. J. Łojek (Warsaw, 1971), 90. Cf. Beales, *Joseph II*, vol. 1, 98–9.

[51] Lubomirski, *Pod władzą księcia Repnina*, 68–85, 89–92.

[52] Staszewski, 'Pomysły reformatorskie czasów Augusta II', 749. Idem, *August III*, 99–100, 280.

[53] Rymszyna, *Gabinet*, *passim*.

At the beginning of the reign, however, the most important decisions were made at a 'ministerial council' (a continuation of the *Familia* councils). It consisted of the king, Michał and August Czartoryski, Zamoyski, Lubomirski, Antoni Przeździecki (the Vice-Chancellor of Lithuania), Jacek Ogrodzki as secretary, and the king's brothers. The most important issues were discussed and decided upon at its meetings, which were held several times a week. Although the king was not bound to heed the advice given him, in most cases he did so, and in practice the council functioned as an unofficial cabinet council, closer than the cabinet proper to both Augustus II's *conseil du cabinet* and the English cabinet.[54] Much has been written on the young king's quarrels with the Czartoryskis. Given his uncles' wealth, birth, and experience on the one hand and Stanisław's ambition on the other, harmony was not to be expected. Repnin and the king's brothers, particularly Kazimierz, tried to sow discord. The Czartoryskis wished to govern in the hard-nosed spirit of party, giving favours only to those of proven loyalty, and excluding the Saxon party rather as the Whigs had starved Tories after 1715. Stanisław August wanted to behave generously to former opponents, as befitted a monarch. Yet despite the tension and some disagreements over policy, a common front was kept up, and from 1764 to 1766 Poland received her first taste of what may fairly be called co-ordinated cabinet government.[55]

Certainly, at the outset of his reign, Stanisław August's enthusiasm was unbridled. He still believed that Catherine would support real reform in Poland, and between his election and coronation he enjoyed a 'honeymoon period'. He soaked up the applause of the crowds and letters of congratulation, and it appeared as though most of his opponents were reconciled to him. Wroughton, who a year earlier had written that Poniatowski's haughtiness had made him 'inconceivably unpopular', now wrote

[54] Konopczyński, *Geneza i ustanowienie Rady Nieustającej*, 94–5. Michalski, 'Problematyka aliansu', 697–8, and Zielińska, 'Początek rosyjskiej niełaski Czartoryskich i "słabość" Stanisława Augusta', in *Trudne stulecia; studia z dziejów XVII i XVIII wieku*, show that the advice of the Czartoryskis was usually decisive. Staszewski, 'Pomysły reformatorskie', 756–7, 761–3 traces the similarity of the 'ministerial council' to a plan by Bishop Szaniawski in 1715 (see above, p. 66). In *August III*, 280, he makes an analogy between Stanisław August's early system and Augustus III's 'ministerial system'. This seems overdrawn, if only because Stanisław August was on the spot and did not delegate policy-making. In the 1760s, Stanisław August did not retreat from reform at the first hint of trouble.

[55] e.g. Konopczyński, *Dzieje Polski nowożytnej*, vol. 2, 180, Lukowski, *Liberty's Folly*, 187–8, Zamoyski, *Last King*, 123–5. Both the king's (*Mémoires*, vol. 1, 525–6, 531–3), and Lubomirski's (*Pod władzą księcia Repnina, passim*) accounts of the conflicts were written later and blighted by mutual recrimination. Repnin tried to play off the 'good' king against his 'bad' uncles, a judgement and strategy questioned by Panin. See Zielińska, 'Początek rosyjskiej niełaski Czartoryskich'.

that 'His Majesty seems so entire a master of His Subjects' hearts and
confidence that He may prosecute any measures for the honour & prosperity of His Country that he thinks proper to adopt.'[56] On the other
hand, Stanisław August was careful to explain to his friends in England
and France the enormous obstacles presented by prejudice. Such letters
served their political purpose; they tried to dampen the extravagant hopes
placed in him by the luminaries of the Enlightenment and justified his
fence-sitting on the dissident question. But they also served as a kind of
safety valve, through which he vented his fears and frustrations. It is worth
quoting a letter to Charles Yorke:

Oui mon cher ami. La devise est bonne: *Patience et Courage*: Elle m'a conduit ou
Je suis. Mais je vous dis avec verité, que j'en ai plus besoin que Jamais. Il me
faut *Le Courage* de *tout* entreprendre, car *tout* est à faire dans ma Patrie, et il me
faut la *Patience* et meme la Resignation de ne me promettre d'autre prix de mon
travail, que la *Croyance* qu'un autre receuillera après ma mort le fruit de l'arbre
que j'aurai planté. Car il est impossible de faire vite et bien de grandes choses,
dans un Pays affaibli par la licence et le desordre de deux Siècles, ou l'on veut
conserver la liberté, et qui est entouré de voisins jaloux et puissans. Haec
superanda![57]

We notice the stern critique of the golden freedom, which comprehended
the entire period of elective kings. What is really striking, though, is that
Stanisław August was already resigned to the idea that another would
harvest the fruits of renewal. It was a metaphor that would give him suc-
cour in the most difficult moments of his reign.[58] That he should employ
it three days after his coronation shows that the popularity he had
acquired since his election had not gone to his head. The opinion of the
papal nuncio, Antonio Visconti, that Stanisław August was possessed of
'a burning desire to reform the country in one day—if only he could—
and the entire nation, in order to bring it up to the level of other, more
advanced nations,' is usually quoted to show the king's frenetic ambition.
Yet it is also worth noting the caveat.[59]

After his coronation, Stanisław August took over from his uncles in
forcing the pace of change. The afore-mentioned mint commission was

[56] Wroughton to Sandwich, 13 Oct. 1763, PRO SP 88/87. Ditto, 3 Nov. 1764 and
Sept.–Dec., *passim*, PRO SP 88/89. Zamoyski, *Last King*, 99–100.
  [57] SA to C. Yorke, 28 Nov. 1764, BL Add. 35349, f. 67. Also SA to Lyttelton, [Nov.?
1764], Zb. Pop. 177, f. 154, and SA to Mme Geoffrin, 22 Dec. 1764, 6 Mar. 1765, 25 May
1765, *Correspondance*, 135–6, 144, 154–5. See Nieć, *Młodość ostatniego elekta*, ch. 12.
  [58] See below, p. 226.
  [59] Visconti to Cardinal Torrigani, 24 Sept. 1766, quoted after Lukowski, 'Towards
partition: Polish magnates and Russian intervention in Poland during the early reign of
Stanisław August Poniatowski', *HJ*, 28 (1985), 557.

established to strike new coins and repair the damage done by Frederick II in the Seven Years' War. A commission *boni ordinis* was created to improve Warsaw. Stanisław August set up a cadet school and a cannon foundry. With Zamoyski he energetically prepared legislation for the Seym of 1766. He wanted to widen the breach made in the *liberum veto* by treating new taxes and an increase in the army as 'economic matters'. He also proposed the joining of the Crown and Lithuanian military and treasury commissions. Although radical and over-optimistic, such plans were hardly the stuff of absolutism. Only the project to allow the king to exploit mineral deposits in the entire country, rewarding the possessor of the land but not requiring his consent, was an attack on property rights going beyond the prerogative of the King of England.[60]

Even Stanisław August's own propaganda was equivocal. While Stanisław wanted his image to be that of a true monarch, descended through his mother from the Jagiellons, he also wanted to project himself as a citizen king, who like his father had risen through his own merit.[61] The result, predictably, was confusion. The stiff etiquette of the court of Augustus III, which had helped clothe that monarch in regal dignity, was virtually abandoned. Charles Lee was delighted that a king could be 'easy, civil and totally unceremonious', but Stanisław Lubomirski found the king's table uncomfortably democratic.[62]

An inveterate, not to say fanatical opponent of monarchical power and David Hume, Charles Lee gave an interesting assessment of Stanisław August's political outlook. He wrote to the Earl of Charlemont on 1 June 1765:

For God's sake, you patriot few at home, *principiis obstate*; for absolute power is a serpent of that wriggling, penetrating kind, that, if it can but introduce its head, it is in vain to pull at the tail. It is curious to hear me converse on these subjects with the King; to hear me advance my doctrines, not the most favourable to monarchy, to defend even the beheading of the martyr Charles; but it is still more curious to hear his opinions, which are singular for a crowned head; in short he is as warm for the natural rights of mankind as was Algernon Sidney himself.[63]

Algernon Sidney was revered by radical Whigs as a martyr, for he had been executed for treason by Charles II. His *Discourses on Government*,

---

[60] Czaja, *Lata wielkich nadziei*, 84–7. Lukowski, *Liberty's Folly*, 188–9. Lubomirski, *Pod władzą księcia Repnina*, 91–3.

[61] SA to Mme Geoffrin, 9 Sept. 1764, *Correspondance*, 101–2. Pokora, *Obraz Najjaśniejszego Pana*, 34, 47–9.

[62] Lee to C. Yorke, Warsaw, 27 Mar. 1765, BL Add. 35637, f. 154. Also Lee to G. Colman, Warsaw, 8 May 1769, *Lee Papers*, vol. 1, 83. Lubomirski, *Pod władzą księcia Repnina*, 97. Staszewski, *August III*, 169–70, 246, 249. Zamoyski, *Last King*, 108–10.

[63] *Lee Papers*, vol. 1, 41.

published posthumously, attacked Filmer's divine right theories and allowed the right of resistance, but in the name of the 'ancient constitution' rather than the social contract. Stanisław August possessed English and French editions.[64] Lee told Charles Yorke that the king was 'a sincere friend to the rights of mankind in general'.[65] Naturally, Stanisław August wanted Lee to pass on a favourable image to his correspondents in England, and the king was hardly likely to confide any schemes to increase royal power to a firebrand like Lee, who could not even refrain from openly criticizing the King of Poland's brother monarch, George III. It is also true that Lee had a penchant for exaggeration and was dependent upon Stanisław August for his upkeep. Lee directed his venom at the tyranny of the *szlachta*. Nevertheless, he was clearly taken aback by the force of Stanisław August's words, and the fact that Stanisław August wanted to create such an image in England cannot be explained merely as a political confidence trick.

In a letter to Stanisław August in October 1767, Lee expressed his sympathy for the American colonists. The Stamp Act would have made them slaves, with their property 'at the mercy of the Crown's Minister, or (what is pretty much the same thing) at the mercy of his tools the House of Commons'. Another such attempt would shake the nation to its foundation. Stanisław August's reply sheds light on his conception of the state:

Je vous demande encor de me dire pourquoi n'accorde t'on point à vos Colonies le droit d'avoir des representans au Parlement Brittanique? Representation et taxation croient alors un pas egal, et la Connexion entre la Mere et les filles reviendroit indissoluble. Au lieu que sans cela je ne connois que l'alternative de l'oppression ou d'independance.

Creating American parliaments would be a mistake, he went on, as the Dutch example demonstrated that the government of a federal republic of seven equal provinces with conflicting interests was slow and defective.

Le pis de tout seroit si les volontes du Parlement d'Angleterre pour être executées en Amerique avoient besoin de la Sanction du Parlement Americain, lequel deviendroit ainsi peu a peu le Souverain de celui d'Europe. Ce seroit le meme abus qu'on voit en Pologne ou la Dietine de Prusse veut arroger le droit de confirmer ou rejeter, ce que la Diette du Royaume de Pologne a statuée.[66]

[64] 'Catalogus Bibliothecae . . . 1783', AKsJP 268, ff. 13, 15. It is impossible to establish whether the king acquired them before or after meeting Lee.

[65] Constantinople, 27 Apr. 1766, BL Add. 35636, f. 454.

[66] Lee to SA, 20 Oct. 1767, SA to Lee, 20 Nov. 1767/Mar. 1768, Zb. Pop. 177, ff. 69–71, *Lee Papers*, vol. 1, 55–9, 62–6.

Stanisław August had cut to the heart of the dilemma that was shortly to tear the British Empire asunder—the indivisibility of the sovereignty of Parliament. Like most contemporary English thinkers, he could not conceive of a satisfactorily functioning federal state. Sovereignty could have only one source.[67] He was thus a determined foe of the claims of the general *seymik* of Polish Prussia. Although purely dynastic unions were common enough in eighteenth-century Europe, Stanisław August seems not to have considered the possibility regarding the British Empire. At the same time, he declared his allegiance to the great principle of no taxation without representation.

In his first letter to Joseph and Charles Yorke after his election, Stanisław August wrote: 'j'ai le noble et ardent desir de faire ce qu'il [Montesquieu] a écrit.'[68] Catherine II might have written the same, but the task before Stanisław was radically different from Catherine's wish to introduce modern judicial principles into her empire. For Stanisław August, the separation of powers entailed not the creation of a legislature or judiciary independent of the monarch, but the establishment of a proper executive, which would not be subordinated directly to the Seym. Stanisław August, let us recall, saw in the English constitution an effective executive under royal direction, and a healthy Parliament, neither of them subordinate to the other, but mutually dependent. Stanisław August had no prospect of achieving more and was well aware of the fact. Nor, on the basis of the above evidence, did he want to. There is no suggestion that he wished to restrict either the *legislative* power of the Seym, or its exclusive right to vote taxes. That cuts him off from ambitions of absolutism, understood in any meaningful sense, and keeps him within the sphere of mixed or limited monarchies such as the English one. The idea of a would-be absolutist disingenuously professing his belief in the natural rights of mankind is unlikely, to say the least. A comparison of reform in Poland and the absolutist states would no doubt prove illuminating, but we cannot call Stanisław August a would-be enlightened absolutist.

IV

Before proceeding to the fate of the early attempts to reform the Commonwealth, let us consider the propagation of English models in support of reform, and their reception by the *szlachta*. The royal camp's main

---

[67] See Pocock, '1776: The revolution against parliament', in *Virtue, Commerce and History*.
[68] 6 Oct. 1764, BL Add. 35433, f. 74.

instrument was *Monitor*. After his election, Stanisław August turned to Adam Kazimierz Czartoryski and Ignacy Krasicki to set up a periodical which would campaign for reform in all areas of Polish life. The first number of *Monitor* appeared in March 1765. Setting aside for the moment its links with the *Spectator*,[69] let us take a look at the role played by England in *Monitor*'s political propaganda in the first years of its existence, when it enjoyed the full backing of Stanisław August.[70]

In its fifth and sixth numbers, *Monitor* boldly attacked the lack of social mobility in Poland. Economic development depended on the freedom and education given to plebeians. For example, in the greatest powers of Europe—England and France—most lawyers were townsmen. The seventh number explained that Polish townsmen lacked any incentive to gain the education and expertise necessary for a successful legal career—in contrast to the power and wealth achieved by their Dutch counterparts. The author's recollection of his own voyage to Holland identifies him as the king.[71] A few months later, Felix Łoyko used arguments formulated by the English economic theorist Josiah Tucker to demonstrate that the population and riches of a country depended on its laws, and in particular the rights given to its various social estates.[72] At the beginning of the new year, Łoyko marshalled an array of statistics to demonstrate Poland's fiscal and military weakness compared to other European states, of which he considered England the most powerful. He saw the source of England's spectacular economic growth and abundance of money in mercantilist legislation, especially export bounties on wheat, and in the welcome given to the Huguenots after the revocation of the Edict of Nantes. If only Poland had done the same . . .[73] In general, Łoyko expressed in print what Andrzej Zamoyski had decided to leave unsaid at the Convocation Seym.

Łoyko's praise of England, particularly in connection with religious toleration, provoked a furious reply from within the episcopate. An *Antimonitor* rolled off the press, which denounced the 'newly fashionable

[69] See below, pp. 187–9.

[70] What follows is based mainly upon G. Chomicki, 'Rola propagandowa obrazu Anglii w publicystyce politycznej "Monitora" (1765–1785)', *ZNUJ*, 943 (1990), and idem, 'Wpływy angielskie' (n. 4), 66–106.

[71] *'Monitor' 1765–1785: Wybór tekstów*, ed. E. Aleksandrowska (Wrocław, 1976), 1765, nos. 5–7. E. Aleksandrowska, 'Na tropie autorstwa króla w "Monitorze"', *Pam. Lit.*, 82 (1991), no. 2, 189–92, also advances stylistic evidence in support of the royal authorship of no. 7.

[72] *Monitor*, 1765, nos. 36 and 37. Łoyko made use of a French translation of Tucker's *The Elements of Commerce and Theory of Taxes* (1755).

[73] *Monitor*, 1766, nos. 2–13.

logic': '*Monitor* likes that nation the most, although it seems that it is a sewer of all sects, errors, and heresies.' God grant, it continued, that Catholics in Britain would suffer no more persecution than dissidents in Poland. A letter from 'Prawdzicki' ('Trueman') made much the same point.[74] The charge was not without justice, and using England as a model of religious toleration was foolhardy. Sarmatia's traditional antagonism towards Protestant England had recently been aggravated by Britain's representations on behalf of the dissidents at the Coronation Seym.[75] It was further inflamed when, despite Wroughton's reservations, Britain joined Prussia, Sweden, and Denmark in supporting Russia's demands for the political equality of the dissidents at the Seym of 1766.[76] One author wrote that England would not accept Catholics even as humble soldiers, and that the four powers had no moral right to interfere.[77]

In August 1765, Adam Kazimierz Czartoryski praised English schools and suggested that Polish Piarists and Jesuits might be sent for further studies not only to France and Italy, but also to England. He was careful to add that he was sure that they would not be 'Lutheranized' or 'Calvinized' and would only bring back to Poland that which was good and useful, and that youth would not fall prey to heresy. Nevertheless, Johann Heyne, the agent of Prince Xavier of Saxony, reported from Warsaw that 'clergymen and laymen alike are unhappy with this article.'[78]

The 'economic comments' at the end of the *Kalendarz warszawski na rok 1765* ('Warsaw almanac for the year 1765') proposed the abolition of serfdom in order to impove the state of the economy, and quoted the example of England in support. Ludwik Osieńko, an enraged 'patriot', sent a letter to be read out at the *seymik* of Brańsk in 1766, which copied it virtually word for word into its instruction: 'after the destruction of the noble estate, a peasant third estate will be formed in imitation of

---

[74] *Antimonitor Monitora albo refleksje na pólarkuszek Monitora tegorocznego na kszalty logika nowomodnego 1766 . . .*, quoted after Chomicki, 'Wpływy angielskie', 93. Johann Heyne, the correspondent of Prince Xavier of Saxony, thought that the author was either Stanisław Grabowski, Bishop of Warmia, or Józef Załuski, Bishop of Kiev. '*Monitor' 1765–1785: Wybór*, p. xxxiii.

[75] Wroughton to SA, 28 Nov. 1764, 20 Dec. 1764, Zb. Pop. 216, ff. 35–7. Wroughton to Sandwich, 28 Nov. 1764, 5 Dec. 1764, PRO SP 88/90.

[76] Copies of the declaration in Zb. Pop. 216, ff. 42–3, 45–6. Wroughton to Conway, 23 July 1766, 24 Sept. 1766, 8 Oct. 1766, 15 Oct. 1766, 1 Nov. 1766, Conway to Wroughton, 19 Aug. 1766, 7 Oct. 1766, 17 Oct. 1766, PRO SP 88/92.

[77] *List anonyme do jednego ex Collegio Episcopati* (1767), cited after G. [J.] T. Lukowski, *The Szlachta and the Confederacy of Radom, 1764–1767/68: A Study of the Polish Nobility* (*Antemurale* 21; Rome, 1977), 112.

[78] *Monitor*, 1765, nos. 31, 32. E. Aleksandrowska, 'Relacje Jana Heyne'a agenta księcia Ksawerego saskiego o "Monitorze" (1765–1770)', *Pam. Lit.*, 67 (1976), no. 3, 177–8.

the English, and in consequence the liberty won by the blood of our ancestors will fall and this happy realm will perish.' Although most of the *seymiki* elected envoys supporting the king or the Czartoryskis in 1766, many instructions explicitly forbade the abolition of serfdom.[79]

Without doubt, Krasicki was conscious of the hostile reception that English models had encountered when he adapted fragments of *De l'esprit des lois* in a series for *Monitor* in 1768. He left out all of Montesquieu's comments on the English constitution in Book 11. Instead, he inserted his own opinion that the English Parliament and Polish Seym were very similar. Elsewhere though, he repeated Montesquieu's approval of the proportionality of punishment to the crime in the English judicial system, and joined Montesquieu's praise of the liberties of the English with his maxim that it is worth paying heavy taxes for political freedom.[80]

From Zamoyski's speech to Krasicki's adaptations, the royal circle thus avoided openly recommending the English constitution as a model. This was partly because *Monitor* did not concern itself much with constitutional questions. The wish not to alarm Catherine II may also have played a part. The main reason, however, was probably the fear of offending the *szlachta*. *Monitor*'s early boldness in attacking sacred cows provoked a strong reaction from conservative circles. The idea that Poland might take a lesson in toleration from England caused particular umbrage. It would seem that the reformers realized that, despite the resonance of Konarski's work, the use of the English model to promote constitutional change might well put off rather than convince potential supporters; hence the caution.

V

The Seym of 1766 heralded the shipwreck of Stanisław August's early ambitions. Even before it opened, Catholic fanatics led by the Bishop of Cracow, Kajetan Sołtyk, had stirred the *szlachta* into a ferment against any concessions to the dissidents. Against the advice of the Czartoryskis, who advised winding up the General Confederacy, and Wroughton, who was dismayed at his 'impolitick and ill-timed heroism', Stanisław August pressed on with the plan to exclude the *liberum veto* from the passing

[79] 'Za zniszczeniem stanu szlacheckiego uformowany trzeci stan chłopski zostanie i tak angielski *imitabitus* zwyczaj, *per consequens* wolność krwią antecessorów naszych nabyta upadnie et *sic felix peribit regnum*.' Michalski, 'Propaganda konserwatywna w walce z reformą w początkach panowania Stanisława Augusta', *PH*, 42 (1952), 539–42.

[80] *Monitor*, 1768, nos. 64, 69, 71. Chomicki, 'Rola propagandowa', 46. Aleksandrowska, 'Montesquieu i d'Alembert na łamach Monitorowych', *Pam. Lit.*, 79 (1988), no. 3, 158–60. Cf. *Esprit des lois*, Book VI, ch. 3, XI 1–6, XIII 12, XIX 27.

of new taxes and increases in the army, under the illusion that Austria would resist any Russian attempt at coercion. Zamoyski introduced the bill on 11 October. Repnin and his Prussian colleague, Gédéon Benoît, threatened war. The Czartoryskis gave way, leaving the king isolated, and the Seym reluctantly passed a law explicitly safeguarding the *veto* from further limitation on 22 November. Stanisław August tearfully told Wroughton that it was the 'Death's wound for the Republick'. The General Confederacy was dissolved a week later. Although the Seym passed some other reforms, including the extension of majority voting to most of the *seymiki*, the most fundamental reform of all was delayed for a generation.[81]

Catherine was enraged by the Seym's defiance of her over the dissidents, and Repnin organized two confederacies of dissident nobles who obediently demanded their rights. In order to win over the Catholic *szlachta*, Repnin encouraged rumours that Stanisław August intended to introduce *absolutum dominium* on the back of a peasant rebellion. Such fears were given credence by some vigorous articles in *Monitor* that year. He also set up a Catholic confederacy at Radom with Karol Radziwiłł as marshal.[82] The Radomians hoped to dethrone the hated 'tyrant' Poniatowski, and overturn the reforms passed since 1764. To their dismay, at the extraordinary Seym of 1767–8 Repnin brutally forced them to pass legislation granting the hated dissidents political equality, to acknowledge Stanisław August as king, and even to swallow some minor improvements in the condition of the peasants (the lord lost his power to sentence his peasants to death, and the death penalty was introduced—theoretically—for nobles who murdered peasants). The king picked up the confederate leaders' idea of a permanent council, aiming to turn it into an effective organ of central government, but Russia eventually vetoed the idea at Prussian insistence. Russia imposed and guaranteed a new settlement, effectively freezing the constitution. Cardinal laws, which included the *veto* and the basic liberties of the *szlachta*, were to be immutable. *Materiae status*, including the army, taxes, and foreign and commercial relations, were to be decided unanimously. Other matters, termed 'economic', were subject to majority voting. At least the *liberum rumpo* was gone, and Stanisław August had managed to save the treasury and military commissions and his powers of nomination. Those *seymiki* left untouched by the legislation

[81] Michalski, *Historia sejmu*, 356–9. Idem, 'Problematyka aliansu', 715–19. Rostworowski, 'Edukacja ostatniego króla', in *Popioły i korzenie*, 69–71. Czaja, *Lata wielkich nadziei*, 94–6. Konopczyński, *Liberum Veto*, 413–15. Madariaga, *Russia in the Age of Catherine*, 196–9. Wroughton to Conway, 12 Nov. 1766, 26 Nov. 1766, PRO SP 88/92.
[82] Michalski, 'Propaganda', 543–4.

of 1764 and 1766 were now to introduce majority voting. A brake had been put on constitutional reform, but it had not been put into reverse.[83]

Renewal was spreading tentatively to most areas of Polish life. The courts functioned more speedily and justly, endemic lawlessness began to wane, and many magnates felt the foundation of their power—the dependency of the lower and middling *szlachta* on rich and powerful protectors —beginning to subside. The abuses of the hetmans had been curbed, if not yet eliminated. The treasury commissions and commissions *boni ordinis* set about beginning to create what we would call infrastructure. The economy was growing. The process of enlightenment continued in education, accelerated by the patronage of the new king. Despite the Russian guarantee and the entrenched conservatism of the *szlachta*, the spirit of reform bid fair to 'create anew the Polish world'.[84] However, Catherine's pride had got the better of her sense in the dissident affair, and she had overplayed her hand. She had never understood Roman Catholicism, and even before the Seym ended, a confederacy was proclaimed in defence of the faith and liberties of the *szlachta* at Bar in Podolia on 29 February 1768. The confederacy engulfed the entire Commonwealth in anarchy for over four years, and provoked war between Russia and Turkey, setting off an international chain reaction that culminated in the First Partition of Poland. Sarmatia's fond illusions about its assured place in the European state system were shattered, and Stanisław August was cured of his youthful impetuousity. The conditions for reform were henceforth to be very different.

What was the role of the English constitution as a model for reform up to 1768? Its influence on the constitutional reforms that the Czartoryskis and Stanisław August actually enacted was minor. The model for the treasury and military commissions was probably the colleges functioning in many European states. Most of the other reforms were straightforward repairs of obvious deficiencies, which required no foreign example. Russia would permit no more. The English model was central, however, to the fundamental overhaul of the Commonwealth that the reformers wished to undertake. The Seym was to be restored to health by English medicine—by the adoption not only of majority voting, but also of procedure

---

[83] Lukowski, *Confederacy of Radom*, 64–257. Madariaga, *Russia in the Age of Catherine*, 199–202. Michalski, *Historia sejmu*, 359–69. Czaja, *Lata wielkich nadziei*, 97–103. Konopczyński, *Liberum Veto*, 415–19. Idem, *Geneza i ustanowienie Rady Nieustającej*, 105–24. Lityński, *Sejmiki ziemskie*, 32–4.

[84] Czaja gives a notably optimistic assessment of the results of reform up to 1772. *Lata wielkich nadziei*, 106–18.

based on the English. It would always be ready to assemble, and its members would represent the entire Commonwealth, not merely their electors. Beyond this common ground, Konarski, the Czartoryskis, and Poniatowski all interpreted the English constitution differently. Konarski was a political kinsman of the Country opposition, the Czartoryskis may well have fancied themselves in the role of the 'Old Corps' Whigs, while Stanisław noted the strength of the royal prerogative and the possibilities such a constitution created for the harmonious co-operation of king and nation. Whatever mistakes he can be accused of making in the first years of his reign, Stanisław August did not become a putative absolutist. He remained faithful to the English model.

After Konarski, the English constitution was not used as an argument to support reform for many years. This was most probably because Sarmatia's traditional suspicions of England remained to be overcome. 'The English are less secure than the others, as they are esteemed the arch-enemies of the holy faith,' wrote Charles Lee from Warsaw during the Confederacy of Bar.[85] The violent reaction in 1767–72 against Stanisław August, the Czartoryskis, and their reforms showed that fundamental constitutional reform was not only blocked by Russia. The mentality of the *szlachta* would have to be transformed before the nation could work out an effective form of government for itself. The Russian guarantee re-imposed after 1772 allowed that transformation time to take effect.

[85] Lee to G. Colman, 8 May 1769, *Lee Papers*, vol. 1, 81.

8

Stanisław August and English Literature

His Majesty had hitherto talked French but now he did me the honour to converse with me in English, which he speaks remarkably well. . . . He is familiarly acquainted with our best authors, and his enthusiastic admiration of Shakespeare gave me the most convincing proofs of his intimate acquaintance with our language, and his taste for the beauties of genuine poetry.[1]

William Coxe's encomiums are often quoted to demonstrate Stanisław August's knowledge and love of the English language and literature, and they fit into the picture of a poet king that Jean Fabre tried to turn on its head. Fabre and others have attributed the impression of Coxe and other travellers partly to flattery and partly to Stanisław August's extraordinary memory of books he had not read since his youth.[2] Certainly, literature was but one of the king's many interests. Out of more than 15,000 volumes in the Royal Library at the castle, there were 2,000 of modern literature. History, with 2,500 volumes, law, theology, philosophy, natural history, geography, art, and the classics were also present in strength.[3] Stanisław August would have digests read to him on various topics as he was being dressed in the morning. Belles-lettres were reserved for evenings or for short breaks at his hunting lodge at Kozienice.[4] The impact of English thought on Stanisław August and his cultural activity was wideranging, and reinforced by his command of English, which was of an unusually high standard.

I

In 1765 Charles Lee wrote to his sister:

[The king] knows the English language perfectly, altho' from want of practice, he does not speak it fluently. He is intimately conversant with all our best writers, and swears by Shakespeare, upon which subject you will readily imagine I shall

[1] Coxe, *Travels*, vol. 1, 174.

[2] Fabre, *Stanislas-Auguste Poniatowski*, 165, 378–9, 606, 650. J. Pawłowiczowa, 'Jeszcze o Teatralskim', *Pamiętnik Teatralny*, 15 (1966), 177.

[3] *Biblioteka Stanisława Augusta na zamku warszawskim: Dokumenty*, ed. J. Rudnicka (Archiwum Literackie, 26; Wrocław, 1988), 218–19.

[4] Zamoyski, *Last King*, 241.

not quarrel with him. Prince Czartorinsky [*sic*] with whom I live, speaks and writes English fluently and critically. He has almost every book in our language at his fingers ends.[5]

The comparison is not unfair. Adam Kazimierz Czartoryski's literary activity included adapting his friend David Garrick's farce *A Miss in her Teens* for the theatre of the cadet school as *Panna na wydaniu* (1774). His erudite introduction, strongly influenced by Addison's essays in the *Spectator*, was of vital importance for the formation of Polish theatrical criticism.[6] Czartoryski's English letters, apart from the archaism of using 'þe' for 'the', shine in their fluency and accuracy.[7]

Czartoryski had time enough for scholarship, whereas Stanisław August had not. Particularly in the early years of his reign, the king would most often write to his English correspondents in French, but was happy to receive their letters in either language. Later, when he had the services of Lewis Littlepage, the American would sometimes translate the king's French into English.[8] Returning from Grodno after the 1784 Seym, Stanisław August excused himself to Harris for not writing in English: 'Pardon, si Je ne Vous repond pas en Anglois. Mon Boyer est egaré, et Je suis pressé de Vous écrire. Mais je Vous entend parfaitement, et je serai toujours charmé de Vous lire en Anglois.'[9] Boyer's *Dictionnaire royal* was one of a number of English dictionaries and grammars acquired for the royal library, of which the most substantial were Dr Johnson's two folio volumes.[10] Stanisław August's own English drafts are more stilted than Czartoryski's, more dependent upon French, and contain the occasional mistake. In one letter, we find 'positif', 'caracter', 'Englisch', and 'the Major Green' instead of 'Major Greene'.[11] The following letter, written to the Marquess of Lansdowne in 1786, is short enough to be quoted in full, and is representative of the king's efforts. The improvement since his first 'billet' to Charles Yorke is noticeable.

[5] Warsaw, 3 Apr. 1765, *Lee Papers*, vol. 1, 38.

[6] Garrick's and Czartoryski's texts are compared by Bernacki, *Teatr, dramat i muzyka*, vol. 2, 17–22. Czartoryski's introduction is reprinted in vol. 1, 21–47. Also see Klimowicz, *Oświecenie*, 207–9, and Z. Wołoszyńska, 'Adam Kazimierz Czartoryski', in T. Kostkiewiczowa and Z. Goliński (eds.), *Pisarze polskiego Oświecenia* (vol. 1; Warsaw, 1992), 399–431.

[7] e.g. Czartoryski to R. M. Keith, 10 May 1785, BL Eg. 3501, ff. 86–7, 3 Apr. 1786, BL Add. 35356, f. 195.

[8] e.g. SA to Lord Wycombe 21/23 Feb. 1787, Zb. Pop. 183, ff. 646–7.

[9] Białystok, 26 Nov. 1784, Zb. Pop. 182, f. 254.

[10] *Biblioteka Stanisława Augusta*, 103, 82, 108, 213. 'Catalogus Bibliothecae . . . 1783', AKsJP 268, ff. 39–41. 'Katalog wszelkich . . . w Łazienkach . . . książek', AKsJP 270, f. 5, 24.

[11] SA to Harris, 5 June 1786, Zb. Pop. 182, ff. 255–6.

A Mylord Marquis of Lansdown.

I thank you Mylord for your having procur'd me the acquaintance of Mylord Wycombe and Major Greene. Verily these are not common Travellers. You have by that acquired right to my gratitude, which I do add most gladly to the sentiments of high esteeme, your reputation has inspird me, since you have renderd to your Country the very best Service, she was able to receive in the most difficult Circumstances, in which she was involvd, at the time of your Administration.

I wish Heaven may bestow constantly upon Your Son as much happiness, as he is like to bestow upon your Paternal heart. His fellow traveller seems to me a very [*illegible word*] and agreable Person.

I am truly [*illegible*—Mylord?]

> Your most affectionate
> [Stanislaus Augustus K.][12]

Stanisław August was therefore much happier reading and listening in English (when the poor accent of his librarian and reader Marc Reverdil spoiled his enjoyment of *Tristram Shandy*, he consoled Reverdil that perhaps next time he would do better)[13] than writing, and had most trouble in speaking. His English improved rather than worsened with age. Nevertheless, when he read primarily for pleasure, as at Kozienice, he preferred a French translation to an English original.[14]

Among the Polish aristocracy, Stanisław August's knowledge of English was surpassed only by Czartoryski, and perhaps by Jan Potocki. His cousin Izabella Lubomirska had been taught English in her youth by Stormont, but read English literature only in French translation.[15] English works were present in the libraries of the Prince-Bishop of Warmia, Ignacy Krasicki (the 'prince of poets'), and Ignacy Potocki only in French. A study of novels and other representative texts of the Enlightenment in various library inventories and booksellers' catalogues by Zofia Sinko confirms this verdict. Apart from the king and Czartoryski, the poet Kajetan Węgierski had a good selection of English books, Professors Jan Kanty Bogucicki and Jacek Przybylski (a translator of Pope and Milton) possessed a number of works in English, and Seweryn Potocki bought a few titles when in England in 1785. Booksellers offered English originals far

---

[12] Warsaw, 7 June 1786, Zb. Pop. 182, f. 340.

[13] A. Kraushar, *Dwa szkice historyczne z czasów Stanisława Augusta* (2 vols.; Warsaw, 1905), vol. 1, 33–4. In 1767 the king insisted that Reverdil take English lessons with one William Ignatius Arundel, a correspondent of Bishop J. A. Załuski. *Biblioteka Stanisława Augusta*, 37.

[14] 'Biblioteka Kozienicka Stanisława Augusta', ed. J. Wojakowski, *Z badań nad polskimi księgozbiorami historycznymi: Szkice i materiały*, 5 (1981), 105.

[15] *Mémoires*, vol. 1, 361–2. Majewska-Maszkowska, *Mecenat Izabelli Lubomirskiej*, 24–5, 295–6.

less frequently than French translations.[16] After encountering the Polish élite at the Grodno Seym of 1784, Georg Forster told a correspondent that all of them spoke French, one German, and a few ('ein paar') English.[17] Due to a lack of teachers, the situation could not improve quickly. John Lind taught a limited amount of English for a few years at the cadet school, but he had no successor. Father Julian Antonowicz taught English at the Basilians' school at Włodzimierz, and wrote the first English grammar in Polish. He lamented the general lack of knowledge of English in the bilingual dedication. This he offered at Stanisław August's desire to Charles Whitworth, who accepted the book during a journey to Kaniów to meet Catherine II in 1787.[18] The main foreign languages taught in the schools of the Commission for National Education were French, German, and Latin. Nor did English feature on the curricula of the reformed universities of Cracow and Wilno, although, as we have seen, some of the professors knew the language.[19] Wider knowledge of English was not a priority for Stanisław August. Despite his insistence that foreign languages form the basis of the education of his natural son Stanisław Grabowski, the boy was not taught English.[20]

[16] *Inwentarz Biblioteki Ignacego Krasickiego z 1810 r.*, ed. S. Graciotti and J. Rudnicka (Wrocław, 1973). Rudnicka, *Biblioteka Ignacego Potockiego* (Wrocław, 1953), 21, 32, 38, 59, 63. Z. Sinko, 'Powieść zachodnioeuropejska w Polsce stanisławowskiej na podstawie inwentarzy bibliotecznych i katalogów', *Pam. Lit.*, 57 (1966), 581–624, table between 620 and 621. Cf. Rudnicka, 'W związku z artykulem Zofii Sinko "Powieść w Polscc stanisławowskiej"', *Pam. Lit.*, 58 (1967), which stresses the difficulties of generalization, especially from booksellers' catalogues.

[17] Forster to T. Heyne, 18 Nov. 1784, quoted by Maurer, *Aufklärung und Anglophilie*, 383. Forster, who was a professor at Wilno in 1784–7, was among those who borrowed works in English from the Royal Library between 1785 and 1791. The others were Prince Stanisław Poniatowski, the king's mistress Elżbieta Grabowska, Sobolewska, Alexandrowicz, Joseph Duhamel, Puzyna, the king's secretary Florian Dembowski, and Littlepage. *Biblioteka Stanisława Augusta*, 149–206.

[18] *Grammatyka dla Polakow chcących się uczyć angielskiego języka* (Warsaw, 1788). *Powitanie Nayiaśnieyszego Stanisława Augusta Krola i Pana naszego przeieżdżaiącego przez Włodzimierz do Kaniowa od szkoł tamecznych pod dozorem Bazylianow . . . roku 1787 dnia 7 marca z aktow szkolnych wyięte* (Warsaw, 1787). J. I. Kraszewski, *Podróż króla Stanisława Augusta do Kaniowa w r. 1787 podlug listów Kazimierza . . . Platera, starosty inflantskiego* (Wilno, 1860), 53.

[19] K. Mrozowska, *Szkoła Rycerska Stanisława Augusta (1765–1794)* (Wrocław, 1961), 81, 148. A. Jobert, *La Commission d'Éducation Nationale en Pologne (1773–1794): Son oeuvre d'instruction civique*, 261, 303–4. Chamcówna, *Uniwersytet Jagielloński, passim*. Jan Śniadecki learned English in Göttingen in order to read works on geometry. 'Jana Śniadeckiego zycie, przez niego samego opisane', in *Korespondencja Jana Śniadeckiego*, vol. 1, ed. L. Kamykowski (Cracow, 1932), 12. See also several letters written in English to Tadeusz Bukaty in vol. 2, ed. M. Chamcówna and S. Tync (Wrocław, 1954). Andrzej Trzciński translated Joseph Priestley from English. See below, p. 243.

[20] See I. Szybiak, 'Edukacja Stanisława Grabowskiego w świetle korespondencji Stanisława Augusta', *Wiek Oświecenia*, 9 (1993).

II

The Royal Library's collection of English literature was extensive and of a high standard. It contained Shakespeare's *Works* in Pope and Warburton's 1747 edition (possibly part of Charles Yorke's present in 1754), George Stevens's 1791 edition, and Le Tourneur's French translation of 1776–83.[21] Shakespeare's contemporaries were represented by Spenser and Jonson, in English. Apart from the most famous and popular authors—Milton, Dryden, Pope, Addison, Swift, Gray, Young, Richardson, Fielding, and Sterne—generally present in both English and French, either as complete *Works* or individually, the library was also notable for its holdings of Restoration drama—all in English. The periodicals included the *Spectator*, *Guardian*, and *Freeholder*, and the current *Monthly Review* and *Critical Review*. Stanisław August also possessed Defoe's *Robinson Crusoe* and MacPherson's *Poems of Ossian*, both in English and French, Chesterfield's *Letters*, and Horace Walpole's *Castle of Otranto*. There were Polish translations of Milton's *Paradise Lost*, Pope's *Essay on Man* and *Essay on Criticism*, Mrs Sheridan's *Memoirs of Miss Sidney Bidulph*, Young's *Poem on the Last Day*, and Chesterfield's *Indian Philosopher*. Also worthy of note are Pope's Homer and Dryden's Virgil in English, and Dr Johnson's *Lives of English Poets*.[22]

The poetry of the ancients remained closest to Stanisław August's heart. In 1785–91, the king himself borrowed no novels from the library, only poetry. He took out Theocritus, Terence, Plautus, Ovid, Virgil, Zanoni, and Racine, all in French, and Milton's *Paradise Lost . . .* in Latin.[23] The library at Kozienice 'was without doubt of a recreational nature' in which belles-lettres, often of a frivolous nature, predominated. Nevertheless, Rousseau and Voltaire took the lead, with nine and six works respectively out of 149 in September 1785. Apart from a French translation of James Thomson's *The Seasons*, there was no English poetry or drama. *Clarissa*, *Tom Jones*, *Sentimental Journey*, and *Tristram Shandy*, together with Eliza Haywood's *Betsy Tatless*, all in French, did something to redress the balance. One or two French sentimental romances on English themes were also present, and the less elevated side of Stanisław August's reading is

---

[21] Bernacki, *Teatr, dramat i muzyka*, vol. 2, 167. The library also possessed *Shakespeare Illustrated, or the Novels and Histories on which the Plays are Founded, Collected and Translated from the Original Authors with Critical Remarks . . . by* [Charlotte Lennox] (3 vols.; London, 1753–4).

[22] *Biblioteka Stanisława Augusta*, 67–8, 76–80, 99–100, 144–5, 162–6, 193–4. AKsJP 268, ff. 48–62. AKsJP 270, ff. 10–23.

[23] *Biblioteka Stanisława Augusta*, 164–5.

conveyed by Anthony Hamilton's *Mémoires de la vie du cte de Grammont, contenant particulièrement l'histoire amoureuse de la cour de l'Angleterre sous . . . Charles II.*[24] A further clue to the king's own tastes lies in the part of his library he took to St Petersburg. From his collection of English literature he selected Pope's *Works* in both English and French, and *Paradise Lost* in French.[25]

Stanisław August's ability to quote *aptly* suggests something deeper than the memory of his youthful reading. In 1779 he told August Sułkowski to make the most of his stay in Paris, in studying the spectacle of the fallen power of the Bourbons: 'On peut vraiment Vous dire cequel Milton fait dire par l'ange à Adam, dans son vision Prophetique: Look, look, because you have much to see.'[26] When away from Warsaw in 1777, reflecting on the amount of correspondence coursing between himself and his cabinet, Stanisław August wrote to Ogrodzki: 'Vous scavez que Swift a dit, il y a longtems, que les gens qui habitent les Capitales sont sujets à oublier quelquefois leurs amis qui sont à la Campagne, mais que jamais les Campagnards n'oublient leurs amis en ville. Et c'est ce qui fait que depuis trois Semaines, vous recevez beaucoup plus d'estafettes que ci-devant.'[27] He did not expect Grimm to send 'quatre graves dissertations' every month. 'Une Chanson, une mauvaise Chanson—a produit le Chef d'Oeuvre d'un Inconnu: et vous connoitrés sans doute le beau sermon de Yorick qu'on trouve au milieu de tout le fatras de Tristram Shandy.'[28]

If Stanisław August enjoyed *Tristram Shandy* despite its chaotic structure, he was plainly dismissive about MacPherson's *Poems of Ossian*. The king wrote in an exasperated tone to Mazzei: 'Le Cte Jean Potocki a deja été en Angleterre, mais au lieu de bien étudier ce qui pourroit être util à imiter pour nous dans ce gouvernement, il est allé puisque dans les îles orcades, pour y verifier les traces des pretendus poemes d'Ocean [*sic*].'[29] This was more than the grumbling of an older generation unable to come to terms with the latest youthful crazes, although it is noteworthy that MacPherson did not fool him. Nor was his disapproval primarily aesthetic.

[24] 'Biblioteka Kozienicka', 106. [25] *Biblioteka Stanisława Augusta*, 144–5.

[26] 11 Aug. 1779, BCzart. 712, f. 385. Also quoted by Fabre, *Stanislas-Auguste Poniatowski*, 650 n. 46.

[27] 20 Sept. 1777, BCzart. 799, vol. 3, ff. 2321–3. Also quoted by Fabre, *Stanislas-Auguste Poniatowski*, 650 n. 47.

[28] 9 May 1770, Zb. Pop. 221, ff. 338–9.

[29] 26 Feb. 1791, PAU 8, f. 132. Also quoted by Fabre, *Stanislas-Auguste Poniatowski*, 371. According to Fabre, 650 n. 48, the Potocki in question was not in fact Jan, but his brother Seweryn.

The king's views were pluralist enough, and it was the paladin of Polish classicism, Krasicki, who first attempted a Polish translation of Ossian.[30] Nothing could express Stanisław August's didactic priorities better. Young men should travel to England to learn, so that they could be useful to their own country in future, and not to indulge their imagination. Moreover, England's main value was in her constitution, not her literature.

Stanisław August's admiration of Shakespeare presents us with the most problems. In Jean Fabre's opinion, the king hardly ever read him, and contented himself with collecting editions of his works and putting up a statue of him at the amphitheatre at Łazienki (to which one might add his medallion in the theatre in the Orangerie alongside Sophocles, Racine, and Molière, and some engravings sent from England in 1792).[31] Certainly, Stanisław August was not forthcoming with references to Shakespeare in his correspondence, and his absence from the selection taken to St Petersburg is striking. If Shakespeare was the English author most honoured by the king, then Milton was probably the most read. Yet Stanisław August's elaborate homage to the Bard was surely more than a diplomatic gesture to visiting Englishmen. Let us remind ourselves of the king's opinion of Shakespeare:

Je me sentais très attaché, très amusé et souvent très bien prêché et je conclus que je pouvais retirer du plaisir et de l'utilité même d'une pièce, qui est censée durer plus d'un jour et dont la scène est supposée se transporter dans plus d'un lieu, pourvu que l'auteur connaisse bien les moeurs, les passions, les travers des hommes et aussi les vertus dont ils sont capables; qu'il fasse parler ses acteurs d'une manière qui augmente à mes yeux le prix de la vertu, de la bonté et de la sagesse et que le tout me soit rendu avec le plus de vraisemblance possible. Or, je pense que les détails, dont les pièces anglaises, et surtout celles de Shakespeare sont remplies et qui servent si fort à constater le costume de temps et du pays que la pièce représente, me font beaucoup plus d'illusion que cette uniformité toujours élevée, et par la même boursouflée du style des tragédies françaises. Or, sans illusion, il n'est point de plaisir théatral.[32]

Stanisław August's contemporaries praised Shakespeare's genius but severely censured his methods. Czartoryski, in his introduction to *Panna na wydaniu*, admired Shakespeare's talents but criticized his neglect of the rules:

---

[30] Sinko, 'Ignacy Krasicki tłumaczem Osjana', *Pam. Lit.*, 61 (1970).

[31] Fabre, *Stanislas-Auguste Poniatowski*, 378. M. Kwiatkowski, *Stanisław August: Król-architekt* (Wrocław, 1983), 209, 220. *Biblioteka Stanisława Augusta*, 131.

[32] *Mémoires*, vol. 1, 112–13. The passage was added in the margin in or after 1775.

Nature endowed him generously with the most exquisite talents. Learning he did not call to their aid. For this reason also, his works lack the regularity and control which ensue from the knowledge and reasonable application of the rules, but what a rare gift of expression![33]

Czartoryski's wife Izabella went so far in her enthusiasm for Shakespeare and his untamed genius as to buy two pieces of his reputed chair, while visiting his house in Stratford-upon-Avon. Nevertheless, even she did not spare him:

It is true that in his works it is possible to perceive the joining of the most beautiful thoughts with the basest expressions. His plays are miraculously beautiful, mixed with absurdities, which display serious inabilities and vulgar boorishness, but all this is to be attributed rather to the taste of his age, than to the author . . .[34]

Ignacy Krasicki thought much the same: 'sometimes among the crudest errors there are such gems, that they raise the workman above a master.'[35] The list could be extended, although not far. In general, the shadow of Voltaire dominated what Polish Shakespeare criticism there was until the end of the eighteenth century. Shakespeare was a genius, but also a barbarian, and he should certainly not be imitated. The unknown author of the novel *Polak w Paryżu* (1787)—itself an adaptation of the Irishman James Rutlidge's *La Quinzaine anglaise à Paris* (1776)—was exceptional in writing that, thanks to Shakespeare, English tragedies were free from the cold, static, and boring 'action' of the French and instead followed nature.[36]

English critics from Dryden to Johnson saw in Shakespeare a symbol of national pride to rival the prestige of Corneille, Racine, and Molière. Voltaire's censures were patriotically rebutted. The tendency was for criticism of Shakespeare's 'faults' to diminish over time. Nevertheless Dr Johnson, excepting the first two unities, continued to excuse rather than defend them. In general, adherence to the three unities was recommended to young dramatists, but, as Addison put it in the *Spectator* (number 592), 'Our inimitable Shakespeare is a stumbling block to the whole tribe of these rigid critics. Who would not rather read one of his plays, where there is not a single rule of the stage observed, than any production of a

---

[33] Bernacki, *Teatr, dramat i muzyka*, vol. 1, 35.

[34] Quoted after Bernacki, *Shakespeare w Polsce do końca XVIII wieku* (Cracow, 1914), 23. See also Gołębiowska, 'Podróż Izabeli i Adama Jerzego Czartoryskich', 138.

[35] Quoted after Bernacki, *Shakespeare w Polsce*, 31.

[36] Bernacki, 'Shakespeare w Polsce do końca XVIII wieku' (2nd version), in *Teatr, dramat i muzyka*, vol. 2, 168–75. Klimowicz, *Oświecenie*, 260.

modern critic, where there is not one of them violated!' Shakespeare's gravest sins were not his breaking the unities of time and place, but his rambling plots, his figurative language—which contradicted the Augustan ideals of simplicity and clarity—his vulgar jokes, his mixing noble 'tragic' characters with low-born 'comic' ones, and above all, his failure to explicitly propagate virtue. These faults were attributed to the need to appeal to the unrefined taste of his age.[37]

Stanisław August does not fit the role of a revolutionary Shakespeare critic, a precursor of Wordsworth or Goethe. His opinions were remarkably close to those of Dr Johnson. Analysing the king's opinion given in his *Mémoires*, we find the same heavy emphasis upon the propagation of virtue as in Johnson's 1765 preface to Shakespeare's *Works*, even if the king does not criticize Shakespeare on this score, but instead, rather halfheartedly, hides behind the stipulation 'pourvu que l'auteur . . . augmente à mes yeux le prix de la vertu'. It is Shakespeare's knowledge of human nature which both praise the most. The 'heresy' is likewise the questioning of the *necessity* of the unities of time and place and the argument that true illusion is best conveyed by costumes and other details of the time and place in which the play is set. Stanisław August does not seem to have owned Johnson's edition of Shakespeare. He probably became familiar with the preface from the free translation in the *Gazette Littéraire de l'Europe* on 15 November 1765. Only nine months later, on 13 August 1766, a letter by 'Theatralski' was published in *Monitor*. It was a translation of a part of Johnson's remarks on the unities of time and place, apparently in reply to the two previous numbers, which had adopted the traditional standpoint: that a comedy which showed one of the characters sent on a journey from Warsaw to Lwów in the first act and returned in the third or fifth would be imperfect. If the audience could imagine itself in Alexandria for the first act, argued Johnson/ Theatralski, then why could it not imagine itself in Rome for the second? However, Theatralski left out Johnson's opinion that, on closer inspection, the unities should lose the weight and glory they had enjoyed since Corneille, and that perhaps they gave more problems to authors than pleasure to audiences.[38]

'Theatralski' was identified as Krasicki by Bernacki on the basis of a note of Krasicki's with the introduction to the letter in Krasicki's editorial papers. However, does the similarity of Stanisław August's views to

[37] P. A. W. Collins, 'Shakespeare Criticism', in *From Dryden to Johnson*, 376–90.
[38] *'Monitor' 1765–1785: Wybór*, 1766, nos. 63–5, 111–23.

Johnson's clinch the case for royal authorship? The argument of a necessary knowledge of English has been disproved, but that does not rule out Stanisław August. Elżbieta Aleksandrowska has plausibly interpreted the pseudonyms 'Josephus' and 'Rex' in Krasicki's papers, referring to numbers 63–65, as Józef Minasowicz and Stanisław August. As we know that the king wrote a number of articles for *Monitor*, it is probable that Stanisław August made the excellent translation from the French himself.[39] Without doubt, Minasowicz's articles and Theatralski's letter alike were echoes of the discussion between Stanisław August, Czartoryski, Bohomolec, and others over the form of the Polish National Theatre, then newly called into existence. One conclusion of such discussions would have been that the first two unities were a theatrical convention which might be followed with profit, but which should not be adhered to slavishly.[40]

Fabre's view that Stanisław August's taste for Shakespeare, although almost revolutionary in mid-century, had lost its novelty by the 1780s, requires some qualification. Certainly, on a European scale, admiration of Shakespeare raised no eyebrows. Nevertheless, compared with Germany, the reception of Shakespeare in Poland was negligible. Stanisław Trembecki translated Hamlet's soliloquy from Voltaire's French.[41] The few productions of Shakespeare in eighteenth-century Poland came mainly from German sources. A Viennese troupe played *King Lear* in Thorn in 1701, and they may well have also played to the German-speaking patriciates of other towns as well.[42] *Romeo and Juliet* was performed in Warsaw by visiting Germans in 1774 and 1775, and by Frenchmen in 1778. *Macbeth* and *King Lear* were played in German in 1793. *The Merry Wives of Windsor* was the first play to appear on the stage in Polish, in 1782, after suffering due classicization at the hands of Collot d'Herbois, who himself used Le Tourneur's French translation. No further plays appeared in Polish until after the Third Partition.[43] Stanisław August's public glorification of Shakespeare did not entail his propagation on the national stage, although adaptations and originals of French pieces abounded. The king

---

[39] S. Ozimek, 'Kto był Theatralski?', *Pamiętnik Teatralny*, 5 (1956) suggested royal authorship, an idea dismissed by Pawłowiczowa, 'Jeszcze o Teatralskim'. Aleksandrowska, 'Na tropie autorstwa króla', 186–8, re-opened the case.

[40] Pawłowiczowa, 'Jeszcze o Teatralskim', 177. Klimowicz, *Oświecenie*, 98–9.

[41] S. Trembecki, *Pisma wszystkie*, ed. J. Kott (2 vols.; Wrocław, 1953), vol. 2, 58.

[42] J. Komorowski, 'Polskie szekspiriana', *Pamiętnik Teatralny*, 40 (1991), 5–11. Ozimek, 'Kto był Theatralski?', 394–9.

[43] Bernacki, 'Shakespeare w Polsce', in *Teatr, dramat i muzyka*, vol. 2, 177–9. Komorowski, '"Makbet" Shakespeare'a w Polsce: Spis premier 1793–1990', *Pamiętnik Teatralny*, 40 (1991), 76.

assembled a fine collection of engravings depicting scenes and personalities from the English theatre, including two of Garrick as King Lear and Macbeth, and a *Recueil des estampes pour servir aux oeuvres de Shakespear*,[44] but English influence on the National Theatre is hard to discern. The three unities predominated, although there were exceptions. One might say that the rules had to be learnt before they could be broken. It was after all at the end of his reign that Stanisław August gave public, sculptural expression to his taste, not at the beginning, when the National Theatre was born. Essentially, Shakespeare was neither didactic nor polished enough to be useful in the fight with Sarmatian prejudice.[45]

Stanisław August's taste for English literature was characterized above all by its catholicity; Shakespeare, Milton, and Pope, with Swift, Sterne, Richardson, Fielding, and perhaps Young, Gray, and Thomson. Such a selection defies classification. The 'metaphysical', the 'Augustan', and the 'sentimental' are inadequate terms and make awkward bedfellows. It would be misleading to read anything strongly pre-romantic into the choice of Shakespeare and Milton, whose popularity gained strength in Poland only from the 1790s. As with the visual arts, Stanisław August refused to be tied down to any one style, and instinctively reacted against aesthetic dogmatism of any kind. Like Pope's ideal critic, he was 'blest with a taste exact, yet unconfin'd'.[46]

III

Stanisław August's taste for English literature remained largely a private matter. The king gave his backing to Polish translations of Montesquieu, Blackstone, Locke, and to Adam Naruszewicz's Horace, not to translations of English novels or poetry. The disproportion is evident from the catalogue of the king's 'Bibliotheca Polona'. Translations of English literature appeared independently of the king.[47] Jan Albertrandi's translation of *Robinson Crusoe* in 1769 swiftly followed Feutry's 1766 French translation.[48] The other main novels appeared much later: *Gulliver's Travels* in 1784, *Roderick Random* in 1785, *Memoirs of Miss Sidney Bidulph*

[44] J. Wyleżyńska, 'Mezzotinta angielska', in *Polska i Anglia: Stosunki kulturalno-artystyczne*, 53–5. 'Catalogue du Cabinet des Estampes (1793)', AKsJP 214, ff. 21, 52, 130. 'Livres demandées à M. Bukaty', BCzart. 938, f. 503.

[45] Ozimek, 'Kto był Theatralski?', 394, 399–400. Klimowicz, *Oświecenie*, 98–9, 214. See also K. Wierzbicka-Michalska, *Teatr w Polsce w XVIII wieku* (vol. 1 of T. Sievert (ed.), *Dzieje teatru polskiego*) (Warsaw, 1977), 75–6, 95, 143, 154, 219–20.

[46] Collins, 'Shakespeare Criticism', 384.

[47] APP 139. On the difficulties in establishing the role of patrons in the choice of works translated, see J. Ziętarska, 'Przekład—adaptacja' in *Słownik literatury polskiego Oświecenia*, 478.

[48] See above, p. 54.

in 1786, *Joseph Andrews* and *Amelia* in 1787, and *Tom Jones* in 1793, all scarred along the way to a greater or lesser degree by efforts to refine them for French taste. Richardson and Sterne (and translations from English) had to wait until the next century.[49] Pope's *Essay on Criticism* was first translated into Polish by Franciszek Podoski in 1787. Three years later, Professor Jacek Przybylski rather ponderously translated it directly from the English, publishing the original opposite the translation. Ignacy Bykowski translated the *Rape of the Lock* in 1788. Five translations of *Eloisa to Abelard* appeared between 1784 and 1795. The *Essay on Man* was translated by Podoski in 1787, by Father Antoni Cyankiewicz in 1788, and into prose by J. Targoński in 1789.[50] Franciszek Dmochowski translated Young's *Poem on the Last Day* in 1785 and Przybylski translated Milton's *Paradise Lost* in 1791.[51] Whether in Polish or French, however, the fashion for English literature in Poland owed little or nothing to the efforts of Stanisław August. It was a general phenomenon of the Enlightenment, and at least to start with, an expression of the power of French cultural models on the Polish aristocracy.

Stanisław August's own literary programme was given its clearest expression in *Zabawy Przyjemne i Pożyteczne* ('Pastimes pleasant and instructive'), Poland's first literary magazine, which appeared at the beginning of 1770. The erudite Albertrandi was the first editor, and his aim was to print translations of foreign literature, mixed with some old Polish classics. In 1771 Naruszewicz took over and *Zabawy* became the official organ of the king's Thursday Dinners. Naruszewicz's panegyrics to Stanisław August defended the king and, often using historical motifs, expounded the idea that the state could be revived only by a strengthened monarchy and the spread of education. On such themes, writes Julian Platt, the royal inspiration amounted to more than patronage. As with the visual arts, the king laid down the content of poems, which were given expression by his Parnassus of poets. The end of the magazine in 1777 may be ascribed to Naruszewicz's increasing historical preoccupations, and the consequent lack of editorial authority.[52]

---

[49] Sinko, *Powieść angielska . . . a powieść polska*, 17–57. Klimowicz, *Oświecenie*, 260–2.

[50] M. Dadlez, *Pope w Polsce w XVIII wieku* (Cracow, 1923), 8, 13, 17–18, 27–8.

[51] Sinko, 'Z zagadnień recepcji "Sądu ostatecznego" i "Myśli nocnych" Edwarda Younga', *Pam. Lit.*, 65 (1974), part 2, 95–6. Eadem, *Twórczość Johna Miltona w Oświeceniu polskim* (Warsaw, 1992), 9–29.

[52] J. Platt, *'Zabawy Przyjemne i Pożyteczne' 1770–1777: Zarys monografii pierwszego polskiego czasopisma literackiego* (Gdańsk, 1986), 10–16, 117–72, esp. 148, 172. The Thursday Dinners gathered literati and educational reformers during the 1770s and early 1780s. See R. Kaleta, 'Obiady czwartkowe', in *Słownik literatury polskiego Oświecenia*, 318–22.

Very little English literature found its way onto its pages. Three *Dialogues of the Dead* by Stanisław August's friend George Lyttelton were translated from French and published in the first volume of *Zabawy* in 1770, and again in 1777. One contained a typical enlightened and Stanislavian theme, condemning the conquerors Charles XII and Alexander the Great. Another contained an interesting confrontation of aristocratic vice in the form of an English duellist, and barbarism as personified by a North American Indian. The Indian boasted of killing men, women, and children, which horrified the duellist, but could not understand why the Englishman had killed his best friend over a trifle. Mercury pronounced the duellist worse, for his upbringing could not excuse him. The choice of dialogue represents a dose of common sense applied to the popular image of the noble savage. There is no evidence that either Albertrandi or the king knew the identity of the author, as the French translation used, like the first three English editions, was anonymous. Lyttelton does not seem to have sent Stanisław August a copy of his work, and the king made no reference to the translation when he wrote to Lyttelton in 1772.[53]

Two of Pope's poems were translated: a pastoral on *Winter* (without the name of the author) and an *Ode on Solitude* (by Ignacy Chołoniewski). One of John Gay's fables found its way in via the collection *Abeille du Parnasse, ou recueil de maximes tirées des poètes françaises*. The last volume of *Zabawy* contained eleven fragments of Young's *Night Thoughts*, badly rendered from Le Tourneur's 1769 translation, possibly by a student, in order to fill up a few numbers.[54] Franciszek Dionizy Kniaźnin translated thirty-one of John Owen's Latin epigrams. Four anonymous pieces and a fragment of Brydon's *Tour through Sicily and Italy* complete the modest English input. The Roman and Greek classical poets dominated the translations, with significant contributions coming from French and Polish-Latin literature. The total number of pieces published in *Zabawy* was 915. Fifty-five of those were by Horace and twenty-seven by La Fontaine, Stanisław August's favourite authors. *Zabawy Przyjemne i Pożyteczne* did not do much to popularize English literature in Poland.[55]

[53] Albertrandi also translated and published a fourth dialogue from Lyttelton's volume, by Elizabeth Wortley Montagu. Sinko, *Oświeceni wśród pól elizejskich*, 147–65. Lyttelton, *Dialogues of the Dead*, in *Works* (vol. 1; London, 1774). R. Phillimore, *Memoirs and Correspondence of George, Lord Lyttelton* (2 vols.; London, 1845), vol. 2, 780–2.
[54] E. Aleksandrowska, *Zabawy Przyjemne i Pożyteczne 1770–1777: Monografia bibligraficzna* (Wrocław, 1959), 43, 186, 32, Platt, *'Zabawy Przyjemne i Pożyteczne'* 73–5, Sinko, 'Z zagadnień recepcji . . . Edwarda Younga', 132–5.
[55] Platt, *'Zabawy Przyjemne i Pożyteczne'*, 21–75, 147–8. Aleksandrowska, *Zabawy Przyjemne i Pożyteczne*, 68–72, 40–1, 88, 219–20.

From 1782 to 1792, the most wide-ranging, radical, and successful Polish periodical was *Pamiętnik Historyczno-Polityczny* ('Historical and political recorder'), edited by the ex-Jesuit Piotr Świtkowski. It included informative accounts of foreign countries, foreign news, articles on Polish affairs, and reports of new inventions and discoveries. Particular weight was given to economic and social problems. Świtkowski also brought out *Magazyn Warszawski* in 1784–5, which focused upon literary and artistic matters, and in 1785–6, *Wybór Wiadomości Gospodarskich* ('A selection of economic news'), devoted to agriculture. Taking most of his material from German periodicals such as Archenholtz's *Annalen der Brittischen Geschichte*, Świtkowski was one of the most enthusiastic Anglophiles in Stanislavian Poland. He propagated English models in government, commerce, manufacturing, agriculture, and philosophy, to which we shall return later, and literature.[56]

Pamiętnik Historyczno-Polityczny, *Magazyn Warszawski*, and even *Pamiętnik*'s short-lived successor, *Zabawy Obywatelskie* ('Citizens' diversions'), included synthetic articles on the literature of foreign countries. Świtkowski particularly recommended English and German literature to readers for their 'freshness'.[57] English poetry, he wrote, showed

great and strongly expressed sensibility but little delicacy. Its beauties come from diverse knowledge and experience, not from learned consultation. Compared to the beauties of foreign writings, they are like an English park set against a garden laid out in the French taste. Much in it appears to be disorder and the irregularity is conspicuous—and yet it is a masterly imitation of nature! Only a wise mind will appreciate Milton, a great heart and sensibility Shakespeare, and a keen observer of people of various classes Fielding.[58]

Świtkowski, although praising the force of English literature, was also pointing out the consequent loss of delicacy, and was not attacking the use of rules, but rather opening his readers' minds to other possibilities. Elsewhere, Linguet's criticism of Shakespeare was dismissed as coming from a Frenchman,[59] and a description of the ceremonies organized by Garrick in honour of Shakespeare at Stratford in 1769 was included in an article about the pastimes of the English.[60]

---

[56] I. Homola Dzikowska, *Pamiętnik Historyczno-Polityczny Piotra Świtkowskiego 1782–1792* (Cracow, 1960).

[57] Ibid., 18, 22. The first number of *Zabawy Obywatelskie* featured a translation of Georg Forster's 'Geschichte der englischen Literatur vom Jahr 1788', first published in Archenholtz's *Annalen*. See Maurer, *Aufklärung und Anglophilie*, 389–92.

[58] *Magazyn Warszawski*, 1784, 272–3, quoted by Bernacki, 'Shakespeare w Polsce', in *Teatr, dramat i muzyka*, vol. 2, 169.

[59] *PHP*, 1786, vol. 1, 92–3, quoted by Bernacki, 'Shakespeare w Polsce', vol. 2, 169–70.

[60] *PHP*, 1786, vol. 4, 182–6, quoted by Bernacki, 'Shakespeare w Polsce', vol. 2, 170–1.

As Świtkowski's correspondence and editorial materials are no longer extant, it is difficult to be categorical about his relationship with Stanisław August. The ex-Jesuit began his career as a writer under the wing of the brothers Sułkowski, who were not then on the best of terms with the monarch. Nevertheless, Świtkowski dedicated his first book, *Budowanie wieyskie* ('Building in villages'), to the king in late 1782, and received a gold *Merentibus* medal early in the next year. Although the king headed the list of subscribers from the start, Świtkowski financed his periodicals himself. In February 1788 he appealed to Stanisław August for financial help, and the Commission of National Education promptly raised his salary as a 'retired' professor.[61] On one occasion, some letters from Paris by the Rector of the Jagiellonian University, Felix Oraczewski, were inserted at the king's request. Until the beginning of the Four Year Seym, *Pamiętnik Historyczno-Polityczny* spared no pains to praise the king's activity, and it took his side in politics. The series of articles on England in 1786, particularly those which dealt with the system of government, must have greatly pleased Stanisław August. In 1788–9 Świtkowski began to work closely with the writers grouped around Hugo Kołłątaj, known as the Forge, paying the king less attention.[62] Thus Świtkowski supported Stanisław August and his programme until 1788, but his periodicals were never royal organs, in the way that *Zabawy Przyjemne i Pożyteczne* and *Monitor* were. His propagation of English literature was not, we may conclude, inspired by Stanisław August.

The great exception to this general conclusion, that Stanisław August did not play a significant role in the diffusion of English literature in Poland, is *Monitor*. The king set up this twice-weekly periodical at the beginning of his reign as one of his three main cultural initiatives—alongside the National Theatre and the cadet school. Its purpose was to spread Enlightenment among the *szlachta*. For three years *Monitor* boldly combated Sarmatian prejudice, but the periodical had the stuffing knocked out of it by the Confederacy of Bar, and it retreated from political controversy. Although it went through better and worse periods until 1785, it ceased to play a role in Stanisław August's programme. Stanisław August's closest collaborators were Ignacy Krasicki, then his chaplain, and Czar-

---

[61] Homola Dzikowska, *Pamiętnik . . . Piotra Świtkowskiego*, 12–14, 26–8. The lack of incentive for peasants to improve their dwellings was a frequent topic of enlightened criticism in late 18th-century Europe.

[62] Ibid., 38–9, 154–62. The 1786 cycle on England was largely translated from Archenholtz's *Reise durch England und Italien* (Leipzig, 1785). Libiszowska, *Życie polskie*, 12, 270 nn. 11–12. See Maurer, *Aufklärung und Anglophilie*, 187–91.

toryski. Each prepared a plan for the journal late in 1764, and the king chose Krasicki's.[63]

It has become a commonplace that *Monitor* was modelled on the *Spectator*, but Czartoryski did *Monitor* an injustice years later by dismissing it as nothing more than a poor imitation.[64] The total number of articles borrowed in greater or lesser degree from the *Spectator* was 234 out of 2,162 over the entire period 1765–85, excluding reprints of earlier articles. The total number of articles in the *Spectator* was 635, of which 417 were available to Krasicki in his edition of *Le Spectateur*. Of those, 102 made up practically the entire year of 1772. In *Monitor*'s heyday of 1765–7, when Stanisław August stood four-square behind it, there were not more than thirty-nine adaptations from the *Spectator*. Moreover, the charge of imitation is not only disproved numerically. Zofia Sinko's monograph reveals that the articles taken from the *Spectator* were almost always adapted to Polish needs, sometimes to such an extent that their relationship to the original is difficult to establish.[65]

A periodical established to polish the merchants of London and satirize aristocratic vice could not be transferred to the noble Commonwealth unaltered. *Monitor* had more to accomplish. No merchant was personified in the pages of *Monitor* except in the exotic guise of the *Spectator*'s Sir Jędrzej (Andrew) Fre(e)port; a Polish merchant would have been unthinkable. It was all that *Monitor* could do to explain the importance of merchants and promote trade and industry. The *Spectator*'s Sir Roger de Coverley was a worthy but rather ridiculous figure, and his old-fashioned charity was challenged by Freeport's more industrious spirit. The peasants of Krasicki's Baron de Kowerli were happy and well-treated rather than his servants, and the virtuous and diligent landowner had to be treated more seriously in the Polish context. The *Spectator* proposed better treatment of servants; *Monitor* urged the abolition of serfdom. Most of Addison's natural theology was left out, but superstition was more vigorously combated and religious toleration more enthusiastically promoted. *Monitor* gave less attention to literary matters and to women, but was more preoccupied with the need to promote the arts and sciences and education. Both campaigned for clarity and simplicity in language, but *Monitor* had the task of rescuing Polish from over a century of neglect. In general, *Monitor* was more overtly patriotic and concerned to propagate public

[63] '*Monitor*' *1765–1785: Wybór*, pp. vii–x and *passim*.
[64] '*Monitor*' *1765–1785: Wybór*, p. xiii.
[65] This paragraph and much of the following two are based upon Sinko, '*Monitor*' *wobec angielskiego 'Spectatora*' (Wrocław, 1956).

virtue—a reflection of the greater strength of republicanism in Polish political culture.

The *Spectator*'s programme was closest to *Monitor*'s in its drive to improve
manners and morals, while steering clear of religious puritanism.[66] Both
periodicals encouraged politeness and good manners, but criticized super-
cilious Frenchified 'beaus'. They applied Virtue to everyday life. Noble-
born idlers and profligates were mercilessly satirized, and the value of
time was frequently recalled. They taught the art of conversation, aiming to replace stubbornness with rational and open-minded argument.
Monitor in addition declared war on drunkenness. The improvement of
the manners of the *szlachta* was one of the main elements of Stanisław
August's programme. In some ways, Warsaw played an analogous role to
Addison's 'town' in polishing the 'country', although Polish conditions
could not yet permit a full interaction between the 'country' and the 'city',
such as that between Coverley and Freeport. The 'Country' republicanism which demonized the capital was far more deeply rooted in Poland
than in England, and was more susceptible to the 'patriotic' campaigns
of the Puławy set in the 1780s than to Bolingbroke's and Cobham's in
the 1730s.[67] The English debate over manners was undoubtedly of great
relevance to Stanisław August, as the account of his visit to England in
his *Mémoires* shows. *Monitor* thus drew upon an ideal source for promoting their improvement. So was it the king who pointed to the *Spectator*
as a particularly fruitful source of material for the campaign to improve
manners?

Krasicki actually wrote most of the adaptations from the *Spectator*,[68]
but there is nothing in his biography up to that point to indicate a particular interest in the English essay periodical. Czartoryski, however, had
both knowledge and experience. From Danzig in August and September
1763, Czartoryski brought out a few numbers of a folio broadsheet,
Monitor, whose name and, in part, content, were borrowed from the *Monitor,
or British Freeholder*, a periodical appearing at that time in London. He
made use of a French translation in *Nouvelles Extraordinaires de Divers*

---

[66] On this point, see J. Jack, 'The Periodical Essayists', in *From Dryden to Johnson*, 186–9
and Pocock, 'Clergy and Commerce', vol. 1, 533–41. The *Spectator*'s campaign is to be distinguished from that of the contemporary 'Societies for the Reformation of Manners', which
concentrated on prosecuting the vices of the lower orders in magistrates' courts. See Burtt,
Virtue Transformed, ch. 3.

[67] Michalski, '"Warszawa", czyli o antystołecznych nastrojach w czasach Stanisława
Augusta', *Studia Warszawskie*, 12 (1972).

[68] Sinko, *'Monitor' wobec angielskiego 'Spectatora'*, 34–45.

Entroits of Leyden of 12 April 1763. His *Monitor* served the *Familia* as a propaganda organ at the end of the reign of Augustus III.[69] In its first number in March 1765, *Monitor* 'the son' paid explicit tribute to its 'father' of 1763. Clearly, Czartoryski would have played a crucial advisory role, but the few articles attributable to his pen do not include any adaptations. Bohomolec's style and favoured subject-matter of manners and morals were closest to that of the *Spectator*, which he often used as a source, but he was involved closely only from 1767.[70] And Stanisław August himself? He would almost certainly have been made acquainted with the *Spectator* by Williams, and whilst in England in 1754. He possessed both the English and French versions, although *Le Spectateur* in seven volumes entered the royal library only at some point between 1767 and 1775.[71] Later, the king praised Addison to his nephew, Prince Stanisław.[72] But there is more compelling evidence. Johann Heyne, the Warsaw agent of Prince Xavier of Saxony, wrote on 13 April 1765: 'He wishes in this way to imitate the English and show the whole world his wit, as well as his absorption by zeal for the splendour of the state, and by the same token he desires to gain immortal fame for himself.'[73] Heyne's source was well-informed; Minasowicz was *Monitor*'s corrector and censor. The previous *Monitor*, number 4, contained reflections on the use of time, translated rather than adapted from *Le Spectateur*. It continued the theme from number 3, a looser adaptation by Krasicki. Number 4 was marked with the cryptonym 'R'—probably 'rex' or 'roi'.[74]

English literature, in particular Pope, Swift, Defoe, Young, and Ossian, left their mark on the development of Polish literature during the reign of Stanisław August and the first years of the nineteenth century. The first Polish novel, Krasicki's *Mikołaja Doświadczyńskiego przypadki* ('The adventures of Mikołaj Doświadczyński') (1776), while dependent upon Voltaire and Rousseau for its philosophy, was modelled structurally on *Gulliver's Travels* and *Robinson Crusoe*. Krasicki's *Historia na dwie xięgi podzielona* ('History divided into two books') (1779) was an explicit extension and adaptation of Gulliver's visit to Glubbdubdrib and

---

[69] Rudnicka, 'Z genealogii "Monitora" z roku 1763', *Pam. Lit.*, 46 (1955). J. Szczepaniec, 'Metryka wydawnicza "Monitora" z 1763 roku', *Pam. Lit.*, 57 (1966), *'Monitor' 1765–1785: Wybór*, pp. x–xii.

[70] *'Monitor' 1765–1785: Wybór*, pp. xviii–xxvi.

[71] *Biblioteka Stanisława Augusta*, 67.   [72] Fabre, *Stanislas-Auguste Poniatowski*, 378.

[73] Johann Heyne to Prince Xavier of Saxony, 13 April 1765, *'Monitor' 1765–1785: Wybór*, p. ix. Translated from a Polish translation of the original German.

[74] Aleksandrowska, 'Na tropie autorstwa króla', 194–6.

Luggnagg, combined with the use of Sterne's technique of breaking off the 'manuscript'.[75]

There is no evidence that Stanisław August played a significant role in the process. He did not mention English literature in his letters to Krasicki, Naruszewicz, or Trembecki.[76] It was no royal scholarship that brought Kajetan Węgierski his stay in England, his knowledge of the English language, or his collection of English literature. A begging letter written in English from London drew no reply from the king.[77] The approved 'models' in both drama and poetry in the king's cultural programme were distinctly classical. Literature had a mission—to clear away confused Sarmatian verbiage in the name of reason, order, and purity—and Stanisław August's eclectic personal taste in English literature did not fit into that framework. Only the *Spectator* was directly useful in the assault on Sarmatism. From that source, the essay periodical with moralizing essays, columns, and letters, was introduced into Poland. Krasicki showed himself a master of the art, and the literary training he received bore fruit in his later prose writing. The attributes of 'Baron de Kowerli' (but not of Sir Roger) became those of the model landowner *Pan podstoli* (1778).[78] If the practical consequences of Stanisław August's taste for English literature were of restricted scope, they were nevertheless of great value.

---

[75] Dadlez, *Pope w Polsce, passim*. Sinko, *Powieść angielska . . . a powieść polska, passim*. Eadem, 'Z zagadnień recepcji . . . Edwarda Younga'. Eadem, 'Osjanizm' and 'Youngizm', in *Słownik literatury polskiego Oświecenia*, 368–74, 681–6.

[76] *Korespondencja Ignacego Krasickiego: Z papierów Ludwika Bernackiego*, eds. Z. Goliński *et al.* (2 vols.; Wrocław, 1958). *Korespondencja Adama Naruszewicza: Z papierów po Ludwiku Bernackim*, eds. J. Platt and T. Mikulski (Wrocław, 1959). S. Trembecki, *Listy*, eds. J. Kott and R. Kaleta (2 vols.; Wrocław, 1954). See Z. Libera, 'Stanisław August Poniatowski—opiekun i milosnik literatury' in *Życie kulturalne i religijność*.

[77] Węgierski to SA, 8 June 1784, Zb. Pop. 181, f. 385, and 20 July 1784, BCzart. 694, f. 147. See Libiszowska, *Życie polskie*, 203–9, for an account of Węgierski's stay in England.

[78] Sinko, *Powieść angielska . . . a powieść polska*, 58–71. Eadem, *'Monitor' wobec angielskiego 'Spectatora'*, 92. P. Cazin, *Le prince-évêque de Varmie: Ignace Krasicki 1735–1801* (Paris, 1940), 133.

9

Stanisław August and English Art

No aspect of Stanisław August's cultural policy has been studied so intently as his patronage of the visual arts. Władysław Tatarkiewicz first wrote of a distinct 'style of Stanisław August' or 'Stanislavian style' in architecture, which, in contrast to the 'Louis seize' or 'Georgian' styles, arose directly from the taste of the monarch. Although the precise definition of the Stanislavian style has provoked much discussion,[1] the fact of its existence is unquestioned. Marek Kwiatkowski compared Stanisław August to the conductor of an orchestra of architects and decorators, and titled his monograph on the king's architecture *Stanisław August: Król–architekt*.[2] Most recently, Andrzej Rottermund has stressed that the completed interiors and the plans for the rebuilding of the Royal Castle should not be interpreted primarily in aesthetic, but rather in functional and ideological terms. The architecture formed the stage for the theatre of court ceremonies and political life in the Commonwealth, including the meetings of the Seym, and these considerations predominated at the design stage.[3] For example, the ceiling of the ballroom showed 'Jupiter bringing the world out of chaos', an unmistakable allusion to Stanisław August and Sarmatia. It was an age more responsive to allegory than our own. 'Architecture' was often understood in the eighteenth century to comprehend the entire exterior and interior, including the floor, paintings, sculptures, and furniture. Nor was the park or garden outside excluded. Stanisław August insisted that every element should form an integral part of the whole and contribute to its message.

---

[1] Tatarkiewicz introduced the term 'styl Stanisława Augusta' in his *Budowa pałacu w Łazienkach* (Warsaw, 1916), and later defined the pure Stanislavian style as that art commissioned by the king in his own individual style, after 1783. Tatarkiewicz, 'Sztuka Stanisława Augusta a klasycyzm', in *Klasycyzm: Studia nad sztuką polską XVIII i XIX wieku* (Wrocław, 1968), 7, 13. Stanisław Lorentz preferred a wider definition, to include all art commissioned by the king, as the king's taste underwent constant evolution, without any particular watershed. S. Lorentz and A. Rottermund, *Klasycyzm w Polsce* (2nd edn., Warsaw, 1984), 18–30. The Polish 'klasycyzm' is roughly equivalent to the English 'neoclassicism', but it also includes Palladianism.

[2] *Stanisław August: Król–architekt* (Wrocław, 1983), 258.

[3] *Zamek warszawski w epoce Oświecenia: Rezydencja monarsza: Funkcja i treści* (Warsaw, 1989).

Stanisław August was convinced that the flourishing of the arts was necessary to the renewal of political life in the Commonwealth. He had, however, to create a Polish school of painting and sculpture from scratch. He therefore imported foreign masters to teach youngsters, as well as to execute commissions for himself; he sent promising young artists on scholarships abroad, and ultimately he sought to create a national gallery of art in which all the best models would be represented, and from which young artists could learn. If originals were too expensive for the king's limited means, copies or engravings of great paintings and sculptures acted as substitutes. The royal collections included tens of thousands of engravings, antiquities, medals, coins, and gems, as well as scientific items (*naturalia* and *artificialia*) such as animals, plants, semi-precious stones, machines, and mathematical instruments.[4] Stanisław August expressed his aims to his friend August Moszyński, who for twenty years was the unofficial head of his collections: 'Mes estampes et mes médailles sans doutes ne sont qu'un amusement en comparaison du reste . . . cependant Vous sçavez que j'y envisage un côté utile, et que je voudrais rendre utile même à ceux qui jouiront de cela après ma mort.'[5] There were other collectors in eighteenth-century Poland who were more passionate and more expert in certain areas,[6] but the king's collecting and patronage was on a wider scale and had more far-reaching aims than those of any of his contemporaries during his reign. Granted, to a degree art, like literature, was for Stanisław August a pleasant diversion from political misfortunes. Building at the Royal Castle and at Ujazdów Castle was not halted by the Confederacy of Bar, and work carried on at Łazienki after the king's departure from Warsaw in 1795. Nor was royal patronage, particularly at first, free from the traditional self-glorification typical of baroque rulers. Nevertheless, any attitude of 'l'état, c'est moi' was out of the question, and the campaign to increase royal power was harnessed to the ideology of the Enlightenment. Stanisław August identified himself with Casimir the Great, as a legislator, patron of learning and the arts, founder of towns,

[4] T. Mańkowski, *Galerja Stanisława Augusta* (Lwów, 1932). Idem, 'Mecenat Stanisława Augusta' and 'Kolekcjonerstwo Stanisława Augusta w świetle korespondencji z Augustem Moszyńskim', in idem, *Mecenat artystyczny Stanisława Augusta* (Warsaw, 1976). Kwiatkowski, 'Mecenas—twórca', in *Życie kulturalne i religijność*. Rottermund, *Zamek warszawski*, 190. Idem, 'Stanislaus Augustus as Patron of the Arts', in *Treasures of a Polish King: Stanislaus Augustus as Patron and Collector* (Catalogue of an exhibition at the Dulwich Picture Gallery, 1992). Lorentz and Rottermund, *Klasycyzm w Polsce*, 16–18, 40–3.
[5] Quoted by Mańkowski, 'Kolekcjonerstwo Stanisława Augusta', 23.
[6] Such as S. K. Potocki. See Mańkowski, 'O poglądach na sztukę w czasach Stanisława Augusta', 112–22, in *Mecenat artystyczny Stanisława Augusta*.

and protector of peasants, rather than as a warrior.[7] Stanisław August's activity went beyond purely humanistic patronage, as well as the vain-glorious or fashionable. It was intended to serve the interests of the state and the nation.

I

What role did English art play in Stanisław August's activity? It would be helpful first to review the impact of English art on eighteenth-century Poland up to 1795. The distinctive characteristics of the king's Anglo-philia will then be set in clearer relief. The fashion for things English appeared first (and very early by European standards) in furniture, at the courts of Augustus II and the Sieniawski family. In 1713, Augustus bought twelve English chairs from Zofia Sieniawska. Saxon hunting lodges and *maisons de plaisance*, where a simpler effect was desired than in royal palaces, were from this time furnished with English mahogany furniture. The impress-ive English mirrors from about 1730, which still adorn Wilanów, could have been bought either by Augustus II or Zofia Sieniawska-Czartoryska (from whom the king rented the palace). In Amsterdam in 1759, her son-in-law Stanisław Lubomirski paid seven ducats for 'une table angloise'.[8]

English furniture was imported to Poland via Danzig, but 'English-pattern' furniture (*angielskim fasonem*) also began to be made in Poland, and was sometimes passed off as 'English'. Danzig furniture itself showed some English influence in the course of the century, at first via Han-seatic trade, and later from the example of Chippendale's chairs and sofas. Shops sprang up, selling both imported and locally made furniture. In Warsaw the most famous was run by Henryk Jarzewicz. Antoni Magier remembered:

Anglomania reached such a degree, that already in Warsaw, just as in London, it was possible to obtain blocks of mahogany, from which floors, furniture, internal doors, and window frames were made, all *massif*, that is, entirely from mahogany.

By 1786, English-pattern furniture was being made in provincial Lublin and could even be obtained in distant Volhynia.[9]

---

[7] The king's self-identification with Casimir was also expressed in Naruszewicz's *Historia Narodu Polskiego*. See A. F. Grabski, *Myśl historyczna polskiego Oświecenia* (Warsaw, 1976), ch. 4.

[8] Majewska-Maszkowska, *Mecenat Izabelli Lubomirskiej*, 25. Lorentz, 'Stosunki artysty-czne', 15–16.

[9] B. Maszkowska, *Z dziejów polskiego meblarstwa okresu Oświecenia* (Wrocław, 1956), 6–9, 11–13, 23, 63. F. Schulz, *Podróże Inflantczyka z Rygi do Warszawy i po Polsce w latach 1791–1793*, trans. J. I. Kraszewski, ed. W. Zawadzki (Warsaw, 1956), 82.

These shops did not only sell furniture. English fireplaces, musical instruments, materials, wallpaper, and every conceivable kind of domestic appliance from table silver and porcelain to spectacles were not only available, but even, as Friedrich Schulz noted, (alongside French goods) *de rigueur* in fashionable society. According to Magier, 'one dressed from head to foot entirely in English clothes.'[10] Aristocratic tourists to England filled up ships to Danzig with crates of shopping; English carriages were especially esteemed. Prince Stanisław Poniatowski persistently troubled Bukaty, and was known for his English dress.[11] Among those who had particularly impressive collections of English furniture and wares were Izabella Lubomirska, Michał Poniatowski, and Izabella Czartoryska.[12]

The mid-eighteenth century was a period of rapid growth in the furnishing of the residences of the magnates and richer *szlachta* and townsmen, and taste was not yet outraged by the placing of white or gilted *Louis quinze-* or *Louis seize*-style sofas next to mahogany English-pattern chairs and old-fashioned Danzig cupboards, with Turkish or Persian tapestries on the walls.[13] The principle of a harmonious and unified interior took some time to catch on. Izabella Lubomirska was one of the pioneers. Her colonnaded hall at Łańcut showed the influence of Robert Adam in its floral motifs, while her 'Chinese apartment' was inspired by the newest interiors she had seen in England.[14] At the Mielżyńskis' Pawłowice in Great Poland, Johann Christian Kamsetzer based his plastered ceilings of 1789–92 on the work of Robert Adam, although Kamsetzer interpreted similar floral and grotesque motifs in his own, richer style.[15]

The impact of English external architecture in Poland should not be measured in terms of the one unexecuted project for a villa which Robert Adam drew up for Izabella Lubomirska.[16] English models in architecture first became known in Poland thanks to illustrated publications. Later,

---

[10] Quoted after Maszkowska, *Z dziejów polskiego meblarstwa*, 9. Schulz, *Podróże Inflantczyka*, 82.

[11] Libiszowska, *Życie polskie*, 226–7. Lorentz, 'Stosunki artystyczne', 11–12.

[12] Majewska-Maszkowska, *Mecenat Izabelli Lubomirskiej*, 116–17, 136, 267, 327, 348–50. A. Morawińska, 'Kolekcjonerstwo polskie i Anglia w dobie Oświecenia: Kontakty artystyczne Stanisława Augusta i Michała Poniatowskich z Noelem Desenfansem', in *Polska i Anglia: Stosunki kulturalno-artystyczne*, 23. Schulz, *Podróże Inflantczyka*, 64. Gołębiowska, 'Podróż Izabeli i Adama Jerzego Czartoryskich', 134.

[13] Maszkowska, *Z dziejów polskiego meblarstwa*, 27–31, 45, 61, 63.

[14] Majewska-Maszkowska, *Mecenat Izabelli Lubomirskiej*, 143, 266–72.

[15] N. Batowska and Z. Batowsci and M. Kwiatkowski, *Jan Christian Kamsetzer: Architekt Stanisława Augusta* (Warsaw, 1978), 197–201. See G. Beard, *The Work of Robert Adam* (London, 1978).

[16] Majewska-Maszkowska, *Mecenat Izabelli Lubomirskiej*, 242–3 (illustrations 136–8).

aristocrats saw English country houses for themselves. Colen Campbell's *Vitruvius Britannicus* helped to ensure that Palladio's path to Poland led through early eighteenth-century England. It should be stressed, however, that the first two volumes of *Vitruvius Britannicus*, which appeared in 1715 and 1717, largely contained Stuart architecture. It was the third volume of 1725 that properly represented early eighteenth-century Palladianism. Two further volumes were brought out by other authors in 1767 and 1771. As in England, the Villa Rotonda near Vicenza inspired few adaptations. Among them was Carlo Thomatis's 'Królikarnia' (rabbits had formerly been bred on the site), designed by Domenico Merlini (1782–6). The square villa was too impractical to be widely imitated.[17]

On the other hand, the type of layout represented by the Villa Badoer in Fratta Polesine was far more popular in both England and Poland; more so, in fact, than anywhere else in Europe. A rectangular house was connected by quarter-circular or straight galleries with pavilions housing kitchens and other service functions. The front was dominated by a giant order portico, and the rear often featured a projecting circular or octagonal saloon. Such an arrangement was both convenient and impressive, and appealed to the taste of both the English and Polish aristocracy. The first Polish examples from the middle of the eighteenth century merely added the layout to existing baroque architecture, but the Primate's Palace, begun in 1777 for Primate Ostrowski by Ephraim Schroeger, saw the first use of the layout in neoclassical form. Carl Langhan's Pawłowice (1779–87) is strikingly reminiscent of early eighteenth-century English forms, not just in its layout, but also in its slightly projecting side 'towers' and its portico not projecting from the façade, but mounted on the ground floor, with the entrance beneath it not accented at all.[18] More usually, however, the main reception rooms were on the ground floor, and the giant order portico was based directly on the ground. The projecting portico, topped by a triangular pediment, was much more common than the recessed type with a balustrade, as introduced by Szczęsny Potocki at Tulczyn in the Ukraine in 1775–82. Although *Vitruvius Britannicus* contained Inigo Jones's uses of the recessed portico,[19] the models for Tulczyn were almost certainly two designs in Neufforge's *Recueil élémentaire*

---

[17] T. S. Jaroszewski, 'Ze studiów nad problematyką recepcji Palladia w Polsce w drugiej połowie XVIII wieku', in *Klasycyzm*, op. cit. (n. 1), 139–54. In a square villa, entrance halls and porticos take up a disproportionate amount of space.

[18] Jaroszewski, *Klasycyzm*, 144–50. Lorentz and Rottermund, *Klasycyzm w Polsce*, 79, 96–100. B. Knox, *The Architecture of Poland* (London, 1971), 127. D. Cruikshank, *A Guide to the Georgian Buildings of Britain and Ireland* (London, 1985), 63.

[19] *Vitruvius Britannicus*, vol. 1, pls. 14 and 15.

d'architecture.[20] The projecting portico based on the ground was characteristic of later eighteenth-century English architecture, as fewer imposing
'power houses' were built than earlier in the century.[21]

The English garden appeared in the environs of Warsaw in the early
1770s, soon after Rousseau's *Nouvelle Héloïse* (1761) and the first English-
style gardens in France and Germany. Another important role was played
by the trip of Adam and Izabella Czartoryski to England in 1768–71.
Immediately after their return to Poland, work began at Powązki on an
irregular sentimental garden. The basis of the composition was a lake
with two islands, on which were situated 'ancient' ruins and 'primitive'
huts with exquisitely furnished interiors for all the members of the family. The programme at Ermenonville was reflected most clearly at Izabella
Lubomirska's Mokotów, begun in 1772. The Gothick dove tower, put
up in 1780, was modelled on the tower of the church at Vévey, the setting of the *Nouvelle Héloïse*. Alongside the cults of nature, primitivism,
and antiquity appeared exotica in the form of various Chinese, Turkish,
and even North American pavilions and bridges. Exotica ran riot at
Kazimierz Poniatowski's gardens at Solec, Książęce, and 'na Górze'.
At Książęce, a large minaret dominated the view, a small mosque with
minarets formed the kitchen, and an underground passage led from a
grotto with a waterfall to a village hut which formed a magnificent ban-
queting hall. Classical antiquity was at first the dominant accent at Helena
Radziwiłł's 'Arkadia', begun in 1778 near Łowicz. Mention should also
be made of Alexandra Ogińska's 'Alexandria' at Siedlce, Stanisław Kostka
Potocki's 'Olesin' near Kurów, the Mniszechs' Dęblin, Michał Poniatowski's Jabłonna, and Fryderyk Brühl's Młociny. The early 'English'
gardens in Poland were settings for entertainments, especially *fêtes cham-
pêtres*, inspired by French rococo paintings. The painter Jean-Pierre Norblin, whose style was closest to the rococo, helped to design Powązki,
and later immortalized it on large, languid canvases. Coxe was enchanted
by such *soirées* given by Izabella Czartoryska and Kazimierz Poniatowski
in 1778.[22] For such purposes, exotica were particularly appropriate. Many
of the buildings were taken from models in Chambers's *Designs of Chinese
Buildings* and *Plans, Elevations, Sections and Perspective Views of . . . Kew*,

---

[20] *Vitruvius Britannicus*, vol. 4, pls. 261 and 458. See Jaroszewski, 'Pałac w Tulczynie i
początki architektury klasycyzmu na Ukrainie', *Przegląd Wschodni*, 1 (1991), 87–90.

[21] Lorentz and Rottermund, *Klasycyzm w Polsce*, 110–11 and *passim*. Jaroszewski, 'Ze
studiów nad problematyką recepcji Palladia', 148–57. Cruikshank, *Georgian Buildings*, 72–3.

[22] Coxe, *Travels*, vol. 1, 175–81. Coxe possibly to Chreptowicz, Smolensk, 23 Aug. 1778,
BCzart. 2725, f. 63.

the Halfpennys' *Rural Architecture in the Chinese Taste*, and Le Rouge's prints of *jardins anglo-chinois*. All the above gardens except Olesin were laid out or at some stage modified by Szymon Bogumił Zug.[23]

Zug worked together with August Moszyński when the latter wrote his 'Essay sur le Jardinage Anglois', completed in January 1774.[24] Moszyński's primary aim was to propose a plan for the laying out of the wilderness below Ujazdów Castle. Nevertheless, he intended his essay for a wider readership. Although it was not published, Zug's co-operation meant that many of the ideas were used in the gardens listed above.[25] The content of Moszyński's essay was drawn for the most part from Thomas Whately's *Observations on Modern Gardening* (1770). Moszyński made use, however, of the 1771 French translation by Latapie, who added excerpts from Chambers's *Designs of Chinese Buildings*[26] and his own introduction and comments. Moszyński criticized an excess of buildings, but in his plan he included an array of exotica. The English, he wrote, exaggerated in their rejection of regularity, and he proposed that the part of the garden nearest the building be laid out symmetrically with trimmed hedges. Moszyński was well aware that the huge scale and cost of English parks was impractical near Warsaw. He preferred Kent's and Chambers's concept of the garden as a series of scenes, each of which had to be deciphered, to Brown's vast and completely asymmetrical re-creations of an idealized nature.[27] Moszyński chose from Whately what he found appropriate, and rejected that which was 'plus propre au caractère anglais qu'au notre'.[28]

The 1780s saw the beginning of a shift in the programme of Polish gardens, although it would only reach fruition after the Third Partition. It was connected above all with the Czartoryskis' removal from Warsaw to Puławy. Puławy became the seat of political opposition to Stanisław August and a rival literary and artistic centre—more sentimental, and

[23] Majewska-Maszkowska, *Mecenat Izabelli Lubomirskiej*, 176–86. I owe the information on the tower of Vévey to Dr B. Majewska-Maszkowska. Lorentz and Rottermund, *Klasycyzm w Polsce*, 36–7, 56, 80, 89, 92–3, 116–19. K. Sroczyńska, *Podróże malownicze Zygmunta Vogla* (Warsaw, 1980), 76–7, 104–11, 114–17, 176–7, 208–9. Zamoyski, *Last King*, 255–6.

[24] BCzart. MNK 118. Most of it has been published in Polish translation by A. Morawińska, 'Nieznany traktat Augusta Fryderyka Moszyńskiego o ogrodach angielskich', in J. Białostocki (ed.), *Myśli o sztuce i sztuka XVII–XVIII wieku* (Warsaw, 1970).

[25] Lorentz and Rottermund, *Klasycyzm w Polsce*, 34–6. Majewska-Maszkowska, *Mecenat Izabelli Lubomirskiej*, 180.

[26] *Designs of Chinese Buildings, Furniture, Dresses, Machines and Utensils . . . to which is annexed a Description of their Temples, Houses, Gardens &c.* (London, 1757, in English and French), 15–19.

[27] See D. Jacques, *Georgian Gardens: The Reign of Nature* (London, 1983).

[28] BCzart. MNK 118, f. 6.

characterized by a strident patriotism. The gardens began to be transformed into a picturesque park, and as time passed, it filled up with mementoes of the national past—echoing the monuments to liberty at Stowe. In England in 1790, Izabella Czartoryska engaged a gardener, James Savage. Over the years, Arkadia also took on a more romantic aspect. After touring England together in 1787, Stanisław Kostka Potocki modified Olesin and drew up plans for his brother Ignacy's Kurów, while his mother-in-law Izabella Lubomirska created a picturesque English-style park at Łańcut.[29]

The first large-scale Gothick building in Poland was Prince Stanisław Poniatowski's palace at Korsuń in the Ukraine. Although the setting on an island among rivulets was picturesque, the Gothick detailing was superficial and the architect, Jan Lindsay (a little-known Pole of Scottish ancestry) was clearly unhappy in the style. Without doubt, Prince Stanisław was inspired by the Gothick and picturesque residences that he had seen in England. He may also have been influenced by Johann Heinrich Müntz, a Swiss painter, architect, and engineer who had engraved Chambers's Gothick 'cathedral' at Kew, and who laid out the garden at Korsuń in 1782. The prince took his uncle over the site and gave him some plans in 1787, and the palace was finished by 1789. It was an isolated, pioneering use of Gothick for a residential building.[30]

Very few English paintings and even fewer sculptures found their way into Polish collections. While in England, some Polish aristocrats—Izabella Lubomirska, Izabella Czartoryska, Michał Kleofas Ogiński and his wife—had their portraits painted by Maria and Richard Cosway. Also dating from Izabella Lubomirska's visit in 1787 is a bust of the young Prince Henryk Lubomirski by Anne Seymour Damer. Peter Francis Bourgeois painted portraits of Izabella Czartoryska and Franciszek Bukaty, and executed at least two and possibly three versions of a group portrait of eminent Poles in the Polish ministry in London for Primate Poniatowski, Ogiński, and (possibly) Izabella Czartoryska.[31] Nevertheless, if

---

[29] Lorentz and Rottermund, *Klasycyzm w Polsce*, 37–8. Gołębiowska, 'Podróż Izabeli i Adama Jerzego Czartoryskich', 134. Majewska-Maszkowska and Jaroszewski, 'Podróż Stanisława Kostki Potockiego w 1787 roku w świetle jego korespondencji z żoną', *Biuletyn Historii Sztuki*, 34 (1972), 212–13. Majewska-Maszkowska, *Mecenat Izabelli Lubomirskiej*, 120, 255–6. Sroczyńska, *Podróże Vogla*, 178–87.

[30] Jaroszewski, *O siedzibach neogotyckich w Polsce* (Warsaw, 1981), 39, 57, 152, 218–20. Idem, *Architektura doby Oświecenia w Polsce: Nurty i odmiany* (Wrocław, 1971), 188–91.

[31] Majewska-Maszkowska, *Mecenat Izabelli Lubomirskiej*, 302, 304, 311. Gołębiowska, 'Podróż Izabeli i Adama Jerzego Czartoryskich', 136. Libiszowska, *Życie polskie*, 242–5 (illustrations between pp. 128 and 129, 208 and 209). *The Polish Road to Democracy: The Constitution of May 3 1791* (Catalogue of an exhibition at the Polish Cultural Institute in London, Warsaw, 1991), 31.

English paintings were sparse, English influence reached Polish painting through Giuseppe Grassi, who painted numerous portraits of Polish aristocrats during his stay in Poland in 1791–2. His free composition, unconventional poses, and lyrical landscape backgrounds are reminiscent of the best English portraitists.[32] The relative lack of influence of English painting was balanced to some extent by the popularity of English engravings. Prince Stanisław Poniatowski began his huge collection in England in 1771–3.[33]

The *mode à l'anglaise* was filtered almost in its entirety through France. It is questionable how deep it really penetrated in Poland. Just as it became a *grande dame* to weep over Rousseau's grave at Ermenonville, so it was the done thing to create one's own sentimental little landscape back home, in which to read the latest pseudo-English novels from Paris and think 'philosophically'. Only with the fall of the Commonwealth was the English garden linked with patriotic motifs. Stanisław August was more discriminating in his use of English art.

II

Before proceeding to an analysis of English influence upon Stanisław August's architecture (including interiors and gardens), we should examine its possible channels, beyond the king's own memories of his stay in England. Stanisław August kept abreast of all the latest novelties. Writing his *Mémoires* in 1775, he noted the spectacular development of Bath since 1754, and in December 1789 he asked General Jan Komarzewski to get him some drawings of that city and other English buildings. Komarzewski sent the king an illustrated plan of Bath in the new year.[34] Michał Poniatowski made contact with the highest artistic circles during his stay in England in 1790–1, and Sir Joshua Reynolds gave the primate his *Discourses* to pass on to the king.[35] The main channel was the enormous royal cabinet of engravings. It contained several hundred illustrated volumes on ancient and modern architecture, which were used by the royal architects for reference. Among the volumes on ancient architecture (which gave a great impetus to the neo-classicist movement), alongside Winckelmann and Piranesi were Robert Wood's *Ruines de Palmyre* and *Ruines de Balbec*, James Stuart's *Antiquities of Athens*, Adam's *Ruins of the*

[32] Morawińska, 'Malarstwo', in A. Zahorski (ed.), *Warszawa w wieku Oświecenia* (Wrocław, 1986), 275–7 (illustrations 13, 340, 342).

[33] Libiszowska, *Życie polskie*, 193, 227.

[34] *Mémoires*, vol. 1, 119. SA to Bukaty, 12 Dec. 1789, 30 Jan. 1790, BCzart. 849, ff. 129, 221.

[35] SA to Bukaty, 30 Mar. 1791, BCzart. 849, f. 363.

Palace of Diocletian at Spalatro, Chandler's *Antiquités d'Ionie* and Thomas Major's *Ruins of Paestum*.[36] The works on modern architecture included *The Designs of Inigo Jones*, the first volume of the Adam brothers' *Works in Architecture*, *A Description of the Library at Merly in the County of Dorset*, and views of London and Oxford. English buildings also figured on loose mezzotints. The earlier catalogue lists only one volume of *Vitruvius Britannicus*, and the later one three, but Komarzewski sent the king a set of five volumes in 1790. Also present was Thomas Chippendale's *Guide du tapissier*.[37]

English gardens and garden architecture were represented by the Halfpennys' *Rural Architecture*, Chambers's *Plans . . . of . . . Kew* and *Designs of Chinese Buildings*, and Ixnard's *Recueil d'architecture*, which included several views of English-style gardens in France and Germany.[38] The strong representation of *chinoiserie* and the lack of any publication with views of any English garden besides Kew is striking. This gap was partly filled in the library proper by Horace Walpole's *Anecdotes of Painting and Engraving*, which contained *An Essay on the Art of Gardening*. The acquisitions of Joseph Farington's *Views of the Lakes &c. in Cumberland and Westmorland* (1789), J. Gardner's views of Rhine castles, and Thomas Hearne's *Antiquities of Great Britain, illustrated in Views of Monasteries, Castles and Churches* (1786), together with a collection of 160 landscapes by Claude Lorrain suggest that Stanisław August developed a taste for the picturesque in the 1780s. Hearne's book included views of Richard Payne Knight's Downton Castle and its grounds, begun in 1772, which had initiated the picturesque style.[39] Hearne's work may have inspired Stanisław August to send Zygmunt Vogel on a tour of southern Poland to paint watercolours of ruined castles in the summer of 1787. Vogel painted ruins visited earlier that year by Stanisław August during his journey to and from Kaniów. Many of them were associated with Casimir the Great. The king enlisted the help of the Gothic past to put across his political message, which in this case went beyond the general cult of his predecessor. At Kaniów he had proposed an anti-Turkish alliance to Catherine.

[36] 'Nombres des Estampes et Livres d'Estampes' (undated but probably from the early 1780s), AKsJP 216, ff. 17–23. 'Catalogue du Cabinet d'Estampes' (1793), AKsJP 215, ff. 70–5.

[37] AKsJP 216, ff. 44–62. AKsJP 215, ff. 58–9, 141–74. SA to Bukaty, 31 July 1790, BCzart. 849, f. 169. Bukaty to SA, 11 May 1790, 20 Aug. 1790, PAU 1658, ff. 14, 25.

[38] AKsJP 216, ff. 43–52. AKsJP 215, ff. 141–86.

[39] *Views taken on and near the River Rhine . . .* (London, 1788). *Recueil de 160 paysages de Claude Lorrain gravé par R. Earlom.* AKsJP 215, ff. 104, 171, 173. Cruikshanks, *Georgian Buildings*, 16, 78–9.

FIG. 3   The Marble Room at the Royal Castle

Casimir's defence of his frontiers chimed in with Stanisław August's plan to stimulate a revival of Poland's military traditions.[40]

III

The first plans commissioned by the king for the rebuilding of the Royal Castle and his projected residence of Ujazdów Castle display a monumental style, derived both from the latest Parisian fashion and from the seventeenth-century 'classical baroque' architecture, which he had seen in Paris in 1753–4. The proposals for the Royal Castle have a powerful flavour of Versailles, and emphasized the strengthening of royal power, a mark of Stanisław August's early ambitions. The gallery of Polish kings in the 'Marble Room', laid out in 1769–70, was dominated by Marcello Bacciarelli's portrait of Stanisław August in his coronation robes (Fig. 3), which was reminiscent of Rigaud's *Louis XIV*, and was reflected in a mirror for good measure.[41]

Several months before his election, Stanisław sent an agent to Paris to buy furniture for the Royal Castle, which, apart from the chamber

[40] Sroczyńska, *Podróże Vogla*, 20, 24, 82–97. Jaroszewski, *Architektura doby Oświecenia*, 177–8.
[41] Kwiatkowski, *Król–architekt*, 18, 26–7, 40, 58, 61, 70. Rottermund, *Zamek warszawski*, 74–5, 105–11. Fabre, *Stanislas-Auguste Poniatowski*, 226.

of envoys and the senate, had been neglected for a century. Madame Geoffrin also made purchases for the king and assisted in the commissioning of historical paintings from the leading French painters—J. M. Vien, J. F. Lagrénie, and Noel Hallé (Carl Van Loo, Stanisław August's first choice, died in 1765). Also at her recommendation, Victor Louis, one of the top Parisian architects, came to Warsaw to draw up plans for the castle, and later sent the finished designs from France. Although his plans were not carried out, some of his ideas for the interiors were adopted, and specially designed furniture arrived in Warsaw up to 1779.[42] The 1769 inventory of the castle reveals a great deal of furniture, including 159 chairs, described as 'Parisian' or 'à la grecque'. The latter was an overpowering, almost brutal style which was all the rage in Paris in the 1760s.[43]

Against the dominant French fashions, traces of English influence are thin on the ground. One of the triumphal arches put up for Stanisław August's coronation was probably the first Gothick structure in Poland.[44] Marshall claimed to have seen the castle in 1770, and wrote that some of the apartments were 'new fitted in the English manner, being executed by London artists, brought from thence at the king's expence,'[45] but this statement is not confirmed by other evidence. According to the later inventories of the castle, the 'Marble Room' contained twelve 'English' chairs and two armchairs, covered in red leather. The choice of room is significant. In a setting where white and gilt French furniture would have appeared frivolous, English mahogany harmonized with the dark tones of the marble and provided a suitably grave and solid accompaniment to the portraits. The date of their placement is not known, however.[46] The 1769 inventory records two English long-case clocks, one of them bought in Warsaw, two English lanterns in a guard room, an English ink-well, and that the billiard table was covered in English cloth.[47] 'English-pattern' windows are mentioned in many of the rooms. The curators of the Royal Castle have established that this meant that wood was used instead of lead to divide the window-panes, thanks to the use of putty. A carpenter's bill from 1777 for three pairs of 'double English windows'

---

[42] Kwiatkowski, *Król–architekt*, 22–38. Rottermund, *Zamek warszawski*, 74. SA, Mme Geoffrin, *Correspondance*, *passim*.

[43] AKsJP 134, *passim*. P. Thornton, *Authentic Decor: The Domestic Interior 1620–1920* (New York, 1984), 91. S. Eriksen, *Early Neo-Classicism in France* (London, 1974), *passim*.

[44] Jaroszewski, *Architektura doby Oświecenia*, 186. The only illustration was lost during the Second World War.

[45] Marshall, *Travels*, vol. 3, 260.   [46] AKsJP 181, ff. 30, 149. AKsJP 185, f. 131.

[47] AKsJP 134, ff. 194, 247, 347, 350, 352.

and for double 'English' doors, together with 'oak frames' (*futra dębowe*)
reveals that they were ordered by Stanisław August, although some may
have already been in the castle under the Saxons.[48] To this short list we
may add the palm motifs in Schroeger's plans for Ujazdów, which had
been used by Inigo Jones at Greenwich and in 1763 by John Vardy for
Lord Spencer in Green Park,[49] and a project by Jakub Fontana for a new
façade of the collegiate church of St John the Baptist, which adjoined the
castle. Tadeusz Jaroszewski established that the model for the two-storey
portico was St Paul's Cathedral in London.[50]

In the wake of the Partition, the king abandoned Ujazdów Castle
and shifted his attention to the wilderness below. He now sought a calm
retreat just outside the city.[51] Nevertheless, the king's gardens differed
greatly from his contemporaries' and little of Moszyński's advice was followed. The wilderness began to be transformed in 1774 into gardens which
were called 'Łazienki' after the old bath pavilion ('Łazienka') at their
heart. There was no departure from French regularity. Sculptures and
fountains were placed symmetrically. Densely planted trees pierced by
straight avenues created vistas closed by architectural features. Visual tricks
like progressively widening vistas with progressively lighter coloured
trees were taken from English practice.[52] Owing to the wet terrain, a multitude of canals was necessary, which were crossed by small bridges, many
of them 'Chinese'. One crossed in front of the waterfall created in 1779.
Kamsetzer's project for a 'Chinese gate' across one of the main avenues,
particularly his first draft, was modelled on a design in Chambers's *Designs
of Chinese Buildings*. It was built in 1779–80. A *Trou-Madame*, used both
for playing that game (similar to billiards) and as a small theatre, had a
green 'Chinese' roof, and murals of trees on the walls.[53] The dominant
theme in the garden was *chinoiserie*, but a small cylindrical house variously called the 'reservoir', 'water tank', or 'bastion' (*baszta*) was begun
in 1777. Rejecting the older view that it was from the first a copy of a
Roman tomb, Kwiatkowski called it the first Gothick building in Poland,
but the apparent absence of Gothick ornament suggests that the model,
as for the contemporary castellated style in England, was the medieval

---

[48] BCzart. 909, f. 22. I owe this reference to Dr B. Majewska-Maszkowska and her assistants.
[49] Tatarkiewicz, *Łazienki warszawskie* (Warsaw, 1972), 22.
[50] Jaroszewski, *Architektura doby Oświecenia*, 83–4.
[51] Tatarkiewicz, *Łazienki*, 32–3. Kwiatkowski, *Król–architekt*, 97, 266.
[52] Such tricks of perspective fascinated Pope. Jacques, *Georgian Gardens*, 26–9.
[53] Tatarkiewicz, *Łazienki*, 61, 67–9, 96–101, 105–6 (illustrations 38–41, 48, 65, 69, 81, 85, 86, 88). Kwiatkowski, *Król–architekt*, 114–20, 214–15. Chambers, *Designs of Chinese Buildings*, pl. vii.

buildings painted by Claude Lorrain. Appropriately, the 'reservoir' closed a vista.[54] The profusion of exotica that featured in Moszyński's *Essay*, and which overran the fashionable gardens of Warsaw, was absent at Łazienki. Although Stanisław August's taste was pluralistic, he strove above all for harmony. His gardens were not a succession of surprises, and contained no temples, huts, gloriettes, follies, or monuments.

Chinoiserie was also present in the pavilion built in 1774–6, called the White House (*Biały Dom*). Jan Bogumil Plersch painted one room with views of Chinese cities. He painted a view of Canton in the cabinet of the bath pavilion. His source has not yet been identified.[55] The villa of Myślewice was built on the other side of the garden in 1774–8. The plan was an interesting variation on the Palladian layout. A central corpus was joined to side pavilions by galleries curving through forty-five degrees. The entrance featured an apse, an element used in several grand English interiors. Inside Plersch painted murals of Italianate idealized landscapes.[56] Despite the contrast between them, the external architecture of both the White House and Myślewice owed most to French sources, not English ones.

The interiors from the 1770s show little sign of English influence, as far as their architecture is concerned. Only the senatorial antechamber or Canaletto Room at the Royal Castle, in which white and gilt architecture richly but discreetly framed Bernardo Bellotto's views of Warsaw, may be compared to English practice.[57] Nevertheless, it is from the 1770s that we may safely date the large-scale introduction of English and English-pattern furniture into Stanisław August's interiors. Scarcely anything has survived. The evidence of inventories and notes is certainly imperfect. The 1793 inventory of the Royal Castle hardly describes anything as 'English' or 'English-pattern',[58] but many of the same items were so described in 1795. Moreover, while 'English-pattern' furniture was certainly made in Poland, 'English' furniture may have been as well. The many pieces described as 'mahogany' could also have been influenced by

[54] The water tank only received classical ornament in the nineteenth century. Kwiatkowski, *Król–architekt*, 111. Cf. Tatarkiewicz, *Łazienki*, 57–8 (illustration 248). Cruikshank, *Georgian Buildings*, 78–9.

[55] Kwiatkowski, *Król–architekt*, 100–1, 113. Tatarkiewicz, *Łazienki*, 37, 53–4, 62–3 (illustrations 72–4). Lorentz and Rottermund, *Klasycyzm w Polsce*, 27.

[56] Jaroszewski, 'Ze studiów nad problematyką recepcji Palladia', 151. Kwiatkowski, *Król–architekt*, 103–7. Tatarkiewicz, *Łazienki*, 59–60, 65. Lorentz and Rottermund, *Klasycyzm w Polsce*, 26, 86–7 (illustrations 40–1).

[57] Kwiatkowski, *Król–architekt*, 129. Rottermund has explained the ideological meaning of the pictures. *Zamek warszawski*, 112–21.

[58] AKsJP 184.

English designs. Fortunately, our purpose is to investigate English *influ-ence*, so determining the exact provenance of particular items may be left to the curators. What is important is that the style was considered English.

The 1795 inventory records that the twelve mahogany English chairs covered with red leather in the king's *garderobe* were 'déjà vieilles'. A mahogany English-pattern fire-screen, gilded and inlaid with satinwood, was also 'déjà vieux' in 1795. So too was the fitted carpet of English moquette in the king's personal chapel. By 1783, the royal cabinet had been carpeted in English moquette, and it was noted in 1800 that the carpeting had been renewed three times.[59] The dining-room at the White House contained eighteen English mahogany chairs, and an English *escri-toire* and English dressing-tables were placed upstairs.[60] More English and English-pattern chairs were placed in the bath pavilion (including twenty-four in the dining-room) and in another pavilion, the 'Hermitage'. Myślewice was richly endowed with English and English-pattern furni-ture: forty chairs, a bureau, an *escritoire*, and two fire-dogs.[61] Courtiers also had some English furniture in their apartments. Moszyński had two English-pattern sofas and twenty-two English chairs, while Maria Teresa Tyszkiewicz had three English tables. Twelve English chairs were placed in General Komarzewski's chancellery.[62] In the villa built for Maurice Glayre in 1778 at Koszyki (later given to Maria Teresa Tyszkiewicz), an English light green striped fabric was used to upholster the library fur-niture.[63] French and French-pattern furniture (closer to the *à la grecque* style than *Louis seize*), usually painted and gilded, continued to predom-inate, however.

The library was built in 1778–82. Separate rooms housed the ever-growing royal collections of engravings, medals, gems, minerals, and math-ematical instruments. The exterior was in a fairly severe neoclassical style. In the opinion of Bożenna Majewska-Maszkowska, the library was the most English of all the Castle interiors (Fig. 4). Broken up by columns, it resembled an English long gallery, as adapted by British architects dur-ing the eighteenth century (Stanisław August had the Adams' *Works in*

[59] AKsJP 181, ff. 14, 21, 24, 120. AKsJP 183, ff. 19–20, 56. AKsJP 185, ff. 14, 16, 21.

[60] 1788 Inventory of Łazienki, AKsJP 162, ff. 51, 63–4, 71, 73. AKsJP 196, f. 13.

[61] AKsJP 162, ff. 10, 15, 19, 24, 83, 85, 90, 97, 109–10, 123.

[62] 'Memble [*sic*] ab Anno 1776 ab annum 1785 sprawione kosztem JKMci z wyrażeniem komu oddane', AKsJP 180, ff. 5, 12–13.

[63] AKsJP 171, f. 8. The material may have been introduced much later, as the invent-ory was drawn up in 1794. Kwiatkowski, *Król–architekt*, 238–9.

FIG. 4   The Library at the Royal Castle

Architecture—including Syon House—in his collection). Twelve English-pattern chairs covered in yellow moquette were placed in the library, six more in one of the smaller rooms, and twelve covered in black leather in the cabinet of medals.[64] The colonnaded ballroom or Assembly Hall, built after much deliberation over the plans in 1777–83, was the largest and most monumental Stanislavian interior. Apollo (for beauty) with the features of Stanisław August, and Minerva (for wisdom), who bore a resemblance to Catherine II, flanked the ceremonial entrance. This was in the form of an apse, similar to the external entrance at Myślewice (Fig. 5). Apses and colonnades were likewise to be found in many English halls and ballrooms.[65]

The other senatorial antechamber, called the Knights' Hall (*Sala Rycerska*), built from 1781 to 1786, was a visual counterpart of the 'dialogues of the dead' and a pantheon of national glory. Six huge historical canvases by Bacciarelli and busts and portraits of Polish heroes proclaimed Stanisław August's enlightened programme; the military exploits of Sobieski and some of the old hetmans were not elevated above the nation's scientific and cultural achievements. The judiciously represented *magnateria*

[64] Kwiatkowski, *Król–architekt*, 153–7. Rottermund, *Zamek warszawski*, 190–8. AKsJP 190, ff. 1–3.
[65] Kwiatkowski, *Król–architekt*, 133–43. Rottermund, *Zamek warszawski*, 199–208.

FIG. 5   The Ballroom at the Royal Castle

was joined on equal terms by astronomers, historians, poets, and Stanisław Konarski. The motto, inscribed around the frieze, was taken from Virgil's *Aeneid*, as it was at the Temple of British Worthies at Stowe:

Hic manus ob patriam pugnando vulnera passi quique sacerdotes casti dum vita manebat quique pii vates et phoebo digna locuti inventas aut qui vitam excoluere per artes quique fui memores alios secere merendo.

F IG. 6   The Knights' Hall at the Royal Castle

(Here are those who shed blood fighting for the fatherland; those who were priests
of unblemished lives; bards, whose songs were worthy of Phoebus; or those who
ennobled life by discovering truths, and those who by their service have won
remembrance among men.)[66]

The furniture was kept to benches around the edge of the hall, as befitted
a large antechamber. They were covered in floral-patterned green English
moquette. The Knights' Hall was the first interior in which Kamsetzer,
who returned from England in 1782, played an important part in the
design. The Hall is the classic example of Stanisław August's ideal of
harmony between painting, sculpture, and architecture in the service of
his programme (Fig. 6).[67]

French and Italian magnificence set an appropriately regal tone in
the new throne room, finished in 1786.[68] English mahogany would have
been inappropriate. Adjacent was a small *chambre de conférence* (Fig. 7),
in which Stanisław August proclaimed his fraternal equality with Europe's
monarchs by seven portraits: of Catherine II, Joseph II, Pius VI, Louis

---

[66] *Aeneid*, VI, lines 660–4. Rottermund, 'Stanislaus Augustus', 31.
[67] Rottermund, *Zamek warszawski*, 123–44. Kwiatkowski, *Król–architekt*, 176–83. AKsJP
181, f. 14. AKsJP 185, f. 5.
[68] Rottermund, *Zamek warszawski*, 156–62. Kwiatkowski, *Król–architekt*, 174–6.

FIG. 7 The *Chambre de Conférence* at the Royal Castle, showing Gainsborough's *George III* on the right

XVI, Frederick II, Gustavus III, and George III.[69] Stanisław August commissioned Thomas Gainsborough to paint the King of England in 1782.
Gainsborough kept Stanisław August waiting three years, and the impatient monarch peppered the Bukatys with requests for the painter to hurry
up. He finally received the portrait on 5 August 1785, just as he was
about to send off another reminder.[70] As if to revenge himself, Stanisław
August took as long to settle the bill. In December 1788, Gainsborough's
widow, unable to get any satisfaction from Tadeusz Bukaty, had to write
to Stanisław August, demanding payment of 60 guineas. Although Gainsborough's work is indicated by the correspondence, Polish art historians
have not agreed with Tadeusz Bukaty's enthusiasm for the 'delicacy of
the brushwork' (*delikatność pęzla* [*sic*]). The stiff pose, expressionless face,
and conventional brushwork incline them to suspect that it is the work,
at least in part, of a pupil.[71] Stanisław August was not content with a
mere representation of his fellow monarchs. He wished to possess portraits of the highest quality (he tried unsuccessfully to persuade Mengs
to paint the Pope).

In 1782, Kamsetzer drew up a plan for rebuilding the old Saxon chapel
at the castle. The overall simplicity of the strongly architectural design,
with columns and a stuccoed ceiling, has been linked by Kwiatkowski to
interiors in England, whence the architect had just returned. The king
decided, however, to convert the chapel into a court theatre.[72] Later, the
theatre reverted to its original use. The mahogany organ in the chapel
was 'fait en Angleterre'.[73] Ten years later, Kamsetzer drew up plans for
a new bedroom and cabinet for Stanisław August, in which was to be
hung a part of the king's picture gallery. Rottermund has observed the
similarity of the plan, with the architecture and the furniture discreetly
framing the densely hung pictures, to English interiors. In particular, the
chairs designed by the architect show distinct English influence (Fig. 8).[74]

[69] Rottermund, *Zamek warszawski*, 178–89.
[70] Bukaty to cabinet, 22 Jan. 1782–25 July 1783, BCzart. 3998, ff. 46–96, *passim*. Dept.
to Bukaty, 20 June 1783, 13 Sept. 1783, AKP 80, ff. 277, 286. Bukaty to dept., 14 Oct.
1783, AKP 80, f. 104. T. Bukaty to dept., 17 May–22 July 1785, AKP 81, ff. 168–84, *passim*. SA to T. Bukaty, 5 Aug. 1785, BCzart. 849, ff. 33, 36.
[71] M. Gainsborough to SA, 16 Dec. 1788, Zb. Pop. 185, f. 24. See also Libiszowska,
Życie polskie, 110. On the artistic value of the portrait, see I. Kołoszyńska, 'Malarstwo
angielskie w polskich zbiorach: Katalog', in *Polska i Anglia: Stosunki kulturalno-artystyczne*,
107–8. B. Majewska-Maszkowska thought that the lifeless appearance of the portrait might
be the result of botched cleaning.
[72] Kwiatkowski, *Król–architekt*, 185–6.   [73] AKsJP 185, f. 1. AKsJP 181, f. 11.
[74] Lorentz and Rottermund, *Klasycyzm w Polsce*, 72–3.

F IG. 8   J. C. Kamsetzer, plan for the king's bedchamber and study at the Royal Castle, 1792

1784 marked the beginning of the transformation of both the gardens and the bath house at Łazienki. In that year Stanisław August himself sketched a bold plan centred on an irregular lake (Fig. 9). Opposite the bath house he located a theatre in the form of a pantheon, and on a wooded artificial hill to the east a viewing pavilion, in the form of a square Palladian villa with a tetrastyle portico. The main rooms were on the first floor to give a better view. Unfortunately, the plan was not executed, perhaps because the pantheon was an unsuitable form for a theatre, but the picturesque location of the pavilion and the pantheon, reflected in the water, the asymmetry of the composition, and the homage paid to classical antiquity all show a shift in Stanisław August's taste. Perhaps he felt his gardens were old-fashioned in comparison with the others around Warsaw. The king was no slave to fashion, but he could not ignore it. He was now considering a water-centred park similar to Stourhead, where the key architectural element was the pantheon, modelled on that in Claude Lorrain's *Aeneas at Delos*.[75]

The changes that actually took place in 1784 express Stanisław August's more positive disposition towards the English landscape garden, but they also delineate its limits. The king employed Johann Christian Schuch, a Saxon architect who had studied gardening in Holland, France, and England, and who had laid out the garden at Dęblin for the Mniszechs. Stanisław August ordered irregular lakes to be dug on both sides of the bath house. An island was created in the southern lake. A higher third lake was joined to the southern lake by the waterfall, which in 1788 was given rocks designed by Kamsetzer. The inspiration was probably

---

[75] Kwiatkowski, *Król–architekt*, 187–9. Jaroszewski, 'Ze studiów nad problematyką recepcji Palladia', 143. See Batey and Lambert, *The English Garden Tour*, 190–5.

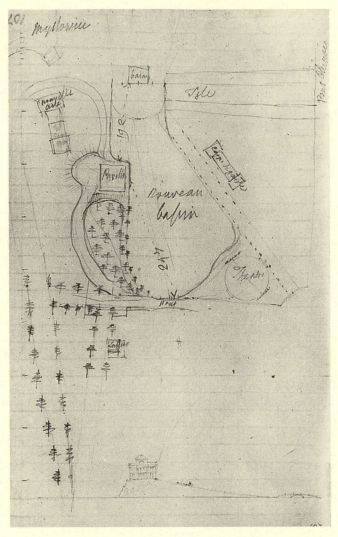

FIG. 9   Stanisław August's plan for Łazienki, 1784

the Falls of Tivoli, which Kamsetzer had painted for Stanisław August
during his Italian tour. The basic north–south axial composition was
retained. Furthermore, in 1788, the shoreline of the northern lake was
straightened to open up the view of the new statue of Sobieski. From 1784,
trees were planted more irregularly, with clearings and meadows, and

meandering paths. The main avenues remained straight. Stanisław August still held symmetry to be an essential element of garden composition.[76]

Stanisław August expressed his views to Horace Walpole, from whom he had just requested and received Walpole's *Anecdotes of Painting and Engraving* and *Essay on the Art of Gardening*:

You will be glad, I think, to be informed that Your lessons do thrive in this Country; and as it is but a short time since we do here creep out of the Servitude of Symmetry, we have not yet had time to come to the opposite excess, against which You endeavour to guard Your Country.[77]

Walpole's taste would not in fact have given the king much encouragement, as it was firmly Brownian. Stanisław August's continuing liking for symmetry is shown by the geometrical garden in front of the Orangery at Łazienki, and by the plans for a large west wing to the bath house (by now the 'palace on the island', Fig. 10), whose foundations were laid in 1794. Adjacent to the building, the garden was entirely geometrical, but further away it was more irregular. This was in accordance with Moszyński's principles, but already in England taste was reacting against Brown and the return of a degree of formality was imminent.[78]

A simple stage was erected in 1785 on the island. Stanisław August needed a larger theatre, however, for the various public performances he wished to stage. A larger stage and amphitheatre were built in 1790–2. The king gave the job to Kamsetzer because of his knowledge of models from classical antiquity, but the architect also made use of illustrated works from the cabinet of engravings. The stage on the island had broken columns based on those at Baalbek (Heliopolis) as drawn by Wood, and trees were planted among them, a picturesque effect probably taken from Piranesi. The amphitheatre across the water contained both Greek and Roman elements, but the closest model was at Herculaneum, as depicted by Piranesi. The overall effect mixed antiquity with the picturesque, and may be counted among the most avant-garde works of Polish architecture in the late eighteenth century (Fig. 12, p. 216).[79]

[76] Tatarkiewicz, *Łazienki*, 98–102 (illustration 114). Kwiatkowski, *Król–architekt*, 214–18. 'Ordre laissé à Bacciarelli', 16 Aug. 1784, Zb. Pop. 368, ff. 19–22.

[77] 7 June 1786, *Horace Walpole's Correspondence*, vol. 43, 164. Draft (6 June), in Zb. Pop. 183, f. 633. See above, p. 136.

[78] Kwiatkowski, *Król–architekt*, 210, 212, 216. Tatarkiewicz, *Łazienki*, 109–13 (illustration 139). Jacques, *Georgian Gardens*, 127–9, 162–3.

[79] Kwiatkowski, *Król–architekt*, 219–20, 265. Tatarkiewicz, *Łazienki*, 75–82. Batowska, Batowski, Kwiatkowski, *Kamsetzer*, 225.

F IG. 10   The north façade of the palace on the island, Łazienki

A first floor had already been added to the bath house in 1777, but in 1784 it was enlarged to the south. The long dining-room so created was, like the library at the castle, broken up by columns. Merlini's new façade featured a tetrastyle recessed portico, a device which had been pioneered in Poland by Szczęsny Potocki at Tulczyn two years earlier. The main influences on the light, almost playful south façade were French and Italian.[80] In 1788, new wings were added to the palace and the new façade was placed further north. Kamsetzer's northern façade (Fig. 10) was more static, monumental, and disciplined than the southern, as befitted the fact that the main approach was from the north. Nevertheless the balustraded attic, the pilasters, and the use of the Corinthian order ensured that the overall effect was far from austere. Several designs for a long recessed portico were drawn up, virtual copies of Tulczyn, which the king had admired in 1787. Such a solution would, however, have given too little light, and so a projecting tetrastyle portico was chosen instead. The style was a mix of French and English neoclassicism. The Palladian character of the palace was strengthened in 1792–3 by the building of side pavilions and colonnaded bridges. The form of these bridges was reminiscent

[80] Kwiatkowski, *Król–architekt*, 190–3.

FIG. 11   The Ballroom at Łazienki

of those at Wilton and Stowe, which the king had seen almost forty years previously.[81]

The interiors, with the north façade, represent the last artistic achievements of Stanisław August. The neoclassical ballroom (Fig. 11), completed in 1793, was light and airy in white stucco. The dominant accents were the fireplaces at each end. Above them were niches for copies of antique statues of Apollo defeating savagery and darkness, and Hercules (virtue) overcoming stupidity and pride. The strongly architectural fireplaces were broadly similar to those favoured by the early eighteenth-century English Palladians. Merlini's rich golden 'Hall of Solomon' was the pendant to Kamsetzer's ballroom. Together they show the pluralism of Stanisław August's taste, and his individual blend of Palladianism, early and mature neoclassicism, and French classical baroque. The styles were

---

[81] Ibid., 194–9, 210. Tatarkiewicz attributed the design mainly to Merlini. *Łazienki*, 39–46. Jaroszewski, 'Pałac w Tulczynie' (n. 20), 90, 104–5. The Wilton bridge appeared in the fifth volume of *Vitruvius Britannicus*, pls. 88–9. Stanisław would not have seen the bridge at Prior Park, as it was built in 1755, but Sir Ralph Allen might have spoken about his plans during Stanisław's visit. See T. Mowl, *Palladian Bridges: Prior Park and the Whig Connection* (Bath, 1993).

FIG. 12   The stage on the island at Łazienki

appropriately fused together in the last Stanislavian interior, the Rotunda at the centre of the palace.[82]

The final phase of Stanislavian architecture saw an increased use of English sources, but the boundaries of their influence remained strictly drawn. Most of the planned or executed buildings and interiors were the work of Kamsetzer, who alone of the royal architects had toured England. The increased English influence is, however, ultimately a manifestation of Stanisław August's evolving taste. The king readily agreed to Kamsetzer's request to travel, and thereafter made heavy use of an architect well versed in English practices and solutions. Stanislavian architecture showed a pronounced shift towards neoclassicism, but the king liked a strong, almost baroque plasticity. Perhaps for this reason, Stanisław August probably found English Palladian interiors, whose strong architectural accents betrayed some influence of the Italian baroque,[83] and the 'movement' of Robert Adam's grand 'Roman' style, more to his taste than the Scottish architect's more usual repertoire of pastel colours and flat

[82] Kwiatkowski, *Król–architekt*, 200–4. Tatarkiewicz, *Łazienki*, 84–7. See the sections of Wanstead and Houghton in *Vitruvius Britannicus*, vol. 1, pl. 26, vol. 3, pl. 34. Thornton, *Authentic Decor*, 88–9. For the programme of the ballroom, see below, p. 228.

[83] Thornton, *Authentic Decor*, 89.

surfaces. Kamsetzer's ceilings were more influenced by the delicate Adam style at Pawłowice and in the Tyszkiewicz palace in Warsaw than in his work for the king. The mature Stanislavian style was closer to the work of James Gibbs, who 'ploughed an individual furrow between Palladianism and baroque'. However, Gibbs's *Book of Architecture* seems not to have been in the royal collection.[84]

Kamsetzer also laid out and designed a number of interiors in accordance with English practice, even designing English-style furniture. English furniture, upholstery, and carpets maintained their presence in the royal residences, but did not challenge French-pattern furniture, luxury French fabrics, and elaborate parquets for predominance. The 1795 inventory of Łazienki even suggests that mahogany English-pattern chairs lost some ground after 1788.[85] This is difficult to verify, not only because of the inadequacy of the descriptions in the inventories, but also because furniture was constantly being moved around. Perhaps the chairs bought or made in the 1770s were now old-fashioned, or just plain old, and needed replacement. For all its grace, the English furniture of the 1780s and 1790s had lost much of its distinctive character, and French influence was at its height. Lacquered or inlaid satinwood began to edge out carved mahogany in fashionable residences.[86] Thus the new furniture made in Warsaw for the king was less likely to follow English models. Likewise, Stanisław August transformed the gardens at Łazienki into a water-centred park after 1784, with an English flavour, but he retained symmetry in the general layout, and geometry continued to hold sway close to the buildings. The king made use of the fashion for England, but did so with discernment.

IV

English paintings formed a tiny proportion of Stanisław August's gallery. The Dutch school, including several reputed Rembrandts, constituted the majority of the 2,289 paintings and groups of paintings mentioned in the catalogue. Apart from Gainsborough's portrait of George III, the only other indisputably English pictures were a portrait of Sir Isaac Newton by Sir Godfrey Kneller, a view of the fort in Agra by William Hodges, *Romeo and Juliet* by Benjamin West, the *Arch in Heaven* by Bourgeois, and two 'peintures angloises' of hunting scenes. Besides those, a number

[84] Cruikshank, *Georgian Buildings*, 13. See T. Friedman, *James Gibbs* (New Haven and London, 1984).

[85] AKsJP 164.

[86] P. MacQuoid, *A History of English Furniture* (2nd edn., London, 1988), 300, 344–53, 380–4, 395.

of portraits may have been by English artists; of Charles II and his queen (Catherine of Braganza), the first Duke of Marlborough, Lord and Lady Payne, Lord Herbert, Lady Montagu, and Lady 'Gilfort' [Guildford?]. The gallery also contained pictures connected with two great artists who spent much of their careers in England: portraits of Henry VIII and Anne Boleyn supposedly by Holbein, and copies of Van Dyck's portraits of Charles I and the young Charles II and James II.[87]

The portrait of Newton was a gift from Michał Poniatowski in 1792. The primate had been advised to present the portrait to the king by a leading London art dealer, Noel Desenfans, whom he had met in 1790. When the primate was forced abroad during the Four Year Seym, Stanisław August asked him to investigate the possibilities of buying major works of art, in order to start a national gallery.[88] This was not the first time that the king had sought to purchase pictures in England. He had instructed Tadeusz Burzyński to look for Van Dycks in 1770. Burzyński discovered that nothing was on the market, nor likely to be so in the near future, and was advised that Van Dycks were easier to come by in Holland.[89] In 1790, Stanisław August judged that the market might be more favourable. After the outbreak of the French Revolution, aristocratic émigrés had begun to sell off their collections. The primate met Desenfans and his friend, the painter Peter Francis Bourgeois. Michał Poniatowski ordered numerous pictures and other items for himself, as the surviving copies of Desenfans's letters to him show, but the king's commission to buy paintings was on a far greater scale. The pictures were not sent to Poland. Desenfans and Bourgeois later bequeathed part of the collection to found the Dulwich Picture Gallery. Some were exhibited at the Royal Castle in 1992. Desenfans spent £9,000, but received only £1,300. He also had to pay the Bukatys' debts. Stanisław August consoled him as best he could, with the honorary title of Consul of His Polish Majesty.[90]

[87] Mańkowski, *Galerja Stanisława Augusta*, 51–60, 235, 275, 280, 289, 353, 363, 373, 375, 398, 401–2, 416, 442, 449 and *passim*. Bukaty wrote on 4 Nov. 1785 that he had sent the portrait of Marlborough to Danzig. AKP 81, f. 214.

[88] See the king's letters to the primate from 1790–1 in Zb. Gh. 801b.

[89] Burzyński to SA, 15 Sept. 1770, Zb. Pop. 216, ff. 129–30.

[90] Morawińska, 'Kontakty Stanisław Augusta i Michała Poniatowskiego z Noelem Desenfansem', 21–34. G. Waterfield, 'Galeria obrazów w Dulwich' and 'Fakty, plotki i dwieście skrzyń przedniego węgierskiego wina: Listy Noela Desenfansa do prymasa Polski', *Kolekcja dla Króla* (Catalogue of the exhibition of paintings from the Dulwich Picture Gallery at the Royal Castle, Warsaw, 1992), 15–23, 49–50. Libiszowska, *Życie polskie*, 109–13. SA to T. Bukaty, St Petersburg, 24 Nov. 1797, Kor. SA 3a, f. 158. The two extant letters from Desenfans to SA do not mention the pictures: 4 Apr. 1794, PAU 6, f. 90, 22 Jan. 1795, Kor. SA 3a, ff. 381–2.

The content of the collection assembled by Desenfans is worth attention, but it was dictated in the first place by the state of the market, which
abounded in Dutch and Flemish paintings. Practically the only evidence
available is the catalogue produced by Desenfans for the auction of some
of the pictures in 1802, and the dealer had continued to buy and sell since
1795, when it had become clear that he would never receive his money.
Although many of the attributions have since been corrected, they show,
as far as the market allowed, what the king wanted to possess.[91] Nothing
was from the fifteenth century and little from the eighteenth. Among the pictures Desenfans bought were a Titian, two Veroneses, a Tintoretto, three
Salvator Rosas, three Velázquezs, five Murillos, a Holbein, six Rubens,
six Van Dycks, a Jordaens, a Rembrandt, a Hobbema, two Jacob van Ruis-
daels, seven Cuyps, six Poussins, five Claude Lorrains, and two Watteaus.
Desenfans mentioned in the catalogue that Stanisław August particularly
wanted young landscapists to use Gaspard Dughet as a model. He was
only able to buy one picture by Dughet—a view of Tivoli.[92] Dughet ranked
behind Claude as an inspiration for English gardens. The fifteen English
pictures were all contemporary. Two were by Reynolds and seven were
by Bourgeois, who was a good landscapist and a reasonable portraitist,
but unsuited to large-scale historical scenes.[93] Stanisław August must have
thought well enough of his brother's paintings by Bourgeois, as he invited
Bourgeois to become 'painter to His Majesty'. Stanisław August had previously granted the same distinction to Bourgeois's master Philip de
Loutherbourg, who had offered the king two pictures in 1783. He also
ennobled Bourgeois (enabling the painter to use the title of 'Sir' in England) and sent him a gold *Merentibus* medal. Like the collection, Bourgeois
never reached Poland. At first he delayed his departure because of growing
successes at home, and later, Poland ceased to be an attractive proposition.[94]

As originals were rare and costly, and the primary purpose of the pictures was to instruct young artists, Stanisław August frequently made do
with copies and reproductions. English painting was better represented

[91] N. Desenfans, *A Descriptive Catalogue . . . of some Pictures of the Different Schools, Purchased
for His Majesty the Late King of Poland . . .* (3rd edn., 2 vols.; London, 1802).

[92] Desenfans, *Catalogue*, vol. 1, 153–4.

[93] Morawińska, op. cit. (n. 12), 33–43. Waterfield, 'Galeria obrazów', 28–31. After some
consideration, the primate decided not to purchase a nymph by Reynolds in 1791 for the
king. SA to M. Poniatowski, 19 Jan., 22 Jan., 29 Jan., 5 Mar. 1791, Zb. Gh. 801b, ff. 120,
123, 124, 137.

[94] SA to Bourgeois, 16 Feb. 1791, Zb. Pop. 186, f. 177. Bourgeois to SA, 11 Mar. 1791,
Zb. Pop. 207, f. 245. Bukaty to dept., 19 Aug. 1783, dept. to Bukaty, 13 Sept. 1783, AKP
80, ff. 104, 286. SA to M. Poniatowski, 29 Jan., 9 Apr. 1791, Zb. Gh. 801b, ff. 124, 152.
Morawińska, op. cit. (n. 12), 23–5. Libiszowska, *Życie polskie*, 110–11. Waterfield, 'Galeria
obrazów', 18, 21. *Kolekcja dla Króla*, 134.

in the cabinet of engravings than in the picture gallery. The *Works of Hogarth* were present in two volumes, with eighty plates. Most of the reproduced English paintings, however, were portraits, arranged by subject and not by author. They do not indicate any artistic preference. It is symptomatic that Stubbs was entered under *The Anatomy of the Horse*. The proportion of English engravings was very high, as in the art of the mezzotint England was renowned. Among the more frequently named engravers in the inventory were Ardell, Bartolozzi, Dickinson, Earlom, Elliott, and Spooner.[95] Stanisław August was excited to hear about the invention of polygraphic reproduction in 1789, as the full size of the original might be reproduced, and Bukaty and Komarzewski bought reproductions for the king in England.[96] It was no doubt for a similar didactic reason that Stanisław August asked his brother to send him details of the recently invented manufacture of artificial stone for statues.[97]

Antiquities *per se* formed but a small part of the royal collections, and they were subordinated to medals and gems in the classification, which is a further indication that Stanisław August was no fanatical neoclassicist. Moszyński wanted to buy more 'Etruscan' vases for him in Italy in 1785–6, but the king refused permission, as he thought the fourteen that decorated the library enough. About 8,000 of the medals were listed as ancient. The king acquired the medal collection of General Jan de Witte in 1787. As commander of the border fortress of Kamieniec Podolski, de Witte had exchanged casts with the British envoy in Constantinople, Sir Robert Ainslie.[98] According to two French visitors, none of the king's gems was worth attention, but Johann Bernoulli thought some of them very pretty.[99] Be that as it may, Stanisław August showed his serious interest by instructing Bukaty to obtain one of only fifty copies of an illustrated book of the Duke of Marlborough's gems.[100]

---

[95] AKsJP 215, ff. 101, 210, and *passim*.

[96] SA to Bukaty, 26 Aug. 1789, 30 Jan. 1790, BCzart. 849, ff. 109, 221. Bukaty to SA, 26 Feb. 1790, PAU 1658, f. 6.

[97] Stanisław August wanted to know whether it matched the polish and whiteness of marble. He was probably referring to Coade stone, which was produced from 1769. See J. Proudfoot, 'Artificial stone' and A. Kelly, 'Coade, Eleanor', in J. Turner (ed.), *The Dictionary of Art* (34 vols.; London, 1996), vol. 2, 540–2, and vol. 7, 480. SA to M. Poniatowski, 5 Mar., 12 Mar. 1791, Zb. Gh. 801b, ff. 138, 142.

[98] A. Abramowicz, *Dzieje zainteresowań starożytnych w Polsce: Część II: Czasy stanisławowskie i ich pokłosie* (Wrocław, 1987), 17–32, 63–97, 129–32.

[99] *Polska stanisławowska w oczach cudzoziemców*, ed. W. Zawadzki (2 vols., Warsaw, 1963), vol. 1, 406, vol. 2, 681.

[100] Dept. to Bukaty, 10 May 1783, Bukaty to dept., 27 May 1783. AKP 80, ff. 85–6, 275. 'Choix de pierres gravées du cabinet du Duc de Marlborough, gravées par Bartolozzi (2

Stanisław August made use of his friendship with Wroughton and his brother, Edward Montagu, to have his coronation medal struck in England by Thomas Pingo, who had earlier struck the medal for George III's coronation. The medals were despatched to Poland by the end of 1764.[101] Stanisław August had other medals and coins struck for him in England, and he was exacting about quality. Those made by R. Wood were not up to scratch, he told Bukaty on one occasion, and asked the envoy to find out if Pingo or MacCartney and Bayley could undertake the work instead.[102] The medals made for Stanisław August in Poland were struck by English steel stamps, and were similar in format to contemporary English medals. The king's head adorned the obverse, with an inscription the reverse.[103]

Like his contemporaries, Stanisław August purchased extensively in England. One British merchant wrote: 'It is now *two years* since I sent to Poland goods consisting of Coaches, hard ware, prints and sundry other articles to the amount of near *two Thousand Pounds* . . . the greater part of them . . . for *the use of His Majesty.*' The merchant, needless to say, was as yet unpaid and in severe financial trouble. A further £2,300 worth of goods was as a result being held up.[104] Stanisław August's taste for things English extended to his dress. Stanisław Lorentz noticed that Bellotto depicted the king in an olive-brown *redingotte*.[105] Stanisław August also wore English elastic garters.[106] Wedgwood sent Stanisław August a service, a set of 'Etruscan' vases, and a medallion bearing the king's head, as part of an advertising campaign, but not much of the king's porcelain

vols., 100 plates)', in the 1793 catalogue of engravings. AKsJP 215, f. 69. The duke later gave the second volume to Bukaty to send to the king. Bukaty to SA, 10 June 1791, BCzart. 3998, f. 136.

[101] Montagu to Wroughton, London, 29 Oct. 1764, Zb. Pop. 179, f. 204. Wroughton to SA, Warsaw, [mid-Nov. 1764?], Zb. Pop. 179, ff. 206–7. SA to Wroughton, 23 Nov. 1764, Zb. Pop. 179, f. 208. Wroughton to SA, undated [Dec. 1764?], Zb. Pop. 177, f. 281. See Libiszowska, *Życie polskie*, 42–3.

[102] SA to Bukaty, 13 June 1789, BCzart. 849, f. 93. Bukaty replied on 14 July 1789 that MacCartney and Bayley were dead, but Pingo was ready to do the job. BCzart. 3998, f. 314.

[103] SA to Bukaty, 13 June 1789, BCzart. 849, f. 97. SA to M. Poniatowski, 16 Mar. 1791, Zb. Gh. 801b, f. 144. L. Brown, *British Historical Medals 1760–1920* (London, 1980). I owe this reference to Dr Jacek Strzałkowski.

[104] H. Hoffmann to J. Lind, London, 11 June 1777, Zb. Pop. 160, ff. 33–4. Lind to SA, 4 July 1777, Zb. Pop. 161, ff. 16–17.

[105] Lorentz, 'Stosunki artystyczne', 12–13. See M. Wallis, *Canaletto: malarz Warszawy* (7th edn., Warsaw, 1983), illustration 1.

[106] Stanisław August asked Bukaty on 8 July 1781 to send him 'znowu kilka par takich sprężyn Elastik garters' [several pairs of such elastic garters again], BCzart. 849, ff. 5–6.

and china was English. Meissen and Sèvres were much more numerous. English models influenced Polish production, though; the king possessed two small vases 'faites sur un model anglois de la fabrique du Prince Stolnik Czartoryski'.[107]

The political messages conveyed by Stanisław August's architecture and interiors made use of the universal symbols of monarchy and of Polish history. The one general political inference that might be drawn from his choice of English models and fashions is their association with simplicity, nature, and informality; suitable perhaps for the enlightened king of a *res publica*. The king's move from symmetry towards irregularity in his gardens might be paired with the scaling down of the monarchical content in successive plans to rebuild the Royal Castle, and extended into a symbolic evolution of his political views. However, the analysis of Stanisław August's early political plans has refuted any suggestion of a would-be absolutist. Increasing English influences on Stanisław August's architecture and collections were rather the result of his evolving taste. In retrospect, his visit to England in 1754 seems to have been overshadowed completely from an artistic point of view by his stay in Paris. The first few years of his reign were dominated by artistic currents from France, which submerged English ones. Subsequently, the king responded to the tide of Anglomania that washed across Poland, but set his own course at a distance from the fashionable Warsaw aristocracy. He introduced some English and English-pattern furniture—mainly chairs—into his residences. In the middle years of his reign he embellished his gardens and pavilions with *chinoiserie*. Later, he created his own more regular variation on the theme of the landscape garden. Of the various strains in English architecture in the eighteenth century, it was Palladianism that most suited his taste for monumentality. Stanisław August had a rare gift for achieving harmony from disparate styles—neoclassicism, Palladianism, the baroque, and the picturesque. He was neither a slave to fashion nor bound by tradition. In the creation of Stanislavian harmony, English art played an increasingly significant role, but never the leading one.

[107] Lorentz, 'Stosunki artystyczne', 15. Reilly, *Wedgwood*, 218–19. AKsJP 181, f. 118. AKsJP 185, f. 87. The *stolnik* of the Crown was Prince Józef Czartoryski. AKsJP 183, ff. 3, 41.

Sapere Aude

Sapere auso: 'To him who dared to be wise'. On a medal struck in 1765, Stanisław August honoured Stanisław Konarski with the Horatian motto of the Enlightenment.[1] If Sarmatia was to be fully liberated from the chains of its self-imposed immaturity and enabled to think for itself, then the blinkered mentality of the late Counter-Reformation had to give way to the enlightened spirit of enquiry and criticism. The second half of the eighteenth century witnessed the flowering of experimental science in Poland, but empiricism did not vanquish superstition and scholasticism unaided or overnight. In Chapter 3 we saw that the pioneers of the 'newer philosophy' sewed together snippets of Wolff, Leibniz, Descartes, Newton, Locke, and others with the remnants of scholasticism, in order to strengthen religious orthodoxy rather than to weaken it. Such eclecticism was a long way from a full-blooded embrace of English empiricism, whose slow progress in Poland is readily comprehensible if we remember that the majority of scientists and philosophers remained Roman Catholic clerics, for whom the defence of the Copernican solar system was still an act of bravery. Nevertheless, in the last quarter of the century, Locke and Condillac became the leading philosophical authorities for most Polish academics.[2]

Władysław Smoleński's account of an 'intellectual revolution' in eighteenth-century Poland, for all its erudition and verve, was flawed by his a priori conviction that orthodox Christianity is the antithesis of empirical reasoning and incompatible with it. While the unenlightened of eighteenth-century Poland would have agreed, the vast majority of the enlightened would not. As a result, Smoleński's dialectic of Christianity versus Enlightenment sat askew with the evidence he uncovered of an Enlightenment, which, especially to start with, was led by the Roman Catholic clergy. Towards the end of the reign of Augustus III, a tide of godlessness began to overrun the aristocracy (including the higher clergy) and it reached high-water mark after the First Partition. Nevertheless,

---

[1] *Mémoires*, vol. 2, 209.
[2] Smoleński, *Przewrót umysłowy*, 101–4.

loose morals and a decline in traditional piety were at first no handicap to religious fanaticism (Bishop Sołtyk openly ate meat on Fridays).[3] In eighteenth-century France, the libertinism of the Regency broke many taboos and opened the way to an open intellectual onslaught on Christian doctrine. In Poland, despite the fears of traditionalists, widespread godlessness and fashionable enthusiasm for Voltaire and Rousseau did not lead to a similar assault.[4]

The authority of Stanisław Konarski buttressed religious orthodoxy. In 1769 he denounced the deist 'religion' of *honnêtes hommes* as contrary to morality, virtue, and common sense. Konarski approvingly cited Warburton's defence of reason, criticized superstition, praised the progress of science, and gave praise where it was due to pagan philosophers. At the same time, he robustly defended revelation as the basis of Christianity.[5] So too did Michał Karpowicz, the leading preacher of Stanisław August's reign. An outspoken supporter of social and political reform, Karpowicz was strongly influenced by the physiocrats, and even used the authority of 'Hume-Anglik' in order to show that religion and the Church were useful to the State and society. He roundly denounced *irreligia* and *libertyństwo*.[6] When *Monitor* demonstrated the existence of God the master clockmaker, Voltaire could not have disagreed with the substance of the argument, which included the statement that Nature invariably follows the rules of mechanics, but the tone was that of a sardonic attack on sceptics.[7]

The above remarks apply in particular to Stanisław August. The king's undisguised admiration of Voltaire (whose statue by Houdon took the

[3] Smoleński did not distinguish sufficiently between godlessness and intellectual deism or atheism, and was reduced to asserting that atheism was widespread among the élite, but hidden for fear of the reaction of the unenlightened *szlachta* masses. It is no coincidence that Smoleński found much of his evidence in the outbursts of scandalized traditionalists. *Przewrót umysłowy*, 159–98, and *passim*. Cf. J. Pasierb, 'Religijność polska w okresie Oświecenia', in *Życie kulturalne i religijność*.

[4] Neither Smoleński nor J. Snopek, *Objawienie i Oświecenie: Z dziejów libertynizmu w Polsce* (Wrocław, 1986), notes more than a handful of cases of open hostility to Christian belief. Snopek defines libertinism as philosophical hostility to the Christian religion, including its sexual morality. I prefer Stanisław's distinction between *philosophie* and a *libertinage* that centred on sexual freedom (see above, p. 109).

[5] *Myśli chrześciańskie o religij poczciwych ludzi* (repr. Cracow, 1887), esp. 81–5. On the refutation of deism, libertinism, etc., see Snopek, *Objawienie*, ch. 5.

[6] L. Gruszczyński, 'Z problematyki politycznej w kazaniach katolickich okresu stanisławowowskiego', *Acta Universitatis Lodziensis*, Folia Historica, 49 (1993), 18. M. Ślusarska, 'Problematyka polityczno-społeczna w polskim kaznodziejstwie okolicznościowym w latach 1775–1795' (unpublished doctoral thesis, Warsaw, 1992), 159 and *passim*, refutes charges of Karpowicz's 'rationalist reductionism'.

[7] *Monitor*, 1777, no. 81, cited after Z. Prószyńska, *Zegary Stanisława Augusta* (Warsaw, 1994), 111.

place of honour in the Royal Library) and his sexual laxity make it all
too easy to characterize his personal religiosity in generalizations about 'a
century more irreligious and libertine than any other'.[8] Emanuel Rostworowski was the first to consider the king's religiosity in the context of
the Catholic Enlightenment. The influence of Anglican Christianity upon
Stanisław August is discussed for the first time below.[9] The king played
a central role in the diffusion of English science in Poland, both by contacts with English scientists and by encouraging the introduction of its
main tenets into education in Poland. In no way, however, did he aim to
weaken the Christian religion.

I

Sarmatian traditionalists linked English influence and Stanisław August
with the apparent advance of godlessness, heresy, and deism in Poland.
In one satirical 'dialogue of the dead', 'Augustus III' alleged: 'he wanted
to reduce the [Catholic] faith in the English way, by introducing freedom of belief', while 'Stanisław Leszczyński' feared that he would die in
the English way as well (i.e. by committing suicide).[10] However, any English
influence on Stanisław August's religious and philosophical outlook was
certainly not reflected in his outward piety, which was appropriate for
the king of a Roman Catholic state. During his visit to Cracow in 1787,
he kissed the relics of St Stanisław, took part in a procession to the place
of his martyrdom, and visited all the more important churches in the
city.[11] Every year on Maundy Thursday, he made his confession kneel-
ing in the middle of the church to a priest sitting in front of the high
altar, washed the feet of twelve old men, gave them new clothes and shoes,
and personally served them dinner at the royal castle. Even Father Jędrzej
Kitowicz, a bitter critic, allowed that the king was prodigal in his charity and that he heard masses and sermons 'with exemplary modesty'.[12]

[8] Nuncio Giuseppe Garampi, quoted by L. Wolff, *The Vatican and Poland in the Age
of the Partitions: Diplomatic and Cultural Encounters at the Warsaw Nunciature* (Boulder,
Col., 1988), 246–7.

[9] Rostworowski, 'Religijność i polityka wyznaniowa Stanisława Augusta', in *Życie
kulturalne i religijność*. I discuss the issue in slightly more detail in 'Stanisław August Poniatowski
as a religious latitudinarian', in *Christianity in East Central Europe and its Relations with the
West and the East* (proceedings of the CIHEC congress in Lublin, 2–6 Sept. 1996, forthcoming, with a Polish version in *Wiek Oświecenia*, forthcoming).

[10] Quoted after Sinko, *Rozmowy zmarłych*, 177. See above, p. 121.

[11] 'Dyaryusz Przyiazdu . . . Stanisława Augusta . . . do Miasta Stołecznego Krakowa . . .
spisany . . . przezemnie Ignacego Labajewskiego', PAU 995, ff. 5, 32 and *passim*.

[12] J. Kitowicz, *Pamiętniki, czyli historia polska*, eds. P. Matuszewska and Z. Lewinówna
(Warsaw, 1971), 673–5. Rostworowski, 'Religijność i polityka wyznaniowa', 13.

However, Kitowicz was not alone in suspecting that Stanisław August's piety was mainly for show. The confederates of Bar and their friend the papal nuncio, Angelo Durini, condemned the king as a libertine and a deist or heretic.[13]

At the age of 24 Stanisław composed a literary self-portrait, which he later included in his *Mémoires*. Regarding his religion, he wrote: 'Je ne suis pas ce qu'on appelle dévot, et tant s'en faut, mais j'ose dire que j'aime Dieu et m'adresse très souvent à lui, et j'ai cette idée flatteuse qu'il aime à nous faire du bien, quand nous le lui demandons.'[14] At the heart of Stanisław August's religious beliefs was Divine Providence, which enabled him to retain a reserve of irrational optimism in even the worst crises, clinging to his motto, *Patience et Courage*. Surely God would not have given him such an ardent desire to make his people happy in vain? He interpreted his deliverance from the assassination attempt of 3 November 1771 as a sign from God, that he was after all predestined to do great things for his nation. He would sow the seeds of regeneration in Polish life, although another would harvest the crop.[15] Reflecting upon the enactment of the Constitution of 3 May, which had been pushed through by a determined *coup d'état*, Stanisław August was convinced that the uncharacteristic decisiveness and sang-froid he had shown were the gifts of Divine Providence: 'A toutes ces questions, je ne trouve d'autre réponse sinon: Dieu l'a voulu.'[16] The king campaigned for the confirmation of the constitution by the *seymiki* in February 1792 by describing it as a miracle of Divine Providence,[17] and on the first anniversary of the constitution he laid the foundation stone of the Church of Divine Providence at Ujazdów, next to Łazienki.[18]

Stanisław August always invoked 'God' in his correspondence, not Christ or the Holy Spirit, let alone the Blessed Virgin Mary or the saints.

[13] Konopczyński, *Konfederacja barska*, vol. 2, 859, 864, 866. Wolff, *Vatican and Poland*, 28.

[14] *Mémoires*, vol. 1, 177.

[15] Rostworowski, 'Religijność i polityka wyznaniowa', 14–15; e.g. SA to J. Yorke, 20 Mar. 1768, BL Add. 35433, ff. 93–4, Zb. Pop. 179, ff. 288–9; SA to Mme Geoffrin, 7 Oct. 1769, 23 Oct. 1771, 18 Dec. 1771, *Correspondance*, 358–60, 410–11, 423–4; SA to Naruszewicz, 21 Aug. 1775, *Korespondencja Naruszewicza*, 42; and SA to Mazzei, 21 Nov. 1789, Oss. 9751/I, f. 7.

[16] SA to Glayre, 25 June 1791, SA and M. Glayre, *Correspondance relative aux partages de la Pologne*, ed. E. Mottaz (Paris, 1897), 252. Rostworowski corrected the date from 21 June on the basis of the original. The king expressed himself similarly to Deboli, Mazzei, and Bukaty.

[17] e.g. SA to the Castellan of Liw, Krzysztof Cieszkowski, 6 Feb. 1792, BCzart. 920, f. 571.

[18] Rostworowski, *Maj 1791–maj 1792: Rok monarchii konstytucyjnej* (Warsaw, 1985), 17–18.

He found the dispute between the Orthodox and Catholic Churches over whether the Holy Spirit proceeded from the Father alone or from both the Father and the Son (*filioque*) rather ridiculous. He wrote to Madame Geoffrin about the peasant revolt in the Ukraine known as the *kolivshchyna*:

Quelques fanatiques ont menacé les paysans de notre Ukraine de toutes sortes de maux s'ils ne promettaient de cesser d'être grecs nons unis pour être grecs unis, c'est à dire s'ils ne cessaient d'expliquer la Trinité comme on l'explique à Petersburg pour l'expliquer à la façon romaine. Jugez si ces malheureux paysans y entendent quelque chose![19]

A rigorous theologian would probably suspect Stanisław August of deism. In the eighteenth century, however, the word 'deist' had aggressive connotations of an attacker of all revealed religion and Christian doctrine, like John Toland or, above all, Voltaire. Stanisław August never expressed any doubt as to the divinity of Christ. He simply did not find the matter important. Stanisław August's open admiration of Voltaire does not mean that he shared the *philosophe*'s religious views. In a conversation with the papal nuncio, Antonio Visconti, at the beginning of his reign, the king held that Voltaire was less dangerous to revealed religion than Rousseau, because Voltaire's own works, whatever Voltaire might wish, demonstrated the existence of Divine Providence and the immortality of the soul.[20] This implies that Stanisław August himself believed in them, and thus rejected one of the main tenets of eighteenth-century deism.

A more helpful description of Stanisław August's religious outlook is that suggested by Rostworowski, of a 'latitudinarian' (*latitudynarysta*), more sensitive to points of agreement than differences.[21] Warburton, a leading mid-century Anglican latitudinarian, had made a great impression on Stanisław in England. In 1797, the ex-king took his works with him to St Petersburg. Among the Royal Library's thousand volumes of theology (at the end of the reign) were the works of Tillotson and another rational apologist for Christianity William Sherlock.[22] Hugh Blair was the Scottish equivalent of a latitudinarian and Stanisław August received a copy of his *Sermons* from James Harris's sister in 1784. The king

[19] 6 July 1768, *Correspondance*, 343–4.

[20] Rostworowski, 'Religijność i polityka wyznaniowa', 16. No doubt the king's argument contained a dose of diplomacy, but it is worth noting that Visconti, unlike his rabid successor, Durini, was on good terms with Stanisław August. Lukowski, *Confederacy of Radom*, 104–5.

[21] Rostworowski, op. cit., 21.

[22] *Biblioteka Stanisława Augusta*, 139, 113. AKsJP 268, ff. 7–10, 30. See above, pp. 113–14.

told Harris that they were 'déjà traduits dans Ma langue, et que je compte bientôt les faire precher devant Moi, ainsi indigenés.'[23] The library also contained less orthodox works: by Conyers Middleton and William Wollaston, and Locke's *Reasonableness of Christianity* (in French). Stanisław August's religiosity was similar in many ways to that he had encountered in Williams and his other English friends in the 1750s; in its outward forms faithful to tradition, while in matters of doctrine unexacting, with the emphasis laid on ethics, 'Dieu', and Divine Providence, rather than grace and the Holy Trinity.

It would be unrealistic to expect Stanisław August to have shared the preoccupation of the latitudinarians with making the Newtonian universe the cornerstone of their theology, in order to ward off rationalistic deism on the one hand and sacerdotal Jacobitism on the other. Stanisław August's admiration for Newton was more personal. He possessed the *Principia*, and to help him understand it, the explanations of 's Gravesande, Pemberton, Algorotti, Voltaire, and others. In addition, he owned Newton's *Arithmetica Universalis, Treatise of the System of the World, Chronology of the Ancient Kingdoms*, and *Observations on the Prophecies of Holy Writ*.[24] The decoration of the ballroom at Łazienki was in part a philosophical reflection upon the Newtonian universe, whose harmony and order were represented by the signs of the zodiac and Raphaelite grotesques depicting the elements, the seasons, the ages of man, the Fates, and day and night. Placed above them was a symbolic clock, and above that, its maker, Saturn, shown with an hourglass. This was not the distant, impersonal master clockmaker of the deists, for like Newton, Stanisław August believed in divine intervention to maintain the marvellous mechanism of the cosmic clock. Moreover, Saturn was Stanisław August's ruling planet, and for the Roman poets, his rule on earth had been a golden age. The king linked the astrological predictions that had attended his birth with implacable Divine Providence, and fervently hoped that his destiny was to restore the Saturnian golden age in Poland.[25]

II

Besides Newton, the Royal Library contained the classics of English empirical philosophy—the *Works* of Bacon, Shaftesbury, and Locke, as well as

    [23] Białystok, 26 Nov. 1784, Zb. Pop. 182, f. 254.

    [24] AKsJP 268, ff. 7, 27–35, 103. AKsJP 270, f. 20.

    [25] Prószyńska, *Zegary Stanisława Augusta*, 103–19. W. Dobrowolski, 'Program Sali Balowej Pałacu Łazienkowskiego', in *Curia Maior: Studia z dziejów kultury ofiarowane Andrzejowi Ciechanowieckiemu* (Warsaw, 1990).

Condillac. Descartes and Wolff were also strongly represented, however. Stanisław August did keep Locke's *Works* at Łazienki, and took them to St Petersburg in 1797.[26] The royal picture gallery contained portraits of Bacon and Newton.[27] Beyond this, Stanisław August seems not to have expressed his views on English empiricism overtly, so we must see how his allies did so in print. The main royal propaganda organ at the beginning of the reign, *Monitor*, encouraged science and combated superstition. In 1766, Krasicki satirized the adherents of scholasticism:

With them Gassendi and Descartes are worth nothing. Why? Because they were French, and what is more, they did not write in set forms. Galileo? An Italian. As for Newton, Leibniz, Locke, Wolff, why, God forbid that they should be even mentioned, they were heretics excommunicated from God's Church![28]

The manner was reminiscent of Voltaire, but the message was more equivocal. The time was not yet ripe to come out in full support of Locke and Newton. When Krasicki adapted one of Addison's discourses on the omnipresence of God, where Addison had written 'the noblest and most exalted way of considering this infinite space is that of Sir Isaac Newton, who calls it the sensorium of the Godhead,' Krasicki replaced 'Newton' with *filozof*. In an essay on the Universe and the creations in it, adapted from the *Spectator*, a long quotation from Locke's *Essay on Human Understanding*, wondering if more perfect creations than ourselves exist elsewhere, was replaced by Krasicki with the pious remark that God knows best. In the fourth number, Stanisław August omitted Locke's name from a quotation on the relativity of the feeling of time passing, so perhaps he was responsible for the policy.[29] However, in another adapted number, Krasicki wrote that Locke had alleged that ghosts and apparitions had no more connection with the night than with the day, and that people learned in childhood to associate fear with the dark from the stories of simple people. Krasicki followed the *Spectator* in refusing to deny the existence of apparitions, but cautioned against belief in silly tales.[30] In 1773, *Monitor* commented that Descartes and Gassendi had overcome Plato and Aristotle, only to be defeated in turn by Newton, Leibniz, and Wolff, so it was better to teach the philosophy of them all.[31]

---

[26] *Biblioteka Stanisława Augusta*, 77, 78, 112, 143, 156. AKsJP 268, ff. 26–35, 133. AKsJP 270, ff. 3, 20.

[27] T. Mańkowski, *Galerja Stanisława Augusta* (Lwów, 1932), 401.

[28] '*Monitor' 1765–1785: Wybór*, 1 Mar. 1766 (no. 18), 81–2.   [29] See above, p. 189.

[30] Sinko, *'Monitor' wobec angielskiego 'Spectatora'*, 117–18, 140–1. *Monitor*, 1772, nos. 15, 69, and 72.

[31] Smoleński, *Przewrót umysłowy*, 99–100. *Monitor*, 1773, no. 69.

Zabawy Przyjemne i Pożyteczne represented the royal circle in the 1770s. One article in 1770 sang the praises of Descartes and Bacon. The latter's achievements were set against the darkness of his age. A piece on 'genius' by Michał Jerzy Mniszech in 1774 included the following: 'The immortal Newton, aided by you, [O genius,] thought to trace the paths and properties of curves with calculus, he first discovered and used the advantages of prisms.'[32] But an apotheosis of the empirical method was lacking. Świtkowski's *Pamiętnik Historyczno-Polityczny* did much to promote the newer philosophy and publicize scientific experiments and discoveries (the voyages of Captain Cook, for example), but it still tended to call in the support of all modern philosophers indiscriminately in the fight against ignorance and superstition. Proclaiming philosophy 'the daughter of experience' (*corka doświadczenia*), it declared that even in Spain, Locke, Helvétius, Montesquieu, d'Alembert, Diderot, Wolff, and Leibniz were well known.[33]

Stanisław August and his camp thus paid discreet and careful homage to the theorists of empiricism, but alongside other modern philosophers. The king's real interest, however, was in science and its application. Captain Cook's companion Georg Forster recorded that at a dinner in Grodno in 1784, Stanisław August, Michał and Stanisław Poniatowski, the king's sister Izabella Branicka, his niece Konstancja Tyszkiewicz, Szczęsny Potocki, and others conversed about comets, William Herschel's telescopes, and bison.[34] Stanisław August tried out lightning conductors at Ujazdów Castle after hearing of Franklin's experiments, and installed a conductor at the Royal Castle on 6 July 1784, an event enthusiastically reported by *Pamiętnik Historyczno-Polityczny*.[35] No sooner had the king read about a new scientific instrument or machine than he would instruct Bukaty to find out more about it, and, if it could be useful, despatch it to Poland. For example, in 1785, he asked about the purpose and the price of an 'aequatorial instrument', new improved muskets, and a water-resistant leather container described in the *St James's Chronicle*.[36] The king's 'physical cabinet' contained models of English machines made in Warsaw, taken from those depicted in Hennequin's *Recueil de différentes machines*

---

[32] Smoleński, *Przewrót umysłowy*, 344. *ZPP*, 9, part I, 280.

[33] Homola Dzikowska, *Pamiętnik Historyczno-Polityczny*, 137–41. Smoleński, *Przewrót umysłowy*, 145–58, 355. *PHP*, Jan. 1783, 6–7, 1786, vol. 2, 303–13, 399–412.

[34] G. Forster, 'Dziennik podróży po Polsce', in *Polska stanisławowska*, vol. 2, 88.

[35] Zamoyski, *Last King*, 241. Smoleński, *Przewrót umysłowy*, 148–50.

[36] SA to Bukaty, 26 Nov. 1785, 7 Dec. 1785, 31 Dec. 1785, BCzart. 849, ff. 41–3, 45, 49.

fait pendant le voyage d'Angleterre (1772), which formed part of the cabinet of engravings.[37]

Astronomy claimed its fair share of Stanisław August's attention, and his astronomical and mathematical instruments were by no means the Cinderella of his collections. Their inventory, drawn up in 1782, runs to sixteen pages in quarto. The majority of them were made by renowned London optical firms; most of the rest were from Paris. There were quadrants, clocks, and refracting and reflecting telescopes from Dollond, Nairne and Blunt, Watkins, Hadley, Shelton, Webster, and Ramsden.[38] Stanisław August nominated Canon Jowin Bystrzycki astronomer royal in 1773, and soon afterwards work started on an observatory at the Royal Castle. From 1775, Bystrzycki's observations, often carried out in the presence of Stanisław August, were reported in the Warsaw press. The observatory was extended in 1788.[39]

Stanisław August's enthusiasm for astronomy was partly motivated by its practical application. At the start of his reign, he granted the Jesuits' observatory at Wilno the title 'royal', and invited Marcin Poczobut and other Jesuits to work on establishing the latitude and longitude of various places in Poland, as part of his grand design to produce the first accurate atlas of the Commonwealth. The Jesuits determined the location of a number of towns in 1767, and Poczobut ordered some more instruments in England in 1769. After the dissolution of the order, however, work only proceeded sporadically, and the atlas was never completed.[40]

Although increasingly the preserve of gentlemen amateurs, the Royal Society could still boast the likes of Franklin and Priestley, and symbolized the fame of English science. It opened its arms to the young King of Poland and his scientists. Through the offices of Edward Montagu (and perhaps also of Hardwicke and Charles Yorke), the Royal Society elected Stanisław August a Fellow in December 1766. As a token of

[37] Bernoulli, 'Podróż po Polsce', in *Polska stanisławowska*, vol. 1, 406–8. Mańkowski, 'Kolekcjonerstwo Stanisława Augusta', 28. AKsJP 216, f. 43, AKsJP 215, f. 153.

[38] 'Catalogus Instrumentor Mathematicor . . .', BCzart. 1493. SA to Bukaty, 8 July 1781, 12 Oct. 1785, BCzart. 849, ff. 5–6, 38. Bukaty to dept., 4 Nov. 1785, AKP 81, f. 214. The king asked the primate to buy a telescope in 1791. SA to M. Poniatowski, 29 Jan. 1791, Zb. Gh. 801b, f. 126.

[39] Smoleński, *Przewrót umysłowy*, 134–5. Libiszowska, *Życie polskie*, 246–7. Kwiatkowski, *Król-architekt*, 125. W. Olszewicz, 'Bibljoteka Stanisława Augusta', *Przegląd Bibljoteczny*, 5 (1931), 40. *Korespondencja Śniadeckiego*, vol. 2, 201–13.

[40] Smoleński, *Przewrót umysłowy*, 133–4. Jobert, *Commission d'Éducation Nationale*, 131. *Mémoires*, vol. 2, 209–10. B. Bieńkowska, 'Kultura umysłowa', in *Warszawa w wieku Oświecenia*, 136–7. The king expressed his regrets to Kazimierz Plater in 1787. Kraszewski, *Podróż Stanisława Augusta do Kaniowa*, 24–6.

his thanks, the king sent the Society a *Merentibus* medal, which was so admired by the luminaries of London that their president, the Earl of Morton, asked for a similar medal for himself. The medal was duly delivered by Montagu.[41] Stanisław August next sent the Royal Society a detailed plan for a medical and veterinary academy in Poland that would include an 'œconomical society' to advance 'a more flourishing state of agriculture and the whole science of Oeconomy, of commerce, of manufactures, and in general of everything relating to industry'. Part of it was read out on 10 November 1768, but the rest of the paper, which was to have been read out at a later date, was withdrawn. The plans were probably shelved because of the cancellation of that autumn's Seym.[42]

In December 1768, Stanisław August recommended Poczobut to the Society. Through the offices of Dr Matthew Maty, both Poczobut and Burzyński attended meetings, and Burzyński was elected a Fellow, supported by Maty, Brühl, Hardwicke, James Harris, and Charles Morton. The next year, the Royal Society communicated to Burzyński a request for the king's portrait. Stanisław August, graciously replying in the affirmative, asked that Poczobut be elected a Fellow, and the Society was pleased to comply. In 1778, Bystrzycki presented the Society with a letter from Poczobut and a medal struck in his honour, and a report of observations at Wilno.[43] In that same year, the Royal Society, alongside the Paris Academy of Sciences, readily agreed to the naming of the new constellation discovered in 1775 by Poczobut 'le Taureau Royal des Poniatowski', and entered it onto its celestial charts. Stanisław August, however, did not wish 'le Taureau' to be compared with the adjoining constellation, *Scutum Sobescianum*, because, as he explained to Naruszewicz, Sobieski's shield had defended the Commonwealth, and his had not.[44] The Danzig astronomer and physician, Nathaniel Matthias Wolf, sent the Society several papers

[41] Journal Book of the RS, 11 Dec. 1766, vol. 25, 976, 12 Nov. 1767, 28 Jan. 1768, vol. 26, 357–8, 435. Copy of certificate, 11 Dec. 1766, Morton to SA, 26 Feb. 1767, SA to Morton, 27 June 1767, Morton to SA, 10 Mar. 1768, Morton to Montagu, 11 Mar. 1768, Montagu to SA, 15 Mar. 1768, note of a request to Wroughton, 13 Apr. 1768, Zb. Pop. 177, ff. 284–97. Libiszowska, *Życie polskie*, 43.

[42] 'A Specimen of Regulations for the Institution of an Academy at Warsaw', RS, Letters and Papers, vol. 5, 42. Journal Book, vol. 26, 544.

[43] Journal Book, 8 Dec. 1768–11 May 1769, vol. 26, 560–646 *passim*, 7 Nov. 1771, vol. 27, 118–19. SA to RS, 14 Dec. 1768, Zb. Pop. 179, f. 201. SA to Wroughton, 14 Dec. 1768, Zb. Pop. 179, f. 225. Burzyński to SA, 21 July 1770, Zb. Pop. 93, f. 2, BCzart. 847, f. 179. SA to Maty, 15 Aug. 1770, Maty to SA, 10 June 1771, Zb. Pop. 395. Libiszowska, *Życie polskie*, 43, 246–7.

[44] Naruszewicz to SA, 10 Aug. 1775, SA to Naruszewicz, 21 Aug. 1775, Poczobut to Naruszewicz, 5 Sept. 1778, Naruszewicz to SA, 11 Oct. 1778, SA to Naruszewicz, 11 Oct. 1778, *Korespondencja Naruszewicza*, 34, 42, 123–8.

from 1766, and was elected a Fellow in 1777.[45] Stanisław August commissioned his brother Michał to complete the Royal Library's set of the *Philosophical Transactions*, and the primate also became a Fellow in 1791.[46]

Nevertheless, with time the Royal Society apparently lost interest in the king of Poland, for in 1784 Stanisław August thanked one of its Fellows, Alexandre Aubert, for having wanted to 'reparer à Mon égard l'espece d'oublie que la Société Royale de Londres a faite de son associé dans Ma Personne'. A few years earlier, Aubert had assisted Poczobut's assistant, Father Andrzej Strzecki, to buy in London the latest instruments for the Wilno observatory. The king had sent Aubert a *Merentibus* medal in 1780, and the London astronomer sent in return a medal struck by the Royal Society to commemorate Captain Cook, and an illustrated edition of his last *Voyage*. Thanking Aubert, Stanisław August wrote that he wished not to 'négliger aucune occasion, qui représentera d'approprier à Mon Pais toutes les connoissances utiles dont la Société Royale de Londres ne cesse d'enrichir la Science'.[47]

Cook's *Voyages* was among the most frequently borrowed books in the Royal Library, and the king himself is recorded to have taken out three volumes in 1787. Stanisław August looked at the plates together with Georg Forster in 1784. The library also contained other prominent works of travel literature, including the voyage of Anson.[48] The king collected animal, plant, and mineral specimens, of which the minerals, encompassing all the main rocks found in the Commonwealth, were the most impressive.[49] Among the illustrated works on natural history in the cabinet of engravings was Hamilton's *Observations on the Volcanoes of the Two Sicilies*.[50]

Stanisław August lacked the financial means to rival Catherine II in sending young men to study in England (and elsewhere), but he did what he could, and took a keen interest in their activity. Tadeusz Bukaty kept him informed of Śniadecki's observations with Herschel, and passed on an account of Herschel's telescopes and a message that the 'volcanoes' on

---

[45] RS, Letters and Papers, vol. 4, 336, 414, vol. 5, 32, vol. 6, 213, 236, vol. 7, 87, 233. Journal Book, 10 Apr. 1777, vol. 29, 36.

[46] SA to M. Poniatowski, 29 Jan. 1791, 30 Apr. 1791, Zb. Gh. 801b, ff. 126, 163.

[47] Aubert to SA, 24 Aug. 1784, SA to Aubert, 26 Nov. 1784, Zb. Pop. 182, ff. 31–3. Bukaty to Cabinet, 29 Aug. 1780, BCzart. 3998, f. 1.

[48] *Biblioteka Stanisława Augusta*, 158–61. Forster, 'Dziennik podróży po Polsce', in *Polska stanisławowska*, vol. 2, 85. The king's niece, Konstancja Tyszkiewicz, followed her uncle's example a few days later. Ibid., vol. 2, 88.

[49] Mańkowski, 'Kolekcjonerstwo Stanisława Augusta', 38. Fortia de Piles and Boiseglin de Kerdu, 'Podróż dwóch Francuzów', in *Polska stanisławowska*, vol. 2, 682.

[50] AKsJP 216, f. 60. AksJP 215, f. 206. *Biblioteka Stanisława Augusta*, 106.

the moon they had observed together should also be visible through the Dollond telescope at the Royal Castle observatory.[51] When Śniadecki, having returned to Poland, reported the progress of astronomy in England to Poczobut, he sent the letter unsealed via Joachim Chreptowicz, who in turn showed it to the king.[52] A few Poles studied at Oxford and Cambridge, despite the oaths which hindered Roman Catholics from matriculating or taking degrees. One Wąsowicz arrived back in Poland in 1768 with letters recommending him to the king from David Durell, the Oxford Vice-Chancellor, and Thomas Hornsby, reader in experimental philosophy and Savilian Professor of Astronomy, whose lectures Wąsowicz had attended. Stanisław August sent them his thanks via Wroughton.[53] Soon afterwards, two royal scholars, Zukowski and Glazer, were sent to Oxford, with a request for Burzyński to look after them. In 1782, Bukaty received a positive reply from the Foreign Secretary to a request for protection and help for Polish students.[54] Prince Stanisław Poniatowski spent the winter of 1772–3 with his tutor John Lind at Cambridge. The prince returned to Poland in the company of Professor Robert Barker of Queens' College, whom Stanisław August warmly welcomed. Barker later wrote a letter to Stanisław August, asking for financial help before his marriage.[55]

The most wide-ranging of the scientific visitors to England was General Jan Komarzewski, the head of the king's military chancellery, who was forced abroad at the beginning of the Four Year Seym. Via the king and Chreptowicz, Komarzewski's information on mathematics and astronomy was sent to Poczobut at Wilno. The general quickly struck up a lifelong friendship with Herschel. Komarzewski sent the king a detailed account of his observatory, and was accompanied by Herschel on three voyages. Herschel, his wife, and his sister even learned to toast the health of the king of Poland in Polish, and the astronomer wrote to Stanisław August, thanking him for his interest. Stanisław August sent Herschel a medal, and wrote to Bukaty:

[51] T. Bukaty to dept., 10 Sept. 1787, AKP 82, ff. 213–14, Muz. Nar. 76, ff. 120–2.

[52] Śniadecki to Poczobut, 14 Feb. 1788, Śniadecki to Chreptowicz, 10 Mar. 1788. *Korespondencja Śniadeckiego*, vol. 2, 8–19, 30–5.

[53] Durell to SA, 15 Feb. 1768, Hornsby to SA, 17 Feb. 1768, Zb. Pop. 177, ff. 287–9. Note of SA, after 13 Apr. 1768, Zb. Pop. 177, f. 285. On Durell and Hornsby see *The History of the University of Oxford*, vol. 5, *The Eighteenth Century*, eds. L. S. Sutherland and L. G. Mitchell (Oxford, 1986), 154, 165, 486, 670–2, 675, 680–1, 734.

[54] Libiszowska, *Życie polskie*, 216, 254–5.

[55] Stanisław Poniatowski, *Pamiętniki synowca Stanisława Augusta*, trans. and ed. J. Łojek (Warsaw, 1979), 49–51. *Alumni Cantabrigiensis*, Part II (Cambridge, 1940, repr. 1978), vol. 1, 153. Libiszowska, *Życie polskie*, 192–3. Barker to SA, London, 23 Sept. 1781, Zb. Pop. 180, ff. 36–7.

Wielce mnie uciesza pomyślny skutek applikacyi Komarzewskiego, ieżeli się tak
wydarzy, że Herschelowi nawet pomoże do ieszcze głębszego w niebie rozpatrzenia
się.

(The successful outcome of Komarzewski's application greatly pleases me, if it
happens that he can help Herschel to see even further into the heavens.[56])

Astronomy was for the general something of a diversion. He concentrated on physics and chemistry, and travelled to Paris to meet Lavoisier,
Fourcroy, and Charles. Komarzewski studied the extraction of metals with
an eye to the modernization of the copper mines at Miedziana Góra, for
which he planned to use English machines. During his peregrinations,
Komarzewski visited tin mines in Cornwall and Matthew Boulton's factory in Birmingham, where he was shown the steam engines, which, he
told the king, did the work of 180 to 200 people. Wilkinson even gave
the general a cannon from his foundry. Komarzewski was no mere dab-
bler; his scientific achievements were substantial and his election as a Fellow
of the Royal Society in 1792 was thoroughly merited. Driven out of the
army he had himself reformed, he wrote himself into the history of Polish
science.[57]

Komarzewski was accompanied on some of his journeys by an enthusiastic young scholar from Wilno, Franciszek Zaliwski, whom he found
an 'exceptional genius in mechanics'. Stanisław August gladly informed
his brother the primate that Zaliwski was to act as his guide and interpreter during his stay in England, and show him the academies, observatories, and factories previously visited by Komarzewski.[58] The king's
personal interest in English developments is demonstrated by his receipt
in 1792 of the *Transactions of the Society for the Encouragement of Arts and
Commerce*.[59] Among the other Poles who toured factories were Izabella

[56] Komarzewski to SA, 4 Dec. 1789, 27 Apr. 1790, 10 June 1790, 25 June 1790, 3 Aug.
1790, 16 Oct. 1792, BJag. 3510 (unpaginated). Bukaty to SA, 26 Feb. 1790, 9 Apr. 1790,
PAU 1658, ff. 5, 9. Ditto, 25 Dec. 1792, BCzart. 3211, f. 35. SA to Bukaty, 14 Dec. 1789,
19 May 1790, 21 Aug. 1790, 21 Mar. 1792, BCzart. 849, ff. 137, 145, 185, 587. I have not
found Herschel's letter of 21 June 1790, but the king acknowledged it to Bukaty on 14 July
1790, BCzart. 849, f. 161. SA to M. Poniatowski, 23 Oct. 1790, Zb. Gh. 801b, f. 90.
Komarzewski to Herschel, Meissen, 20 Sept. 1799, RS 3.35. See Libiszowska, 'Podróże naukowe
Generała Jana Komarzewskiego', *ZNUŁ*, Ser. I, 88 (1972), and eadem, *Życie polskie*, 251–4.
[57] Komarzewski to SA, 27 Apr. 1790, 5 Dec. 1790, 14 Feb. 1791, 11 Oct. 1791, 16 Oct.
1792, BJag. 3510. Bukaty to SA, 1 May 1792, BCzart. 3998, ff. 173–4. RS Journal Book,
vol. 34, 9 Feb. 1792. Komarzewski was proposed by Herschel.
[58] Bukaty to SA, 9 Apr. 1790, PAU 1658, ff. 9–10. SA to Bukaty, 3 Nov. 1790, BCzart.
849, ff. 213–24. Bukaty to SA, 10 May 1791, BCzart. 3998, f. 127. SA to M. Poniatowski,
23 Oct. 1790, Zb. Gh. 801b, f. 90.
[59] *Biblioteka Stanisława Augusta*, 131. BCzart. 938, f. 503.

and Adam Jerzy Czartoryski and the primate's natural son, Piotr Maliszewski, who undertook a range of economic studies.[60]

The most ambitious industrial complex in the Commonwealth was created on the royal estate of Grodno by the court treasurer of Lithuania,
Antoni Tyzenhauz. Tyzenhauz wished to make use of the latest foreign
techniques, and so he sent Tadeusz Downarowicz to western Europe in
1773–5. In London and Manchester, Downarowicz examined factory
machinery. In 1778, Tyzenhauz himself was in England with a team, each
of which was to gather information on different subjects. The astronomer
royal Bystrzycki was one. In the treasurer's own crowded programme were
various museums, observatories, a glassworks, the exhibits of inventions,
machines in the halls of the Society for the Encouragement of Manufacture and Trade, and institutions for orphans and invalids.[61] Tyzenhauz's
schemes at Grodno were vast. They encompassed the manufacture of wool,
linen, silk, lace, hats, iron, firearms, paper, candles, and carriages, as well
as a botanical garden under the Frenchman Jean Gilibert, an observatory
with English instruments, and a medical academy. The results were
mixed. The wool, linen, leather, and candles made profits, but the other
enterprises ran at a loss, suffering from under-investment, an under-
developed market, and the unsuitability of their conscripted peasant labour
forces. In 1780 Tyzenhauz fell from grace, a victim both of the intrigues
of his enemies and of his own restless ambitions. Only the most competitive of his factories survived him. The charge of over-ambition also
applies to Stanisław August, who stuck to Tyzenhauz as long as he could,
and placed great hopes in him. Unfortunately, Stanisław August was not
blessed with commercial acumen. None of his many ventures in mining,
porcelain, or firearms can be described as a resounding success. He was
not alone in his poor results, but some magnates, notably Józef Czartoryski
and 'Prot' Potocki, did better.[62]

No less than industrial development, the modernization of Polish agriculture was a goal of the Polish reformers, and the enlightened press gave
details of English and Dutch crop rotations.[63] One Polish botanist, named

---

[60] Gołębiowska, 'Podróż Izabeli i Adama Jerzego Czartoryskich', 138–41. Libiszowska,
Życie polskie, 241, 255.

[61] S. Kościałkowski, Antoni Tyzenhauz, podskarbi nadworny litewski (2 vols.; London 1970–1),
vol. 1, 380, vol. 2, 340–54. Libiszowska, Życie polskie, 12, 196–9.

[62] Kościałkowski, Tyzenhauz, vol. 1, 225–314, 499–521. W. Kula, Szkice o manufakturach w Polsce XVIII wieku (2 vols.; Warsaw, 1956), vol. 1, 309–448 and passim. Korzon,
Wewnętrzne dzieje, vol. 2, 230–81. Zamoyski, Last King, 244–53. Coxe, Travels, vol. 1, 207,
211–24.

[63] Lukowski, Liberty's Folly, 53–4.

Au (!), sent Stanisław August some cotton and indigo seeds from England via Bukaty in 1790, with the hope of their cultivation in southern Poland.[64] The Bishop of Wilno, Ignacy Massalski, one of the keenest disciples of the physiocrats, was the first Pole to visit the agronomist Arthur Young.[65] During his years in England, Franciszek Bukaty acquainted himself with modern agricultural techniques and got to know the leading authorities. In 1793 he informed Stanisław August that a parliamentary commission on agriculture had been set up, and that its chairman, Sir John Sinclair, had given him a copy of the Act establishing the commission for the king. The previous year, Bukaty had sent a pamphlet by Sinclair to the king, the primate, and Mniszech.[66] Bukaty sent his own nephew Aloyzy to Young at Bradfield, but the youth did not show much enthusiasm, and swiftly returned to Poland. Thanking Young for his trouble, Bukaty informed him that the King and the Primate of Poland, hearing of his fame,

wish to see you once in that Country, whose natural riches consisting in agriculture, might be essentially improved by your transcendent Knowledge therein. It was already their intention to establish there a Society of agriculture, had it not been for the present political circumstances, which necessarily take up all their time and attention. I would be exceedingly happy, Sir, to know, when you will be present in town, in order to have some conversation on the subject.

Bukaty also asked Young where he might obtain the threshing machine, a drawing of which his nephew had taken back to Poland. On another occasion, Bukaty informed Stanisław August that he had recommended young Sobolewski to Young 'to examine English agriculture'. A further Polish student of Young's was Adam Kołaczkowski, who later attempted to put his ideas into practice on his estate of Wełna near Poznań, without much success.[67] That verdict may be applied generally. Despite the interest in English agricultural methods, their practical impact in Stanislavian Poland, including the king's own estates, was virtually zero. The necessary investment in draining, marling, or manuring was prohibitively

[64] The king was bemused by the unexpected seeds and asked Bukaty to explain. He was eventually enlightened by Au himself in Warsaw. Bukaty to SA, 11 May 1790, 20 Aug. 1790, PAU 1658, ff. 14, 25. SA to Bukaty, 31 July 1790, 18 Aug. 1790, 8 Sept. 1790. BCzart. 849, ff. 169, 181, 193.

[65] J. Włodek, *Dwa szkice z historji stosunków polsko-angielskich w dziedzinie agronomji* (Cracow, 1921), 11–12. Jobert, *Magnats polonais et physiocrates français* (Paris, 1941).

[66] Bukaty to SA, 15 Mar. 1793, BCzart. 3211, f. 50. *Biblioteka Stanisława Augusta*, 131.

[67] Libiszowska, *Życie polskie*, 213–14, 217, 256–7, 264. Bukaty to Young, 27 May 1789, BL Add. 35126, f. 457.

expensive, and peasants stubbornly resisted enclosure. The entire serf economy would have to be transformed before agricultural innovation went
beyond the expensive experiments of a few enthusiasts.[68]

Stanisław August and his circle believed that science should be subordinated to economic utility. A good example is the plan submitted to
the Royal Society for an academy. Nevertheless, the king's approach to
economics was in practice characterized more by curiosity and an enthusiasm for novelty, in a word, by the dilettantism typical of the age. Any
suggestion of a co-ordinated 'economic policy' would be inappropriate.
For this reason, economics have been discussed at the end of the section
on science. Dilettantism was no bad quality for a patron of science, but
Poland's economic development in the late eighteenth century owed little
to Stanisław August's *direct* initiatives (the permanent presence of the
Court indisputably furthered the rapid growth of Warsaw). Poland was
not Prussia. In the decentralized and relatively unregulated Commonwealth, the market was left largely to itself. The king's efforts to kick-
start industrial development were ineffectual, but also unnecessary. The
biggest obstacle was, even more than the commercial warfare waged by
Frederick II, the basic social structure, and no amount of royal factory-
founding or propaganda on crop rotations could change it. Let us now
see how the royal enthusiasm for English science affected education in
Poland.

III

Stanisław August's unflattering comments in his *Mémoires* on the traditional education of young Englishmen were written in 1775, when the
Commission for National Education was still deliberating over the form
of schooling in Poland. We therefore know what the king wished to avoid—
rote learning of Latin with the liberal assistance of the lash, and a neglect
of common civility (with overbearing pride and political egoism as its consequence). Most of his comments might have just as well applied to traditional Jesuit schooling. Stanisław August's caustic views contrast with the
praises lavished upon English schools in *Monitor*, probably by Czartoryski, emphasizing that no nation knew the classics so well as the English.[69]

---

[68] Lukowski, *Liberty's Folly*, 54–5. M. Wachowski, 'L'agriculture polonaise dans l'orbite
des influences internationales de 1750 à 1830', in *Actes du XIe Congrès International
d'Histoire des Sciences . . .* (Wrocław, 1968), vol. 5, 365–8, cites no English influence on Polish
agricultural *practice*.

[69] *'Monitor' 1765–1785: Wybór*, 21 July 1765, 34–6. Krasicki also praised English schools
in *Pan podstoli*. Krasicki, *Pisma wybrane*, eds. T. Mikucki *et al.* (5 vols.; Warsaw, 1954),
vol. 3, 249–50.

Nevertheless, a French translation of Locke's *Thoughts on Education* was in the Royal Library,[70] and a look at the king's own cadet school shows the predominant influence of *progressive* English pedagogical theory and practice.

Since 1632, the kings of Poland had been obliged in their *pacta conventa* to found a military school for the education of noble youth. Stanisław August was the first to keep his promise. Soon after his election, he set about organizing a cadet school (*szkoła rycerska* or *korpus kadetów*), which opened in 1765. The king nominated Czartoryski commandant. In addition to giving the school its general enlightened and patriotic ethos, summed up in his *Katechizm kadetów*, Czartoryski was a generous benefactor. He supplied the bulk of the library of 10,000 volumes, one of the most modern in Poland. Among the many French translations of English works were Hume's *Political Discourses*, Pope's *Works*, Fielding's *Tom Jones*, and a number of mathematical titles. However, Czartoryski's interest waned in later years and he eventually resigned his post in 1785. Although the school was theoretically funded by the Commonwealth, the king bore the initial costs himself, including the purchase of its building, and for three decades, despite the continual shortages in his own pocket, he helped the school struggle through one financial crisis after another. In addition, Stanisław August paid the expenses of some cadets, and if they showed promise, like Tadeusz Kościuszko, he sent them abroad for further study. The king read the cadets' reports, examples of their work, and was present at all the most important school ceremonies. His involvement extended to the recruitment of professors.[71]

In its first years, the cadets were unruly youths in their late teens or early twenties, whose conduct did not always add lustre to the school's reputation. Academic work was placed on a lower plane than military training. Stanisław August appointed John Lind director of studies in 1767, and the Englishman promptly set before the king a plan of reform, effected in 1768–9. Lind took as his model the best English private academies, which featured a similar general curriculum, stressing languages and using Lockean methods. Boys, drawn in the main from the middling *szlachta*, were to enter at the relatively unspoilt age of 8 to 12, and a modern curriculum was introduced, which had as its aim the schooling not only of army officers, but also of future state functionaries. Lind expected

[70] *Biblioteka Stanisława Augusta*, 192.
[71] Mrozowska, *Szkoła Rycerska Stanisława Augusta Poniatowskiego (1765–1794)* (Wrocław, 1961), 7, 9, 12, 21–2, 26, 43–59, 130–2. J. Wojakowski, *Biblioteka królewskiego Korpusu Kadetów w Warszawie* (Warsaw, 1989).

that the first two classes would teach the boys to read and write in Polish, Latin, French, and German, and the basics of arithmetic. The next three would give them a general education, with the addition of history and geography. The last two classes placed the emphasis on military and civil architecture and law. Throughout the school, drawing, fencing, and dancing were taught, in order to make the youths into gentlemen.[72]

Under the influence of Locke and Rousseau, Lind abandoned rote learning completely and sought to work on the pupils' understanding. He made far greater use than Konarski of visual aids—portraits of illustrious Poles, maps, globes, measuring instruments, collections of animals and plants, and even an orrery (a machine demonstrating the Copernican solar system), bought in England for 1,000 ducats by Czartoryski. Languages, including Latin, were taught directly by practising speech and writing. Grammar, wrote Lind, should be used like a dictionary, and not learnt by heart—an idea taken from Locke's *Thoughts on Education*. The aim was to enable pupils to read foreign literature and so obtain useful information—another Lockean idea. Lind wanted teaching to be in Polish as far as possible, but most teachers were at first foreigners out of necessity. Fortunately, some had studied Polish at Königsberg. Both the strongly moral tone of lessons in history and literature, and the minimal corporal punishment in the school (although not on the military side of the corps) were consequences of Lind's belief that the malleable *tabula rasa* could yield virtuous and patriotic servants of the Commonwealth.[73]

Lind himself did not stay long as director of studies, as he accompanied Prince Stanisław Poniatowski to England in 1771. His curriculum proved in practice to be rather too ambitious, and his successors paid more attention to basics, but in its essentials it remained untouched until the closure of the school in 1794. A compulsory reading list of twenty-eight works was introduced for senior cadets in 1781. It included French translations of Hume's *History of England* and William Robertson's *Charles V*. The teaching in the cadet school was therefore an adaptation of progressive English educational thought and practice to Polish conditions by John Lind, the trusted friend of Stanisław August.[74]

The Commission for National Education ('Kommissya Edukacyi Narodowey') was set up by the Partition Seym in 1773. The idea of using the wealth of the suppressed Jesuit order to finance a system of national education was dear to Stanisław August, and his first victory was over

---

[72] Mrozowska, *Szkoła Rycerska*, 80–2, 143. The plans are in Zb. Pop. 366 and 367.
[73] Ibid., 83, 86–7, 112–19, 148.
[74] Ibid., 80, 83–5, 147. Wojakowski, *Biblioteka Korpusu Kadetów*, 73–6.

the papal nuncio, who wanted the estates handed over to the episcopate. However, the Seym cut the king off from direct control over the commission, and Adam Poniński and his cronies helped themselves to a third or more of the Jesuit inheritance under the cover of a so-called 'inventory'. The pillage was only halted in 1776. As a result, funds were always short, and the projected University of Warsaw remained on paper. Nevertheless, in practice, a compromise was worked out between the king and the first president of the commission, Ignacy Massalski. The king concluded his first meeting with the commissioners on 18 October 1773 with the somewhat muddled hope that 'with time this Polish educational commission would equal the Free Company (*Kompania Wolna*) [Royal Society?] in England, which has as its aim the spread of all types of arts and sciences.'[75] Stanisław August, as patron, exerted much influence on the commission through some of its members, notably his brother Michał, who was president from 1778, and Chreptowicz. From 1776 the king nominated all new members, who included Prince Stanisław Poniatowski and Mniszech. The king unfailingly marshalled his political forces to defend the commission from Sarmatian critics, who would seize its assets, in order to avoid paying taxes for an augmented army, and return all schooling to the ex-Jesuits.[76]

The cadet school, although the king defended its autonomy, served the commission in many ways as a practical model. Lind's successors as directors of studies, Christoph Pfleiderer and Michael Hube, were active in the Society for Elementary Textbooks (*Towarzystwo do Xiąg Elementarnych*). The curriculum in the commission's schools (*szkoły wojewódzkie*) was similar, although less time was given to modern languages and more to sciences. The final class devoted most time to Polish public law. Teaching methods were similarly based on Locke. Rote learning was replaced (at least in the better schools) by observation, analysis, and explanation. Many schools had impressive collections of instruments and other visual aids. Experiments became the basis of physics lessons, and in order to enlighten parents, they were sometimes performed on open days. Locke's *Thoughts on Education* was translated into Polish by the Piarist, Edmund

---

[75] 'Z czasem ta Kommissya Edukacyina Polska wyrówna Kompanii Wolney w Anglii będącey, maiącey za cel przez szerzenia wszelkiego gatunku kunsztów y sciencyi.' W. M. Grabski, 'Pierwsza audiencja "ministrów" KEN u Stanisława Augusta Poniatowskiego', *ZNUŁ*, Ser. I, 88 (1972), 60.

[76] Jobert, *Commission d'Éducation Nationale*, 164–74, 217–34. Mrozowska, *By Polaków zrobić obywatelami*, 2–15. The finances of the commission are the subject of W. M. Grabski's monograph, *U podstaw wielkiej reformy: Karta z dziejów Komisji Edukacji Narodowej* (Łódź, 1984).

Truskolawski, and published in 1781.[77] Condillac was invited to write a primer in 1777, but the resulting *Logique* was thought too materialistic to be used in schools. The main theological content in teaching was the demonstration of God's beneficence in the Creation, with no appeal to revelation. The Piarist, Antoni Popławski, proposed the use, among others, of Derham's *Physico-Theology* and Condillac's *Comment l'homme acquiert la connaissance de Dieu*. In accordance with physiocratic thought (Dupont de Nemours was secretary to the commission in 1774) and the needs of a republican system of government, the emphasis was placed on the education of virtuous and useful citizens.[78]

The slumbering academies of Cracow and Wilno were reformed under the auspices of the commission, which turned them into 'main schools' (*szkoły główne*) for the Crown and Lithuania respectively. One of their main functions was to train teachers, who were to form a separate 'academic estate'. The reform of Wilno University was handicapped by its Jesuit foundation. The professors were embittered and the academy had vegetated since 1773 until its refoundation in 1781. Poczobut was appointed rector, but he neglected the natural sciences for Latin poetry. Nevertheless, astronomy continued to flourish; the collection of mostly English instruments astounded Forster, and in the rector's opinion rivalled that of the observatory in Oxford. The physical museum also contained a great many English instruments, and Newtonian mathematics were taught by Franciszek Narwoysz after his return from England in 1783. Stanisław August generously endowed the medical faculty with a collection of surgical equipment and a cabinet of natural history.[79]

[77] *Xiążka o edukacyi dzieci z francuskiego na polski język przełozona* (Warsaw, 1781).
[78] Jobert, *Commission d'Éducation Nationale*, 176, 197–202, 284–90, 302–23. Idem, 'Tradition et nouveauté dans l'oeuvre de la Commission d'Éducation', and I. Stasiewicz-Jasiukowa, 'Wartości wychowawcze podręczników do nauki moralnej', in K. Mrozowska and R. Dutkowa (eds.), *W kręgu wielkiej reformy: Sesja naukowa . . . w dwusetną rocznicę powstania Komisji Edukacji Narodowej* (Warsaw, 1977), 21–5, 219–32. C. Majorek and T. Słowikowski, 'Wkład pijarów w teorię wychowania patriotycznego i obywatelskiego w Polsce w XVIII wieku', in I. Stasiewicz-Jasiukowa (ed.), *Wkład pijarów do nauki i kultury w Polsce XVII–XIX w.* (Warsaw and Cracow, 1993), 443–4. Mrozowska, *Szkoła Rycerska*, 152, 223–6. Eadem, *By Polaków zrobić obywatelami*, 41–51. For a rare comparative perspective, see Rostworowski, 'Polski głos w edukacyjnym koncercie wieku Oświecenia', in *Popioły i korzenie*.
[79] Jobert, *Commission d'Éducation Nationale*, 253–61. Smoleński, *Przewrót umysłowy*, 274. Lukowski, *Liberty's Folly*, 228. Z. Pawlikowska-Brożek, 'Matematyka w szkołach głównych Komisji Edukacji Narodowej', in *W kręgu wielkiej reformy*, 145–6. Mrozowska, *Z Polaków zrobić obywatelami*, 16–31. Forster to C. G. Heyne, 20 Nov. 1784, cited after Maurer, *Aufklärung und Anglophilie*, 382.

First as visitor, and then as Rector of the Jagiellonian University, Hugo Kołłątaj was more successful than Poczobut.[80] He was able to fill the reduced number of chairs with local talent, such as Jan Śniadecki, Józef Bogucicki, and Antoni Cyankiewicz, a translator of part of Locke's *Essay on Human Understanding*.[81] Scholasticism was finally laid to rest, but Newtonian physics still coexisted with the systems of Wolff, Descartes, and Leibniz. From 1784 Franciszek Scheidt included Priestley's experiments on gases in lectures for first-year physics students, and in 1786 he demonstrated a Nairne electrical machine. His colleague Andrzej Trzciński, an enthusiastic Anglophile, translated Priestley's account of the impregnation of water with 'fixed air' (the artificial carbonation of water).[82] Michał Poniatowski paid for the chemical laboratory. An astronomical observatory and a botanical garden were established, although the former was not opened until 1791. Stanisław August contributed by arranging for the purchase of chemical and astronomical instruments in England, and by presenting the professor of mathematics and astronomy, Śniadecki, with a Dollond telescope and a pneumatic pump from his own collections. After his trip to England in 1787, Śniadecki ordered books and further astronomical and physical instruments from London via Tadeusz Bukaty.[83] In 1787, during his visit to Cracow, apart from taking part in numerous religious ceremonies, Stanisław August gave the university his demonstrative support. He planted herbs and bushes in the botanical garden, saw experiments performed before him, was shown the collections of the *Collegium Physicum*, and listened to Trzciński's dissertation extolling the growth of science 'through the spirit of observation'.[84]

Stanisław August was himself no theologian, no philosopher, no scientist, no economist, and no pedagogue. It did not matter. As king he saw his role in the opening of minds. How could a society that for a century and a half had viewed the universe through the meniscus of a literal interpretation of Genesis, some distorted precepts of Aristotle, and a strong

[80] Chamcówna, *Uniwersytet Jagielloński*, 36, 48, 83–129, 158–200 and *passim*. Jobert, *Commission d'Éducation Nationale*, 248–52. Smoleński, *Przewrót umysłowy*, 273–4, 285–6.

[81] *Logika czyli myśli z Lokka o rozumie ludzkim wyięte* (Cracow, 1784).

[82] *Nauka o napuszczaniu wody powietrzem kwaskowem . . . z dzieł oryginalnych sławnego Prystleia . . . wyięta* (Cracow, 1787), a translation of *Directions for Impregnating Water with Fixed Air . . .* (London, 1772). See R. E. Schofield, 'Priestley, Joseph', in *Dictionary of Scientific Biography* (New York, 1975), vol. 11, 144–5.

[83] Bystrzycki's remarks on the instruments in the 1782 catalogue, AKsJP 276, ff. 1–3. *Korespondencja Śniadeckiego*, vol. 1, 322–7, 340, vol. 2, 55–133, *passim*.

[84] PAU 995, ff. 20–3, 31, 41, 63–4.

dose of superstition, be expected to question in political and social affairs the maxim *omnia mutatio nociva*? Stanisław August did not begin the work of re-educating the *szlachta*. Others accomplished a great deal during his reign independently, and the process carried on after his death. Nevertheless, his tireless if unsystematic patronage gave the Polish Enlightenment its greatest single forward impetus. By taking such a keen personal interest in science, the king contributed to the raising of its prestige in society. Giving Copernicus the place of honour in the Knights' Hall at the Royal Castle was a revolutionary gesture. Stanisław August gave the proponents of modern philosophy and science moral support in their battle with scholasticism and superstition, while at the same time strengthening by his own example the bridges between Enlightenment and Catholicism. Both in its respect for tradition and its open-minded approach to doctrine, his religiosity owed not a little to Anglican latitudinarianism. This did not go deep enough, however, for him to grasp and pass on to enlightened Polish clerics the insight that Newtonian physics offered the theological foundations on which to build the rational, tolerant, and practical Christianity which they expounded in the schools of the Commission for National Education. Nor is it likely that it should have done.

Stanisław August also gave generous material assistance to institutions of learning, providing part of the plethora of English instruments with which experimental science was carried out, and he helped Polish scientists to make contact with their colleagues in western Europe. He was particularly fascinated by astronomy, and it was in astronomy that Anglo–Polish co-operation was most fruitful. The king's cadet school set new standards in Polish schooling. With its Lockean methods, it sent its enlightened graduates back into the provinces, met with the general approval of the *szlachta*, and provided a model for the schools of the Commission of National Education. Stanisław August's role in the propagation of science, especially English science, in Poland was therefore significant both symbolically and practically.

'Less Showy Means':
From the Confederacy of Bar to
the Four Year Seym

The Confederacy of Bar gave a stimulus to thought on the future shape of the Polish government. Under the supervision of Stanisław August, Adam Naruszewicz wrote a pamphlet, *Suum cuique*, which argued on historical grounds that the prime source of Poland's ills was the hallowed right of free election, which prevented the king from giving an effective lead and afforded neighbouring powers the opportunity to interfere in Poland's affairs. Andrzej Zamoyski looked to England when he proposed a hereditary throne and a governing cabinet, although the Polish king's powers were to be more circumscribed. Meanwhile, some of the confederate leaders were prepared to abolish the veto and offer the throne on a hereditary if emasculated basis to the Elector of Saxony, if by doing so they could dethrone Poniatowski.[1] The agent of the confederacy in France, Michał Wielhorski, approached Gabriel Mably and Jean-Jacques Rousseau, and asked them to draw up plans, based on the information he supplied them with. The results were Mably's *Du gouvernement et des lois de Pologne* and Rousseau's *Considérations sur le gouvernement de Pologne*. Later Wielhorski drew upon their reflections (Rousseau's rather than Mably's) and his own thoughts when he wrote *O przywróceniu dawnego rządu Rzeczypospolitey* ('On the restoration of the ancient government to the Commonwealth'), whose sole concession to modernity, the abolition of the *veto*, was hedged about with the strictest guarantees of the sovereignty of the *seymiki* and the impotence of the elective king.[2] All

---

[1] *Suum cuique*, ed. R. Pilat, repr. in *Przegląd Polski*, 14 (Oct.–Dec. 1869), 423–36. See A. F. Grabski, *Myśl historyczna*, 157–60, which reviews the evidence on the authorship of *Suum cuique*; Zielińska, 'O sukcesyi . . .', 14–18; Michalski, 'O rzekomych i rzeczywistych pismach Andrzeja Zamoyskiego'; *PH*, 60 (1970); idem, 'Gdyby nami rządziły kobiety. (Poglądy Amelii Mniszchowej na reformę Rzeczypospolitej)', in *Wiek XVIII: Polska i świat*; Konopczyński, *Geneza i ustanowienie Rady Nieustającej*, 125–43; idem, *Konfederacja barska*, esp. vol. 2, 891–2; and idem, *Polscy pisarze polityczni*, 286–9.

[2] See Michalski, *Rousseau i sarmacki republikanizm* (Warsaw, 1977); idem, *Sarmacki republikanizm w ozach Francuza: Mably i konfederaci barscy* (Wrocław, 1995); idem, 'Z problematyki

these projects went for nothing. The Commonwealth's fate was now beyond their authors' control.

While fighting Turkey, Russia lacked the manpower to stamp out the rebellion in Poland. Once suppressed in one place it flared up in another, like an irritating but hardly lethal bout of acne. While the pretext for the First Partition of Poland was Austria's seizure of the *starostwo* of Spisz (Zips), its immediate cause was Austria's insistence that Russia return the conquered provinces of Moldavia and Wallachia to the Turks. In the event of war between Austria and Russia, Russia would have to reward Prussia with a slice of Poland for her aid. Until January 1771, Frederick II was sceptical about the chances of a partition, but he was emboldened by the Austrian stand. Frederick had already shown a willingness to negotiate with Austria, and even if, as Catherine guessed, the Austrian bellicosity was a bluff, she did not relish the task of getting Frederick to relinquish what he had already occupied in Polish Prussia. Catherine preferred to settle for gains on the northern shore of the Black Sea and in Polish Belorussia, paid for by Austrian and Prussian shares of Poland. The Austrian triumvirate decided not to go to war (Kaunitz was sensibly overruled by Maria Theresa and Joseph), and as Frederick refused to countenance giving up part of Silesia, they joined in the partition, rather than be left with nothing. The three powers reached agreement in August 1772, just as the confederacy finally burnt itself out.[3] The Commonwealth was stripped of nearly a third of its territory and more than a third of its population, and was disabled economically by Prussian control of the lower Vistula.

The general lines of the new constitutional settlement were dictated by Catherine II personally. Austria and Prussia had conflicting views on the matter, but were too concerned to extend their shares of the spoils to put up any significant resistance on the form of government. The details were therefore contested between the king and the hirelings used by Catherine's new ambassador, Otto Magnus Stackelberg, to force the

republikańskiego nurtu w polskiej reformatorskiej myśli politycznej w XVIII wieku', *KwH*, 90 (1983), 330–2; Konopczyński, *Konfederacja barska*, vol. 2, 907–29; Leśnodorski, 'Idee polityczne J. J. Rousseau w Polsce', in *Wiek XIX: Prace ofiarowane Stefanowi Kieniewiczowi* ... (Warsaw, 1967); J. Grobis, 'Sukcesja tronu w publicystyce Sejmu Czteroletniego' (unpublished doctoral thesis, Łódź, 1975), 66–78; A. Walicki, *The Enlightenment and the Birth of Modern Nationhood: Polish Political Thought from Noble Republicanism to Tadeusz Kościuszko* (Notre Dame, Ind., 1989), 11–16; and Lukowski, 'Recasting Utopia: Montesquieu, Rousseau and the Polish constitution of 3 May 1791', *HJ*, 37 (1994), 70–1. I am grateful to Dr Lukowski for a typescript.

[3] This interpretation of the Partition largely follows Madariaga, *Russia in the Age of Catherine*, 219–36, Beales, *Joseph II*, vol. 1, 280–300, Cegielski and Kądziela, *Rozbiory*, 102–28, and Rostworowski, 'Gra Trzech Czarnych Orłów', in idem, *Popioły i korzenie*.

ratification of the partition treaties through the specially convened Seym. Before returning to that battle, in order to analyse any English influence on the new constitutional arrangements eventually established in 1775 and 1776, let us examine Stanisław August's views of the English constitution at this time.

I

On 6 August 1772, Stanisław August sent an anonymous article to Manzon's *Journal du Bas-Rhin*, titled 'Extrait d'un lettre des frontières de Pologne et sur l'État du Royaume'.[4] The news of the Partition had just broken, and the Austrian envoy Reviczky was expected shortly. While the Partition looked unavoidable, Stanisław August hoped that the Commonwealth might be able to trade its ratification of it for an improved form of government, and that Austria would support his stand: 'On sent que ce ministre soit specialement chargé de faire tous ses efforts . . . de changer la forme du Gouvernement et d'établir un sur le modèle de celui d'Angleterre.' The king's hopes were not altogether without foundation; Kaunitz was inclined to make the rest of Poland as strong as possible, and described the *liberum veto* as 'ein politisches monstrum'.[5]

The 'letter' opened with the statement that 'les Polonois instruits' might support reform if it were shown to be in their own interests. The Polish nobility had shown its patriotism in resisting foreign oppression,

mais il faudrait qu'elle fut moins légere, et moins inconstante pour Son Roy, qu'au lieu d'exciter des troubles, de fermenter la division, Elle chercha les moyens d'assurer la tranquillité Publique au dedans, surtout qu'elle prouvait le cas qu'elle fait de la liberté en la rendant à ceux qui dépendent d'elle.[6]

It was a call for a shift in political culture. 'Tranquillity', understandably enough, was a watchword of the article. Stanisław August followed up with a devastating attack on the existing state of affairs; it was 'un Gouvernement bizarre, le plus défectueux de tous ceux qui existent', 'un mélange monstrueux de servitude et de grandeur', 'rempli d'Inconsequences et d'absurdités', 'un amas confus de puissances qui se heurtent sans cesse', and 'une machine politique dont tous les rouages n'ont aucun raport les uns et les autres, dont tous les ressorts sont sans harmonie'. Here the

---

[4] A draft is in Zb. Pop. 177, ff. 185–7. On the king's relations with Manzon, see J. Łojek, *Polska inspiracja prasowa w Holandii i Niemczech w czasach Stanisława Augusta* (Warsaw, 1969), ch. 4.

[5] Konopczyński, *Geneza i ustanowienie Rady Nieustającej*, 177, 182, 191.

[6] Zb. Pop. 177, f. 185.

king made clear his preference for a government constructed logically and working harmoniously. Above all, 'la Pologne est une Republique qui a un chef sans autorité.' Birth, not wisdom or experience, was the qualification in the 'conseil national' (the Seym), which was at the mercy of the caprice of a single member, because of the *liberum veto*. There was no country with more contrasts, between a Crown and a republic, between an outward love of liberty and the manners of courtiers, between luxury and poverty, between taste and the lack of useful or agreeable arts, and between bravery and indiscipline.[7]

Stanisław August contrasted the situation of the kings of France and Poland. The former was free to make himself loved. The latter, 'toujours contrarié, toujours surveillé, perpetuellement contredit, souvent même il est attaqué', was forced by his situation to attempt to subvert liberty, and make himself feared rather than loved. He had a modest income, but in *starostwa* and other graces the means to corrupt. 'On peut dire qu'il n'a pas un grand pouvoir, mais de grands moyens d'en exercer un tres grand.' Stanisław August then presented the traditional Polish ideal of a king:

Notre Roi, disent les Polonois, ne peut être heureux qu'autant qu'il renonce au desir d'eteindre nos privilèges, de transgresser nos Loix. S'il respecte les uns et les autres, il est chéri de Ses Peuples, il a leur Confiance, il règne sur les Esprits, parce qu'il règne sur les Coeurs. Tout plie de ses ordres, s'il n'en donne que plie notre bonheur. Il dispose de l'armée, si nous savons qu'il ne s'en servira que pour notre defense. S'il ne trouble pas les Conseils pour ses intrigues, Ces Conseils prennent ses avis, et les servirent. Les Tribunaux qui le voient respecter la Loi, veillent à ce qu'elle soit observée. Les Ministres de l'État ne cherchent point à le contraire, ni à le flatter parce qu'ils savent que ses bienfaits seront le prix de leur zèle et de leur vigilance. Le Senat enfin, qui voit en Luy le Père de la Patrie n'est point en garde contre son influence.[8]

The Poles had possessed 'ce Roi cheri' in Stanisław Leszczyński; they had dethroned him (hardly the whole truth!). They had him in Stanisław August. No king had ever tried harder to reign over his people's hearts, but he could only aspire to making himself feared. Stanisław August judged that this idyllic vision was rendered impossible by the vices of the constitution, which might, however, be righted at the forthcoming 'pacification' Seym. The tribute to Leszczyński was a clue to the provenance of the passage, which was taken almost word for word from the French edition

---

[7] Stanisław August referred to these 'paradoxical' contrasts in the same manner as did travellers from western Europe. See Wolff, *Inventing Eastern Europe*, 17–31.

[8] Zb. Pop. 177, ff. 185–6.

of *Głos wolny*.[9] Stanisław August was engaging in an extended polemic with his namesake before European public opinion. He took issue with both Leszczyński's blaming of successive monarchs for the absence of 'tranquillity', and his call to reduce the monarchy to an honorific role, totally dependent upon the will of the nation.[10]

Supposedly the duties of the king were to lead the army, see that justice was dispensed to all, make proper use of the state revenues, and keep the peace. But these duties had become abuses in the hands of ministers. If their function was to stop the king attacking liberty, why was the king allowed to appoint whomsoever he liked? 'Si d'un autre coté il faut pour le bien de l'Etat qu'ils maintiennent la Liberté dans ses justes bornes et l'y feront rentrer quand Elle est immoderée,' why were they practically undismissable? It would be better for them to be chosen for a few years at a time by the king, senate, and chamber of envoys jointly. At present, their incapacity, ignorance, intrigues, and indolence enfeebled the entire life of the state. The notion that liberty has proper limits and should be forced back within them when 'immoderate', while taken from Leszczyński, became for Poniatowski an attack on the root of *aurea libertas*.

At the end of the article, the king noted that

Jean-Jacques Rousseau a formé un Plan de Legislation pour le Royaume et l'a communiqué à plusieurs Polonais qui sont en France, on dit que c'est le plus beau Roman politique qui ait encore paru, une Éducation Nationale est la base. En suivant ce Plan, la noblesse s'était divisée en trois Classes et aurait 'chacqu'une une marque distinctive, et l'on tirait au soit du Corps de Senateurs; trois sujets donc l'un serait du Roi'. Il y a bien de la difference entre ce Plan et celui de former le Gouvernement sur le Modèle du Gouvernement de la Grande Bretagne.[11]

Stanisław August had been sent a copy of Rousseau's *Considérations sur le gouvernement de Pologne* in February 1772 by Grimm, who scathingly called it 'une barbouilleuse de papier, quelque eloquent qu'il pouvait être'. When he found time to reply a year later, Stanisław August regretted that 'Rousseau n'a voulu voir, ni reconnoitre, d'ennemis ni de dangers, pour la Pologne, que dans la personne de son Roi,' but he reserved his real bile for those 'Philosophes qui prodiguent l'encens à l'oppresseur

---

[9] *La Voix libre du citoyen, ou observations sur le gouvernement de Pologne* (Paris, 1749), 37–8.

[10] Ibid., 32–9. I deal with this polemic more fully in 'Two views of the Polish monarchy in the eighteenth century: the polemic of Stanisław August Poniatowski with Stanisław Leszczyński', *OSP*, new series, 30 (1997).

[11] Zb. Pop. 177, f. 187.

heureux'. No doubt Grimm felt the sting of the rebuke. Stanisław August compared Rousseau's *Considérations* to Raphael's grotesques at the Vatican —sublime, but bizarre and far removed from reality. If Rousseau had had other sources, 'il eut écrit tant différement.'[12] The king too put his hopes in national education and could certainly appreciate the power and beauty of the *Considérations*. He judged its author generously and was reluctant to criticize him, but he could not but realize its utter impracticability as a blueprint for government. His comparison of it with the English system of government was mild, but pointed.

Rousseau's prediction that England would fall because of its want of public virtue in the face of the corruption of the Crown, may have been in Stanisław August's mind when he came to relate his stay in England in his *Mémoires* in 1775. By then, he had been disappointed by the British government's failure to defend Poland from dismemberment and he saw England heading for disaster in America. Stanisław August, however, detected some signs of hope, where Rousseau would have seen the certainty of impending disaster, in the polishing and even the Gallicization of the manners of the English. Two decades after his visit, English ladies now closely followed their French neighbours. Whereas traditionalists saw in this trend only 'une approximation vers l'esprit monarchique', Stanisław August saw the mutual good of both nations in the increasing contact and lessening of hostility between them:

Les Français sont devenus un peu plus penseurs et moins légers, et les Anglais, croyant n'adopter que par complaisance pour les femmes de leur pays une partie de manières françaises, corrigeront peut-être le défaut de leur éducation nationale, qui en les affranchissant trop, les rend ensuite par un effet de plusieurs conséquences trop dépendants de leurs passions.

Stanisław August's view of the causes of English decline was therefore basically the opposite of Rousseau's—an excess of English individuality was responsible for the corruption of their political culture, not their captivation by luxury and French manners. The progressive polishing of English manners over the course of the century was a highly positive development to the civilized king, a near teetotaller, who still carried with him the dreadful memory of fraternizing with the drunken *szlachta* in order to be elected to the Seym. Politer manners were essential to the rejuvenated Poland he so fervently desired.[13]

---

[12] Grimm to SA, undated [late 1771/early 1772], 22 Feb. 1772, SA to Grimm, 17 Apr. 1773, Zb. Pop. 221, ff. 375, 380, 381–3.
[13] *Mémoires*, vol. 1, 124–5. See *The English Satirical Print*, vol. 3, 37, 180–1.

Whatever his disenchantment with the policies of His Britannic Majesty's government, whatever his distaste for blatant political corruption, whatever his sympathy for Rousseau, the English constitution remained Stanisław August's preferred model for Poland. Even his avowed abandonment of 'cet enthousiasme de jeunesse' in 1779, intended for consumption at Versailles, applied to the English king and the English nation, and not the constitution.[14] He remained attached to the same basic programme as in 1763—an end to the *liberum veto*, the curbing of the old-style ministers, an effective central government, the creation of mutual confidence between king and people, and a hereditary throne. He had developed the concept, similar to Montesquieu's, that liberty must sometimes be restrained by submission to the law, if it were not to slide into licence and anarchy. Let us now look at the settlement of 1775.

II

Catherine II was now determined to exclude all Prussian or Austrian influence from the remains of the Commonwealth. She had learnt that stirring up Sarmatian prejudice against the king could swiftly reduce the entire country to chaos and open the way to a further partition. A minimum of order was required in Poland, and so the Seym called in 1773 to ratify the partition treaties was also to enact a new form of government. Catherine sensibly consented to the scaling down of the dissidents' political rights from those passed in 1768. In any case, most of the dissident *szlachta* now found themselves under the benevolent rule of that champion of the Protestant cause, Frederick II. The King of Prussia aimed at the greatest possible partition, and the worst possible government for the Commonwealth. Austria was disposed, as we have seen, to aid Stanisław August, but not at the price of a lesser share of the spoils.[15]

Stanisław August's hopes of strengthening royal power and abolishing the *veto* in exchange for ratification of the Partition were soon deflated. Catherine rightly suspected him of scheming to make Poland strong, and in the long run independent. She resolved to shackle him by transferring most of his powers, including the *ius distributivum*, to a Permanent Council under the control of her ambassador. Stackelberg worked through a band of hired lackeys, headed by Adam Poniński, Crown Grand Chancellor Andrzej Młodziejowski, and Stanisław August's erstwhile friend August Sułkowski. Stackelberg dubbed him 'le Cromwell de la Grande Pologne',

---

[14] SA to Gen. François de Monet, 3 Nov. 1779, in SA, M. Glayre, *Correspondance*, 169. See also 26 Aug. 1772, ibid., 29–30.

[15] Konopczyński, *Geneza i ustanowienie Rady Nieustającej*, 180–4.

and indeed, Sułkowski wanted to turn the king into a cipher.[16] As the ex-confederates and the *Familia* either boycotted the Seym or were excluded from it, Stackelberg's creatures secured a majority over the king's supporters in the Seym which opened on 19 April 1773. Like Repnin before him, Stackelberg used a delegation of the Seym to force through the partition treaties and the form of government, but not all its members proved as obsequious as anticipated. Stanisław August manoeuvred as best he could. He realized that neither internal nor international circumstances were favourable enough for him to emulate Gustavus III's coup. He was careful not to appear to accept the partition in exchange for any benefit to his purse or prerogative. When the treaties were finally ratified in September 1773, the battle over the form of government could begin in earnest.[17]

At first, the king stuck to the rights granted him by the *pacta conventa*. He was forced to capitulate in December 1773 by an ultimatum that the three powers would quarter their armies across the country, and print leaflets blaming the king's attachment to his prerogatives for the ensuing misery. Unofficially, Stanisław August had been negotiating for some time on the extent of his nominative power.[18] His position began to improve in the new year. The law on the Commission for National Education having been passed, it could no longer be used to threaten or tempt him into concessions. His resistance to the partition and the forced renunciation of his prerogatives had won him sympathy both within and without the Seym, while the popularity of Poniński and Sułkowski continued to plunge. Having forced Stanisław August's acceptance of the outline of the settlement, Stackelberg was now prepared to be more accommodating over the details, and the king set about winning the ambassador's confidence. Stanisław August's position was weakened, however, by his financial straits and he too became tarnished by the general scramble for plunder which was the chief occupation of the delegates.[19] He was finally [?] compensated for his lost revenues (mainly the salt from Wieliczka) by a civil list that topped his income up to a reasonable, but hardly prodigious 7 million złotys a year.

---

[16] Konopczyński, *Geneza i ustanowienie Rady Nieustącej*, 155–6, 160–70, 197. SA to Mme Geoffrin, 5 June 1773, *Correspondance*, 444–50.
[17] Konopczyński, *Geneza i ustanowienie Rady Nieustającej*, 174–80, 227, 237. *Mémoires*, vol. 2, 11. See M. Roberts, '19 August 1772: An ambivalent revolution', in *L'étà dei lumi*, vol. 1.
[18] Konopczyński, *Geneza i ustanowienie Rady Nieustającej*, 204–69. SA to S. Lubomirski, 3 Aug. 1774, APP 184, ff. 28–9 and BCzart. 799, ff. 763–6.
[19] Konopczyński, *Geneza i ustanowienie Rady Nieustającej*, 204–69.

The new arrangements, which were finally enacted in April 1775, were a bitter disappointment to the king. The Permanent Council (*Rada Nieustająca*)[20] replaced the senate council. It was to consist of the king, eighteen senators and eighteen envoys elected by the Seym for a two-year term, and a non-voting secretary. In the event of opposition to royal proposals, all matters were to be decided by majority vote. One of the envoys was to be elected the council's marshal; Sułkowski was the first. Three of the senators were to be bishops (the primate would sit in alternate councils) and four, ministers. Of the rest, two more might be ministers. Moreover, the three provinces of Great Poland, Little Poland, and Lithuania were to be equally represented (a breach in Lithuanian separatism). No family could have more than one envoy and one senator in the council. Exactly one third of the outgoing council was to be re-elected, in order to ensure both continuity and new blood. These arrangements were too inflexible to allow the development of any serious political responsibility to the Seym, and it is not surprising that elections proved extremely time-consuming.

The council was divided into five departments, whose protocols were to be read out at plenary sessions. The police, military, treasury, and justice departments each consisted of eight councillors, and were chaired by the relevant minister or, in the justice department, the first in rank. The department of foreign affairs had four councillors, including one of the chancellors, and was chaired by the king, who had two votes. Each department was provided with a secretary and a chancellery, whose members were chosen at plenary sessions, but the king was to choose the secretary and officials of the department of foreign affairs. One of the councillors for foreign affairs was to accompany the king on journeys, a provision that was probably taken from the Swedish requirement that two senators accompany the king on longer journeys (as noted by Konarski). Resolutions were to be made in the name of the king 'after the opinion of the Permanent Council', rather like those of the King of England in the Privy Council. When the King of England met with foreign rulers or ministers, a secretary of state had to be present. Thus the law of 1775 was, consciously or unconsciously, a step towards the English convention that the king cannot act by himself.

The king lost the greater part of his nominative and distributive powers. He was to choose from three candidates presented by the council for

---

senators and ministers. He could no longer promote officers. Seniority was to prevail except on the recommendation of a hetman to the council. The king was also deprived of his four guard regiments. The Crown estates attached to non-judicial *starostwa* were henceforth to be auctioned off on fifty-year leases, as their current holders died off.[21] The king was thus reduced to the chairman of the highest executive body, much as the King of Sweden had been before 1772, but with even fewer rights. This flawed collegiate system was borrowed (and deliberately worsened) from Sweden.[22] Although the act creating the Permanent Council was cloaked in the language of old laws in order to mollify the *szlachta*, it also showed the influence of Montesquieu. The council was forbidden to interfere in the legislative and judicial processes, and councillors were banned from attending election and deputational *seymiki*, and the openings of tribunals. On the other hand, the Seym could overturn its resolutions at will. As an executive body, it was seriously hamstrung by the vagueness of its powers and competences, and its inability to command obedience from the treasury and military commissions. The departments could only issue reminders or bring the commissions before the Seym. This too, however, was a point on which Montesquieu's advice that power should check power found common ground with traditional *szlachta* suspicions of the executive. Contrary to the hopes of Stanisław August, the possible influence of the English model was confined to a one-sided move in the direction of ministerial responsibility. The king could no longer act alone, but he had very little say in the choice of councillors, and those councillors had no real administrative clout.

The months following the Seym showed that the system was unworkable. Power was checking power only too effectively. The projected budget proved far too optimistic, and the treasury department was continually squabbling with the treasury commissions. Crown Grand Hetman Xawery Branicki, having won control of the Crown military commission, engaged in a trial of strength with the military department. He made the Crown army swear an oath to him, and together with the much-weakened *Familia*, now led by Stanisław Lubomirski, agitated for the abolition of the council.

---

[21] A. Stroynowski, 'Emfiteutyczna reforma królewszczyzn', *Czasopismo Prawno-Historyczne*, 33 (1981). The *starostwa* were divided into judicial (*grodowe*) and non-judicial (*niegrodowe*) *starostwa*. The former carried with them the judicial and administrative charge of royal towns. The latter did not, but were in general more lucrative and thus a more dangerous source of royal corruption. Lukowski, *Liberty's Folly*, 67–8.

[22] Konopczyński, *Geneza i ustanowienie Rady Nieustającej*, 356–60. See M. Roberts, *The Age of Liberty: Sweden 1719–1772* (Cambridge, 1986). Wroughton referred to 'all colleges and dicasters' on 11 Sept. 1776. PRO SP 88/111.

Relations with Hetman Michał Kazimierz Ogiński's Lithuanian commission were no better. The minimum of order in the Commonwealth required by Russia was threatened, and the safest bet now seemed to be Stanisław August. The king managed to convince Stackelberg and Catherine to allow the strengthening of both the council and his own position. The election *seymiki* were the scenes of clashes between Branicki's soldiers and Russian troops. The Seym was confederated to allow the passing of controversial legislation, and to make sure, opponents were excluded at the doors. Several salutary changes were made to the Permanent Council. The subordinate executive bodies were bound to obey the council's directives, and in cases of doubt, the department of justice was to be able to interpret the law. The police department was given charge of all the royal towns and empowered to make commercial contracts over the heads of the judicial starostas. The military commissions were abolished altogether, and their powers given to the departments. The hetmans might choose to chair the department in rotation, but were otherwise superfluous. The king recovered his guard regiments and his rights to promote officers and distribute four of the largest non-judicial *starostwa*. Stanisław August had finally broken the power of the hetmans, although he had not yet exorcized their ghost.[23]

On 23 September 1776, Stanisław August defended the bill widening the powers of the Permanent Council in an important speech to the Seym. It was translated into French for the *Courier de Pologne* and also printed in French as a pamphlet. Stanisław August copied it into his *Mémoires* years later.[24] This treatment was reserved only for keynote speeches, intended for a wider audience than the envoys and senators to whom they were delivered. He began by asserting the Commonwealth's right to change its own laws. He challenged the 'Cardinal Laws' of 1768, which restricted that right, by reminding the Seym that political equality for the dissidents, established in 1768, had been trimmed back in 1775. Still less had anyone the right to challenge on legal grounds the restitution of some of the royal prerogatives taken away in 1775, for they had been solemnly guaranteed to the king by the *pacta conventa*. He then went on to answer the fears of the *szlachta* that the king would become too powerful, and

---

[23] D. Stone, *Polish Politics and National Reform 1775–1788* (Boulder, Col., 1976), 14–28. Czaja, *Lata wielkich nadziei*, 129–34. Lukowski, *Liberty's Folly*, 210–11. SA to Grimm, 18 Nov. 1776, Zb. Pop. 221, f. 431.

[24] Copies of both the pamphlet and the gazette were sent to London on 9 Oct. 1776 by Wroughton, PRO SP 88/111, ff. 205–6, 209–10. *Mémoires*, vol. 2, 353–9. Quotations are from the Polish original, *Mowa Krola JMci na seymie dnia 23 Septembris 1776 miana* (Warsaw, 1776).

that he would devour liberty. Among the restituted powers, was there one not promised to him by the *pacta conventa*? Were they not only the third part of what he had lost? Were not the augmented powers of the hetmans over promotions dangerous to the balance *inter maiestatem ac libertatem*? And since the late sixteenth century, when the hetmans began to hold their office for life, and royal authority started to decline, had the extent of the Commonwealth's frontiers and its standing in Europe increased or decreased?

The king now reached for another argument:

Takowe obawiania łatwo odrzuci, ktokolwiek uczynić zechce komparacyą Naszego Rządu do tego, ktory *tandem*, powszechnym ziednoczeniem Całey Europy, iest uznanym za nayprawdziwiey Wolny, oraz za nayszczęśliwszy. Wszak każdy widzi, że o Anglii mowię.

(These fears will be readily dismissed by anyone who wishes to compare our government with that, which in the opinion of all Europe, is recognized as the most truly free, as well as the happiest. Everyone sees that I speak of England.)

The Polish monarch went on to list the ways in which the King of England's powers exceeded his own. The King of England could confer and take away all ecclesiastical, civil, and military employments according to his will, commute sentences of death, pardon offenders, conclude treaties, declare war, and make peace. The king disposed of the army, the fleet, and the public finances,

A wolność iednak cała! przy ktorey ta iedna, ale dostateczna warowność, że na Rok tylko ieden Podatki bywaią stawione, ktorych gdyby Krol użył nie do smaku Narodu, Panem iest tenże Narod odmowić Krolowi onych odnowienia.

(and yet freedom is still intact! with this one, but sufficient safeguard, that taxes are established for one year only, and should the king's use of them be not to the taste of the nation, the nation is free to refuse their renewal.)

Stanisław August exaggerated the King of England's rights of patronage, particularly ecclesiastical, but his analysis of the foundation of English freedom was unerring. It was true that the House of Commons was extremely reluctant even to threaten to refuse subsidies, because the country would be left defenceless and the normal business of government would be paralysed, and George III was able to exploit this in maintaining William Pitt in office in 1784. Nevertheless, the possibility that subsidies *might* be refused forced the king to abandon ministers, such as Walpole, Granville, and North, who had palpably lost the confidence of both the House and the nation, and ruled out any thoughts of absolutism.[25] Stanisław August met the objection that taxes were established in perpetuity in Poland with the reminder that the Seym met every two years, and should the king or the Permanent Council fail to call it, the nation could assemble itself and abolish whatever taxes it chose. Stanisław August also made the point that the civil list in England, amounting to the equivalent of 40 million złotys (nearly six times his own revenue) was founded upon a one-off grant. It was only for the expenses of the fleet and the army that the king needed the annual consent of the nation. Here again, Stanisław August was slightly inaccurate. The inadequacy of George III's civil list to pay for the civil administration and maintain his growing family and court resulted in rising debts which, although paid by Parliament in the end, repeatedly exposed him to wounding criticism, and led after 1782 to the pruning of the sinecures which were a valuable source of patronage.[26]

Having disposed of 'these phantoms', the king then attacked the excesses of the ministers, comparing them to overgrown cedars which no longer provided shade and refreshment in the Commonwealth's constitution, but blocked out the sunlight and rain for smaller plants. Finally, Stanisław August countered fears that his successor might abuse the 'new' powers by reminding the envoys that the next king would be the nation's choice, and bound by the *pacta conventa* it would prescribe. This was probably the only occasion on which Stanisław August himself made use of the English example in a speech to the Seym. The Seym of 1776 was the most docile of his reign. Yet the speech shows how Stanisław August's first concern was to reassure the *szlachta* that he did not threaten its liberty. In this context he used England as an example, not to argue that the powers of the King of England be given to himself, but to demonstrate that, despite royal power stronger than in Poland, English liberty was safe. England, moreover, was one of many arguments, the main one being that the powers now being restored were only a third of those which had been taken away. Stanisław August identified the real threat to liberty as the ministers, especially the hetmans. At the modest height of his command of Polish politics, Stanisław August was on the ideological defensive.

Stanisław August's praise of England is not evidence of English influence on the revised constitutional settlement, although he believed that the gap between his powers and those of the English king had been narrowed again. The one feature of the settlement that did provoke

[25] See Cannon, *Fox–North Coalition*, 144–233.

[26] Brooke, *George III*, 89, 202–8. R. Pares, *King George III and the Politicians* (Oxford, 1953), 189, 198.

barbed analogies to the English 'prime ministership' was the raising of the dignity of the marshal of the Permanent Council above all the lay senators and ministers, a sop to the vanity of Sułkowski.[27] In general, the post-Partition settlement owed very little indeed to the example of England. The most influential foreign model was the Swedish one, but the settlement was essentially the outcome of Russia's balancing between Stanisław August and his enemies, in order to secure a Poland that was both manageable and innocuous.

III

The outcome of the Seym of 1776 cheered the king. He sent his 22-year-old nephew, Prince Stanisław, to St Petersburg to try to obtain permission for further changes at the next Seym. The Prince returned empty-handed but the warmth of his welcome from Catherine II augured well. There was some truth in the suspicions of many contemporaries that the king's ultimate aim was to secure the succession for his nephew. He also tried to re-establish diplomatic relations with France and Turkey. The plans for rebuilding the Royal Castle drawn up at this time show the symbolism of strong royal power alongside national traditions. Even Wroughton, although he continued to prophesy the final partition of the country sooner or later, and regretted the violent means used to effect the changes, expressed the hope that 'as there is now a probability of good order, & a firm Government', the new councillors would 'calm the apprehensions of the Public, & convince them of His Polish Majesty's desire of rendering this Country as happy & flourishing as its local position will admit of'.[28]

The main hope of this second wind of reform was in the work of legal codification, entrusted by the Seym of 1776 at royal prompting to Andrzej Zamoyski. While the *szlachta* were enthusiastic for a simple codification, the royal circle saw the opportunity for legal and social reform by the back door. Zamoyski's brief included an instruction not to follow the letter of old laws, but to promote natural justice. Zamoyski collected together a team of helpers who included Joachim Chreptowicz. Frequent conferences took place at the Royal Castle, and work proceeded at such a tempo that the code was ready for presentation to the Seym of 1778.[29]

---

[27] Czaja, *Lata wielkich nadziei*, 133. Wroughton later referred to the marshal as 'prime minister'. Wroughton to Suffolk, 15 Apr. 1778, PRO SP 88/114.

[28] SA to Grimm, 18 Feb. 1777, Zb. Pop. 221, ff. 436–7. Michalski, 'Dwie misje księcia Stanisława', in *Księga pamiątkowa 150-lecia AGAD*. Stone, *Polish Politics*, 29–30. Rottermund, *Zamek warszawski*, 85–6, 89. Wroughton to Suffolk, 28 Sept. 1776, 23 Oct. 1776 and *passim*, PRO SP 88/111.

[29] E. Borkowska-Bagieńska, *'Zbiór praw sądowych' Andrzeja Zamoyskiego* (Poznań, 1986), 20–60.

Zamoyski and Chreptowicz were both known for their Anglophilia, but the question of the extent of English influence on the code is most easily approached through the works of Józef Wybicki, the most active member of the committee. Wybicki was a former confederate of Bar who had made his peace with the king. In April 1776 he sent his first work, *Myśli polityczne o wolności cywilney* ('Political thoughts on civil freedom'), to Stanisław August via the king's agent in Danzig, Aleksy Husarzewski. This strongly monarchist book was a radical departure from his past, and Husarzewski explained that Wybicki had gone to Leiden to study law at the end of the Confederacy. 'Il avait grande envie de voir également l'Angleterre, mais ayant compté avec sa bourse il a été contraint d'y renoncer,' added Husarzewski. Called to Warsaw by Zamoyski, Wybicki soon received marks of royal favour—the title of *szambelan* and an invitation to discuss the proposals at the Thursday Dinners. He wrote his *Listy patryotyczne do . . . Andrzeja Zamoyskiego* ('Patriotic letters to Andrzej Zamoyski') in 1777–8 to win public support for the changes proposed in the code.[30]

Wybicki's *Myśli polityczne* was probably the first work in Polish to show the strong influence of *De l'esprit des lois* and to expound Rousseau's social contract. In a display of classical learning, Wybicki cited the traditional advantages of effectiveness that monarchies enjoyed over republics. Although he admitted that republics necessitated a lesser loss of natural freedom than monarchies, he argued that the anarchy resulting from freedom poorly understood was worse than despotism, and that the source of Poland's misery and partition was an immoderate love of liberty that did not respect the law. Polish liberty was in practice confined to the magnates, he declared. Without good political laws, civil freedom and economic development were impossible. A 'novemvirate' should therefore be appointed to draw up new ones. As the Seym could not save the state from impending ruin, a hereditary monarchy and an extended prerogative, but not 'the rule of one person' (*jednowładztwo*), were necessary. He cited England and Holland, which enjoyed freedom despite their hereditary rulers and heavy taxes. Wybicki closed with a stirring quotation from Bolingbroke's *Patriot King*:

The profound politician Bolingbroke surveying the unhappy state of his country said: 'My country, a true patriot king might save thee.'

---

[30] Rostworowski, ' "Myśli polityczne" Józefa Wybickiego, czyli droga od Konfederacji Barskiej do obiadów czwartkowych', in A. Bukowski (ed.), *Józef Wybicki: Księga zbiorowa* (Gdańsk, 1975), 12–17, repr. as the introduction to J. Wybicki, *Myśli polityczne o wolności cywilnej*, ed. Z. Nowak (Wrocław, 1984), 5–14.

Desirous of seeing my country saved, at the end of my thoughts which have its survival as their aim, I use the opinion of that great citizen.[31]

The *Listy patryotyczne* was essentially a continuation of the *Myśli polityczne*. Once again, Wybicki used Montesquieu to stress that the rule of law was the foundation of civil liberty. He also made use of Hume's *Political Discourses* to depict the lowly condition of Poland.[32] He made quite extensive use of the English example, but he took a detached view of the various types of government. He censured the jealousies inherent in mixed government and even quoted a 'certain politician' (Walpole?) on the necessity of the king corrupting the Commons to prevent the country sliding into democracy.[33] Criticizing serfdom, he argued that England's prosperity and populousness was the result of the freedom and security of *all* its inhabitants, based on habeas corpus and the right of everybody to buy land. Wybicki also praised export bounties on wheat and enclosures. Having discovered that a certain drink was killing the common people, the English suppressed it. This reference to the gin laws was particularly barbed in Poland, because the vodka monopoly (*propinacja*) was one of the main sources of *szlachta* income.[34] He vaguely praised the jury system on the basis of *De l'esprit des lois*, and used Blackstone's account of Edward I's legislation to propose that the monarch should approve all papal bulls prior to their publication. Notwithstanding his sympathies for the Americans, who in his eyes were vindicating English freedoms, the English were the freest people in the world.[35]

If, apart from the detailed recommendations lifted from Blackstone, Wybicki's use of England was rather conventional, his overall message was anything but. The rottenness of the entire nation had led to the present plight of the Commonwealth, and perhaps not even English-style mixed government could turn it round. The exigencies of the present situation demanded a hereditary monarchy with extensive prerogatives. 'Immoderate liberty' might then become true civil freedom. Stanisław August must have been struck by the closeness of many of Wybicki's

---

[31] Rostworowski, '"Myśli polityczne" Wybickiego', 17–34. Wybicki, *Myśli polityczne*, esp. 49–53, 75–6, 80, 82, 143, 161–233. The original was not as pithy. *The Idea of a Patriot King*, in *The Works of Lord Bolingbroke, with a Life* (4 vols.; London, 1844), vol. 2, 375, 429.

[32] Rostworowski, '"Myśli polityczne" Wybickiego', 23. See also Chomicki, 'Wpływy angielskie', 107–23. *Listy patriotyczne*, ed. K. Opałek (Wrocław, 1955), 54, 203–4.

[33] *Listy patriotyczne*, 42–4.

[34] Ibid., 81–3, 157–8, 176–7, 208, 139–40, 146–7, 118. See Lukowski, *Liberty's Folly*, 29–32.

[35] *Listy patriotyczne*, 106, 282, 292–6, 314. *Esprit des lois*, Book IV, ch. 3.

ideas to his own, expressed in his 'Extrait d'une Lettre', and the theme of a 'patriot king' was bound to appeal to him (he owned Bolingbroke's *Works*). A few years later, Wybicki wrote to the king: 'if the nation over which Your Majesty reigns has not yet stood in the state and power which become it, then the people's inborn dislike, as it were, of its kings and love of domestic confusion are the causes.'[36]

Wybicki's arguments naturally went much further than the code itself. Nevertheless, some of his recommendations found their way into its provisions. Among the most controversial were the prohibition of the publication of papal bulls without the consent of the Permanent Council, and the end of Rome's appellate jurisdiction. Together with substantial restrictions on the right of the clergy to acquire property, this part of the code has rightly been viewed in the context of Josephism.[37] Yet Wybicki's *Listy* reveals that Blackstone's account of the relations of medieval England with the papacy was also important. Wybicki's call for more houses of correction and prisons may also have been influenced by information from Blackstone. Ewa Borkowska-Bagieńska suggests that the information sent by Bukaty on poor relief in England may have inspired the code's proposals to combat vagrancy (instead of ineffectually forcing vagrants to return to their own villages, they would be set to work). However, this information was sent in the autumn of 1780, too late to have played a role.[38] Beyond this, English influence is hard to discern. The main sources of the code were the *Volumina Legum* and the Third Lithuanian Statute of 1588. Old laws were interpreted, renewed, or jettisoned on the basis of natural justice, as in the proposals to relax the rigours of serfdom and afford peasants some legal protection. Some humanitarianism tempered the old laws, and there was some move to a corrective function of punishment, but as in the Austrian *Nemesis Theresiana* of 1768, punishments of mutilation were retained. This and other codes in absolutist states were the main inspirations for Zamoyski and his team.[39] The very idea of a code was alien to the English tradition.

Although a group of political laws was in the end omitted, the code aroused the wrath of the *szlachta* for presuming to touch a nobleman's

---

[36] Wybicki to SA, Poznań, 14 Nov. 1784, BCzart. 694, f. 505, printed in *Archiwum Wybickiego*, ed. A. Skałkowski (2 vols.; Gdańsk, 1948–50), vol. 1, 106. 'Catalogus', AKsJP 268, f. 133.

[37] Borkowska-Bagieńska, '*Zbiór praw sądowych*', 324–6. Rostworowski, *Historia powszechna*, 771.

[38] *Listy patriotyczne*, 246. Borkowska-Bagieńska, '*Zbiór praw sądowych*', 70, 137–9. See below, pp. 263–4.

[39] Borkowska-Bagieńska, '*Zbiór praw sądowych*', 265–88.

power over his peasants. The *szlachta*'s fears were astutely stirred up by the papal nuncio, Giovanni Archetti, while Stackelberg was piqued at not having been consulted on the limited extension proposed to the king's powers of pardon, and he gave Archetti his support. The opposition to the code was so great at the Seym of 1778 that Stanisław August had consideration of it postponed to 1780. The intervening two years did not sweeten the *szlachta*'s temper, and the king's efforts to procure the acquiescence of Rome failed. The Seym of 1780 demanded that the code never be brought before it again, and the frenzied envoys trampled copies underfoot.[40]

1780 marked a watershed for Stanisław August. He was now bitterly aware that he stood isolated between the whims of Stackelberg, whom he compared to a proconsul of ancient Rome,[41] and Sarmatian fanaticism, whipped up by the magnate opposition. It was particularly galling that Stanisław Lubomirski had led the fervid assault on the Zamoyski Code. Stanisław August tried to win a measure of independence from Stackelberg by extending his own personal following among the middling and wealthier *szlachta* through the copious distribution of gracious letters, orders, minor offices, and even castellanies, but the process took time, and would never bring full emancipation. The king had no alternative to humiliating Russian protection and realized that any major change must wait until the international situation altered.

IV

The five Seyms from 1778 to 1786 were 'free'; that is, they were not confederated, and were vulnerable to the *liberum veto*. It was a notable success that the *veto* was not used, but the threat alone allowed individuals to frustrate useful measures, explained Stanisław August to Wroughton in 1778. The proposals from the throne amounted to a programme of unspectacular but essential administrative, economic, and military reform, but much of it was 'talked out'. The Seyms passed some useful legislation, particularly that of 1784, held in Grodno, which limited the purchase of commissions in the army until after fifteen years' service. However, the unruly Seym of 1786 threw out the plan to impose discipline on the anarchic, part-time 'national cavalry' and excluded foreign and non-noble officers. Whitworth wrote that 'the king has the wish but not the power to serve his Country.'[42]

[40] Borkowska-Bagieńska, '*Zbiór praw sądowych*', 317–18. Stone, *Polish Politics*, 33–6. Wolff, *Vatican and Poland*, 126–9.

[41] *Mémoires*, vol. 2, 298.

[42] Stone, *Polish Politics*, 29–67. Rostworowski, *Sprawa aukcji wojska*, esp. 136–60. Whitworth to Camarthen, 4 Nov. 1786, PRO FO 62/2. SA to Wroughton, 10 Dec. 1778, Zb.

More could be achieved by administrative than by legislative means. Despite the election of some of his opponents to the Permanent Council, Stanisław August (with Stackelberg's tacit consent) managed to dominate it, and turn it into a useful organ of central government, the first that Poland had ever known. A modest diplomatic service was properly organized. Despite the growing subservience of the department of foreign affairs to the king, the cabinet continued to handle the most sensitive information. The story was similar in the military department. The real centre of power lay in General Komarzewski's chancellery. Careful budgeting allowed the army to increase from 16,100 in 1778 to 18,300 in 1786, well short of the permitted 30,000, and still disproportionately heavy in cavalry (43 per cent) and officers. Stanisław August could not resist the temptation to create even more sinecures as a source of patronage. The treasury department remained an essentially supervisory body. The right to interpret the law allowed the justice department to develop it in a more logical and humanitarian direction. The use of the army to enforce verdicts and sentences quelled lawlessness, but did nothing to calm the *szlachta*'s fear of *absolutum dominium*. The Permanent Council lacked legitimacy. It was all a long way from England's anomalous yet flexible and effective administration.[43]

If Stanisław August had to put away all thought of modelling the Polish constitution as a whole on the English, England might still provide models for individual improvements. It was in June 1780 that the department of foreign affairs instructed Franciszek Bukaty to write some reports on factories and especially on hospitals 'whose establishment or improvement is necessary at home'.[44] Bukaty sent in a well researched account of the provisions made in England for dealing with the poor and vagrants, from medieval charity through draconian Tudor legislation to the poor rate, and a description of a typical poorhouse near London. Bukaty criticized the harshness of the old laws, which made magistrates reluctant to execute them, and resulted in a patchy network of poorhouses and houses of correction. He praised moves to build houses serving more than one parish.[45] When Michał Jerzy Mniszech thanked Bukaty, on behalf of the

---

Pop. 179, ff. 226–7. SA to Harris, Białystok, 26 Nov. 1784, Zb. Pop. 182, f. 253. It seems that, despite the demise of the *liberum rumpo* in 1768, the king still feared efforts to break up the Seym altogether.

[43] Czaja, *Lata wielkich nadziei*, 137–56. Rymszyna, *Gabinet*, 101–39. Rostworowski, *Sprawa aukcji wojska*, esp. 55–76.

[44] 'Ktorych u nas założenie lub wydoskonalenie iest potrzebne'. Instruction, June 1780, Zb. Pop. 216, f. 234, point 9.

[45] Bukaty to dept., 15 Sept. 1780, 6 Oct. 1780, AKP 79, ff. 35–49.

department, he added: 'it will be able to serve us as a model for a similar establishment sometime, but it will be easier to carry out instructions given to us, than to contrive adequate funding.'[46] So it proved. The department of police tried to introduce forced labour for able-bodied vagrants, and restrict relief to the parish of origin. However, the building of hospitals for the old, sick, and invalid hardly got off the ground for lack of money, and the department had to accept a system of licensed begging. In the countryside, parish priests bore the burden of organization. Constant disputes with the judicial starostas and urban authorities it was supposed to supervise diminished the effectiveness of the department in royal towns.[47]

Bukaty's next report was on the English militia. He explained that the 1673 Militia Act had fallen into neglect, but had been reinvigorated in the Seven Years' War. The militia could only be used for home defence, and could not be sent abroad. The total number of militiamen was over 30,000, who served for three years. Musters (twenty-eight days a year) were presided over by the lords lieutenant, who, stressed Bukaty, were appointed at royal pleasure. The lords lieutenant nominated their subalterns, subject to royal confirmation. Bukaty also noted the exemptions and the pay. Mniszech wrote back that 'this model should encourage us to imitate the means used in this measure all the more, because these less showy means would be less suspect for the neighbours surrounding us.'[48]

It is interesting that Bukaty should stress the royal control of the militia. In the 1720s and 1730s the Country opposition had demanded the militia's reactivation, but had been opposed by Walpole, who preferred regular troops. After the embarrassments of the 1745 rising, the militia issue was linked to dynastic legitimacy, and lost its anti-Court connotations. The 1757 Militia Act added to the formal powers of the Crown.[49]

---

[46] 'Będzie nam mogło służyć kiedyś za wzor w podobnym ustanowieniu, łatwiey jednak przyidzie rozporządzeń nam podane wprowadzić niż dostateczny Fundusz tym końcem obmyślić.' Dept. to Bukaty, 11 Oct. 1780, 4 Nov. 1780, AKP 80, ff. 212–13.

[47] M. Poniatowski, *Do uniwersału Nayiaśnieyszego Krola JMci za zdaniem Rady Nieustającej, względem żebraków wydanego stosowny list pasterski do diecezyi krakowskiey* (1786). Czaja, *Lata wielkich nadziei*, 142–8. Idem, *Między tronem . . .* , ch. 6. Zahorski, *Centralne instytucje policyjne w Polsce w dobie rozbiorów* (Warsaw, 1959), 34–58.

[48] Bukaty to dept., 28 Nov. 1780, AKP 79, ff. 55–63. 'Wzor ten tym bardziey powinien nas zachęcać do naśladowanie użytych w tey mierze środkow, że te sposoby mniey okazałe, stały by sie y mniey podeyrzanemi otaczającym nas sąsiadom.' Dept. to Bukaty, 30 Dec. 1780, AKP 80, f. 214.

[49] E. H. Gould, 'To strengthen the king's hands: dynastic legitimacy, militia reform and ideas of national unity in England 1745–1760', *HJ* 34 (1991). See also J. R. Western, *The English Militia in the Eighteenth Century: The History of a Political Issue 1660–1802* (London, 1965, repr. 1994).

In contrast, *Pamiętnik Historyczno-Polityczny* printed a more 'republican' account of the English militia in April 1786.[50] Stanisław August, despite what he had written in his 'Anecdote Historique', combated all attempts to revive the general levy of the *szlachta*, which he feared would become a tool in the hands of provincial magnates. The militia he had in mind would be an instrument of royal control, through the judicial starostas. It would not be chiefly for home defence, as in England, but would police the towns and enforce court verdicts, which would let the army concentrate on soldiering. He proposed such a militia at the Seyms of 1784 and 1786. However, the popularity of ideas for reviving the general levy, which now occasionally included the peasantry and townsmen under *szlachta* command, meant that the king lost the initiative. Some palatinates set up militias, from which the king was hard put to extract an oath of loyalty.[51] Stanisław August experienced yet again the gulf between English and Polish political culture.

In August 1781, Bukaty sent in an 'Etat de toutes les Debtes publiques de la Grande Brétagne' (amounting to £168 million). Mniszech asked how much more was held by foreigners. Bukaty explained that they were usually represented by correspondents or companies among the official holders of the debt.[52] He despatched all the annual fiscal estimates since 1775, which were examined by the department and the king. For 1779–80 and 1780–1, he noted the swiftly rising debt, and admired the fact that the nation's credit remained firm. He put the total military establishment, including the navy, auxiliaries, militia, and soldiers of the East India Company at no less than 391,090 in 1780–1. English goods had been made very expensive by the war, but maintained their markets in Europe through export bounties and their high quality.[53] The king and the department then requested Bukaty to send further information on the income and expenses of the English government. He did so in February 1782. First he explained the traditional revenues formerly belonging to the Crown, from Crown estates to royal fish. Then there was permanent income— customs and excise, stamp tax, and other fees. The land tax, sugar tax, the provision for the sinking fund (supposedly to pay off the debt), and borrowing were set every year by Parliament. In his next despatch, Bukaty described the civil list. George III had accepted £800,000 a year in return for the old 'hereditary revenues', had run up huge debts, and

---

[50] *PHP*, Apr. 1786, 314–20.   [51] Rostworowski, *Sprawa aukcji wojska*, 161–76.
[52] Bukaty to dept., 31 Aug. 1781, 23 Oct. 1781, AKP 79, ff. 113, 130–1. Dept. to Bukaty, 26 Sept. 1781, AKP 80, f. 228.
[53] AKP 79, ff. 151–78, 193–202.

was forced to ask for a pay rise, which was acrimoniously agreed to by Parliament. Plainly, nearly £1 million was not enough to pay for the court, the royal family, the salaries of ministers, diplomats, judges, royal expenses, building works, and the secret expenditure to win friends in Parliament. Two weeks later, Bukaty sent a relation of state expenditure, writing: 'its rise in wartime, and during this war in particular, is astonishing, as are the taxes raised.' Another fortnight later, he detailed how the English had lately been increasing the national debt by £12 or £13 million a year, and explained the difference between unfunded debt (based on the sinking fund) and funded debt (based on tax assignments). Bukaty was suitably impressed by the fiscal-military English state. His reports won the approval of his superiors and the king. They asked for clarification regarding fines, the land tax, customs and excise, and bills of exchange.[54] They were unable to alter the Commonwealth's slender budget.

Bukaty also filed a report on the organization of the Admiralty, which, being a collegiate body or 'in commission', was relevant to the military department.[55] He wrote about parliamentary procedure to the cabinet. He noted that the royal prerogative of veto had fallen into abeyance, as ministers could always rely on one of the two houses to defeat any measure which he opposed. The king had no power of emendation, and no formal right of legislative initiative, but in practice he enjoyed it via his ministers. The Lords had the right to vote by proxy, and could enter *vota separata* in a book, giving their reasons. If one house wished to amend bills passed by the other, a joint delegation was formed to try to reach agreement. If that failed, the bill was lost for that session. The Commons had the sole right to pass taxes; the Lords could not amend, but only accept or reject money bills. Through his member, wrote Bukaty, every citizen indirectly assented to taxation. The absence of such representation had caused the Americans to rebel. The members were representatives of the entire people, not just their own electors. Bukaty then went through the rules for elections (without delving into borough franchises), noting the property qualifications for members, the poll books, and other arrangements before moving on to procedure proper, explaining the three readings and committee stages in both houses, and the royal assent.[56] In 1789, Bukaty sent the king another report which distinguished between

---

[54] 'Wzrost onych w Czasie Woyny, a osobliwie teraźnieyszey, jest do podziwienia, rownie jak y Podatki utworzone.' Bukaty to dept., 19 Feb.–28 June 1782, AKP 79, ff. 210–95, *passim*. Muz. Nar. 76, ff. 42–53. Dept. to Bukaty, 23 Jan.–12 June 1782, AKP 80, ff. 228–55, *passim*.

[55] Bukaty to dept., 31 Dec. 1782, AKP 80, ff. 41–2.

[56] Bukaty to cabinet, 14 Jan. 1783, Muz. Nar. 76, ff. 86–97, BCzart. 3998, ff. 73–84.

public and private bills (for roads, canals, naturalization, etc.), and dealt with curiosities such as the hats used to attract the Speaker's attention, giving way, and the satisfaction required for insults. He noted that the chambers could adjourn their sittings for short periods, but only the king could prorogue Parliament.[57]

In his despatches, Bukaty would frequently make passing comments on the constitution; for example, that the Mutiny Act was the basis for the existence of the fleet and army.[58] He wrote of the provisions for civil magistrates to use soldiers to quell riots (George III had personally instructed them to restore order during the Gordon riots).[59] Frequent changes of ministry were not as fatal to the country as might be imagined, he explained, because the experienced administrators stayed on in every department. The genesis of the Fox–North coalition (which he thought insincere and likely to be short-lived) allowed him to generalize: 'the aim is to form a ministry which would be pleasant to the king and have enough credit in Parliament to outweigh all the parties; the construction of such a combination is very difficult.' It is worth noting that Bukaty used the word 'party' to refer to groups within Parliament who were to be overcome, as intrinsically hostile to the king. This reflects the fact that the Rockingham Whig 'party' justified its existence in principled opposition.[60]

The department frequently reacted to Bukaty's information on events in Britain by asking him to clarify points of the constitution, for example, regarding the status of the Irish Parliament in respect of the British. In Bukaty's opinion, through the reform of 1782, Ireland had become a kingdom allied rather than united to Great Britain. Nevertheless, Irish laws were still subject to the veto or emendation of the king, and the Irish, he wrote, felt keenly their continuing dependence on the British Parliament for defence and trade. The Polish envoy drew attention to the oppressive situation of the Catholic majority, many of whom had been driven to emigrate.[61] Bukaty enlightened the department as to Lord North's sitting in the Commons—his father, the Earl of Guildford, was

---

[57] Bukaty to cabinet, 24 July 1789, 31 July 1789, Muz. Nar. 76, ff. 225–36, 240–4.

[58] Bukaty to dept., 18 Apr. 1783, AKP 80, f. 68.

[59] Bukaty to dept., 17 Jan. 1783, AKP 80, f. 46.

[60] 'Rzecz idzie o uformowanie Ministerii ktoreby krolowi było przyiemne y dosyć maiące kredyt w Parlamencie do przeważenia wszystkich partyi, Takiego zbioru układ bardzo iest trudny.' Bukaty to dept., 4 Mar. 1783, 11 Apr. 1783, AKP 80, ff. 59, 66–7. See F. O'Gorman, 'Party in the Later Eighteenth Century', in J. Cannon (ed.), *The Whig Ascendancy: Colloquies on Hanoverian England* (London, 1981).

[61] Bukaty to dept., 29 Mar. 1782, 24 May 1782, 28 May 1782, AKP 79, ff. 245–53, 281, 283–4. Dept. to Bukaty, 8 May 1782, AKP 80, f. 253.

still alive. Should the Prime Minister sit in the Lords, the Chancellor of the Exchequer would handle treasury business in the Commons. North had combined the posts.[62] On another occasion, Mniszech asked how Parliament could authorize the king to make peace with the Americans, since the king alone had the prerogative of doing so. Bukaty explained that the king indeed possessed that prerogative, but Parliament had empowered him to alter trade regulations, which fell within Parliament's legislative competence. The royal prerogative, he went on, was differently interpreted by the 'Whigs' and 'Tories'. The former were more republican in spirit and would allow Parliament to advise on war and peace, making the king responsible to the nation. The latter insisted that ministers only should advise the king, and ministers only were responsible to Parliament, as the king could do no wrong. This classification follows that of the Rockinghamites, who called themselves Whigs and smeared their opponents as Tories. This may be a clue to Bukaty's contacts, but not his sympathies at this stage; he was sorry for George III, and defended him from the charges of stubbornness and vengefulness, while he believed that Rockingham's repeal of the Stamp Act had only encouraged the Americans to rebel.[63]

Bukaty gave an account of Pitt the younger's proposals for parliamentary reform in May 1783. As Pitt wished to increase the number of county members, Bukaty explained that electoral corruption was particularly rife in small boroughs. As the purchase of votes was forbidden, candidates would give presents to voters' wives and children, pay for goods and services at inflated prices, and deliberately lose bets. The tariff for borough seats started at £2,000 or £3,000. No one was surprised, wrote the envoy, that Pitt's bill was rejected as hopelessly idealistic. Two years later, Tadeusz Bukaty sent information about Pitt's second attempt at parliamentary reform, which also failed.[64] Although not altogether free from bias (it was only to be expected that the abuses of the unreformed electoral system would strike him more than its advantages), Bukaty's despatches and reports provided the king and his circle with a reasonably objective and detailed picture of the English system of government. In at least two cases—the provisions for the poor and the militia—Bukaty's information

[62] Dept. to Bukaty, 15 Mar. 1783, AKP 80, f. 273. Bukaty to dept., 4 Apr. 1783, AKP 80, ff. 64–5.
[63] Dept. to Bukaty, 10 July 1782, AKP 80, f. 257. Bukaty to dept., 2, 16 Aug. 1782, AKP 80, ff. 1, 3, 5–6.
[64] Bukaty to dept., 13 May 1783, AKP 80, ff. 81–2. T. Bukaty to dept., 22 Apr. 1785, AKP 81, ff. 161–2.

bore upon the Permanent Council's efforts at reform. His account of parliamentary procedure had, as we shall see, an influence during the Four Year Seym.

Naturally, the king continued to inform himself from other sources. He had the volumes of *Parliamentary History* bought for him.[65] Lord Lansdowne sent him a book in French describing parliamentary procedure.[66] By 1783, the Royal Library contained over a hundred titles in English and French on British politics, jurisprudence, and history, including Hume's *Political Discourses* and *History of England*, Blackstone's *Commentaries*, de Lolme's *De la constitution d'Angleterre*, Raynal's *Histoire du Parlement*, *Proceedings in the House of Peers*, Catherine Macaulay's *History of England*, John Fortescue's *De laudibus legum*, Rapin's *Histoire d'Angleterre*, and Robertson's *History of Scotland*.[67]

It was in the 1770s and 1780s that an admittedly hazy knowledge of the English constitution began to spread more widely among the public. Anna Grześkowiak has pointed out that the word *oppozycya* came to denote a group of envoys in the Seym formally opposed to the policies of the Court.[68] Important roles were played by translations into Polish, and by articles in journals. Voltaire's *Lettres philosophiques* came out as *Listy o Angielczykach* in 1773.[69] In 1777, the first full Polish translation of Montesquieu's *De l'esprit des lois* was published. The translator, Mateusz Czarnek, was a secretary in the cabinet and he dedicated the work to the king, with the hope that it would be useful to those then engaged in preparing the code.[70] In 1786, part of Blackstone's *Commentaries* was translated into Polish from French by the Piarist, Teodor Ostrowski. In his extensive notes, Ostrowski noted the similarity of the English constitution to the Polish, and argued that English criminal law was far more relevant to Poland than that of Ancient Rome. He praised bail, the jury system, and the differentiation of punishments, as well as humanitarian principles, going beyond Blackstone in his opposition to the death penalty. However, England's lack of censorship was less to his taste, and he edited out some anti-Catholic phrases.[71]

---

[65] T. Bukaty to dept., 10 Aug. 1787, AKP 82, ff. 191–2. Dept. to T. Bukaty, 20 Sept. 1786, 15 Sept. 1787, AKP 82, ff. 3, 50.

[66] Bukaty to SA, 1 Apr. 1791, PAU 1658, ff. 41–2.   [67] AKsJP 268, ff. 13–17, 121–4.

[68] Grześkowiak, 'Publicystyka', 151.   [69] Smoleński, *Przewrót umysłowy*, 176.

[70] *Duch czyli treść praw, albo o stosowności, które powinny mieć prawa z ustawą rządu każdego* (Leipzig and Dresden, 1777). Smoleński, *Monteskjusz w Polsce wieku XVIII* (Warsaw, 1927), 54–6, 71.

[71] *Prawo kryminalne angielskie przez Wilhelma Blakstona zebrane a przez X. T. Ostrowskiego S. P. wytłómaczone i z uwagami do prawa polskiego stosownemi pomnożone* (2 vols.; Warsaw, 1786).

Polish writers also paid more attention to the English constitution between the partitions. The lawyer Wincenty Skrzetuski backed his call for a hereditary throne with the English and Dutch examples in 1773.[72] Polish readers could glean information from Karol Wyrwicz's *Geografia powszechna* (1773), Antoni Mikucki's *Mowy o kształcie i własnościach różnych kraiowych rządów* ('On the form and properties of various governments') (Wilno 1774), Kajetan Skrzetuski's *Historia polityczna dla szlachetney młodzi* ('Political history for noble youth') (1775), and Konstanty Bogusławski's *O doskonałym prawodawctwie* ('On perfect legislation') (1786). Part of the fourth volume of Konarski's *O skutecznym rad sposobie* was reissued as *Opisanie formy obrad rzeczypospolitych* ('Description of the forms of deliberation in republics') in 1783. Montesquieu, either at first or second hand, was a major source. Probably the most important disseminator of information was Świtkowski's *Pamiętnik Historyczno-Polityczny*, which ran a long series of articles about England in 1786 and 1787. They included Archenholtz's description of London and the Bank of England. Świtkowski was concerned to show that a hereditary throne did not necessarily lead to despotism. Not everything they wrote was favourable, however. Even its admirers admitted that Parliament was corrupted by the king. Kajetan Skrzetuski polemicized with Voltaire and saw in the Septennial Act the triumph of royal tyranny. Oscillating between insolence and baseness, and drowning in debt, the English were headed for a revolution. He reiterated the traditional message that the Reformation had unleashed destructive forces of discord. The third volume of Norbert Jodłowski's detailed *Historya angielska* (1789–91), written for the Commission of National Education, included an account of the American war.[73]

The American Revolution could not but reflect badly on the British government. The ex-Jesuit Stefan Łuskina's *Gazeta Warszawska* printed information on the events across the Atlantic 'with an unconcealed aversion to England, and eagerly noted all of Albion's defeats'.[74] An informative German work, passionately justifying the Americans, was translated into Polish by Paweł Kollacz and published in 1778,[75] while Franciszek

---

[72] *Mowy o głównieyszych materyach politycznych*. See Grześkowiak, 'Publicystyka', 151.

[73] Grześkowiak, 'Publicystyka', 151–4, 162. Grześkowiak-Krwawicz, '*Rara avis*', 174–5, 179–80. Libiszowska, 'Model angielski', 5. Idem, *Życie polskie*, ch. 1. Idem, *Opinia polska*, 128. Konopczyński, *Polscy pisarze polityczni*, 422–4. P. Komorowski, *Historia powszechna w polskim piśmiennictwie naukowym czasów stanisławowskich i jej rola w edukacji narodowej* (Warsaw, 1992), chs. 2 and 3. *PHP*, Jan. 1783, 1786–7, *passim*. Skrzetuski, *Historya polityczna* (2nd edn., Warsaw, 1777), 117–50, 310–39.

[74] Libiszowska, *Opinia polska*, 16.

[75] *Rewolucya teraźnieysza Ameryki Północnej . . . jarzmo Wielkiey Brytanii zrzucających . . .* (Poznań, 1778). Libiszowska, *Opinia polska*, 45. Of the hundreds of German works on the

Siarczyński's translation of the part of Raynal's *Histoire* dealing with the American Revolution appeared in 1783.[76] However, Świtkowski grew disillusioned with the republican experiment of the confederated states, and in *Pamiętnik Historyczno-Polityczny* pronounced the English constitution superior. He later changed his mind after the publication of the American constitution.[77] Siarczyński published a full Polish translation in 1790. In general, events across the Atlantic did not resonate in political debate until the Four Year Seym. It was only then that the Declaration of Independence was translated into Polish, although a French translation had reached Poland in 1776.[78]

V

By the opening of the Four Year Seym, the ground had been prepared for the outburst of controversy on the English constitution that was to follow. Stanisław August was vastly more knowledgeable than nearly all of his countrymen. His correspondence with Filippo Mazzei, who told Stanisław August that he thought English liberty was an illusion,[79] provoked the king to some reflections upon England and France, which allow us to analyse his mature views on the English constitution. We have already noted Stanisław August's gloomy prognoses for England as the crisis in America worsened. Interestingly, in 1775 he blamed the elder Pitt's agitation of the colonists for the government's sad alternative 'd'une indulgence qui tiendrait de la faiblesse et ferait tort à tous ces droits ou d'une sévérité qu'on est toujours tenté d'appeler cruelle et qui peut devenir aisément fatale'.[80] He 'showed a particular interest in these American affairs',[81] and was kept informed on the course of the American revolutionary war by Bukaty and foreign newspapers. He had Paine's *Common Sense* and Dickinson's *Letters from a Farmer in Pennsylvania* by 1783. Mazzei

American Revolution listed and discussed by Horst Dippel, the most likely candidate seems M. C. Sprengel's *Briefe den gegenwartigen Zustand von Nord Amerika betreffend* (Göttingen, 1777). *Germany and the American Revolution*, 13, 51.

[76] *Historya polityczna Rewolucyi Amerykańskiey teraźnieyszey przez sławnego Rainala* ... (Warsaw, 1783). Libiszowska, *Opinia polska*, 46, 52–3.

[77] *PHP*, Mar., May 1784, Sept. 1785, Jan. 1787, Apr. 1789. See Libiszowska, *Opinia polska*, 118–24.

[78] See Libiszowska, *Opinia polska*, esp. 49–52, 127. Stanisław August's French copy of the Declaration of Independence is in Zb. Pop. 213, ff. 48–51.

[79] *Biblioteka Stanisława Augusta*, 114. Mazzei to SA, 13 Oct. 1788, 27 Apr. 1789, *Lettres de Philippe Mazzei et du roi Stanislas-Auguste de Pologne*, eds. J. Michalski *et al.* (vol 1; Rome, 1982), 56–8, 246.

[80] *Mémoires*, vol. 1, 125.

[81] 'Objawiał osobliwą w tych okolicznościach amerykańskich ciekawość'. Dept. to Bukaty, 15 Nov. 1775, AKP 78, f. 20. Libiszowska, *Misja polska*, 63.

later sent Stanisław August his *Recherches . . . sur les États Unis de l'Amérique*, Jefferson's *Notes on Virginia*, and John Stevens's anti-Federalist *Examen de la constitution d'Angleterre comparée à celle des États-Unis*.[82] From the political point of view, the king had wanted the British to crush the rebellion swiftly, in order to reinstate Britain in the European balance of power.[83] On the other hand, he had some sympathy for the Americans, and later had statuettes of Franklin and Washington put into his study at Łazienki. He told Mazzei in 1790: 'Je crois de plus en plus que Washington, et ceux qui pensent comme lui dans son pays, deviendront les meilleurs précepteurs du genre humain.'[84] He applauded the Americans' decision 'de restreindre une trop grande indépendance les uns et les autres, et qu'ils ont reconnus le besoin d'un chef, qui fut le point de réunion'.[85] We note once more his dislike of loose federations.

Stanisław August initially greeted the French Revolution with an enthusiasm that is revealing of his priorities. After the 'mémorable réunion des trois ordres des États Généraux', he wrote:

C'est sans contredit un des événements les plus remarquables que l'histoire ait jamais produits et des plus surprenants, qu'une si grande révolution, une transition si considérable de l'absolutisme à une liberté raisonnable et modérée ait pu s'opérer dans une nation si grande et vive, sans effusion de sang, et par un effet réel d'une saine philosophie et d'une vraie vertu, tant de la part de la nation que du Roi.[86]

He saluted the night of 4 August 1789 as 'la meilleur preuve que ce 18e siècle mérite d'être appelé celui de la philosophie'. However, with time, it became obvious that the liberty of the French Revolution was becoming less and less 'raisonnable et modérée', and the king grew steadily more critical, although for a long time he did not lose hope that moderation would prevail.[87]

Stanisław August retained his faith in England. After Mazzei had reported approvingly some critical remarks on England by La Croix, the king reminded his agent that 'les belles maximes de liberté et de l'égalité', if pushed beyond a certain point, would necessitate all the inconveniences of Plato's *Republic*. He went on to sum up his views on England:

---

[82] Mazzei to SA, 1 Aug. 1788, *Lettres*, 11–12. See Venturi, *The End of the Old Regime in Europe 1776–1789*, vol. 1, 137–43. The translation of Stevens's work was heavily annotated by Mazzei, Dupont de Nemours, Condorcet, Piattoli, and Gallois.

[83] Libiszowska, *Opinia polska*, 37, 40, 68–9, 94, 127. Dept. to Bukaty, 4 Nov. 1776, 25 Mar. 1779, AKP 78, ff. 27, 47.

[84] AKsJP 162, f. 33. SA to Mazzei, 17 Apr. 1790, Oss. 9751/I, f. 29.

[85] SA to Mazzei, 22 July 1789, *Lettres*, 324.   [86] Ibid.

[87] Michalski, 'Stanisław August obserwatorem Rewolucji Francuskiej', *KwH*, 97 (1990). Fabre, *Stanislas-Auguste Poniatowski*, 509–22.

Je conviens sans doute que les Nations Angloises et Irlandoises se feraient un grand honneur, si elles abolissaient leurs loix trops sevères contre les non-conformistes à leur Religion dominante; mais je pense en même temps que le gouvernement apres avoir vu tres différens essais (dont quelques recents) que la pluralité du peuple n'est pas encore mure pour cet acte de tolerance, que le gouvernement, dis-je, a fait sagement de ne pas le précipiter encore. Je conviens de même que la jurisprudence civile en Angleterre a besoin de beaucoup de corrections, mais je crois sa jurisprudence criminelle tres parfaite, et si on n'a pas aboli expressement les supplices anciennement institués pour châtiment de haute trahison nous voyons que dans la practique rien n'est moins cruelles que leurs supplices. Je conviens leur indulgence pour les voleurs de grands chemins, et la quantité de mendians qu'on voit en Angleterre malgré leur immenses établissements de charité sont des tâches à leur administration. Il y en a bien d'autres que je connois; mais en total c'est pourtant la Nation la plus heureuse, ou du moins dans la quelle il y a (proportion gardée des nombres relatifs) le moins de malheureux et le moins d'opprimés.[88]

Stanisław August could sympathize with the position of enlightened English statesmen after the Gordon riots. Lord Mansfield had had his house burnt down by the mob. The tone of pessimism from before the American war has vanished. Evidently the British state had survived and was once again flourishing. This opinion was formed from a wealth of information—Bukaty's despatches, Blackstone, conversation with Englishmen, and his own recollections. It was not the enthusiasm of a starry-eyed youngster, but the considered judgement of an experienced and practical statesman.

The years between the Confederacy of Bar and the Four Year Seym were the least exciting of Stanisław August's reign. From outside, the truncated Commonwealth appeared to have been subsumed into the Russian Empire, and to have fallen into a deep apathy which was occasionally shaken by petty squabbles. It was easy to write off Stanisław August, as did Wroughton, Wraxall, and their superiors, as a broken reed. Yet, although it was not apparent from *seymiki* instructions, these were the years when real inroads were made into the Sarmatian cast of mind. Political journalism and education slowly did their work. The law was enforced, religious fanaticism abated, Warsaw grew, nobles engaged in trade, manners were polished, and peace brought back prosperity. This progress did not, however, redound wholly to the benefit of Stanisław August. The virtuous patriotism promoted by his educational initiatives was completely at odds

[88] SA to Mazzei, 25 Aug. 1790. I am grateful to Prof. Jerzy Michalski for sending me a copy of this letter made by Jean Fabre.

with his inglorious policy of submission to Russia and the vice that was rampant in Warsaw. Cultural factors played their part too. A generation born after 1750, increasingly susceptible to romantic sensibility, grew impatient with Stanisław August's generation's rational acceptance of the inevitable. By the later 1780s, the combination of enlightened but hot-headed zeal, still powerful Sarmatian prejudice, and aristocratic ambition had become increasingly difficult to control.[89]

Stanisław August had hoped to realize at least part of his old dream of an English-style constitution, first formulated in his 'Anecdote Historique', as a sort of compensation for the Partition. He was rapidly disillusioned as the Permanent Council was set up to emasculate him. Stanisław August managed, however, to bring it to heel, and to curb the hetmans at last. The council became an agency of unspectacular but important reform. However, reform initiatives were always piecemeal and often unsuccessful. The 'free' Seyms achieved very little indeed. The English example influenced a few clauses of the abortive Zamoyski Code, the efforts of the police department to deal with vagrancy, and the royal plans for a militia. At the same time, the English constitution re-entered political discussion for the first time since Konarski, and knowledge of it slowly spread, encouraged by the king. Wybicki, Świtkowski, and the translations of Montesquieu and Blackstone probably played the most important roles. Stanisław August and his closest associates, notably Mniszech, became very well informed about the English system of government. Stanisław August was critical of some aspects of English government, but applauded others. His forebodings of English collapse vanished. He continued to think the English constitution the best in Europe, based upon a wise and moderate liberty that afforded security to all. It was not a vision that was shared by many of his compatriots. Polish political culture remained firmly republican, albeit with some signs of modernization by the late 1780s,[90] and when Russian control was lifted, the king's carefully built system came crashing down.

---

[89] Czaja, *Lata wielkich nadziei*, 169–76, 185–7. Zamoyski, *Last King*, 265–83.
[90] See Michalski, 'Z problematyki republikańskiego nurtu', 333–4.

12

The Influence of the English Constitution on the Constitution of 3 May 1791

A change in the international order was heralded by Russia's switch from a Prussian to an Austrian alliance in 1781. The long anticipated war with Turkey broke out in 1787. Prussia and England, isolated at the beginning of the decade, gravitated towards each other after the death of Frederick II, while the Prussian intervention in the Netherlands proved that France was financially and politically bankrupt after the War of American Independence. At Kaniów on the Dnieper in 1787, Stanisław August offered Catherine Polish troops to fight the Turks in return for fiscal reform and an increase in the army. Up-river in Kiev, a loose coalition of magnates led by Xawery Branicki and Ignacy Potocki tried to outbid him. Catherine gave only a tardy and partial acceptance of Stanisław August's offer, but haughtily dismissed his opponents. Amid rising anti-Russian sentiments in Poland, the disappointed Potocki began to look to Prussia. The political temperature rose through 1788. The Seym, which was confederated to pass the Russian alliance, promised to be the stormiest in years. When the Prussian envoy Buchholtz read out a note from Frederick William II warning against an alliance with Russia and offering help, Stanisław August lost control. His majority evaporated, and the Seym decreed an army of 100,000 in scenes of delirious enthusiasm, without any consideration of how it was to be paid for. Having prolonged itself indefinitely, the Seym went on to abolish the hated military department, the department of foreign affairs, and in January, the Permanent Council itself. It had become a 'ruling Seym' (*Seym rządzący*). After destroying the old order, it could begin to think about constructing a new one. On 3 May 1791, after a long and winding road, a new constitution was passed.[1]

---

[1] On the international background, see T. C. W. Blanning, *The Origins of the French Revolutionary Wars* (London, 1986), 45–60, and R. H. Lord, *The Second Partition of Poland* (Cambridge, Mass., 1915). Much has been written on the opening of the Four Year Seym and the lead up to it, but the standard work remains Kalinka, *Sejm Czteroletni*. Also see Dembiński, *Polska na przełomie*; Rostworowski, *Ostatni król*, 114–54; idem, *Sprawa aukcji wojska*, 177–266; Michalski, 'Sejmiki poselskie 1788 roku', *PH*, 51 (1960); and idem, 'Zmierzch prokonsulatu Stackelberga' and 'Opozycja magnacka i jej cele w początkach Sejmu

From the moment in which the proposed Law on Government (*Ustawa Rządowa*) was read out to the Seym by Stanisław Małachowski, the extensive influence of both the English and American systems of government upon the Constitution of 3 May 1791 has been asserted. For Małachowski said:

In this age we have two most famous republican systems of government; the English, and the American, which corrected the faults of the former. But that, which we are to establish today, will be still more perfect, because it unites in itself, whatever in both systems is best and most proper to be in our own.[2]

Małachowski's statement, however, glossed over the fundamental differences in aim between the main authors of the Constitution—Stanisław August, Ignacy Potocki, and Hugo Kołłątaj. From the political point of view, it was as well for Małachowski to minimize the 'monarchical' elements in the constitution; the more 'republican' it could be made to look in the eyes of the noble nation, the better.[3]

That the marshal of the Seym should praise the American constitution somewhat at the expense of the English is in itself evidence, not only of Polish sympathy for the American cause, but also of the suspicions which advocacy of an English-style constitution could continue to arouse in some quarters.[4] In the course of the fierce debate over the shape of the future form of government during the Four Year Seym, critics of the English model were not lacking. As this subject has already attracted the attention of historians,[5] it is not necessary to provide a comprehensive

Czteroletniego' in J. Kowecki (ed.), *Sejm Czteroletni i jego tradycje* (Warsaw, 1991). Askenazy, *Przymierze polsko-pruskie*, and Łojek, *Geneza i obalenie Konstytucji 3 Maja* (Lublin, 1986) should be treated with great caution, as they try to prove that the Prussian alliance offered Poland a real opportunity, which was wasted by the 'cowardice' of Stanisław August. The term *sejm rządzący* was used by Kalinka as the title of Book III of *Sejm Czteroletni*. See Michalski, 'Kilka uwag o koncepcji Sejmu rządzącego w XVIII w.', *Śląski Kwartalnik Historyczny Sobótka*, 37 (1982).

[2] Quoted by Rostworowski, *Maj 1791–maj 1792*, 5.

[3] A point also made by Michalski, *Konstytucja 3 Maja* (Warsaw, 1985), 49.

[4] Stanisław August was at pains to deny rumours in St Petersburg that he, the king, had recommended any foreign constitutions. SA to Deboli, 4 June 1791, Zb. Pop. 413, f. 113.

[5] See Grześkowiak, 'Publicystyka'; Grześkowiak-Krwawicz, 'Obce wzory ustrojowe w dyskusjach publicystycznych Sejmu Czteroletniego' in *Sejm Czteroletni i jego tradycje*, 85–6; Libiszowska, 'Model angielski', 5–10; Rostworowski, 'Republikanizm polski i anglosaski', 100–3; R. Pilat, *O literaturze politycznéj Sejmu Czteroletniego (1788–1792)* (Cracow, 1872), 68–70; Konopczyński, 'Polscy pisarze polityczni XVIII w.', vol. 2 (unpublished typescript in BJag Akc. 52/61), *passim*; Leśnodorski, *Dzieło Sejmu Czteroletniego* (Wrocław, 1951), 59–64; Grobis, 'Sukcesja tronu', esp. 78–88; Zielińska, 'Publicystyka pro- i antysukcesyjna w początkach Sejmu Wielkiego', in *Sejm Czteroletni i jego tradycje*; eadem, *'O sukcesyi . . .'*, 24–41.

analysis. Nevertheless, in order to understand the difficulties encountered by Stanisław August and his fellow reformers in agreeing and forcing through the Constitution of 3 May, a review of the uses made of the English model in the polemical battles of the Four Year Seym will be helpful. From the outset those battles were dominated by the issue of hereditary succession to the throne. On that score, the publication of Stanisław Staszic's *Uwagi nad życiem Jana Zamoyskiego* ('Considerations on the life of Jan Zamoyski') in 1787, which argued that granting the Polish crown with hereditary succession to a foreign prince was a price worth paying for a 'natural ally', put the spark to the tinder.[6] In the ensuing debate, the English example was used as a tool in political polemics. Objectivity was in short supply.[7]

I

Among the critics, a few die-hard 'old republicans', as well as some enthusiastic, Rousseau-quoting supporters of the French Revolution like Gabriel Taszycki and Wojciech Turski,[8] denied that a hereditary monarchy, whether in England or anywhere else, was compatible with freedom. The appearance in 1789 of Rousseau's *Considérations sur le gouvernement de Pologne* in Polish translation undoubtedly encouraged opponents of the English model. 'English freedom' was a fiction! At best, it was restricted to elections. So stated Seweryn and Adam Rzewuski, Tadeusz Czacki, and the anonymous author of *Uwagi nad rządem angielskim y inne dla wolnego narodu użyteczne* ('Considerations on the English government and other considerations useful to a free nation'). One reason was that no safeguards existed to prevent the king breaking the law and ruling tyrannically, in the manner of Henry VIII. Blackstone and Filangieri were ransacked to prove the point.[9] If the English enjoyed any freedom at present, it was because the Hanoverian kings were weak. The second reason

---

[6] Zielińska, 'Publicystyka pro- i antysukcesyjna', 109–12. Eadem, '*O sukcesyi . . .*' 24–5.

[7] Grześkowiak, 'Publicystyka', 151.

[8] Turski is listed as a radical by Libiszowska, 'Model angielski', 8 and Rostworowski, 'Republikanizm polski i anglosaski', 102, but Grześkowiak places him closer to the old republicans, 'Publicystyka', 156 n. 37. This shows how blurred the boundaries could become.

[9] Konopczyński, 'Polscy pisarze polityczni', vol. 2, 134, 145, 174–5, 182. Zielińska, *Republikanizm spod znaku buławy: Publicystyka Seweryna Rzewuskiego z lat 1788–1790* (Warsaw, 1988), 116–17. Walicki, *The Enlightenment and the Birth of Modern Nationhood*, 21, 23. The author of *Uwagi nad rządem angielskim y inne dla wolnego narodu użyteczne* (1791) added to one of his footnotes citing Blackstone (no. 5) that 'dobrze jest wiedzieć, ze ten sławny Pisarz jest naywiększym wielbicielem Konstytucyi swego Kraju' ('It is as well to know that this famous writer is the greatest admirer of his country's constitution').

was that the king of England had so corrupted Parliament by his powers of patronage that he did as he pleased without having to resort to tyranny. The much vaunted responsibility of ministers to Parliament was therefore worthless. In general, 'a man would have difficulty in deciding if it would be better for him to be a citizen in England, or a subject under despotic rule.'[10] The American colonists had evidently come to that conclusion and had revolted against royal tyranny. Why should not the Poles follow their example and suppress the institution of monarchy altogether?

Such confidence, whether apparent or real,[11] was not shared by all the old republicans. Faced with the authority of Montesquieu, other opponents of the English model preferred to argue in the manner of Montesquieu that while the English enjoyed freedom, the English constitution was unsuitable for transplantation to Poland. One author, Olizar Wołczkiewicz, devoted 320 pages to this very subject.[12] The islanders' famed love of liberty (attributed by Montesquieu to the incommodiousness of their climate)[13] was turned into an argument against the introduction of a hereditary throne in Poland. The English national character had led to civil wars against would-be absolute kings. The Poles, having, it was alleged, a milder temperament, would soon allow themselves to be enslaved, should the throne be made hereditary.[14] Stanisław August, it may be recalled, had less faith in the proverbial English love of liberty. Other reasons advanced for the survival of English freedom included the country's island situation—no foreign monarch could help the English king become a despot. The threat posed by the Pretenders forced the monarchs to seek the support of the nation, and the dependence of the economy on overseas trade supposedly inhibited royal efforts to seize the wealth of the citizens, as landed estates were easier to confiscate. Other hypotheses included the part allegedly played by the 'common people' (*pospólstwo*) in the legislature, the populousness of London, which deterred the use of a standing

[10] Probably S. Rzewuski, *Uwagi nad wyborem między elekcyą a sukcessyą tronu w Polszcze* (1791), 35, quoted after Grześkowiak-Krwawicz, 'Obce wzory', 93 n. 27.

[11] The sincerity of their denial of English freedom was immediately questioned by Kołłątaj, *Uwagi nad pismem . . . Seweryna Rzewuskiego . . . o sukcessyi tronu w Polszcze rzecz krótka* (Warsaw, 1790), 100, and latterly by Grześkowiak-Krwawicz, '*Rara avis* czy wolni wśród wolnych', 175–6.

[12] *Co ma uważać Rzeczpospolita Polska w prawodawstwie, tak przed dopuszczeniem jako i po dopuszczeniu składu rządu angielskiego. Stanu politycznego różnice i podobieństwa między sobą tych dwóch wolnych państw stosując. Przez L. W. O.* (1791).

[13] *Esprit des lois*, Book XIV, ch. 13.

[14] Grześkowiak, 'Publicystyka', 158. Grześkowiak-Krwawicz, '*Rara avis*', 175–80. Rostworowski, 'Republikanizm polski i anglosaski', 100. The author of 'Myśli o Sukcessyi Tronu lub Elekcyi Króla', which remained in manuscript, put the number of civil wars as 'około [about] 40', following K. Skrzetuski's *Historya polityczna*, 327. APP 197, f. 149.

army, and even the role of the king as head of the Church—he was forced to obey the voice of conscience![15]

The influence of the English model, however, was such that one writer used the name of 'Lord Burke' (*sic*) to warn against its adoption, especially as regarded hereditary succession to the throne. Although he declared that England and Poland were animated by the same spirit of freedom, different in its philosophy from that of the French Revolution (an attempt at authenticity), he counselled: 'do not take any example either from our form of government in England; for being separated from all our neighbours by seas, it is absolutely necessary that we should have a different system of government from you.'[16]

Opinion as to the merits of the English constitution had undergone a sea change. While Hetman Rzewuski and his supporters could still appeal to provincial anti-English prejudices, in the more enlightened capital their arguments lacked credibility. Rzewuski himself wrote that he heard the English constitution constantly praised and set before the Poles as a model.[17] Hence the caution of other critics, and hence also the extensive use made of the popular American cause. That the English constitution reconciled hereditary monarchy with freedom had become a commonplace. Konarski's old dictum to that effect was often quoted.[18] In the Seym on 16 September 1790, Julian Niemcewicz backed up his call for a hereditary throne by citing the English example: 'you have no freer nation under the sun.' In reply, the conservative Wojciech Suchodolski did not deny the reconciliation of freedom with hereditary succession in England, but instead cited the examples of Hungary, Bohemia, Denmark, and Sweden, where the introduction of a hereditary monarchy had, in his opinion, led to slavery.[19] At the beginning of 1791, Niemcewicz's comedy, *Powrót posła* ('The return of the envoy'), did more than any pamphlet to make opponents of a hereditary throne and the English system of government look ridiculous. Jan Suchorzewski's outraged protests only produced outbursts of laughter in the Seym.[20]

[15] Grześkowiak, 'Publicystyka', 158–9, 161. Libiszowska, 'Model angielski', 8.

[16] *Lord Burke do Polaków. Pismo z angielskiego przełożone* (1791), not paginated. See Libiszowska, 'Lord Burke do Polaków', in *Kultura średniowieczna i kultura staropolska: Studia ofiarowane Aleksandrowi Gieysztorowi* . . . (Warsaw, 1991).

[17] Zielińska, 'O sukcesyi . . .', 41. Grobis, 'Sukcesja tronu', 79.

[18] See above, pp. 148–9. Grześkowiak, 'Publicystyka', 157.

[19] Grześkowiak, 'Publicystyka', 157. Kalinka, *Sejm Czteroletni*, vol. 2, 386.

[20] *Powrót posła*, ed. Z. Skwarczyński (Wrocław, 1981), introduction, *passim*, act II, scene iv, lines 134–60, act III, scene v, lines 127–32, 219–20. SA to M. Poniatowski, 22 Jan. 1791, Zb. Gh. 801b, f. 123. SA to Deboli, 19 Jan. 1791, 22 Jan. 1791, Zb. Pop. 413, ff. 13–14, 16. Printed in *Rok nadziei i rok klęski 1791–1792: Z korespondencji Stanisława Augusta z posłem polskim w Petersburgu Augustynem Debolim*, ed. J. Łojek (Warsaw, 1964), 29–30.

Thus far we have made no nice distinction between 'the English system of government' and 'hereditary succession to the throne'. Nor did many of those who cited the English example. Among the leaders of the reform camp in the Seym, and also in diplomatic circles, the two had become virtually coterminous.[21] This vagueness enabled the proponents of a hereditary throne to put to one side the question of the actual prerogatives of the King of England, which were uncomfortably closer to those attributed to him by Rzewuski and his supporters than they cared to admit.[22] Kołłątaj shunted the issue into a long endnote of his answer to the hetman, where he argued cogently enough that England guaranteed perfect civil liberty to *all* its citizens and was therefore distasteful to the magnates. Political liberty was adequately guarded from the king by the division of the legislative power between king, Lords, and Commons, and by the right of the Commons to withhold taxes. Yet at least until 1791, Kołłątaj paid only lip-service to the separation and balance of the legislative, executive, and judicial powers, and his proposals would have resulted in a 'ruling Seym'.[23] Kołłątaj and Tadeusz Morski reconciled their admiration for the Americans with the English model by holding that the Americans had only claimed the rights of Englishmen.[24] The 'patriot' leaders and publicists rejected the American-style king-less republic proposed by Rzewuski and Szczęsny Potocki by denying its applicability in Polish conditions. Poland had no ocean to defend her, and the loose federal system envisaged by the old republicans would mean the rule of each province by a magnate kingling. Moreover, as Kołłątaj reminded Rzewuski, in America there were no subjects or social estates, only men.[25]

Practically the whole current of reformist thought in the first half of the Four Year Seym flowed in fact towards further 'republicanization' of the form of government. The king would be stripped of most of his remaining powers in favour of a 'ruling Seym'. There was some hesitation over

[21]   See Zielińska, '*O sukcesyi . . .*', 71, 73, 79, 81.

[22]   The use of Blackstone is revealing. For Blackstone's monarchist credentials and further conservative views on the extent of the royal prerogative in England, see Dickinson, *Liberty and Property*, 43–9, 96–100, 130–2, 154–7, 273–9; Clark, *Dynamics of Change*, 449–53; and idem, *English Society*, 201–16.

[23]   Kołłątaj, *Uwagi nad pismem . . . Rzewuskiego*, 99–113. *Listy Anonima*, in *Wybór pism politycznych*, ed. B. Leśnodorski (Wrocław, 1952), 102. M. Pasztor, *Hugo Kołłątaj na Sejmie Wielkim 1791–1792* (Warsaw, 1991), ch. 5.

[24]   Rostworowski, 'Republikanizm polski i anglosaski', 101–2. T. Morski, *Uwagi o chłopach*, in *Materiały do dziejów Sejmu Czteroletniego*, vol. 1, eds. J. Woliński, J. Michalski, and E. Rostworowski (Wrocław, 1955), 104.

[25]   Kołłątaj, *Uwagi nad pismem . . . Rzewuskiego*, 65–77. Libiszowska, *Opinia polska*, 129–34. Rostworowski, 'Republikanizm polski i anglosaski', 101–2. Konopczyński, 'Polscy pisarze polityczni', vol. 2, 140–1.

whether it should be constantly in session (*trwały*) or merely reconvenable (*gotowy*). While neither idea was foreign to Polish republicanism, the former was associated by both the king and some of his opponents with the English model. Stanisław Kostka Potocki thought that premature in Polish conditions and insisted on a reconvenable Seym.[26] Any central executive body would have a purely supervisory function. In other words, the 'shame' of 1776 would be avenged.[27] Within this framework, the responsibility of ministers to Parliament and the absence of the King of England from the cabinet, occasionally recommended by reformers, would help to reduce royal influence to nil (this appealed to old republicans as well).[28] The new 'enlightened republicanism' was the product of traditional *szlachta* republican thought under the heady influence of Rousseau, combined with a craving to throw off the Russian shackles.[29] The bitter experience of chaos, corruption, and foreign intervention during interregna, although it knocked away the intellectual props of royal elections, was not the primary source of the 'patriot' leaders' desire to make the Crown hereditary. More pressing was the need to secure the Commonwealth against future aggression. This was to be done by making an alliance with another power. The bargaining counter was to be the offer of the Polish crown with hereditary succession. Too often, however, the reformers failed to appreciate that neither the Elector of Saxony nor anyone else would accept the Polish throne if its prerogatives were to be yet further whittled down. Nevertheless, the illusion persisted, even after 3 May 1791.[30]

[26] SA to Deboli, 5 Nov. 1788, Zb. Pop. 417, ff. 618–19. S. K. Potocki, *Myśli o ogólnej poprawie rządu krajowego* (1789), repr. in *Kołłątaj i inni: Z publicystyki doby Sejmu Czteroletniego*, ed. Ł. Kądziela (Warsaw, 1991), 57–8. The annual sessions of the British Parliament actually averaged about five months in the later 18th century.

[27] This emerges particularly clearly from *Myśli o ogólnej poprawie* . . . , 51–3. See Michalski, 'Opozycja magnacka', 56–7, and Kalinka, *Sejm Czteroletni*, vol. 1, 159–62, 262.

[28] Czaja, *Między tronem* . . . , 350.

[29] Szczygielski, 'Konstytucja 3 maja', in *Konstytucja 3 Maja w tradycji i kulturze polskiej*, 10–13 and *passim*. Rostworowski, 'Marzenie dobrego obywatela', 407–10. Both Pilat, *O literaturze politycznej*, 14–15, 60, and Lukowski, 'Od Konarskiego do Kołłątaja—czyli od realizmu do utopii', in *Trudne stulecia*, 187–94, have negatively assessed Rousseau's influence as doctrinaire and utopian.

[30] A point made by Stanisław August to M. Poniatowski on 24 Nov. 1790, Zb. Gh. 801b, f. 108, and by Hailes to Grenville on 19 May 1791. PRO FO 62/4. See Zielińska, 'O sukcesyi . . .', esp. 222–3. K. Zienkowska has argued that the main motive of the 'patriots' was to create in a hereditary monarch a symbol of national unity and sovereignty; 'Sukcesja tronu w Ustawie Rządowej 3 Maja 1791 roku—koncepcja władzy, czy symbol suwerenności?', in *Konstytucja 3 Maja. Prawo—Polityka—Symbol*. Cf. Z. Zielińska (in the discussion), ibid., 114–15. The symbolic role played by the king *after* the passing of the constitution is unquestioned, but the evidence for it as a primary motive beforehand is scratchy. For the later hopes of the 'patriots', see Rostworowski, 'Marzenie dobrego obywatela', 462–3.

The Polish 'patriots' therefore interpreted 'the English form of government' very much as it suited them. For the most part they would graft a hereditary throne onto a republican system of government, and justify it by citing 'England'. When they looked a little closer, they took their view of the English constitution from the opposition Whigs and from Montesquieu, whose common source was the Country or 'patriot' opposition to Walpole.[31] Nevertheless, it was Montesquieu that royalists quoted in order to defend the Permanent Council from the 'ruling Seym'.[32] 'Monarchist' recommendations of the English example, that is, calling for an extension to the royal prerogative, were far rarer. Surprisingly, the most telling monarchist work of all, Józef Pawlikowski's *Myśli polityczne dla Polski* ('Political thoughts for Poland') (1789), made no mention of England.[33] Defending the Permanent Council, Roch Lasocki argued that

England has a hereditary king, who has control over the army and the power to make war or peace, and the nation, perhaps even more jealous than ourselves of its rights and liberties, does not complain about it; it has its tranquillity secured, without feeling the burden and power of the army, which the king controls, and which is the cause of its great importance in Europe.[34]

The best tract written about the English constitution was Ignacy Łobarzewski's *Zaszczyt wolności polskiey angielskiey wyrownywaiący* ('The honour of Polish freedom equalling the English'), which was followed by a project for a 'republican' form of government, *Testament polityczny*.[35] Their interest for us is heightened by the facts of Łobarzewski's having worked in a department of the Permanent Council until it was abolished in January 1789, and his receipt of a royal pension from the middle of that year.[36] It is unlikely that Stanisław August was directly responsible for the works; he would not have agreed, as we shall see, with the proposal that members of the 'custodial council', or *Straż*, should be elected

---

[31] See above, pp. 50–1, and also B. Bailyn, *The Ideological Origins of the American Revolution* (Cambridge, Mass., 1967), ch. 2, and Dickinson, *Liberty and Property*, 207–10, 169–92.

[32] Czaja, *Między tronem . . .* , 347, 357–8. Also see Kalinka, *Sejm Czteroletni*, vol. 1, 222.

[33] In the same author's *O poddanych polskich* (1788), we find only a short mention that England has a free government, but as that freedom was denied to the Americans, they rebelled and are now free. In *Materiały do dziejów Sejmu Czteroletniego*, vol. 1, 16. J. Lukowski wonders if the English monarchy was strong *enough* for Pawlikowski.

[34] 3 Nov. 1788, quoted after Czaja, *Między tronem . . .* , 351.

[35] *Zaszczyt wolności polskiey angielskiey wyrownywaiący z uwagami do tego stosownemi i opisaniem rządu angielskiego* (Warsaw, 1789). *Testament polityczny synowi oyczyzny zostawiony z planem beśpieczney formy republikantskiego rządu* (Warsaw, 1789).

[36] Konopczyński, 'Polscy pisarze polityczni', vol. 2, 163. Zielińska, 'Publicystyka pro-i antysukcesyjna', 113. Also see J. Kowecki's article on Łobarzewski in *PSB*, 18 (1973), 370–1.

by the chamber of envoys but should not take part in the deliberations of the Seym.[37] Nevertheless, he was clearly pleased by them,[38] and so in some measure they may be taken as an expression of the attitude of the king and his circle to the English constitution.

Łobarzewski had toured England in 1786 with his late patron, August Sułkowski; he knew English, and was better informed than his rivals. He even brought back eighteen volumes of *Parliamentary History* for Stanisław August,[39] but nevertheless he idealized the English constitution, especially parliamentary elections,[40] and borrowed heavily from Montesquieu. He appealed to sentiments of noble equality and severely castigated the magnates. Apart from advocating a hereditary throne (although freedom was to be safeguarded by a short interregnum between the death of the old king and his successor's taking the oath),[41] Łobarzewski proposed the extension of the royal prerogative to correspond with that of the king of England. In the legislative sphere, he urged that the king and the senate should each have a full power of veto. The apparent similarity of the three estates of the Seym to the king in parliament was, he wrote, fictitious, because in Poland the chamber of envoys had usurped all the legislative power to itself. (A similar view was expressed by the author of a project presented to the Seym deputation for the form of government in late 1789.) Quoting Montesquieu, Łobarzewski argued that a 'ruling Seym' would lead inevitably to tyranny, as was already the case in that old *szlachta* favourite, Venice.[42] He stressed the importance of the responsibility of ministers, not the king, to Parliament,[43] and that members of the House of Commons were not bound by instructions. As a result, they acted as the representatives of the entire nation, and not merely of their constituents.[44] He accompanied such proposals with a comprehensive account of the progress of liberty in England, seeing in the Commons' control of the purse-strings liberty's source and guarantee.[45] One strong influence

---

[37] *Testament*, 78–83.

[38] 'Łobarzewski,' wrote Stanisław August to Deboli on 22 June 1791, 'pisał kilka książek wcale użytecznych w duchu naszey Rewolucyi; y lubo był wychowankiem nieboszczyka Sułkowskiego, względem mnie y Oyczyzny, wcale dobrze się zachowywał od śmierci tegoż' ('wrote some very useful books in the spirit of our revolution, and although brought up by the late Sułkowski, since his death he has conducted himself extremely well as regards myself and the country'). Zb. Pop. 413, f. 126.

[39] T. Bukaty to dept., 1 Sept. 1786, AKP 81, f. 277. Libiszowska, *Życie polskie*, 255.

[40] *Zaszczyt wolności* . . . , 107–9.   [41] Ibid., 244–53.

[42] Ibid., 10, 18, 147–51. Prospekt do ulepszenia formy rządu w Polszcze', APP 98, ff. 172–6, cited by Zielińska, 'O sukcesyi . . .', 106.

[43] *Testament*, 118–21. Grześkowiak, 'Publicystyka', 164.

[44] *Zaszczyt wolności* . . . , 105, 194–5.   [45] Ibid., 38–41, 118–39. *Testament*, 128–32.

of Montesquieu was in the definition of English freedom as submission to the law. Łobarzewski held up the English judicial system as a paradigm of humanity and fairness, and made much of the execution of Lord Ferrers in 1760 for murdering his servant. He urged that, as in England, the king should be able to commute the death sentence.[46] Many of these points also found expression in Stanisław August's programme.

The English example also served writers urging the extension of political rights to burghers, and the abolition of serfdom. The flourishing of England's trade and agriculture was attributed to the lack of a noble monopoly of political power and the absence of serfdom. Was the English nobility any less well off than the Polish as a result? 'And what is the cause of this wealth? Freedom,' wrote one author.[47] It was difficult for Polish writers to grasp the informal and conditional control of England by the aristocracy. There was some exaggeration of English social mobility. One writer alleged that a tailor could rise to be a minister if he had the talent. The name of the House of 'Commons' caused confusion. Perhaps Staszic came closest, stating that it was composed of representatives of both the '*szlachta*' and the towns.[48] Świtkowski wrote that if agriculture were to flourish, apart from freedom, farmers must have the incentive of the comforts provided by flourishing town life. He described, rather sanguinely, the lot of the English tenant farmer, who

lives like a prosperous Polish nobleman, he dresses and feeds himself honestly, he has the best horses, oxen, ploughs, and carts, and on holidays drinks English beer from a large silver beaker, and this is to be seen not just around London, but throughout the entire country.[49]

On social questions, therefore, the use made of the English model did not rise to as high a plane as in the debate over the nature of the monarchy. At its base, England's social structure differed too greatly from Poland's to be of much relevance.

---

[46] *Zaszczyt wolności . . .* , 145, 160–82. Smoleński, *Monteskjusz w Polsce*, 80.

[47] *PHP*, Oct. 1789, repr. in *Materiały do dziejów Sejmu Czteroletniego*, vol. 1, 148.

[48] Grześkowiak, 'Publicystyka', 160–1. *Nie wszyscy błądzą. Rozmowa Bartka chłopa z panem rzecz całą objaśni* (1790), repr. in *Materiały do dziejów Sejmu Czteroletniego*, vol. 1, 354. Staszic, *Przestrogi dla Polski*, in idem, *Pisma filozoficzne i społeczne*, ed. B. Suchodolski (Warsaw, 1954), vol. 1, 296. Idem, *Uwagi nad życiem Jana Zamoyskiego*, ibid., vol. 1, 47. Staszic's approval of England's social structure was mixed with criticism of its 'despotic' foreign policy and the conviction that such a government would turn Poland into a despotism.

[49] 'Jak wiele od pomyslności miast zawisła powszechna szczęśliwość kraju i jak wiele rząd starać się powinien o ich zakwitnienie', *Pamiętnik Historyczno-Polityczno-Ekonomiczny*, Mar.–Apr. 1790, repr. in *Materiały do dziejów Sejmu Czteroletniego*, vol. 3 (Wrocław, 1960), 256.

The polemics about England were therefore dominated by the question of whether a hereditary throne could be reconciled with freedom. Seweryn Rzewuski and a few others stated that it could not, and that 'English freedom' was a fiction. Other opponents of hereditary succession did not deny English freedom, but argued that a hereditary throne in Poland would lead to slavery. The majority of the reformers justified a hereditary throne by citing England, but also wished to reduce the royal prerogative yet further. Those advocating an increase in the prerogative to correspond with that of the King of England found themselves in a small minority. The noble nation's suspicion of any form of strong executive remained intense.

II

The Constitution of 3 May was the outcome of a *rapprochement* between the king and the leaders of the 'patriots'. Although the king had always trusted Stanisław Małachowski and, to a lesser extent, Kołłątaj, bringing together Stanisław August and Ignacy Potocki was not easy. Potocki had little regard for Stanisław August's ability or character, and suspected that the monarch harboured despotic ambitions. In 1788–9 he had been the chief tribune of the 'ruling Seym' that had reduced the king to a virtual cipher. Stanisław August also remembered Potocki's wounding attacks upon him during the 1780s, and feared being compromised in the eyes of the nation. The achievement of any sort of trust between them was extraordinarily difficult.[50] The experience of the chaotic first two years of the Seym nevertheless forced Potocki to acknowledge that the road from old republicanism to 'enlightened republicanism' was maddeningly slow. Cracks soon began to appear in the opposition between the progressive elements and the filibustering supporters of the hetmans. For his part, Stanisław August refused to 'reconfederate' the country against the Seym as Stackelberg desired, and dropped his opposition to the Prussian alliance in order to preserve national unity and prevent a confrontation that might lead to Prussian intervention and a new partition. Trying to moderate rather than reverse the flow, he made full use of his powers of oratory in the Seym and steadily rose in authority.[51] His powers of nomination were restored to him after much debate in September 1790.[52] As

[50] Rostworowski, 'Marzenie dobrego obywatela', 285–6, 298–9. SA to Deboli, 11 Mar. 1789, Zb. Pop. 414, f. 125, 10 Mar. 1790, Zb. Pop. 420, f. 761, 2 Feb. 1791, Zb. Pop. 413, f. 23.
[51] See Rostworowski, *Ostatni król*, 150–92.
[52] SA to M. Poniatowski, 1 Sept.–15 Sept. 1790, Zb. Gh. 801b, ff. 52–66, *passim*.

that year wore on, it became evident to Potocki that while it had been easy to overthrow the Permanent Council and the ambassadorial-royal duopoly, the 'patriots' were not strong enough by themselves to force constitutional reform through the Seym. Only with royal support was progress towards a new constitution possible. In fact, tentative efforts to effect a reconciliation began in the summer of 1789. The role played by the radical democrat Scipione Piattoli was crucial. He was originally sent to the castle to spy on the king, but while retaining the trust of Potocki, he became increasingly attached to Stanisław August.[53] The last straw for Potocki was the conservative attitude of the provincial *szlachta* revealed by the instructions of the November 1790 *seymiki*. Stanisław August's old distrust of the *seymiki* was underscored. A majority of the instructions defended free royal elections. Proposals to sequester the funds of the Commission for National Education and return schooling to monastic orders distressed both the king and Potocki. Stanisław August deplored 'cette renaissance de barbarisme',[54] but was consoled by the electoral success of his own supporters and, it may be added, by Potocki's discomfort. On 4 December 1790, Potocki visited Stanisław August at the castle, and invited the king to draw up his own project for a new constitution.[55]

Potocki's change of heart was not just forced upon him by political necessity. He also underwent an ideological conversion. In 1789, he had been the chief author of the 'Principles for the correction of the form of government' (*Zasady do poprawy formy rządu*)—the first step taken by the Seym towards the creation of a new constitution. This was a logical conclusion of traditional republican political thought which also showed the strong influence of Rousseau and the phraseology of the French National Assembly, as Stanisław August discerned. Naturally, the organs of executive power were to 'emanate' from the Seym, despite the endorsement of the separation of powers. Nevertheless in legislation, even the concept of the 'ruling Seym' did not suffice, as all laws and taxes were to be passed by a simple or qualified majority (and in the case of 'cardinal laws' by all) of the *seymiki* instructions. It was through the *seymiki* that the 'general will' of the nation was expressed.[56] Now, on 4 December 1790, Potocki

---

[53] Rostworowski, 'Marzenie dobrego obywatela', 283–342. Zielińska, '*O sukcesyi* . . .', 125, 132–6, 167, 170–2, 186–8, 197. Michalski, *Konstytucja 3 Maja*, 39.

[54] SA to M. Poniatowski, 20 Nov. 1790, Zb. Gh. 801b, f. 106.

[55] Zielińska, '*O sukcesyi* . . .', 207–19. Rostworowski, 'Marzenie dobrego obywatela', 343–6. Kowecki, 'Posłowie debiutanci na Sejmie Czteroletnim', in *Wiek XVIII: Polska i świat*, 203. SA to Deboli, 17 Nov. 1790, 20 Nov. 1790, 27 Nov. 1790, Zb. Pop. 420, ff. 1085–9, 1091–3, 1099–1102. SA to Bukaty, 24 Nov. 1790, BCzart. 849, ff. 265–7.

[56] Rostworowski, 'Marzenie dobrego obywatela', 290–1, 295–8.

was proposing 'une monarchie limitée'. Evidently, the results of the November *seymiki* had shaken his faith in pure noble democracy. He now thought that until such time as the nation could be enlightened, a compromise with the monarch would be better than trusting either the Seym or the *seymiki*.[57] Kołłątaj's views underwent a similar evolution from his extreme republicanism in his *Listy anonima* ('Letters of an anonymous correspondent') to his acceptance of a stronger executive in his work on the final form of the constitution.[58] Both, however, continued to fear royal power.

The example of England played a role in the sparring between the king and the 'patriots' in 1789–90. As has been shown, the 'English constitution' was used very loosely by the latter. It is quite likely that this very vagueness of expression gave both the 'patriot' leaders, especially Potocki, and the king a flexible and respectable cover under which they could fence on the sensitive subject of the royal prerogative, which, if confronted directly, might have produced a swift rupture. Stanisław August used the *pacta conventa* in a similar way. During a conversation on 27 July 1789, Potocki was not yet in a mood for compromise, and the discussion was robust. After discussing which powers of nomination should be left in royal hands, Stanisław August asked: 'Do you wish, Sir, to leave the king the right of veto, as has the king of England?' Potocki answered categorically: 'Oh no!'[59] On 8 December 1789, the king conversed with the Prussian envoy Lucchesini, who was in close contact with Potocki:

W teyże konwersacyi gdy *naturalnie* [my italics] upadła pochwała Rządu Angielskiego, to mi dało powód powiedzenia: '. . . Szczęśliwym bym się zaiste sadził, gdyby moy los był przyrownany losowi Krola Angielskiego; ale się tego nie spodziewam.' On na to zwrocił dyskurs na inszą materyę.

(In that conversation, *naturally* it came to pass that the English system of government was praised, which gave me an occasion to say '. . . I would consider myself truly happy, if my fate were to be compared with the fate of the King of England, but that I do not expect.' At that he turned the discussion to other material.)[60]

The 'respectable cover' is well illustrated by the next incident. On 20 December 1789 the king pressed Potocki and Małachowski about his powers of nomination.

---

[57] Ibid., 317, 318, 322–3, 343–54, 458–9.   [58] Pasztor, *Kołłątaj*, 164–5.

[59] 'Czy chcesz WPan krolowi zostawić facultatem vetandi, iak ią ma Krol Angielski?', 'Oh nie!', SA to Deboli, 29 July 1789, Zb. Pop. 414, f. 388.

[60] SA to Deboli, 9 Dec. 1789, Zb. Pop. 414, f. 569. Also partly quoted by Rostworowski, 'Marzenie dobrego obywatela', 292.

Potocki po wielu nieiasnych wyrazach, między innemi y to powiedział, że w koncu roboty ja będę miał prawie tyle władzy iak Krol Angielski. Ja na to: 'Nie czyn WPan żartow, a to wyraznie powiedz czy przynaymniey Pacta Conventa będą mi dochowane?' Na to on, znowu generalnościami nieiasnemi odpowiedział.

(After many unclear expressions Potocki among other things also said this, that at the end of the work I will have almost as much power as the King of England. In reply I said 'Don't joke, Sir, and tell me clearly: will at least my rights in the *pacta conventa* be kept?' Again he replied in vague generalities.)[61]

When, in August 1790, Stanisław August via Piattoli sent his comments to Potocki upon the Seym deputation's 'Project for the form of government' (*Projekt do formy rządu*), he did not pick up the gauntlet on the key questions of royal power and the composition and competence of the highest executive body, the *Straż Praw* (Custodial Council of the Laws). Instead, he raised a host of minor questions which tended to improve the day-to-day functioning of the Seym, showing himself a man of 'great experience and knowledge of arcane political life in the Commonwealth, who sees the practical importance of apparent trivialities'.[62] Stanisław August greatly admired the procedure in the English Parliament. As he told Deboli,

I always say, that in the procedure of the Seym, it would be best simply to adopt the English method, as only that is equally free from unnecessary delay and verbosity, and from unnecessary haste.[63]

He made use of his extensive knowledge of English parliamentary practice to suggest a number of beneficial amendments. Again via Piattoli, Potocki sent his replies back to Stanisław August, so that the exchange of views has been preserved.[64]

The king objected to rigorous measures to enforce attendance at the Seym, and recommended a low quorum of forty, as in the House of Commons. If important matters were at stake, then the English example might again be followed, and summonses could be sent to those envoys present in the city, with fines for unjustified absence. Potocki thought that the matter might be so resolved during discussion in the Seym. The French National Assembly's practice of voting by standing up, proposed by the deputation, met with royal suspicion. Perhaps mindful of the agitation from the public galleries common to both the French and Polish

---

[61] SA to Deboli, 26 Dec. 1789, Zb. Pop. 414, ff. 606–7. Also quoted by Rostworowski, 'Marzenie dobrego obywatela', 292–3.

[62] Rostworowski, 'Marzenie dobrego obywatela', 332.

[63] SA to Deboli, 16 Mar. 1791, Zb. Pop. 413, f. 53.

[64] Oss. 9675/I, ff. 243–57. Rostworowski, 'Marzenie dobrego obywatela', 328–32.

assemblies, Stanisław August objected that the practice could lead to genuine or deliberate mistakes in counting votes. Much better, he wrote, was the English method of voting 'par Sécéssion'. Potocki, however, feared the English model, though he did not rule out other solutions. The English example may also be detected, although it is not explicit, in Stanisław August's proposal that members of the outgoing *Straż Praw* (who were to be changed every two years at ordinary Seyms) should take part in the deliberations of the Seym if they were ministers, senators, or envoys, so as to share the benefits of their experience. To this Potocki objected on the grounds that members of the executive should be excluded from the legislature until their conduct had been approved, fearing royal corruption of the senate. Ignacy Potocki was capable though of using the English model against Stanisław August. When the king complained that unlimited freedom of speech in the Seym meant licence to slander the innocent, Potocki riposted that personal insults might be dealt with by 'la police de la Chambre'. The example provided by the continual insults in the English Parliament might make things clearer, he added.

Stanisław August's detailed knowledge and understanding of the English constitution, and particularly of the parliamentary process, stand out against the general run of publicists and politicians. To win support, he had Franciszek Bukaty's second report on parliamentary procedure published as *Opisanie porządku seymowania w parlamencie angielskim* in 1790. Naturally, there were others who were well oriented in the English system of government, such as Ignacy Potocki—in his case without feeling much enthusiasm for it. Even Stanisław August's erudition might have to take a bow to that of Adam Kazimierz Czartoryski. In general, however, the 'English model' served as a pretext or even as a synonym for certain reforms, especially for the introduction of hereditary succession to the throne. No Polish statesman understood so acutely, not merely from theoretical knowledge, but from hard political experience, how individual details of the English constitution might be adapted to Poland's advantage, as King Stanisław August.

III

With the king and the 'patriot' leaders fully committed to co-operation in writing the new constitution, it is now appropriate to raise the question of the influence of the English constitution on the Constitution of 3 May. This is probably best answered by considering in turn each part of the Law on Government of 3 May 1791, and, where relevant, the associated detailed legislation, together with Stanisław August's wishes, and thence seeking to assess the extent of English influence. Two statements in particular are highly revealing of Stanisław August's wishes and intentions. In his first draft of the constitution, probably dictated to Piattoli on 20 December 1790,[65] regarding the form of projects, debates, and legislation in the Seym, he simply recommended 'la ressemblance la plus grande que possible entre le Parlement d'Angleterre et notre Diete'.[66] On 19 March, after Potocki had insisted upon further changes to the king's final version, Stanisław August wrote tiredly to Deboli: 'and so patching up now as best we can, though going round in circles, we will still get in the end to the English system of government.'[67] Stanisław August's intentions are not in doubt. As far as possible, he wanted to model the general shape of the Polish constitution upon the English.

The idea of a set of fundamental laws, grouped together in one document is the hallmark of a modern constitution. Contemporaries used the word *konstytucya* to describe the Law on Government, not only in the old Polish sense as any law passed by the Seym, but also in the modern sense of a single document.[68] The English understanding of the word as being that which 'constitutes' the system of government was also current, and with the American, Polish, and French, the English constitution was listed as one of *Cztery przednieysze konstytucye narodów wolnych* ('four foremost constitutions of free nations').[69] The fact of a single document, however, marks out the Polish constitution from the English, and shows the possible influence of the American.

The notion of a preamble[70] is, obviously, likewise alien to the English constitution and probably taken from American usage. Nevertheless, the first words clearly show the difference between the old world and the

[65]   Rostworowski, 'Marzenie dobrego obywatela', 401–2.

[66]   APP 98, f. 775. Quoted in Polish translation by Rostworowski, 'Marzenie dobrego obywatela', 429, and *Ostatni król*, 212.

[67]   'Azali łataiąc teraz iak można, choć okrążaiąc, trafiemy iednak na koniec do angielskiego rządu.' Zb. Pop. 413, f. 54. Also quoted by Rostworowski, 'Marzenie dobrego obywatela', 369.

[68]   Z. Szcząska, 'Ustawa Rządowa 3 Maja', *Niepodległość*, 3/4 (1991), 42; e.g., 'le plan de la nouvelle Constitution, proposé il y a plus d'un an', SA to Glayre, 9 May 1791, *Correspondance*, 247.

[69]   In the Piarists' almanac, *Kalendarzyk polityczny na rok przestępny* (1792).

[70]   I have made use of J. Kowecki's critical edition, *Konstytucja 3 Maja* (Warsaw, 1981). All quotations are from *Konstytucja 3 Maja 1791: Faksymile rękopisu z Archiwum Głównego Akt Dawnych w Warszawie* (Wrocław, 1991), in order to retain the original spelling. Both include the Law on Royal Towns. I have consulted F. Bukaty's translation, *New Constitution of the Government of Poland* (London, 1791), repr. in the *Annual Register* (1791) and elsewhere, but owing to its imperfections and omissions I have in many places made my own translation.

new. 'In the name of the one God in the Holy Trinity, Stanisław August, King of Poland, Grand Duke of Lithuania, Ruthenia, Prussia, Mazovia . . . together with the confederated estates representing the Polish nation'[71] contrasts vividly with 'We the people'. The declared aims were, however, similar—the general good and the salvation of the country.[72] In Article I, concerning religion, it is difficult to find any English influence, beyond the general role of the Enlightenment in reaffirming the Commonwealth's traditions of toleration. We have seen that Stanisław August was critical of English treatment of Catholics and dissenters.[73] The king wished to safeguard the Roman and Greek Catholic faiths by insisting that the children of mixed marriages be brought up as Catholics, while the Law on Government followed the deputation project and threatened punishment for apostasy in an equally unenlightened manner.[74] Articles II, III, and IV, regarding social relations, merely serve to underline the huge gulf between England and Poland. The same is true of the ultimately unsuccessful attempts to reform Polish Jewry.[75]

Article III stated simply that the Law on Royal Towns, passed on 18 April 1791, was part of the constitution. According to that law, all public offices, commissions in the army, except for the 'national cavalry', and clerical situations bar bishoprics were opened to townsmen. The law of 1775 enabling the *szlachta* legally to engage in trade without the loss of noble status was confirmed. The opening of municipal office to nobles, the ability of townsmen to purchase landed estates, and the opening of wide possibilities of ennoblement through landowning or public service, might in the long run have contributed to the blurring of the border between the landowning classes and the higher strata of merchants and manufacturers, as in England. Kołłątaj's ultimate aim was a nation based on property rather than birth. Behind his rhetoric was a phenomenon

[71] 'W imię Boga w Troycy Świętey jedynego, Stanisław August z Bożey Łaski y Woli Narodu Król Polski, Wielki Xiążę Litewski, Ruski, Pruski, Mazowiecki . . . , wraz z Stanami Skonfederowanemi . . . Naród Polski reprezentuiącemi.'
[72] I. Rusinowa, 'Wpływ konstytucji Stanów Zjednoczonych Ameryki Północnej na Konstytucję 3 Maja', *Niepodległość*, 3/4 (1991), 112.
[73] See above, p. 273.
[74] SA to Bukaty, 20 Apr. 1791, BCzart. 849, f. 388. Rostworowski, 'Marzenie dobrego obywatela', 412–13.
[75] Vol. 6 of *Materiały do dziejów Sejmu Czteroletniego*, ed. J. Woliński, J. Michalski, E. Rostworowski, and A. Eisenbach (Wrocław, 1969), devoted to the Jewish question, contains only one comparison. Envoy Butrymowicz told the Seym in 1789 that in England, Holland, and other countries, Jews differed from other citizens only in their religion (p. 81). See Eisenbach, *The Emancipation of the Jews in Poland 1780–1870* (Oxford, 1991), 1–112.

of the upper and middling *szlachta* absorbing the richest and most able townsmen into its ranks, while arrogating to itself the best opportunities for enterprise and office in royal towns. The limited powers of the 'plenipotentiaries' (as opposed to envoys) who were to represent the towns at the Seym indicate that the *szlachta* was to remain firmly in charge. Nevertheless, the inevitable price of improved career opportunities was the hallowed idea of the exclusively noble nation. Stanisław August's thoughts were rather traditional, and affected by political considerations. He wished to grant the estate of townsmen extensive rights, and to include noble- and church-owned towns within the scope of the law, but had no wish to see the gradual fusing of the townsmen with the *szlachta* through mass ennoblement; as a separate estate the townsmen would tend to side with the king against the *szlachta*.[76]

The Law on Royal Towns conferred the *szlachta* privilege of *neminem captivabimus nisi iure victum*, equivalent to the English habeas corpus, on townsmen able to provide bail, with the exception of bankrupts. A later administrative decision extended it to Jews. Article II of the Law on Government confirmed all the *szlachta*'s privileges, including 'personal security and personal freedom'.[77] Recent studies of protection against arbitrary arrest have revealed certain tendencies to limit the extent of *neminem captivabimus* in exceptional cases,[78] but no one in Poland would have dared propose the English practice of a general suspension in times of national emergency.

Moving on to the general form of government, Article V declared that 'all power in human society should derive from the will of the nation,'[79] a clear sign of the common ground between Rousseau's *Contrat social* and noble republicanism. The interpretation of the word 'nation' was kept deliberately vague. The declaration was added by Kołłątaj to Stanisław

---

[76] K. Zienkowska, *Sławetni i urodzeni: Ruch polityczny mieszczaństwa w dobie Sejmu Czteroletniego* (Warsaw, 1976), *passim*. Pasztor, *Kołłątaj*, 71–85, 109–10, 156–7. Rostworowski, 'Marzenie dobrego obywatela', 414–19. James Durno expressed the hope in his 'Letter' (ch. 6, n. 78) that 'the time is not far distant when the *mercantile* and *monied* interests will be here allowed, as in England, through the medium of the principal Towns and Cities, that *direct* and individual representation.' Durno to Grenville, 11 May 1791, PRO FO 62/4, f. 137.

[77] 'Bespieczeństwa Osobistego, y wolności Osobistey'.

[78] M. Mikołajczyk, 'Z badań nad zagadnienieniem nietykalności osobistej w okresie Sejmu Czteroletniego', in A. Lityński (ed.), *W dwusetną rocznicę wolnego Sejmu. Ludzie—państwo—prawo czasów Sejmu Czteroletniego* (Katowice, 1988). Lityński, 'Tradycje i nowości w ustawodawstwie karnym Sejmu Czteroletniego (ze szczególnym uwzględnieniem Kodeksu Stanisława Augusta)', in *Konstytucja 3 Maja: Prawo—Polityka—Symbol*, 40–4.

[79] 'Wszelka władza w społeczności ludzkiey początek swoy bierze z woli narodu.'

August's project. Then Montesquieu received his homage. Three powers, the legislative, executive, and judicial, 'in balance for always', were necessary to safeguard the integrity of the state, the liberty of citizens, and social order.[80] In his final Polish version, Stanisław August added the clause 'three powers should constitute the government of the Polish nation,'[81] in order to guard against the domination of the executive by a 'ruling Seym'.[82]

Article VI encompassed the Seym or the legislative power. Stanisław August gave up his own status as a separate estate of the Seym, but fought hard for the senate, over which he was to preside. He wished to make the rights of the chamber of envoys and the senate as equal as possible. The agreement of both houses, voting separately by simple or qualified majority, should be necessary to pass legislation. In the Law on Government, the senate received only a suspensive veto until the next ordinary Seym. Stanisław August was not merely concerned with his own influence over the Seym; he attached particular weight to the mutual *correction* of projects, which would reduce the necessity for the use of the veto,[83] and greatly regretted the omission of this provision in the Law on Government. He told Glayre that 'si au *veto* suspensif du Sénat on avait ajouté une forme de discussion réciproque entre les deux Chambres, nous nous serions rapproché davantage de la Constitution anglaise.'[84] Stanisław August always valued the role of the House of Lords, and saw in the upper house of a parliament a place of calmer, maturer deliberation. He wrote to Mazzei that the 'défaut radical' of the French was 'd'avoir fait une seule Chambre de l'Assemblée Nationale, et d'avoir anéanti absolument les prérogatives de la noblesse,' and reminded his agent of 'l'utilité d'une Chambre Haute'.[85] Another reverse suffered by Stanisław August was the joint voting on all matters except general laws. The senate was only half the size of the chamber of envoys. In England, peers could accept or reject, but not amend money bills, while in Poland permanent taxes were removed altogether from the scope of the suspensive veto of the senate by the two laws concerning the Seym passed on 12

---

[80] 'W rowney wadze na zawsze'.

[81] 'Trzy władze Rząd Narodu polskiego składać powinny'.

[82] Rostworowski, 'Marzenie dobrego obywatela', 419. Pasztor, *Kołłątaj*, 158.

[83] In a speech to the Seym on 5 Oct. 1790, Stanisław August argued openly for a power of correction. SA to Deboli, 6 Oct. 1790, Zb. Pop. 420, f. 1019.

[84] SA to Glayre, 25 June 1791, Stanisław August, M. Glayre, *Correspondance*, 263. Stanisław August wrote in the same tone to Mazzei, 1 June 1791, Oss. 9751/I, f. 65. Rostworowski, 'Marzenie dobrego obywatela', 429–31. Pasztor, *Kołłątaj*, 159.

[85] SA to Mazzei, 16 June 1790, 25 Aug. 1790, quoted after Fabre, *Stanislas-Auguste Poniatowski*, 511.

and 16 May.[86] Thus the House of Lords was much more powerful. James Durno thought the senate so emasculated that he preferred to compare it with the Privy Council.[87]

The Seym was ordinarily to meet every two years for ten weeks (an increase of four). If the king failed to convene the Seym, the marshal of the last Seym was empowered to do so. It could be reconvened in its current complement up to the end of the two-year term. Thus the idea of the permanent Seym, associated by the leading reformers with England, bowed to that of the reconvenable Seym. It was expressly provided for that the Seym could be reconvened against the will of the king,[88] which was not the case in England. However, long annual sessions in England had been put beyond any doubt by the wars and massive debt-financed expenditure of 1739–63. At the same time, the amount of local and commercial parliamentary legislation increased to such a degree that Parliament became the natural forum of the nation's business. Dispensing with Parliament was now unthinkable. A friendly Parliament could be kept for seven years. The king remained free, however, to dissolve a Parliament and call a new one before then, if he wished.[89] Thus the King of England possessed the weapon of an appeal to the electorate at any moment, should the Commons be against him. The Polish legislators, in contrast, envisaged a reversion to biennial Seyms with fixed dates of elections; extraordinary Seyms (in the same complement) were reserved for emergencies. It is possible, however, that with the growth of business over time, a similar practice to the English might have evolved.

Article VI abolished those old bugbears, the *liberum veto* and confederacies. Nevertheless, the Laws on Seyms laid down that decisions were to be taken by simple majority vote only in matters of civil legislation. Criminal and political laws, together with declarations of war, the contracting of debts, and the making of alliances required the agreement of two-thirds, and new taxes . . . of three-quarters.[90] 'Old habits died hard.' Despite Konarski's labours, the English model of simple majority voting remained out of reach.[91]

Stanisław August lost his struggle, first to include the senate in the legislative initiative, and then to equal the King of England's virtual

[86] Michalski, *Historia sejmu polskiego*, vol. 1, 409.
[87] 'Letter', loc. cit. (n. 76), ff. 136–7.
[88] Michalski, *Historia sejmu polskiego*, vol. 1, 410.
[89] Langford, *Polite and Commercial People*, 704.
[90] Michalski, *Historia sejmu polskiego*, vol. 1, 410.
[91] Lukowski, *Liberty's Folly*, 251. Idem, 'Od Konarskiego do Kołłątaja', 188.

monopoly of it, but he did secure priority for royal proposals in deliberation.[92] The king enjoyed a near-complete success, however, concerning
the *seymiki*. The Law on *Seymiki* of 24 March, reaffirmed by the Law
on Government, excluded *impossessionati* from participation, striking a
blow at the power of the magnates. The king also wished to insist upon
literacy. 'Dangereux et choquant,' commented Ignacy Potocki. Stanisław
August ensured that elections took place *before* the drawing up of instructions. The effects of the opposite procedure in November 1790 had been
that candidates had agreed to anything in order to get themselves elected.
The vital issue for Stanisław August, however, was that the instructions
should not be binding on the envoys. Although in the Law on *Seymiki*,
the mandatory nature of instructions remained, in the Law on Government instructions were not mentioned at all. The envoys were declared
to be 'representatives of the entire nation,'[93] endowed with a plenitude
of legislative power, a clear allusion to English theory and practice.[94]

Article VII, on the executive power, was the most doggedly contested
battlefield of all. Stanisław August's proposed title of the article, 'The
king, that is, the executive power', was even watered down by Kołłątaj
to 'The king, the executive power'.[95] Stanisław August was responsible
for the first three sentences, explaining to the *szlachta* the need for a strong
executive:

Żaden Rząd naydoskonalszy bez dzielney Władzy Wykonawczey stać niemoże.
Szczęśliwość Narodów od Praw sprawiedliwych, Praw skutek od Ich wykonania
zależy. Doświadczenie nauczyło, że zaniedbanie tey części Rządu, nieszczęściami
napełniło Polskę.

(The most perfect system of government cannot be upheld without an effective
executive power. The happiness of nations depends upon just laws, but the good
effects of laws depend upon their execution. Experience has taught us that the
neglect of this part of government has overwhelmed Poland with disasters.)[96]

---

[92] Rostworowski, 'Marzenie dobrego obywatela', 426–9.

[93] *'Reprezentanci Całego Narodu'*.

[94] F. S. Jezierski explicitly distinguished between the Polish *poseł*, bound by instructions,
and the English *reprezentant*, unbound by them. *Niektóre wyrazy porządkiem abecedła
zebrane* (1791) in Jezierski, *Wybór pism*, eds. Z. Skwarczyński and J. Ziomek (Warsaw, 1952),
244–5. Rostworowski, 'Marzenie dobrego obywatela', 425–6; Lityński, 'Status posła po
Konstytucji 3 Maja' in H. Kocój (ed.), *Pierwsza w Europie: 200 rocznica Konstytucji 3 Maja
1791–1991* (Katowice, 1989); K. Baran and A. Partyka, 'Rozwój angielskiego systemu rządów
parlamentarnych a Konstytucja 3 Maja w Polsce', *ZNUJ*, 625 (1982), 107, 112, 124.
Bukaty's translation, *New Constitution*, 18, completely omitted this important declaration.

[95] 'Król czyli Władza Wykonawcza' became 'Król, Władza Wykonawcza'.

[96] Rostworowski, 'Marzenie dobrego obywatela', 431–2. Pasztor, *Kołłątaj*, 160–1.

The introduction of hereditary succession to the throne was the riskiest part of the constitution, in view of its rejection by the November *seymiki*. To assuage *szlachta* prejudices it was disguised as 'elective in regard to families',[97] and extensively justified by reference to the subversion of government and foreign intervention during interregna, by the memory of Poland's greatness and happiness under 'families reigning continuously,'[98] and the necessity of diverting the ambitions of foreigners and powerful Poles from the throne. The actual order of succession was the outcome of a purely political compromise between Ignacy Potocki and Stanisław August. The Elector of Saxony was named successor, and his 9-year-old daughter—'*infantka*'. As it was clear, despite the provisions for a male heir, that the elector would have no more children, there was to be no lasting reunion of Poland and Saxony (which besides an alliance, might have counted for something in a dynastic Europe). Stanisław August hoped that his nephew, Prince Stanisław Poniatowski, might win the hand of the *infantka*, while Ignacy Potocki was still hoping for a Hohenzollern. As the Seym was to approve the elector's choice of husband for his daughter, another election was, *de facto*, foreordained.[99] So much for the rhetoric about interregna? No part of the Constitution of 3 May has drawn so much criticism,[100] yet had Stanisław August's dreams come to pass and had Stanisław III ascended the throne, Poland would have enjoyed the rule of an enlightened yet ruthlessly clear-headed monarch, the protoplast of a native Polish dynasty.[101]

The formula 'elective in regard to families' bears a certain analogy to the English Act of Settlement of 1701, in which the already wounded principle of *indefeasible* divine hereditary right received a mortal blow. Parliament designated the mother of the Elector of Hanover heir presumptive to the throne of England, overriding the claims of numerous Catholics and even some Protestants, who by blood were nearer the succession. This time no convenient fiction, such as talk of James II's 'abdication', was available to camouflage the irreparable breach. Thus the Kings of England, succeeding hereditarily by right of Parliament, were set apart from the absolutist monarchs of much of the Continent. The

---

[97] 'Elekcyinym przez familie'.   [98] 'Familij ciągle panuiących'.

[99] Libiszowska, 'Międzynarodowe powikłania sukcesji saskiej', in *Konstytucja 3 Maja: Prawo—Polityka—Symbol*. Rostworowski, 'Marzenie dobrego obywatela', 432–5.

[100] Notably Korzon, *Zamknięcie dziejów wewnętrznych za Stanisława Augusta* [1899], repr. in idem, *Odrodzenie w upadku: Wybór pism historycznych*, eds. A. F. Grabski and M. H. Serejski (Warsaw, 1975), 330, and Kalinka, *Sejm Czteroletni*, vol. 2, 527–9.

[101] See J. Łojek's thought-provoking speculation in *Pamiętniki synowca Stanisława Augusta*, 7.

Kings of Poland were henceforth to be in the same category, and Stanisław August's old aim was to be achieved. Nevertheless, it should be stressed that in England, justifications abounded of George III's hereditary right to rule by the *divine right of Providence*. On this, English and Polish political culture still differed significantly.[102] The symbolic authority of the monarch was stressed, as it was in England. All public acts and judgments were to be made in the king's name, and all seals and coins were to bear his head or arms. Soldiers, officials, and diplomats swore their oath of loyalty to him as well as to the Commonwealth and the constitution. After 3 May, laudations of Stanisław August and votes of thanks flooded in from the provinces.[103] The road was opened, although it was not an aim, for transforming the Polish monarchy into the symbolic, ceremonial embodiment of national unity; a process initiated by George III in Britain and consummated in the house of Windsor.[104]

Supreme executive power was vested in the king in the *Straż Praw*. All other bodies were to obey its directives. Stanisław August envisaged a 'Conseil du Cabinet' or 'Conseil privé', composed of the king as president, one of the marshals as head of police, the chairman of the military commission, one of the chancellors as head of justice, one of the treasurers as head of finances, the minister of foreign affairs, and the primate as head of the Church and chairman of the Commission for National Education. Each was to preside in his own department, and each was to have a deputy. The king proposed no alternation, but a free choice between the Lithuanian and Crown ministers, and in the case of the Crown chancellors, between the layman and the cleric. Stanisław August also proposed scrapping the Crown–grand duchy duality in ministers, thereby removing half of them, but on this he was overruled. It would seem as though Stanisław August was edging towards removing the life terms of the old-style dignitaries—hetmans, marshals, chancellors, and treasurers—confusingly also called ministers. No doubt he would have preferred the free choice of person enjoyed by the King of England, but accepting the old-style ministers as the ministerial pool was better than letting the Seym elect counsellors into the *Straż*, as Potocki wished. The new-style ministers were to serve in the *Straż* for two years, extendable by the king for further terms of two years indefinitely. Decisions were to be taken by

[102] Clark, *English Society*, 173–89.
[103] Durno, 'Letter', f. 136. Szczygielski, 'Konstytucja 3 Maja', 18. The point is made rather too strongly by Zienkowska, Sukcesja tronu . . . symbol suwerenności?'. See above, n. 30.
[104] Colley, *Britons*, ch. 5.

majority vote. Various arrangements of two votes for the king, or a casting vote were considered.[105]

The end result, in the Law on Government and the Law on the *Straż Praw*, was, from the point of view of effective government, an unsatisfactory compromise. The king was to choose the members from the old-style ministers, without deputies. Ignacy Potocki objected to a ministry of justice as contrary to the principle of the separation of powers. Nevertheless, Crown Grand Chancellor Jacek Małachowski sat in the *Straż* with the portfolio of the 'seal' (*pieczęć*). The marshal of the Seym was added to the *Straż* as a republican sentinel. Unlike the Permanent Council, the *Straż* could not interpret the law. Ministers were not allowed to preside over their relevant commissions. Worse, those hetmans, marshals, and treasurers not chosen for the *Straż*, that is, the discontented ones, were to preside in rotation over the military, police, and treasury commissions, of which the Seym was to elect the membership. The *Straż* was not to be a flexible and informal English-style inner cabinet of directing ministers (*pace* Durno),[106] but a legislatively defined body which was always likely to be in conflict with the theoretically subordinate commissions. Jerzy Lukowski has stressed that for Ignacy Potocki and his allies, this was the very point. The idea of a 'guardian of the laws' (the literal translation of *Straż Praw*) was common to virtually all their proposals since the start of the Seym. Power was to check power, as Montesquieu had recommended. What is more, the Laws on Seyms enabled the Seym directly to instruct both the *Straż* and the commissions, and to annul their resolutions. Luckily, the ministry of foreign affairs (under Chreptowicz) was made independent of the Seym, and the primate's direction of education was strengthened.[107] In practice, the *Straż* functioned reasonably smoothly, but it was never tested by a hostile Seym.[108]

A last-minute change of mind on the part of the 'patriots' led to the full and consequential expression of a principle that was implicit in the earlier projects of the constitution, that of the responsibility of ministers to the Seym. As the 'patriot' leaders trusted the king more than the likely members of the *Straż*, majority voting was replaced by the enactment that after all opinions had been expressed, the will of the king was to

[105] Rostworowski, 'Marzenie dobrego obywatela', 438–45.
[106] Durno, 'Letter', f. 138.
[107] Rostworowski, 'Marzenie dobrego obywatela', 444–7. Michalski, *Historia sejmu polskiego*, vol. 1, 409–10. Pasztor, *Kołłątaj*, 160–1. Szcząska, 'Ustawa Rządowa', 45. Szczygielski, 'Konstytucja 3 Maja', 17–18. Lukowski, 'Recasting Utopia', 75–7. *Esprit des Lois*, Book V, ch. 7.
[108] See J. Wojakowski, *Straż Praw* (Warsaw, 1982).

'prevail' (*przeważać*), with the proviso that one of the ministers should countersign the resolution. The person of the king was after the English fashion declared inviolable; the king was held 'not to act by himself in anything,' and could not 'be responsible to the nation for anything'.[109] This was based upon the medieval principle that the 'king can do no wrong'. The recurrent consequence had been action against 'evil counsellors'. For his counter-signature, the minister was answerable to the Seym. If he broke the law, then a majority of both houses joined together could commit him to be tried by the Seym Court. This was similar to the English process of impeachment, also adopted by the Americans. The example of Warren Hastings was still fresh in the minds of the Poles. An English minister could not even plead an express royal order; Danby's impeachment in 1679 had settled the matter.[110]

The Law on Government also introduced, again on the English model, the principle of the *political* responsibility of ministers to the Seym. If two-thirds of the secret votes of both houses joined together so decreed, the king was bound to replace any minister in the *Straż* with another. This was a drastic and inflexible method enshrined in legislation. In England, if taxes were to be voted, the general business of the country to be carried on, and ultimately, the Mutiny Act to be passed, the king's ministers as a whole had to be able to command the acceptance of the House of Commons. Failure to keep a majority generally meant resignation.[111] It should be stressed, though, that more ministers fell as a result of the loss of royal favour than as a result of losing votes in the House of Commons. Parliament could not *compel* the king to dismiss his ministers. There was scope for flexibility, as George III's dismissal of Fox and North and maintenance of Pitt in office in the face of a hostile—but shrinking—parliamentary majority demonstrated in 1783–4.[112] The notion among independent backbenchers, as well as among the electorate at large, that they should support the king's ministers unless there was an overwhelming reason *not* to do so was deeply ingrained.[113] That was not the case in Poland. Despite the requirement of a two-thirds majority,

---

[109] 'Nic sam przez Się nieczyniący, za nic w odpowiedzi Narodowi bydź niemoże.'

[110] Durno, 'Letter', f. 136, made the analogy very strongly. Baran and Partyka, 'Rozwój angielskiego systemu . . .', 114–15, 122. Szcząska, 'Odpowiedzialność prawna ministrów w państwach konstytucyjnych XVIII–XIX w.', in *Wiek XVIII: Polska i świat*, 340–3, 354. Idem, 'Ustawa Rządowa', 34, 45.

[111] Baran and Partyka, 'Rozwój angielskiego systemu . . .', 115–16, 122–3.

[112] Kołłątaj praised George III's actions as necessary in an emergency and justified by public support. *Uwagi nad pismem . . . Rzewuskiego*, 110.

[113] Dickinson, *Liberty and Property*, 178–9.

therefore, the principle of political responsibility was a good deal more threatening to royal ministers in Poland than in England.

Stanisław August fought hard for the royal prerogative, especially that of nomination. Like the King of England, he retained the right to nominate bishops and lay senators, but in the latter case only for life. The Laws on Seyms laid down that his successors were to choose from two candidates presented by the appropriate *seymik* (so that, for example, the Wilno *seymik* would present candidates for the Palatine and Castellan of Wilno). Whether the Elector of Saxony would have agreed to such a condition is another matter. The Law on Government laid down that the *pacta conventa* to be negotiated with the elector would cover royal prerogatives. Stanisław August, trying to defend the prerogative from erosion, had wanted the Constitution to be modified only with each new reign, but the concept of the 'patriots' prevailed, and a special constitutional Seym was to revise the Law on Government every twenty-five years.[114] In the event, less than a month after 3 May, the king had already lost a part of his prerogative. The Law on Government had laid down that the king, 'to whom ought to be left every power of doing good, shall have the right of pardoning those condemned to death, except for crimes against the state'.[115] This was soon to be severely limited to the right to commute the death sentence to life imprisonment, and only then if the order was counter-signed by a member of the *Straż*. Moreover, those sentenced by the Seym Court or a court martial, as well as murderers and thieves of public funds, were excluded from all clemency.[116] The King of England's prerogative of pardon was, in contrast, very wide. Only those sentenced by impeachment could not be rescued, although, from 1689, the king could not suspend the law or dispense individuals from it, as James II had done.[117]

Article VIII reformed the judicial power. The retention of the Seym Court as the forum of political trials was broadly analogous to (but not taken from) the role played by the House of Lords, except that in Poland, members of the lower house were among the judges chosen by lot. The rest of the system showed little obvious English influence. Judges of the *szlachta* courts of the first instance were henceforth to be elected at *seymiki*,

[114] Rostworowski, 'Marzenie dobrego obywatela', 436–7, 455–60. SA to Deboli, 14 May 1791, Zb. Pop. 413, ff. 92–3.

[115] 'Któremu wszelka moc dobrze czynienia zostawiona być powinna, mieć będzie *Ius agratiandi* na śmierć wskazanych, prócz *in Criminibus Status*.'

[116] Rostworowski, 'Marzenie dobrego obywatela', 437–8. SA to Deboli, 14 May 1791, 1 June 1791, Zb. Pop. 413, ff. 92–3, 112. SA to Mazzei, 15 June 1791, Oss. 9751/I, f. 66.

[117] Declaration of Rights, clauses 1 and 2, in Holmes, *Making of a Great Power*, 426.

and the king's proposal that they should be confirmed by himself was overruled by the 'patriots'. Royally appointed 'Justices of the Peace' (*Sędziowie Pokoju*), proposed by Stanisław August, were also rejected. Town courts of appeal were to include an eleven-man jury, which was probably taken from the English model. The promise of a civil and criminal code was a typical expression of the Enlightenment, and a negation of the English example. Work soon started on the 'Code of Stanisław August', and among its principles was equality before the law—although any English influence requires separate investigation.[118]

Article IX, concerning regency, laid down a clear procedure, in contrast to the chaos and controversy which surrounded the issue in England in 1788–9, during George III's illness, of which Stanisław August had been well informed.[119] Article X, on the education of royal children, introduced the interference of the Seym into their upbringing, which would have been unthinkable in England.

Article XI contained flighty rhetoric about the obligation of all citizens to defend the country and its freedoms (the thin end of the wedge against noble exclusiveness), the respect due to the army from the nation, and the duty of the army to protect the frontiers and public order (as was also the case in England). Stanisław August's renewed attempt to create a militia for internal policing was rejected.[120] Article VII had left to the king the right to commission and promote officers, and appoint them to their regiments, and to nominate the commanders in time of war—although the Seym could overrule him on the last point. The overall command of the army was granted to the king in wartime only. It peacetime the Seym-elected military commission, nominally under the *Straż*, had to be reckoned with.

The King of England enjoyed greater power over the military. Apart from overall command and a monopoly over appointments, still guarded from ministers by George III, the King of England could formally make war and peace of his own accord, being limited of course by the need

[118] Szcząska, 'Ustawa Rządowa', 45–6. Szczygielski, 'Konstytucja 3 Maja', 20–1. Pasztor, *Kołłątaj*, 160–2. Lityński, 'Tradycje i nowości' (n. 78). Idem, 'Z zagadnień reformu prawa karnego', 192–3.

[119] Not just by Tadeusz Bukaty, but also by Mazzei. Mazzei to SA, 22 Dec. 1788–29 May 1789, SA to Mazzei, 25 Feb. 1789, *Lettres de Philippe Mazzei et du roi Stanislas-Auguste*, vol. 1, 123–272, *passim*, esp. 185. The king thought that Fox would adopt a less anti-Russian policy than Pitt. SA to Deboli, 29 Nov. 1788, 31 Dec. 1788, Zb. Pop. 417, ff. 653, 687.

[120] L. Ratajczyk, 'Sprawa wojska i obronności w Konstytucji 3 Maja', in *Konstytucja 3 Maja: Prawo—Polityka—Symbol*. Rostworowski, 'Marzenie dobrego obywatela', 450–1. Stanisław August continued, without success, to press for a militia. SA to Deboli, 24 Aug. 1791, 12 Nov. 1791, Zb. Pop. 413, ff. 175, 235a. Also see Pasztor, *Kołłątaj*, 82–4.

for funds. The prohibition by the 1689 Bill of Rights of raising and keeping a standing army in time of peace without the assent of Parliament was no obstacle in practice to an average *peacetime* establishment after the Seven Years' War of 45,000, small by Continental standards, but easily multiplied in wartime and as large as the 45,000 that Poland could put into the field in 1792. For defence, there was in any case the fleet. The royal prerogative was kept from unwanted ministerial interference by the absence of anything resembling a ministry of defence. Control over the army was split between a bewildering array of different ministers and boards, although the admiralty was somewhat more logically ordered. It should be noted, however, that (as in Poland) the prevalence of jobbery in the army, especially the right to purchase commissions, in practice limited the patronage powers of the king. Under George III, old fears of a standing army in royal hands had virtually vanished.[121]

We have seen how, regarding the problem of the American colonists, Stanisław August, like contemporary British thinkers, had difficulty even in conceiving how a federative state could properly function. Likewise, from the start of his reign, he aimed at turning the Commonwealth of the Two Nations into a single state. In one of his constitutional projects, filled out by Piattoli from the initial outline dictated by the king, the two nations 'ne seront désormais qu'une seule et même nation', and all duplications between the Crown and Lithuania in offices and administrative bodies were to go. This met with the opposition of Ignacy Potocki, the Grand Marshal of Lithuania, who had a vested interest. The subject was not mentioned in the Law on Government, and some passages hint at a unitary state, prompting some historians to sing a requiem mass over the Polish-Lithuanian union. In fact, whatever the integrationist wishes of Stanisław August, avoidance of the subject was essential to buy the support of the Lithuanian Marshal of the confederated Seym, Kazimierz Nestor Sapieha, a hothead who opposed the hereditary throne and distrusted executive power in general. During the debate on 3 May, Sapieha was won over, his marshal's signature was attached to the document, and the bill remained to be paid. Paid it was. The Laws on Seyms reserved every third Seym to Grodno, Sapieha entered the *Straż Praw*, two separate

[121] Brewer, *Sinews of Power*, 29–34, 42–5, 60. Langford, *Polite and Commercial People*, 208, 687–9. Brooke, *George III*, 31–3, 180–3. Taswell-Langmead, *English Constitutional History from the Teutonic Conquest to the Present Time* (11th edn., London, 1960), 450–1, 461, 596, 673–4. D. L. Keir, *The Constitutional History of Modern Britain 1485–1951* (5th edn., London, 1951), 274, 303, 304–7. Stanisław August wished to end the purchase of commissions but lacked the funds. SA to Deboli, 1 June 1791, Zb. Pop. 413, f. 111.

codification commissions were established (the Lithuanians were very proud of the 1588 Third Lithuanian Statute), the police commission was named that of the Two Nations, and a third of its members were to be Lithuanians, while half the members of the treasury and military commissions were to come from the grand duchy. Lithuanian and Crown treasurers and hetmans would head them alternately. On 20 October 1791, these concessions were enshrined into a solemn law called the 'Mutual Assurance of the Two Nations' (*Zaręczenie wzajemne obojga narodów*), which was to form part of the future *pacta conventa*. Among the other provisions were reaffirmation of duality among the old-style ministers, and a separate Lithuanian treasury and treasury court. Stanisław August naïvely stressed to Deboli that the new law, passed unanimously, solemnly reiterated the Law on Government and therefore those envoys who still opposed the Constitution of 3 May would be contradicting themselves. Another factor was the attitude of the Lithuanian *szlachta* in the approaching international crisis. It is impossible to state whether separate Lithuanian identity was actually fostered, but it was certainly not weakened by the strengthened bond between the two nations.[122] The Anglo-Scottish Union was always more unequal. Scotland could never have driven as hard a bargain, and its government was effectively grafted onto England's. Like the Lithuanians, however, Scotland's political élite after the Act of Union did not hanker after a separate Parliament, but the separate law and national identity of Scotland was preserved, and many Scots set the English an example in Enlightenment and industry.[123]

IV

The news of the Constitution of 3 May was enthusiastically received in England. Edward Tatham, the Rector of Lincoln College, Oxford, was among those who pointed out that the Poles had taken the English constitution for their model. James Durno, in his enthusiasm to prove that the Poles had done so in almost every particular, exaggerated the monarchical content of the Law on Government. Above all, Edmund Burke set the Polish revolution against the French in a long passage in his *Appeal*

---

[122] See Michalski, 'Zagadnienie unii polsko-litewskiej w czasach panowania Stanisława Augusta', *Zapiski Historyczne*, 51 (1986), 112–25; J. Bardach, 'The Constitution of May Third and the mutual assurance of the Two Nations', *Polish Review*, 36 (1991); and Rostworowski, 'Marzenie dobrego obywatela', 451–3. SA to Deboli, 22 Oct. 1791, Zb. Pop. 413, f. 215.

[123] A huge subject. Frost, *After the Deluge*, 7. See Holmes and Szechi, *Age of Oligarchy*, ch. 15; Pocock, 'Clergy and Commerce', and the literature cited therein; and in general, T. C. Smout, *A History of the Scottish People 1560–1830* (1969, repr. London, 1985).

from the New to the Old Whigs in August 1791. He stressed that 'this great good, as in the instant it is, contains in it the seeds of all further improvement; and may be considered as in a regular progress, because founded on similar principles towards the stable excellency of a British constitution.' Nothing could have been closer to Stanisław August's heart. The comparison was translated into Polish by Julian Niemcewicz and published in two Warsaw newspapers on 3 September.[124] The resonance of Burke's praises reached distant Owrucz in the Ukraine, where a dinner was held in his honour.[125] Replying to Tadeusz Czacki's criticism of the constitution, Ignacy Potocki quoted Burke's opinion that the constitution was 'probably the most pure and defecated [i.e. purified] public good which has ever been conferred on mankind,' and reminded his readers of Burke's defence of the Americans. He went on to deny the stark contrast between a republic and a monarchy. It was as if Czacki did not know

that in the forms of government there is a middle way between a monarchy and a republic, that a republic moderated by monarchy is consistent with liberty, that the English constitution is the incontrovertible proof of it, and that the present Polish constitution approaches the English.

Potocki then quoted Burke's passage on the 'similar principles' as evidence. He had come a long way since 1789.[126]

Was Potocki's abandonment of the quest for the republican Holy Grail part of a more general shift in political culture? The Law on Government ushered in a year of harmony and unity unparalleled in the Commonwealth's history. Stanisław August was lauded as never before. His slogan of 'the king with the nation, the nation with the king' (*król z narodem, naród z królem*), which summed up his old aims of mutual trust and dependency, scored a general triumph. At virtually all the *seymiki* in February 1792, the *szlachta* voted thanks for the Constitution, and at a comfortable majority of them (73 per cent), pledged or swore to defend it. The new procedures for the *seymiki* were followed, despite their inconvenience. The new order clearly enjoyed the support of the nation. The Seym worked at unprecedented speed, a result not only of the new mood,

---

[124] See above, Ch. 6, n. 89. Libiszowska, 'Polska reforma w opinii angielskiej', in *Sejm Czteroletni i jego tradycje*, 68–71. Eadem, 'Odgłosy Konstytucji 3 Maja na Zachodzie', in *Konstytucja 3 Maja w tradycji i kulturze polskiej*, 76–9. Eadem, 'Edmund Burke a Polska', 69–70.

[125] Szczygielski, *Referendum trzeciomajowe: Sejmiki lutowe 1792 roku* (Łódź, 1994), 261.

[126] *Na pismo, któremu napis O Konstytucji 3 Maja do JWW Zaleskiego . . . i Matuszewica . . . odpowiedź* [1791], repr. in *Za czy przeciw Ustawie Rządowej: Walka publicystyczna o Konstytucję 3 Maja: Antologia*, ed. A. Grześkowiak-Krwawicz (Warsaw, 1992), 110–15.

but also of an important procedural reform, influenced by English practice. The discussion of every clause of a bill was abolished in favour of
drafting in committee, with the Seym voting to accept, reject, or send
back the bill for amendment.[127] Did all this amount to a significant shift
in Polish political culture in an 'English' direction? Towards greater trust
in the monarch, greater support for a strong monarchy at the head of an
efficient executive, and a readiness to pay heavier taxes and admit the
'monied' and mercantile interests (in the Polish context, townsmen) into
political partnership with the landed *szlachta*? The question is beset by
the problems of measuring 'political culture', which is only a historian's
term of convenience.

The polemics for and against the Constitution after it was passed were
written to influence rather than to reflect the opinion of the *szlachta*.
Nevertheless, the issues on which debate centred offer some valuable clues.
Apart from the hysterical outbursts of Jan Suchorzewski, the issue of hereditary succession was scarcely raised by the constitution's opponents,
whose fears were aroused by the *extent* of royal power. The 'surrender'
of the executive to the king, his role in the legislature and his unanswerability
all seemed to herald despotism, if not under Stanisław August, then under
his successors. Even some of the constitution's supporters felt uncom-
fortable about the power granted to the king, and suggested its limitation. Others countered by emphasizing the restrictions placed on the king.
They preferred to argue that the constitution had replaced the unrestricted
licence of the magnates with 'ordered liberty' (*rządna wolność*). On this
point the reformers seem to have scored a success. A large number of
seymiki witnessed speeches denouncing the abuses of the magnates and
rejoicing in the end of 'anarchy', and many *seymiki* expressed such sentiments in their resolutions. The inability of the magnates to bring in
cart-loads of illiterate, landless nobles led to a noticeable decline in corruption, drunkenness, and disorder, and an improvement in the standard
of deliberations.[128]

The English model was less central to the debate than before 3 May,
but it continued to provoke controversy. One author cited Filangieri on
England, rousing the spectre of Henry VIII to demonstrate that in a 'mixed

[127] Kądziela, 'Rok realizacji reform majowych (1791–1792)', in T. Kostkiewiczowa (ed.),
'Rok Monarchii Konstytucyjnej': Piśmiennictwo polskie lat 1791–1792 wobec Konstytucji 3 Maja
(Warsaw, 1993), 17–18, 22. Szczygielski, *Referendum*, is the definitive monograph on the
reaction of the *seymiki* to the Constitution. Also see Lityński, *Sejmiki ziemskie*, 132–40.
[128] Grześkowiak-Krwawicz, 'Walka publicystyczna o Konstytucję 3 Maja: Maj 1791–maj
1792', in *Sejm Czteroletni i jego tradycje*, 102–4. Szczygielski, *Referendum*, 161, 194, 202,
227, 263, 285, 288, 310–11, 314–15, 322–5, 370–2.

government' the king could oppress the nation.[129] Tadeusz Czacki and the author of the afore-mentioned *Uwagi nad rządem angielskim y inne* were trenchantly critical of the English constitution, especially regarding ministerial responsibility.[130] Tomasz Dłuski, the 79-year-old chamberlain of Lublin, berated the adoption from England of ministerial responsibility and royal inviolability, but also argued that liberty was better secured in England than Poland, by the hereditary House of Lords.[131] Stanisław August himself replied that ministerial responsibility was 'the greatest shield of liberty',[132] as ministers needed the good opinion of the nation to survive. The King of Poland was limited in his appointments to the senate to filling vacancies, and the nation chose the treasury and military commissioners. The Seym, and not the king, decided on war and peace, as well as taxes and new laws. Stanisław August took Dłuski to task over the English constitution. He repeated his contention of 1776 that the King of England could appoint to, and dismiss from, all military, civil, and ecclesiastical positions. He reached for another argument from 1776, that the civil list was six times greater than the King of Poland's income, and he corrected Dłuski's assertion that it was renewed annually; in fact it was voted for life. Stanisław August refuted the contention that England had no 'empty offices'.[133] On the contrary, lucrative sinecures were the English equivalent of *starostwa* as the 'bread of the deserving', with the difference that the king could take them away at will. He cited the Keeper of the Green Cloth, who in former centuries had laid green cloth before

---

[129] *Zastanowienie się nad nową Konstytucją polską* [1791], repr. in *Za czy przeciw Ustawie Rządowej*, 144–6. The author used the 1786 French edition of *La scienza della legislazione*.

[130] [Czacki], *O Konstytucji Trzeciego Maja 1791 do JWW Zaleskiego trockiego i Matuszewica brzeskiego litewskiego posłów* (1791), repr. in *Za czy przeciw Ustawie Rządowej*, 94, 98, 101–4.

[131] *JW. JP. Tomasza Dłuskiego ... usprawiedliwienie się przed publicznością z manifestu przeciwko Ustawie dnia 3 maja*, repr. ibid., 62. The author of *Myśl obywatela o nowej Konstytucji* (1791), also noted the hereditary upper house; repr. ibid., 47.

[132] 'Naywiększa tarcza wolności'. *Uwagi nad pismem ... Usprawiedliwienie się JW. Dłuskiego ... z manifestu, przeciwko Ustawie 3 Maja 1791* (1791). The pamphlet is signed 'Jeden z tych, którzy zaprzysięgli Konstytucyę 3 Maia' ('One of those who swore to uphold the Constitution of 3 May'). Konopczyński, 'Polscy pisarze polityczni', vol. 2, 391 n. 6, noted that the example in the Biblioteka Jagiellońska bears a late 18th-century annotation that the king was the author. On this basis, Stanisław August's authorship has been taken as probable by Grześkowiak-Krwawicz, *Za czy przeciw Ustawie Rządowej*, 14. The use of very similar arguments and rhetoric as in Stanisław August's speech to the Seym on 23 Sept. 1776 (the repetition of 'po staremu Anglia jest wolna' ('and still England is free') in the place of 'a wolność iednak cała' ('and yet freedom is still intact'), combined with the absence of any panegyric to the monarch, permit the establishment of Stanisław August's authorship as certain. See above, p. 256.

[133] 'Czcze urzędy'.

the king when sitting in council. Yet England was free. Finally, Stanisław August rather mischievously informed Dłuski that the English Tower (of London) had not been destroyed like the Bastille, and that not even habeas corpus could save a Member of Parliament from imprisonment in it, if he 'rose up against the form of government'.[134]

Perhaps the key argument was that by strengthening the state, the constitution had somehow 'saved' the Commonwealth from the threats of her neighbours. On important state and ecclesiastical occasions, preachers eulogized Stanisław August, condemned anarchy, pleaded for unity, and above all, demonstrated the beneficent workings of Divine Providence. The vast majority of poetry inspired by the constitution carried the same message. Ceremonies in honour of the constitution, particularly on 3 May 1792, allowed the reform camp to deploy a theatrical and rhetorical armoury to which the *szlachta* was extremely susceptible. Unfortunately, the unwarranted optimism, not to say naïvety, about the international situation was shared by the Commonwealth's leaders, including the king. The national mood of euphoria and unity led the Seym to work faster, and helped 'sell' the constitution to the *szlachta*, but a more realistic assessment of the situation might have stimulated yet greater urgency, as well as a real financial sacrifice to raise, equip, and train a larger army.[135]

Preachers and poets tended to exalt Stanisław August, but their royalism did not translate into monarchism. On the contrary, many saw in the constitution a return to the best traditions of the Commonwealth. This was more than reassuring propaganda. Although the *liberum veto* had been abolished, the desire for unanimity remained. This was particularly evident at the *seymiki*. Appeals to the minority to accept the will of the majority and accept the constitution despite their misgivings were often successful. The most spectacular individual conversion was Wojciech Turski's.[136] The 'Society of the Friends of the Constitution' (*Zgromadzenie Przyjaciół Konstytucji Rządowej*), formed in mid-May to

---

[134] 'Przeciwko Formie Rządu powstawał'.

[135] See M. Ślusarska, 'Konstytucja 3 Maja w kaznodziejstwie okolicznościowym lat 1791–1792'; Kostkiewiczowa, 'Sławni poeci polscy XVIII wieku wobec Konstytucji 3 Maja'; K. Maksimowicz, 'Konstytucja 3 maja w anonimowej poezji politycznej lat 1791–1792'; F. Sawicka, 'Uroczystości dla uczczenia pierwszej rocznicy Konstytucji 3 Maja'; Kądziela, 'Rok realizacji', 18–25, all in *'Rok Monarchii Konstytucyjnej'*; Gruszczyński, 'Z problematyki politycznej w kazaniach', 22–7; Michalski, ' "Wszystko pójdzie wyśmienicie": (O politycznym optymizmie po 3 Maja), in *Losy Polaków w XIX–XX w.: Studia ofiarowane Profesorowi Stefanowi Kieniewiczowi . . .* (Warsaw, 1987); and Rostworowski, *Maj 1791–maj 1792*, 14–19.

[136] Szczygielski, *Referendum*, 51–68, 374, 377, 379 and *passim*. Kądziela, 'Rok realizacji', 22–3. Grześkowiak-Krwawicz, 'Publicystka lat 1791–1792 wobec Konstytucji 3 Maja', in *'Rok Monarchii Konstytucyjnej'*, 147.

defend the constitution and work for its implementation, has often been called Poland's first modern political party, as it discussed issues and voted together.[137] That would be a move in the English direction. However, it can also be viewed as the confederacy renascent.

The urban issue remained unresolved in May 1792. On the one hand, the leading townsmen and their *szlachta* allies (notably Kołłątaj and Wybicki) pressed to extend the rights granted on 18 April 1791. Many noblemen, led by Stanisław Małachowski, were received into the urban estate amid public demonstrations of fraternity. On the other hand, efforts to enlarge the political role of the towns ran into the opposition of most envoys, who feared the French example. The position of townsmen remained far weaker than in England, but the nation was no longer exclusively noble.[138]

The English influence upon the Constitution of 3 May was less than Stanisław August would have wished. The king himself was most interested in the English example in the key spheres of the Seym and the royal prerogative. He laid particular emphasis on the role of the senate, inspired by the House of Lords, but in that matter he was almost entirely unsuccessful. The king retained his powers of nomination, broadly comparable to those of the English king, but only for life. His fellow authors aimed to remove most of them from his successors. The apparent similarity of the *Straż Praw* to the English cabinet was fatally weakened by the lack of flexibility in its composition, and especially by the inability of most of the ministers to chair their own commissions. Effectiveness was sacrificed on jealous liberty's altar. However, the king was to preside over the *Straż*, which the King of England chose not to do, and Stanisław August's strong political (though not constitutional) position gave him the prospect of personally directing policy. The clearest case of English influence attributable to the king was the declaration that envoys represented the entire nation. The English model also played a central role in the introduction of the legal and the political responsibility of ministers to the Seym, and strengthened the case for the establishment of a reconvenable Seym. The pressure in these cases came as much from the 'patriots' as from the king, as they were expressions of the supremacy of the legislative over the executive power. For that modicum of independence

---

[137] See Kowecki, 'Pierwsze stronnictwo polityczne w Polsce XVIII w.', in *Dzieje kultury politycznej w Polsce: Prace XI Powszechnego Zjazdu Historyków Polskich* (Warsaw, 1977).
[138] Kądziela, 'Rok realizacji', 11–14. Zienkowska, *Sławetni i urodzeni*, part 3. Pasztor, *Kołłątaj*, 71–110. W. Zajewski, *Józef Wybicki* (3rd edn., Warsaw, 1989), 136–9.

possessed by the executive, Poles were indebted to Stanisław August and his English inspiration. The limits of this achievement resulted from the *szlachta*'s almost pathological fear of royal power. This is amply demonstrated by the polemics about the English constitution. A hereditary throne, justified by the English example, certainly did not entail the wide prerogatives of the King of England. It seems justified to argue that Polish political culture moved significantly in an English direction in 1791–2, but the gap remained substantial. Comparing the noble nation's shackling of its king at the outset of the Four Year Seym with the trust and power Stanisław August enjoyed at its close, the Constitution of 3 May must be reckoned a very great victory indeed.

Conclusion

The Prussian minister Ewald von Hertzberg reacted to the Constitution of 3 May with alarm. 'Les Polonois viennent de donner le coup de grâce à la monarchie prussienne, en rendant le royaume héréditaire et en se donnant une constitution qui vaut mieux que celle d'Angleterre.'[1] The validity of Hertzberg's comparison may be open to question; the degree of *Angst* in Berlin is not. From the beginning, Prussia had been playing a game of provocation, in order to acquire more Polish territory. The prospect of a strong and independent Poland, its government modelled on the English, was too awful to contemplate. The agreement with Austria at Reichenbach in 1790, and the British government's about-turn in the Ochakov crisis, removed the last bases for any short-term Prusso-Polish co-operation whatsoever. For her part, Catherine II denounced the constitution to Grimm as both Jacobinical and absolutist, and settled down to plan her revenge. Once she had made peace with the Turks, she sent her army into Poland in May 1792, under cover of a confederacy of Polish malcontents, led by Szczęsny Potocki, Seweryn Rzewuski, and Xawery Branicki—Targowica. Despite some successes, the heavily outnumbered Polish forces stood no chance. Supported by a majority of an expanded *Straż Praw*, Stanisław August acceded to the confederacy on 24 July 1792, in an attempt to save as much as possible of the constitution. Unfortunately, Catherine was determined to restore the Commonwealth to its former impotence. A partition was not inevitable, but Catherine wished to keep both Austria and Prussia fighting France. She offered Danzig, Thorn, and Great Poland to Prussia, on condition that the war be continued. Embattled Austria was fobbed off with vague promises of gains from France or in the *Reich*. Catherine helped herself to a huge slice of the Polish Ukraine and Belorussia, and the last Seym in the Commonwealth's history was called to approve the Partition in the summer of 1793. To the rump of the Commonwealth Catherine dictated the

[1] Hertzberg to Lucchesini, 12 May 1791, *Źródła do dziejów drugiego i trzeciego rozbioru Polski*, ed. B. Dembiński, vol. 1, *1788–1791* (Lwów, 1902), 451.

outlines of a government theoretically better than any before 1791, but in practice an instrument of her will. Stanisław August still hoped to salvage something from the wreckage, but an insurrection broke out in the spring, led by Tadeusz Kościuszko. The insurgents took some pressure off the French, but had no chance of success themselves. Russia parcelled out the spoils. Stanisław August's abdication on 25 November 1795 formally ended the Commonwealth's existence.[2]

The shift in Polish political culture was abruptly halted by Stanisław August's accession to the confederacy of Targowica. The wishful thinking that had helped win over the *szlachta* to the Constitution now served to deepen its sense of betrayal.[3] The king's popularity plummeted, and with it sank that of the English constitution. As Rostworowski wrote, 'Poland, which had so reluctantly and so recently set off down the road of constitutional parliamentary monarchy, turned again towards republicanism.'[4] During the Kościuszko insurrection, while moderates wished to restore the Constitution of 3 May, radicals demanded revolutionary terror and a general mobilization of all social estates to achieve victory, and a democratic republic thereafter. Kościuszko himself was a consequential republican; he disliked the English constitution, and privately criticized the Law on Government as far too monarchical.[5]

The dying Commonwealth left two political testaments to the stateless Polish nation of the nineteenth century: the constitution and the insurrection.[6] As a basis for the government of a restored Polish state, the former was propagated by Adam Jerzy Czartoryski and his circle. Czartoryski was a profound admirer of the English constitution.[7] However, his aspirations for a constitutional monarchy in the Congress Kingdom of Poland after 1815 eventually proved incompatible with the nature of the Tsarist autocracy, and his failure to achieve the resurrection of a Polish state by diplomacy and negotiation meant that, in the long run, the inheritance of the insurrection proved stronger. The insurrectionary tradition benefited from a wider social base. It drew its main strength

---

[2] Cegielski and Kądziela, *Rozbiory Polski*, 213–325. Madariaga, *Russia in the Age of Catherine*, 420–51. Lord, *Second Partition*.
[3] Michalski, 'Wszystko pójdzie wyśmienicie'. Zienkowska, 'W obliczu klęski—czyli co warto ratować? Epizod warszawsko-grodzieński', in *Trudne stulecia*, 80–5.
[4] Rostworowski, 'Czasy saskie i Oświecenie', 370.
[5] Idem, 'Republikanizm polski i anglosaski', 102–3.
[6] Idem, 'Czasy saskie i Oświecenie', 368–9.
[7] See W. H. Zawadzki, *A Man of Honour: Adam Czartoryski as a Statesman of Russia and Poland 1795–1831* (Oxford, 1993), 21, 46, 51n., 66, 115, 219, 228, 262, 266, 289, 317–18, and A. Barszczewska-Krupa, 'Stronnictwo księcia Adama Czartoryskiego wobec dziedzictwa Konstytucji 3 Maja', in *Konstytucja 3 Maja w tradycji i kulturze polskiej*.

from the poor and *déclassé szlachta*, the seed-bed of the modern Polish urban intelligentsia. In the programme of the revolutionary Polish Democrats, the traditions of noble republicanism—egalitarianism, the confederacy, and the general levy—mixed with the slogans of the French Revolution and an awareness of the need to involve the peasantry in the work of national liberation. The insurrectionary ethos aimed at national independence; it did not prepare Polish society to govern itself. On the other hand, the ethos of 'organic work', which gained support after the crushing of the 1863–4 uprising, could contribute little to Polish *political* culture in the face of severe Russian and German repression. Only in Austrian Galicia after 1867 could Poles gain significant experience in parliamentary politics and statecraft without renouncing all national aspirations. The consequences for the twentieth century have been unfortunate. Both in 1918 and in 1989, Poles have had to create a parliamentary political culture almost from scratch. It is to be hoped that the Third Republic proves more successful in this respect than the Second.

The Third Partition altered but did not arrest the cultural and intellectual trends of the Polish Enlightenment, while the heroic failure of the insurrection contributed powerfully to Polish Romanticism. This was reflected, for example, in architecture and gardens, which became crowded with shrines to the national past—notably at Puławy. The neo-Gothic style, symbolizing the venerable Polish state, spread widely in the first half of the nineteenth century, while the landscape park attained maturity. Not that Anglomania shed its superficial aspect. Many wealthy aristocrats adopted the fox-hunting attire and lifestyle which their successors would retain, evoked by the paintings of Wojciech Kossak, until the Second World War. At the same time, however, Shakespeare began his real career in Poland, Sterne and Ossian reached the height of their popularity, Sir Walter Scott was widely read, and Lord Byron heavily influenced Adam Mickiewicz. The long life of Julian Niemcewicz (1757–1841) wove together Enlightenment and Romanticism as it did literature and politics. Alone in his Russian prison cell after the insurrection, he translated Pope's *Rape of the Lock* into Polish. Released by Tsar Paul, he emigrated to America, only to return when Napoleon created the grand duchy of Warsaw. He also translated Gray, Byron, and English 'ballads' into Polish. These inspired him to write his own ballad-like poems on the history of Poland. Under the influence of Scott, he wrote the first historical novel in Polish, *Jan z Tęczyna* (1825). He failed to persuade the British government to support the uprising of 1830–1, and died an exile in Paris.[8] Niemcewicz was an exceptional Anglophile, but not an isolated one. English influences in culture attained their zenith in the thirty-five years after 1795.

By this time, Anglophilia and Anglomania were slowly declining in most European countries, bar Russia and Hungary.[9] As with the Enlightenment as a whole, Anglophilia had affected Poland later than France, Germany, and Italy. The philosophical Enlightenment slowly permeated into Poland from a mixture of Italian, German, and French sources from the 1730s. The English components—Locke's educational thought and Newtonianism—were generally imported from France, but direct contacts between Poland's social and intellectual élites and England began in the 1750s, and grew rapidly from the 1780s. In literature, art, and fashion, Poland was subject to the Francophone Anglomania typical of the entire European aristocracy. As in Russia and Bohemia, there was no struggle between Gallomania and Anglomania. The Gallophobic *bürgerlich* Anglophilia typical of Germany was absent from Poland—except possibly among the Germanophone patriciates of the north-western cities. Polish townsmen were simply too weak to develop any rival culture to that of the *szlachta*. Nor, despite the polemics of Kołłątaj and Łobarzewski, was there any possibility of Anglophilia taking on an anti-magnate aspect among the wealthier and middling *szlachta*. After a century of almost unbroken isolation, Poland experienced the intellectual and cultural currents of the entire eighteenth century compressed into its second half.[10] Anglomania joined rather than supplanted Gallomania among the fashionable élite (which by no means corresponded to the *magnateria*—the semi-literate Karol Radziwiłł was born in the same year as Adam Kazimierz Czartoryski) before the majority of the *szlachta* had even begun to stir from its Sarmatian slumber. Conservative critics of

---

[8] Lorentz and Rottermund, *Klasycyzm*, esp. 38–9. Jaroszewski, *O siedzibach neogotyckich*. Sinko, *Powieść angielska . . . a powieść polska*, chs. 6–8. Miłosz, *History of Polish Literature*, 170–4, ch. 7. Niemcewicz, *Pamiętniki*, *passim*.

[9] Cross, '*By the Banks of the Thames*', 271. Országh, ' "Anglomania" in Hungary'. Maurer, *Aufklärung und Anglophilie*, 430–47.

[10] Adam Zamoyski expressed this insight in *The Polish Way: A Thousand-Year History of the Poles and their Culture* (London, 1987), 231–5, but seems to have gone back on it in *The Last King of Poland*, 278–83, where he rules too clean a line between the 'enlightened' rationalism of the 1760s and the 'romantic' sensibility of the 1780s. While I broadly share his view of the political and cultural significance of the Czartoryskis' move to Puławy, and naturally agree that Anglophilia deepened over time, there is a danger of being dazzled by Izabella Czartoryska. She is better described as a Francophone Anglomaniac than as a Gallophobic Anglophile, a characterization which applies a fortiori to other Polish aristocrats.

Enlightenment lumped all foreign novelties together. The Polish Enlightenment did see a patriotic reaction against cosmopolitanism; it was neither
Gallophobic nor Anglophile, but neo-Sarmatian. In 1788 Jan Potocki, who
spoke better French than Polish, appeared at Court in a *kontusz*, and caused
a sensation. Later that year Izabella Czartoryska ceremonially cut off the
powdered locks of Kazimierz Sapieha.[11]

The discussion of England as a social model was on a far lower plane
than, for example, in Germany, while the interest in English economic
achievements was part of a general European pattern. By far the most
notable feature of Polish Anglophilia was its reception of the English
constitution. From the time of the pioneers until the Four Year Seym,
the basic problem under discussion was whether England might offer a
model of more effective government without risking Polish freedom. Using
the example of England, Stanisław Konarski forcefully argued that the
abolition of the *liberum veto* would not mean the end of liberty, but its
renewal. Later, especially during the Four Year Seym, England was used
to demonstrate that a hereditary throne bespoke no peril. However, very
few authors called for an increase in the royal prerogative to correspond
with that of the King of England; most demanded its further limitation.
In the Continental monarchies, the basic problem was reversed. England
was used to show that increased liberty was compatible with a successful state. In France, this generally meant the intellectual construction
of constitutional barriers to royal despotism. In Germany and Italy, it
entailed pressure for more legal rights, in order to moderate princely
absolutism. In Russia, however, Catherine II interested herself in aspects
of English jurisprudence and legal administration, with the intent of
strengthening her rule. Polish Anglophiles had to answer two questions.
The first was whether England was truly free. To begin with, faced with
the hostility of the *szlachta*, they asserted the general similarity of the
English constitution to the Polish (in Hungary, similar comparisons were
made in 1790, during the revolt against Joseph II). Later, they argued
that England was in fact freer than Poland.[12] The second question was
whether, if England was free, the English model was suitable for application in the Commonwealth. These same questions occupied critics of
absolute monarchy in France, and to some extent in Italy and Germany
also. If the ends of the debates differed, the arguments were often similar
and sometimes identical. The Polish discussion owed much to Continental

---

[11] Kalinka, *Sejm Czteroletni*, vol. 1, 69, 206. Rostworowski, *Ostatni król*, 119–23, 170.
[12] See Grześkowiak-Krwawicz, 'Rara avis', and Orszāgh, 'Anglomania', 169.

authors such as Montesquieu, de Lolme, Rousseau, and Filangieri. However, the Poles also referred to French translations of English sources, notably Blackstone, and some to their own impressions of England.

Continental Anglophilia may be compared to a system of prisms. Some of the 'light from the north'[13] was broken down into its components, mixed with light from other sources, magnified, and projected onwards by the first and most important prism—France. The refracted light was skewed further by prisms placed further away: Germany and Italy. Finally the light reached the outer prisms: Poland, Russia, and Hungary. The pattern of the prisms shifted over time. France initially received nearly all her light through a prism of Huguenot exiles in England and Holland. More light reached the middle and outer prisms unrefracted. And finally, one more task for our hard-worked optical metaphor: after a number of refractions, a clear shaft of light becomes indistinct and eventually diffuses imperceptibly into darkness. However, an inverted second prism refracts light back towards its original direction and restores some of its clarity. Poles and Englishmen shared an agenda of preserving political liberty rather than achieving it.

The Anglophilia of Stanisław August expressed his own enlightened and cosmopolitan patriotism. Unlike many Polish and European aristocrats, Stanisław August was no shallow and indiscriminate Anglomaniac. His knowledge and appreciation of England transcended his contemporaries', chiefly because of his unique friendship with Sir Charles Hanbury Williams, his unusually perceptive observations of England in 1754, and his constant communion with Englishmen and English thought thereafter. He was able to accept, reject, or adapt elements of English culture in his efforts to 'create anew the Polish world', as the requirements of his taste and his programme dictated. English influence was perforce greater upon some aspects of his activity than others. In his patronage of letters, English literature played a minor role, despite the love of Milton, Shakespeare, Pope, Swift, and others he acquired in his youth. The exception was the use of the *Spectator* as a model for *Monitor*, because in the improvement of manners, both periodicals had a similar aim, and the task was one to which Stanisław August attached great weight. In the visual arts, English influences played an increasingly important but always supporting role. Stanisław August's religiosity was similar to and influenced by Anglican latitudinarianism, but the king faced problems of a different order in religious affairs. He fostered strong links between English and

---

[13] The title of ch. 3 of Hazard, *The European Mind*.

Polish science. Notwithstanding his criticism of traditional English education, Stanisław August presided over the introduction of progressive English pedagogy in his own cadet school, which provided a model for the Commission of National Education.

Stanisław August's interest in the English constitution was no mere academic curiosity. The king sought remedies for particular problems in Polish government. His enquiries flowed thickest regarding the powers of the Crown and parliamentary procedure, but extended to the militia and poor relief. Stanisław August was an avid reader of Blackstone and admired the English criminal law, but criticized other elements of the judicial system. He recognized that despite a hereditary throne, majority voting in Parliament, and a somewhat greater royal prerogative than in Poland (he tended to exaggerate it sometimes), English freedom was safe because of the House of Commons' control of the purse strings. Stanisław August also grasped the political culture that underpinned the constitution. His opinion was by no means entirely favourable, and he deplored egoism and Walpolean corruption. Yet the advance of politeness in England also pointed the way to overcoming the problem. Politeness and religious moderation were central to both the English and Polish Enlightenments. A polite and reasonable citizen was more likely to see the necessity of compromising liberty in the interests of the state. For Stanisław August, therefore, English political culture represented a *via media* between excessive fear of government and excessive subservience to it.

Before his election, Stanisław August defined the aims he was consistently to pursue: a hereditary throne, the modest expansion, or at least the retention of the royal prerogative, majority voting in the Seym, an end to binding instructions, and the replacement of the abuses of the old ministers, particularly the hetmans, with an effective executive under royal direction. There is no evidence to indicate that Stanisław August ever aimed at absolute rule. He sympathized with the French *parlements*, the American colonists, and the French Revolution in its early stages. He wished to rule with the consent of the nation, and to win its trust. His aims might be compared to the co-operation between Sigismund Augustus and the executionists in the 1560s, which gave birth to the *monarchia mixta*. The reform of Crown estates and the curbing of the magnates, the legislative omnipotence of the Seym, at which in practice decisions were taken by the majority, and the control of the executive by the king all found analogies in Stanisław August's plans. Stanisław August knew his history well, and knew how to use it as propaganda. He defended the rights left to him by the *pacta conventa*. Yet he found no inspiration in the 1560s. His hero was Casimir the Great, and he was deeply critical of Polish history since the sixteenth century, focusing on the *liberum veto*, royal elections, and uncontrollable ministers. The evidence of his plans and correspondence is unequivocal: in all of his constitutional aims, Stanisław August was influenced or fortified by the example of England.

English examples played a minor role in the reforms effected in 1764–6, and virtually none at all in the constitutional changes of 1767–8 and 1775. The first reason was that the king and his supporters worked under a Russian guarantee that set the limits of reform and reined it back as it saw fit. Stanisław August's intentions for the Commonwealth were ultimately at total variance with those of Catherine II. The second reason was the *szlachta*'s continuing fear of any increase in the effectiveness of government. In 1776, Stanisław August defended the recovery of a modest part of his lost prerogatives by citing the English example. A year later, he sponsored a Polish translation of Montesquieu, and the royal camp's praise of the English constitution gradually grew bolder. This offensive in print culminated in the first half of the Four Year Seym. As a result, many of the king's opponents were as willing to appeal to the English example as the royalists, especially regarding a hereditary throne. The establishment of the English constitution as common currency between the king and his more enlightened opponents was of crucial importance in the negotiations that led to the Constitution of 3 May. However, Stanisław August was only partially successful in his aim to model the new Polish system of government as closely as possible on the English. His constitutional position remained weaker than that of George III, but in 1791–2, Stanisław August's political position was stronger.

In that *annus mirabilis*, it looked as if the conflict *inter maiestatem ac libertatem* had lost much of its potency. The Seym, unrecognizable as its former self, hurried to repair the neglect of centuries. The *szlachta* signalled its approval, and a large measure of mutual trust between king and nation was achieved. It would seem that between 1790 and 1792, Polish political culture moved significantly in an English direction, but remained distinctly more republican. The propagation of English models since the 1760s had not visibly weakened doctrinaire republicanism by 1789, despite the popularity of the English example. It required the demonstration of republicanism's shortcomings and Stanisław August's political skill to bring the 'patriot' leaders round to the 3 May compromise, and astute propaganda to convince the bulk of the *szlachta*, creating in the process the basis of a new political culture.

We cannot help asking if the Constitution of 3 May would have enabled Poland to evolve in a direction similar to that of nineteenth-century England. Would the Commonwealth have gradually extended the franchise, reduced the role of the Crown in favour of a cabinet at the head of a parliamentary majority, and witnessed the growth of party discipline? For Rostworowski, the reformable institutions created by the Four Year Seym brought Poland into the group of states (Great Britain, Sweden, the Netherlands, and Switzerland), whose main constitutional problem in the nineteenth and twentieth centuries was the struggle for universal suffrage.[14] It is easy to list objections. The links between the *Straż Praw* and the commissions were weak, and the system of political responsibility inflexible. But all the shortcomings of the Constitution might have been remedied later, and none would have ruled out an evolution towards England. Had the rejuvenated Commonwealth been allowed to live and flourish, the concept of a backward 'Eastern Europe' might have been strangled at birth.

Darker clouds, however, loomed ahead for the Commonwealth if by some miracle it had avoided partition. While the fraternization of the *szlachta* and the townsmen boded well, the *szlachta* remained unwilling to contemplate change in agrarian relations. The Commonwealth would have faced the problem of an increasingly restless peasantry. The problems might have been surmountable in Roman Catholic, Polish-speaking areas, but the potential for upheaval among the Ruthenian peasantry would have been immense. The perspective from Warsaw was very different from that from Volhynia. But perhaps the truly insuperable problem was this: an English-style Commonwealth would have been as intolerable to the 'Holy Alliance' as was its prospect to the enlightened monarchies of the late eighteenth century.

The constitution was not given the chance to prove itself. Given the realities of Central and Eastern European power politics in the 1790s, it is difficult to see how it could have been otherwise. From the earliest anniversaries of 3 May 1791, Poles have celebrated a glorious symbol of national sovereignty and defiance of 'the shameful commands of foreign violence',[15] rather than the legislative and constitutional merits of the Law on Government.[16] Stanisław August's efforts to 'get in the end to the English system of government'[17] and so transform Polish political

---

[14] Rostworowski, *Maj 1791–maj 1792*, 11.

[15] 'Z hańbiących Obcey przemocy Nakazów'. From the preamble.

[16] See Kowecki (ed.), *Sejm Czteroletni i jego tradycje*, part II, and Barszczewska-Krupa (ed.), *Konstytucja 3 Maja w tradycji i kulturze polskiej.*

[17] See above, Ch. 12, n. 67.

culture have been, in the long term, a failure. That cannot be said of his endeavours to renew Polish culture in the wider sense. Polish culture was rescued from terminal decline, and the Polish nation from possible extinction, by the determined efforts of enlightened Poles of varying political persuasions. Foremost among them was Stanisław August Poniatowski. His patronage of Polish art, literature, learning, and education constitute some of the most important chapters in the history of the Polish Enlightenment. The English contribution to the renewal of Polish culture was substantial and, on the whole, beneficial.

BIBLIOGRAPHY

MANUSCRIPT SOURCES

Warsaw

Archiwum Główne Akt Dawnych (AGAD)

Zbiór Popielów (Zb. Pop.)

93	Summary of the diplomatic correspondence of Tadeusz Burzyński, 1769–1771.
160	Letter of H. Hoffmann to John Lind.
161	Letter from Lind (to Stanisław August).
165	Correspondence (of Stanisław August) with James Harris, H. Johnson, and others. Memoir regarding Filippo Mazzei.
173	Letter from Lord Chesterfield.
174	Letter from Lady Essex.
176	Correspondence with Archibald Gibson, the Duchess of Gordon, Thomas Greather, Harris, and others.
177	Correspondence with Charles Lee, Lord Lyttelton, Lord Mansfield, Edward Montagu, Thomas Wroughton, Lord Morton, David Durrell, Thomas Hornsby, and others. 'Extrait d'une Lettre des frontieres de la Pologne et sur l'État du Royaume', sent to the *Journal du Bas-Rhin*, 1770.
178	Correspondence with Lord Stormont. Notes from Lady Caroline Petersham and Lady Mary Capel. Letter from Lord Thanet.
179	Correspondence with Wroughton, and Charles and Joseph Yorke.
180	Letter from Robert Barker.
181	Letters from John Hyam and Kajetan Węgierski. Correspondence with Mary Lind. Letter (of Stanisław August) to Lord Stormont.
182	Correspondence with Alexandre Aubert, Harris and Lady Harris, and Lord Lansdowne. Letters from Littlepage and Stormont.
183	Letter to Sir Robert Murray Keith. Letters from Sir Ralph and Lady Payne. Correspondence with Horace Walpole and Lord Wycombe.
184	Correspondence with Harris and Mary Lind.
185	Letters from Lord Dalrymple and Margaret Gainsborough.

186	Correspondence with Joel Barlow and William Coxe. Letter to Peter Francis Bourgeois. Letters from Edmund Burke, Henry William Cole, James Durno, and Romuald Mikłaszewski. Letter of Andrew Johnson to Franciszek Bukaty.
187	'Tableau de ce qu'on appelle le Commerce ou le Jeu d'actions en Hollande'.
206	Letters from Thomas Christie, Cole, Durno, and others. Correspondence with Dalrymple.
207	Letters from Barlow, Bourgeois, and others. Polish translation of the letter from Edmund Burke.
213	Particulars of the trial of the Duchess of Kingston. Materials relating to the public finances and system of public credit of Great Britain. Articles of Confederation of the thirteen colonies. French translation of the Declaration of American Independence.
215	Miscellanea Anglica.
216	Miscellanea Anglica. Correspondence with Burzyński, Mansfield, Charles and Joseph Yorke, Lord Shelburne, Stormont, Lind, and Franciszek Bukaty. Letter to George III.
221	Correspondence with Maurice Glayre and Friedrich Melchior Grimm. Letters from Lord George Gordon, and Le Grand.
222	Letter from Richard Rigby. Correspondence with Sir John Sinclair. Draft of a letter to George Washington.
318	Letters from Sir Charles Hanbury Williams, the Duchess of Gordon, C. Yorke, Stormont, and Mme de Broglie. Letter of Williams to Stanisław Poniatowski.
368	'Bâtiments et jardins'.
413, 414, 417, 420	Letters to Deboli 1788–1792.

Archiwum Królestwa Polskiego (AKP)

78, 79, 80, 81, 82	Correspondence of Franciszek and Tadeusz Bukaty with department of foreign affairs, 1775–88.

Archiwum Księcia Józefa Poniatowskiego i Marii Teresy Tyszkiewiczowej (AKsJP)

5	Letters from Konstancja Poniatowska to her sons. Letters from S[tanisław] A[ntoni] Poniatowski to Konstancja Poniatowska. Letter from Williams to Stanisław Poniatowski.
134	Inventory of the Royal Castle (1769).
162	Inventory of Łazienki (1788).
164	Inventory of Łazienki (1795).

171, 172   Inventories of the villa at Koszyki (1794, 1808).
179, 180   Inventories of furniture bought by the king for the Royal Castle (1766–8, 1766, 1785).
181   Inventory of the Royal Castle (in Polish, 1795).
183   Inventory of the furniture magazine at the Royal Castle (1785).
184   Inventory of the Royal Castle (1793).
185   Inventory of the Royal Castle (in French, 1795).
186, 187   Inventories of the furniture magazine at the Royal Castle (1795).
188   Specification of furniture moved from the furniture magazine to the chambers of the Royal Castle (1808).
189   Furniture in the Royal Castle (*c*.1770?).
190   Furniture in the library of the Royal Castle (1795).
192   Inventory of the Palace 'pod Blachą' (1793).
195   Notes on the 1783 inventory of Ujazdów Castle (1785).
196   Furniture moved from Ujazdów Castle (1771–82).
214, 215, 216   Catalogues of engravings (1783, 1793, early 1780s?).
268   Catalogue of the Royal Library (1783).
270   Catalogue of the books at Łazienki (after 1792).
271   Summary of the collections in the Royal Library (*c*.1790).
273, 274   Project for a historical index. Catalogue of medals (1783).
276   Remarks on the 1782 inventory of mathematical instruments.

Archiwum Masońskie

Box 3, 2/1   Resolution of the Grand Orient Lodge of London, legalizing the Grand Orient of Poland, 1780, in French and German, with a Polish translation.

Archiwum Publiczne Potockich (APP)

98   Stanisław August's first draft of the Constitution of 3 May.
139 'Bibliotheca Polona Stanislai Augusti' (catalogue, after 1792).
184 Letters to Stanisław Lubomirski.
197 'Uwagi polityczne krotko zebrane względem Reformy Rządu Polskiego, Roku 1789'. 'Myśli o Sukcessyi Tronu lub Elekcyi Krola'.

Archiwum Rodzinne Poniatowskich (ARP)

373 i, ii   Poniatowski family correspondence.

Korespondencja Stanisława Augusta (Kor. SA)

3a   Letter from Noel Desenfans. Correspondence with William Gardiner.

Zbiór Ghigottiego (Zb. Gh.)

514   Correspondence with Gaetano Ghigotti.
801b Letters to Michał Poniatowski, 1790–1.
905   Letter to Wroughton.

Zbiory z Muzeum Narodowego (Muz. Nar.)
76 Diplomatic papers of F. and T. Bukaty.

Cracow

Biblioteka książąt Czartoryskich (BCzart.)
694 Letter from Węgierski. Correspondence with Wybicki.
712 Correspondence with the Sułkowskis.
798 Letters to August Sułkowski from Paris and London. Letter of Sir Luke Schaub to Stanisław and Konstancja Poniatowski. 'Anecdote Historique'.
799 Letter to S. Lubomirski, 1774. Correspondence with Jacek Ogrodzki.
847 Index of Burzyński's diplomatic correspondence.
849 Letters to F. and T. Bukaty 1781–94.
909 Bill for work done at the Royal Castle.
911 School exercises of S. A. Poniatowski.
920 Letter to Krzysztof Cieszkowski.
937 Various letters to and papers of Stanisław Poniatowski.
938 Letter from Thomas Christie. 'Livres demandées à M. Bukaty'.
940a Speech of S. A. Poniatowski to the *seymik* of Warsaw, 1764.
1493 Catalogue of mathematical and astronomical instruments (1782).
1983 Extracts of British diplomatic correspondence from the PRO (1728–46).
2725 Letter of Coxe, probably to Joachim Chreptowicz.
2770 'Souvenirs Anglois', collected by Adam K. and Izabella Czartoryski.
3211 Correspondence with F. Bukaty 1789–93.
3429 Letters of Michał and August Czartoryski to Ogrodzki.
3972 Letters of Stanisław and Konstancja Poniatowski to Ludwika Zamoyska.
3998 Copies of letters of F. Bukaty to Stanisław August and the cabinet 1780–92.

BCzart. Muzeum Narodowe w Krakowie (BCzart. MNK)
118 A. Moszyński's 'Essay sur le Jardinage Anglois'.

Biblioteka Jagiellońska (BJag.)
3091 Copies of correspondence with T. Bukaty.
3510 Extracts of letters from General Jan Komarzewski.
5992 Letters of F. Bukaty to O. Prozor.

Biblioteka Polskiej Akademii Umiejętności (PAU)
6 Letter from Desenfans.
8 Letter to Mazzei. Letter from Tadeusz Mostowski to a friend.
995 'Dyaryusz Przyiazdu . . . Stanisława Augusta . . . do . . . Krakowa' (1787).
1658 Correspondence with F. Bukaty 1790–3. Letter from Hubert Croft.
1660 Letter from John Anderson. Letter of Edmund Burke to F. Bukaty.
2647, 2648 Correspondence with Scipione Piattoli.

Wrocław

Biblioteka Zakładu Narodowego imienia Ossolińskich (Ossolineum) (Oss.)

9675/I Copies of letters from Piattoli.
9751/I Extracts from letters to Mazzei.

London

British Library (BL)

Additional Manuscripts (Add.)

Coxe Papers
9261 Papers of W. Coxe relative to Poland.

Buckingham Papers
22358 'Caractère du roi de Pologne'.

Newcastle Papers
32984 Letter of Ludwika Poniatowska to the Duke of Newcastle.

West Papers
34728 Letter of Izabella Czartoryska to James West.

Young Papers
35126 Letter of F. Bukaty to Arthur Young.

Hardwicke Papers

35349	Letters of Stanisław August to Charles and Joseph Yorke.
35350	Letters of Montesquieu to C. Yorke.
35353	Letters of C. Yorke to the 1st Earl of Hardwicke.
35356	Letters of J. Yorke to the 1st Earl of Hardwicke.
35367	Letters of J. Yorke to Lord Royston (later 2nd Earl of Hardwicke). Copy of J. Yorke's letter to Stanisław August. Copy of a note from Stanisław August to Wroughton.
35385	Letters of J. Yorke to C. Yorke.
35404	Letters of C. Yorke to William Warburton.
35433	Letters of Stanisław August to J. Yorke.
35484, 35485	Letters of Adam Kazimierz and August Czartoryski to R. Keith.
35526, 35527	Letters of A. K. Czartoryski to Sir R. M. Keith.
33536	Letters of A. K. and Izabella Czartoryski to Sir R. M. Keith.
35633	Correspondence of C. Yorke with Thomas Potter. Letters of J. Jeffreys to C. Yorke.
35634	Letters of S. A. Poniatowski to C. Yorke. Letters of Jeffreys to C. Yorke.

35635   Letters of S. A. Poniatowski to C. Yorke.
35636   Letters of Charles Lee to C. Yorke.
35637   Letter of Edward Montagu to C. Yorke.
35639   Letters of Stanisław August to C. Yorke. Letters of Richard
             Owen Cambridge to C. Yorke.

Liverpool Papers

38224 Letter of F. Bukaty to Lord Liverpool.

Holland House Papers

51392, 51393 Letters of Williams to Henry Fox. Letter of Harry Digby to
             Williams.

Egerton Manuscripts (Egerton)

1952 Letters of Warburton to C. Yorke.
3419 Diplomatic correspondence of Williams.
3501 Letter of A. K. Czartoryski to Sir R. M. Keith. Letter of Keith to Lord
     Camarthen.

Public Record Office (PRO)

State Papers, Poland (SP 88)

69–89, 91–2, 94, 96, 98, 100,   Diplomatic correspondence of Williams
102, 104, 106–8, 110–11, 114   1747–55, Stormont 1756–61, and Wroughton
                                 1762–78.

Foreign Office Papers, Poland (FO 62)

1–9 Diplomatic correspondence of Dalrymple 1782–5, Whitworth 1785–8,
    Hailes 1788–92, Durno 1790–2, and Gardiner 1792–6.

Royal Society (RS)

Letters and Papers,   'A Specimen of Regulations for the institution of an
Various vols. 4–7   Academy at Warsaw'. Papers from Dr N. M. Wolf.
RS 3.35   Letter from Komarzewski to Herschel.
The Journal Book of the Royal Society, vols. 25–34 (1763–93).

Oxford

Bodleian Library (Bodl.)

Dep. Bland Burges

32   Letters of F. Bukaty to James Bland Burges. Letter of Bland Burges to
      F. Bukaty for Prince Stanisław Poniatowski.
35   Letters of Gardiner to Bland Burges.
45   Letter of Michał Poniatowski to Bland Burges. Letter of Kenelm Digby
      to Bland Burges.
47, 48 Letters of Bland Burges to Gardiner and F. Bukaty.

Newport, Gwent

Central Library

Hanbury Williams Papers

qM 411 012 'Journal begun at Berlin in 1750'.

Farmington, Connecticut

The Lewis Walpole Library (Yale University) (LWL)

Sir Charles Hanbury Williams Manuscript Collection (CHW)

50–10918, 54–10910, 55–10877, Letters of Stanisław Antoni, Stanisław,
57–10904, 58–10907, 59–10908, Konstancja, Kazimierz, and Andrzej
60–10903, 61–10913, 62–10895, Poniatowski, and Michał, August, Adam
64–10911, 95–10892. Kazimierz, and Maria Zofia Czartoryski to
Williams.

In addition, Professor Jerzy Michalski kindly lent me a transcript of one of Stanisław August's letters to Filippo Mazzei made by Jean Fabre from the copies in MS 37 of the *Bibliothèque Polonaise* in Paris, which were burnt in Warsaw in 1944. So far one volume of the correspondence between Stanisław August and Mazzei has been published by Professor Michalski *et al.*, but the rest has been held up due to lack of funds.

PRINTED SOURCES

Primary Sources

Addison, J., 'The spacious firmament on high', *The New English Hymnal* (Norwich, 1986), no. 267.

Antonowicz, J., *Grammatyka dla Polakow chcących się uczyć angielskiego języka* (Warsaw, 1788).

Austen, J., *Northanger Abbey* [1803] (Harmondsworth, 1972).

'Biblioteka Kozienicka Stanisława Augusta', ed. J. Wojakowski, *Z badań nad polskimi księgozbiorami historycznymi: Szkice i materiały*, vol. 5 (1981).

Biblioteka Stanisława Augusta na zamku warszawskim: Dokumenty, ed. J. Rudnicka, (Archiwum literackie, 26; Wrocław, 1988).

Blackstone, W., *Commentaries on the Laws of England* (5th edn., 4 vols.; Oxford, 1773).

—— *Prawo kryminalne angielskie przez Wilhelma Blakstona zebrane a przez X. T. Ostrowskiego S. P. wytłómaczone i z uwagami do prawa polskiego stosownemi pomnożone* (2 vols., Warsaw, 1786).

Bolingbroke, Henry St John, Viscount, *The Idea of a Patriot King*, in *The Works of Lord Bolingbroke, with a Life* (vol. 2; London, 1844).

Burges, J. B., 'Angielskie świadectwo pomysłów reformatorskich Stanisława Augusta. List J. B. Burgesa do W. Bukatego', ed. S. W. Jackson, *KwH*, 73 (1966).

Burke, E., *An Appeal from the New to the Old Whigs* . . . (London, 1791).
—— *The Correspondence of Edmund Burke*, eds. L. S. Sutherland *et al*. (10 vols.; Cambridge, 1957–78).
Campbell, C. *et al*., *Vitruvius Britannicus, or The British Architect, Containing the Plans, Elevations and Sections of the Regular Buildings both Publick and Private in Great Britain* (5 vols.; London, 1715–71).
Catherine II and Williams, C. H., *Correspondance de Catherine Alexéiévna grande duchesse de Russie et de Sir Charles H. Williams, ambassadeur de l'Angleterre 1756–1757*, ed. S. Goryainov (Moscow, 1909).
Chambers, Sir William, *Designs of Chinese Buildings, Furniture, Dresses, Machines and Utensils. Engraved by the Best Hands from the Originals Drawn by Mr Chambers, Architect . . . to which is Annexed, a Description of their Temples, Houses, Gardens &c.* (London, 1757).
—— *Plans, Elevations, Sections and Perspective Views of the Gardens and Buildings at Kew in Surry* . . . (London, 1763).
Chesterfield, P. D. Stanhope, 4th Earl, *The Letters of Philip Dormer Stanhope, 4th Earl of Chesterfield*, ed. B. Dobrée (6 vols.; London, 1932).
—— *Letters to His Son and Others*, ed. R. K. Root (London, 1929, repr. 1986).
Chlebowski, W., *Wolność złota Korony Polskiey nad insze pod słońcem narody* . . . (Cracow, 1611).
Chmielowski, B., *Nowe Ateny, albo akademia wszelkiey sciencyi i pełna na różne tytuły, iak na szkolne classes podzielona. Mądrym dla memoriału, idiotom dla nauki, politykom dla praktyki, melancholikom dla rozgrywki, erigowana* (8 vols.; Lwów, 1756).
Chróścikowski, S., *Fizyka, doświadczeniami potwierdzona* . . . (Warsaw, 1764).
—— *Filozofia chrześciańska o początkach praw naturalnych przeciwko deistom czyli teraźnieyszego wieku mędrkom* . . . (Warsaw, 1766).
Coxe, W., *Travels into Poland, Russia, Sweden and Denmark* (2 vols.; London, 1784).
—— *An Historical Tour in Monmouthshire* (2 vols.; London, 1801).
—— *Catalogue of the Valuable Library of the late Rev. Archdeacon Coxe* (Salisbury, 1828).
Craven, Elizabeth, *A Journey through the Crimea to Constantinople in a Series of Letters From . . . Elizabeth Lady Craven to . . . The Margrave of Brandenbourg, Anspach and Bareith* (London, 1789).
Defoe, D., *The Dyet of Poland, a Satyr, by Anglipoloski* . . . (Danzig [i.e. London], 1705).
Desenfans, N., *A Descriptive Catalogue . . . of some Pictures of the Different Schools, Purchased for His Majesty the Late King of Poland* . . . (3rd edn., 2 vols.; London, 1802).
Diderot, D., *Oeuvres complètes*, ed. R. Lewinter (15 vols.; Paris, 1969–73).
Diderot, D., and d'Alembert, J. (eds.), *L'Encyclopédie, ou dictionnaire raisonné des sciences, des arts et des métiers* (27 vols.; Paris and Neuchâtel, 1751–72).
Dodington, G. B., *The Political Journal of George Bubb Dodington*, eds. J. Carswell and L. A. Dralle (Oxford, 1965).
The English Satirical Print (7 vols.; Cambridge, 1986), vol. 3, *The Englishman and the Foreigner*, ed. M. Duffy.

Frederick II, 'Essai sur les formes de gouvernement et sur les devoirs des souverains' [1777], in *Oeuvres de Frédéric le Grand*, ed. J. D. E. Preuss (vol. 9; Berlin, 1848).

Garczyński, S., *Anatomia Rzeczypospolitey Polskiey* . . . (Warsaw, [1751]).

Goślicki, W., *The Accomplished Senator in Two Books, Written Originally in Latin, By Gozliski, Done into English, from the Edition Printed at Venice, in the Year 1568. By Mr Oldisworth* (London, 1733).

Great Britain. *Historical Manuscripts Commission; Reports on Manuscripts in Various Collections*, vol. 6 (1909).

Helvétius, C.-A., *Correspondance générale d'Helvétius* (vol. 3; Toronto and Oxford, 1991).

Historia Polski 1764–1795: Wybór tekstów, ed. J. Michalski (Warsaw, 1954).

Jezierski, F. S., *Niektóre wyrazy porządkiem abecedła zebrane* (1791) in Jezierski, *Wybór pism*, eds. Z. Skwarczyński and J. Ziomek (Warsaw, 1952).

Jodłowski, A. N., *Historya angielska* . . . (3 vols.; Warsaw, 1789–91).

Kant, I., *Kant's Political Writings*, ed. H. Reiss (Cambridge, 1971).

Karwicki, S. Dunin, *Dzieła polityczne z początku XVIII wieku*, eds. A. and K. Przyboś (Wrocław, 1992).

Kitowicz, J., *Pamiętniki czyli historia polska*, eds. P. Matuszewska and Z. Lewinówna (Warsaw, 1971).

Kołłątaj, H. S., *Wybór pism politycznych*, ed. B. Leśnodorski (Wrocław, 1952).

—— *Uwagi nad pismem* . . . *Seweryna Rzewuskiego* . . . *o sukcessyi tronu w Polszcze rzecz krótka* (Warsaw, 1790).

Kołłątaj i inni: Z publicystyki doby Sejmu Czteroletniego, ed. Ł. Kądziela (Warsaw, 1991).

Konarski, S., *O skutecznym rad sposobie, albo o utrzymaniu ordynaryinych seymów* (4 vols.; Warsaw, 1760–3, repr. 1923).

—— *Myśli chreściańskie o religij poczciwych ludzi* [1769] (Cracow, 1887).

Konstytucja 3 Maja, ed. J. Kowecki, intr. B. Leśnodorski (Warsaw, 1981).

Konstytucja 3 Maja 1791: Faksymile rękopisu z Archiwum Głównego Akt Dawnych w Warszawie, eds. J. Płocha, intr. J. Michalski (Wrocław, 1991).

Krasicki, I., *Korespondencja Ignacego Krasickiego 1743–1801: Z papierów Ludwika Bernackiego*, eds. Z. Goliński, M. Klimowicz, R. Wołoszyński, and T. Mikulski (2 vols.; Wrocław, 1958).

—— *Pisma wybrane*, ed. T. Mikucki *et al.* (5 vols.; Warsaw, 1954).

—— *Inwentarz Biblioteki Ignacego Krasickiego z 1810 r.*, eds. S. Graciotti and J. Rudnicka (Wrocław, 1973).

Kraszewski, J. I., *Podróż króla Stanisława Augusta do Kaniowa w r. 1787 podług listów Kazimierza* . . . *Platera, starosty inflantskiego* (Wilno, 1860).

Lee, C., *The Lee Papers, Collections of the New York Historical Society* (4 vols.; New York, 1871–4).

Locke, J., *An Essay Concerning Human Understanding* [1690], ed. P. H. Nidditch (Oxford, 1975).

Lord Burke do Polaków. Pismo z angielskiego przełożone (1791).

Lubomirski, S., *Pod władzą księcia Repnina: Ułamki pamiętników i dzienników historycznych (1764–1768)*, ed. J. Łojek (Warsaw, 1971).

Lyttelton, George, 1st Baron, *The Works of George, Lord Lyttelton* (London, 1774).

—— *Memoirs and Correspondence of George, Lord Lyttelton, from 1734 to 1774*, ed. R. Phillimore (2 vols.; London, 1845).

Łobarzewski, I., *Zaszczyt wolnosci polskiey angielskiey wyrownywaiący, z uwagami do tego stosownemi i opisaniem rządu angielskiego* (Warsaw, 1789).

—— *Testament polityczny synowi oyczyzny zostawiony z planem beśpieczney formy republikantskiego rządu* (Warsaw, 1789).

Łubieński, W., *Świat we wszystkich swoich częsciach większych i mniejszch . . .* (Breslau, 1740).

Majchrowicz, S., *Trwałość szczęśliwa krolestw albo ich smutny upadek wolnym narodom przed oczy stawione, na utrzymanie nieoszacowaney szczęśliwości swoiey* (4 vols.; Lwów, 1764).

Malmesbury, James Harris, 1st Earl, *Diaries and Correspondence of James Harris, First Earl of Malmesbury, edited by his Grandson, the Third Earl* (4 vols.; London, 1844).

Marshall, J., *Travels through Holland, Flanders, Germany, Denmark, Sweden, Lapland, Russia, the Ukraine and Poland in the Years 1768, 1769 and 1770* (3 vols.; London, 1772).

Materiały do dziejów Sejmu Czteroletniego, eds. J. Woliński, J. Michalski, E. Rostworowski, and A. Eisenbach (6 vols.; Wrocław, 1955–69).

'Monitor' 1765–1785: Wybór, ed. E. Aleksandrowska (Wrocław, 1976).

Montesquieu, C. L. de, *Oeuvres complètes* (Paris, 1963).

—— *Duch czyli treść praw, albo o stosowności, które powinny mieć prawa z ustawą rządu każdego*, trans. M. Czarnek (Leipzig and Dresden, 1777).

Naruszewicz, A., *Korespondencja Adama Naruszewicza 1762–1796: Z papierów po Ludwiku Bernackim*, eds. J. Platt and T. Mikulski (Wrocław, 1959).

—— with Stanisław August(?), *Suum cuique* [1771], ed. R. Pilat, repr. in *Przegląd Polski*, 4 (Oct.–Dec. 1869).

New Constitution of the Government of Poland, trans. F. Bukaty (London, 1791).

Niemcewicz, J. U., *Pamiętniki czasów moich*, ed. J. Dihm (2 vols.; Warsaw, 1957).

—— *Powrót posła* [1790], ed. Z. Skwarczyński (Wrocław, 1981).

Pamiętnik Historyczno-Polityczny, ed. P. Świtkowski (1782–92).

Pawlikowski, J., *Myśli polityczne dla Polski* (Warsaw, 1789).

Polska stanisławowska w oczach cudzoziemców, ed. W. Zawadzki (2 vols.; Warsaw, 1963).

Poszakowski, J., *Historya o początku odszczepieństwa Kościoła Anglikańskiego y weyściu do niego herezyi kalwińskiey . . .* (Warsaw, 1748).

Poniatowski, M., *Do uniwersału Nayiaśnieyszego Krola JMci za zdaniem Rady Nieustającej, względem żebraków wydanego stosowny list pasterski do diecezyi krakowskiey* (1786).

Poniatowski, S., *List ziemianina do pewnego przyjaciela z inszego województwa* [1744], repr. in K. Kantecki, *Stanisław Poniatowski, kasztelan krakowski, ojciec Stanisława Augusta* (2 vols.; Poznań, 1880).

Poniatowski, Prince Stanisław, *Pamiętniki synowca Stanisława Augusta*, trans. and ed. J. Łojek (Warsaw, 1979).

Powitanie Nayiaśnieyszego Stanisława Augusta Krola i Pana naszego przeieżdżaiącego przez Włodzimierz do Kaniowa od szkoł tamecznych pod dozorem Bazylianow . . . roku 1787 dnia 7 marca z aktow szkolnych wyięte (Warsaw, 1787).

Priestley, J., *Nauka o Napuszczaniu Wody Powietrzem Kwaskowem . . . z Dzieł oryginalnych sławnego Prystleia . . . wyięta*, trans. A. Trzciński (Cracow, 1787).

Raynal, G. T., *Histoire philosophique et politique des établissemens et de commerce des Européens dans les deux Indes* [1781] (10 vols.; Paris, 1820).

Rousseau, J.-J., *Oeuvres complètes*, eds. B. Gagnebin and M. Raymond (3 vols.; Paris, 1959–64).

—— *Uwagi nad rządem polskim oraz nad odmianą, czyli reformą onego projektowaną*, trans. M. F. Karp (Warsaw, 1789).

Rulhière, C. C. de, *Histoire de l'anarchie de Pologne et du démembrement de cette république . . . suivie des anecdotes sur la révolution de Russie, en 1762, par le même auteur* (4 vols.; Paris, 1807).

The Saints' Liberty of Conscience in the New Kingdom of Poland Proposed for the Consolation of the Distressed Brethren (Warsaw [i.e. London], 1683).

Schulz, F., *Podróże Inflantczyka z Rygi do Warszawy i po Polsce w latach 1791–1793*, trans. J. I. Kraszewski, ed. W. Zawadzki (Warsaw, 1956).

A Short View of the Continual Sufferings and Heavy Oppressions of the Episcopal Reformed Churches, formerly in Bohemia, and now in Great Poland and Polish Prussia (London, 1716).

Skrzetuski, K. J., *Historya polityczna dla szlachetney młodzi . . .* (2nd edn., Warsaw, 1777).

Śniadecki, *Korespondencja Jana Śniadeckiego: Listy z Krakowa*, vol. 1, *1780–1787*, ed. L. Kamykowski (Cracow, 1932), vol. 2, *1787–1807, ze spuścizny po Ludwiku Kamykowskim*, eds. M. Chamcówna and S. Tync (Wrocław, 1954).

Stanisław I Leszczyński, *Głos wolny wolność ubespieczaiący* (Nancy, 1733/43).

—— *La Voix libre du citoyen, ou observations sur le gouvernement de Pologne* (Paris, 1749).

Stanisław August, *Mowa Krola JMci na seymie dnia 23 Septembris 1776 miana* (Warsaw, 1776).

—— *Uwagi nad pismem . . . usprawiedliwienie się JW. Dłuskiego . . . z manifestu, przeciwko Ustawie 3 Maja 1791* (1791).

—— *Mémoires du roi Stanislas-Auguste Poniatowski*, eds. S. Goryainov et al. (vol. i; St Petersburg 1914, vol. ii; Leningrad 1924).

Stanisław August and Deboli, A., *Rok nadziei i rok klęski 1791–1792: Z korespondencji Stanisława Augusta z posłem polskim w Petersburgu Augustynem Debolim*, ed. J. Łojek (Warsaw, 1964).

Stanisław August and Geoffrin, M.-T., *Correspondance inédite du roi Stanislas-Auguste Poniatowski et de Madame Geoffrin (1764–1777)*, ed. C. de Mouy (Paris, 1875).

Stanisław August and Glayre, M., *Correspondance relative aux partages de la Pologne*, ed. E. Mottaz (Paris, 1897).

Stanisław August and Mazzei, F., *Lettres de Philippe Mazzei et du roi Stanislas-Auguste de Pologne*, eds. J. Michalski *et al.* (vol. 1; Rome, 1982).

Staszic, S., *Pisma filozoficzne i społeczne*, ed. B. Suchodolski (2 vols.; Warsaw, 1954).

Trembecki, S., *Pisma wszystkie*, ed. J. Kott (2 vols.; Wrocław, 1953).

—— *Listy*, eds. J. Kott and R. Kaleta (2 vols.; Wrocław, 1954).

Uwagi nad rządem angielskim y inne dla wolnego narodu użyteczne (1791).

Vigée-Lebrun, E., *Souvenirs*, ed. C. Herrmann (2 vols.; Paris, 1984).

Voltaire, F. M. A. de, *Lettres philosophiques* [1734] (Paris, 1964).

—— *L'ABC* [1768], in *Oeuvres complètes* (vol. 27; Paris, 1879).

Walpole, H., *Horace Walpole's Correspondence*, eds. W. S. Lewis *et al.* (48 vols.; New Haven, 1938–83).

Williams, Charles Hanbury, *Works* (3 vols.; London, 1822).

Wraxall, N. W., *Memoirs of the Courts of Berlin, Dresden, Warsaw and Vienna, in the Years 1777, 1778 and 1779* (2 vols.; London, 1806).

Wybicki, J., *Myśli polityczne o wolności cywilnej* [1775–6], ed. Z. Nowak, intr. E. Rostworowski (Wrocław, 1984).

—— *Listy patriotyczne* [1777–8], ed. K. Opałek (Wrocław, 1955).

—— *Archiwum Wybickiego*, vol. 1, *1768–1801*, ed. A. Skałkowski (Gdańsk, 1948).

Za czy przeciw Ustawie Rządowej: Walka publicystyczna o Konstytucję 3 Maja: Antologia, ed. A. Grześkowiak-Krwawicz (Warsaw, 1992).

Źródła do dziejów drugiego i trzeciego rozbioru Polski, vol. 1, *1788–1791*, ed. B. Dembiński (Lwów, 1902).

Secondary Sources

Abramowicz, A., *Dzieje zainteresowań starożytnych w Polsce: Część II: Czasy stanisławowskie i ich pokłosie* (Wrocław, 1987).

Acomb, F., *Anglophobia in France 1763–1789: An Essay in the History of Constitutionalism and Nationalism* (Durham, NC, 1950).

Aleksandrowska, E., *Zabawy Przyjemne i Pożyteczne 1770–1777: Monografia bibliograficzna* (Wrocław, 1959).

—— 'Relacje Jana Heynego agenta księcia Ksawerego saskiego o "Monitorze" (1765–1770)', *Pam. Lit.*, 67 (1976).

—— 'Montesquieu i d'Alembert na łamach monitorowych', *Pam. Lit.*, 79 (1988).

—— 'Na tropie autorstwa króla w "Monitorze"', *Pam. Lit.*, 82 (1991).

Almagor, J., *Pierre Des Maizeaux (1673–1745), Journalist, and English Correspondent for Franco-Dutch Periodicals, 1700–1720* (Amsterdam, 1989).

Alumni Cantabrigiensis, Part II, vol. 1 (Cambridge, 1940, repr. 1978).

Anderson, M. S., 'Some British influences on Russian intellectual life and society in the 18th century', *SEER*, 39 (1960).

Askenazy, S., *Przymierze polsko-pruskie* (2nd edn., Warsaw, 1901).

Bailyn, B., *The Ideological Origins of the American Revolution* (Cambridge, Mass., 1967).

Bałuk-Ulewiczowa, T., 'The Senator of Wawrzyniec Goślicki and the Elizabethan Counsellor', in S. Fiszman (ed.), *The Polish Renaissance in its European Context* (Bloomington, Ind., 1988).

Bańkowski, P., *Archiwum Stanisława Augusta* (Warsaw, 1958).

Baran, K. and Partyka, A., 'Rozwój angielskiego systemu rządów parlamentarnych a Konstytucja 3 Maja w Polsce', *ZNUJ*, 625 (1982).

Barber, W. H., 'Voltaire and Samuel Clarke', in *Voltaire and the English, Studies on Voltaire and the Eighteenth Century*, 179 (1979).

Bardach, J., 'The Constitution of May Third and the Mutual Assurance of the Two Nations', *Polish Review*, 36 (1991).

Barszczewska-Krupa, A., 'Stronnictwo księcia Adama Czartoryskiego wobec dziedzictwa Konstytucji 3 Maja', in A. Barszczewska-Krupa (ed.), *Konstytucja 3 Maja w tradycji i kulturze polskiej* (Łódź, 1991).

Batey, M., and Lambert, D., *The English Garden Tour* (London, 1990).

Batowska, N., Batowski, Z., and Kwiatkowski, M., *Jan Christian Kamsetzer: Architekt Stanisława Augusta* (Warsaw, 1978).

Beales, D., *Joseph II*, vol. 1, *In the Shadow of Maria Theresa 1741–1780* (Cambridge, 1987).

—— 'Social Forces and Enlightened Policies', in H. M. Scott (ed.), *Enlightened Absolutism: Reform and Reformers in later Eighteenth-Century Europe* (London, 1990).

Beard, G., *The Work of Robert Adam* (London, 1978).

Berlin, I., 'Two Concepts of Liberty', in *Four Essays on Liberty* (Oxford, 1969).

Bernacki, L., 'S. A. Poniatowski tłumaczem Szekspira', *Pam. Lit.*, 2 (1902).

—— *Shakespeare w Polsce do końca XVIII wieku* (Cracow, 1914).

—— *Teatr, dramat i muzyka za Stanisława Augusta* (2 vols.; Lwów, 1925).

Bianco, B., 'Wolffianismus und katholische Aufklärung: Storchenaus' Lehre von Menschen' in H. Klueting (ed.), *Katholische Aufklärung—Aufklärung in katholischen Deutschland* (Studien zum achtzehnten Jahrhundert, 15; Hamburg, 1993).

Bieńkowska, B., 'Kultura umysłowa', in A. Zahorski (ed.), *Warszawa w wieku Oświecenia* (Wrocław, 1986).

Black, J., *The British Abroad: The Grand Tour in the Eighteenth Century* (Stroud, 1992).

—— *British Foreign Policy in an Age of Revolution 1783–1793* (Cambridge, 1993).

Blanning, T. C. W., *The Origins of the French Revolutionary Wars* (London, 1986).

—— 'Frederick the Great and German Culture', in R. Oresko *et al.* (eds.), *Royal and Republican Sovereignty in Early Modern Europe: Essays in Memory of Ragnhild Hatton* (Cambridge, 1997).

Bogucka, M., *Staropolskie obyczaje w XVI–XVII wieku* (Warsaw, 1994).

Bonno, G., *La Culture et la civilisation britanniques devant l'opinion française de la Paix d'Utrecht aux "Lettres Philosophiques" 1713–1734*, Transactions of the American Philosophical Society, new series, 38 (1948).

—— *Les relations intellectuelles de Locke avec la France* (Berkeley, Calif., 1955).

Borkowska-Bagieńska, E., *'Zbiór Praw Sądowych' Andrzeja Zamoyskiego* (Poznań, 1986).

Borowy, W., *O poezji polskiej w wieku XVIII* (2nd edn., Warsaw, 1978).

Borucki, M., *W kręgu króla Stanisława* (Warsaw, 1984).

Brewer, J., *The Sinews of Power: War, Money and the English State 1688–1783* (London, 1989).

Brockliss, L. W. B., *French Higher Education in the Seventeenth and Eighteenth Centuries: A Cultural History* (Oxford, 1987).

Bromley, J. S., 'Britain and Europe in the eighteenth century', *History*, 66 (1981).

Brown, A. H., 'S. E. Desnitsky, Adam Smith and the *Nakaz* of Catherine II', *OSP*, new series, 7 (1974).

Brown, L., *British Historical Medals 1760–1920* (London, 1980).

Brooke, J., *King George III* (London, 1972).

Brooke, J., 'The God of Isaac Newton' in J. Fauvel *et al.* (eds.), *Let Newton Be!* (Oxford, 1988).

Brunet, P., *L'introduction des théories de Newton en France au XVIIIe siècle*, vol. 1, *Avant 1738* (Paris, 1931).

Bulloch, J. H., 'The Gordons in Poland', *Scottish Notes and Queries*, 12 (1898).

—— 'Polish alliances with the Gordons', *Scottish Notes and Queries*, 2nd series, 4 (1902–3).

Burtt, S., *Virtue Transformed: Political Argument in England 1688–1740* (Cambridge, 1992).

Butterwick, R. J., 'The visit to England in 1754 of Stanisław August Poniatowski', *OSP*, new series, 25 (1992).

—— 'Od kpiarza do wielbiciela: Horace Walpole wobec Polski w dobie rozbiorów', in *Oświeceni wobec rozbiorów Polski* (proceedings of a conference in Łódź, 8–9 Nov. 1995; Łódź, forthcoming).

—— 'Two views of the Polish monarchy in the eighteenth century: the polemic of Stanisław August Poniatowski with Stanisław Leszczyński', *OSP*, new series, 30 (1997).

—— 'Stanisław August Poniatowski as a religious latitudinarian', in *Christianity in East Central Europe and its Relations with the East and the West* (proceedings of the CIHEC congress in Lublin, 2–6 Sept. 1996, forthcoming).

Cannon, J., *The Fox–North Coalition: Crisis of the Constitution 1782–4* (Cambridge, 1969).

—— *Aristocratic Century: The Peerage of Eighteenth Century England* (Cambridge, 1984).

—— 'The English Nobility 1660–1800', in H. M. Scott (ed.), *The European Nobilities in the Seventeenth and Eighteenth Centuries*, vol. 1, *Western Europe* (London, 1995).

Carpanetto, D. and Ricuperati, G., *Italy in the Age of Reason 1685–1789* (London, 1987).

Cazin, P., *Le Prince-Évêque de Varmie: Ignace Krasicki 1735–1801* (Paris, 1940).

Cegielski, T., *'Ordo et chao': wolnomularstwo i światopoglądowe kryzysy XVII i XVIII wieku*, vol. 1, *'Oświecenie Różokrzyżowców' i początki masonerii spekulatywnej 1614–1738* (Warsaw, 1994).

—— and Kądziela, Ł., *Rozbiory Polski: 1772–1793–1795* (Warsaw, 1990).

Chamcówna, M., *Uniwersytet Jagielloński w dobie Komisji Edukacji Narodowej: Szkoła Główna Koronna w okresie wizyty i rektoratu Hugona Kołłątaja 1777–1786* (Wrocław, 1957).

Champion, J. A. I., *The Pillars of Priestcraft Shaken: The Church of England and its Enemies, 1660–1730* (Cambridge, 1992).

Chaussinand-Nogaret, G., *The French Nobility in the Eighteenth Century: From Feudalism to Enlightenment* (Cambridge, 1985).

Chomicki, G., 'Rola propagandowa obrazu Anglii w publicystyce politycznej "Monitora" (1765–1785)', *ZNUJ*, 943 (1990).

Cieślak, E., *Stanisław Leszczyński* (Wrocław, 1994).

Clark, J. C. D., *The Dynamics of Change: The Crisis of the 1750s and English Party Systems* (Cambridge, 1982).

—— *English Society 1688–1832: Ideology, Social Structure and Political Practice during the Ancien Régime* (Cambridge, 1985).

Colley, L., *Britons: Forging the Nation 1707–1837* (New Haven, 1992).

Collins, P. A. W., 'Shakespeare Criticism', in B. Ford (ed.), *From Dryden to Johnson* (The New Pelican Guide to English Literature, 4; Harmondsworth, 1991).

Colombo, R. M., *Lo Spectator e i giornali veneziani del settecento* (Bari, 1966).

Crocker, L., 'John Toland et le matérialisme de Diderot', *Revue de l'histoire littéraire de la France*, 53 (1953).

Cross, A. G., *'By the Banks of the Thames': Russians in Eighteenth-Century Britain* (Newtonville, Mass., 1980).

Cruikshank, D., *A Guide to the Georgian Buildings of Britain and Ireland* (London, 1985).

Cynarski, S., 'The ideology of Sarmatism in Poland (16th–18th centuries)', *Polish Western Affairs*, 33 (1992).

Czaja, A., *Między tronem, buławą a dworem petersburskim: Z dziejów Rady Nieustającej 1786–1789* (Warsaw, 1988).

—— *Lata wielkich nadziei: Walka o reformę państwa w drugiej połowie XVIII w.* (Warsaw, 1992).

Czapliński, W., 'Sejm w latach 1587–1696', in *Historia sejmu polskiego*, vol. 1, *Do schyłku szlacheckiej Rzeczypospolitej*, ed. J. Michalski (Warsaw, 1984).

Dadlez, M., *Pope w Polsce w XVIII wieku* (Cracow, 1923).

Davies, N., *God's Playground: A History of Poland* (2 vols., Oxford, 1981).

—— '"The Languor of so remote an Interest": British attitudes to Poland, 1772–1832', *OSP*, new series, 16 (1983).

—— *Heart of Europe: A Short History of Poland* (Oxford, 1984).

—— 'Cztery strony i serce', *Gazeta Wyborcza* (2–3 Sept. 1995).

—— *Europe: A History* (Oxford, 1996).

Dedieu, J., *Montesquieu et la tradition politique anglaise en France: Les sources anglaises de 'L'Esprit des Lois'* (Paris, 1909).

Dembiński, B., *Polska na przełomie* (Lwów, 1913).

—— 'William Gardiner, ostatni minister Wielkiej Brytanii na dworze Stanisława Augusta', in *Księga pamiątkowa ku czci L. Pinińskiego* (2 vols.; Lwów, 1936).

—— 'The Age of Stanislas Augustus and the National Revival', in W. F. Reddaway (ed.), *The Cambridge History of Poland*, vol. 2, *1696–1935* (Cambridge, 1941).

Dickinson, H. T., *Liberty and Property: Political Ideology in Eighteenth-Century Britain* (London, 1977).

Dickson, P. G. M., *The Financial Revolution in England: A Study in the Development of Public Credit 1688–1756* (London, 1967, repr. with revisions 1993).

Dieckmann, H., *Le Philosophe: Texts and Interpretation* (St Louis, Mo., 1948).

Dippel, H., *Germany and the American Revolution, 1770–1800; A Sociohistorical Investigation of Late Eighteenth-Century Political Thinking* (Wiesbaden, 1978).

Dobrowolski, W., 'Program Sali Balowej Pałacu Łazienkowskiego', in *Curia Maior: Studia z dziejów kultury ofiarowane Andrzejowi Ciechanowieckiemu* (Warsaw, 1990).

Drozdowski, M. M. (ed.), *Życie kulturalne i religijność w czasach Stanisława Augusta Poniatowskiego* (Warsaw, 1991).

Dunn, J., *Locke* (Oxford, 1984).

Dzięgielewski, J., *Izba poselska w systemie władzy Rzeczypospolitej w czasach Władysława IV* (Warsaw, 1992).

Ehrman, J., *The Younger Pitt*, vol. 2, *The Reluctant Transition* (London, 1983).

Eisenbach, A., *The Emancipation of the Jews in Poland 1780–1870* (Oxford, 1991).

Eriksen, S., *Early Neo-Classicism in France* (London, 1974).

Evans, A. W., *Warburton and the Warburtonians: A Study in some Eighteenth-Century Controversies* (London, 1932).

Evans, R. J. W., 'Über die Ursprünge der Aufklärung', in *Das achtzehnte Jahrhundert und Österreich, Jahrbuch der österreichischen Gesellschaft zur Erforschung des achtzehnten Jahrhunderts* (vol. 2; Vienna, 1985).

Fabre, J., *Stanislas-Auguste Poniatowski et l'Europe des lumières: Étude de cosmopolitanisme* (Paris, 1952).

Fairbairn, A. W., 'Dumarsais and *Le Philosophe*', *Studies on Voltaire and the Eighteenth Century*, 87 (1972).

Feldman, J., *Stanisław Leszczyński* (3rd edn., Warsaw, 1984).

Fleming, J., and Honour, H., *The Penguin Dictionary of Decorative Arts* (London, 1989).

Friedman, T., *James Gibbs* (New Haven and London, 1984).

Friedrich, K., 'Gottfried Lengnich (1689–1774) und die Aufklärung in Preußen königlich-polnischen Anteils', in H. Schmidt-Glinzer (ed.), *Förden und bewahren: Studien zur europäischen Kulturgeschichte der frühen Neuzeit* (Wiesbaden, 1996).

Frost, R. I., ' "Liberty without Licence?": The Failure of Polish Democratic Thought in the Seventeenth Century', in M. P. Biskupski and J. S. Pule (eds.), *Polish Democratic Thought from the Renaissance to the Great Emigration* (Boulder, Col., 1990).

—— *After the Deluge: Poland-Lithuania and the Second Northern War 1655–1660* (Cambridge, 1993).

—— 'The Nobility of Poland-Lithuania, 1569–1795', in H. M. Scott (ed.), *The European Nobilities in the Seventeenth and Eighteenth Centuries*, vol. 2, *Northern, Central and Eastern Europe* (London, 1995).

Garms-Cornides, E., 'Un trentino tra Impero, antichi stati italiani e Gran Bretagna: l'anglomane Carlo Firmian', in C. Mozzarelli and G. Olmi (eds.), *Il Trentino nel settecento fra Sacro Romano Impero e antichi stati italiani* (Bologna, 1985).

Gascoigne, J., *Cambridge in the Age of the Enlightenment: Science, Religion and Politics from the Restoration to the French Revolution* (Cambridge, 1989).

Gawerski, A., 'Stanisław August Poniatowski w Paryżu', in A. Mączak *et al.* (eds.), *Francja-Polska XVIII–XIX w: Studia z dziejów kultury i polityki poświęcone Profesorowi Andrzejowi Zahorskiemu* . . . (Warsaw, 1983).

Gay, P., *Voltaire's Politics: The Poet as Realist* (2nd edn., New Haven, 1988).

Gierowski, J. A., 'U źródeł polskiego Oświecenia', in A. Zahorski (ed.), *Wiek XVIII: Polska i świat: Księga poświęcona Bogusławowi Leśnodorskiemu* (Warsaw, 1974).

—— 'Rozkład państwowości szlacheckiej w czasach saskich' in T. Chynczewska-Hennel *et al.* (eds.), *Między Wschodem a Zachodem: Rzeczpospolita XVI–XVIII w.: Studia ofiarowane Zbigniewowi Wójcikowi* . . . (Warsaw, 1993).

Gillies, A., 'Herder's Essay on Shakespeare: "Das Herz der Untersuchen"', *Modern Language Review*, 33 (1937).

Gołębiowska, Z., 'Anglia w planach wychowawczych Adama Kazimierza Czartoryskiego w świetle instrukcji dla syna z roku 1789', *Rocznik Lubelski*, 21 (1979).

—— 'Podróż Izabeli i Adama Czartoryskich do Wielkiej Brytanii (1789–1791)', *Annales Universitatis Marie Curie-Skłodowska*, 38/39, Sectio F Historia (1983/84).

Gould, E. H., 'To strengthen the king's hands: dynastic legitimacy, militia reform and ideas of national unity in England 1745–60', *HJ*, 34 (1991).

Gömöri, G., 'Polish Authors in Ben Jonson's Library', *Polish Review*, 38 (1993).

Grabski, A. F., *Myśl historyczna polskiego Oświecenia* (Warsaw, 1976).

Grabski, W. M., 'Pierwsza audiencja "ministrów" KEN u Stanisława Augusta Poniatowskiego', *ZNUŁ*, Seria I, 88 (1972).

—— *U podstaw wielkiej reformy: Karta z dziejów Komisji Edukacji Narodowej* (Łódź, 1984).

Graf, A., *L'anglomania e l'influsso inglese in Italia nel secolo XVIII* (Turin, 1911).

Granpré Molière, J. J., *La théorie de la constitution anglaise chez Montesquieu* (Leiden, 1972).

Grieder, J., *Anglomania in France 1740–1789: Fact, Fiction and Political Discourse* (Geneva, 1985).

Gruszczyński, L., 'Z problematyki politycznej w kazaniach katolickich okresu stanisławowskiego', *Acta Universitatis Lodziensis*, Folia Historica, 49 (1993).

Grześkowiak, A., 'Publicystyka polska lat 1772–1792 o angielskim systemie rządów', *Przegląd Humanistyczny*, 29, nos. 5–6 (1985).

Grześkowiak-Krwawicz, A., 'Obce wzory ustrojowe w dyskusjach publicystycznych Sejmu Czteroletniego' in J. Kowecki (ed.), *Sejm Czteroletni i jego tradycje* (Warsaw, 1991).

—— 'Walka publicystyczna o Konstytucję 3 Maja: Maj 1791–maj 1792', in J. Kowecki (ed.), *Sejm Czteroletni i jego tradycje* (Warsaw, 1991).

Grześkowiak-Krwawicz, A., 'Publicystyka lat 1791–1792 wobec Konstytucji 3 Maja', in T. Kostkiewiczowa (ed.), *'Rok Monarchii Konstytucyjnej': Piśmiennictwo polskie lat 1791–1792 wobec Konstytucji 3 Maja* (Warsaw, 1992).
—— *'Rara avis* czy wolni wśród wolnych?', in Ł. Kądziela *et al.* (eds.), *Trudne stulecia: Studia z dziejów XVII i XVIII wieku ofiarowane Profesorowi Jerzemu Michalskiemu* . . . (Warsaw, 1994).
Grzybowski, S., 'Z dziejów popularyzacji nauki w czasach saskich', *Studia i materiały z dziejów nauki polskiej*, seria A, 7 (1965).
Guerlac, H., *Newton on the Continent* (Ithaca, NY, 1981).
Haikala, S., *'Britische Freiheit' und das Englandbild in der öffentlichen deutschen Diskussion in ausgehenden 18. Jahrhundert* (Studia Historica Jyväskyäensia, 32, Jyväskyla Yliopisto, 1985).
Hans, N., 'Polish Protestants and their Connections with England and Holland in the 17th and 18th Centuries', *SEER*, 37 (1958–9).
Hazard, P., *The European Mind (1680–1715)* (London, 1953).
—— *European Thought in the Eighteenth Century* (Harmondsworth, 1965).
Hołdys, S., 'Sejm polski, Parlament angielski', *PH*, 71 (1980).
Holmes, G., *The Making of a Great Power: Late Stuart and Early Georgian Britain 1660–1722* (London, 1993).
Holmes, G., and Szechi, D., *The Age of Oligarchy: Pre-Industrial Britain 1722–1783* (London, 1993).
Homola Dzikowska, I., *Pamiętnik Historyczno-Polityczny Piotra Świtkowskiego 1782–1792* (Cracow, 1960).
Horn, D. B., *Sir Charles Hanbury Williams and European Diplomacy 1747–58* (London, 1930).
—— *British Diplomatic Representatives 1689–1789* (Camden Society, 3rd series, 46; London, 1932).
—— *British Public Opinion and the First Partition of Poland* (Edinburgh, 1945).
Hulliung, M., *Montesquieu and the Old Regime* (Berkeley, Calif., 1976).
Humphreys, A., 'The Literary Scene', in B. Ford (ed.), *From Dryden to Johnson* (The New Pelican History of English Literature, vol. 4; Harmondsworth, 1991).
Ilchester, G. S. H. Fox-Strangways, 6th Earl, and Mrs. Langford-Brooke, *The Life of Sir Charles Hanbury Williams, Poet, Wit and Diplomatist* (London, 1929).
Iwaszkiewicz, J., 'Chreptowicz, Joachim', *PSB* (vol. 3; Cracow, 1937).
Izdebski, H., 'Political and Legal Aspects of the Third of May Constitution', in M. Rozbicki (ed.), *European and American Constitutionalism in the Eighteenth Century* (Warsaw, 1990).
Jack, J., 'The Periodical Essayists', in B. Ford (ed.), *From Dryden to Johnson* (The New Pelican Guide to English Literature, vol. 4; Harmondsworth, 1991).
Jacob, M. C., *The Radical Enlightenment: Pantheists, Freemasons and Republicans* (London, 1981).
—— *Living the Enlightenment: Freemasonry and Politics in Eighteenth-Century Europe* (Oxford, 1991).

Jacobson, D., *Chinoiserie* (London, 1993).

Jacques, D., *Georgian Gardens: The Reign of Nature* (London, 1983).

Janeczek, S., *Oświecenie chrześcijańskie: Z dziejów polskiej kultury filozoficznej* (Lublin, 1994).

Jaroszewski, T. S., 'Ze studiów nad problematyką recepcji Palladia w Polsce w drugiej połowie XVIII wieku', in *Klasycyzm: Studia nad sztuką polską XVIII i XIX wieku* (Wrocław, 1968).

—— *Architektura doby Oświecenia w Polsce: Nurty i odmiany* (Wrocław, 1971).

—— *O siedzibach neogotyckich w Polsce* (Warsaw, 1981).

—— 'Pałac w Tulczynie i początki architektury klasycyzmu na Ukrainie', *Przegląd Wschodni*, 1 (1991).

Jasnowski, J., *England and Poland in the XVIth and XVIIth Centuries (Political Relations)* (London, 1948).

Jobert, A., *La Commission d'Éducation Nationale en Pologne (1773–1794): Son oeuvre d'instruction civique* (Paris, 1941).

—— *Magnats polonais et physiocrates francais* (Paris, 1941).

—— 'Tradition et nouveauté dans l'oeuvre de la Commission d'Éducation' in K. Mrozowska and R. Dutkowa (eds.), *W kręgu wielkiej reformy: Sesja naukowa na uniwersytecie Jagiellońskim w dwusetną rocznicę powstania Komisji Edukacji Narodowej* (Warsaw, 1977).

Kądziela, Ł., 'Rok realizacji reform majowych (1791–1792)', in T. Kostkiewiczowa (ed.), *'Rok Monarchii Konstytucyjnej': Piśmiennictwo polskie lat 1791–1792 wobec Konstytucji 3 Maja* (Warsaw, 1992).

—— *Między zdradą a służbą Rzeczypospolitej: Fryderyk Moszyński w latach 1792–1793* (Warsaw, 1993).

Kaleta, R., 'Obiady czwartkowe', in T. Kostkiewiczowa (ed.), *Słownik literatury polskiego Oświecenia* (2nd edn.; Wrocław, 1991).

Kalinka, W., *Sejm Czteroletni* [1880–8] (4th edn., 2 vols.; Warsaw, 1991).

Kantecki, K., *Stanisław Poniatowski, kasztelan krakowski, ojciec Stanisława Augusta* (2 vols.; Poznań, 1880).

Kaplan, H. H., *The First Partition of Poland* (New York, 1962).

Keir, D. L., *The Constitutional History of Modern Britain 1485–1951* (5th edn., London, 1951).

Kelly, A., 'Coade, Eleanor', in J. Turner (ed.), *The Dictionary of Art* (34 vols.; London, 1996), vol. 7.

Klimowicz, M., *Oświecenie* (4th edn., Warsaw, 1980).

Knox, B., *The Architecture of Poland* (London, 1971).

Kolekcja dla króla: Obrazy dawnych mistrzów ze zbiorów Dulwich Picture Gallery w Londynie (Catalogue of the exhibition at the Royal Castle, Warsaw, 1992).

Kołłątaj i wiek Oświecenia (*PH*, Warsaw, 1951).

Kołoszyńska, I., 'Malarstwo angielskie ze zbiorów polskich: Katalog', in J. Białostocki and I. Kołoszyńska (eds.), *Polska i Anglia: Stosunki kulturalno-artystyczne: Pamiętnik wystawy sztuki angielskiej* (Warsaw, 1974).

Komorowski, J., 'Polska szekspiriana', *Pamiętnik Teatralny*, 40 (1991).

—— '"Makbet" Shakespeare'a w Polsce: Spis premier 1793–1990', *Pamiętnik Teatralny*, 40 (1991).

Komorowski, P., *Historia powszechna w polskim piśmiennictwie naukowym czasów stanisławowskich i jej rola w edukacji narodowej* (Warsaw, 1992).

Konopczyński, W., *Geneza i ustanowienie Rady Nieustającej* (Cracow, 1917).

—— *Liberum Veto* (Cracow, 1918).

—— *Stanisław Konarski* (Warsaw, 1926).

—— *Dzieje Polski nowożytnej* [1936] (3rd edn., 2 vols.; Warsaw, 1986).

—— *Konfederacja barska* [1936–8] (2nd edn., 2 vols.; Warsaw, 1991).

—— 'Czartoryski, August', *PSB* (vol. 4; Cracow, 1938).

—— 'Czartoryski, Michał', *PSB* (vol. 4; Cracow, 1938).

—— 'Anglia a Polska w XVIII wieku', *Pamiętnik Biblioteki Kórnickiej*, 4 (1947).

—— *Polscy pisarze polityczni XVIII wieku* (vol. 1; Warsaw, 1966).

Koropeckyj, R., 'The Kiev Mohyla Collegium and seventeenth-century Polish-English literary contacts: a Polish translation of Henry Montagu's *Manchester al Mondo*', *Harvard Ukrainian Studies*, 8 (1984).

Korzon, T., *Wewnętrzne dzieje Polski za Stanisława Augusta (1764–1794): Badania historyczne ze stanowiska ekonomicznego i administracyjnego* (2nd edn., 6 vols.; Cracow, 1897–8).

—— *Odrodzenie w upadku: Wybór pism historycznych*, eds. M. H. Serejski and A. F. Grabski (Warsaw, 1975).

Kościałkowski, A., *Antoni Tyzenhauz, podskarbi nadworny litewski* (2 vols.; London, 1970–1).

Kostkiewiczowa, T., 'Sławni poeci polscy XVIII wieku wobec Konstytucji 3 Maja', in T. Kostkiewiczowa (ed.), *'Rok Monarchii Konstytucyjnej': Piśmiennictwo polskie lat 1791–1792 wobec Konstytucji 3 Maja* (Warsaw, 1992).

Kowecka, E., *Dwór 'najrządniejszego w Polszcze magnata'* (Warsaw, 1991).

Kowecki, J., 'Łobarzewski, Ignacy', in *PSB* (vol. 18; Wrocław, 1973).

—— 'Posłowie—debiutanci na Sejmie Czteroletnim', in A. Zahorski (ed.), *Wiek XVIII: Polska i Świat: Księga poświęcona Bogusławowi Leśnodorskiemu* (Warsaw, 1974).

—— 'Pierwsze stronnictwo polityczne w Polsce XVIII w.', in *Dzieje kultury politycznej w Polsce: Prace XI Powszechnego Zjazdu Historyków Polskich* (Warsaw, 1977).

Kozłowski, W. M., 'Karol Lee w służbie Stanisława Augusta', *Przewodnik Naukowy i Literacki*, 2 (1911).

Kraushar, A., *Dwa szkice historyczne z czasów Stanisława Augusta* (2 vols.; Warsaw, 1905).

Kriegseisen, W., *Ewangelicy polscy i litewscy w epoce saskiej (1696–1763): Sytuacja prawna, organizacja i stosunki międzywyznaniowe* (Warsaw, 1996).

Kroll, R., *et al.* (eds.), *Philosophy, Science and Religion in England 1640–1700* (Cambridge, 1992).

Król, G., 'Anglia wobec wydarzeń toruńskich 1724 roku', *Zapiski Historyczne*, 56 (1991).

Kroupa, J., *Alchymie štěstí: Pozdní osvícenství a moravská společnost* (Brno, 1987).
Kuchowicz, Z., *Człowiek polskiego baroku* (Łódź, 1992).
Kula, W., *Szkice o manufakturach w Polsce XVIII wieku* (2 vols.; Warsaw, 1956).
Kurkowski, J., *Warszawskie czasopis ma uczone doby Augusta III* (Warsaw, 1994).
Kwiatkowski, M., *Stanisław August: Król-architekt* (Wrocław, 1983).
—— 'Mecenas-twórca', in M. M. Drozdowski (ed.), *Życie kulturalne i religijność w czasach Stanisława Augusta* (Warsaw, 1991).
La Harpe, J. de, *Le Journal des Savants et l'Angleterre 1702–1789* (Berkeley, Calif., 1941).
Langford, P., *A Polite and Commercial People: England 1727–1783* (Oxford, 1989).
Lawson, P., *George Grenville: A Political Life* (Oxford, 1984).
Lelewel, J., 'Panowanie Stanisława Augusta' [1845], in *Dzieła* (vol. 8; Warsaw, 1961).
Leśnodorski, B., *Dzieło Sejmu Czteroletniego* (Wrocław, 1951).
—— 'Mowa Andrzeja Zamoyskiego na konwokacji 1764 r.', in *Księga pamiątkowa 150-lecia AGAD w Warszawie* (Warsaw, 1958).
—— 'Idee polityczne Jana Jakuba Rousseau w Polsce', in *Wiek XIX: Prace ofiarowane Stefanowi Kieniewiczowi . . .* (Warsaw, 1967).
Lewitter, L. R., 'Intolerance and foreign intervention in early eighteenth-century Poland–Lithuania', *Harvard Ukrainian Studies*, 5 (1981).
Libera, Z., 'Stanisław August Poniatowski—opiekuń i miłosnik literatury', in M. M. Drozdowski (ed.), *Życie kulturalne i religijność w czasach Stanisława Augusta* (Warsaw, 1991).
Libiszowska, Z., 'Echa burżuazyjnej rewolucji angielskiej w Polsce', *Przegląd Nauk Historycznych i Społecznych*, 3 (1953).
—— *Opinia polska wobec rewolucji amerykańskiej w XVIII wieku* (Łódź, 1962).
—— *Misja polska w Londynie w latach 1769–1795* (Łódź, 1966).
—— 'Model angielski w publicystyce polskiego Oświecenia', *Sprawozdania z Czynności i Posiedzeń Naukowych Łódzkiego Towarzystwa Naukowego*, 23, no. 10 (1969).
—— 'Edmund Burke a Polska', *KwH*, 77 (1970).
—— 'Lee, Karol', *PSB* (vol. 16; Wrocław, 1970).
—— 'Lind, John', *PSB* (vol. 17; Wrocław, 1972).
—— 'Littlepage, Lewis', *PSB* (vol. 17; Wrocław, 1972).
—— 'Podróże naukowe Generała Jana Komarzewskiego', *ZNUŁ*, Ser. I, 88 (1972).
—— *Życie polskie w Londynie w XVIII wieku* (Warsaw, 1972).
—— 'James Durno i jego misja w Polsce', *PH*, 44 (1973).
—— 'Prasa i publicystyka angielska wobec drugiego rozbioru Polski', *Rocznik Historii Czasopiśmiennictwa Polskiego*, 12 (1973).
—— 'Misja Ogińskiego w Londynie', in A. Zahorski (ed.), *Wiek XVIII: Polska i świat: Księga poświęcona Bogusławowi Leśnodorskiemu* (Warsaw, 1974).
—— 'Jakobin brytyjski obrońcą Polski', *ZNUJ*, 753 (1986).
—— 'Les voyages scientifiques aux temps des lumières', *ZNUJ*, 870 (1989).

342   *Bibliography*

Libiszowska, Z., 'England–Poland during the XVIIIth Century', in *The Polish Road to Democracy: The Constitution of May 3 1791: Exhibition in the Polish Cultural Institute in London, April 18–June 18 1991* (Warsaw, 1991).

—— 'Lord Burke do Polaków', in *Kultura średniowieczna i kultura staropolska: Studia ofiarowane Aleksandrowi Gieysztorowi . . .* (Warsaw, 1991).

—— 'Odgłosy Konstytucji 3 Maja na Zachodzie', in A. Barszczewska-Krupa (ed.), *Konstytucja 3 Maja w tradycji i kulturze polskiej* (Łódź, 1991).

—— 'Polska reforma w opinii angielskiej', in J. Kowecki (ed.), *Sejm Czteroletni i jego tradycje* (Warsaw, 1991).

—— 'Międzynarodowe powikłania sukcesji saskiej', in A. Grześkowiak-Krwawicz (ed.), *Konstytucja 3 Maja: Prawo—Polityka—Symbol: Materiały z sesji Polskiego Towarzystwa Historycznego na Zamku Królewskim w Warszawie 6–7 maja 1991* (Warsaw, 1992).

—— 'Joel Barlow wobec rewolucji francuskiej i polskiej reformy', *Wiek Oświecenia*, 9, *Pamięci Profesora Emanuela Rostworowskiego* (1993).

—— 'Insurekcja kościuszkowska widziana z Anglii', in H. Kocój (ed.), *200 rocznica powstania kościuszkowskiego* (Katowice, 1994).

Link-Lenczowski, A., 'Poniatowska, Konstancja', *PSB* (vol. 27; Wrocław, 1983).

—— 'Poniatowski, Stanisław', *PSB* (vol. 27; Wrocław, 1983).

Lipoński, W., 'The Influence of Britain on Prince Adam Jerzy Czartoryski's Education and Political Activity', *Polish–Anglo-Saxon Studies*, 1 (1987).

Lityński, A., *Sejmiki ziemskie 1764–1793: Dzieje reform* (Katowice, 1988).

—— 'Status posła po Konstytucji 3 Maja', in H. Kocój (ed.), *Pierwsza w Europie: 200 rocznica Konstytucji 3 Maja 1791–1991* (Katowice, 1989).

—— 'Tradycje i nowości w ustawodawstwie karnym Sejmu Czteroletniego (ze szczególnym uwzględnieniem Kodeksu Stanisława Augusta)', in A. Grześkowiak-Krwawicz (ed.), *Konstytucja 3 Maja: Prawo—Polityka—Symbol: Materiały z sesji Polskiego Towarzystwa Historycznego na Zamku Królewskim w Warszawie 6–7 maja 1991* (Warsaw, 1992).

—— 'Z zagadnień reformy prawa karnego w Polsce (1764–1794)', *Wiek Oświecenia*, 9, *Pamięci Profesora Emanuela Rostworowskiego* (1993).

Łojek, J., *Polska inspiracja prasowa w Holandii i Niemczech w czasach Stanisława Augusta* (Warsaw, 1969).

—— *Siedem tajemnic Stanisława Augusta* (Warsaw, 1982).

—— *Geneza i obalenie Konstytucji 3 Maja: Polityka zagraniczna Rzeczypospolitej 1787–1792* (Lublin, 1986).

Lord, R. H., *The Second Partition of Poland* (Cambridge, Mass., 1915).

Lorentz, S., 'Stosunki artystyczne polsko-angielskie w dobie Oświecenia' in J. Białostocki and I. Kołoszyńska (eds.), *Polska i Anglia: Stosunki kulturalno-artystyczne: Pamiętnik wystawy sztuki angielskiej* (Warsaw, 1974).

Lorentz, S., and Rottermund, A., *Klasycyzm w Polsce* (2nd edn., Warsaw, 1984).

Lukowski, G. [J.] T., *The Szlachta and the Confederacy of Radom 1764–1767/8: A Study of the Polish Nobility* (*Antemurale*, 21; Rome, 1977).

Lukowski, J. T., 'Towards partition: Polish magnates and Russian intervention in Poland during the early reign of Stanisław August Poniatowski', *HJ*, 28 (1985).

—— *Liberty's Folly: The Commonwealth of Poland–Lithuania in the Eighteenth Century* (London, 1991).

—— 'Od Konarskiego do Kołłątaja—czyli od realizmu do utopii', in Ł. Kądziela *et al.* (eds.), *Trudne stulecia: Studia z dziejów XVII i XVIII wieku ofiarowane Profesorowi Jerzemu Michalskiemu . . .* (Warsaw, 1994).

—— 'Recasting Utopia: Montesquieu, Rousseau and the Polish Constitution of 3 May 1791', *HJ*, 37 (1994).

Mackiewicz, S., *Stanisław August* (3rd edn., Warsaw, 1991).

MacManners, J., *Death and the Enlightenment: Changing Attitudes to Death among Christians and Unbelievers in Eighteenth-Century France* (Oxford, 1981).

MacQuoid, P., *A History of English Furniture* [1904–8] (2nd edn., London, 1988).

Madariaga, I. de, *Russia in the Age of Catherine the Great* (1981, repr. New Haven, 1990).

Majewska-Maszkowska, B., *Mecenat artystyczny Izabelli z Czartoryskich Lubomirskiej 1736–1816* (Warsaw, 1976).

—— and Jaroszewski, T. S., 'Podróż Stanisława Kostki Potockiego do Anglii w roku 1787 w świetle jego korespondencji z żoną', *Biuletyn Historii Sztuki*, 34 (1972).

Majorek, C., and Słowikowski, T., 'Wkład pijarów w teorię wychowania patriotycznego i obywatelskiego w Polsce w XVIII wieku', in I. Stasiewicz-Jasiukowa (ed.), *Wkład pijarów do nauki i kultury w Polsce XVII–XIX w.* (Warsaw and Cracow, 1993).

Maksimowicz, K., 'Konstytucja 3 Maja w anonimowej poezji politycznej lat 1791–1792', in T. Kostkiewiczowa (ed.), *'Rok Monarchii Konstytucyjnej': Piśmiennictwo polskie lat 1791–1792 wobec Konstytucji 3 Maja* (Warsaw, 1992).

Mańkowski, T., *Galerja Stanisława Augusta* (Lwów, 1932).

—— *Mecenat artystyczny Stanisława Augusta* (Warsaw, 1976).

Markiewicz, M., 'Rady Senatu za Augusta III', *ZNUJ*, 614 (1985).

—— *Rady senatorskie Augusta II (1697–1733)* (Wrocław, 1988).

Mason, S., 'Montesquieu on English Constitutionalism Revisited: A Government of Potentiality and Paradoxes', *Studies on Voltaire and the Eighteenth Century*, 278 (1990).

Maszkowska, B., *Z dziejów polskiego meblarstwa okresu Oświecenia* (Wrocław, 1956).

Maurer, M., *Aufklärung und Anglophilie in Deutschland* (Göttingen and Zürich, 1987).

Michalski, J., 'Propaganda konserwatywna w walce z reformą w początkach panowania Stanisława Augusta', *PH*, 43 (1952).

—— 'Plan Czartoryskich naprawy Rzeczypospolitej', *KwH*, 63 (1956).

—— 'Dwie misje księcia Stanisława', in *Księga pamiątkowa 150-lecia AGAD w Warszawie* (Warsaw, 1958).

Michalski, J., 'Sejmiki poselskie 1788 roku', *PH*, 51 (1960).
—— 'Les diétines Polonaises au XVIIIe siècle', *APH*, 12 (1965).
—— 'O rzekomych i rzeczywistych pismach Andrzeja Zamoyskiego', *PH*, 61 (1970).
—— '"Warszawa" czyli o antystołecznych nastrojach w czasach Stanisława Augusta', *Warszawa XVIII wieku*, 12 (1972).
—— 'Sarmatyzm a europeizacja Polski w XVIII wieku', in Z. Stefanowska (ed.), *Swojskość i cudzoziemszczyzna w dziejach kultury polskiej* (Warsaw, 1973).
—— 'Gdyby nami rządziły kobiety: (Poglądy Amelii Mniszchowej na reformę Rzeczypospolitej)', in A. Zahorski (ed.), *Wiek XVIII: Polska i świat: Księga poświęcona Bogusławowi Leśnodorskiemu* (Warsaw, 1974).
—— *Rousseau a sarmacki republikanizm* (Warsaw, 1977).
—— 'Kilka uwag o koncepcji Sejmu rządzącego w XVIII w.', *Śląski Kwartalnik Historyczny Sobótka*, 37 (1982).
—— 'Poniatowski, Stanisław', *PSB* (vol. 27; Wrocław, 1983).
—— 'Z problematyki republikańskiego nurtu w polskiej reformatorskiej myśli politycznej w XVIII wieku', *KwH*, 90 (1983).
—— 'Problematyka aliansu polsko-rosyjskiego w czasach Stanisława Augusta: Lata 1764–1766', *PH*, 75 (1984).
——'Sejm w czasach saskich' and 'Sejm w czasach panowania Stanisława Augusta', in *Historia sejmu polskiego*, vol. 1, *Do schyłku szlacheckiej Rzeczypospolitej*, ed. J. Michalski (Warsaw, 1984).
—— 'Stanisław August Poniatowski', in *Poczet królów i książąt polskich* (2nd edn., Warsaw, 1984).
—— *Konstytucja 3 Maja* (Warsaw, 1985).
—— 'Zagadnienie unii polsko-litewskiej w czasach panowania Stanisława Augusta', *Zapiski Historyczne*, 51 (1986).
—— '"Wszystko pójdzie wyśmienicie" (O politycznym optymizmie po 3 maja', in *Losy Polaków w XIX–XX w.: Studia ofiarowane Profesorowi Stefanowi Kieniewiczowi* . . . (Warsaw, 1987).
—— 'Stanisław August obserwatorem Rewolucji Francuskiej', *KwH*, 97 (1990).
—— 'Opozycja magnacka i jej cele w początkach Sejmu Czteroletniego', in J. Kowecki (ed.), *Sejm Czteroletni i jego tradycje* (Warsaw, 1991).
—— 'Zmierzch prokonsulatu Stackelberga', in J. Kowecki (ed.), *Sejm Czteroletni i jego tradycje* (Warsaw, 1991).
—— 'Fryderyk Wielki i Grzegorz Potemkin w latach kryzysu przymierza prusko-rosyjskiego', in T. Chynczewska-Hennel *et al.* (eds.), *Między wschodem a zachodem: Rzeczpospolita XVI–XVIII w.: Studia ofiarowane Zbigniewowi Wójcikowi* . . . (Warsaw, 1993).
—— 'Sprawa przymierza polsko-rosyjskiego w dobie aneksji Krymu', in Z. Wójcik *et al.* (eds.), *Z dziejów polityki i dyplomacji polskiej: Studia poświęcone pamięci Edwarda hr. Raczyńskiego* . . . (Warsaw, 1994).
—— *Sarmacki republikanizm w oczach Francuza: Mably i konfederaci barscy* (Wrocław, 1995).

Mierzwa, E. A., *Anglia a Polska w pierwszej połowie XVII wieku* (Warsaw, 1986).
—— *Anglia a Polska w epoce Jana III Sobieskiego* (Łódź, 1988).
Mikołajczyk, M., 'Z badań nad zagadnieniem nietykalności osobistej w okresie Sejmu Czteroletniego', in A. Lityński (ed.), *W dwusetną rocznicę wolnego Sejmu: Ludzie—państwo—prawo czasów Sejmu Czteroletniego* (Katowice, 1988).
Miłosz, C., *The History of Polish Literature* (2nd edn.; Berkeley, Calif., 1983).
Morawińska, A., 'Nieznany traktat Augusta Fryderyka Moszyńskiego o ogrodach angielskich', in J. Białostocki (ed.), *Myśli o sztuce i sztuka XVII–XVIII wieku* (Warsaw, 1970).
—— 'Kolekcjonerstwo polskie i Anglia w dobie Oświecenia: Kontakty artystyczne Stanisława Augusta i Michała Poniatowskich z Noelem Desenfansem', in J. Białostocki and I. Kołoszyńska (eds.), *Polska i Anglia: Stosunki kulturalnoartystyczne: Pamiętnik wystawy sztuki angielskiej* (Warsaw, 1974).
—— 'Malarstwo', in A. Zahorski (ed.), *Warszawa w wieku Oświecenia* (Wrocław, 1986).
Mowl, T., *Palladian Bridges: Prior Park and the Whig Connection* (Bath, 1993).
Mrozowska, K., *Szkoła Rycerska Stanisława Augusta Poniatowskiego (1765–1794)* (Wrocław, 1961).
—— *By Polaków zrobić obywatelami* (Dzieje narodu i państwa polskiego, vol. 2, part 37; Cracow, 1993).
Müller, M. G., *Polen zwischen Preussen und Russland: Souveränitätskrise und Reformpolitik 1736–1752* (Berlin, 1983).
—— *Die Teilungen Polens: 1772–1793–1795* (Munich, 1984).
Nieć, J., 'Stanisława A. Poniatowskiego plan reformy Rzeczypospolitej', *Historja*, 3 (1933).
—— *Młodość ostatniego elekta: St. A. Poniatowski 1732–1764* (Cracow, 1935).
Nowak-Dłużewski, J., *Stanisław Konarski* (1951, 2nd edn., Warsaw, 1989).
O'Gorman, F., 'Party in the Later Eighteenth Century', in J. Cannon (ed.), *The Whig Ascendancy: Colloquies on Hanoverian England* (London, 1981).
—— *Voters, Patrons and Parties: The Unreformed Electorate of Hanoverian England 1734–1832* (Oxford, 1989).
O'Keefe, C. B., *Contemporary Reactions to the Enlightenment (1728–1762)* (Paris, 1974).
Olszewicz, W., 'Bibljoteka króla Stanisława Augusta', *Przegląd Bibljoteczny*, 5 (1931).
Opaliński, E., 'Między "liberum veto" a głosowaniem większościowym: Funkcjonowanie semu w latach 1587–1648', in T. Chynczewska-Hennel *et al.* (eds.), *Między wschodem a zachodem: Rzeczpospolita XVI–XVIII w.: Studia ofiarowane Zbigniewowi Wójcikowi . . .* (Warsaw, 1993).
Országh, L., '"Anglomania" in Hungary, 1780–1900', *New Hungarian Quarterly*, 22 (1981).
Owen, J. B., *The Rise of the Pelhams* (London, 1957).
—— 'George II Reconsidered', in A. Whiteman *et al.* (eds.), *Statesmen, Scholars, and Merchants* (Oxford, 1973).
Ozimek, S., 'Kto był Theatralski?', *Pamiętnik Teatralny*, 5 (1956).

Palmer, R. R., *The Age of the Democratic Revolution* (2 vols., Princeton, NJ, 1959–63).

Pares, R., *King George III and the Politicians* (Oxford, 1953).

—— *Limited Monarchy in Great Britain in the Eighteenth Century* (Historical Association pamphlet, London, 1957).

Pasierb, J. S., 'Religijność polska w okresie Oświecenia', in M. M. Drozdowski (ed.), *Życie kulturalne i religijność w czasach Stanisława Augusta* (Warsaw, 1991).

Pawlikowska-Brożek, Z., 'Matematyka w szkołach głównych Komisji Edukacji Narodowej', in K. Mrozowska and R. Dutkowa (eds.), *W kręgu wielkiej reformy: Sesja naukowa na uniwersytecie Jagiellońskim w dwusetną rocznicę powstania Komisji Edukacji Narodowej 24–26 Października 1973* (Warsaw, 1977).

Pawłowiczowa, J., 'Jeszcze o Teatralskim', *Pamiętnik Teatralny*, 15 (1966).

Pilat, R., *O literaturze politycznéj Sejmu Czteroletniego (1788–1792)* (Cracow, 1872).

Platt, J., *'Zabawy Przyjemne i Pożyteczne' 1770–1777: Zarys monografii pierwszego polskiego czasopisma literackiego* (Gdańsk, 1986).

Pocock, J. G. A., *Virtue, Commerce and History: Essays on Political Thought and History, chiefly in the Eighteenth Century* (Cambridge, 1985).

—— 'Clergy and Commerce: The Conservative Enlightenment in England', in R. Ajello *et al.* (eds.), *L'età dei lumi: Studi storici sul settecento europeo in onore di Franco Venturi* (vol. 1; Naples, 1985).

Pokora, J., *Obraz Najjaśniejszego Pana Stanisława Augusta (1764–1770): Studium z ikonografii władzy* (Warsaw, 1993).

Pomeau, R., *D'Arouet à Voltaire 1694–1734* (*Voltaire et son temps*, vol. 1; Oxford, 1985).

—— *'Écraser l'infâme' 1759–1770* (*Voltaire et son temps*, vol. 4; Oxford, 1994).

—— *On a voulu l'enterrer 1770–1791* (*Voltaire et son temps*, vol. 5; Oxford, 1994).

Porter, R., 'The Enlightenment in England', in R. Porter and M. Teich (eds.), *The Enlightenment in National Context* (Cambridge, 1981).

Prószyńska, Z., *Zegary Stanisława Augusta* (Warsaw, 1994).

Proudfoot, J., 'Artificial stone', in J. Turner (ed.), *The Dictionary of Art* (34 vols.; London, 1996), vol. 2.

Przeździecki, R., *Diplomatic Ventures and Adventures: Some Experiences of British Envoys at the Court of Poland* (London, 1953).

Przyboś, A., 'Gordon de Huntlej, Henryk', *PSB* (vol. 8; Wrocław, 1959–60).

Quest-Ritson, C., *The English Garden Abroad* (London, 1992).

Raeff, M., 'The Empress and the Vinerian Professor: Catherine II's projects of government reforms and Blackstone's *Commentaries*', *OSP*, new series, 7 (1974).

Rattansi, P., 'Newton and the Wisdom of the Ancients' in J. Fauvel *et al.* (eds.), *Let Newton Be!* (Oxford, 1988).

Ricken, U., *Linguistics, Anthropology and Philosophy in the French Enlightenment: Language Theory and Ideology* (London, 1994).

Roberts, M., '19 August 1772: An Ambivalent Revolution', in R. Ajello *et al.* (eds.), *L'età dei lumi: Studi storici sul settecento europeo in onore di Franco Venturi* (vol. 1; Naples, 1985).

—— *The Age of Liberty: Sweden 1719–1772* (Cambridge, 1986).

Robertson, J., 'Franco Venturi's Enlightenment', in *Past and Present*, 137 (1992).

Roos, H., 'Ständewesen im parlamentarische Verfassung in Polen 1505–1772', in D. Gerhard (ed.), *Ständische Vertretungen in Europa im 17. und 18. Jahrhundert* (Göttingen, 1969).

Rose, W. J., *Stanislas Konarski, Reformer of Education in XVIIIth Century Poland* (London, 1929).

Rosner, A., 'Mniszech, Michał Jerzy', *PSB* (vol. 21; Wrocław, 1972).

—— 'Wolność polska rozmową Polaka z Francuzem roztrząśniona', in A. Mączak *et al.* (eds.), *Francja–Polska XVIII–XIX w: Studia z dziejów kultury i polityki poświęcone Profesorowi Andrzejowi Zahorskiemu . . .* (Warsaw, 1983).

Rostworowski, E., *Sprawa aukcji wojska na tle sytuacji politycznej przed Sejmem Czteroletnim* (Warsaw, 1957).

—— *Legendy i fakty XVIII wieku* (Warsaw, 1963).

—— *Ostatni król Rzeczypospolitej: Geneza i upadek Konstytucji 3 Maja* (Warsaw, 1966).

—— '"Myśli polityczne" Józefa Wybickiego, czyli droga od konfederacji barskiej do obiadów czwartkowych', in A. Bukowski (ed.), *Józef Wybicki: Księga zbiorowa* (Gdańsk, 1975).

—— 'Republikanizm polski i anglosaski w XVIII wieku', *Miesięcznik Literacki*, 11, nos. 7–8 (1976).

—— *Historia powszechna: Wiek XVIII* (1977, 3rd edn., Warsaw, 1984).

—— 'Czasy saskie i Oświecenie', in J. Tazbir (ed.), *Zarys Historii Polski* (Warsaw, 1980).

—— *Maj 1791–maj 1792: Rok monarchii konstytucyjnej* (Warsaw, 1985).

—— *Popioły i korzenie: Szkice historyczne i rodzinne* (Cracow, 1985).

—— 'Ilu było w Rzeczypospolitej obywateli szlachty?', *KwH*, 94 (1987).

—— 'Religijność i polityka wyznaniowa Stanisława Augusta', in M. M. Drozdowski (ed.), *Życie kulturalne i religijność w czasach Stanisława Augusta* (Warsaw, 1991).

Rottermund, A., *Zamek warszawski w epoce Oświecenia: Rezydencja monarsza: Funkcje i treści* (Warsaw, 1989).

—— 'Stanislaus Augustus as Patron of the Arts', in *Treasures of a Polish King: Stanislaus Augustus as Patron and Collector* (Catalogue of the exhibition at the Dulwich Picture Gallery, 1992).

Roszkowska, W., 'Polacy w rzymskiej "Arkadii" (1699–1766)', *Pam. Lit.*, 56 (1965).

Rudnicka, J., *Biblioteka Ignacego Potockiego* (Wrocław, 1953).

—— 'Z genealogii "Monitora" z roku 1763', *Pam. Lit.*, 46 (1955).

—— 'W związku z artykułem Zofii Sinko "Powieść w Polsce stanisławowskiej"', *Pam. Lit.*, 58 (1967).

Rusinowa, I., 'Wpływ Konstytucji Stanów Zjednoczonych Ameryki Północnej na Konstytucję 3 Maja', *Niepodległość*, 3/4 (1991).

Rymszyna, M., *Gabinet Stanisława Augusta* (Warsaw, 1962).

Salmonowicz, S., 'The Toruń Uproar of 1724', *APH*, 47 (1983).

Bibliography

Salmonowicz, S., 'Prawa człowieka w Konstytucji 3 Maja a tradycje wolnościowe demokracji szlacheckiej', in A. Grześkowiak-Krwawicz (ed.), *Konstytucja 3 Maja: Prawo—Polityka—Symbol: Materiały z sesji Polskiego Towarzystwa Historycznego na Zamku Królewskim w Warszawie 6–7 maja 1991* (Warsaw, 1992).

Sawicka, F., 'Uroczystości dla uczczenia pierwszej rocznicy Konstytucji 3 Maja', in T. Kostkiewiczowa (ed.), *'Rok Monarchii Konstytucyjnej': Piśmiennictwo polskie lat 1791–1792 wobec Konstytucji 3 Maja* (Warsaw, 1992).

Schama, S., *Citizens: A Chronicle of the French Revolution* (London, 1989).

Schlegel, D. B., *Shaftesbury and the French Deists* (Chapel Hill, NC, 1956).

Schofield, R. E., 'Priestley, Joseph', in *Dictionary of Scientific Biography* (vol. 11; New York, 1975).

Scott, H. M., 'France and the Polish Throne 1763–1764', *SEER*, 53 (1975).

—— 'Great Britain, Poland and the Russian Alliance 1763–1767', *HJ*, 19 (1976).

—— *British Foreign Policy in the Age of the American Revolution* (Oxford, 1990).

Scott, H. M. (ed.), *Enlightened Absolutism: Reform and Reformers in later Eighteenth-Century Europe* (London, 1990).

Serczyk, W., *Kultura rosyjska XVIII wieku* (Wrocław, 1984).

Shackleton, R., *Montesquieu: A Critical Biography* (Oxford, 1961).

Shklar, J., *Montesquieu* (Oxford, 1987).

Shvidkovsky, D., *The Empress and the Architect: British Architecture and Gardens at the Court of Catherine the Great* (New Haven and London, 1996).

Sidorowicz, S., 'Czartoryska, Izabella z Morsztynów', *PSB* (vol. 4; Cracow, 1938).

Sinko, Z., *'Monitor' wobec angielskiego 'Spectatora'* (Wrocław, 1956).

—— *Powieść angielska osiemnastego wieku a powieść polska lat 1764–1830* (Warsaw, 1961).

—— 'Powieść zachodnioeuropejska w Polsce stanisławowskiej na podstawie inwentarzy bibliotecznych i katalogów', *Pam. Lit.*, 57 (1966).

—— 'Ignacy Krasicki tłumaczem Osjana', *Pam. Lit.*, 61 (1970).

—— 'Z zagadnień recepcji "Sądu ostatecznego" i "Myśli nocnych" Edwarda Younga', *Pam. Lit.*, 65 (1974).

—— *Oświeceni wśród pól elizejskich: Rozmowy zmarłych: Recepcja—twórczość oryginalna* (Wrocław, 1976).

—— 'Polskie przekłady *Pilgrim's Progress* Johna Bunyana', *Pam. Lit.*, 68 (1977).

—— 'Kontakty literackie z zagranicą', in T. Kostkiewiczowa (ed.), *Słownik literatury polskiego Oświecenia* (2nd edn., Wrocław, 1991).

—— 'Osjanizm', in T. Kostkiewiczowa (ed.), *Słownik literatury polskiego Oświecenia* (2nd edn., Wrocław, 1991).

—— 'Youngizm', in T. Kostkiewiczowa (ed.), *Słownik literatury polskiego Oświecenia* (2nd edn., Wrocław, 1991).

—— *Twórczość Johna Miltona w Oświeceniu polskim* (Warsaw, 1992).

Smoleński, W., *Przewrót umysłowy w Polsce wieku XVIII: Studia historyczne* [1890] (4th edn., Warsaw, 1979).

—— *Monteskjusz w Polsce wieku XVIII* (Warsaw, 1927).

Smout, T. C., *A History of the Scottish People 1560–1830* (1969, repr. London, 1985).

Snopek, J., *Objawienie i Oświecenie: Z dziejów libertynizmu w Polsce* (Wrocław, 1986).

Sroczyńska, K., *Podróże malownicze Zygmunta Vogla* (Warsaw, 1980).

Spurr, J., '"Latitudinarianism" and the Restoration Church', *HJ*, 31 (1988).

Stasiewicz-Jasiukowa, I., 'Wartości wychowawcze podręczników do nauki moralnej', in K. Mrozowska and R. Dutkowa (eds.), *W kręgu wielkiej reformy: Sesja naukowa na uniwersytecie Jagiellońskim w dwusetną rocznicę powstania Komisji Edukacji Narodowej 24–26 Października 1973* (Warsaw, 1977).

Staszewski, J., 'Pomysły reformatorskie czasów Augusta II', *KwH*, 82 (1975).

—— *Polacy w osiemnastowiecznym Dreźnie* (Wrocław, 1986).

—— 'La Culture polonaise durant la crise du XVIIIe siècle', *APH*, 55 (1987).

—— *August III Sas* (Wrocław, 1989).

—— 'Reformowanie Rzeczypospolitej przed Sejmem Wielkim', in A. Grześkowiak-Krwawicz (ed.), *Konstytucja 3 Maja: Prawo—Polityka—Symbol: Materiały z sesji Polskiego Towarzystwa Historycznego na Zamku Królewskim w Warszawie 6–7 maja 1991* (Warsaw, 1992).

—— 'Między Wiedniem a Petersburgiem: Uwagi na temat międzynarodowego położenia Rzeczypospolitej w XVII–XVIII w.', in T. Chynczewska-Hennel *et al.* (eds.), *Między Wschodem a Zachodem: Rzeczpospolita XVI–XVIII w. Studia ofiarowane Zbigniewowi Wójcikowi . . .* (Warsaw, 1993).

—— 'Co się wydarzyło na sejmie w Grodnie w 1744 roku?', in K. Iwanicka *et al.* (eds.), *Parlament, Prawo, Ludzie: Studia ofiarowane Profesorowi Juliuszowi Bardachowi . . .* (Warsaw, 1996).

Stone, D., *Polish Politics and National Reform 1775–1788* (Boulder, Col., 1976).

Stroynowski, A., 'Sprawa reform królewszczyzn w kulturze polskiego Oświecenia', *Acta Universitatis Lodziensis. ZNUŁ*, Seria I, 8 (1978).

—— 'Emfiteutyczna reforma królewszczyzn', *Czasopismo Prawno-Historyczne*, 33 (1981).

Sutherland, L. S. and Mitchell, L. G. (eds.), *The History of the University of Oxford*, vol. 5, *The Eighteenth Century* (Oxford, 1986).

Swann, J., 'The French Nobility 1715–1789', in H. M. Scott (ed.), *The European Nobilities in the Seventeenth and Eighteenth Centuries*, vol. 1, *Western Europe* (London, 1995).

Sykes, N., *Church and State in England in the XVIIIth Century* (Cambridge, 1934).

Szcząska, Z., 'Odpowiedzialność prawna ministrów w państwach konstytucyjnych XVIII–XIX wieku', in A. Zahorski (ed.), *Wiek XVIII: Polska i świat: Księga poświęcona Bogusławowi Leśnodorskiemu* (Warsaw, 1974).

—— 'Ustawa Rządowa 3 maja', *Niepodległość*, 3/4 (1991).

Szczepaniec, J., 'Metryka wydawnicza "Monitora" z 1763 roku', *Pam. Lit.*, 57 (1966).

Szczygielski, W., 'Polska kultura republikańska XVI–XVIII wieku', *Rocznik Łódzki*, 32 (1982).

Szczygielski, W., 'Konstytucja 3 Maja', in A. Barszczewska-Krupa (ed.), *Konstytucja 3 Maja w tradycji i kulturze polskiej* (Łódź, 1991).
—— *Referendum trzeciomajowe: Sejmiki lutowe 1792 roku* (Łódź, 1994).
Szybiak, I., 'Edukacja Stanisława Grabowskiego w świetle korespondencji Stanisława Augusta', *Wiek Oświecenia*, 9, *Pamięci Profesora Emanuela Rostworowskiego* (1993).
Ślusarska, M., 'Konstytucja 3 Maja w kaznodziejstwie okolicznościowym lat 1791–1792', in T. Kostkiewiczowa (ed.), *'Rok Monarchii Konstytucyjnej': Piśmiennictwo polskie lat 1791–1792 wobec Konstytucji 3 Maja* (Warsaw, 1992).
Targosz, K., *Jan Heweliusz: uczony—artysta* (Wrocław, 1986).
—— *Jan III Sobieski mecenasem nauk i uczonych* (Wrocław, 1991).
Taswell-Langmead, *English Constitutional History from the Teutonic Conquest to the Present Time* (11th edn., London, 1960).
Tatarkiewicz, W., *Łazienki warszawskie* (Warsaw, 1968).
—— 'Sztuka Stanisława Augusta a klasycyzm', in *Klasycyzm: Studia nad sztuką polska XVIII i XIX wieku* (Wrocław, 1968).
—— *O filozofii i sztuce: W setną rocznicę urodzin* (Warsaw, 1986).
Tazbir, J., 'Stosunek do obcych w dobie baroku', in Z. Stefanowska (ed.), *Swojskość i cudzoziemszczyzna w dziejach kultury polskiej* (Warsaw, 1973).
—— 'Wazowie i Barok', in J. Tazbir (ed.), *Zarys Historii Polski* (Warsaw, 1980).
—— 'Elżbieta I Tudor w opinii staropolskiej', *Odrodzenie i Reformacja w Polsce*, 34 (1989).
Thacker, C., 'Voltaire and Rousseau: Eighteenth-Century Gardeners', *Studies on Voltaire and the Eighteenth Century*, 90 (1972).
Thornton, P., *Authentic Decor: The Domestic Interior 1620–1920* (New York, 1984).
Torrey, N. L., *Voltaire and the English Deists* (1930, repr. Oxford, 1963).
Vaillot, R., *Avec Madame du Châtelet 1734–1749* (*Voltaire et son temps*, vol. 2; Oxford, 1988).
Venturi, F., *Utopia and Reform in the Enlightenment* (Cambridge, 1971).
—— *Italy and the Enlightenment: Studies in a Cosmopolitan Century* (London, 1972).
—— *The End of the Old Regime in Europe 1768–1776: The First Crisis* (Princeton, NJ, 1989).
—— *The End of the Old Regime in Europe 1776–1789*, vol. 1, *The Great States of the West*, vol. 2, *Republican Patriotism and the Empires of the East* (Princeton, NJ, 1991).
Wachowski, M., 'L'agriculture polonaise dans l'orbite des influences internationales de 1750 à 1830', in *Actes du XIe Congrès International d'Histoire des Sciences . . .* (vol. 5; Wrocław, 1968).
Wade, I. O., *The Clandestine Organization and Diffusion of Philosophic Ideas in France from 1700 to 1750* (Princeton, NJ, 1938).
—— *The Structure and Form of the French Enlightenment* (2 vols.; Princeton, NJ, 1977).
Walicki, A., *The Enlightenment and the Birth of Modern Nationhood: Polish Political Thought from Noble Republicanism to Tadeusz Kościuszko* (Notre Dame, Ind., 1989).

—— *Trzy patriotyzmy* (Warsaw, 1991).

Wallis, M., *Canaletto: malarz Warszawy* (7th edn.; Warsaw, 1983).

Wasylewski, S., *Na dworze króla Stasia* (Lwów, 1919).

Waterfield, G., 'Galeria obrazów w Dulwich' and 'Fakty, plotki i dwieście skrzyń przedniego węgierskiego wina: Listy Noela Desenfansa do prymasa Polski', in *Kolekcja dla Króla* (Catalogue of the exhibition of paintings from the Dulwich Picture Gallery at the Royal Castle, Warsaw, 1992).

Western, J. R., *The English Militia in the Eighteenth Century: The History of a Political Issue 1660–1802* (London, 1965, repr. 1994).

Wierzbicka-Michalska, K., *Teatr w Polsce w XVIII wieku* (vol. 1 of T. Sivert (ed.), *Dzieje teatru polskiego* (Warsaw, 1977).

Wilson, A. M., *Diderot* (London, 1973).

—— 'The Enlightenment Came First to England', in S. B. Baxter (ed.), *England's Rise to Greatness 1660–1760* (Berkeley, Calif., 1983).

Włodek, J., *Dwa szkice z historji stosunków polsko-angielskich w dziedzinie agronomji* (Cracow, 1921).

Wojakowski, J., *Straż Praw* (Warsaw, 1982).

—— *Biblioteka królewskiego Korpusu Kadetów w Warszawie* (Warsaw, 1989).

Wójcik, Z., *Jan Sobieski 1629–1696* (Warsaw, 1983).

Wolff, L., *The Vatican and Poland in the Age of the Partitions: Diplomatic and Cultural Encounters at the Warsaw Nunciature* (Boulder, Col., 1988).

—— *Inventing Eastern Europe: The Map of Civilization on the Mind of the Enlightenment* (Stanford, Calif., 1994).

Wołoszyńska, Z., 'Adam Kazimierz Czartoryski' in T. Kostkiewiczowa and Z. Goliński (eds.), *Pisarze polskiego Oświecenia* (vol. 1; Warsaw, 1992).

Wyleżyńska, J., 'Mezzotinta angielska', in J. Białostocki and I. Kołoszyńska (eds.), *Polska i Anglia: Stosunki kulturalno-artystyczne: Pamiętnik wystawy sztuki angielskiej* (Warsaw, 1974).

Yolton, J. W., *Locke and French Materialism* (Oxford, 1991).

Yorke, P. C., *The Life and Correspondence of Philip Yorke, Earl of Hardwicke, Lord High Chancellor of England* (3 vols.; Cambridge, 1913).

Żaboklicki, K., *Ferdynand Galiani (1728–1787): Życie i Twórczość* (Wrocław, 1966).

Zahorski, A., *Centralne instytucje policyjne w Polsce w dobie rozbiorów* (Warsaw, 1959).

—— *Stanisław August polityk* (2nd edn., Warsaw, 1966).

—— *Spór o Stanisława Augusta* (Warsaw, 1988).

Zajewski, W., *Józef Wybicki* (3rd edn., Warsaw, 1989).

Zamoyski, A., *The Polish Way: A Thousand-Year History of the Poles and their Culture* (London, 1987).

—— *The Last King of Poland* (London, 1992).

Zawadzki, W. H., *A Man of Honour: Adam Czartoryski as a Statesman of Russia and Poland 1795–1831* (Oxford, 1993).

Zgorzelska, A., *Powrót króla* (Warsaw, 1991).

Zielińska, Z., 'Poniatowski, Michał', *PSB* (vol. 27; Wrocław, 1983).

Zielińska, Z., *Walka 'Familii' o reformę Rzeczypospolitej 1743–1752* (Warsaw, 1983).
—— *Republikanizm spod znaku buławy: Publicystyka Seweryna Rzewuskiego 1788–1790* (Warsaw, 1988).
—— *'O Sukcesyi Tronu w Polszcze' 1787–1790* (Warsaw, 1991).
—— 'Publicystyka pro- i antysukcesyjna w początkach Sejmu Wielkiego' in J. Kowecki (ed.), *Sejm Czteroletni i jego tradycje* (Warsaw, 1991).
—— 'Rzewuski, Wacław', *PSB* (vol. 34; Wrocław, 1992).
—— 'Początek rosyjskiej niełaski Czartoryskich i "słabość" Stanisława Augusta', in Ł. Kądziela *et al.* (eds.), *Trudne stulecia: Studia z dziejów XVII i XVIII wieku ofiarowane Profesorowi Jerzemu Michalskiemu . . .* (Warsaw, 1994).
Zienkowska, K., *Sławetni i urodzeni: Ruch polityczny mieszczaństwa w dobie sejmu Czteroletniego* (Warsaw, 1976).
——'Sukcesja tronu w Ustawie Rządowej 3 Maja 1791 roku—koncepcja władzy czy symbol suwerennosci?', in A. Grześkowiak-Krwawicz (ed.), *Konstytucja 3 Maja: Prawo—Polityka—Symbol: Materiały z sesji Polskiego Towarzystwa Historycznego na Zamku Królewskim w Warszawie 6–7 maja 1991* (Warsaw, 1992).
—— 'W obliczu klęski—czyli co warto ratować? Epizod warszawsko-grodzieński', in Ł. Kądziela *et al.* (eds.), *Trudne stulecia: Studia z dziejów XVII i XVIII wieku ofiarowane Profesorowi Jerzemu Michalskiemu . . .* (Warsaw, 1994).
Ziętarska, J., 'Przekład—adapcja', in T. Kostkiewiczowa (ed.), *Słownik literatury polskiego Oświecenia* (2nd edn., Wrocław, 1991).

Unpublished secondary sources

Barnouw, J., 'The Contribution of the English—and English—to Voltaire's Enlightenment' (paper delivered at the conference *Voltaire et ses combats*, Oxford, 30 Sept. 1994, to be published in *Studies on Voltaire and the Eighteenth Century*).
Chomicki, G., 'Wpływy angielskie w publicystyce politycznej obozu reform w Rzeczypospolitej od wydania "O skutecznym rad sposobie" do upadku Kodeksu Zamoyskiego (1761–1780)', MA thesis (Cracow, 1984).
Gołębiowska, Z., 'Wpływy angielskie na Puławach na przełomie XVIII i XIX wieku', doctoral thesis (Marie Curie-Skłodowska University, Lublin, 1982).
Grobis, J., 'Sukcesja tronu w publicystyce Sejmu Czteroletniego', doctoral thesis (Łódź, 1975).
Haupt, K., 'Recepja poglądów Johna Locke'a przez Stanisława Konarskiego', MA thesis (Łódź, 1964).
Israel, J., 'Who began the European Enlightenment: The English or the Dutch?' (paper given at the Early Modern Europe seminar in Oxford, 13 Oct. 1995).
Konopczyński, W., 'Polscy pisarze polityczni XVIII wieku', vol. 2 (unpublished typescript in BJag. Akc. 52/61, microfilm lent by Professor Z. Zielińska).
Ślusarska, M., 'Problematyka polityczno-społeczna w polskim kaznodziejstwie okolicznościowym w latach 1775–1795', doctoral thesis (Warsaw, 1992).

INDEX

absolute monarchy, absolutism 15, 163, 165, 278, 314
  see also despotism; enlightened absolutism; France, absolutism
Achenwall, Gottfried 47
Act of Settlement (1701) 296
Acta Eruditorum 39
Adam, James 200, 205
Adam, Robert 194, 200, 205, 216–17
Adams, John 140
Addison, Joseph 41 n., 43–5, 53, 98, 173, 179–80, 187–8, 229
aesthetics 70
Ainslie, Sir Robert 220
Aix-la-Chapelle, peace of (1748) 82
Albemarle, William, 2nd Earl of 104
Albertrandi, Jan 183–4
Aleksandrowska, Elżbieta, historian 166 n., 181
Alembert, Jean le Rond d' 49, 230
Alexander the Great 184
Alexandria 180
Alexandria, garden 196
Alexandrowicz 175 n.
Algarotti, Francesco 49, 228
Allaire, Jacques, Abbé 80–2
Allen, Sir Ralph 98, 113, 215 n.
America:
  Constitution 271, 276, 290–1, 299
  Indians 184
  Polish reaction to Revolution 164–5, 265, 270–2, 278, 280, 282 n.
  Revolution, War of Independence 58, 61–3, 130, 140–1
Amsterdam 43, 193
Anglophilia, Anglomania:
  in Europe 43–64, 89, 108, 313–15
  in Poland 9–11, 65–73 *passim*, 76, 136, 137, 182–3, 185, 193–9, 243, 312–15, 319
Anglophobia 60–1, 68–70, 73
Anhalt-Dessau, Leopold III Frederick, Prince of 55
Anne, Queen of England 17
Anne Boleyn, Queen of England 218
Annet, Peter 48

Anson, George, Admiral 111–12, 117, 233
Antonowicz, Julian 175
Apollo 82, 206, 215
Arcadian Academy 68
Archenholtz, Johann Wilhelm von 58, 185, 186 n., 270
Archetti, Giovanni, nuncio 262
architecture 68–9, 191, 194–6, 198, 201–17, 240
Ardell 220
Aristotle 38, 229, 243
Arkadia, garden 196, 198
Artois, Charles, Count of 53
Arundel, William Ignatius 174 n.
Askenazy, Szymon, historian 7, 276 n.
assessory courts (*assessoria*) 157
astronomy 72, 232–6, 242–4
atheism 42, 50, 224 n.
Atterbury, Francis, Bishop 98
Au, botanist 236–7
Aubert, Alexandre 233
Augustus II, King of Poland (1697–1706, 1709–33) 24, 27, 32, 160, 193
  and the *Familia* 73–4
  reform plans 66, 68
Augustus III, King of Poland (1733–63) 20, 66–7, 88, 118, 149, 155, 161 n., 163
  and the *Familia* 75–6, 148, 154
Austen, Jane 99
Austria, Habsburg Monarchy:
  and England 91, 97, 126–7
  Nemesis Theresiana (1768) 261
  and Poland 25 n., 76–7, 126–7, 155, 169, 246–7, 251, 312
  and Russia 275, 310–11

Baalbek (Heliopolis) 199, 213
Bacciarelli, Marcello 201, 206
Bacon, Francis 29, 38, 49, 71, 228–9
Bank of England 23, 153, 270
Bar, confederacy of (1768–72) 6, 170, 192, 245–6
  propaganda *vs* Stanisław August 86, 97, 121
Barker, Robert 234

Barlow, Joel 141, 145
baroque 26, 80, 192, 195, 201, 215–16
Barrington, William, Viscount 107, 108
Bartolozzi, engraver 220
Basilian order 175
Bastille 47, 307
Bath 113, 117, 199
Bath, Earl of, *see* Pulteney
Bayle, Pierre 37
Beaujeu, Count 112 n.
Beccaria, Cesare 61
Bedford, John, 7th Duke of 115
Beefsteak club 133
Bellotto, Bernardo (known in Poland as
    Canaletto) 204, 221
Belorussia viii, 246, 310
Benedict XIV, Pope 71
Benoît, Gédéon 169
Bentley, Richard 39
Berlin 87
Bernacki, Ludwik, historian 9, 81, 180
Bernoulli, Johann 220
Białłozor, Mateusz 67 n.
Białystok 68, 91
Bibliothèque universelle 40
Bignon, abbé 38
Birmingham 235
Black Sea 246
Blackstone, William 59, 62
    influence in Poland 182, 260–1, 269,
    273, 274, 277
Blair, Hugh 227–8
Bogucicki, Jan Kanty 174, 243
Bogusławski, Konstanty 270
Bohemia 19, 23, 279
Bohemian Brethren 29
Bohomolec, Franciszek 69, 181, 189
Bolingbroke, Henry, 1st Viscount 51,
    107 n., 188, 259–60, 261
Bolingbroke, Frederick, 2nd Viscount
    107
booksellers 12, 68–9, 174–5
Borkowska-Bagieńska, Ewa, historian 261
botanical gardens 236, 243
Boulainvilliers, Henri de 26, 45
Boulton, Matthew 235
Bourgeois, Sir Peter Francis 198, 217–19
Boyer, Abel 37, 43, 173
Boyle, Robert 38, 39, 41–2
Brancas, Adelaide Geneviève Félicité,
    Duchess of 104
Branicka, Izabella, née Poniatowska 136,
    230

Branicki, Jan Klemens, Hetman 68, 91,
    121, 156, 157
Branicki, Xawery, Hetman 130, 254–5,
    275, 310
Brewer, John, historian 18
Brissot de Warville, Jacques-Pierre 61
British Empire 3, 165
Broglie, Marquise de, née Besenval 105 n.
Brown, Lancelot, 'Capability' 54, 114,
    197, 213
Brożek, Jan 30
Brühl, Fryderyk 196
Brühl, Heinrich, Count 76, 83, 92, 148,
    155
Brühl, Moritz 131, 232
Brühl, Countess, née Bielińska 88, 104
Brutus, Marcus Julius 98
Brydon 184
Buchholtz, Ludwig von 275
Buffier, Claude 41
Bukaty, Franciszek 100, 133–4, 137, 139,
    142–4, 198, 218, 234–5, 290 n., 295 n.
    commissions for king and others 133,
    194, 210, 220–1, 230, 237
    reports on English government and
    society 261, 263–9, 273, 289
Bukaty, Tadeusz 133–4, 210, 218, 233,
    243
Bulgaria 3 n.
Bunyan, John 33
Burges, James Bland 139–40, 142
Burke, Edmund 142–5, 303–4
    'Lord' 279
Burtt, Shelley, historian 19 n.
Burzyński, Tadeusz 131–3, 218, 232, 234
Butrymowicz, Mateusz 291 n.
Bykowski, Ignacy 183
Byron, George Gordon, Lord 64, 312
Bystrzycki, Jowin 231–2, 236

cabinet (English) 151, 160–1, 281, 298,
    318
cabinet (*gabinet*) 160–1, 263, 266
cadet school 130, 163, 173, 186, 239–40,
    241, 316
Calais 105
Cambridge 30, 119, 139, 234
Cambridge, Richard Owen 113
cameralism 67
Cameron, Charles 55
Campbell, Colen 195
Canaletto, *see* Bellotto
Cannon, John, historian 10, 48 n.

cannon foundry 163
Canterbury 105
Canton 204
cardinal laws 169, 255
Carteret, Viscount (later Granville) 50,
    108, 118, 256
Cartesianism, *see* Descartes
Carthage 61
Casimir III the Great, King of Poland
    (1333–70) 5, 192–3, 200–1, 317
Cassiobury 110
Catherine of Braganza, Queen of England
    218
Catherine II the Great, Tsaritsa of Russia
    138–9, 160, 165
    Anglophilia of 55, 59–60, 233, 314
    policy towards Poland: (1762–8) 147–8,
        155–8, 168–70; (1768–88) 246, 251,
        255, 258; (1788–96) 275, 310–11,
        317
    affair with S. A. Poniatowski 86, 93–4, 147
    relations with Stanisław August 128,
        144, 161, 206–8, 249–50, 251, 255
    meeting with Stanisław August at
        Kaniów (1787) 138, 200, 275
Catholicism, Catholics, Roman Catholic
    Church:
    and the Enlightenment 40–3, 46, 56,
        68–73, 223–9, 241–4
    challenges to in Poland 67, 166–70
    hegemony in Poland 26, 29–34, 37
    place in reformed Commonwealth
        240–1, 264, 291, 298, 307
    situation of in Britain 29–33, 77, 133–4,
        167, 267, 273
Chambers, Sir William 196–8, 200, 203
chancellors 20, 150, 157, 297
Chandler 200
Charlemont, James, 1st Earl of 163
Charles I, King of England 98, 163, 218
Charles II, King of England 18, 32, 163,
    177, 218
Charles XI, King of Sweden 159
Charles XII, King of Sweden 70, 73, 159,
    184
Charles, Jacques-Alexandre 235
Chartres, Philippe, Duke of 53
Châtelet, Madame du 49
Chatham, 1st Earl of, *see* Pitt the elder
chemistry 235
Chernyshev, Alexander 132
Chesterfield, Philip, 4th Earl of 50, 53,
    108–9, 117, 120, 176

chinoiserie 55, 114, 194, 196–7, 200,
    203–4, 222
Chippendale, Thomas 193, 200
Chiswick 54
Chlebowski, Wawrzyniec 31
Chmielowski, Benedykt 33
Chreptowicz, Joachim 131, 134, 234, 241,
    258–9, 298
Christ 226–7
Christianity 48–50, 97, 223–8, 244
Christie, Thomas 142–3
Chróścikowski, Samuel 71–2
Church of England 25–6, 48, 114, 225,
    227, 244, 279
Churchill, Sir Winston 3 n.
Chute, John 109
Cicero, Marcus Tullius 80, 98
Cieszkowski, Krzysztof 226 n.
Cirey 49
civil list 169–70, 278–9, 289, 334
Cizes, Emmanuel de 51
Clarendon, Edward, 1st Earl of 98
Clark, Jonathan, historian 10
Clarke, Samuel 39, 41, 48–9
classical republicanism 5, 19
classicism (literature) 178, 190
    for art, *see* neo-classicism
Coade stone 220
Cobham, Richard, 1st Viscount 117–18,
    188
cock-fights 102, 106–7
collegiality 151, 155, 157, 170
Collegium Nazarenum 70
Collegium Nobilium 70–2
Collins, Anthony 41, 42, 43
Collot d'Herbois, Jean Marie 181
Commission of Foreign Affairs (est. 1789)
    160
Commission for National Education 175,
    186, 240–4, 270, 286, 298
Commission of Public Accounts (English)
    18
commissions *boni ordinis* 163, 170
Commons, House of 18–19, 22–3, 116,
    118, 164, 294
    as a model for Europe 47–8, 50–2,
        62
    as a model for Poland 150, 152–3, 256,
        260, 266–8, 280, 283–4, 288, 316;
        see also Parliament
Communism 2, 3 n.
Condillac, Etienne Bonnet de 49–50,
    63–4, 223, 229, 242

Condorcet, Marie-Jean-Antoine-Nicolas Caritat de 62, 272 n.
confederacies 294, 308
Constantinople 130, 136, 140, 220
Constitution of 3 May 1791 226, 275–6
  analysis 289–303, 308–9, 318
  consequences 310–12, 318–19
  genesis 285–90, 317
  polemics for and against 304–8
  reaction abroad 133, 138, 140, 141–4, 303–4, 310
Cook, James, Captain 230, 233
Copernicus, Nicolaus 38, 71, 223, 244
Coppenhole, Mr 105
Corneille, Pierre 54, 70, 179, 180
Cornwall 235
corruption 16, 84
  English criticism of 18, 95
  European criticism of in England 45, 51, 60–1, 140, 250
  Polish fears of 32, 152–3, 248
  Polish views of in England 32, 117, 120, 152, 250–1, 260, 266, 268, 270, 278
cosmopolitanism 36–8, 53, 64, 78, 85, 122
Coste, Pierre 37, 39–40, 49
Cosway, Maria 198
Cosway, Richard 198
Counter-Reformation 26, 223
Country ideology 16–19, 188, 264–5
  influence on Konarski 152, 155
  influence on Montesquieu 50–1, 282
Court ideology 50–1
Coxe, William 55, 135, 172, 196
Cracow 1, 2, 225
  Jagiellonian University 72–3, 175, 242–3
Craven, Elizabeth, Lady 136
Crell (Crellius), Jan 30
Cromwell, Oliver 31, 98
Crown estates 21–2, 153, 158, 248, 254, 255, 306, 316
Cruikshanks, Eveline, historian 10
Culloden, battle of (1746) 107 n.
Cumberland 200
Cumberland, William, 'Butcher', Duke of 96, 107
Cuyp, Aelbert 219
Cyankiewicz, Antoni 183, 243
Czacki, Tadeusz 277, 304, 306
Czaja, Aleksander, historian 170 n., 253 n.
Czarnek, Mateusz 269
Czartoryska, Izabella, née Flemming 125, 134, 179, 194, 196–8, 235–6, 314

Czartoryska, Izabella, née Morsztyn 73–4, 78
Czartoryska, Zofia, née Sieniawska, 1 voto Denhoff 74, 193
Czartoryski, Adam Jerzy 125, 134, 236, 311
Czartoryski, Adam Kazimierz 124–6, 134, 146–8, 173–4, 289, 313
  and the cadet school 239–40
  in England 76, 122 n., 134, 197
  and *Monitor* 166–7, 186–9, 238
  and the theatre 173, 178–9, 181
Czartoryski, August 74–9, 94, 103, 125–6, 147, 161
Czartoryski, Kazimierz 73–4
Czartoryski, Józef 222, 236
Czartoryski, Michał 74–9, 83, 88 n., 161
Czartoryskis 10, 21; (1754) 92, 111, 121; (1763–8) 147–8, 161–2, 168–9
  reform plans 146–58, 170–1; *see also Familia*
Częstochowa 25

Dalrymple, John, Viscount (later 6th Earl of Stair) 137–8
Damer, Anne Seymour 198
Danby, Earl of 299
dancing 99, 240
Danzig (Gdańsk) 30, 68, 232, 259
  and British merchants 28, 69
  furniture 193
  Poniatowskis in 79–80
  Prussian designs on 138, 139, 310
Darnley, John, 4th Earl of 136
Dartmouth, William, 2nd Earl of 104
Davies, Norman, historian 3 n.
Dęblin 196, 211
Deboli, Augustyn 13, 288, 290, 303
deductive reasoning (a priori) 50, 53
Defoe, Daniel 32
  Robinson Crusoe 44, 54, 176, 182
deism, deists 30, 41–3, 48–9
  and Poland 72, 97, 224–7
Dembiński, Bronisław, historian 7, 8
Dembowski, Antoni, Bishop 66
Dembowski, Florian 175 n.
democracy 61–2
Denhoff, Stanisław 74
Denmark 60, 167, 279
Derham, William 42, 242
Des Maizeaux, Pierre 37, 42, 44
Desaguliers, Jean 45
Descartes, René, Cartesianism 38–41, 50
  and Poland 71–2, 223, 229–30, 243

Desenfans, Noel 218–19
Desnitsky, S. E. 59
despotism 118, 259, 270, 278, 284 n.
  European criticism of 47, 52, 60, 314
  fear of in Poland 157, 159–60, 285
Dickinson, engraver 220
Diderot, Denis 42–3, 50, 59–61, 230
Digby, Harry 88–9, 96, 98, 99–100, 140
Digby, Kenelm 140
Diplomatic Revolution 93–4, 97, 117
dissident question 127, 158, 167, 168–70,
  251
Divine Providence 25, 34, 80, 226–8,
  307
  church of (Warsaw) 226
divine right 19, 42, 94, 181, 323
Dłuski, Tomasz 306
Dmochowski, Franciszek 183
Dnieper, river 275
Dodington, George Bubb 106–7
'Dogrumowa affair' 125–6
Dollond 231, 234, 243
Dominican order 71
Dover 105
Downarowicz, Tadeusz 236
Downton Castle 200
drawing 240
Dresden 67, 69, 89, 90, 91, 109, 126
drunkenness 16, 84–5, 119, 188, 250, 260,
  305
Dryden, John 176, 179
duelling 184
Dughet, Gaspard 219
Duhamel, Joseph 175 n.
Dulard, Paul 42
Dulwich Picture Gallery 218
Dumarsais 43
Dupont de Nemours, Pierre Samuel 262,
  296 n.
Durell, David 234
Durini, Angelo, nuncio 226, 227 n.
Durno, James 140, 292 n., 294, 298,
  299 n., 303
Dussert de Bourgogne 112 n.

Earlom, engraver 220
East Anglia 67
'Eastern Europe' 3, 318
eclecticism 40, 71, 223
Edward I, King of England 260
Edward III, King of England 82
Edward VI, King of England 33
Effen, Justus van 43–4

Elbing (Elbląg) 30
elections, royal, *see* monarchy
Elizabeth, daughter of Frederick, Elector
  Palatine 48
Elizabeth, Tsaritsa of Russia 77, 147
Elizabeth I, Queen of England 29, 33
Elliott, engraver 220
empiricism 38–43, 48–50, 53, 71–3, 223,
  228–30
Encyclopédie 49, 50, 52–3, 60
England, Great Britain 10, 28
  agriculture 59, 67, 131, 156–7, 166,
    236–8, 260, 284
  aristocracy 15–16, 22–3, 115, 155,
    187–8, 195, 284
  armed services 18, 117, 265–6, 282,
    301–2
  art 89, 135, 315; *see also* architecture,
    furniture, gardens, painting
  and Austria 91, 97, 126–7
  Civil War 23, 31, 98
  constitution 15–19, 22–4, 27–8;
    European views of 45, 47–8, 50–3,
    57–64, 314–15; Polish views of 32–4,
    67–8, 73, 76, 125, 146–58, 168,
    170–1, 245, 257–8, 259–61, 266–309
    passim; Stanisław August and 316–19,
    (–1754) 82, 96, 102, 118, (1763–8)
    146–7, 149–55, 159, 164–5, 170–1,
    177–8, (1771–87) 247, 249–51,
    256–7, 263, 269, (1788–) 271–4,
    282–4, 287–309 *passim*
  'decline' 60–2, 120, 250, 273
  dress 194, 221
  education 109, 119–20, 167, 238–9,
    250, 316
  experience of warfare 23–8, 294
  'fiscal-military state' 18, 23–4, 27–8,
    166, 265–6
  Glorious Revolution 17, 26, 31, 95–6,
    300, 302
  heretical 31, 33–4, 167, 171, 270
  horses 53
  industry 59, 64, 235–6
  ladies 109, 144, 250
  legal system: Polish views of 131, 166,
    260–2, 269, 273, 284; European views
    of 52, 59, 60–1
  literature 43–4, 53–7, 63; influence in
    Poland 173, 177–90, 312; *see also*
    Stanisław August
  militia 170, 264–5, 316
  mobs 107–8, 273

England, Great Britain (*cont.*):
  national character 44–5, 105, 107, 250, 278
  newspapers 142
  place in Enlightenment 10–11, 37–8, 63–4
  policy regarding Poland (–1756) 28, 77–8, 87–8, 91–2, 111; (1756–97) 126–9, 137–40, 142, 144, 156, 167
  Polish visitors to 10, 125, 130–1, 134–5, 194–9, 210, 216, 220, 232–7
  political culture 17–19, 23–4, 27–8, 31, 297, 299, 305; Stanisław August and 82, 95, 102, 119–20, 250, 264–5, 278, 316, 317
  S. A. Poniatowski in (1754) 63, 81, 92, 97–8, 102–124, 188, 189, 199, 222, 273, 315
  poor relief 131, 261, 263–4, 273, 316
  'prime minister' 258, 268
  and Prussia 93–4, 96–7, 124, 138–9, 275
  radicals 142–3
  religiosity 25–6, 115, 228, 244; *see also* latitudinarianism
  and Russia 93–4, 97, 126–9, 138–9, 156, 310
  sailors 108
  sinecures 306–7
  social structure 15, 48, 139, 291–2; Polish views of 166, 188, 260, 284
  trade 15, 166, 265, 268, 278, 284
  trade with Poland 28, 138–40
English language 3, 47, 187
  knowledge of in Europe 37, 38–9, 56, 63
  knowledge of in Poland 110–11, 145, 191–6, 203, 211
engravings 182, 192, 199–200, 219–20, 230–1
enlightened absolutism 159–60, 165, 318
Enlightenment 34–8, 63–4, 68, 223, 291
  Catholic; *see* Catholicism
  Dutch 37, 39–40, 41–5, 315
  English 38, 115, 345
  French 36, 38–53, 59–63, 68, 224, 313–15
  German 40, 46–7, 57–8, 313–15
  Italian 40, 58, 68, 313–15
  'national Enlightenments' 11, 36–8
  Polish 65–6, 68–73, 183–90, 192–3, 222–44, 281, 312–19
  Russian 59–60, 314–15

Scottish 11, 57, 331
Swiss 44, 58–9
  transmission of 36–8, 68–9, 73, 315
envoys, chamber of 5, 16, 151–2, 283
  in Constitution of 3 May 293–5, 300
  chamber 201–2
Ermenonville 54, 196, 199
Eschenburg, Johann Joachim 57
esprit 44, 90, 99, 134
esprit de système 40, 53
Essex, William, 4th Earl of 89, 97, 123
Essex, Charlotte, Countess of, née Williams 110
Eugene of Savoy, Prince 42
Euthanasius, Victorinus 29
excise 18, 23, 265–6
executionist movement 316–17

Fabre, Jean, historian 7–8, 9, 81, 83 n., 100, 103 n., 127, 172, 178, 181
Familia 73–9, 119, 161, 189
  (1748–56) 83–97 *passim*, 103
  (1756–64) 124, 146–8, 156–8
  (1773–80) 252, 254
  see also Czartoryskis
Farington, Joseph 200
fencing 240
Ferguson, Adam 11
Ferney 54
Ferrers, Lord 284
Feutry 182
Fielding, Henry 98, 99, 109, 176, 183, 185, 239
Filangieri, Gaetano 62, 277, 305, 315
Filmer, Sir Robert 115 n., 164
Finch, Edward 77
Firmian, Carlo, Count 89–90
Flemming, Jacob Heinrich, Field-Marshal 66
Flemming, Jerzy, Count 91
Flernet, Jean 72
Florence 58, 132
Fontana, Jakub 203
Forster, Georg 175, 230, 233, 242
Fortescue, John 269
Fourcroy, Antoine-François de 235
Fougeret de Montbron, L.-C. 53 n.
Fox, Charles James 62, 267, 299, 301 n.
Fox, Henry 93, 95–6, 99, 116
frac, *see* frock coat
France:
  absolutism, monarchy 19, 45, 52, 112, 248, 272

Academy of Sciences 38
Anglophilia/Anglomania in 45, 53–5,
    108, 313–15
  conservatives 52–3, 60, 61–3
  crisis of late 1780s 62–3, 275
  cultural distance from Poland 3
  cultural hegemony challenged 56, 63
  drama 81, 108, 179
  dress 69, 80
  ladies 104, 109, 250
  nobility 45, 48, 51
  Poles' contacts with 68–74, 102–5,
    181–4, 194, 199, 235
  policy regarding Poland 78, 111, 126,
    155
  S. A. Poniatowski in (1753–4) 92,
    103–5, 109, 110–11, 121, 201, 222
  as a prism 11, 73, 176–7, 181–3,
    196–9, 315
  reception of English thought in 38–43
  Revolution and revolutionary wars 46,
    64, 218, 310–11; English reaction to
    139, 142–3, 160, 303–4; Polish
    reaction to 277, 279, 286, 290, 308,
    312; Stanisław August and 272–3,
    288, 293
  rivalry with England 37, 53, 56, 61–2,
    117, 155
  towns 166
Francis Stephen, Emperor 46
Franklin, Benjamin 62, 140–1, 230, 231,
    272
Fratta Polesine 195
Frederick, Elector Palatine, 'Winter King'
    of Bohemia 148
Frederick, Prince of Wales 117–18
Frederick II the Great, King of Prussia
    61, 96–7, 124, 160, 210
  and England 57, 59
  and Poland 257; (1744–56) 77, 84, 94,
    (1756–64) 147, 156, 158, 163,
    (1768–) 138, 246, 251; *see also*
    Prussia
Frederick Augustus III, Elector of Saxony
    245, 281, 296, 300
Frederick Christian, Elector of Saxony
    155
Frederick William II, King of Prussia 275
freedom of the press 57, 58
Freeholder 43, 82 n.
freemasonry 36, 45–6, 112
  in Saxony and Poland 69, 78, 130,
    136–7

Freeport, Sir Andrew 43, 187, 188
freethinking 35, 37, 42, 43, 63, 115
French language 37–45 *passim*, 49, 54–5,
    105, 108–9, 119, 313
  knowledge of in Poland 68–74 *passim*,
    175, 181, 183–4, 239–40, 269
  Stanisław August's knowledge of 81,
    97, 172–7, 181
frock coat (*frac*) 53, 106
furniture 193–4, 202, 204–10, 217, 222

Gainsborough, Margaret 210
Gainsborough, Thomas 210, 217
Galiani, Ferdinando, abbé 58
Galicia 312
Galileo Galilei 38, 71, 229
Gallois, Gauvin Jean-Antoine 272 n.
Gallophilia, Gallomania 56, 106, 108–9,
    119–20, 313
Gallophobia 56, 119–20, 313–14
Garampi, Giuseppe, papal nuncio 225 n.,
    241
Garczyński, Stefan 67–8
gardens:
  Dutch 114, 211
  English 113, 114–15, 185, 200, 207–8,
    215
  French 185, 197, 203, 211–13
  influence of English on European 53–5,
    196–7, 200
  influence of English on Polish 196–8,
    200, 203–4, 211–3, 312
Gardiner, William 140, 144
Gardner, J. 200
Garrick, David 173, 182, 185
Gassendi, Pierre 71, 229
Gay, John 184
Gazeta Warszawska 270
Gazetteer and New Daily Advertiser 107
Gdańsk, *see* Danzig
General Confederacy (1764–6) 158,
    169
general customs system (1764–5) 158
general levy (*pospolite ruszenie*) 32, 154,
    265
Geneva 61
Genoa 153
Genovesi, Antonio 71
Geoffrin, Marie-Thérèse 12, 104, 106,
    123, 144, 202, 227
Geoffroy, Etienne 39
geography 70, 172, 240
George I, King of England 22, 77

George II, King of England 22–3, 91, 107 n., 117, 153
  Stanisław August on 96, 110–11, 117–18
George III, King of England 130, 135, 164, 221
  'Farmer' 59
  and Poland 137, 144
  political role 23, 132, 267, 268, 297, 301–2, 317; and the civil list 153, 265–6; and the Fox-North coalition 62, 299
  portrait of 210, 217
German language 99, 137, 175, 240, 313
  Stanisław August's knowledge of 80
Germany 23, 45, 48, 73
  Anglophilia/Anglomania in 42–7 *passim*, 55–8, 313–15
  as a prism 185, 186 n., 193, 270, 315
  see also Holy Roman Empire
Ghigotti, Gaetano 134
Gibbs, James 217
Gierowski, Józef Andrzej, historian 4 n.
Gilibert, Jean 236
Girardin, Marquis of 54
Glasgow 59
Glayre, Maurice 12, 137, 141, 160, 205, 293
Glazer, student 234
Glemp, Józef, Primate 2
Glinka, Antoni 84
God 41, 42, 49, 72, 82, 224, 226–9, 242
  see also Christ; Christianity; Trinity
Goethe, Johann Wolfgang von 56, 57, 180
'golden freedom' 19, 26, 162, 249, 259–60
'good sense' 44, 90
Gordon, Alexander, Duke of 110
Gordon, Catherine, Lady, *see* Morsztyn, Catherine
Gordon, Fabian 134
Gordon, George, Lord 110, 133
  riots 108 n., 133, 267, 273
Gordon, Katherine, Duchess of 109–10
Gordons (Polish) 134
Goślicki (Goslicius), Wawrzyniec, Bishop 31
Gothic novels 54
gothick style 198, 202
Göttingen 46–7, 175 n.
Grabowska, Elżbieta 175 n.
Grabowski, Stanisław, Bishop 167 n.
Grabowski, Stanisław, natural son of Stanisław August 175

Grabski, Andrzej Feliks, historian 245 n.
Graces, the 82, 108, 134
Graham, Macaulay 142
Grand Tour 109, 119–20, 130
Granville, Earl of, *see* Carteret
Grassi, Giuseppe 199
Gravesande, Willem Jacob 's 39, 228
Gray, Thomas 56, 176, 182, 312
Great Northern War 6, 24–5, 27, 73
Great Poland (Wielkopolska) 21, 194, 253, 310
Greek Catholic (Uniate) Church 291
Greek literature and drama 81, 119, 172
Green Park 203
Greene, Major 136, 173–4
Greenwich 203
Gregory, David 39
Grenville, George 114
Grenvilles 114, 116–17, 118–19
Grey, Marchioness, later Countess of Hardwicke 114
Grimm, Friedrich Melchior von, Baron 59, 177, 249–50, 310
Grodno 91, 173, 230, 236, 302
  see also Seym
Grześkowiak (-Krwawicz), Anna, historian 269, 277 n., 278 n., 306 n.
Guardian 43, 82 n.
Guildford, Lady 218
Gulliver's Travels, see Swift
Gustavus III, King of Sweden 159–60, 210, 252

habeas corpus 16, 52, 57, 260, 292, 307
Habsburg Monarchy, *see* Austria
Habsburgs 1
Hadley 231
Hague, The 91, 103, 116 n., 127, 137
Hailes, Daniel 139, 140
Halfpenny, William and John 197, 200
Halle 68, 71, 72
Hallé, Noel 202
Halley, Edmond 30, 38
Hamburg 46–7
Hamilton 233
Hamilton, Anthony 177
Handel, George Frederick 110
Hanover 16, 46–7, 59, 90–1, 118
  house of 96, 277, 296
  S. A. Poniatowski in (1753) 91
Hanseatic cities 46, 57, 193
Hardwicke, Philip, 1st Earl of, Lord Chancellor 103, 111–12, 116

Hardwicke, Philip, 2nd Earl of (formerly Royston) 111, 114, 127, 231–2
Harrach, Rosa, Countess 89
Harrington, William, 1st Earl of 78
Harris, Sir James, later 1st Earl of Malmesbury 59, 130, 136–8, 173, 232
Harris, Lady 137
Harris, Miss 137, 227
Hartley, Dr 143
Hartlib, Samuel 30
Harwich 121
Hastings, Mr 81
Hastings, Warren 299
Haywood, Eliza 176
Hearne, Thomas 200
Helvétius, Claude Adrien 61, 230
Hennequin 230–1
Henry VII, King of England 82
Henry VIII, King of England 33, 62, 218, 277, 305
Herbert, Lord 135, 218
Herculaneum 213
Hercules 215
Herder, Johann Gottfried von 57
Heriot, John 142 n.
Herschel, Sir William 230, 233–5
Hertzberg, Ewald von 310
hetmans 20, 74, 285
  criticism and reforms of 150–1, 157, 254–7, 297–8, 303
Hevelius, Johann 30
Heyne, Johann 167, 189
Histoire des ouvrages des sçavans 39
history 70, 80, 119, 172, 206–8, 240
Hobbema, Meindert 219
Hodges, William 217
Hogarth, William 107 n., 220
Hohenzollerns 1, 296
Holbach, Paul Henri Thiry, Baron d' 49–50, 60
Holbein, Hans 218, 219
Holland, *see* the Netherlands
Holy Alliance 318
Holy Roman Empire (*Reich*) 16, 21, 24, 68, 126, 310
Holy Spirit 226–7
Homer 44, 176
Hooke Robert 38
Horace (Quintus Horatius Flaccus) 98, 182, 184, 223
Hornsby, Thomas 234
Houdon, Jean Antoine 224

Houghton Hall 46, 216 n.
Hube, Michael 241
Hubertusburg 88
Huguenots 36–7, 41, 45, 63, 166, 315
humanitarianism 35, 261, 263, 269
Hume, David 11, 60, 163, 224
  History of England 240, 269
  Political Discourses 239, 260, 269
Hungary 3 n., 279, 313, 314, 315
Huntly, Lewis, 3rd Marquess of 74
Husarzewski, Aleksy 259
Hutchinson, John 115 n.

impeachment 150, 299, 300
India 136
inductive reasoning (*a posteriori*), *see* empiricism
innoculation 55
instruments, scientific 71, 72, 133, 192, 230–3, 236, 240–4
interior decoration 55, 68
Ionia 200
Ireland 3 n., 61, 267, 273
Israel, Jonathan, historian 37 n.
Italian language 81
Italian opera 104
Italianate landscapes 204
Italy 19, 24, 68, 120
  Anglophilia/Anglomania in 40, 42, 44, 56, 58, 314–15
  Criticism of England in 61, 62
  Polish travellers to 68, 70, 212, 220
Ixnard 200

Jabłonna, garden, palace 196
Jacob, Margaret, historian 38 n., 45
Jacobinism 142, 144, 145, 310
Jacobites, Jacobitism 23, 33, 45, 69, 96, 228
Jagiellonian University, *see* Cracow, university
Jagiellons 5, 163
James I, King of England 29, 82
James II, King of England 18, 27, 218, 296, 300
James Francis Edward, Prince, the 'Old Pretender' 27, 77, 278
Janeczek, Stanisław, historian 71 n.
Jaroszewski, Tadeusz, historian 203
Jarzewicz, Henryk 193
Jaucourt, Louis, Chevalier de 52–3
Jefferson, Thomas 141, 272
Jeffreys, J., Dr 112 n.

Jesuit order 29, 33, 41, 71, 167, 185, 231, 240–1
colleges 26, 72, 238, 242
Jews 133, 291, 292
Jodłowski Norbert 270
John II Casimir, King of Poland (1648–68) 148 n.
John III Sobieski, King of Poland (1674–96) 20, 24, 30, 32, 74
Stanisław August and 206, 212, 232
Johnson, Edward 142 n.
Johnson, Samuel, Dr 179–81
Jones, Inigo 195, 200, 203
Jordaens, Jacob 219
Joseph II, Emperor 56, 160, 208, 246, 314
Josephinism 261
Journal des Sçavans 39, 40, 41–2, 54
Journal Encyclopédique 54
Journal Littéraire 39, 44
Jupiter 82, 191
jury system 52, 57, 301
Justices of the Peace 51, 107, 301

Kądziela, Łukasz, historian 14 n.
Kalinka, Walerian, historian 7, 275 n.
Kalkoen, Count 88
Kamieniec Podolski 220
Kamsetzer, Johann Christian 194, 203, 210–17
Kaniów (Kaniv) 138, 175, 200, 275
Kant, Immanuel 35, 50, 64, 66
Karpowicz, Michał 224
Karwicki, Stanisław Dunin 66–8
Kaunitz, Wenzel Anton, Count 246–7
Keill, John 39
Keith, Sir Robert 89–90
Keith, Sir Robert Murray 125, 126 n.
Kent, William 197
Kew 196, 198, 200
Keyserling, Hermann, Count 70, 87, 147–8, 156, 158
Kiciński, Pius 160
Kiev (Kyiv) 29, 275
Kievan Rus' 5
Kitowicz, Jędrzej 225–6
Kneller, Sir Godfrey 217
Kniaźnin, Franciszek Dionizy 184
Knight, Richard Payne 200
Kołaczkowski, Adam 237
kolivshchyna 227
Kollacz, Paweł 270

Kołłątaj, Hugo 186, 280, 299 n., 308, 313
and Constitution of 3 May 276, 285, 287, 291–2, 295
and the Jagiellonian University 243
Komarzewski, Jan, General 125 n., 199, 205, 220, 234–5, 263
Komenský (Comenius), Jan Amos 29
Komorowski, Cypryan 71
Konarski, Stanisław 69, 207, 223, 224
educational reforms 70–3, 240
O skutecznym rad sposobie 146–55, 156, 253, 314; impact of 67, 168, 171, 270, 274, 279, 294
Königsberg 33, 240
Konopczyński, Władysław, historian 7, 9, 76 n., 306 n.
Korsuń, palace 198
Korzon, Tadeusz, historian 7
Kościuszko, Tadeusz 141, 239, 311
Insurrection (1794) 6, 14, 144, 311–12
Kossak, Wojciech 312
Koszyki 205
Kotulinský, Angelika, Countess 90 n.
Kozienice 172, 174, 176
Kraków, *see* Cracow
Krasicki, Ignacy, Prince-Bishop 174, 178, 179, 189–90
and *Monitor* 166, 168, 180–1, 186–90, 229
Królikarnia, palace 195
Krzystanowicz, Stanisław 29
Książęce and 'na Górze', gardens 196
Kurów, garden 196, 198
Kwiatkowski, Marek, historian 191, 203, 210
Kysil (Kisiel), Adam 29

La Croix 272
La Fontaine 184
La Mettrie, Julien Offraye de 49
Lagrénie, J. F. 202
Łańcut, palace and park 194, 198
land tax 18, 23, 265–6
Langford, Paul, historian 10, 22 n.
Langhan, Carl Gotthard 195
Lansdowne, William, 1st Marquis of (formerly Shelburne) 132, 136, 145, 173–4, 269
Łaski, Jan (John a Lasco) 29
Lasocki, Roch 282
Latapie 197

Latin 36, 37, 69, 242
  in schools 26, 70, 119, 175, 238, 240
  Stanisław August's knowledge of 81,
    98, 176, 184
latitudinarianism, latitudinarians 25–6, 30,
    41–3, 45
  influence on Stanisław August 113–15,
    227–8, 244, 315
Lavoisier, Antoine de 235
law, laws 119, 166, 172, 240, 251, 259–60,
    273, 284
  of Poland 70, 158, 241, 254, 258,
    261–2, 263, 273, 299
Law on Government, *see* Constitution of
    3 May 1791
Law on Royal Towns (1791) 142, 291–2,
    308
Łazienki 100, 178, 192, 203–5, 211–17,
    228, 272
Le Rouge 197
Le Tourneur, Pierre 54, 176, 181, 184
Leclerc, Jean 40
Lee, Charles 12, 129–30, 131, 163–4, 171,
    172–3
Leibniz, Gottfried Wilhelm von 41, 50,
    71, 80, 223, 229, 230, 243
Leiden 39, 259
Leipzig 39, 68, 71
Lengnich, Gottfried 70, 80
Leningrad, *see* St Petersburg
Leominster 110
Leopold II, Emperor 159
Lessing, Gotthold Ephraim 56
Leszczyński, Stanisław, *see* Stanisław I
    Leszczyński
Leszno 29
Lewitter, Lucjan, historian 25 n.
liberalism 64
libertinism 109, 224
liberty 17, 27, 31, 34, 52, 96, 249,
    259–60, 272, 314
  see also England, constitution and
    political culture; Poland, constitution
    and political culture
liberum rumpo 20, 66, 175, 188
liberum veto 20, 27, 247–8, 262
  abolition of (1791) 294, 307
  plans to abolish 66, 146, 151–2, 154–5,
    245, 251, 343, 346
  plans to restrict 66, 75–6, 156, 163,
    168–9
  restriction of (1764, 1768) 158, 169–70
  uses of 74, 77, 84–5, 87, 91, 147

Libiszowska, Zofia, historian 9, 129 n.,
    132, 142 n., 270
Ligne, Charles Joseph, Prince de 37
limita, see prorogation
limited monarchy 35, 52, 165, 287
Lind, John 129 n., 130, 132–3, 136, 175,
    234, 239–40
Lindsay, Jan 198
Linguet 185
Lipoński, Wojciech 102 n.
Lithuania, Grand Duchy of 21, 253
  duality of offices etc. 150–1, 163, 297,
    302–3
  Third Lithuanian Statute (1588) 261,
    303
  Union with Poland 5, 19, 302–3
Little Poland (Małopolska) 253
Littlepage, Lewis 140, 173, 175 n.
Liverpool 139
Łobarzewski, Ignacy 282–4, 313
Locke, John:
  educational theory 40, 70, 73, 182,
    239–42, 244
  philosophy 39–41, 49–50, 63–4, 71,
    182, 223, 228–30
  political theory 10, 50, 58
  religious views 30, 40–1, 228
logic 80
Łojek, Jerzy, historian 8, 86, 88 n., 90 n.,
    93, 276 n.
Lolme, Jean de 58–9, 62, 269, 315
Łomża 84
London 82, 126, 133, 188, 203, 263, 270,
    278
  Grand Orient lodge 69, 137
  Poles in 71, 131–5, 190, 194–9, 251–2,
    232–3
  Polish contacts with 72, 193, 200, 218,
    231–3, 243
  S. A. Poniatowski in 105–23
  Tower of 307
Lords, House of 62, 111, 153, 308
  as a model for Europe 47, 51–2
  as a model for Poland 266, 268–9, 280,
    293–4, 300, 306
Lorentz, Stanisław, historian 191 n., 221
Lorrain, Claude 114, 200, 204, 211, 219
Louis XIII, King of France 82
Louis XIV, King of France 18, 27, 201
Louis XV, King of France 105
Louis XVI, King of France 208–10, 272
Louis, Victor 202
Loutherbourg, Philip 219

364

Index

Łowicz 196
Łoyko, Felix 166
Lublin 193
  Union of (1569) 5, 19
Lubomirska, Izabella, née Czartoryska
  103, 134, 174, 194, 196, 198
Lubomirski, Henryk 198
Lubomirski, Stanisław 160, 161, 163, 193,
  254, 262
Lucchesini, Girolamo 287
Lukowski, Jerzy, historian 15 n., 281 n.,
  282 n., 294, 298
Łuskina, Stefan 270
Lutherans 30, 68, 167
Lwów (Lviv, Lemberg) 72, 180
Lyons 112 n.
Lyttelton, Sir George, later 1st Baron
  113, 116, 127, 184

Mably, Gabriel Bonnot de 60–1, 245
Macaulay, Catherine 269
MacCartney and Bayley 221
MacKintosh, James 142
MacPherson, James 56, 176, 177–8
Madrid 140
Magazyn Warszawski 185
Magier, Antoni 193–4
magnates, magnateria 206–7, 313, 316
  criticism of 66, 152, 259, 280, 283, 305,
    313
  cultural role 30, 68–70, 194–5
  'oligarchy' 21–2
  opposition to Stanisław August 125,
    262, 265, 275
  power base weakened 170, 295, 305
  rise of 19
Majchrowicz, Szymon 34
Majewska-Maszkowska, Bożenna, historian
  205, 210 n.
Major, Thomas 200
Maków, starosta of 84
Małachowski, Jacek 298
Małachowski, Stanisław 276, 285, 287, 308
Malebranche, Nicolas 39
Maliszewski, Piotr 236
Malmesbury, 1st Earl of, see Harris, James
Manchester 236
manners 344
  English and French 44, 99–100, 108–9,
    119–20, 250
  Polish 69, 70, 134, 188
Mansfield, William, 1st Earl of 126,
  131–2, 273

Maria Antonina, Crown Princess of
  Saxony 88
Maria Luiza Gonzaga, Queen of Poland
  148
Maria Theresa, Empress 46, 56, 127,
  246
Marie-Antoinette, Queen of France 53,
  54
Marlborough, John, 1st Duke of 218
Marlborough, George, 4th Duke of 220
Mars 159
Marshall, Joseph 135, 202
marshals 20, 150, 297–8
Mary, Blessed Virgin 25, 226
Martinelli, Vicenzio 58
Marxism 65
Massalski, Ignacy, Bishop 237, 241
Massalski, Michał, Hetman 157
materialism 42, 49–50
mathematics 70, 72, 119, 239–42 passim
Maty, Matthew, Dr 232
Maupertuis, Louis de 39
Mazovia (Mazowsze) 84
Mazzei, Filippo 140–3, 177, 271–2, 293
medals 133, 221
medicine 242
Meissen 222
Memel 140
Mémoires de Trévoux 41, 49, 55
Mengs, Anton Raphael 100–1, 210
mercantilism 62, 166
Mercury 184
Merentibus medals 142, 143, 186, 219,
  232, 233, 234
Merlini, Domenico 195, 214
metaphysics 71, 80
Michalski, Jerzy, historian 8, 161 n.,
  276 n.
Mickiewicz, Adam 312
Middleton, Conyers 98, 228
Miedziana Góra 235
Mielżyńskis 194
Mikucki, Antoni 270
military commissions:
  (1764–1776) 157–8, 163, 169, 254–5
  (1788–1792) 297–8, 301, 303
Milton, John 44, 56
  influence in Poland 174, 183, 185, 315
  Stanisław August and 98, 176–7, 182,
    315
Minasowicz, Józef Epifani 81, 181, 189
Minerva 159, 206
'ministerial council' 161

ministerial responsibility 149–50, 253–4, 256–7
  in Constitution of 3 May 1791 298–300, 308
  discussion of 278, 281, 283, 306
ministers:
  in England 18–19, 22–3, 150–1, 155, 256–7, 266–8, 297–300
  in Poland 20–2, 67, 69; criticism of 66, 150–1, 247–9, 251, 256–7, 317; reform of 157–8, 253–5, 258, 297–300, 308
ministry of foreign affairs (1791–2) 298
mint 160, 162–3
Mirabeau, Honoré de 61
mixed government 31, 35, 260, 304–6
Młociny, garden 196
Młodziejowski, Andrzej, Bishop 251
Mniszech, Amalia, née Brühl 76
Mniszech, Jerzy 147
Mniszech, Michał Jerzy 131, 196, 211, 230, 237, 241, 263–5, 268, 274
Mniszech, Urszula, née Zamoyska 131, 137, 196, 211
modern languages 70, 239, 241
Mohyla Academy, Kiev 29
Mokotów, garden 196
Moldavia 246
Molière, Jean Baptiste Poquelin 70, 178, 179
monads 72
Monitor 166–8, 169, 180–1, 186–90, 224, 229, 238, 315
Montagu, Lady 218
Montagu, Edward, Lord 128, 131, 221, 231–2
Montagu, Elizabeth Wortley 184 n.
Montagu, Henry, Earl of Manchester 29
Montesquieu, Charles Louis de Secondat, Baron 40, 46, 58, 59–60, 68, 78, 113, 114
  and the English constitution 50–3, 57, 63, 112
  influence in Poland 156, 168, 230, 254, 259–60, 269–70, 274, 278, 282–3, 293, 298, 315
  and Stanisław August 104, 165, 182, 251, 269, 317
moquette 55, 205–6, 208
Morellet, André 61
Morski, Tadeusz 280
Morsztyn, Catherine, lady, née Gordon 84, 122, 148

Morsztyn, Jan Andrzej 74
Morton, Charles 232
Morton, George, 16th Earl of 134, 136, 232
Moszyński, August 192, 197, 203–4, 205, 213, 220
Merly 200
Müntz, Johann Heinrich 198
Muralt, Beat 44
Muratori, Lodovico 40
Murillo, Bartolomé 219
music 69
muslin 53
Myszkowski, Zygmunt 28

Naigéon 43
Nairne and Blunt 231, 243
Nantes, revocation of Edict of (1685) 166
Napoleon 312
Naruszewicz, Adam, Bishop 182, 183, 190, 193 n., 232, 245
Narwoysz, Franciszek 242
Nassau-Siegen, Charles, Prince of 140
natural history 172, 233, 242
natural law 35, 40
natural rights 35, 163, 165
natural theology 187
'nature' 35, 49, 53–4, 63, 115, 185, 197, 224
Nazis 1–2
Neelov, Vasilii 55
neminem captivabimus, privilege of 16, 292
neo-classicism 69, 199, 205, 211–16, 220, 222
neo-gothic style 312
  see also gothick style
Netherlands, the 30, 130–1, 218, 275, 291 n.
  as a channel for English thought 37, 39–45, 63, 315
  constitution 67, 76, 148, 153, 164, 259, 270, 318
  contrast with Poland 3, 83, 166, 236
  S. A. Poniatowski in (1748, 1753) 83, 91–2, 166
Neufforge 195–6
Newcastle, Thomas, 1st Duke of 91, 95, 115–18, 131
Newton, Sir Isaac, Newtonianism 30, 38, 43, 128 n.
  influence in Europe 39–42, 48–9, 53
  influence in Poland 40, 71–2, 229–30, 242–3
  Stanisław August and 217–18, 228–9, 244

Nieć, Julian, historian 86 n., 102 n.,
    118–19, 146 n.
Niemcewicz, Julian Ursyn 10, 133, 279,
    304, 312–13
Norblin, Jean-Pierre 196
Norfolk, Thomas, 8th Duke of 46
North, Frederick, Lord (later 2nd Earl of
    Guildford) 23, 62, 104, 132, 256,
    267, 299
Notizie del mondo 58, 61
Nowogródek 72

Ochakov crisis 138–9, 310
O'Connor, Bernard, Dr 32
'oecomical societies' 59, 232
Ogińska, Alexandra, née Czartoryska (wife
    of Michał Kazimierz) 196
Ogińska, Izabella, née Lasocka (wife of
    Michał Kleofas) 198
Ogiński, Michał Kazimierz, Hetman 134,
    255
Ogiński, Michał Kleofas 198
Ogrodzki, Jacek 88 n., 161, 177
Old Sarum 59, 113
Oldisworth, William 31–2
Olesin, garden 196–7, 198
Olizar Wołczkiewicz, Leonard 278
Oraczewski, Felix 186
'organic work' 7, 312
Orkney islands 177
Orthodox Church, Orthodoxy 148, 227
Osieńko, Ludwik 167
Ossian 11, 56, 176–8, 189, 312
Ossoliński, Jerzy 28
Osten, Adolf 148
Ostróg affair 92, 111, 121
Ostrowski, Antoni, Primate 195
Ostrowski, Teodor 269
Ovid (Publius Ovidius Naso) 98, 176
Owen, John 184
Owrucz 304
Oxford 10, 114, 115, 119, 131, 200, 242, 303
    Poles at 234

Paine, Thomas 142–3, 271
painting 53, 69, 191–2, 206–8, 217–19
    influence of English in Poland 198–9,
    217–20
    influence of French in Poland 196,
    201–2
Palladio, Andrea del 195
Palladianism 191 n., 195, 204, 211,
    214–17, 222

Palmyra 199
Pamiętnik Historyczno-Polityczny 185–6,
    230, 265, 270–1, 284
Pangloss, Dr 36
pantheism, pantheists 41–3
papal bulls 260–1
Paris 37, 39, 128, 140, 141, 142, 145, 177,
    186
    centre of Enlightenment culture 36, 42,
    49, 108, 112, 199, 201–2, 232, 235
    instruments from 72, 231
    Poles in 68, 70, 71, 74, 78
    S. A. Poniatowski in 92, 104–5, 110,
    120, 201, 222
Parkinson, John 135 n.
parlements 51, 104–5, 316
Parliament 15, 18, 27, 150, 257, 294, 299,
    318
    elections 22, 84, 116, 152, 266, 268
    European opinion of 47, 50–2, 59–60,
    62
    king in 16, 23, 51, 280, 283
    Polish opinion of 32, 148–9, 151–2,
    155, 156, 164–5, 168, 170–1, 265–70,
    278, 280–3, 288–90, 306, 316
    procedure 156, 170–1, 266–7, 288–9,
    290
    and the succession 17, 82, 296
    see also Commons, Lords
patriotism 37–8, 53, 122, 128, 137, 153,
    198, 199
'patriots' 70, 122 n., 163, 167, 188, 259–61
    party at Four Year Seym 280–2,
    285–9, 300, 308
Paul I, Tsar of Russia 1, 90 n., 144, 312
Pawlikowski, Józef 282
Pawłowice 194, 195, 217
Payne, Sir Ralph 136, 218
Payne, Lady 136, 218
peasants 15, 227, 236, 260, 318
    calls to improve condition of 67–8, 169,
    186 n., 193, 312
Pelham, Henry 22, 95, 115–16, 118
Pemberton, Henry 49, 228
Permanent Council 261, 263–9, 274, 282
    abolition of (1788–9) 275, 282, 286
    creation and reform of (1773–6) 251,
    253–8
    department of foreign affairs 162,
    263–8, 275
    idea of 169
Perry, James 142 n.
Peter I the Great, Tsar of Russia 6, 24, 59

Peter III, Tsar of Russia 86, 147
Petersham, Caroline, Lady 106, 121
Pfleiderer, Christoph 241
philanthropy 43, 45
philosophia recentiorum 70–3, 223
philosophes 37, 43, 53, 60–2, 63, 112, 159, 249–50
philosophy 63–4, 119, 191, 272
physical education 70
physics 71–2, 235, 241–4
physiocrats 62, 224, 237, 242
Piarist order 70–3, 167, 241–2
Piattoli, Scipione 272 n., 286, 288, 290, 302
picturesque 198, 200, 213, 222
pietism 68
Piotrków 83
Pilat, Roman, historian 281 n.
Piłsudski, Józef, Marshal 1
Pingo, Thomas 221
Piranesi 199, 213
Pitt the elder, William, later 1st Earl of Chatham 116–17, 271
Pitt the younger, William 23, 62, 138–9, 256, 268, 299, 301 n.
Pius VI, Pope 208–10, 262
Plantier, Jacques 42
Plater, Kazimierz 231 n.
Platt, Julian, historian 183
Plato 229, 272
Plautius Titus Maccius 176
Plersch, Jan Bogumil 204
Płock 70
Pluche, Abbé 42
pocket and rotten boroughs 51, 59, 84, 268
Pocock, J. G. A., historian 19 n.
Poczobut, Marcin 231–3, 242
Podlasia (Podlasie) 68
Podolia (Podole) 170
Podoski, Franciszek 183
Poestum 200
Poland, Poland–Lithuania, Commonwealth of 2, 4–6
    affected by foreign fashions 3, 68–9, 188, 193–9
    army 24, 67, 74–5, 153, 187, 188, 254–5, 263, 275, 291, 301–2, 307
    atlas of 231
    commercial relations with England 28, 138–40
    condition 4, 23, 29, 73, 78, 83–5, 170, 247–9, 259–60, 273–4

constitution (unreformed) 16–22, 52, 96, 165, 248–9, 256
    diplomatic relations with England 28–9, 33, 77–8, 87, 91, 92, 125–9, 131–4, 137–40, 144, 167
    distributive power 21–2, 66, 153, 248, 253–5; *see also* Crown estates
    economy 65–7, 169, 156, 189, 222, 232, 235–8, 246, 273
    education 26, 29–30, 68–83, 175, 238–44, 250, 273, 319
    effects of war on 24–5, 27
    English travellers to 129–30, 135–7, 190–3, 202
    hereditary throne 148–9, 245, 251, 260, 270, 277–85, 296–7, 305, 309, 314, 316–17
    image of in England 29–33, 96, 123, 128, 135–6, 142–3, 303–4
    international situation 6, 24–5, 66, 75, 77, 97, 126–7, 131, 155–6, 170, 258, 273–5, 281, 307, 318
    interregna 19, 148, 281, 283, 296
    ladies 136, 137, 199
    legal system 158, 166, 263, 300–1
    literature 183–90, 319
    monarchia mixta 16, 36, 316
    monarchy 248–9, 295–300, 304–5
    nation 319
    nominative power 20, 66, 154, 158, 165, 188, 249, 253–4, 285, 287, 297–8, 300, 306
    pacta conventa 16, 252, 255–6, 257, 287, 300, 303, 316
    partitions 1, 2, 6, 158, 199, 348–9; first (1772) 127, 132, 170, 246–7, 251–2; second (1793) 310; third (1795) 197, 311, 312
    plans for reform of (before 1760) 66–8, 75–7, 96; (1760s) 146–57, 168–71; (*c.*1770–88) 245, 247–9, 258–65, (1788–91) 280–9
    political culture 16, 20, 27, 32, 34, 188, 247–9, 265, 274, 297, 299; transformation of (1790–2) 286–7, 304–9, 311, 317, 319
    poor relief 261, 264
    prospects of in 19th century 318
    reception of English thought in 70–3, 166, 223–4, 227–30, 239–44, 270
    reforms of (1764–8) 157–8, 169–70, 317; (1775–6) 251–5, 262–4, 317; *see also* Constitution of 3 May 1791

Poland, Poland–Lithuania, Commonwealth
of (*cont.*):
religiosity 25–6, 223–5
renewal of culture 319
revenues 252, 257, 306
royal elections 16, 66, 245, 257, 281
royal prerogative 16, 66, 148–51,
154–5, 188, 245, 251–7, 260, 262,
280–3, 287–8, 300, 301, 305–8, 314,
316–17
social structure 15, 166–7, 187, 284,
291–2, 311–12, 318; see also szlachta,
magnates, peasants
towns 15, 66–7, 75, 166, 189, 193, 255,
264, 284, 291–2, 308, 312, 318
vivente rege elections 91, 296
Poland:
Congress Kingdom of (1815–64) 311
1830–31 uprising 312
1863–64 uprising 7, 312
Poland, Second Republic of (1918–39) 1, 312
Poland (Polish People's Republic,
1944–89) 1–2
Poland, Third Republic of (1990–) 2–3, 312
police commission (1791–2) 298, 303
Polish Brethren, see Socinians
Polish Democratic Society 312
Polish language 26, 69, 70, 79, 175
translations into 176, 178, 180–1,
182–5, 241–2, 243, 269–71, 304, 312,
317
politeness 19, 43–5, 99–100, 108–9,
188–9, 250, 316
Poltava, battle of (1709) 25, 74
Polybius 50
Poniatowska, Konstancja, née Czartoryska
73, 78–80, 83, 86–94 passim 102,
106, 121, 163
Poniatowski, Alexander 79, 80, 82, 103
Poniatowski, Andrzej 79, 128, 130, 161
Poniatowski, Franciszek 79, 80
Poniatowski, Józef, Prince 6–7
Poniatowski, Kazimierz, Prince 76, 79, 80,
82, 83, 103, 128, 130, 161, 196
Poniatowski, Michał Jerzy, Prince Primate
79, 128, 130, 161, 194, 196, 230, 237,
241, 243, 264 n., 297–8
in England (1791) 131, 134–5, 139, 198,
199, 218–20, 233, 235
Poniatowski, Stanisław 73–9, 84, 87, 126,
163
List ziemianina 15, 67, 68, 75–6, 85,
103
relations with Stanisław Antoni 79,
82–3, 88–9, 90, 92, 94, 96, 99,
103–6, 121
Poniatowski, Stanisław, Prince 139,
175 n., 189, 194, 198, 230, 231
in England (1771–3) 130, 199, 230, 240
and the throne 257, 296
Poniatowski, Stanisław Antoni/August see
Stanisław August Poniatowski
Poniński, Adam 134, 241, 251–2
Pope, Alexander 44, 98, 113, 117–18,
203 n.
influence in Poland 174, 176–7, 182–4,
189, 239, 312, 315
Popławski, Antoni 242
porcelain 55, 194, 221–2, 236
Portalupi, Antonio Maria 70
Porter, Roy, historian 38 n.
Potemkin, Grigory, Prince 138
Potocka, Anna Teofila, née Ossolińska
(wife of Seweryn) 134
Potocka, Julia, née Lubomirska (wife of
Jan) 134
Potocki, Antoni 67, 77
Potocki, Antoni Protazy 'Prot' 236
Potocki, Ignacy 174, 198, 275
and Constitution of 3 May 276,
285–90, 295, 296, 298, 302, 304
Potocki, Jan 134, 174, 177, 314
Potocki, Józef, Hetman 75, 79, 83
Potocki, Seweryn 134, 174, 177 n.
Potocki, Stanisław Kostka 134, 192 n.,
196, 198, 281
Potocki, Stanisław Szczęsny 195, 214,
230, 280, 338
Potocki, Wincenty 136
Potockis 21, 75, 83–4
Poussin, Nicolas 219
Powązki, garden 196
Poznań 72, 237
Prévost, abbé 44, 53
Price, Richard 143
Priestley, Joseph 142–3, 231, 243
Primate's palace 195
Prior Park 113, 215 n.
Privy Council 253, 294
prorogation (in Poland, limita) 32, 152,
267
Protestantism, Protestants 29–34, 45, 56,
68, 75, 77, 148, 296
Prussia 56, 75, 147, 151, 238
alliance with Poland (1790–2) 6, 138,
275, 285, 310

and England 94, 97, 138, 275
  hostility to reform in Poland 77, 84,
    169, 251, 310
  part in partitions of Poland 6, 246, 251,
    310
  and Polish Protestants 33, 167, 251
Prussia, Polish (Royal) 165, 246
Przeździecki, Antoni 161
Przeździecki, Michał 131
Przybylski, Jacek 174, 183
Psarski, Jakub 137
public credit 23
'public sphere' 57
Puławy 136, 147, 188, 197–8, 312,
    313 n.
Pulteney, William, later Earl of Bath 50,
    95
Puzyna 175 n.
Puzyna, Elżbieta 72

Quakers 48

Racine, Jean 176, 178, 179
Radicati di Passerano, Alberto 42
Radom 91
  confederacy of (1767–8) 169
Radziwiłł, Helena, née Przeździecka (wife
    of Michał Hieronim) 196
Radziwiłł, Karol 156, 169, 313
Radziwiłł, Michał, Hetman 72, 91
Radziwiłł, Michał Hieronim 134
Radziwiłłs 21
Raków 30
Ramsden 231
Raphael (Rafaelo Santi) 228, 250
Rapin de Thoyras 45, 98, 269
Raynal, Guillaume-Thomas 61, 271
reason 35, 62, 64
  see also deductive reasoning and
    empiricism
Red Army 2
redingotte 53, 221
Reformation 29–31, 33, 270
Regency crisis (1788–9) 301
Regensburg (Ratisbon) 126
regimentary (regimentarz) 74
Reich, see Holy Roman Empire
Reichenbach, convention of (1790) 310
religious intolerance 25–6, 29–30, 33,
    133–4, 167, 273
religious toleration 29–30, 35, 102, 114,
    134, 244
  calls for 48, 75, 156, 166, 187

Rembrandt van Rijn 217, 219
Repnin, Nikolai 158, 161, 169, 252
Republic of Letters 36–7, 42
resistance, right of 17, 164
revelation 35, 40, 71, 224, 227, 242
Reverdil, Marc 174
Reviczky, Count 247
Reynolds, Sir Joshua 199, 219
Richardson, Samuel 54, 176, 183
Riga, Treaty of (1921) 1
Rigaud 201
Rigby, Richard 100 n.
Robertson, William 11, 240, 269
Robinson Crusoe, see Defoe
Rockingham, Charles, 2nd Marquess of
    23, 268
Rockingham Whigs 132, 145, 268
rococo 196
Rogaliński, Józef 72
Rohan, Chevalier de 47
Rollin, Charles 40, 71
Roman Catholicism, see Catholicism
Romanovs 1
Romanticism 35, 64
  Polish 312–13
Rome 68, 70, 71, 73, 262
  ancient 47, 61, 180
Rosa, Salvator 219
Rossbach, battle of (1757) 56
Rostworowski, Emanuel, historian 8, 9,
    15, 16, 24, 35 n., 38 n., 65, 67 n.,
    146, 150, 155, 225, 227, 288, 311,
    318
rotten boroughs, see pocket and rotten
    boroughs
Rottermund, Andrzej, historian 191,
    204 n., 210
Rousseau, Jean-Jacques 50, 54, 176, 189,
    199, 224, 227, 240, 281, 286
  Considérations sur le gouvernement de
    Pologne 60, 245, 249–51, 277,
    315
  Contrat social 259, 292
  Nouvelle Héloïse 54, 196
Rousset de Missy, Jean 45
Royal Castle, Warsaw 191–2, 195, 201–11,
    218, 225, 230, 258, 286
  ballroom 191, 206–7
  Knights' Hall 206–8, 244
  marble room 201, 224
  observatory 231, 234
  plans to rebuild 159, 191, 201, 210–11,
    222, 258

Royal Library and collections 205–6, 225
  books 172–7, 182, 227–9, 233, 239,
    269, 271–2, 283
  engravings 199–200, 220
  other collections 192, 220–2, 231, 243
Royal Society 38–9, 112, 241
  links with Poles 30, 231–3, 235, 238
Rubens, Sir Peter Paul 83, 219
Ruisdael, Jakob van 219
Rulhière, Claude Carloman de 86, 97
Russia 151, 311–12
  Anglophilia/Anglomania in 43, 55–6,
    58, 59, 313–15
  and England 93, 97, 126–7, 128–9,
    137–9, 156, 167
  and the *Familia* 75–8, 92, 97, 148
  hegemony in Poland 4, 317; (1709–62)
    24–5, 77, 84, 87; (1762–8) 126–7,
    132, 147–8, 155–8, 167, 169–71;
    (1772–88) 246–7, 251–2, 255, 258,
    273–5, 281; (1792–5) 14, 144, 310–11
  invasion of Poland in 1792 1, 6, 310
  part in partitions of Poland 6, 246–7,
    310–11
  S. A. Poniatowski in 86, 90, 92–5,
    98–9, 147
  and Turkey 6, 130, 157, 170, 200–1,
    246, 275, 310
Russian language 81
Ruthenians 318
Rutlidge, James 179
Rutowski, Friedrich August, Count 69
Rymszyna, Maria, historian 159
Ryx, Franciszek 125 n.
Rzewuski, Adam 277
Rzewuski, Seweryn, Hetman 277–80, 285,
    310
Rzewuski, Wacław, Hetman 32

St John the Baptist, collegiate (later
    cathedral) church, Warsaw 1–2, 203
St Paul's Cathedral, London 203
St Petersburg 37, 137, 280
  S. A. Poniatowski in (1755–6, 1757–8)
    86, 90, 92–4, 97–9, 100, 124, 128;
    (1797–1938) 1, 177, 178, 227, 229
saints 226
Salisbury 113
Salmour, Count 88
salons 74, 104
Sapieha, Józef, Bishop 72
Sapieha, Kazimierz Nestor 302, 314
Sapieha, Michał 73

Sapiehas 21
Sarmatism 26–7, 66, 68, 69, 78, 89, 182,
    186, 190, 191, 262, 274, 314
  costume 79–80, 314
Saturn 228
Savage, James 198
Saxon court 66, 68, 69, 73, 87, 126, 163,
    193
  and the *Familia* 74–7, 95–6, 87, 96,
    121, 124, 147–8
Saxon era 4, 65, 67
Saxon party (1763–6) 156, 159, 161
Saxony 68, 92, 94, 151, 160
  house of (Wettins) 76, 147, 203, 296
  S. A. Poniatowski in (1751, 1753) 87–8,
    91
  union with Poland–Lithuania 6, 16, 27,
    296
Schaub, Sir Luke 77, 105–6, 111
Schaub, Lady 106
Scheidt, Franciszek 243
scholasticism 39, 71, 73, 223, 229, 243–4
Schroeger, Ephraim 195, 203
Schuch, Johann Christian 211
Schulz, Friedrich 194
science:
  English 38–9, 49, 63, 72, 89, 131, 225,
    230–6, 240–4, 315–16
  experimental 38–41, 49, 50, 63–4, 71–2,
    223, 230, 241–4
  Polish 30, 70, 205, 230–6, 241–4,
    315–16
Scotland, Scots 11, 28, 96, 134, 269
  union with England 16, 303
Scott, Sir Walter 312
sculpture 191–2, 198, 203, 206–8
Second World War 1–2, 65, 202 n.
Sędziwoj, Michał 30
senate 5, 16, 19–20, 31, 202, 253–4,
    293–5, 308
  proposals to reform 66, 149, 151–2,
    155, 249, 283
senate council 19, 21, 132, 253
sensationism, *see* Locke, philosophy of
sensibility 44, 54, 56, 63, 64, 185, 274,
    313 n.
sentimental novels 53–4, 176, 199
separation of powers 50–1, 156, 165, 280,
    286, 293
Septennial Act (1716) 32, 270
Seven Years War (1756–63) 37, 53, 56,
    69, 93–4, 155, 264, 302
  and Poland 34, 147, 163

Sèvres 222
Seym 5, 16, 27, 32, 168, 191, 248, 257, 269, 296
of 1652 (first of two) 20
of 1669 (coronation) 20
of 1717 ('Dumb') 24, 25
of 1726 33
of 1729, 1730, 1732, and 1733 74
of 1744 (Grodno) 75, 77, 85
of 1748 83
of 1750 83–4, 99–100
of 1752 (Grodno) 84–5, 91
of 1754 92, 121
of 1756 (cancelled) 94
of 1758 and 1760 147
of 1761 126, 147
of 1762 147
of 1764 (convocation) 156–8
of 1764 (coronation) 157, 167
of 1766 163, 167, 168–9
of 1767–8 169–70, 255
of 1768 (cancelled) 232
of 1773–5 (Partition) 129, 240, 247, 251–5
of 1776 255–8, 281
of 1778, 1780, and 1782 262, 274
of 1784 (Grodno) 173, 175, 262, 265, 274
of 1786 262, 265, 274
of 1788–92 (Four Year) 137, 142, 160, 275–309 *passim* 314, 317
of 1793 (Grodno) 14, 310–11
paralysis of 20–1, 24, 76–7, 83
plans to reform 66, 67, 146, 151–5, 156, 170–1, 245, 280–3, 288–9, 316
reform of (1764) 158; (1791) 293–5, 301, 302, 306, 308–9
procedure 158, 288–90, 305
'ruling Seym' 151, 254, 275, 280–3, 286, 293, 298, 301
seym court 299, 300
seymiki 5, 24, 84–5
of Feb. 1750 83 n.
of Sept. 1766 167–8
of Aug. 1776 255
of Nov. 1790 286, 295, 296
of Feb. 1792 226, 304, 305
general *seymik* of Polish Prussia 165
instructions 20, 67, 154, 158, 273, 283, 286, 295, 316
plans to reform 149, 150, 152, 154, 245
reform of 158, 169–70, 254, 295, 300–1
seymik relationis 174

Shaftesbury, Anthony Ashley, 3rd Earl of 42, 49, 53, 228
Shakespeare, William 114
influence in Europe 54–7, 59, 81, 181
influence in Poland 81, 178–82, 185, 312
Julius Caesar 54, 81
and Stanisław August 81, 108, 172, 176, 178–82, 315
Shelburne, 2nd Earl of, *see* Lansdowne
Shelton 231
Sheridan, Mrs 195, 203
Sherlock, William 227
Siarczyński, Franciszek 270–1
Sidney, Algernon 163–4
Siedlce 196
Sieniawskis 193
Sigismund II Augustus, King of Poland (1548–72) 316
Sigismund III, King of Poland (1587–1632) 29, 148
Silesia 246
Sinclair, Sir John 136, 237
Sinko, Zofia, historian 174, 187
Skarga, Piotr 29
Skrzetuski, Kajetan 270, 278 n.
Skzetuski, Wincenty 270
slavery 139
Śliwicki, Piotr 80
Sloane, Hans 38
Ślusarska, Magdalena, historian 224 n.
Smith, Adam 11, 59, 143
Smoleński, Władysław, historian 7, 223–4
Smollett, Tobias 182
Śniadecki, Jan 175 n., 233–4, 243
Snopek, Jerzy, historian 224 n.
Sobieski, Jakub, father of John III 28
Sobieski, Jan, *see* John III
Sobieski, Marek 32
Sobolewska 175 n.
Sobolewski 237
social contract 10, 164
see also Locke, Rousseau
Society for Elementary Textbooks (*Towarzystwo do Xiąg Elementarnych*) 241
Society of the Friends of the Constitution (*Zgromadzenie Przyjaciół Konstytucyi Rządowey*) 307–8
Socinians, Socinianism 30, 37, 41, 48
Solec, garden 196
'Solidarity' 2
Sołtyk, Kajetan, Bishop 168, 224

Sophocles 178
Sorbonne 40
sovereignty of the people 10, 17
Soviet Union 1–3
Spain 52, 230
Spalatro 199–200
Spanish language 108
Spectator 43–4, 55, 98, 99 n., 179–80
    influence in Poland 173, 187–90, 229,
    315
Spencer, Earl 203
Spinoza, Baruch 37, 41, 49
spleen 121
Spooner 220
Sprengel, M. C. 271 n.
Stackelberg, Otto Magnus, Count 246–7,
    251–2, 255, 262, 263, 285
Stalin, Joseph 2
Stamp Act 164, 268
Stanhope, Captain 105
Stanhope, Philip 109
Stanisław, Saint 225
    order of 140
Stanisław I Leszczyński, King of Poland
    (1704–10, 1733–6), Duke of Lorraine
    25, 66, 75, 78, 121, 225
    Głos wolny 67–8, 248–9
Stanisław August Poniatowski, King of
    Poland (1764–95):
    abdication, exile, and death 1, 138, 145,
    177, 178, 227, 229, 311
    ambition to reform Poland 4, 122, 125,
    135, 159–65, 168–9, 201, 226, 228,
    247, 250–1, 289–90, 302, 316–19
    and America 140–1, 164–5, 271–2, 316
    'Anecdote historique' (1763) 146–55,
    159, 170–1, 265, 274
    Anglophilia 4, 9–13, 100–2, 121–2, 135,
    144, 221, 251, 273, 315–19
    and art 83, 159, 172, 182, 191–3,
    206–8, 220–2, 319; architecture
    199–217, 222; gardens 114–15, 200,
    203–4, 211–13, 217, 222; picture
    gallery 210, 217–19, 229
    assassination attempt (3 Nov. 1771)
    226
    birth, baptism, and childhood 1, 78–80
    and Catherine II, *see* Catherine II
    character 79, 90, 92, 99, 123, 128, 161,
    168, 225, 226, 238, 285
    concept of partnership with the 'nation'
    149–50, 155, 247–9, 251, 304, 316,
    317

contacts with Englishmen 81, 84–115,
    121–45, 161–5, 172–5, 184, 218–7,
    221, 227–8, 231–40, 269, 315
    coronation 161–2, 201, 202, 221
    economic ventures 236, 238
    education 79–82, 88
    education policy, *see* Poland, education
    election 6, 127–8, 156, 158–9, 161–2
    and the English constitution, *see*
    England, constitution
    and English education *see* England,
    education
    and English history 82, 97, 102, 117–19
    and English literature 81, 97–8, 108,
    191–211, 315
    and English political culture, *see*
    England, political culture
    and English politics 102, 115–17
    an enlightened absolutist? 159–65, 222,
    316
    envoy to the seym (1750, 1752, 1758,
    1760, 1761, 1762, 1764) 84–5, 87, 91,
    147, 157–8, 250
    'Extrait d'un lettre' (1772) 247–50, 261
    funerals (1798, 1938, 1995) 1–2
    foreign policy 97, 131–4, 137–40, 160;
    (1764–72) 126–7, 168–9; (1772–87)
    247, 258, 262, 274; (1787–95) 200,
    275, 285
    on France 104–5, 109, 248, 272, 293,
    316
    historical reputation 6–8
    image of in England 127–9, 135, 139,
    142–5, 163–4, 273
    joins confederacy of Targowica (1792)
    310–11
    knowledge of English 81, 97–8, 111,
    136, 172–5
    knowledge of other languages 80–1,
    97–8, 136, 172–4
    and legal codification 258–62, 301
    library and collections, *see* Royal
    Library and collections
    manners 99–100, 104, 106, 109, 135,
    163
    and the military 82–3, 153–4, 163, 201,
    254–6, 262–3, 265, 275, 301–2
    and *Monitor* 166–7, 180–1, 186–90,
    315
    'new creation of the Polish world' 4,
    159, 191, 315, 318–19
    own political party 160, 262, 282–4,
    286

plans to create a strong central
government 150–1, 169, 247, 251–2,
255, 274, 295–300, 316–17
and Polish history 162, 192–3, 200–1,
206–8, 248, 316–17
political tactics 4, 8, 252, 262, 285–6
popularity among women 104, 109–10
propaganda 159, 163, 164, 183, 186,
223, 245, 247–9, 255–7, 306–7, 317
relations with parents 79–94 *passim*, 96,
99, 102–6, 121, 163
relations with uncles 79, 83, 94, 103,
121, 154, 161
religiosity 80, 93, 97, 114, 224–8, 244,
315
religious policy 133–4, 162, 166–7,
225–6, 244, 261–2, 273, 291
and science, *see* science, Polish
sources regarding 12–13, 102–3
speech of 23 Sept. 1776 255–7, 306,
317
as starosta of Przemyśl (1753–64) 86,
147
Thursday dinners 183, 259
and towns 166, 292
travels, *see* England; France; Hanover;
London; The Netherlands; Paris;
Russia; St Petersburg; Saxony;
Vienna
unpopularity of 128–9, 161, 169, 245
Uwagi and pismem . . . Dłuskiego (1791)
306–7
youth 63, 80–123 *passim*
Stanley, Hans 106
starostas 254, 264, 265
starostwa, *see* Crown estates
Staszewski, Jacek, historian 25 n., 64,
76 n., 147 n., 161 n.
Staszic, Stanisław 277, 284
Steele, Sir Richard 43
Sterne, Laurence 176, 177, 182–3, 190,
312
Stevens, George 176
Stevens, John 272
Stillingfleet, Edward, Bishop 49
Stockholm 129
Stonehenge 113, 122
Stormont, David, 7th Viscount 126–7,
134, 137, 145, 174
Stourhead 211
Stowe 100 n., 114–15, 117–18, 198,
207–8, 215
Stratford-upon-Avon 179, 185

Strange, Lord 106–8
Straż Praw (custodial council of the laws)
282, 288–9, 297–9, 300, 301, 302,
310, 318
'Strict Observance', masonic network 137
Strzecki, Andrzej 233
Stuart, house of 95–6
Stuart, James 199
Stubbs, George 220
Suchodolski, Wojciech 279
Suchorzewski Jan 279, 305
Suffolk, Henry, 12th Earl of 129
Sułkowski, Antoni 186
Sułkowski, August 121, 134, 177, 186,
251–2, 258, 283
Sweden 24, 25 n., 129, 153, 167, 279, 318
constitution of 151, 253, 254, 258
coup of 1772 28, 60, 159
'Deluge' (1655) 24, 26
Świątkowski, Marcin 72
Swift, Jonathan 44, 98, 176–7, 182, 189,
315
Świtkowski, Piotr 185–6, 230, 265, 274,
284
Switzerland 32, 67, 76, 318
Syon House 206
Szaniawski, Konstanty, Bishop 66, 161 n
Szczygielski, Wojciech, historian 305 n.
szlachta 4–6, 19
and the army 66–7, 75, 154, 241, 265,
307
Catholicism of 26, 29, 34, 69, 168–70,
225–6
conservatism of, *see* Poland, political
culture, and Sarmatism
and Constitution of 3 May 1791 304–5,
307, 311, 317
and education 26, 239, 241, 244
income of 260, 273, 284
Lithuanian 303
manners of 109, 250, 273
middling 160, 239, 262, 313
and the peasantry 15, 164, 167–8, 169,
261–2, 265, 318
poor 152, 312
suspicion of English constitution 28,
32, 34, 156–7, 168, 171, 276, 279,
314
and the towns 66, 265, 291–2, 305, 308,
318

table lands (*dobra stołowe*) 153
Tahitians 50

Targoński, J. 183
Targowica, confederacy of (1792–93) 6,
    145, 310–11
Tarło, Adam 83
Taszycki, Gabriel 277
Tatarkiewicz, Władysław, historian 191,
    215 n.
Tatham, Edward 303
Tatler 43, 82 n.
taxation 164–5, 305
    in England 18, 23, 34, 48, 164, 256–7,
        259, 265–6, 280, 283, 293–4, 316
    in Poland 24, 75, 158, 165, 169, 257,
        294, 306
Taylor, William 126 n., 129 n.
tea 55, 89
Temple, Richard, Lord 114
Terence (Terentius Publius Afer) 176
Theatine order 70, 80
'Theatralski' 180–1
theatre:
    National (established 1765) 181–2, 186
    school productions 70
    unities 54–5, 108, 115, 178–82
Theocritus 176
theology 119, 227, 242, 244
Thomatis, Carlo 195
Thomson, James 176, 182
Thorn (Toruń) 68, 139, 181, 310
    Tumult of (1724) 33, 77
Thundertentronk 36
Tillotson, John, Archbishop 30, 41, 97–8,
    227
Tindal, Matthew 41, 48
Tintoretto, Jacopo 219
Titchfield, William, Marquess of 136
Titian (Tiziano Vecellio) 219
Tivoli 211–12, 219
Tokay 100 n.
Toland, John 41, 42, 227
Tom Jones, see Fielding
Tories 17, 22–3, 30, 32, 115, 161
    ideology 17, 28, 268
Townshend, Charles, 2nd Viscount 50
treasurers 20, 150, 157–8, 297–8, 303
treasury commissions (1764–91) 157–8,
    160, 163, 188–9, 254
treasury commission (1791–2) 298, 303
treasury tribunal (Radom) 91
Trembecki, Stanisław 181, 190
tribunals 149, 154, 248, 254
    of the Crown 83, 147
    of Lithuania 72

Trinity, Holy 40, 226–7
    see also Socinianism
Tristram Shandy, see Sterne
Truskolawski, Edmund 241–2
Trzciński, Andrzej 175 n., 243
Tsarskoe Selo 55
Tucker, Josiah 166
Tulczyn 195, 214
Turin 71
Turkey, Ottoman Empire 3 n., 19, 24, 73,
    138, 258
    wars with Russia 6, 130, 157, 170, 200,
        246, 275, 310
Turski, Wojciech 277, 307
Tuscany 159
Tyszkiewicz, Konstancja, née Poniatowska
    230, 233 n.
Tyszkiewicz, Maria Teresa, née
    Poniatowska 134, 205
Tyszkiewicz palace, Warsaw 194, 217
Tyzenhauz, Antoni 236

Ujazdów Castle 192, 197, 203, 230
Ukraine (Ukraina) viii, 19, 21, 195, 198,
    227, 304, 310
Uniate Church, see Greek Catholic Church
universal suffrage 318
utilitarianism, utility 35
Utrecht, peace of (1713) 39

Van Dyck, Sir Anthony 83, 218, 219
Van Loo, Carl 202
Vardy, John 203
Vatican 250
    see also Benedict XIV; Pius VI; Rome
Velázquez, Diego 219
Venice 31, 32, 61, 67, 76, 283
Venturi, Franco, historian 37–8
Veronese, Paolo 219
Verri, Alessandro 58
Versailles 68, 201
Vicenza 195
Vien, J. M. 202
Vienna 37, 56, 99, 120, 125, 126, 140,
    145, 181
    S. A. Poniatowski in (1751–52, 1753)
        89–91, 99
Villiers, Sir Thomas 78
Virgil (Publius Vergilius Maro) 98, 176,
    207–8
Virginia 141, 272
virtue 19, 57, 178, 180, 188, 215, 224,
    250, 272, 273

Visconti, Antonio, nuncio 162, 227
Vistula 246
Vitruvius Britannicus 195, 200
vodka monoply (*propinacya*) 260
Vogel, Zygmunt 200
Volhynia (Wołyń) 193, 318
Volland, Sophie 60
Voltaire, François Marie Arouet de 41,
   43, 63, 98
  and the English constitution 47–8, 52,
   61, 149, 294
  influence in Poland 69, 70, 71, 81, 181,
   189, 224, 269
  influence on Stanisław August 99, 149,
   176, 224–5
  Lettres philosophiques 47–9, 54, 99, 293
  and Locke 48–9, 247
  and Newton 48–9, 53, 246
  and religion 48–9, 245
  and Shakespeare 54, 81, 179, 181, 201
Volumina legum 70, 261

Wałęsa, Lech, President 2 n.
Wallachia 246
wallpaper 55
Walpole, Horace 54, 106 n., 109–10, 136,
   142, 176, 200, 213
Walpole, Sir Robert 22, 31, 45, 63, 256,
   260, 264, 282
  Stanisław August and 95, 117–18, 122,
   155, 316
Wanstead 215 n.
War of Jenkins' Ear (1739–48) 82
War of the Spanish Succession 37
Warburton, William, Bishop 98, 113–14,
   115 n., 122, 176, 224, 227
Warsaw 1–2, 69, 70, 80, 130, 135–7, 157,
   181, 193, 279, 318
  growth of 163, 238, 273
  palaces and gardens 195–7, 201–17
  press 231, 304
  projected academy 232, 241
  suspicion of in provinces 121, 188,
   273–4
Warsaw, Grand Duchy of (1807–13) 312
Washington, George 140, 272
Wąsowicz, student 234
Wasylewski, Stanisław, historian 8
Watkins 231
Watteau, Antoine 219
Webster 231
Wedgwood, Josiah 21, 55
Węgierski, Kajetan 174, 190

West, Benjamin 217
Westminster, Convention of (1755) 93, 97
Westminster Abbey 98
Westmorland 200
Wettins, *see* Saxony, house of
Whately, Thomas 197
Whigs 45, 63, 115–19, 130, 133, 161, 282
  exiles 30, 42
  ideology 10, 17–19, 31–2, 95–6, 163–4,
   268
  'oligarchy' 22–3, 155; *see also*
   Rockingham Whigs
Whitworth, Charles, later Viscount 138,
   175, 262
Wieland 56
Wielhorski, Michał 245
Wieliczka 252
Wilanów 193
Wilkes, John 52, 58, 60, 140
Wilkinson, John 235
William III, King of England 22, 114
Williams, Sir Charles Hanbury 112 n.
  and English politics 93, 95–6, 116
  and the *Familia* 78, 87–8, 91, 92, 106,
   111
  friendship with S. A. Poniatowski
   86–95, 101, 102–4, 123, 144, 315
  influence on Poniatowski 81, 90,
   95–102, 189, 228
  and international affairs 91, 93, 97
  and manners 99–100, 109
Williams, Lady Frances, née Coningsby
   110
Williams, Frances 110
Wilno (Vilnius, Vilna) 70
  observatory 231, 242
  university 72, 82, 175, 235, 242
Wilson, Arthur, historian 38 n.
Wilton 55, 113, 215
Winckelmann 199
Windsor, house of 297
wiski 53
Wiśniewski, Antoni 71
Witte, Jan de, General 220
Władysław IV, King of Poland (1632–48)
   146, 148–9
Włodzimierz (Vladimir) 175
Wołczyn 1–2, 77, 78
Wolf, Nathaniel Matthias 232–3
Wolff, Christain 40, 68, 70–2, 223, 229,
   230, 243
Wollaston, William 228
Wollstonecraft, Mary 142

Wood, R. 221
Wood, Robert 199, 213
Woodward, George 77–8
Wordsworth, William 180
Wörlitz 55
Wraxall, Sir Nathaniel 135, 273
Wrest Park 114
Wroughton, Thomas 128–9, 135, 137, 156, 157, 161–2, 167, 168–9, 221, 234, 258, 273
Wybicki, Józef 259–61, 274, 308
Wycombe, John, Earl of (later 2nd Marquess of Lansdowne) 136, 173–4
Wyrwicz, Karol 270

Xavier, Prince of Saxony 167, 189
xenophobia 27, 37, 109

Yarmouth, Countess of 91
Yorke, Charles 93, 98, 103, 111–14, 116, 121–32, 144–5, 162, 164, 165, 176, 231
Yorke, Sir Joseph, later Lord Dover 103, 116 n., 121, 122 n., 127–8, 130–2, 165
Yorkes 93, 96, 111, 132

Young, Arthur 237
Young, Edward 56, 176, 183, 184, 189

Zabawy Przyjemne i Pożyteczne 183–4, 186, 230
Zakroczym 84
Zaliwski, Franciszek 235
Załuski, Andrzej Stanisław, Bishop 68–73
Załuski, Józef Andrzej, Bishop 68, 69–70, 81, 167 n., 174 n.
Zamoyska, Ludwika, née Poniatowska 131
Zamoyski, Adam, historian 8, 100, 313 n.
Zamoyski, Andrzej 156–7, 161, 163, 168, 169, 245
code 258, 261–2, 269, 274
Zamoyski, Jan, Hetman 277
Zanoni 176
Zawisza, Barnaba 130–1
Zielińska, Zofia, historian 76 n., 97 n., 161 n.
Zienkowska, Krystyna, historian 281 n.
Zinzendorf, Ludwig Friedrich Julius, Count 89–90
Zug, Szymon Bogumil 197
Zukowski, student 234
Zweibrücken 73